600 New Churches
The Church Building Commission
1818-1856

To the coming generation:

Thomas, Dominic, and Charlotte
Sebastian, JAC, and Benjamin

600 New Churches
The Church Building Commission
1818-1856

M. H. Port

Spire Books Ltd

PO Box 2336, Reading RG4 5WJ
www.spirebooks.com

Spire Books Ltd
PO Box 2336
Reading RG4 5WJ
www.spirebooks.com

This book has been published with the aid of grants from the Marc Fitch Fund,
The Paul Mellon Centre for Studies in British Art, and Queen Mary University
of London.

CIP data:
A catalogue record for this book is available
from the British Library
ISBN 1-904965-08-3
ISBN 978-1-904965-08-4

Designed and produced by John Elliott
Text set in Adobe Bembo

Printed by Alden Group Ltd
Osney Mead
Oxford OX2 0EF

Cover illustrations:
Front: Holy Trinity, Marylebone Road, London (John Soane, 1826-7)
Back: All Saints, Stand, Lancashire (Charles Barry, 1822-5).

Contents

Note on MS transcriptions:

I have not considered it either necessary or desirable to reproduce obsolete conventions of eighteenth-century orthography such as 'y' for 'th', which in a work such as this tend to give the material an undesirable 'olde-worlde' character. The Commission's Minute Clerk was a careless transcriber of letters. I have in general silently expanded abbreviations, supplied necessary punctuation, but (inconsistently if you will) followed the original spelling and capitalisation.

Measure and value:

Measurements are given in feet and inches, the mode employed at the time, and similarly money is referred to as pounds (£), shillings (s.) and pence (d.), 12d. = 1s., 20s. = £1. I have made no attempt to provide modern equivalents, as I regard that as an exercise inevitably imprecise and giving rise to misunderstanding. The wages of a mason were about 5s. a day, a carpenter 4s.6d., but varied from place to place, and employment was not necessarily regular. A clerk of the works (who would normally be employed continuously over the course of a building project) could expect between two guineas and three guineas a week (as a professional man, he was paid in guineas, *i.e.,* 21s.). I am told that such a man would get about £25,000 a year currently. The Commissioners' churches of the 1820s cost on average about £10,000 for 1,500-2,000 worshippers; today a stone-clad church to accommodate (much more amply) some 500 worshippers might cost £6,000,000 to £7,500,000, or about £1,500 per square metre.

Although most of the Commissioners' churches were originally technically chapels of ease, I have referred to them throughout as churches, to avoid any misunderstandings. The Commissioners' officers are distinguished by an upper-case initial, as Surveyor etc.

Foreword
to the 1st Edition

Since the close of the Middle Ages there have been four major church-building episodes in England. The first was occasioned by the Great Fire of London and produced the celebrated churches by Wren. The second, also metropolitan, was inaugurated by the Act for Fifty New Churches of 1711; the presiding architectural genius was Hawksmoor. The third is the subject of this book. The fourth was the High Anglican church-building movement of Victoria's reign which reached its zenith in the 'seventies; the Catholic Pugin was its herald, Butterfield, Street, and Scott were its chief expositors. Now of these four periods only one — the third — has been consistently denied the merit of producing churches of high architectural excellence. This is a very curious fact. It cannot be a question merely of the see-saw of fashion, because today we are almost over-anxious to admire artefacts of the Regency and the decade which succeeded it. It cannot be because money and talent were denied to these churches — they were not always cheap, and the names of Soane, Nash, and Smirke are not without glamour. And yet, somehow or other, the expression 'a Commissioners' church' still tends to be, to say the least, deflationary. Why is this?

The question has always seemed to me as well worth investigation as the question why Wren's churches are glorious, or why Pugin and Butterfield swept all before them a hundred years ago. Clearly, there can be no simple answer – indeed there could be no answer at all short of a thorough, detailed inquiry into the history of the Commissioners and their work. This is what Mr Port has undertaken and is the basis of this book. The tolerance, humility, and exactness with which he unfolds the story enables us to see quite clearly what was right and what was wrong. There was nothing very much wrong, surely, except that neither administrators nor architects, clergy nor laymen possessed conviction about what they were doing. The coolness of the whole undertaking, from beginning to end, is quite remarkable!

But to-day there is something very touching about these Commissioners' churches. Not only because many are being found redundant and demolished, but because when we come to look at them carefully we find so much honest ingenuity in them, so much good workmanship that one feels ashamed of not cherishing them as one cherishes the churches of the 'great' periods. It is not only that the steeples and porticos are often gracefully and sometimes brilliantly composed. Very often the gallery fronts and pews (where they survive), the pulpit, reredos, and organ-case are specimens of quiet, unostentatious design, and joinery of the finest quality. Another point about them is their almost invariably good siting; many a drab suburb is given dignity and coherence by the Commissioners' care in the acquisition of sites. Altogether, these buildings are worth much more than is customarily admitted, and now, thanks to Mr Port, we can not only look at them with sympathy but study them in nicely calculated historical perspective.

John Summerson,
August 1960

Preface

'Commissioners' Church' was a term of disapprobation, and even contempt, for much of the nineteenth and twentieth centuries, and moreover one loosely applied, as have been the labels 'Waterloo' and 'Million' church. One aim of this study, arising out of an Oxford B.Litt. thesis inspired by Howard Colvin, was to establish an accurate terminology; another was to redeem the churches themselves from careless contempt. Hardly was the plaster dry on their walls before there began a great change of emphasis in the Anglican liturgy, away from the Word, towards sacramental worship, which together with developments in architectural style condemned them as 'dreary God-boxes'. But John Betjeman in the mid-twentieth century observed that 'Commissioners' churches ... had a dignity and coherence which we can appreciate today', and there has since been, despite continuing grievous losses, appreciation sufficient for English Heritage currently to commission a survey of the survivors.

I had long been aware of the desirability of revising *Six Hundred New Churches*, and had begun to contemplate tackling it, when Geoff Brandwood suggested to me the possibility of his firm's (Spire Books) re-issuing the work either in its original form or in an enlarged edition. Thus inspired, I agreed to undertake a modest up-dating and augmenting of the text to accompany a seriously increased number of illustrations.

Since 1961 a great deal has been written about almost every aspect of the history of the Church of England, of which I have been able, within the scope of revision, to take account merely of the main features so far as they relate to early nineteenth-century church extension. There does not, however, appear to have been very much more written in respect of the Commissioners' churches themselves, and I have therefore fleshed out the original text in that regard. It has been supplemented, with Spire Books' encouragement, by extensive illustration captions which they encouraged to flourish to an extent made possible by the beneficence of the Marc Fitch Fund, while the deeply-appreciated generosity of the Paul Mellon Foundation, and that of Queen Mary, University of London, and the magnanimity of several custodians of illustrative material (notably the National Monuments Record and the Trustees of Sir John Soane's Museum), have permitted an impressive range of illustrations themselves, unaffordable in the first edition.

To Howard Colvin's guidance and advice in thesis and first edition I was deeply indebted. The readiness of the Church Commissioners for England to put the records of the Church Building Commission freely at my disposal (despite lack of office space at Millbank) alone made the work possible, and the generosity of the Marc Fitch Fund Trustees and the Church Historical Society enabled publication. Others who generously placed their manuscripts at my disposal were the late Earl of Harrowby, the Curator of Sir John Soane's Museum, the Incorporated Church Building Society, and the Librarian of the Royal Institute of British Architects (whose kindness permitted me to make full use of the Goodhart-Rendel index of Victorian churches). The Trustees of the Arnold Historical Essay Fund awarded me a grant in aid of visiting churches in the north of England; the Society of Architectural Historians of Great Britain allowed me to draw from my article on Francis Goodwin (*Architectural History*, 1958); the National Buildings Record (as it then was) and the Church Commissioners provided illustrations; and the staff at the Church Commissioners, at the Public Record Office, and at many libraries gave ready help, as did numerous incumbents of parishes throughout the country. The Rev. B. F. L. Clarke kindly helped to check the lists of churches and architects, and Sir John Summerson most kindly wrote the Foreword reproduced here. The Society for Promoting Christian Knowledge has kindly surrendered all their rights in the first edition.

In the preparation of this new edition I have again received much help. I would like to thank in the first place Geoff Brandwood for the very great help he has given in facilitating it, inducting me in new computer arts and going to the labour of himself scanning the original text. Dr John Elliott has kindly computerised the appendices, a formidable task. For assistance with finding and obtaining illustrative material I should like to thank Charles Hind (RIBA Drawings Collection), Susan Palmer and Stephen Astley (Sir John Soane's Museum), Clare Brown (Lambeth Palace Library), Philip Gale and Sarah Duffield (Church of England Record Centre), Christopher Webster, David Hunt, and Rowland Billington (Bath Preservation Trust). Edward Oliver (Department of Geography, Queen Mary, University of London), has assisted with the maps. Michael Slaughter and Cameron Newham have taken excellent photographs in the field. Study of the illustrations with Professor Christopher Wilson and Ashley Ellis (Wakefield Diocese) afforded me valuable insights, illuminating captions. Correspondents augmenting the first edition included Mr D. N. Griffiths and Mr Frank Smith. In various significant ways Mr Neil Burton, Sir Howard Colvin (originator of this study), Dr Bernard Nurse (Society of Antiquaries), Professor Philip Ogden, Dr Richard Palmer and all his staff (Lambeth Palace Library), Mr Marius Reynolds RIBA, Mrs Margaret Richardson (Curator, Sir John Soane's Museum), Professor Andrew Saint, Mr John Scott RIBA, and Dr Frank Salmon (Paul Mellon Centre) have given valuable help; and my wife has been very tolerant of an undertaking that has absorbed more time than either of us expected at the outset.

Michael Port
Dartmouth Park, NW5
June 2005

Introduction

'Tory reform' is generally held to have commenced after the death of Castlereagh in 1822, and it is often said that the cabinet he dominated had no policy but that of repression. But even during his ascendancy, there were constructive measures. At a time when the cry was all for economy and the reduction of taxation after the burdens of the Napoleonic Wars, the government proposed the grant of a million pounds sterling for the building of new churches to cater for the needs of the new industrial towns. At the same period as the 'Gag Acts' the first moves were made for reforming the Church – both in the aspect of its relations with the people at large, and that of its internal organisation. The government did not itself undertake this difficult task but entrusted it to a commission of churchmen, which was to make an annual report to parliament but was otherwise independent. Even if Church reform was undertaken, as in Metternich's Austria, as safeguarding the established order, it could yet be a means of improving the lot of the labouring poor, whether in the spiritual sense or materially by promoting the building trades.

The churches erected under the aegis of the Commission have not met with much notice or sympathetic criticism, and many of the six hundred and more are neither inspired nor inspiring. But changing liturgical fashions may help us to appreciate the quality of at least the 'Million' churches – those built in the first fine flush of the Parliamentary Grant; and to recognise the importance of the standards laid down for the Commissioners' churches: a vital contribution to rekindling the art of church-building in the Gothic style, and leading to the excellent work of the best Victorian architects in this field.

The Commission was very deeply concerned with architectural problems. At first it sought the technical advice of the Crown Architects, but a number of members were keenly interested in, and considered themselves competent judges of design. They soon found that full-time technical assistance was also necessary, and therefore appointed their own surveyor; and the consideration of the plans of churches occupied a great deal of time of both officials and members of the Commission. I have dealt with these questions at length, describing the methods by which the designs were obtained, how they were approved, some of the churches that were built, contemporary reactions, and the architects and the methods of contracting employed. I believe that these are the aspects of the Commission's work that may be found to be of most general interest.

The Commission also had powers to enable the new churches to function as effectively as possible; in particular by the division and subdivision of parishes, and the provision of endowments. These powers were extended and ramified by successive Acts of great complexity, so that by 1856 Spencer Walpole, himself an Ecclesiastical Commissioner, thought they were in such a state of inconsistency and confusion that nobody could know how to act upon them. I have dealt with these matters only generally. Moreover, in the later years of the Commission's life, they fell increasingly within the purview of the Ecclesiastical Commissioners, who had to consider the whole state of the Church of England. The Church Building Commission was perhaps the model for the later body, and the two were able to work closely together, many members sitting on both, until the older was absorbed into the younger on New Year's Day, 1857. But the story of the Ecclesiastical Commission is both wider and longer. My concern has been with the more limited field of the Church Building Commission in its primary task and the architectural development thereof.

Opposite:
1 St Peter, Ashton-under-Lyne (Francis Goodwin, 1821-4). Brought up in King's Lynn, Goodwin will have known the great medieval churches of the region. His stately and imaginative reinterpretations of Perpendicular Gothic, as seen here, were acknowledged by connoisseurs examining designs for a new House of Commons in 1833 and for new Houses of Parliament in 1835. St Peter's is one of many churches by architects working for the Church Building Commission that give the lie to the idea, common in the twentieth century, that the Commissioners' churches are architecturally deficient, unworthy predecessors of those built under the influence of the Ecclesiologists.

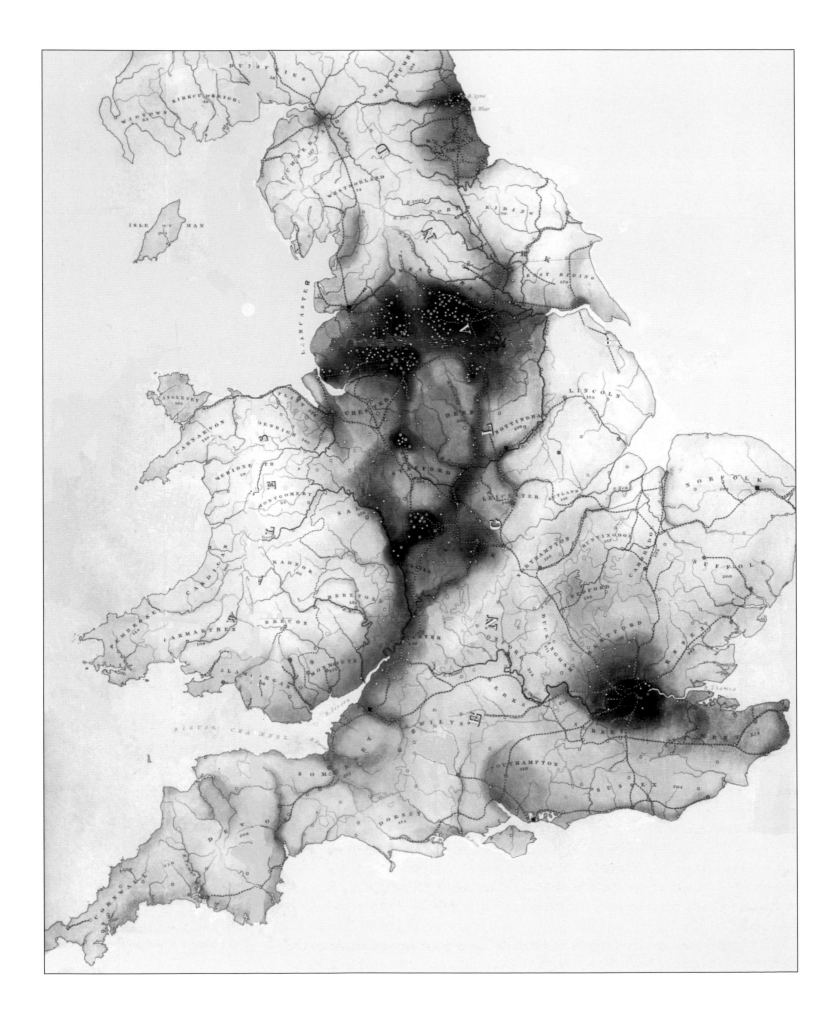

14

1

The Church Building Movement, 1810–1818

The effect of the Revolutionary and Napoleonic wars on England's internal economy, historians have observed, was to increase the pace of industrialization and at the same time to allow it free rein. While manufacturers throve, the industrial poor sank deeper into an ever-spreading morass. Government was too preoccupied with a struggle for national survival to ameliorate by legislation conditions in the industrial areas, even had the contemporary ethos favoured such intervention. What improvements were carried out were the work of individuals, private bodies, or commissioners empowered by local Acts.

Yet if the State would not, one might have expected at least the Church to make some comment on the new conditions. There was a feeling diffused throughout society, particularly since the outbreak of war with revolutionary France, that the influence of the Church and its religious and moral teaching was a bulwark against revolution;[1] a fear that the ignorant and atheistical masses, and indeed those under the sway of the impassioned oratory of the Methodists, would fall an easy prey to revolutionary agitation. Some philanthropists thought that what had previously been done by the Church might better be accomplished by education: but the part supposedly played by the *philosophes* in bringing about the French Revolution had left many profoundly suspicious of education for the mob, at any rate further than the barest rudiments. Yet enlightened spirits saw a glorious opportunity to win the masses for Christ – by education within the Church. A National Society was founded in 1811, 'for the education of the poor in the principles of the Established Church', and the call went forth for more churches to be built, so that the education commenced in the school might reach its climax in the temple, and lest the knowledge acquired should be perverted to false ends.[2]

The eighteenth-century Church of England has a poor reputation. After the failure of the plan in Queen Anne's reign to build fifty new churches in London

Opposite:
2 Map of England and Wales by Augustus Petermann, 1849, showing the distribution of population based on the 1841 census.

3 St Catherine Cree, 1628-31. A characteristic eighteenth-century parish-church interior, filled with pews rented to the inhabitants; a three-decker pulpit, reading desk and clerk's desk in the central aisle in front of the altar.

and its suburbs, it is generally held that there was little church-building before George IV's reign,[3] and that the clergy were for the most part lazy and self-seeking. Existing churches were occupied by the owners of pews to the exclusion of the poor and even, in expanding towns, the middle classes. The clergy were ignorant, like Parson Trulliber, or non-resident, like Sydney Smith for most of his life, or both. Distorted or exaggerated as such views are, undeniably there is a sub-stratum of truth. While 'non-residence' was a technical point, there were in 1812 more than a thousand parishes 'simply unattended by ministers of the Established Church'.[4] Furthermore, some 3,300 livings received less than £150 a year, at least 860 receiving less than £50, thanks in a large degree to the impropriation of rectorial revenues[5] that accompanied the Reformation, bringing pluralism, absenteeism and uneducated and unrespected clergy in its train.[6]

'The church's main function was social control', declares Professor Best forthrightly. 'Very few in the Church of England before the eighteen-thirties … thought that the church, in its function as an established church, could have any higher aim than complementing the work of the civil power and − what it alone could do − toughening the fabric of society.'[7] The old close relationship between the landed gentry and the Church of England had been a fundamental factor in the authority that the Church exercised through the parochial system, but in a revolutionary and industrializing age that alliance was under attack, and eroding − faster in some areas than in others.[8] Parochial organization, moreover, had always been imperfect: in the 'highland' regions of the midlands and north, as Dr Gilbert points out, the diffused settlement patterns of 'scattered communities combining pastoral farming with domestic industry, or engaged in mining or quarrying', and lacking resident gentry, afforded it little or no financial or logistical basis.[9] A church in a once-small (but rapidly growing) market town might be the focus of a 'parish' of perhaps several square miles, with as many as ten or a dozen little townships or villages miles distant, few having even a chapel. The average size of a parish in the diocese of Lichfield and Coventry (which straddled the 'highland' and 'lowland' areas) was 4,275 acres, or about 6.7 square miles. In Cheshire and Lancashire (the two counties that, together with the archdeaconry of Richmond, formed the diocese of Chester), there were only 156 parishes in 1811, with an average area of 11,860 acres:[10] Blackburn with 22 townships, was no less than 14 miles long and ten in breadth, over 48,000 acres; Rochdale, a little smaller at nearly 42,000 acres; Warrington parish, 12½ miles long, with four townships, covered about 16,000 acres; Oldham-cum-Prestwich, with four townships, extended five miles by three, amounting to 10,586 acres:[11] a situation supporting a modern historian's reference to 'great organizational and clerical deficiencies that rendered the urban Church largely invisible and meaningless'.[12] Although current research is uncovering a greater extent of church-building in the Georgian era than once supposed,[13] and organizational defects were being tackled, particularly in the early nineteenth century,[14] the growth of population, and even more significantly, the rapid migration of workers to hitherto sparsely inhabited districts[15] – with which no national church could have coped[16] – did mean that the Established Church was in many places invisible. Such invisibility drove religious enthusiasts to seek their own solutions.

Latitudinarian as many of the clergy might be, the Church had not found itself wide enough to comprehend all the followers of Wesley and Whitfield. This tendency of the enthusiasts to organize in their own societies had irritated several bishops, and some local magistrates (of whom many were clerics)[17] were preventing their itinerant preachers from taking the oaths required under the Toleration Act.[18] There was among the clergy much suspicion of, and even outright hostility, towards the Methodists,[19] although, as Lord Liverpool reminded the Archbishop of Canterbury in 1812, 'a large proportion of this particular Body of Men profess to be Members of the Church of England – They attend Divine Service in the Church, & take the Communion in the Church – But they claim the privilege of Meeting & Associating for Religious Purposes, in other Places & at other Times. ... I think with all their Errors, their occasional Conformity ... is more advantageous than injurious to the Establishment itself.'[20]

But the Established Church was bound to a fixed liturgy and a fixed place; and the parties tended to move further apart.[21] From about 1795 more and more Methodists demanded communion from their own preachers, and the building of Methodist chapels became grounds for zealous Anglicans to demand more churches: Methodism 'thrived in areas of Anglican parochial weakness' and 'gained most [of all the denominations] from the expansion of the English population and economy between 1750 and 1850'.[22] But episcopal concentration on the threat thought to be offered by the Methodists and to a lesser extent by other dissenting congregations obscured a greater problem: the existence of large numbers who, deprived for generations of the facility of worship, had become entirely secular.[23] The Rev. Daniel Wilson, Vicar of Islington, expressed a view widely held among churchmen in the 1820s that 'By a decisive plan of affording church-accommodation, however, there is every hope of keeping the vast bulk of the population in the Church, and of training them in those sentiments of sound religion and those habits of Christian subjection and obedience, which are the best foundations of loyalty in the state, as well of individual piety and virtue'.[24] But it was a delusion to suppose that people did not attend Anglican services simply because there was no room, and that, were room provided, they would flock in. Dissent – particularly the Methodists – and secularism alike were growing. 'The Church, in theory still identified with the nation and controlled by the nation's legislature, had become in fact a sect with fewer instead of more privileges than the other sects.'[25]

Churchmen consequently often had a sense of being under siege. The anti-Christian element of the French Revolution sharpened an awareness that not only were there great numbers of poor, ignorant people whom the Church was not reaching, and growing numbers of dissenters of various colours, but also many hostile to religion in general and specifically to the Church of England as a part of the established order. A petition from Dewsbury (Yorkshire) for additional churches referred to 'the increasing irreligion, and <u>Dissent</u> from the <u>Establishment</u>, and *Disaffection to the State*, which has been gradually occasioned by the want of Church-room', and to 'the <u>dreadful</u> spirit of insubordination and irreligion which so <u>alarmingly</u> prevails throughout this populous manufactoring District'.[26] Such a spirit had however become too widespread to be extinguished by providing church-room, as J. B. Sumner, the Evangelical Bishop of Chester recognized in his 1832 Charge to his clergy: 'infidelity is openly avowed by those who have no knowledge, or only a smattering of knowledge. ... the unbelief of the lower classes in the present day, is not merely the unbelief of vicious practice. Their principles are undermined ... Every man who is not the friend, is the enemy of religion.' Sumner referred to irreligious 'multitudes [who] keep one another in countenance' in the crowded towns.[27]

Recognition of the seemingly irremediable hopelessness of this situation was, however, slow to surface. There were two active parties in the Church,[28] the Evangelicals, (often, as Lord Liverpool indicated, having some sympathy with Methodists), and that High Church party[29] which (fewer in numbers perhaps) still maintained in its worship the tradition of the Caroline divines, and viewed the State as the stick upholding that candle which embodied the light of the world: the Church – though, as Professor Best remarks, 'the spiritual estate had evaporated. ... The clergy had to "acquiesce" in the layman's supremacy'.[30] Nevertheless, committed as they were to the contemporary alliance of Church and State, the High Churchmen could set forth a high doctrine of the Church's rights, as Charles Daubeny, Archdeacon of Salisbury from 1804, did in his *Guide to the Church* (1798).[31] Church and State were mutual supports. Daubeny also promoted (and subscribed to) the building of Christ Church, Walcot, Bath, opened in 1798 as 'the first free and open church in the country'.[32] Daubeny's associates formed a particular group of High Churchmen that was to replenish the Church in the early nineteenth century. Their activities were first seen in the closing years of the eighteenth, when their aid secured for the Scottish bishops the repeal of the unjust laws against the Episcopal Church in North Britain. Daubeny's fellow-Wykehamist, George Isaac Huntingford (1748-1832), praised his work, in an important sermon in 1796, suggesting that the government should encourage similar activities nation-wide.[33] This group leading High Church thought revolved around two personalities: William Stevens (1732-1807)[34] in the first generation; in the second, Joshua Watson (1771-1855),[35] whose wife was Archdeacon Daubeny's niece. Similarly it took shape in two particular forms: the dining club called 'Nobody's' (later 'Nobody's Friends'); and the 'Hackney Phalanx', bonded in worship and social ties, with a power base in the Society for the Promoting of Christian Knowledge (S.P.C.K.), that acted as a powerful pressure group'.[36]

Who these men were and what they accomplished are matters so intimately bound up that they must be considered together. William Stevens founded the dining club called after his nickname 'Nobody', to which belonged a goodly number, both laymen and clerks, of the High Church party. Among the fifteen founder members were Joshua Watson, his brother, the Rev. John James Watson, vicar (and later, rector) of Hackney,[37] and wealthy brother-in-law, the Rev. Henry

4 Christ Church, Bath (John Palmer, 1798), in 1905. Promoted by Charles Daubeny, Archdeacon of Salisbury to provide a free place of worship for the poor.

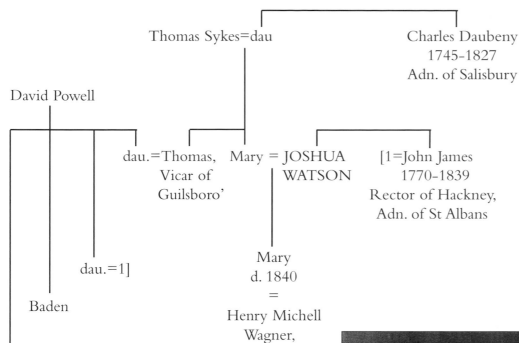

Thomas Sykes=dau

Charles Daubeny
1745-1827
Adn. of Salisbury

David Powell

dau.=Thomas,
Vicar of
Guilsboro'

Mary = JOSHUA
WATSON

[1=John James
1770-1839
Rector of Hackney,
Adn. of St Albans

dau.=1]

Baden

Mary
d. 1840
=
Henry Michell
Wagner,
Vicar of Brighton

dau.=Henry Handley Norris
1771-1850
Curate, later Rector,
of South Hackney

5 Joshua Watson (1771-1855). Wine merchant, High Church theologian, administrator of church charities, and promoter of church extension. Engraving of a portrait by Sir William Ross, R.A.

Handley Norris (1771-1850);[38] Stevens' associates on the committee which had campaigned for the Scottish Episcopal Church, the judges Sir James Allan Park[39] and Sir John Richardson;[40] and the propagandist John Bowdler.[41] During the first year of the club's existence,[42] members admitted included John Bowles,[43] a vigorous opponent of Tom Paine's *The Rights of Man,* Baden Powell,[44] and George, 2nd Lord Kenyon,[45] a pupil of Stevens' great friend Jones of Nayland.[46] The extent to which this club was bound up with the family connexions of the 'Hackney Phalanx' may best be seen in a genealogical table.

Joshua Watson, the nucleus of the Phalanx, was the greatest lay churchman of his day. Of the Church Building Commissioners he was one of the most energetic: during thirty-three years he served on most of the committees, as well as attending the majority of the meetings of the full Board.[47] He was indeed the cornerstone of the Commission. A prosperous wine-merchant in the City, he retired in 1814 in order to devote himself more completely to Church affairs. The significance of his position in the High Church party may be gauged by the very name 'Hackney Phalanx', so called because the Watsons lived at Hackney. Keystone of the High Church party, the 'Phalanx' was the body that 'offered the most principled opposition to the Evangelicals ... and more or less controlled whatever church societies and journals were not in the Evangelical camp'.[48]

One of Watson's closest friends was the Rev. Christopher Wordsworth,[49] brother of the poet, and a domestic chaplain to the Archbishop of Canterbury.[50] It was he who induced the primate to 'treat Watson as his principal lay adviser'.[51] This relationship between Watson and the primate was to be of great service to the church-building movement. Around the archbishop revolved a number of other young chaplains, several of whom became friends of Watson during the second decade of the century, and subsequently Church Building Commissioners: among them Richard Mant, George Owen Cambridge, George D'Oyly and John Lonsdale. Other priests among Watson's friends included the future Commissioners J. H. Pott,[52] William Van Mildert,[53] and F. J. H. Wollaston.[54]

It was by the efforts of Watson and two other members of the Phalanx, John Bowles and H. H. Norris, that the National Schools Society was founded in 1811, with Andrew Bell as superintendent. Watson became its first treasurer – a post he continued to hold until 1842 – by the primate's appointment, inspired, it is said, by H. H. Norris. At the inaugural meeting, the chair was taken by the archbishop; and he, with the Bishop of London, chose the first committee, which included Lord Radstock,[55] Sir John Nicholl,[56] William Davis, Francis Burton,[57] Cambridge, Wordsworth, and Norris. Among prominent supporters were Lord Kenyon, Sir J. A. Park, and Charles Hampden Turner.[58]

Watson increased his authority in the years between the foundation of this society and that of the Church Building Society by his excellent management of the German relief fund of 1814, and the Waterloo widows' fund of 1815. The former involved the administration of a parliamentary grant of £100,000, and was presided over by Archbishop Manners-Sutton; but Watson was his right-hand man, and the effective administrator.[59] The latter was of £500,000, raised by subscription for the dependants of those who fell at Waterloo. Watson was also a leading member of the great Church societies, the Society for the Propagation of the Gospel (S.P.G.) and his power-base, the S.P.C.K. In 1814 he became joint-treasurer with Cambridge of the S.P.C.K., having been proposed by Archdeacon Pott.[60] The transfer of the Indian missions supported by that society to the control of the S.P.G. brought him into close contact with the Bishop of London, William Howley.[61]

Meanwhile, contemporaneously with the founding of the National Society, attention was being called to the deficiency in church accommodation. Great towns had sprung from villages, and, if there were a church at all, the village church was often all the footing the Establishment yet had therein. Frequently most or all of the seats in such churches were rented by the rich to the exclusion of the poor (and, indeed, of many middle-class newcomers),[62] or appropriated to particular properties.[63] When the increase of population is considered, it is the new industrial towns in the north that spring first to mind: William Cleaver, Bishop of Chester, called attention to the discrepancy between church accommodation and population in his 1799 Charge to his clergy.[64] Richard Watson, Dean of St Paul's and non-resident Bishop of Llandaff, wrote to William

6 St Peter, Vere Street, London (James Gibbs, 1721–4). One of the proprietary chapels built as a commercial proposition to provide for the spiritual needs of wealthy Londoners on the Harley-Cavendish estate.

Wilberforce in 1800 (in the hope of his raising the issue with the Prime Minister) to propose building 'free churches' (open to all comers) in London: £100,000 from public funds could, he suggested, build 20 churches.[65] Ignored, the bishop iterated his call in a major sermon in 1804.[66]

Other bishops in sermons and charges began to direct attention to the problem. John Fisher, Bishop of Exeter, in a sermon preached before the House of Lords in 1807 cited statistics of church-room and population in the parishes of west London: 'a melancholy spectacle ... which calls for immediate attention'.[67] John Randolph, Bishop of London from 1809 to 1813, active in the work of the National Society, also expressed the need for more churches in his primary Charge, 1810 (when he attacked the erection of proprietary chapels, restricted to fee-payers, by Evangelicals), but recognized that the necessary legislation could not be undertaken at that time.[68] His learned disputant, the High Church Professor Herbert Marsh (1757-1839), in his seminal Charity Schools' sermon of 1811 (launching-pad of the National Society) called for the Church to have equal freedom with the dissenters in chapel-building.[69]

Ministers were not unaware of the Church's problems, as will be seen below; Lords Sidmouth and Harrowby were particularly concerned, and their efforts secured returns made to the House of Lords in 1816 and 1818,[70] which gave wide publicity to the acute lack of church room. These showed that Stockport, for instance, with a population then calculated at 33,973, had church-room for only 2,500; and Almondbury (Yorkshire), with 13,195 inhabitants had church-room for 2,800. The older northern towns were similarly unprovided: Sheffield had accommodation for 6,280 out of its population of 55,000, Manchester for some 11,000 out of nearly 80,000. But London, as Fisher had argued, was no better served: St Marylebone had 76,624 inhabitants to share seating for 8,700, Shoreditch 2,300 seats among 43,488 inhabitants. In the ports, the story was the same: Stoke Damerel parish (Plymouth) had a population of 32,250: church-room for 5,000. The fashionable watering-places were also crying out. The largest parish in Bath, Walcot, had room in its churches for 4,870 out of 20,560 persons habitually resident; the situation in Brighton was similar.[71] From these returns it was calculated in 1818 that in parishes where the population was 4,000 or more, and the capacity of the churches did not exceed one-quarter of the population, there was throughout England and Wales an excess of population over church-room totalling 2,528,505.

The immediate difficulties of supplying this need were enormous, and the stiffest hurdles, perhaps, were the four Ps: Patron, Parson, Pews, and Parish. To the patron,[72] an advowson, the right of presentation to a living, was convenient capital, easily sold, or used to provide for a relation, as well as conferring social status: 'of all matters [patronage] was the most difficult to do anything about. ... Patrons enjoyed an all but absolute control over their livings'.[73] The more valuable the living, the more valuable the advowson. The parson or incumbent, whether rector, vicar or perpetual curate, was effectively irremovable, save for heinous crimes; his income depended on tithes, surplice fees (for marriages and funerals), any endowment the parish might possess, profits from the glebe or church land, and, in many places, rents from pews or seats in the church, and freewill Easter offerings. Some or all of these were threatened by the coming of a new church. Most country parish churches were pewed: these seats, with lockable doors, were often attached by prescription to particular properties; while, particularly in the towns, many churches charged an annual rent for seats to pay church expenses, including the incumbent's stipend. A new church was only too likely to diminish the rental of an existing church, so that the congregation itself might well be hostile to the idea of a rival. And the parish, whether governed by an open or by a select vestry, would have to bear the cost of services and maintenance of a new church, expenses that would increase the church-rate; so that it was not only parishes where dissenters controlled the vestry that might resist a proposal for a new church. Thus an individual who wished to build a church, even at his own expense, was often faced with hostility from these existing interests – and dissenting chapels were also a financial speculation, so that dissenters might suffer a twofold blow from a new church, in loss of paying worshippers as well as an additional parochial burden.

When the parish itself agreed to provide more accommodation, there was the difficulty of raising funds: church-rates were unpopular, the law regarding them 'confused and uncertain',[74] and they were not a valid security for a loan. If a new church or chapel-of-ease were built, those who worshipped there would still have to pay church-rate to the mother church. For rebuilding a church some money might be raised by brief, which was 'a Royal Warrant authorizing a collection in a place of worship, and sometimes from house to house, for a specified charitable object'.[75] Briefs were granted by the Lord Chancellor, after application had been made to the justices at Quarter Sessions. The whole business of distributing briefs to all the parishes, and collecting the returns, had been conducted since 1799 by John Stevenson Salt, a banker of Lombard Street. The system had been organized by the statute 4 & 5 Ann. c. 14, and subsequently regulated by the Lord Chancellor's directions of 1755 and 1804. The latter ascribed the delays and smallness of the contributions to neglect and carelessness by churchwardens or incumbents.[76] The costs of administration often absorbed two-thirds of the sum collected, and it was usually about three years before the business of a single brief was completed.[77] Between 1805 and 1819, the sum raised by a brief varied from £321 (Audlem, Cheshire, 1816) to £604 (Radford, Nottinghamshire, 1811), though usually between £300 and £400. The collector's salary was about £160, and expenses about £90, so that Audlem church received only £89 and Radford £336.[78] The system was efficient only as a means of providing for several sinecurists. Like other parts of the ecclesiastical organization it was not competent to provide for contemporary needs.

All these factors made it almost indispensable to obtain an Act of Parliament before a church was rebuilt, or a new one built. To divide a parish an Act was essential. This added heavily to the expense. On the other hand, to open a dissenting chapel one had merely to take out a licence, which could generally be obtained without difficulty (though under the menace of the revolutionary wars, some magistrates made difficulties, as noted above).[79] Many well-wishers to the Establishment were ultimately driven to this expedient;[80] and then used in their chapels the Book of Common Prayer with minimal alterations.

Clearly, then, important as the old High Church party was in the church-building agitation, it could have achieved little without governmental support, as was shown by the ineffectiveness of an act of 1803 passed 'to promote the building, repairing, or otherwise providing, of Churches and Chapels, and of Houses for the Residence of Ministers, and the providing of Church-yards and Glebes'.[81] And it was there that the evangelical factor notably came into play. It was ministers associated with the Evangelical wing of the Church, who showed themselves most deeply concerned about the situation of the Church, and put forward measures to reduce abuses. Spencer Perceval, Prime Minister from 1809 to 1812, and hailed as 'the evangelical prime minister',[82] had vainly attempted to improve the lot of stipendiary curates; and in 1809 secured the first of eleven annual augmentations of £100,000 to Queen Anne's Bounty for raising the income of the poorest livings.[83] He was supported by Lord Harrowby,[84] a cabinet minister of Evangelical sympathies, who had long been deeply concerned with clergy-residence bills and similar measures. Convinced of the essential commitment of the mass of Englishmen to the Established Church, Harrowby remarked in the House of Lords on the inadequate number of churches, which drove people to dissenting chapels,[85] calling attention to the disparity between church-room and population in the manufacturing towns.[86] He sought the removal of the obstacles to church-building. If the fetters were struck off the Establishment, the wealth and prosperity of the new towns would, he thought, supply the funds. The existing situation drove the people from the Church to Dissent: a gulf had appeared between Church and People which was growing ever wider. Therefore, when churches were built, a certain space should be set aside for the poor – a suggestion endorsed by Lord Sidmouth.[87]

Another idea put forward by Harrowby was that 'where particular circumstances rendered the erection of new churches too heavy a burden upon local funds, the precedent established by Parliament in the time of Queen Anne, might with great propriety be followed'; which, although local in nature, was the first suggestion of a Commission and parliamentary supply for building new churches. The following day Sidmouth returned to the subject, commenting on the advantages enjoyed by dissenters over the Establishment in the provision of facilities for worship.[88] He moved an address to the Crown praying for a statement of church accommodation in parishes with more than a thousand inhabitants, and the number of dissenting chapels therein.[89] Spencer Perceval himself then took up consideration of the problem, but he was assassinated before he had 'all the details which would enable him to take some active step'.[90] The ministerial crises that followed the murder, and the intensification of the war on the Continent, forced into the distance the prospect of any such step.

But as the victorious Allies drove Napoleon from France itself, four of Watson's friends, Sir J. A. Park, John Bowdler, C. H. Turner, and William Davis wrote to the Bishop of London about the lack of church room, especially in his diocese, 'an Evil of no common magnitude … in many districts in the West and East Parts of the Metropolis, in populous parts of the County of Middlesex, & also in many great towns in other parts of the kingdom, not a *tenth* part of the Church of England population can be accommodated in our churches & Chapels, to worship God after the manner of their forefathers'.[91] The lack of church room was one great cause of the increase of sectarianism and Methodism. Many having exerted their utmost strength to educate the poor in the principles of the Established Church, it would be a 'heavy offence to the sight of God' were they not now to provide free churches for these children when adult 'in which the means of grace, which we have taught them to use, may be dispensed for the supply of their spiritual needs'. A further consideration was that they could not better render thanks to God for victory over 'the most dreadful scourge that ever affected the human race' [Napoleon Bonaparte] than 'by immediately dedicating to his honour and service, a number of free Churches & Chapels [i.e, with all seats free], sufficient to supply the spiritual wants of all his faithful worshippers in the established Church of England'. They proposed that free churches sufficient to supply the needs of all who wished to adhere to the Church of England should be provided as a national thank-offering. (It is noteworthy that these High Church laymen had abandoned the principle that the Established Church should provide room for all.) Such a proposal might be better received coming from laymen, but they had been informed 'that steps have already been taken by our rulers, both in Church and State, upon this important business'. Were this so, such steps would have their most active co-operation. But if nothing were in contemplation, they suggested a private meeting of well-affected clergy, noblemen 'and other excellent Laymen, … to digest some plan, for carrying into immediate execution, for the erection of churches & chapels, a great part of which should be for the accommodation of the poor', which would then be submitted to Howley for transmission to the Regent and his ministers. 'Whether there should be first a Commission, & then a Bill: or an act of Parliament first, & *then* a Commission, as was done in the reign of the pious Queen Anne … must be a matter for future consideration.' But '*now or never* is the time'.

That such steps were unlikely to be taken in the immediate future appears from Lord Sidmouth's reply as Home Secretary to a correspondent pointing out the lack of churches in Manchester: that he had had many conversations with friends of the Church on the subject generally, and that he trusted the attention of parliament would 'at length be awakened to the urgent importance of adopting upon an extensive scale' measures to supply the deficiency.[92] Reasons for this inaction were given by Lord Harrowby to his brother Henry Ryder, the evangelical Dean of Wells:[93] 'I shall be glad to see your friend's plan about churches, but I cannot flatter myself with much hopes this session [i.e. 1814-15]. The expense of winding up the war upon the Continent, and of continuing that with America presses so severely upon our finances, that I doubt whether even Vansittart[94] will have the courage to set his shoulder to any scheme which must cost much money.'[95] He was himself willing to support any scheme brought forward by the bishops, or to bring one forward for them, if they thought it would arouse less hostility coming from a layman.

It is highly probable that Joshua Watson would have been aware of the tenor of this letter, but perhaps from natural modesty he left it to men more distinguished in the public eye to bring the proposal forward. No indication of government action having emerged, it was he, at any rate, who with John Bowdler drew up late in 1815 a memorial to the Prime Minister[96] that is important as giving an explanation of the need for more churches, and the first clear statement of principles in this matter on the part of the High Church group.

They were, they declared, alarmed at 'the danger to which the constitution of this country both in church and state is exposed from the want of places of public worship, particularly for persons of the middle and lower classes,' in many parts of the kingdom, particularly London.[97] Anxious as the High Church leaders were for the spiritual condition of the population, they undoubtedly saw the Church as a pillar of the State, which had a reciprocal duty to support the Church.[98] Morals, the memorialists insisted, could only be inculcated by religious principles, and without them the nation could not prosper: the benefit of the new schools so widely being built must be lost, unless the work of education could be

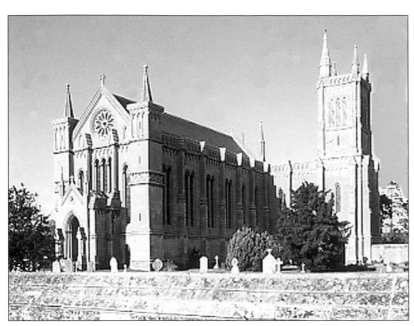

7 Theale Church, Berkshire (E. W. Garbett, 1820-2). An early, remarkably accurate, Early English revival based on Salisbury Cathedral. Tower by John Buckler, 1827-8.

completed in the Church. To illustrate their argument they referred to the condition of fifty parishes in or near London, where there were 'more than a million of inhabitants; and … all the places of public worship in those parishes belonging to the Establishment are not capable of containing one tenth part of that multitude, and even those places chiefly calculated for the higher classes of society'.[99] To provide the necessary churches was beyond the power of private or parochial subscription: 'Parliament alone can do it; and we conceive it to be one of its chief duties to provide places of worship for the members of the established religion.' Here for the first time is a public demand that the legislature should provide funds on a nation-wide scale. The memorial was signed by 120 laymen, including Lord Kenyon, Sir J. A. Park, William Davis, C. H. Turner, Francis Burton MP, George Bramwell, R. H. Inglis,[100] George Gipps MP,[101] and Joseph and William Cotton.[102]

The ground for this widely supported memorial had been laid by pamphlets and letters,[103] most notably a vigorous and influential pamphlet published some months previously in the shape of a letter to Lord Liverpool: *The Church in Danger,* by the Rev. Richard Yates.[104] This contained an exposition of appalling deficiencies in church accommodation. 'For sheer exhaustive honest investigation and methodical exposition, Yates had no rival.'[105] Yates believed that it was essential to keep the tone of society religious - the function of the established church, and particularly of the parochial clergy. Yates's statements were widely quoted, and seriously disputed by none. He saw the answer in terms of the traditional parish: an Act should distribute the population into 'appropriate divisions', supply means of public worship, and provide 'for the useful and efficient discharge of the pastoral offices, in districts not hitherto so provided'. He quoted instances of the difficulties in the way of building churches. He claimed that the societies for educating the poor would prove a menace, and acts for enforcing clergy residence inefficacious, unless more churches were provided in which the poor might be freely accommodated, although some seats might be let to furnish an income for the minister. Finally he proposed that future increases of population might be met by requiring space to be left for a church wherever three or four hundred houses were built. It is clear that he sought a much more radical measure than that passed in 1818, but his ideas were influential. He anticipated possible complaints: already a high poor-rate – the church would contribute to the safety of the rich and the stability of the state; interference with existing institutions – enclosure acts had employed 'compulsatory measures'. He called for the abolition of peculiars and immunities, which might be compensated by the grant of patronage for a new church. The lack of churches was due to the neglect of former legislators: therefore he demanded that at the public cost a sufficient number of small, simple churches, 'within the easy range of the human voice', should be built.

Lord Liverpool, friendly to the Church though he was, seems to have been reluctant to discuss the memorial of December 1815. According to the account

Bowdler gave to a meeting of signatories at the City of London Tavern in May 1817,[106] it was not until the end of the following February that he was able even to ascertain that it had been placed before the Prime Minister, 'and that it formed part of a more extended concern in his Lordship's contemplation'. But nothing further had transpired in the ensuing fifteen months.

That something had been in contemplation, however, perhaps sparked by the letter to Bishop Howley, may be gathered from a confidential letter from Sidmouth, then Home Secretary, to Lord Kenyon, dated 20 November 1815: 'I have now no doubt of Lord Liverpool's determination to submit a proposition to parliament, in the ensuing session, for an augmentation, to be progressively made, of the number of places of worship under the Established Church.'[107] During the autumn Sidmouth had been in correspondence with Christopher Wordsworth about the best means of presenting the matter to the public, a pamphlet being favoured, to be written by Robert Southey, the poet laureate, in preference to Coleridge or William Wordsworth.[108] But the storms that greeted Vansittart's budget proposals of 1816, the resultant abolition of the income tax though there was still a heavy burden of wartime expenditure unpaid, and the consequent diminution in the funds available to government, made any action impossible that year. On 25 June the Commons negatived a motion for free churches to be erected in London as the promised national monuments to the victories of Trafalgar and Waterloo. Vansittart, admitting the lack of churches, stated, 'it was intended to propose some measure next session to remedy the evil'. He disliked 'the idea of appropriating a great number of churches to commemorate our triumphs', and feared that 'the expense would exceed the sum voted'. Prior to the London Tavern meeting, he replied to a parliamentary question, that 'there was no intention on the part of government from the financial difficulties of the country to enter on the consideration of the subject at present'.[109]

Yet the question remained very much in the air.[110] The Dean of Wells, writing to his brother Lord Harrowby, then Lord President of the Council, on 16 November 1816, put a question 'upon the subject of *churches,* which as the Government seem absolutely pledged to bring it forward in the ensuing session, must now I am sure, begin again to occupy your thought'.[111] He was anxious to obtain for Cheltenham a 'real share of the first grant from government', which again implies a series of annual grants on the lines of the current augmentation of Queen Anne's Bounty. And by March 1817 the cabinet was considering the insufficiency of churches. Lord Liverpool replied to a grant-seeking vicar of Sheffield that 'it is in the contemplation of government to submit to Parliament some measures for removing the evil so much felt in most of the populous towns … in respect to the insufficient accommodation for religious worship'.[112] When Vansittart introduced his budget, however, in June, he contemplated a deficit of nearly £16,000,000, and action was again deferred.

Unaware of these inner-circle deliberations, William Davis, in view of Vansittart's earlier reply, had written to John Bowdler, proposing a public meeting to launch a voluntary subscription. If, he suggested, Joseph Cotton were to take the chair, 'it would not only give respectable countenance, but secure in the outset the most liberal subscriptions; for where are we to look for much money but among the opulent and patriotic merchants of London? and where are they to be found but in his society and connection?'[113] Another view was represented by

Christopher Wordsworth, the primate's chaplain, who thought that if government would not act, the friends of the Church should rest silent, because many cries and nothing done begat despair in even the best-disposed. He echoed Harrowby's plea of 1810: 'The only help the Church wants is fair play and more churches; but while dissenters are at liberty, and the Church, by its connection with the state, completely tied up and handcuffed by the very increase of population, things must grow worse', for the animation of religious feeling would benefit the enemies of the Church, whose chapel-building was unimpeded.[114]

Nevertheless, the signatories of the memorial were appealed to, and a meeting held at the City of London Tavern on 23 May 1817, when an account was given of events since 1815.[115] An attempt to delay proceedings until Lord Liverpool had stated his views was defeated. A committee which was appointed to consider the next steps met three days later under Joseph Cotton's chairmanship: it included Bowdler, Kenyon, Davis, Bramwell, Gipps, and a number of Nobody's Friends. They resolved to form a society for 'promoting public worship by obtaining additional church-room for the middle and lower classes'. That this was to be from the High Church standpoint of maintaining the existing order in Church and State, was emphasized by their resolution that: 'No money be advanced … to any parish without the consent of the Ordinary [diocesan bishop], Patron, and Incumbent.' The committee's report was put to a general meeting on 7 June, when it was determined to send a deputation to the Prime Minister to seek his approval. Sir Thomas Dyke Acland[116] was the spokesman of the deputation which, five days later, met Liverpool, who (as they reported on 21 June) approved, subject to the consent of the heads of the Church.[117] The committee was anxious not to interfere with any more comprehensive plan the government might be preparing, but the Prime Minister thought that the proposed society would rather help, and prepare the way for the measures the government had in view, but which the condition of the country had compelled it to defer.

The deputation then waited on the Archbishop of Canterbury, who welcomed such a society as complementing the work of the National Society. He hoped that it would not induce slackness in government, because parliament alone could remedy the magnitude of the evil: an underlining of Christopher Wordsworth's opinion. This hope and fear was in the minds of many, and the promoters endeavoured to make quite clear the limited nature of the functions envisaged. The rules, drawn up by a committee which included Bowdler and Watson,[118] stated that no grant exceeding £500 was normally to be made, nor of a proportion greater than a quarter of the cost. The society itself would not engage in building or extending any church or chapel.[119] These rules received the approval of both Church and State, for Liverpool and the archbishop had particularly requested to be made acquainted with the arrangements of the society before they were finally settled.

Thenceforward the committee met frequently (eight times in July). An address to be circulated with the rules among likely subscribers was prepared by Davis, Watson, and William Cotton. A crisis arose in October, when the Lord Chancellor questioned the legality of such a society, especially fearing that it infringed the rights of patrons and incumbents: the committee replied that the society had no idea of planting churches throughout the country by any authority assumed by itself; but the incident is indicative of the suspicions aroused in legal minds and those of patrons by any attempt to engage in church-building.

8 Charles Manners-Sutton (1755-1828), Archbishop of Canterbury, 1805-28. A key figure in building up the High Church party. Engraving by W. Holl, from a drawing by Thomas Wageman.

During the ensuing months Watson was constantly employed as liaison officer between the committee and Archbishop Manners-Sutton. The arrangements for a great public meeting to launch the society, ultimately held in the Freemasons' Hall on 6 February 1818, were made by the committee, while Watson kept the primate informed, and settled with him what was required from the bishops.[120] In his speech from the Throne, on 27 January 1818, the Regent announced the government's intent to make provision for the building of new churches: this made some doubtful whether the society was necessary. Such waverers were reassured. At the meeting, the Archbishop of Canterbury took the chair, the Duke of Northumberland proposed a motion to form a Church-Building Society, and Lord Kenyon seconded. A committee of thirty-six was then appointed, which included Dr Yates and eight future Church Building Commissioners.[121] The list of vice-presidents included, in addition to the bishops, Lords Kenyon, Radstock, and Grenville, and the Speaker. The ultimate triumph of the Phalanx came about a month later, when the House of Commons went into committee on the government's bill to grant a million pounds sterling for building new churches. An improvement in the revenue afforded the opportunity to present this long-maturing measure, details of which had been agreed between the Prime Minister and the primate early in March, though evidently not altogether to the latter's satisfaction. But Liverpool was determined to proceed, even though the Bill was imperfect.[122] On 16 March 1818 Vansittart moved in the Commons for a committee on the proposal in the Speech from the Throne relating to new churches;[123] and Liverpool himself moved the resultant bill's second reading in the Lords on 15 May.[124]

The Times described the just-published returns[125] on which the bill was based as 'so voluminous as hardly to admit even of a comprehensive abstract'.[126] Parishes with a population over 2,000 and church-room for fewer than half, totalled 4,659,786 inhabitants, and church room for only 929,221; while of those with a population more than 4,000 and church room for less than a quarter, the totals were 2,947,698 and 419,193. The population statistics were of course derived from the 1811 census. Clearly there was a formidable need; 'But in building new places of worship', the paper warned, 'we must not shut our eyes to the glaring fact, that there is, and always will be, a considerable number of dissenters for whom no Church-room need be provided; and farther - painful as the truth may be, we still must not conceal it - that there are, and likewise always will be, a vast body of absentees.' This pointed to a weakness in the Establishment's argument that room must be provided in the national church for all who might wish to attend: a refusal to recognize that there was a considerable population wholly alienated from religious observance of any kind. *The Times* suggested that it should have been ascertained how many did habitually attend the churches that existed, compared with their capacity.

★★★★★

In matters of Church and Charity between 1810 and 1818 it was generally the same men who came forth as leaders; and in the matters more specifically Church – of which the building of new churches was the most important – it was laymen[127] who originated, who showed the way, who stirred up timid clerics and economy-minded statesmen. This fact is significant in showing not that the Church was necessarily moribund spiritually, but that it was so separated from the bulk of the nation that its natural leaders, the bishops, dared claim nothing. As Lord Harrowby remarked: 'Though I meet with some encouragement and general professions, there is no person who will really put his hand to the plow. … no man in lawn sleeves dares to act for himself, and when they talk over such subjects together, there is so much timidity and so much jealousy, that it always ends in giving way to trifling objections, and in contenting themselves with the old mumpsimus, which they hope will last out their time.'[128] Many of the bishops had been appointed for political reasons. By 1815 it was less political than ecclesiastical views which were influencing elevations to the Bench;[129] but the men already there represented a fashion and a generation that were passing; and fearful of stirring up the envy of reformers and radicals, they chose to keep the Church in the very background of the nation's life - it is noteworthy that Lord Liverpool did not think that they ought to dominate the Commission. But events had brought a spiritual re-awakening in the nation; and demanded an extension of Church activity. Consequently the great Christian movements of the time received their impetus from either the Evangelical clergy, or from the laity. In the movements under consideration, the leaders were laymen and mostly members of the old High Church party. Such men had a deep regard for the established order in Church and State; desired to act only with the sanction of the bishops, and to work through the episcopate. So it was that the bishops came to play a larger part in church extension than they deserved, or perhaps expected. So it was that the Church of England was able to resume its historic role as the national Church.

The setting up of the Church Building Commission was the climax of the work on which these men had been engaged since 1811: the foundation of the National Society was duly complemented seven years afterwards by the creation of the two great bodies for church-building; and both movements originated from the pressure exerted largely by the same little group of churchmen. From all their pronouncements it is clear that they regarded the events of 1818 as the necessary sequel to those of 1811 – a sequel essential if the benefit of the work started then was not to be lost.

Of all the laymen, Joshua Watson was ever the most active. Although little in the public eye, his influence with the primate and the Bishop of London was great, and his stature was increased by his long apprenticeship in Church business, in which he had shown himself so capable and painstaking an administrator. It was obviously this man and his collaborators on whom the archbishop would call to administer any parliamentary grant for church-building – a grant he would have played a not inconsiderable part in obtaining. Of the thirty-four members of the first Commission, ten had been closely associated with Watson in his earlier work. When one discounts the provincial clergy and the cabinet ministers or heads of government departments, who would be unlikely to attend frequently at meetings, Watson and his friends form the great majority of those who might be expected to compose the executive nucleus – eleven out of seventeen. Watson was for more than thirty years one of a half-dozen who sat on almost every committee of the Commission, standing or occasional; he devised the form in which the Surveyor reported on tenders and specifications; in 1822 he refers to taking all the tenders from the Office to total up the amounts; he viewed potential sites; he was in correspondence with parish clergy, fellow Commissioners and architects; in close touch with the progress of bills in the Commons; and confidentially discussing a defalcating employee with the Secretary: he was veritably a linchpin of the Commission.[130]

Watson and his associates, then, were the prime movers, many of whom assisted in the continuing work of church-building. The membership of the Commission that was set up to administer the church-building grant was essentially arranged between the primate and the Prime Minister at a meeting at the latter's residence, Fife House, about the beginning of June, 1818, when it was decided that of the bishops, only those whose dioceses were most in need of additional accommodation should be members. But after looking at the eighteenth-century commissions for fifty new churches,[131] Manners-Sutton concluded that more bishops were necessary, and urged that all should be included: after all, they would cost nothing; and though 'the great demand for additional Churches will be confined to a few Dioceses … some want of them, will be found in most.'[132] In a private note, the premier responded wearily that the matter had already been settled, as he had supposed; that it was too late in the session to change things; and that 'the addition of the whole Bench of Bishops together with all the other Ecclesiastics included in the Commission wd give such a decided & large preponderance in point of numbers to the Clerical parts of the Commission, as I shd think by no means expedient.'[133] As well as Watson's immediate associates in the Commission, there were also the politicians and the senior clergy: it was particularly those clergy who had been associated with the Hackney Phalanx in the years since 1810 who, still working with its lay members, were among the 'efficient' Commissioners. Let us then look at the most important members who have not yet been considered.

First in significance we may put William Howley (1766-1848), Bishop of London since 1813,[134] who was closely associated with the Watsons and Norris. A well-informed classical scholar from a country parsonage, but sometime tutor to the Prince of Orange at Oxford, and later Regius Professor of Theology there, he was reserved, conservative, typical of his peers in being unwilling to give a lead. In 1828 he succeeded Manners-Sutton at Canterbury, keeping princely state at Lambeth, escorted in his journeyings by outriders and accompanied by flambeaux-bearers across the palace courtyards. He was too much a man of the *ancien régime* to be the right primate in difficult times, though the clergy were said to have been devoted to him, and he could carry conservatives with him when he supported ecclesiastical reforms.[135] In his first episcopal sermon in the Chapel Royal, however, he had 'urged the necessity of building more churches'; and in his 1818 Charge to his clergy commented on the inadequacy of the new Act in the face not only of a great increase in population in general, but also the transfer of masses to areas ill-provided with churches.[136] Yet Howley's mildness of manner, deliberation of judgment, and notorious inability to express his thoughts orally, masked a resolution that surprised ministers when they later came to embark on major reform of the Church.[137] He was closely concerned in the consideration of the 1818 Bill, which he discussed with several of his clergy,[138] and his surviving

9 William Howley (1766-1848), Bishop of London, 1813-28; Archbishop of Canterbury, 1828-48. A poor speaker who was surprisingly resolute in defending and strengthening the Church. Drawn by W. H. Brooke.

papers include detailed notes on the problems related to the measure, as well as communications from fellow-bishops.[139] As a Commissioner he was constant in attendance, heading committees on drafting legislation, compiling annual reports, and accounts.[140] Rank, relative youthfulness, and location made him a significant figure at the outset of the Commission, though he lacked the passionate conviction of a real reformer.[141]

Charles Manners-Sutton (1755-1828), Archbishop of Canterbury since 1805 (pl. 8), of ducal race, was significant rather for his social and moral influence than for any specific acts of his own, though his role in determining with the Prime Minister the membership of the Church Building Commission was important. It is also noticeable how many of the junior clergy who played a major role in the Commission's work were his protégés. As Harrowby had remarked, the episcopal bench of the day was characterized by timidity,[142] and Manners-Sutton was a clerical statesman whose nature was to temporize rather than stand up to fight for the Church of which he was the chief bishop. Aristocratic, like many of his colleagues,[143] he disliked rabble-rousing and enthusiasm. He owed the primacy to the personal favour of George III, and was highly respected for the sanctity of his life. But he demanded the respect due to his exalted station, and had a horror of becoming a parliamentary accountant. It was this that made Watson so important to those public causes to which the Archbishop was persuaded to lend his name and influence and assist with his advice.

Edward Venables Vernon (1757-1847), Archbishop of York, was a man similar both in origins[144] and life to his brother-primate. He was a good diocesan who took a close interest in the condition of his vast see, and 'regularly spent more than his total income on diocesan improvements';[145] the Commissioners usually awaited his opinion before deciding matters of any importance relating to the diocese. Although he had already entered his seventh decade, he was alert to the needs of his vast diocese and always ready to consecrate a new church and preach the sermon - and give his views on the edifice.

A more yet elderly diocesan, the Hon. James Cornwallis (1742-1824), who had become Bishop of Lichfield and Coventry in 1781, had owed his rapid rise in the Church to his uncle, Frederick, Archbishop of Canterbury from 1768 to 1783. In 1823 he succeeded his nephew as fourth Earl Cornwallis. Soloway's view of Cornwallis as the type of the obstructive older prelate is a misconception: a fuller study of archival material reveals him as anxious to promote church extension. Despite problems with local vested interests in the townships of Stoke-on-Trent, he urged the Board that 'it would be most inexpedient to abandon the plan of building at Fenton as well as Shelton' - though calling for 'a plain church ... Waste of money upon ornament will be quite absurd in such a district'.[146] When invited to become a foundation member of the Commission, he replied to the primate that 'My Diocese is so populous and so much an object for consideration upon this occasion, That I should think myself very blameable, were I to decline to contribute all the assistance, which my great age may enable me to afford, for the furtherance of so excellent a purpose.'[147] He responded rapidly to the call to appoint district boards to examine the church-room needs of his diocese, and he recommended several other church-building proposals, though tending to oppose the division of parishes, with all the consequent complications.[148]

His immediate contemporary, the Bishop of Winchester, Brownlow North

(1741-1820), had notoriously used his position to aggrandize his family, granting his children long leases of the episcopal estates at nominal rents, as well as continuing the tradition of nepotism in which he had been raised,[149] by preferring his sons and grandson to dignities in his presentation. In 1818, aged 77, he expressed a desire to 'be useful on the Church Building Act', but admitted the physical impossibility: 'I am almost wholly blind, and as to business quite so. My deafness is considerably increased and my inability to write continues.'[150] His presence at the Board would only prove an impediment. This was one of the difficulties the Commission and the Church had to contend with in an age when episcopal resignation was unknown and suffragan bishops had passed almost out of memory.

The other two episcopal Commissioners were also beneficiaries of nepotism. The Bishop of Lincoln, George Pretyman Tomline (1750-1827), soon to succeed North at Winchester, had been tutor and later secretary to the younger Pitt, who had failed to place him at Canterbury in 1805. The moderate income of his see was augmented in 1816 by the Deanery of St Paul's. Back in 1800 he had approved the publication of a report by some of his clergy on the state of the Church in 79 Lincolnshire parishes, showing that only about one-sixth of the adult population were communicants.[151] George Henry Law (1761-1845), F.R.S. and F.S.A., son of a former Bishop of Carlisle and a nephew of Lord Chief Justice Ellenborough, ruled as Bishop of Chester over one of the largest dioceses; with relatively few parishes, many of which were exposed to the full blast of industrialization. Keenly interested in church-extension, Law was one of the most active bishops. Apparently the first Commissioner to inquire into the problem of the design of the new churches,[152] he was the patron of Thomas Rickman, just stretching his wings as a church architect. In 1824 Law was translated to Bath and Wells, where there was less scope for his building interests, but he continued active on the Commission.

The bishops were supported by a number of parochial clergy;[153] several, appointed to supervise matters locally, were nominated by their diocesans. Four were incumbents in the provinces, the most celebrated being Thomas Dunham Whitaker (1759-1821), Vicar of Whalley and Blackburn, local historian and antiquary, who had been at St John's, Cambridge, with Archdeacon Pott. The Bishop of Chester thought him the best qualified of his clergy to assist in the work, but his death prevented his contributing much to the Commission. The other provincial clergy – John Eyre (1758-1830), Archdeacon of Nottingham, John Headlam (c.1768-1853), Archdeacon of Richmond, Yorkshire, and Edmund Outram (1765-1821), Archdeacon of Derby – rarely attended the Board, despatching reports on their districts, and service on local committees.[154]

Another six clergymen, drawn from the London region, include some of the most important Commissioners. John Ireland (1761-1842), Dean of Westminster, was the most distinguished, but only attended about a quarter of the meetings up to 1825. He served intermittently on the Building Committee, but resigned as he was unable to attend the meetings.[155] More significant was Richard Mant (1776-1848), rector of the crowded London parish of St Botolph Bishopsgate, and a domestic chaplain to the primate, who had collaborated with Rev. George D'Oyly (rector of Lambeth, and himself a Commissioner from 1825) to produce the Annotated Bible of 1814, for which Watson and Cambridge had selected the plates, a work designed to reach the masses. Mant attended the crucial meeting of the Commissioners at Lambeth on 28 July 1818 to consider how to proceed, and with Watson and Wollaston formed the decisive committee to prepare an abstract of the Act and draw up the draft Order in Council and rules of the Commission. Such intimate involvement was arrested by his elevation to the Irish bishopric of Killaloe in April 1820. He nevertheless remained a Commissioner, attending occasionally, and he did much work for church extension in Ireland. Translated to Down and Connor in 1823, he promoted a diocesan Church Accommodation Society, and as an amateur of church architecture accepted a vice-presidency of the Cambridge Camden Society,[156] publishing a pamphlet in 1843, *Church Architecture Considered*. A minor poet who had grown up with the Romantic movement, Mant may have had leanings to the Gothic style from his early days.

Francis John Hyde Wollaston (1762-1823), Canon of St Paul's and Archdeacon of Essex, rich son of a well-known city clergyman of scientific interests, and brother of an eminent physician and scientist, had enjoyed a brilliant career at Cambridge. Senior wrangler in 1783, he had become successively Taylorian lecturer in mathematics, and Jacksonian professor from 1792 to 1813, lecturing mostly on chemistry. Wollaston was consulted on the bill as it left the Commons, and wrote to the Bishop of London about a number of defects.[157] As a Commissioner he appears purposeful and a 'man of taste', accompanying Watson to view sites, serving on the committee of July 1818, the regulations committee, and several others, including those to consider the inadequacies of the Act (16 February 1819) and to prepare the third annual report (9 July 1822). Above all, he was a stalwart of the Building Committee. His correspondence reveals his anxiety to instil method into the Commissioners' dealings, and to work on some sort of national plan; perhaps the result of his scientific training. But his views appear to have been set aside some time before his death in mid-1823.

Joseph Holden Pott (1759-1847), from 1813 Archdeacon of London, had close experience of populous parishes as rector of St Martin-in-the-Fields (1812-24) and vicar of Kensington (1824-42). He had long been associated with Watson and his friends in the great Church societies.[158] He frequently served on sub-committees on specific issues, being constant in his attendance at meetings of the Board, – present at four-fifths those up to 1825 – as was his close contemporary George Owen Cambridge (1756-1841). Son of the wit and poet Richard Owen Cambridge, he had been Archdeacon of Middlesex since 1806, and proved a key member of the Commission. Along with Wollaston a pillar of the Building Committee, he also helped prepare the annual report, usually in company with Pott: both were appointed to the standing committee established in 1825 to consider pew-rent schedules, the division of parishes, and similar important matters. A Nobody's Friend, Cambridge was joint-Treasurer of the S.P.C.K. with Watson, to whom he had written while the composition of the Commission was yet uncertain: 'My main hope is that I shall find myself by your side, and then I shall know how to act.'[159]

Last of these clergymen was scholarly Christopher Wordsworth (1774-1846), domestic chaplain to the primate since 1805, and Rector of Lambeth 1816-20, when, appointed Master of Trinity College, Cambridge, he exchanged livings with George D'Oyly (1778-1846). Thenceforwards he was less frequently in London, but continued an extensive high-level correspondence upon church-building matters. 'A High Churchman of the old school',[160] he had early been one of Watson's closest associates; and had enjoyed the primate's friendship since he had been tutor to his son, Charles Manners-Sutton (1780-1845), who in 1817 was elected Speaker (and as such became a Commissioner).

The remaining members of the Commission were laymen. Of the members of the Cabinet, the two most important were Nicholas Vansittart (1766-1851), Chancellor of the Exchequer (noted for the complexity of his budgets) until 1823, when he exchanged that for the Duchy of Lancaster and was created Lord Bexley; a keen supporter of Church and religious societies, he was one of the most dutiful Commissioners. 'However inferior in talents Vansittart is, I really believe, a churchman in the *vital* sense of the word' commented the Rev. Henry Ryder to his brother, Lord Harrowby, when Vansittart became Chancellor after Perceval's assassination.[161] Harrowby himself (1762-1847) was probably almost as significant a figure as Liverpool in achieving the Million grant. Lord President of the Council from 1812 to 1827, he had laboured mightily on Curates' Bills to improve their lot, and continued a strong advocate of the Commission's claims in the Cabinet,[162] though attending only occasional Board meetings. Another departmental head was the Surveyor-General, Lt-Col. Benjamin Charles Stephenson (d. 1839), a military engineer who brought technical knowledge to the aid of the Building Committee, which he attended regularly, and ensured the maintenance of amicable relations with Office of Works, which from the outset contributed vital advice. Present at nearly all the Board's meetings up to the end of 1827, thereafter he only occasionally attended, ceasing to be a member when the Office of Works was abolished in 1832. The second Lord Kenyon, younger, but surviving, son of the late Lord Chief Justice, was himself a barrister; years before, the painter Lawrence had found him 'a sensible young man'.[163] A leading member of the St Marylebone Vestry, he had territorial connexions with Chester diocese, and was one of the five key figures in the Commission's Building Committee.

Others who were able to contribute specialized advice were lawyers, essential since the Commission's work so often involved questions of law. Sir John Nicholl (1759-1838) and Sir William Scott (1745-1836) divided between them most high positions in the ecclesiastical courts. Scott (created Lord Stowell 1821), Lord Chancellor Eldon's brother, 'a two-bottle man', who nonetheless delivered luminous judgments, was notoriously conservative: he had wrecked attempts at tithe reform, and led the opposition to a patronage clause in the committee stage of the 1818 Act. His feeble Clergy Residence Act of 1803 he had considered a mere interim measure until clergy incomes could be improved and houses provided where necessary, but it did institute annual returns of non-residence.[164] His sight and voice alike failed in the early 1820s.[165] Francis Burton, K.C. (1744-1832), an old friend of Watson's, had been second justice of Cheshire until 1817, and earlier, Recorder of Oxford, which city he had represented in Parliament from 1790 to 1812. He, too, had long sought church reform, in 1802 introducing a bill to enlist private charity for church maintenance,[166] and supported a number of clergy residence measures.[167] Although of advanced age, and blind, he devoted much attention to the Commission's affairs, and attended its meetings regularly until 1825.

2

The First Church Building Act

At the beginning of 1818, in his speech from the Throne, the Prince Regent had referred to the need for providing new churches. On 16 March the Commons went into committee on the government's proposals to this end. The Whig opposition, weak and divided, did not make any trouble; on the contrary, their leader in the Commons, George Tierney, anticipated Vansittart's proposals by himself giving notice of a motion for applying the grant voted for erecting a victory monument to the building of churches. Ultimately it was some of the Tories who divided the House to force government to withdraw an unpalatable clause. When the bill went to the Lords, Liverpool commented that 'no individual had yet opposed this grant'.[1]

The Chancellor of the Exchequer in moving for a committee on the Regent's statement,[2] seized on Tierney's proposal, to stress that an economical arrangement for building new churches was a very different concept from that of erecting monumental churches on a great scale of ornamental architecture. He pointed out that there had been a shortage of church-room in some places for more than a century; in London fifty new churches had been called for in Queen Anne's time, when the population was only half as numerous. He blamed the delay in acting on continual wars. Even so, government had made grants to augment stipends and so to obtain a resident and respectable ministry; yet these could not supply the deficiency in places of worship. Accounts of the state of parishes laid before the House showed how the situation varied in different parts of the country. Of parishes with a population exceeding 2,000, without church-room for half the inhabitants, there were in London diocese eighty, with an average population of 11,629. In Winchester and Chester dioceses the average parochial population was 8,000; in Oxford only 2,422. Vansittart called attention to the statistics in Yates's pamphlet, *The Church in Danger*, though admitting that it placed the deficiencies in the strongest light. He suggested it would suffice if church-room were provided for a third of the population, as three services could be held in the new churches on Sundays and the more important festivals. It was not only that the people could not worship; the clergy were unable to discharge many of their sacred functions to such huge numbers of parishioners, and frauds relating to civil rights were easily perpetrated (ill-kept

Opposite:
10 St Anne, Limehouse, (N. Hawksmoor, 1714-30), west front. One of the Queen Anne churches criticized in the debates of 1818 for their unnecessary extravagance.

registers were to play a vital role in several Victorian novels). As it was important that, 'in a great public improvement, there should be the least possible interference with private rights', parishes would be divided for ecclesiastical purposes only, and only with the patron's consent. Where there were difficulties, ecclesiastical districts, or chapels of ease, might sometimes be preferable to a complete division. Ministers obviously realized that questions of patronage might form a serious obstacle to new churches.

Vansittart proposed that instead of annual grants of uncertain extent (as currently provided for Queen Anne's Bounty since 1811), a round sum should be given to Commissioners; as had been done for the encouragement of public works in 1817.[3] He thought that 'the public bounty ought only to be given in aid of a fair exertion on the part of the district'; the Commissioners would 'assist rather than ... support the whole charge. ... The greatest exertion of parochial funds and of private liberality, co-operating with the munificence of parliament would be necessary to attain the object.' Nor would the grant be sufficient to aid parishes of fewer than (probably) 10,000 inhabitants. The Church-Building Society would help where the Commission could not. Although, as in proprietary chapels, provision would be made for a minister out of pew-rents, there would be much free seating for the poor. The Church 'which existed for the benefit of all, and derived support from all, was bound to afford accommodation for all'.

In the debate that followed, the idea was again canvassed of a church as a monument for Waterloo, as earlier suggested by Tierney. Sir Charles Monck, a moderate Whig, thought that some of the endowments of the Church should be applied to church-extension (which was also to be Lord Holland's cry in the Lords); and worship should be performed more often in a day; the morality of a town did not depend on its number of churches. Rather than a national fund, he favoured local commissioners for each city, applying to parliament for what funds they could not raise. The ecclesiastical lawyer Joseph Phillimore[4] laid stress on the importance of dividing parishes. *The Times*, remarking that it was not possible to report fully the details of the debate, highlighted an issue raised by ministerialist J. W. Croker, the unhealthy effects of burials within churches, and the need for new burial grounds removed from the city, as in Paris.[5]

The bill received close scrutiny, being considered in committee on 6, 28 and 30 April, and 4 and 6 May. Although it had been amended on the last two occasions, it was again amended on third reading (7–8 May), and then yet again extensively in the Upper House.[6] At one point,[7] the chancellor, in defining the objects of the bill, put first the power of dividing parishes. One of the most important amendments during the committee stage came from Sir William Scott, the principal ecclesiastical judge, who objected, 'and with much earnestness',[8] to a clause enabling 'twelve well-disposed persons to build a church and appoint a minister' with the bishop's consent, because it would infringe on patrons' rights and introduce 'dogmatical sectaries' (i.e. men favourable to the dissenters) into the parishes. He thought the clause would arouse such opposition in the Upper House as would endanger the whole bill. (He also thought that 'It was unworthy, too, in the Church, to depend on private funds for its increase or support.')[9] Vansittart defended the clause as encouraging private liberality, but there was a general hostility expressed, especially to subscribers from outside the parish, an evident fear of some wealthy organization's acquiring patronage, as the evangelical Simeon Trust was doing.[10] Even Vansittart's colleague, Robert Peel, who had been got at by a nervous High Church divine,[11] agreed with Scott, and thought that such a clause should go in a separate bill,[12] Castlereagh and

Phillimore alone supporting the chancellor in their speeches. The clause was rejected by 47 votes to 22. This shows how vital it was for the measure to avoid interfering with perceived property rights.

Memoranda and letters in the surviving papers of Bishop Howley suggest that he had a leading role to play in taking the bill through the Lords. Already, as soon as the bill was published, he had circulated it to some of his clergy.[13] The Bishop of Durham, Barrington, an early supporter of church extension, was concerned that in allotting grants the comparative wealth of parishes should be considered, as well as how much they were prepared to subscribe, and he referred to the complexity of the tithe problem in dividing parishes.[14] He was also concerned about the lack of precise provision for the patronage of new rectories, which, he suggested, might be sold to raise an endowment; and wished the alteration of pew rent schedules to be reserved to the bishop rather than left to the churchwardens.[15] The Bishop of Hereford wanted clarification about the number of services to be provided, and whether marriages might be celebrated in chapels of ease, as well as who was to receive offerings.[16] Other notes criticize the clause allowing the Commissioners to divide parishes 'after consulting with the Bishop', which implied that they could act without the bishop's specific consent; and complain that a reference to 'owners of pews' was 'to introduce an Evil similar to that which is so sorely felt ... in the old Churches, with respect to *permanent property* in pews'.[17]

In the Lords, the prime minister in moving the second reading on 15 May 1818 called the bill 'the most important measure he had ever submitted to their Lordships' consideration'.[18] He had intended to bring it forward long before, but the need for mature deliberation, and the circumstances of the country had alike delayed it. The basic purpose 'was to remove dissent'. Therefore church-room must be provided for one in three or one in four of the population. The specific objects were to grant a million pounds; authorize subscriptions in aid of the grant; and appoint Commissioners to execute the Act. The Million would build a hundred churches,[19] but with the aid of subscriptions he expected a hundred and fifty or two hundred would be built. The great extension of manufacturing towns had exposed their inhabitants to vicious habits and corrupting influences dangerous to public security as well as to private morality. The success of the movement for educating the poor was an additional inducement to provide means for directing that education into a proper course. The dissenters could build without limit: the Establishment had to regard the rights of property and the discipline of the Church. The new Act would put the Church on an equal footing with dissenters. Recalling the experience of the Queen Anne Commission, he pointed out

11 Robert Banks Jenkinson, 2nd Earl of Liverpool (1770-1828). As Prime Minister, 1812-27, he sought to strengthen the Church of England for both religious and secular reasons. Contemporary engraving after a portrait by Sir Thomas Lawrence, P.R.A.

that it would be some years before the Commission could be in full beneficial operation.

Lord Holland, a leading Whig of sceptical disposition, criticized the measure, arguing that a church so rich in endowments as the Church of England should contribute to its own increase; but Lord Harrowby, whose concern for church extension has been referred to above, retorted that the measure was for the advantage, not of the clergy, but of religion in general and the community at large; and emphasized the importance of affording 'a useful channel to the blessings of education'. This was a measure that 'concerned all ages and the interests of immortality', and had been under consideration by the late prime minister (Perceval), who, according to the Archbishop of Canterbury, had been about to 'take some active step' when he was assassinated. The archbishop also controverted criticisms: it was difficult and confusing to multiply services; and Holland's idea of suspending cathedral dignities to appropriate their income would be slow and inefficient.

Nevertheless, Holland persisted with his idea of sequestrating cathedral dignities, referring to a precedent at Lichfield in 1792, so bringing down on his head the ridicule of Lord Grenville, as well as of Liverpool and Canterbury: too local, too slow, and – on any large scale – harmful. One point on which their lordships were all agreed was in deprecating what Lord Grenville called 'useless splendour'. But they were not so clear what was to be understood by this. Lord Liverpool required 'that decent decoration which would mark character of the established Church', but did not want churches like those of the Queen Anne Commission. Lord Holland insisted on the literal meaning of the clause; but Lord Harrowby could never agree that this meant 'merely to erect four walls like a barn'. The Archbishop of Canterbury also interpreted it as implying some ornament; 'even the humble spire of a village church indicated the purposes to which it was dedicated'. One object of the Bill would be lost if the churches which were built 'might be mistaken for places devoted to another use'. He defended, too, the Queen Anne churches, which had been designed as lasting ornaments of their cities; and recommended 'an adherence to that mode of building which characterized the reformed church of England from churches where that reform was carried too far'.[20]

Lord Liverpool was anxious to 'press the matter forwards as rapidly as we can, consistent with decency and the forms of parliament'.[21] He would, he confessed, 'rather even pass the measure with some imperfections than delay it', as none knew when another favourable opportunity might arise, and it would be easy to amend what was difficult to originate. So it is not surprising that the first Church-Building Act[22] was not a very satisfactory piece of legislation. It had to be amended within the year by a further statute[23] of 41 clauses, which itself did not long suffice, although the draft received the benefit of a 'great many marginal notes' by Lord Grenville.

The preamble of the 1818 Act referred to the need to provide free church accommodation for the poor; and its first clause set aside one million pounds in Exchequer bills bearing two per cent interest, which could be drawn upon by Commissioners whom the King was empowered to appoint for executing the Act. The Commission was to continue in force for a maximum period of ten years (s.8). Thus the approach was different from that of the earlier attempt begun under Queen Anne.[24] Instead of having a certain number of churches to build, for which purpose the proceeds of a specific tax were appropriated, the new Commissioners were given a fixed sum of money to be expended as economically as possible within a certain period. The earlier Commission was criticized as extravagant during the debates on the Bill, and it was doubtless thought that the new method would be simpler, speedier, more economical, and more efficacious.

The rest of the Act was devoted to defining the powers and duties of the Commissioners. They were to examine the state of parishes (s.9), to draw up rules for their proceedings and to fix the largest amount to be spent on any one church (s. 12). They might make grants or pay the total cost of new churches, or make loans for this purpose, but this power was restricted to parishes with a population exceeding 1,000 in which there was not church-room for one-fourth; or in which more than 4,000 lived more than four miles from the nearest church (s.13). Part of the expense might be raised by subscription; and the Commissioners were directed in their selection of parishes to favour those furnishing the greatest proportion of self-help; while parishes offering nothing, but of similarly disproportionate accommodation, were to be favoured in the order in which they offered sites (s.15).

The Commissioners were to build on the plans they considered most suitable for providing 'a proper accommodation for the largest number of persons at the least expense' (s.62). It is unfair to blame the Commissioners for the stark appearance of their churches: they had a statutory duty to build as cheaply as possible. It was consequently obligatory upon them to call on architects for designs with the least possible degree of ornament. This insistence upon 'functional' architecture accounts for some of the hostility the churches of the Million era were, within twenty years, to arouse. Yet compared with those built in the cheap church phase which started in the late 1820s, these were elegant and handsome. The Commissioners did not at first discover how cheaply it was possible to build a church.

Within the churches, part of the seating was to be enclosed and rented, part to be for ever open and free (s.62). Thus all classes were to be brought together in worship. Provision for endowing the churches was not omitted: the Commissioners were to establish a scale of pew-rents; from the income a stipend was to be provided for the minister and clerk (s.63) – a power which was to keep the parliamentary grant in existence long after the expiry of the Commission.[25] The lack of a secure provision for ministers was, however, a major defect in the legislation. An annual account was to be laid before parliament showing the progress made (s.81).

Harriet Martineau complained that churches came of religion, not religion of churches: but provision for an improved pastoral care was not omitted. The Commissioners, with the bishop's consent, might divide parishes into either ecclesiastical districts (s.21), or separate ecclesiastical parishes – the consent of the patron then being necessary (s.16). If the accommodation were still inadequate, an afternoon service might be ordered by the bishop, and pews let to provide a stipend for a curate to take it. Patronage of the new districts was normally to belong to the patron of the parish church (s.67). But if a church were built by parish rate (s.68), or left as a simple chapel-of-ease, then the incumbent of the mother church was to have the nomination. This was to be augmented by the Act of 1819, which enabled ecclesiastical districts to be assigned to chapels-of-ease, the right of nomination then remaining in the incumbent (c.134, s.16). Ecclesiastical patronage was regarded as an important class of property, and, as we have seen, the issue was one of the major obstacles to the building of new churches. It was to be a source of difficulty in many of the Church Building Acts, and some proposals in the first Bill had, as mentioned above, aroused hostility. Similarly the incumbent's right to fees for various offices of the Church performed in his parish – particularly marriage and burial – created a problem, the more difficult in that some of the largest parishes were not richly endowed.[26] The Commissioners were therefore given a discretionary power to decide what offices should be performed in the new churches and how the fees should be allotted, care being taken to protect the interests of the then incumbent

12 Dudley Ryder, 1st Earl of Harrowby (1762-1847). A leading politician who strenuously advocated the claims of the Church of England to state aid. Engraving by H. B. Hall from portrait by Mme Meunier.

(ss.24, 27-30). But the new ecclesiastical divisions were not to affect the civil parishes (s.31).

Another vexed question to come pressingly to the fore in succeeding years was that of church-rates.[27] The Act provided for the repair of district churches by a rate levied within the district (s.70); while the districts were also to remain liable to rates for the parish church repairs for twenty years (s.71). No specific provision was made for a fund for the maintenance of the service of the church, the common-law provision doubtless being considered adequate. Thus where the churchwardens were hostile to a new church, it was difficult to obtain payment of the necessary running expenses, and the omission encouraged discord. Rates for the purposes of the Act, or for providing additional church-room by enlargement, were specifically authorized, subject to the consent of a majority of the ratepayers, or select vestry and landowners (ss.56-61).

The Commissioners might accept buildings suitable for conversion, or lands sufficient in any one place for a church and burial ground, and also up to ten acres for a parsonage house and garden (s.33). Bodies politic and the Crown might grant or sell such sites (ss.34, 36). It is perhaps rather surprising to find that the Commissioners were given power to compel parishes either to purchase sites, or to raise the cost (ss.35, 55). If the price of a site could not be settled between the parties, they might have to resort to arbitration by a jury, whose decision should be binding (ss.39, 40). Another unusual power granted to the Commission was that a proper conveyance to it should be a bar to all entails and other rights (s.37); and other special facilities for purchasing sites, including a power of compulsory purchase (except for certain specified classes of land, s.53), were granted (ss.38, 43, 47, 50). The Commission might use these compulsory powers to assist parishes not needing financial aid, but unable to procure sites (s.52). A different kind of privilege was that of free postage.

The parliamentary weakness of the Whigs would have prevented their effectually opposing the Bill, but many of them were in fact as strong supporters of the Establishment as the ministerialists.[28] The expectation that an extension of church influence would promote greater docility and orderly habits among the lower orders was not lost sight of on either side.

Outside parliament, comment was perhaps more strong. *The Times,* after reviewing the publication of the official statistics on church-room, and commenting on the considerable part of the population who would never wish to enter a church,[29] announced that it had received letters about the proposals, but for a variety of reasons it would probably not publish them. Two that it did publish urged the desirability of repairing and enlarging existing churches.[30] The Tory *Quarterly Review* supported the measure: 'The edifices which we have erected are manufactories and prisons, the former producing tenants for the latter … the sure and only way of making the people good subjects is by making them good Christians and good men'. From the high vantage-point of its anonymous review it dealt out impartially praise and criticism to the government: 'Although the grant of the late parliament is far from being adequate to the whole exigencies of the case, no measure of equal magnitude has ever yet been deliberately taken by any government for the interest of religion.'[31] Harriet Martineau's remark about the relationship between religion and churches was met by the comment:

> The causes of the insufficiency of the clergy are to be found in the history of the Reformation, in the decay of discipline … or in circumstances arising from the present state of society, which requiring more than any other in which men have hitherto been placed the restraining and healing influences of religion, places them less within its reach. The erection of new churches and the division of parishes is the first step towards a correction of this evil.

The *New Annual Register,* however, was not 'among those who augur good from this Bill'.[32] It did not think that 'the enactments of the legislature can often be of service to real religion',[33] and attacked the granting of so much money for so uncertain a result at a time of such financial embarrassment. The official statistics were disputed: no account had been taken of the room provided in dissenting chapels; if churches had, in fact, been needed, they would have been built by private effort. (It was partly the difficulty of doing such a thing that had made governmental action necessary.) There was 'not less wealth among the members of the established church than among the richest of the dissenters: why then is there less zeal …?' But 'taking the churches throughout the kingdom, they are not nearly filled'. If the legislature had to interfere, it should have enforced the residence of the clergy:[34] it was only through an improved clergy that persons would be attracted to church. A clinching argument was that the Scottish peasantry were superior to the English because the Scottish clergy were 'real shepherds'.

The *Gentleman's Magazine* seemed favourably disposed towards the measure, but its correspondents, taking the preliminary question as settled, immersed themselves in the Battle of Styles. Its columns were also made the terrain for a campaign for a new church or churches as a national memorial to Princess Charlotte, similar to that earlier demand for a memorial of the Napoleonic wars. It was doubtless from such proposals that the popular misnomer, 'Waterloo Churches',[35] became applied to those built with the aid of the first parliamentary grant.

13 Halifax from the south-east in 1822. Lithograph by John Horner.

Halifax parish was the largest in Yorkshire, extending 17 miles east-west by 11 miles north-south, containing 23 townships and chapelries. It illustrates one of the Commissioners' major problems in allocating grants. The town itself, a major centre of manufacture of woollen cloths, with 1,973 houses in 1802 and nearly 9,000 inhabitants. had two churches, the old parish church (seen on the extreme right) and Holy Trinity, built in 1795-8 (in the distance towards the left), while there were 12 chapels in outlying districts. The parish therefore did not qualify for a grant by the 1818 criteria, although the population of Halifax town alone had grown to 12,628 by 1821. It had to wait for the less restrictive (and smaller) Half-Million grants of 1825.

3

The Church Building Commission: The First Steps

Of all the duties and powers entrusted to the Church Building Commissioners by the 1818 Act, the primary and most pressing was to get churches built in the indigent districts. The first necessary step towards this was the apportionment of the parliamentary grant. Vast as the sum then was, at £20,000 a church it would have built only fifty – the number called for in the Metropolis alone a century before. It was clear that by itself the grant would not be sufficient: therefore the circumstances of the various parishes had to be investigated.

The Commission having been embodied on 20 July 1818, it met in the Privy Council chamber in Whitehall on 28 July, when it appointed a secretary, George Jenner (c.1779-1829),[1] at £250 p.a.; instructed him to hire an office, and obtain the parliamentary returns about church room and any other relevant papers from the Privy Council Office. A memorandum among the Bishop of London's papers,[2] endorsed to the effect that it was copied from 'Lord H[arrowby]'s ms', observes that 'The first question to be determined … seems to be this. By what criteria shall you distinguish the parishes which have a claim to the first share?' There were two sets of returns to the Privy Council: list A, of parishes with a population over 2,000, with church room for less than one half; and list B, of parishes over 4,000 lacking church room for more than one quarter.[3] Harrowby suggested that one might take all parishes with a population of more than, say, 20,000 from list B; or from list A all parishes where there were, say, 20,000 persons for whom there was no accommodation: 'A good deal might be said on both sides.' Fortunately, it appeared that there was little practical difference, 32 parishes fulfilling both conditions.[4] A further eight should be included in the prime list.[5] Harrowby then went into detailed calculations to show that, even if the aim were to provide church room for only one-third of the population (rather than half), a far greater number of churches would be needed than could be supplied from the million pounds available: 'the demand is

45

evidently far beyond all the means which can be brought forward', so that any precise computation were useless.

> Enough, however, has been remark'd, to lead to one *practical* conclusion of great importance, the absolute *necessity* of forming the plan of distribution in such a manner as to call forth by every possible inducement the voluntary exertions of parishes and of subscribers. In doing this, there is only one evil, against which it is necessary to guard viz. claims upon the public fund from places where sums may be offered, either by votes or subscription, but where, altho' there may be a want of accommodation which it would be very desirable to remedy, this want does not affect a population so considerable in its numbers, as to entitle it to the *first* place. If they were now admitted, the whole fund destined for the supply of the most urgent wants might be absorbed. The rules to be laid down for admission to preference will therefore require the greatest consideration: and previously to their being formed, it will be necessary to derive from an accurate examination of the Returns (and from farther inquiry, where they appear doubtful) a comprehensive view of the probable practical result of such rules.

That Howley had Harrowby's memorandum copied is significant, and it was along similar lines that the Commission took its first steps. The Privy Council returns, however, were far from satisfactory. The returns of the capacity of places of worship laid before the House of Lords in 1811 and 1812 was so imperfect that the bishops were required to obtain better information. The 1818 returns were based on their information, but further inquiries had been found necessary, 'in order to approach more nearly to accuracy'; deficiencies were supplied from material held by the Privy Council Office, Queen Anne's Bounty and the 1811 census.[6]

The Board immediately appointed a committee[7] to devise a *modus operandi* that met at Lambeth three days later. Archdeacon Pott reported to Joshua Watson: 'I need not say how much we missed you. The Commission committee met at Lambeth as was determined … alas! empty chair for J. W. Very little was done, but the canvassing two sections in the Act which seem a little repugnant; and counsel's opinion was to be taken.'[8] This was to belittle their activity: seizing on the importance of ensuring local interest, they had prepared a notice for the *London Gazette* (subsequently put in other papers) inviting applications; and proposed the appointment of district boards in each diocese to update information about population, church room, and the ability of parishes to contribute,[9] as the several reports on church room and population made between 1810 and 1818 could serve only as a basis. Up-to-date, full, local knowledge was essential. Most of the bishops responded promptly, setting up boards in their dioceses in August and September.[10]

The points referred to the Crown's Law Officers were also of some importance for the Commissioners' calculations: whether the population restrictions (s.13) applied to parishes where 'a certain proportion of the expence was raised by rate or subscription' (s.14); and whether unconsecrated chapels were to be included in computing church room – a significant point, as there were numerous such proprietary chapels. The Law Officers held that the restrictions were binding in all cases, and defined the rather vague 'accommodation' clause (s.13) as excluding unconsecrated chapels.[11] The need for legal advice about the interpretation of the Act illuminated the inadequacies of the measure; it rapidly became clear that further legislation would be necessary.

Such points settled, and an office obtained at no.12 (later, no.13) Great George Street, Westminster,[12] the next problem was how to handle the applications that already by 2 September were flowing in, all of which needed to be referred to the relevant diocesan. Jenner therefore asked the bishops for details of the most urgent cases – taking Harrowby's criterion of those in which the population exceeded church-room by 20,000 or more, though Jenner's computation from the parliamentary returns amounted to the smaller figure of twenty-five.[13] A small committee (Wollaston, Mant, and Watson) was appointed to draw up an abstract of the regulations in the Act, for the guidance of the bishops. To expedite matters, Jenner was to refer applications to the diocesan without waiting for an instruction from the Commissioners.[14] The committee swiftly reported back on 7 September with an abstract of rules, and it was decided to send details of the Act to interested bishops. The Commissioners were meeting three or four times a month: replies about diocesan district boards continued to flow in, as well as applications for new churches.[15] They resolved to print 500 copies of the abstract, and draft an order-in-council to give judicial authority to their proceedings, so avoiding an immediate need for parliamentary legislation. The committee was instructed to draw up forms of application and enquiry; and obscure points about their funds and about incumbents' fees were referred to the Law Officers.[16]

14 St Philip, Hardman Street, Liverpool (Thomas Rickman, 1815-16). The third of Rickman's Liverpool churches built for the iron-master John Cragg. Its iron framework was clad in brick.

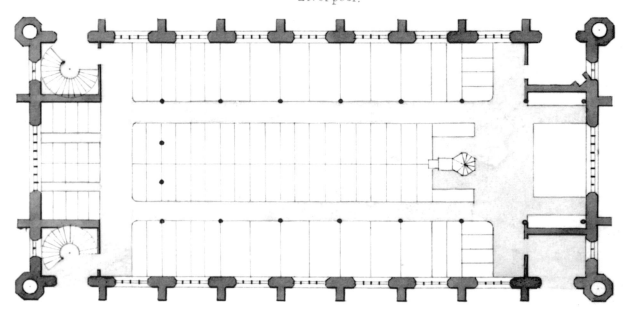

Meanwhile, the Commissioners began to consider the question of the design of the churches they were to pay for. Economy was prescribed by the Act, but at the same time the buildings must be clearly recognizable as those of the Established Church: a tower would be necessary, perhaps even a spire. The Bishop of Chester, G. H. Law, had recommended a protégé of his own, Thomas Rickman, to prepare plans for his own diocese, 'in order that no time might be lost in fixing a plan', and at their third meeting the Commissioners invited Rickman to discuss his designs with the Crown Architects.[17] The Bishop of London, concerned with completing the regulations which the Board as required to make, suggested that the 'most expeditious mode of obtaining from the Crown Architects such information as may enable the Commissioners to determine their maximum of allowance [for each church] … will be a conference between them and a small number of the Commissioners'.[18]

The rules committee reported further on 10 November 1818, when the Commissioners confirmed their lucubrations: a statement of their duties and powers as found in the Act; rules and regulations for their proceedings, arranged under heads, to be embodied in an order-in-council; similarly arranged resolutions which appeared to arise out of the provisions of the Act, or to promise assistance in their execution, but did not need the authority of an order-in-council; a summary statement of regulations, with information for the use of the bishops; and forms of enquiry and petition for the applicant parishes.[19]

The order-in-council[20] provided for regular meetings of the Board, on every Tuesday during the sitting of parliament, and on the second and fourth Tuesdays of each month during the rest of the year. A standing committee of accounts was to be set up,[21] to examine the accounts quarterly and prepare the annual statement to be laid before parliament. The ninth rule specified that the Board should take the census returns and the various reports presented to parliament as the foundations of the enquiry into the state of parishes ordered by the Act. The census of 1811 was recognized as *prima facie* evidence for population; the accommodation in any church or chapel was to be verified by actual admeasurement. Where distance from a church formed the grounds of application, that was to be authenticated by the minister and churchwardens. The Commissioners, in order to decide on any of these points, might obtain information from any source, including bishop, minister, or churchwardens; and should information about the emoluments be required for considering the expediency of dividing a parish, the bishop was to be asked to obtain it.

A crucial decision was how much to allow for building a church. Harrowby in his memorandum had estimated £10,000, and Liverpool, as noted above, had accepted the same figure when introducing the bill in the Lords, doubtless on the basis of estimates from the architects attached to the Office of Works. Their role will be considered in detail in the next chapter; suffice it here to say that the government had addressed this question almost as soon as it committed itself to action, and the 'Attached' or Crown architects had come up with estimates of between £10,000 and £33,000.[22] The Commissioners appointed a committee to obtain from them information to enable them to establish a maximum,[23] the result of which was to adopt a figure of £20,000 with reference 'principally to London, on general view of such cases as are likely to come before the Board', though they recognized that there might be exceptional cases for larger grants.[24] This was accordingly embodied in Rule 10.

Perhaps to reassure those who compared this sum with the higher cost of recent London churches,[25] the next rule stated: 'In every building to be erected under the

Opposite: **15** St Botolph, Boston. The famous tower, made widely known by this plate in Britton's *Architectural Antiquities*, provided a popular model for early nineteenth-century Revival architects.

16 St George, Ramsgate (Henry Hemsley jun. and Henry Edward Kendall, 1824-7) as seen in 1841. A very expensive church (£11.9s. a sitting), in the vein of Boston, to which the Commissioners contributed a grant of £9,000.

authority of this Board, the character be preserved, both externally and internally, of an ecclesiastical edifice for divine worship according to the rites of the united Church of England and Ireland.' The work in any building constructed by authority of the Act, and paid for in any degree by the parliamentary grant, was to be subject to 'such regular inspection of His Majesty's Board of Works on the application of this Board as shall secure the due execution thereof'. Together with certain regulations about accounts and monies, this completed the rules laid down by the order-in-council.[26]

Those rules were extended and interpreted by resolutions of the Board of Commissioners, which incorporated the earlier decision to refer applications in the first instance to the diocesan. The expediency of dividing a parish was to be considered before making any grant or loan, or selecting a site. Loans were to be repaid by an annual rate for a portion of the principal equal to the interest. The greatest economy in construction was to be observed, consistent with maintaining the character of an Anglican church. Where the Commissioners could dispose, they were to provide as many free sittings as the circumstances would permit.[27]

A resolution that influenced the planning of churches directed that in construction and arrangement 'particular regard be had to the ease of the minister in speaking and to the situation of the reading desk and pulpit to the advantage of the congregation in seeing and hearing the officiating minister'. An attempt was made to sustain the old methods of contracting, by a refusal to accept 'general undertakers', and requiring that 'every artificer be separately contracted with to perform the work belonging to his trade'. The implementation of these rules will be discussed below.

Forms of enquiry and petition were to be completed by the parishes applying for aid.[28] When completed both would contain much the same information, but differently presented. The former – to be accompanied by a map - required the name and location of the applicant hamlet (or chapelry, township, etc.), its extent and area; whether there were separate townships in the parish; the population of the parish and its component parts, and divisions for rating assessments; its industries; who was patron, and details of the incumbent's emoluments; location, size and accommodation of existing churches, and likewise of the proposed church; and an extent of financial information about rental value, rates, cost of the proposed church and how much was to be raised by the parish and in what manner.[29] A local committee was to be established to handle matters at the parochial level, and secure subscriptions: their need was early apparent as parishes were riven by proposals for new churches; it was impossible for the Commissioners, or even the bishops, to resolve such strife, and some local organization was essential to fight the case for the Established Church.

Decisions as to sites and architects could prove more acceptable if made by local men; at any rate, the Commission need only intervene when issues had been thoroughly thrashed out.[30] The petition form was the actual application for aid.

There is no record of any discussion of the Bishop of Chester's suggestion of a general plan that could be adopted for all the new churches; such a proposal was hardly likely to stimulate local enthusiasm. At an early date the Board had decided to call on the local committees in applicant parishes to obtain and submit plans, 'with a view to calling forth a general competition, and of bringing forward professional talent in various parts of the country'.[31] Competition was the order of the day: a House of Commons committee had already in 1815 called for competition for designs for all major public buildings, and the full House passed a resolution to that effect in 1819.[32] Competition would, it was believed, bring forth local talent and the best designs, just as competitive tendering would achieve the most economical construction.

Competition, however, proved the tool of the entrepreneurial architect who was prepared to race up, down and across the country in post-chaises on McAdam's and Telford's new roads to interview the key men in local committees and seduce them with delectable coloured sketches of highly ornate churches to be erected at amazingly modest cost.[33]

But it was essential that the new churches should be soundly built: the Commissioners set up a Building Committee because they 'experienced great difficulty in forming any opinion upon the plans submitted to their consideration, with reference to the construction and durability of the buildings'.[34] It was composed of Archdeacons Cambridge and Wollaston, Lords Grenville and Kenyon, Colonel Stephenson, and Joshua Watson;[35] but Grenville played no part; the two archdeacons, Stephenson, and Watson bore the burden of the day, with periodic assistance from Lord Kenyon. The importance of this committee can hardly be exaggerated: although it referred important issues to the Board, and its recommendations were not always accepted *in toto*, it was the real executive of the Commission. Its first function was to examine the plans submitted, particularly the number and arrangement of the sittings, the estimated expense, the tenders for performance of the several works, the contractors' sureties, and similar matters.

17 St James, Louth, Lincolnshire. Another plate from Britton's *Architectural Antiquities* that spread the fame of the tallest parish church spire in England, exciting contemporary architects to emulation.

The Building Committee received the plans when the general character and appearance had been approved by the Board, and in its turn passed them on, 'as a measure of precaution and in order to obtain the best possible assurance of the stability', to the Crown Architects. In their *First Report* the Commissioners commented: 'This arrangement has been attended with the most beneficial consequences; for many instances have occurred in which plans have been altogether rejected, owing to defects which have been pointed out in the proposed construction, and which the Building Committee themselves might have been unable to detect; and other plans have been repeatedly sent back to the architects who prepared them, for correction and amendment.'[36] They were to find, however, that this procedure was not entirely satisfactory, and was a source of long delays. The Crown Architects clearly considered most of the local men as highly incompetent, and were not prepared to accept any responsibility for execution of the plans passed. The Commissioners therefore decided to appoint their own Surveyor.[37] But reference of plans to the Crown Architects continued until the abolition of the old Office of Works in 1832.

Requests for aid, many within, but some without the provisions of the Act were now coming in, together with information from the district boards. But the Commission did not make a general plan covering the whole country for the distribution of the Million. Overwhelmed, perhaps, by the appalling dimensions of their task, they tended merely to respond, though in London they were more pro-active for reasons that may be guessed at – the importance of the church as a means of social control in the capital, the more immediate knowledge of circumstances on the part of most of the more active Commissioners, the rapid development of the suburbs, and sometimes a wealthy community willing to subscribe handsomely. Nationally, their piecemeal grants were often secured by an assiduous minister making early application, by the donation of a site, or promise of a large subscription (though wealthy parishes were the best able to supply their deficiency themselves), or by a Commissioner's personal knowledge of a particular parish. Many populous towns, such as Plymouth and Rochdale, were ignored, while country parishes of comparatively small population, like Christchurch (Hampshire), with 4,650, or Hawarden (Flintshire) with 4,435, were accommodated. These apparently idiosyncratic decisions are more comprehensible viewed in the light of the 1818 parliamentary returns, in which the population figures are derived from the 1811 census, and the particular condition of parishes forming a single city not always recognized. Thus the four parishes composing Plymouth had between them church room for nearly 10,000, against a population of 29,000, thereby disqualifying Plymouth, as not satisfying the criterion of church-room for less than one in four. Rochdale was listed as having a population of 8,217, with church-room for 1,800; whereas in 1821 37,229 inhabitants were counted. Stoke-on-Trent was returned with a population of 8,000; but in the 1821 census it was 29,000; and Wolverhampton in the returns had 3,000 church sittings for 14,000 inhabitants, whereas the 1821 census counted 36,838 inhabitants. But occasionally the Commissioners of their own accord offered churches to some parishes (e.g. Liverpool), or even imposed them on hostile vestries, as at Shoreditch, where the needs were known.

The Commissioners' task was thus complicated by the form of the population returns. Experience and more up-to-date information improved matters in 1825, when the apportionment of the second parliamentary grant was considered, but earlier returns caused miscalculations.[38] Comparison by totals of population alone could mislead, as Harrowby's memorandum had noted in respect of Halifax and Rochdale. Many of the north-country parishes included vast tracts of land, and, as remarked in chapter One, were composed of several townships or villages. These needed a larger number of smaller chapels rather than the large churches that the Commissioners preferred, which were suitable only for the towns with a concentrated population (as at Nottingham, where a general opposition to the enclosure of the open fields and common land prevented for many years the lateral expansion of the town). At Preston, however, where the town was expanding in two directions, the Board was persuaded to build two smaller chapels instead of one large, central church – though only the same grant was allowed.[39]

The second major factor complicating the Commissioners' task was popular hostility to church-rates. The building of a new church naturally entailed some charge on a parish, even if this were no more than the cost of divine worship. This gave the enemies of the Establishment an opportunity to rally round them all the lukewarm, and those disinterested persons who had no objection to anything – so long as their own pockets were not touched. The local hostility was sometimes such as to induce the Commissioners, despite their powers to compel parishes to provide a site (which proved cumbersome and expensive), to give up their intention of building a new church, or to build only one where two had been proposed.[40] This, occurring in parishes where the Establishment was weakest, induced the seeming neglect of some areas most in need of additional church-room.

The Bishop of London reported to his fellow-Commissioners on 24 November 1818 his fears

that in the places where the wants are the greatest very little can be done to meet the Parliamentary grant by voluntary contribution, and still less by rates. There is not a parish of this description to the East of Temple Bar, which from the multitude of its Paupers, and the general low circumstances of the Householders must not in its collective capacity be regarded as Poor. In the parish of St Matthew Bethnal Green, where the number of these exceeds 7,000 forty-two only are assessed at a rent of more than £50 per annum and upwards of 5,000 under ten pounds. There are indeed individuals in affluent circumstances but of these some are Jews or Dissenters from whom nothing can in reason be expected; others are indifferent to the concerns of religion or accustomed to ramble from home on the Sabbath without regard to the purposes of the day and the resources of the more serious Inhabitants who are conscientiously attached to the Church are subject to a regular drain in the maintenance of local Charities. … the imposition of a Rate for building New Churches would seldom be carried in an open Vestry, and if voted in the Vestry would be sanctioned in very few instances by the concurrence of the Proprietors.[41]

He requested the Board to supply churches immediately in five parishes: Shoreditch, St George-in-the-East, Bethnal Green, Whitechapel and Stepney, with a collective population of about 170,000 and church-room for less than 11,000. The Board resolved that the first three of these were fit under the Act for the erection of churches entirely out of the Parliamentary Fund, save for the cost of sites. An informal approach having apparently met with a refusal, on 22 December it was further resolved to give notice to the Shoreditch churchwardens that the Board would build two churches there at New Hoxton and Haggerston, each requiring an acre and a half; and to those at Bethnal Green for two sites, each of one acre. The Shoreditch vestry on 5 January 1819 responded with a resolution of regret, carried 'by a great majority', that the Commissioners were demanding the parish supply two sites, and that they could not comply.[42] A committee consisting of Bishop Howley, Archdeacon Pott and Francis Burton recommended advising the vestry to reconsider, lest the Commission use its compulsory powers, but the Board referred the problem to the Law Officers, to whom a similar hostile response from Bethnal Green was also referred. The Law Officers' opinion was that notice could not be given to a parish to provide two sites at the same time; nor could the Board compel a parish to provide a site for a church for a new district parish until such parish had been created by order-in-council.[43] Eventually the Board decided to pay for sites in Shoreditch.[44]

The Commissioners' reluctance to use such compulsory powers as they did possess was due to the immense difficulty of actually securing from a parish reimbursement for any work done, and exciting hostility against the Church, rather

18 St Barnabas, King Square, parish of St Luke, Old Street, London (Thomas Hardwick, 1822–3). Built by the Commissioners in one of the most deprived London parishes, against the wishes of a powerful party of the inhabitants who succeeded in blocking a second church for many years.

than any scruples about interfering with property rights.[45] The rector of St Luke, Old Street, London, reporting that half of his parish's population of 34,000 were dissenters, and a further quarter 'persons of the most depraved character and habits … [who] never attend any Place of Worship', warned the Commissioners against 'exercising the imperative power' afforded by the Act of compelling the parish to provide sites: a parish rate would 'greatly aggravate the Spirit of Dissent'. Were sites to be provided, voluntary subscriptions might be obtained by selling pews.[46] When the vestrymen of Manchester were whipped up by radicals to vote down a resolution to obtain sites, the Anglican protagonist, the Rev. William Johnson, urged the Commissioners to institute compulsory purchase, it being 'a matter of the first importance for the recovery and support of the salutary Influence' hitherto exercised there by 'the Friends of social order and sound constitutional principles'; but the Bishop of Chester (writing from Kedleston) advised that compulsory measures should be avoided.[47]

Unfortunately, hostility to a new church sometimes extended even to supporters of the Establishment: the Dean of Lichfield reported that the church-goers at Stoke-on-Trent 'had been very divided among themselves' about proposals for two new churches – though opposition from dissenters and radicals had served to unite them.[48] In Manchester, 'supineness in some and an objection to the Patronage of the Warden and Fellows [of the collegiate church] in others', was blamed as partly responsible for the defeat of the proposal to obtain sites.[49] Church-goers already provided for might resent the additional maintenance costs arising from additional churches, particularly if a parish were divided, so that a smaller population would have to carry the charge of the old church. At Shipley in Bradford parish (Yorkshire), there was a 'general fear' of having to pay the new curate's salary.[50] Even the incumbent might not be able to allow the general good to overcome his particular pain in suffering some financial loss, as at Wandsworth (Surrey), where the incumbent demanded £247 p.a. indemnification for the effect of a new church on his interest in the pews of the parish church.[51] Harrowby had remarked on the need for general rules about parish division:

> There will always be so many bad tempers, so many clashing interests, – so many in all parishes are found, who are disposed to blame and resist calls that they do not propose or direct … One great obstacle to a division would be, that one part might consist chiefly of the rich, the other of the poor. To remove this, in some instances, perhaps though divided as to the church, continue jointly to maintain their poor.[52]

The Commissioners' First Report to parliament[53] is dated 3 February 1821, although Archdeacon Pott and Lord Kenyon had been entrusted with its preparation on 30 June 1820 (and Joshua Watson was also deeply involved).[54] It was a comprehensive document, with a series of schedules appended showing the progress that had been made. Eighty-five churches had been provided for, seating 144,190 persons (one-third in free seats), at a cost of £1,068,000. As £88,000 was promised in subscriptions, and £59,000 was allotted for loans to parishes, the Commissioners were left with some £80,000, plus their two per cent interest on Exchequer bonds:[55] The final schedule listed twenty-five applications postponed for want of funds. It was quite obvious that if the Commission were to fulfil its task, another parliamentary subvention would be necessary. The Evangelical Bishop of Gloucester, Henry Ryder, blamed the deletion from the Act of the clause granting a term of patronage to persons building new churches at their own cost. He wrote to his brother, Lord Harrowby:[56]

In assistance of the million afforded by the state only £88000 has been raised by subscription, not therefore 1/12th of the whole sum expended. A much larger sum was allowed on all hands to be expected and acquired from this source and can the disappointment be ascribed to any cause so probable and adequate, as the want of that inducement which temporary patronage would supply? Secondly the necessity ... is no less evident from the contents of the Report. I presume it will not be contended that another million, or indeed any further grant can *at present* be expected from the state.

Has then the *first* million accomplished ... its object? No. There have been 155 applications, and of these only 85 in any measure complied with. 45 it is said, were rejected, but *several* of these, I doubt not from *some* instances which have come to my own knowledge, were cases greatly deserving and requiring the public aid – and are still therefore probably in want. The Commissioners performed their duty, I have no doubt, with every desire and endeavour to do the utmost good *within* the limits of the rules laid down, but one of these rules, viz. *that the subscribers should not receive any return or profit from any portion of the Pews* has been amongst other circumstances proved very naturally an effectual check to contributions. ... 25 were postponed from the state of the fund. And it is surely not improbable that some cases may exist for which, though their circumstances might have qualified them for a grant, application has not *yet* been made, and a multitude of others, where, though their deficiency might not exactly reach the prescribed amount of the Act, encreased accommodation would be most desirable, and where from local peculiarities as to Dissenters, Radicalism etc, the need is more urgent than in some which have received relief.[57]

Ryder's observations were only too shrewd, as succeeding years were to show: nor had the problem been faced of the unrelenting increase in population. He suggested that, as grants of such a large proportion of the cost had not succeeded in awakening public benevolence, it was 'highly expedient' to recur to the granting of advantages to subscribers, 'to secure the completion of one of the most important of all National Works', perhaps through a petition from all the parishes still in need. 'Some such provision as this', he concluded, 'would afford the best, if not the only, hope of securing the Establishment against further encroachments of dissenters and thus support the most certain and efficacious means[?] for inculcating or rather reviving religious feeling[?][57] and right political feeling among the people.' While acceptable to the Evangelicals, this concept, as seen above, alarmed the High Church party.

As the First Report stated, it had been necessary to apply to parliament for an extension of the Commission's powers. In 1819, the exposed inadequacies of the original Act called forth a second, amended in its passage through both Houses,[58] the 59 Geo. III, c.134, of 41 clauses, which moved a step farther in breaking down the old rigid parochial system. Among the most important of these were s.4 which empowered the Commissioners to pay all the expenses of building a church if they found sufficient cause (which overcame the difficulties created when a parish refused to provide a site, more simply than by recourse to their compulsory powers – s.22 specifically authorized the Commissioners to provide sites); and s.5, which recognized the peculiar status of many districts, particularly in the vast northern parishes, and permitted grants for hamlets, chapelries, etc., though these divisions might not have 4,000 inhabitants, or the parish as a whole should have accommodation for more than a quarter of its population. The Commissioners' work was made easier by the provision that grants might be made without a prior decision as to the status of the proposed building, or consideration of the desirability of dividing the parish; and loans could be made similarly (s.7). Contiguous parts of different parishes might be formed into consolidated chapelries (s.6). Districts, remaining under the control of the incumbent of the parish church, but under the pastoral care of a particular curate, might be assigned to chapels (s.16). A provision of importance in the long continuance of the Commission, considered further below, was that the drawback of customs duty and excise upon materials used for church-building under the Acts was to be allowed, upon the Commissioners signifying their approval (s.21). This had the effect of increasing the funds at their disposal, though where they had made no contribution, the drawback was returned to the parish. But it was several years before the Bishop of Gloucester's suggestion of providing an inducement to subscribers was acted upon. Finally, from 1819, church-rates might be levied for rebuilding or enlarging a church; and money borrowed on the security of such rates. But church rates were to prove a source of much dissension.[59]

The First Report had referred also to the Board's regulations for architects and tradesmen,[60] the use of their powers for obtaining sites for parishes not needing financial aid,[61] and the number of applications they had had to defer. It was signed by the Archbishop of Canterbury, the Bishop of London, Lord Kenyon, Sir John Nicholl, Archdeacons Cambridge, Pott and Wollaston, Colonel Stephenson, Joshua Watson, and the Chancellor of the Exchequer. These names largely represent (as signatures to later reports often do not)[62] the effective or executive members of the Commission. The onus inevitably fell on a small group, supported by the Secretary, whose assiduity[63] earned him an increase of salary to £750 p.a. in 1821. If what may be called the 'First Commission' (i.e. from 1818 to the reissue of the Letters-Patent in 1825) be considered, there are eight members who are found to attend more than half the meetings: the Archbishop of Canterbury, Howley, Pott, Cambridge, Wollaston, Burton, Stephenson and Watson. From these the membership of the various committees was almost exclusively drawn. During the first nine months, the Chancellor of the Exchequer, Mant, and Scott could be added to the list; but then Mant was elevated to the Irish Bench, and the others' attendance fell off, though in

St George, Tyldesley, Lancashire (Robert Smirke, 1821-4).

Left: **19** Gothic for a country township; the spire derived from Louth.

Right: **20** Interior, looking north-east. The details are of different periods: quasi-Perpendicular arcade and clerestory, but aisle windows of an earlier character (chancel bay added 1887).

February 1823 Vansittart, relieved of his custody of the national purse, returned as Lord Bexley to a frequent attendance. Joshua Watson's crucial role may be discerned from the frequent references to him by correspondents.

Of the lay peers Lord Kenyon was the most reliable.[64] As a leading member of the St Marylebone vestry, he played an important part in discussions relating to the proposed four churches in that important parish. Members of the government looked in at the Board occasionally, Harrowby the most frequent, averaging about one in three meetings of which records are extant. Liverpool himself had attended the first four meetings, and a further four in November 1818. The Archbishop of York and the Bishop of Chester attended regularly while in London for the sitting of parliament, during the winter months; and the judges, Scott and Nicholl, attended intermittently, averaging (like the Dean of Westminster) one meeting in four. The 'third party' leader, Lord Grenville, a supporter of church extension, attended nine of the first twenty-five meetings. Sidmouth, Eldon, Colchester – the decorative elder statesmen – did not appear at all: nor scarcely the provincial clergy members – Eyre, Outram, Whitaker, Headlam – whose function was specifically to handle matters in key dioceses, where they were busy on diocesan and local committees. The irregular attendance of members of either house of parliament may in some part be ascribed to their parliamentary duties, for even the zealous Bishop Law of Chester wrote lamenting that he had not been able to attend a single Board meeting during a month's stay in London, because of the 'daily call of the House'.[65]

As the Commissioners learned on the job, the need for further legislation became apparent, but parliamentary time was not easy to procure. An amending bill introduced in April 1821, much deferred in the Commons, reached the Lords too late in the session for consideration.[66] In 1822 a third Church Building Act (3 Geo. 4, c.72), that survived the end-of-session hurly-burly,[67] helped further to ease the Commission's work. Public departments and corporations were enabled to grant sites for church-building purposes (s.1). The Commissioners' powers to make loans were clarified (s.5). They could apportion the charitable gifts (and debts) and the surplice fees when dividing a parish (s.11); and convert district chapelries into district parishes (s.16). New churches might be substituted for old (s.30); legal instruments made for the purposes of the Acts were to be free of stamp duty (s.28) - important to small tradesmen contracting for churches; and titles to sites were not to be questioned more than five years after conveyance to the Commissioners (s.29). The new chapels were to be repaired in the same manner as the parish church (s.20) – the usual means being by a church-rate – and freed from having to share the repair costs of other chapels in their parish. This was the last Act in which any reliance was placed on rate levies. Subsequently it was realized that only voluntary subscriptions could be relied upon, and repair funds were secured before churches were consecrated.

21 John Soane. Unexecuted designs of the 1820s for the Church Building Commission, water-colour by J. M. Gandy. The three foreground designs represent proposals for Holy Trinity, St Marylebone: from left to right, Norman and Gothic versions prepared in April 1824 to meet the St Marylebone Vestry's wishes, and an earlier Classical version with clerestory. Behind, in the centre, is St Peter, Walworth, flanked by several abortive schemes.

4

The Crown Architects

When Lord Liverpool decided to embark on a church-building scheme, it was clearly necessary for him to have some idea of what new churches might cost. Economy was the datum, and it seemed common sense that they should be as capacious as was functionally possible. For the requisite information the Treasury naturally turned to the Office of Works,[1] then under the direction of Lieutenant-Colonel Benjamin Stephenson. A Treasury memorandum, dated 2 February 1818, instructed the Surveyor-General to 'Desire each of the Consulting Architects of the Board of Works to consider of the most economical mode of building churches with a view to accommodating the greatest number of persons at the smallest expense, within the compass of an ordinary voice. One half of the number to be free seats for the poor.'[2]

The 'Consulting', 'Attached' or 'Crown Architects' (as they were variously termed), those retained by the Office of Works, were three in number: John Nash (1752-1835), John Soane (1753-1837), and Robert Smirke (1781-1867). Three of the outstanding architects of their generation, each had his merits and his drawbacks. Nash, the Regent's favourite architect, was a master of the Picturesque, whether Classical or Gothic, with a slap-dash attention to detail and an optimistic attitude towards estimating costs. Soane, on the other hand, an idiosyncratic genius, was obsessive about the perfect realization of his projects, with a tendency to sulk. Smirke, a younger man, was noted for his skill in amending others' defective work, and as an architectural designer had a taste for a neo-classical cubism, though prepared to present Gothic were that called for. They were employed by the Church Building Commission in two capacities, as consultant and as executive architects. They assisted at the birth of the Commission, preparing designs for churches at the request of the Treasury in the early months of 1818.[3] They subsequently advised the Commissioners on the plans submitted to them, and were entrusted with the execution of several designs – though not exactly those they had originally prepared.[4]

It was an obvious step for the Commission to invite its consultants to become executants. That they were not more widely employed was probably due to their being already very busy men. This did not prevent accusations of their advising the Commissioners with a view to their own profit.[5] But they were too busy and too

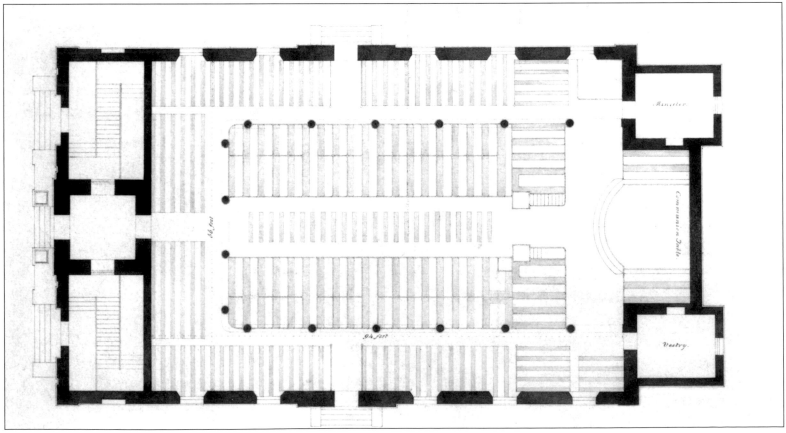

exalted to engage in uncertain competitions for small prizes, and the local committees, who usually chose the architect, tended to employ either local men, or those who seduced them with attractive designs. Soane was invited by a local committee at Manchester, but declined to try to build for the money available.[6]

Following his summons to the Treasury, Stephenson called on the Crown Architects for costings for new churches, writing to them on 14 February to enquire when their plans and estimates 'for the churches proposed to be built by Parliament in the Metropolis' would be completed,[7] as the Treasury was anxious to have them as soon as possible. Smirke and Nash responded by submitting several designs to the surveyor-general in March 1818.[8] In his report, Smirke observed that St Martin-in-the-Fields and St James's, Piccadilly, were large churches, but not well arranged. The new church at Hackney (built by the efforts of Watson's brother-in-law, H. H. Norris) was larger than any in the metropolis, and seated more than 2,000; it was 'built in the most economical manner, the walls being of plain brickwork', with a low, stone steeple and small stone entrance porticoes, and cost £26,000, exclusive of organ, bells, and other fittings. But in some respects the economical execution had been ill-judged, and the structure was not wearing well. He had therefore calculated on the basis of a church of an area some two-thirds of Hackney's 9,000 sq. ft, to hold about 1900 persons, standing in 'a clear surrounding space' for security from fire, as well as for light and ventilation, built of brick covered with roman cement, and 'fitted up in the simplest manner'. Such a church would, Smirke reckoned, cost about £24,000-£25,000, and somewhat more for a tower. Walls of masonry would put the cost quite beyond the indicated bounds: 'I am aware of no eligible means by which the expense could be reduced to a less amount'.[9]

Sending several designs for the proposed churches, Smirke hoped 'they might serve as proper examples for them, and as satisfactory specimens of my endeavours to do justice to the subject.' They showed brick buildings, covered with roman cement, of an area rather greater than St Martin-in-the-Fields or St James's, Piccadilly.[10] He had 'endeavoured to shew … what may be done at the smallest expense consistently with the character and substantial durability proper for such edifices', with the largest capacity that could be within hearing of the minister, not varying 'in any great degree the general arrangements usually adopted in our National Churches' and omitting 'expensive Architectural forms, substituting those which seemed most compatible with simplicity and moderate charge'. Thus they would be inexpensively distinguished from meeting-houses or proprietary chapels. With an area of 6,000-6,500 sq. ft, they would hold about 1,900 persons. The internal arrangement might depend on the particular siting of the building, so he offered several variations, all supposing, however, a clear surrounding space.[11] Smirke feared his estimate about £25,000 without a tower, might be thought high: 'but cannot conscientiously state it at a less sum nor recommend building of a less expensive kind – for the whole amount of superfluous ornament is very small indeed in proportion to their whole cost'.[12] The next day he wrote again to point out that his estimate was based on London prices; and that probably they could build more cheaply in the provinces, in many instances for not more than four-fifths of the estimate.[13]

The designs, all in Smirke's characteristic 'cubical', stripped-down Classical style, are two-storeyed compositions (to allow for the essential galleries), generally rectangular in plan, with western porches containing the gallery stairs; alternatives offer west or east towers, the latter flanked by robing room and vestry, which in the former lie either side of the altar recess. The towers are square, two-stage compositions, the belfry louvres flanked by pilasters, and topped by a depressed

Opposite: Designs by Robert Smirke, for the Commissioners.

22 (above). Perspective elevation for St John, Chatham, 1821, based on one of Smirke's model designs of March, 1818. Cp. p. 94. The two ranges of windows indicate the presence of galleries internally.

23 (below). Plan of Model Church no II (March, 1818), the nave measured 13 x 31ft, and a west tower 13ft square internally. Iron columns support galleries on three sides, reached by stairs on either side of the tower. The pews, within the area left open by the galleries, are surrounded by free seats, and the central aisle is occupied by movable benches. Pulpit and reading desk balance each other exactly, accompanied by double pews (objected to by the Commissioners) for the minister and his family and church officers.

Robert Smirke, Office of Works Model Church III (1818). The concept of a principal entrance on the south side, under a circular portico and tower, Smirke embodied in St Mary, Wyndham Place, St Marylebone, and replicated at Salford. This design obviated the difficulty of combining a tower with a Grecian temple.

Above: **24** Elevation.
Opposite: **25** Plan. Transepts could provide a lot of free seats, but the Commissioners insisted that all must face the altar.

pyramid. A more complex model of intersecting rectangles, with a tower external to the north arm, has nine rows of north- or south-facing seats in the lateral arms, under galleries; the tower is more elaborated, with balustrade crowning the first stage, and a cupola-ed top; the body, too, has a more neo-Grecian than Roman character.

Soane with his customary thoroughness had been studying the problem, without yet arriving at a resolution. He took plans of St James's, Piccadilly (one of Wren's cheapest, and one Wren had himself considered an ideal Protestant church), and estimated the cost of erecting a similar church, which he calculated at £23,587.13s.8d.[14] But such elaborate enquiries were not what was needed at that moment: the Surveyor-General wrote again, more pressingly: 'I have this moment received positive orders from the Treasury, to send as soon as possible some Plans and Estimates for building the New Churches, as a Debate upon this Subject is expected to take Place in the House of Commons this Afternoon … Do pray send me something if it is only One, and if this cannot be done, send me an Estimate of the Probable Expence of your Plan.'[15] Like the modern civil servant, the Crown Architect was required to supply his minister with the requisite departmental

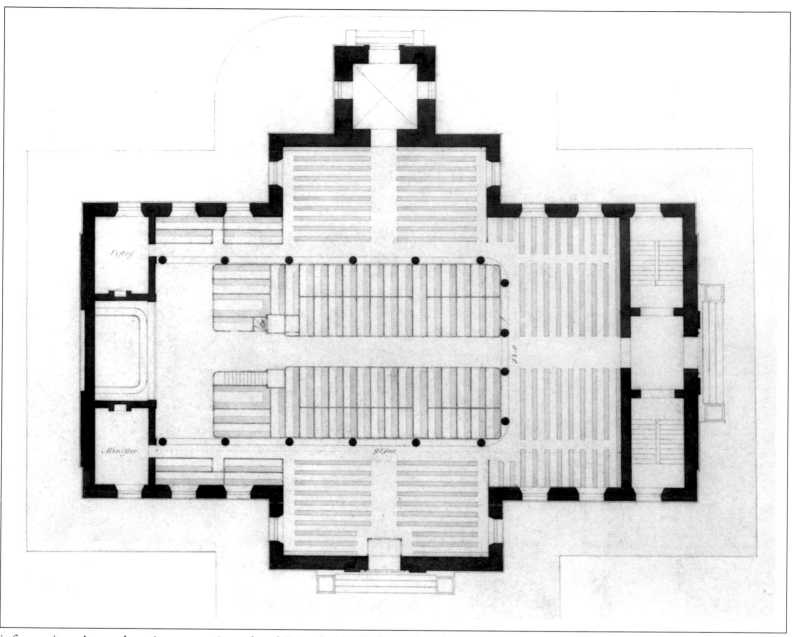

information. A rough estimate survives, dated 'March 1818', for a church for 2,000 persons at £33,000.[16] Whatever Soane may have produced, the chancellor, Vansittart, arranged to see him with his plans on 1 April 1818. Following this interview, Soane sent his written opinion on 3 April:

That the interior of churches, to be within the compass of an ordinary Voice, should not exceed in length ninety feet, and in breadth seventy; that the Square and parallelogram are the most economical forms.

That the Structure as regards the Walls should be of brick, and no greater quantity of Stone used than is required to assist their construction, or to render the exterior Characteristic, and in the requisite pavements. That the Roofings should be covered with Lead, and Eaves or drips every where prevented, and that the water be conveyed away so as to prevent injury and the decay of Walls and foundations.

That the Gallery in small Churches be sustained by Iron Pillars, but in those of large size their supports should be partly of Stone and continued to the roof, and should it be objected that the use of Iron alone has not sufficient Character and apparent stability, it may be enclosed in the manner best adapted to prevent obstruction.

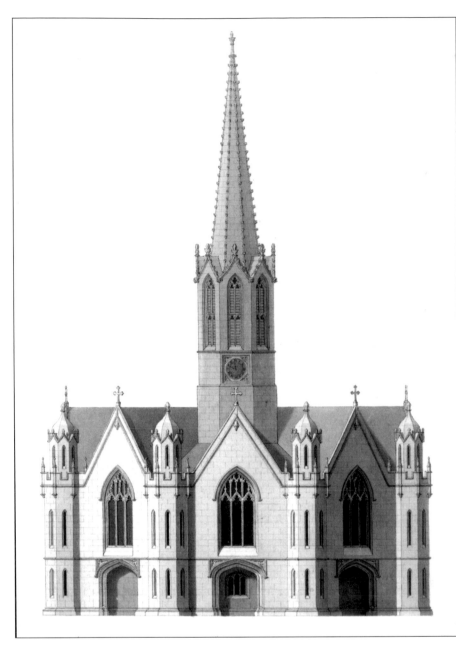

The ceilings should be flat.

The windows should be principally of Iron Glazed in small squares in metal.

The pews and finishings should be generally of Deal and with the Stuccoings painted.

In arranging the interior to accommodate the greatest Number of Persons, ... enclosed Seats or Pews should be as much as possible avoided, that open rising Seats should be substituted, that the Aisles be wide and Benches with backs placed therein. These open seats and Benches would be free for the accommodation of the Poor.

It will be difficult to form an Estimate that shall apply generally as a Scale to compare the probable cost of Churches, differing in size and accommodation and in locality, and differing also perhaps widely as respects their construction and stability, but I apprehend the largest Churches cannot be built with a requisite attention to their Character and durability for a less sum than thirty thousand pounds.[17]

This estimate was much more expensive than the Commissioners were to allow. Soane's insistence upon 'characteristic' appearance – at a necessary price[18] – was to preclude him from building many churches and to cause difficulties over those he did design.[19] Yet Vansittart had said that small churches were 'not likely to be wanted, but those to hold about two thousand persons'; and that they should be different from Methodist chapels, – so that 'towers if they could be added without much additional expence would be preferred on that account'.[20]

Nash was characteristically much more optimistic: he promised estimates averaging £10,000, which included such interior fitments as pulpit, reading desk, clerk's desk, and privy.[21] Shortly afterwards he sent a detailed report. In his usual way, considering the setting

John Nash, Office of Works Model Church (1818), Gothic, octagon. Nash exhibited a neo-classical enthusiasm for unusual plans. Some Dissenting congregations had erected octagonal chapels in the late eighteenth century, e.g., Colegate, Norwich, 1754-6. Nash's turrets, perhaps derived from Henry VII's Chapel, Westminster, were later employed in his church at Haggerston, cp. p. 81. Nash estimated the cost of the church and its fittings at £10,420 plus £1,800 for the tower and spire.

Above: **26** West front.

Below: **27** Left: ground plan; right: gallery plan. A vestry room is placed behind the altar, with pulpit and reading desk on either side of the altar.

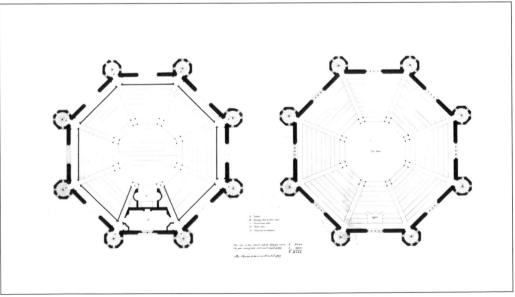

for his work, he emphasized that the locality should influence the design, both in form and arrangements.[22] The ten designs and estimates (now in the R.I.B.A. Drawings Collection) were again drawn for London and its environs, but varied 'that they may suit different scites [sic]', typically of the Picturesque aesthetic that they embodied. Their remarkable diversity led Summerson to suggest that 'anybody in the office was allowed to have a go', though Dr Liscombe argues for a controlling mind,[23] which the uniformity of presentation does suggest. A. C. Pugin was paid for drawing one of the six Gothic designs, almost certainly that now numbered PB471/1, an assemblage of carefully modelled details from late Gothic churches, including western turrets from Henry VII's Chapel, Westminster and a tower with free-standing corner-turrets connected to the central element by flying buttresses, recalling Boston (Lincs) or Lowick (Northants), 'calculated for a Situation where an ornamental Fabrick is required' and costed at £9,300 for the building itself. A much less elaborated design, hardly more than two-dimensional, with a tower terminating in a similar manner to the first, estimated at only £8,000, was the basis of Nash's design for the church he later built at Haggerston. Nash however scarcely played fair in giving an estimate for each building at under £10,000, but adding £1,920 for pews, pulpit and desk. Several of the Gothic styles, whether or not suppressing stylistic features in order to form a composition of greater unity (as Dr Liscombe argues), have that papery thinness familiar in a number of late eighteenth-century Gothic churches. Of the four classical designs, one was a cross between a meeting-house and the Halicarnassus Mausoleum; a Grecian version re-worked the tower Nash had designed in 1816 for St Mary, Northwood, Isle of Wight; a third was akin to Smirke's style, and the fourth an amazing assemblage, a classical body (partly French in derivation) with a medievalist but fluted spire rising from a Grecian colonnade, that was to be embodied in All Souls, Langham Place, Marylebone. Nash makes the tower, that distinguishing feature of the Anglican church, the dominant in all save one of his designs; the lesser turrets have a functional purpose, containing stairs to the galleries.

The plans of these churches are as noteworthy as their elevations; all have massive galleries, none a chancel. The altar, usually recessed between vestry and robing room, would have been invisible to a sizable proportion of the congregation. The first-mentioned Gothic design has the most conventional plan, T-shaped, with a slight eastern extrusion to contain altar, robing room and vestry; another is octagonal (as were some meeting-houses); and several are as wide as they are deep, though varying the back fronts (no orientation being given): two being hemispherical, and one with a projecting feature between turrets, with a semi-circular ground-floor vestry at the centre. Several place the altar under the tower, flanked by entrances. Since none of these unusual plans was executed, it is interesting that the Church Building Society (with several of the Commissioners among its leading members) published in 1819 'Suggestions and Instructions' for church builders that stated: 'The most approved forms are a parallelogram and an octagon; but a polygon or a semi-polygon, or a figure of three straight sides and one polygonal, would bring a large congregation nearer to the Preacher than any other except a circle, which is objectionable, as confounding reticulate sounds'.[24] John Wesley had also advocated polygonal chapels.

Nash remarked that the most economical design for 2,000 persons would be a brick room 80 or 90ft square and 24ft high, covered with slates, floored, plastered, pewed and lighted, and having a gallery. That would not exceed £6,000 in cost: 'but so mean a building … cannot be in contemplation.'

John Nash, Office of Works Model Church (1818), Classical with spire. His estimated cost for the church and fittings was £10,800 plus £1,450 for the 'Spire and Pedestal & Colonade'.

Above: **28** West front. The towers are modelled on Robert Adam's Mistley church (1776); the spire is possibly a classicised version of Patrington (East Yorks). Nash adopted the spire for his All Souls, Langham Place, St Marylebone (p. 80).

Below: **29** Plan. B, C, and D in the left-hand plan indicate the pulpit, the reading and clerk's desk, and the communion rails respectively.

The economy therefore which has regulated these designs is to adapt forms capable of holding the 2,000 persons arranged on two floors in the smallest space, having due consideration to air and ventilation – to make sure of the cheapest but most substantial materials – to adopt no ornaments but such as belong either to the construction of the building itself, or are appropriate to some indispensable purpose belonging to it.

He considered that essential elements included a covered entrance, a belfry and a clock. He suggested the body of the church should be of brick covered with Parker's cement 'coloured and painted as Bath stone or with Dehl's mastic which would have the same effect without being coloured'; the dressings would be of Bath stone.

It can only have been these plans that the Surveyor-General was reported to have submitted to the Commissioners at their first meeting,[25] But there was much to be settled before they could consider plans. These estimates were not used as a basis for determining the maximum grant to be made to any one church. Instead, the committee appointed to consider this was directed to obtain the requisite information from the Crown Architects. They appear to have put questions about materials and their prices to the Architects, judging by a paper endorsed 'Answers to Questions', addressed to the Commissioners, dated 2 September 1818, among Soane's papers.[26] It looks as if the Commissioners wanted to go deeper than the Architects' general conclusions. Soane was active at this time acquiring information about church-building costs: surveyors and architects had sent him their estimates for churches at Bathwick, Egham, Stepney and Clerkenwell, and details of the prices of Bath stone and of labour costs, etc. During a visit to Bath in September, Soane visited the Bathwick church and talked to the builder.[27]

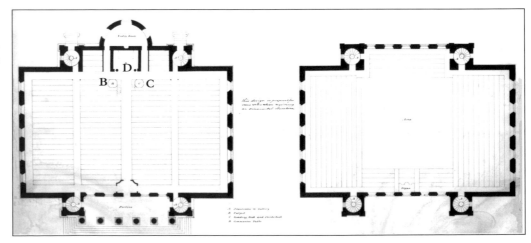

The Surveyor-General asked Soane, and doubtless his two colleagues, to attend a meeting of the Commissioners on 23 September 1818,[28] though the Commissioners' minutes say nothing of the architects' presence. A subsequent meeting was arranged at the Office of Works in Whitehall on 27 October, between the architects and a committee of the Commissioners, 'for the purpose of obtaining from the Architects … such information as may enable the Board to fix, and specify the largest amount of allowances to be granted for building any Church'. Stephenson asked Nash and Soane to meet him an hour previous, as he considered 'some conversation upon the subject' necessary before meeting the committee.[29]

In November 1818, when the Commissioners had set their maximum grant at £20,000, there was a further flurry of estimates. Smirke at their request made 'a very detailed calculation of the expence of building St Andrew's Church in Holborn according to the prices of work allowed at this time by the Office of Works', which, excluding organ, clock and bells, came to £34,000. This large church, seating some 1,400, but capable of holding more, was of Kentish ragstone, cased with Portland, the internal woodwork of wainscot, and the roof covered with lead. Smirke then carefully estimated the cost of a similar church, but built of light stone-coloured brick, with stone dressings, and of a somewhat more economical construction, but again with oak fittings, which he calculated at about £25,500.[30]

The Commissioners were obliged to reject such costings as too high. At £25,000 they could build not Liverpool's one hundred churches, but merely forty. And as Soane's enquiries had shown, churches were building around London at £6,000 or £7,000. In a Utilitarian age, economy was the cry. Economy had caused the postponement of the whole scheme in 1816: now it had to be the lodestar of the Commission. In view of the cheapness of many of the churches of the day, the Commissioners were not ungenerous in fixing their maximum grant at £20,000 (specifically for London churches: £16,000 was normally the provincial maximum – Smirke's 'four-fifths'); and it was probably the weighty views of Smirke and Soane that induced them to set it so high. Nonetheless, Soane's scorn for the whole enterprise was expressed in one of his later Royal Academy lectures:

> Unfortunately for the architecture of this country, instead of the Fifty Churches directed to be built in the reign of Queen Anne, we have erected a series of economical churches, chapels, and meeting houses, in their external appearance indicative rather of buildings designed for mere utility, than those dedicated to the purposes of devotion.[31]

Although the Commissioners had not adopted the designs prepared by the Crown Architects, they depended upon their advice about structural reliability. One of the most important of the Architects' investigations was their scrutiny of Thomas Rickman's design for a church at Liverpool. This was being put forward by Bishop Law of Chester as a potential model church that might be generally adopted, and is considered in more detail in chapter 8. After an intensive examination by all three Attached Architects, their report was decidedly unfavourable, and this may have been one factor in persuading the Commissioners to rely on local enterprise.[32]

Consequently, they were incessantly referring to the Office of Works the plans of local architects. From the number of times that such plans were returned for modification, it would appear that the local talent called forth was of a poor order, but the Crown Architects clearly erred on the side of safety: their judgment had to be made on the drawings put before them, and from their comments the commonest defect appears to have been inadequacy of the drawings. Among the first plans thus referred were those for Blackburn (Lancashire), by John Palmer (1785-1846), an autodidact, apprenticed as a mason, who now practised in Manchester as an ecclesiastical architect.[33] 'They do not afford security and stability to the building and that the defects are not remediable without an entire alteration of the construction,' Nash and Soane reported.[34] On their re-submission, though the strength had been increased by introducing tie-beams to the roof-rafters of the side aisle, 'many things constituting the strength and stability of the building do not appear on the drawings, nor does the specification accompany the plans by which we might judge of those points'.[35] On 5 August 1819 Soane and Smirke complained that 'the drawings are made out in so loose a manner without dimensions and to so small a scale that it is impossible to form any judgement upon them'.[36] At last they received plans 'exhibiting the proposed construction … in more detail'; with their standard saving clause, 'as far as we are able to form an opinion upon them', they remarked that they perceived

> nothing objectionable in the description of the masons work, but that we consider that the roof is framed very injudiciously … the roof and ceiling of the side aisles will appear between two and three feet below the crown of the arches of the nave, no description is given of the manner of forming the gutters and of conveying the water from the roof, but the lead with which the gutters are to be covered is not of sufficient thickness nor can we approve of the manner in which the slates are intended to be secured to the roof.[37]

In March 1820, an attempt to remedy the construction of the aisle roofs was still 'weak and injudicious'; only in May 1820 was the roof approved as well-constructed.[38]

James Foster (c.1748-1823) was a long-established Bristol architect who practised with his sons James and Thomas. Their designs for a small church at Kingswood, Bitton (Gloucestershire), were adjudged as affording sufficient security 'as far as the construction is concerned', reported Nash and Soane, except for 'the principal rafters forming the roof, which we consider as calculated to force out the external walls … additional means should be taken to tie the feet of the principal rafters together'. Three months later, Soane and Smirke decided that 'the drawings of the two roofs submitted to us are not made out with sufficient detail as to the scantlings and manner of framing to enable us to give any opinion'. Finally, on 10 January 1820, the Fosters won approval for their roof 'for a building of this size if properly executed'.[39]

Another experienced architect with a quiver of churches was Thomas Taylor (c.1778-1826), the leading Leeds architect of his day, damned for lack of detailed drawings, and estimates considerably too low to ensure a 'proper and reasonable degree of stability', for his churches at Pudsey, Dewsbury Moor and Hanging Heaton, all outliers of Leeds. A second set of drawings for Pudsey met no better fate: 'it is our decided opinion that the proposed construction is throughout exceedingly weak'. In May Pudsey was still unsatisfactory and the drawings for the Dewsbury chapels insufficient; it was not till June 1820 that Nash and Smirke declared that their principal objections 'in respect to some material parts of the construction are now in a great measure removed, but the designs are not free from defects particularly in the injudicious manner in which the principal timbers are proposed to be arranged'. Finally Taylor won a modicum of praise: 'The proposed construction of his church is now detailed with great care and if executed strictly according to the drawings we conceive it will be in every respect a durable and well constructed building'.[40] Similarly, an architect whose name is not recorded was criticized on three successive submissions for the weakness of the piers of the nave, the arrangement of the roof principals, and the framing of the gallery in his chapel at Farnworth, Lancashire (Bolton being of the same design), among other defects; and though, the fourth time, material defects had been removed, there were still so many defective parts in the drawings that it was doubtful whether the chapels would be properly executed.[41] The Commissioners, in fact, after the third rejection instructed the parishes to obtain other plans, and the churches were ultimately designed by the Architects' colleague in the Office of Works, Thomas Hardwick (1752-1829).[42]

Security and stability were not the only questions to be considered in reviewing the plans submitted: cost was a major factor. And about this the Crown Architects disliked committing themselves: of Bordesley, a design by Francis Goodwin (1784-1835),[43] they wrote: 'With regard to the prices we do not feel ourselves competent to pronounce upon their propriety without local information respecting materials and labour.'[44] Further information was supplied for this and other churches, but the comment was:

> The account of local prices sent to us does not appear to have been made with reference to these buildings. In order to enable us to give an opinion upon the accuracy of calculations it is necessary we should see the details of the estimates and be informed of the prices at which materials and labour are supplied at those respective places.[45]

Of another of Goodwin's plans, that for Kidderminster (similar to the already approved Ashton design), they observed:

> The author of these designs professes that the building will be constructed in every respect according to principles sanctioned by us: we must beg it to be understood that though we have thought it our duty to point out material defects in construction we have by no means intended to convey our approbation of the whole of the constructive part of any one of the designs laid before us; the opinions we are enabled to form upon them must not be considered as involving us in any degree of responsibility in respect to the work.[46]

In the same report, referring to the Erdington (Warwickshire) and Southsea plans, they stated the impossibility of giving a satisfactory judgement on estimates, 'as experience daily shows that in cases of competition for the execution of a building their amounts vary from ten to thirty per cent and still more, though they are each formed upon the same specification'.

A general comment, which seems ultimately to have made its impression on the Commissioners, was called for by James Savage's bold plans for Chelsea new church.[47] Nash and Smirke remarked in their report to the Surveyor-General:

> We feel it incumbent upon us to solicit your attention to the difficult circumstances under which we are placed by a reference of this nature, as well as by many that have been made by you for the information and guidance of the Commissioners for Building New Churches.
> We have always attentively examined the designs you have at their desire laid before us, and have pointed out, as well as was in our power, the defects of construction where they appeared to exist, but the drawings have for the most part been made in the most unskilful manner or have shown only the principle of the design, affording us at best very imperfect grounds whereon to form our judgement, and if any of these works should be executed under a careless superintendence and by ignorant, or dishonest workmen we are rendered very undeservedly liable in the event of their failure to the censure of having sanctioned the defective work. ...

We could not be indifferent to the degree of responsibility we have thus in many instances been called upon to incur, but upon the present occasion it appears to us of so serious a nature that our situation becomes extremely painful.

In these drawings for the church at Chelsea an attempt is proposed to be made to carry into execution a work of extremely difficult construction; with what prospect of success it would be improper in us to venture an opinion without giving to the subject the same degree of attentive study, with the assistance of accurately detailed models as well as drawings which we should think necessary in engaging upon a similar undertaking ourselves - we know too that the best considered instructions cannot in such a work ensure success if they are not carried into execution with equal care and ability.[48]

For Savage was proposing to embark on the unparalleled enterprise of constructing a stone vault!

On a further reference of Savage's designs, Soane and Smirke approved alterations made in the upper part of the tower, but expressed

in the strongest manner our opinion of the insufficient strength and improper construction of the lower part of the building. We consider it highly objectionable that any part of the walls upon the basement story should be less in thickness than they are to be made above it neither can we approve of the manner proposed for connecting brick and stone work in the tower, particularly as shewn in the plan of the western porch.[49]

Even after the Commissioners appointed their own Surveyor, the reference of plans to the Office of Works continued, until its abolition in 1832. Still questions were referred to the Crown Architects that they declined to answer. 'We consider that the measures necessary to be adopted presuming the foundation of a building, depend on many local considerations which must be referred entirely to the experience and judgement of the architect employed.'[50] Still they uttered warnings: 'In giving our approbation of these designs, we think it necessary to repeat an observation we have so often made upon former occasions, that such approbation is confined entirely to those parts of the work which appear upon the drawings, and we always presume that the whole will be done with the best materials and in the most workmanlike manner.'[51] Doubtless such warnings influenced the Commissioners in their demand for bonds of indemnity from architects − another serious professional question upon which the Board sought the views of the Attached Architects (discussed below in chapter 6) − and their various precautions against unsatisfactory tradesmen.[52]

30 St James, West Hackney (Robert Smirke, 1821 3). A deep Doric portico may have been thought more appropriate than Smirke's favourite Ionic for a north-eastern London suburb. Elmes thought the portico a good copy from a Grecian temple, 'but its effect is destroyed by ... the incubus of a bell tower that is riding upon its back' (*Metropolitan Improvements*, p. 163).

★★★★★

In their executive capacity, the Crown Architects were responsible for a dozen of the Commissioners' churches: Smirke headed the list with seven, Soane designed three, and Nash two.[53] Robert Smirke, youngest of the Attached Architects, had in his twenties spent some years in Greece, as well as Italy; his taste was decidedly for the Greek Revival mode, and particularly the Ionic order. Although some of his early country-houses are quasi-medieval, in the day of success he eschewed the Gothick. His churches are severe and rather heavy, but not altogether lacking in elegance. He was very early in the church-building field, those at Chatham and Wandsworth being listed as completed in the Commission's second Report (1822). In both parishes, he was the Commissioners' nomination.[54] At Chatham (pl. 53), following closely one of his 'model church' designs of 1818, it is the severity of the church that is the most striking feature. Smirke approved a site of about 115ft by 100ft offered by the local committee. A building to hold a thousand worshippers, 650 of whom would be seated in pews, could not, he stated, measure less than 60ft by 54ft internally; built of brick, with due attention to durability, without a tower, and 'finished in the plainest manner consistent with the character of the building' it would cost about £8,000 completely furnished, and enclosed with an iron railing. The Commissioners however wanted a church for 2,000 persons, half in free sittings, the interior fittings to be paid for by the parish. Despite a plea from the local archdeacon, the Board clung to its demand for a large church, though agreeing to pay any costs the parish could not discharge.[55] It was built in ragstone, with a small tower over the west front, and measured internally 91ft by 62, and 32ft in height.[56] Wandsworth, though of the same dimensions as Chatham, was built in light-coloured bricks, and dignified with dressings, portico and tower of stone from excellent Sussex quarries.[57]

There seems to have been some idea of displaying the merits of the nation's finest architects in the growing and fashionable suburban parish of St Marylebone, made the more important by Nash's development of the Regent's Park area, and construction of an elegant thoroughfare, Regent Street, from the Park to the Regent's palace, Carlton House. A new parish church had recently been built to the design of the parish architect, Thomas Hardwick (a pupil of Sir William Chambers, and clerk of the works (i.e. architect in charge) at the Crown properties at Hampton Court and Richmond), at a cost of more than £60,000.[58] The opulent but independent-minded vestry offered to find four sites and raise £20,000 if the Commissioners would build four churches each to hold 2,000. As their annual expenditure for ecclesiastical purposes was already £13,000, they asked for a loan of £24,000 for 30 years at three per cent.[59] The Board accordingly invited each of the Crown Architects to design one of the St Marylebone churches,[60] the fourth being awarded to Hardwick. Lord Kenyon, a leading figure in the parish, was closely involved in the negotiations, as was Bishop Law of Chester, also a resident during the parliamentary session. William Huskisson, the minister responsible for Crown lands, pointed out that Nash was architect of the New Street (Regent Street), so that it was desirable that he should be the architect of the church to be located there. The Commissioners agreed. To Soane they allotted the church in Marylebone Park (Regent's Park), in the eastern sector of the parish. To Smirke fell the south-western commission: he was instructed to view possible sites, one being approved on 16 May 1820, and to prepare appropriate plans.

St Mary's, Wyndham Place (pl. 32), is situated in a small square, with its portico and principal entrance on its long south side, facing the road leading to fashionable Bryanston Square. In plan, the church is a parallelogram, and the portico semicircular.[61] In elevation, there are two storeys on account of the galleries inside: the lower windows rectangular, and the upper long and round-headed. Built of brick, it is finished with a cornice and plain parapet. Six Ionic columns, with entablature and an elegant balustraded parapet, compose the portico, above which rises a 110ft high rather spindly cylindrical tower of the 'pepper-pot' variety. Smirke reported that 'I have placed the entrances in the situations where they appeared to me the most convenient on the site selected for the chapel; those to the ground floor are made on the South from Wyndham Place and at the West end; those to the galleries are also on the South and on the East from York Street.' He provided accommodation for

St Mary, Wyndham Place, St Marylebone (Robert Smirke, 1821-3).

Right: **31** View from the east. Smirke's relentlessly 'cubic style' is all too evident.

Below: **32** Portico and tower. 'The beauty of it is obscured by the liberties which have been taken with the architecture', said E. J. Carlos (*Gentleman's Magazine*, 1827, pt 2, p. 9). Another contemporary critic, James Elmes, condemned the novelty of the perforated parapet, instead of a balustrade, and the heaviness of the ill-graduated tower.

about 640 persons in pews and 1,180 in free seats. The walls were to be of brick, 'faced with bricks of a light color', with dressings of stone. On the south, the portico and tower were to be wholly of stone. He reckoned on excavating five feet below ground level for the wall foundations, and eight feet for the tower. The total cost, exclusive of an organ and communion plate, he estimated at £20,000: the church's 'very favorable site appeared to justify in the design as much of the advantage arising from external character as could be given consistently with the views of the Commissioners in respect to its expence'. The Board approved, with the rider that it would not be responsible for any sum beyond £20,000.[62]

Inside, galleries on three sides rest on square piers, while above them slender Doric columns rise to the gently curved ceiling, coffered and painted. Edward John Carlos (1798-1851), who, as 'E. I. C.', wrote a series of articles on new churches in the *Gentleman's Magazine,* regarded St Mary's as 'a handsome building', but (displaying the 'intellectual elegance of the gentleman connoisseur') disapproved of Smirke's free treatment of the detail, of which he said: 'According to the well-known professional dictum, it is "Gothic", since it is anything but Grecian.'[63] The Rev. William Johnson, chairman of the Manchester committee, however, chose the Wyndham Place design for their church at Salford (pl. 86), for which the Board had rejected some other plans. But there it is faced with ashlar, which much improves its appearance. The Commissioners were happy to agree, as there was a resultant saving of 2½ per cent. of the cost – half the architect's usual commission. Building at Salford was also cheaper than at Marylebone, at an estimated £14,850, further reduced by copying Wandsworth's ceilings and roof in place of St Mary's own.[64] Carlos criticized Wandsworth more pertinently, that it suffered from a 'marked frigidity', a charge true of all three churches.[65] The south portico (at both Wyndham Place and Salford) looks like an afterthought, added in a more ornamental style when it was seen how much money had been left after the completion of the main structure. The tower is isolated and undistinguished. As a composition the design is less successful than some of Francis Goodwin's Gothic efforts.

St Anne, Wandsworth, along with St James, West Hackney, and St George, Brandon Hill, Bristol, represents a third pattern by Smirke: these have an impressive western portico of four Doric columns, behind which rises a cupola; while the body of the church is the usual galleried box. There is no attempt to vary the interiors; the design merely consists of manipulation of three features: portico, tower, and body of the church. It is the portico that is the most decorative feature, the most conspicuous, and the only one into which Smirke introduced important variation: it might be of various shapes, and the columns offered a choice basically of three orders, capable of finer variation. But Smirke was a busy man,[66] and the taste of the day saw no objection to the duplication of a design in different and distant parts of the country,[67] as the Salford episode shows. The Board had evidently considered also using Smirke's Chatham plan elsewhere, as the architect expressed his 'most ready compliance' with their desire to make use of it.[68]

Quite different from those, however, was Tyldesley (Lancashire) (pl. 19), a handsome church in mainly thirteenth-century Gothic style, with 'later' clerestory, and west tower crowned by an impressive spire that resembles Louth, connected to the tower pinnacles by flying buttresses.[69] This spire so impressed the Board that, though demanding that Smirke cut his estimate from £13,500 (inclusive of commission, etc.) to the £12,000 reported to parliament, they asked that the spire be retained if possible.[70]

Smirke, renowned for his efficiency and technical skill, was the architect to whom the Commissioners turned in difficulty, asking him, for instance, if he could do two smaller chapels at Preston for the price of a single larger one (his response was 'no', politely phrased).[71] Similarly, it was from Smirke that they sought advice on the vexed question of the comparative cost of Grecian and Gothic churches. In April 1820 they commissioned two designs 'for a Church fit for a considerable provincial Town, giving to one of these the characteristic Style of a Gothic Building'. Smirke was left uncertain whether detailed estimates were required, and on inquiring was told to 'Prepare such detailed estimates and specifications as will enable the Board to judge of their comparative expence'.[72] Unfortunately, we do not have the results. Some years later, he was consulted about repairing the roofs of Francis Bedford's South London churches (discussed in chapter 7). He pleaded pressure of public business, but indicated that in the last resort he would undertake the work, which closed the church for four weeks and cost some £900.[73] Again, in 1833, further problems with Bedford's roofs were referred to Smirke, who supervised the repairs.[74]

33 St Anne, Wandsworth (Robert Smirke, 1820-2). West front. The excessive height of the tower unbalances the front, and the omission of the fascia from the architrave and dentils from the cornice give an air of 'naked frigidity' rather than simplicity to what was a country church. 'How often must the laboring mason blush to perform the task imposed on him by handing down such errors' (E. J. Carlos, *Gentleman's Magazine*, 1829, pt 2, pp. 577-8).

★★★★★

73

John Soane, architect to the Bank of England, and as a Crown Architect nominally responsible for the royal palaces in London, was a far more original architect than Smirke, or indeed than the other architects of his generation. But he was an old man whose creative power had, in Summerson's view, diminished. He had had little experience in church work. As noted above, in 1818 he formed the conclusion that the type of church required for the Commissioners would cost about £30,000; and though he designed churches that were built for considerably less, yet their costs were more than for the general run of Commissioners' churches. He declined a pressing request to design a church at Stand (Lancashire), because of the insufficiency of the funds allotted. In his letter of refusal he set forth his views: he was aware that churches for 2,000 persons had been erected in some districts for £12,000 or less; 'but churches of such a capacity, whether built after the ancient English architecture, or of the more ancient architecture of Greece or Rome, if substantially and characteristically designed and erected, of sufficient size to afford the congregation convenient accommodation and access, cannot … anywhere be built and finished for such sums as have been determined by the Trustees for building additional churches'.[75] He expressed disapproval of the different methods adopted to obtain designs and cheap estimates; and thought that the Commissioners had been misled 'by attending to the suggestions of inexperience and false economy'.

St Peter, Walworth (John Soane, 1823-4).

Above: **34** West front. A strictly 'grammatical' composition: a Roman Ionic portico, with Corinthian columns to the first stage of the tower and Composite to the second stage.

Right: **35** The long east-west free benches in the centre aisle, and those at the sides, did not meet the Commissioners' requirement that ground floor seats should face the altar. The side entrances were changed to windows.

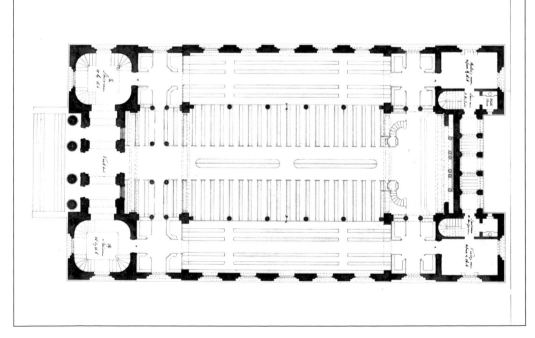

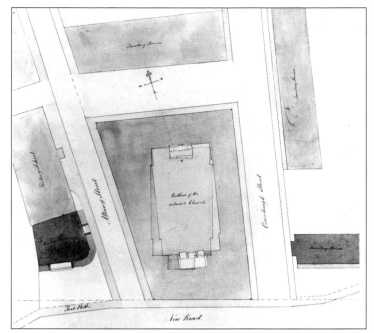

Holy Trinity, St Marylebone (John Soane, 1826-7).

Top left: **36** Ritual west front. Carlos criticized the omission of the pediment to the portico (a solution to the problem of a tower appearing to ride on a Grecian temple roof, which was so often attacked), and objected to brick corners when the rest was stone.

Top right: **37** Site plan, showing changes of axis. The original ordering, east-west, may be faintly discerned; the north-south layout, which allowed space all round, was then given a slight eastward inclination, enough to satisfy the Anglican tradition. The surrounding buildings are all identified as dwelling houses.

Left: **38** Gothic version, 1826, to meet the Vestry's wish. This exercise in Wyatt's Gothic proved too expensive.

Above: **39** Interior, looking towards the altar (ritual east). The arcades imparted something of a Gothic quality to the interior. The gallery pews have their original numbering, a requirement of the Commissioners. Chancel 1876.

This would tend to a deterioration of architecture unlikely to stop at the mere design.

Soane's three churches were in London, and designed at the express invitation of the Commissioners.[76] They are, like Smirke's, similar - a circumstance on which Carlos commented unfavourably.[77] St Peter's, Walworth, was the first to be completed. It lay in a parish, Newington, riven by dissension about a local Act which allowed trustees five years for building new churches. The Commissioners had called for improvements in selected designs, but as one of the two architects had failed to deliver and three years had already elapsed, the local committee asked the Board to appoint an architect.[78] Soane was thereupon requested immediately to provide designs for a church to hold 2,000, with a cost limit of £16,000. His alternative versions ran to £17,800, and - though he suggested that competitive contracts would bring the cost to £16,000 - he was therefore told to make reductions. By reducing the size of vaults under the church, using Bath instead of Portland stone, and substituting grey stocks for white brick he cut off £2,000.[79] Soane resented these limitations, and angrily drafted a letter: 'I have compressed pinched – pared & starved the design in all its parts in substance & quality of materials – & under all these mortifying circumstances the Church may be brought in the limits prescribed'.[80] Tenders opened at the end of April 1823, however, totalled £18,348: the Commissioners were 'very anxious' to have them reduced, but under the pressure of the local Act's time limit, 30 June 1825, rather than obtain new plans, they agreed to split the excess with the local trustees.[81] Because of an 'unavoidable delay' in obtaining Bath stone of the necessary dimensions, Portland stone was ultimately employed for the four giant Ionic columns of the portico, without extra charge (an indication of the profitability of these contracts).[82] Work proceeded rapidly and the church, the cornerstone laid in June 1823, was consecrated on 28 February 1825.[83] The entrance is recessed behind the portico columns, which are in line with the flanking walls of the west front; the problem of the tower on a Grecian temple body Soane resolved (like Gibbs at St Martin-in-the-Fields) by placing it in front of the pitched roof of the church – and also by substituting a balustrade for a pediment over the portico. The interior has a cut-off segmental arch, strengthened with wrought iron, separating the sanctuary from the nave, with portholes pierced through the spandrels; an arcade of slender segmental arches demarcates the gallery fronts.

Holy Trinity, Portland Road, Marylebone, was the most expensive of the four Marylebone churches (£24,708 18s. 8d.) and the church to which the Commissioners gave their largest grant – £19,041[84] – the remainder being subscribed by the parish. As remarked above, although well disposed, the St Marylebone Vestry was keen to have its own way: this involved the Commissioners in tedious negotiations, particularly over the site of the fourth new church (i.e. the one Soane was to design).

Invited by the Commissioners to design a church in the eastern sector of the parish, 'at the top of the Portland Road by the Circus', [85] Soane proposed a neo-classical building with a recessed tetrastyle Doric western portico, clerestory and a central hemispherical dome on a square base,[86] and exhibited three drawings in the 1821 summer exhibition at the Royal Academy.[87] Soane offered alternative designs, one, with clerestory, estimated at about £20,000, but the Commissioners called for their being re-considered, entertaining 'a doubt as to the effect of the building which is proposed to arise out of the centre of the chapel'. But the parish being unable to obtain the proposed site, further consideration was postponed.[88] A nearby site, 'on the South side of the New Road', was fixed upon in March 1822, and the

Commissioners asked Soane for his plans as soon as possible. Soane's subsequent reworkings provided a cylindrical western tower, modelled probably on the Temple of Vesta in the Forum Romanum, which Soane had drawn when in Rome as a tiro.[89] On 22 April 1823 the Board approved a new site obtained by the parish on the north side of the New Road, requested Soane to submit his plans at the next Board, and approved the division of the parish into four district parishes.[90] Lord Kenyon asked Soane to a meeting of the Building Committee on 20 May, but he replied that his drawings were not completed because he was revising those of two years earlier; a week later, he sent two sets of designs, one made to come within the £20,000 allowed, the other (14 drawings and a model)[91] 'to meet the wishes of the parish'.[92] But on 27 May 1823 the Commissioners rejected Soane's proposal at £28,600 as too expensive.[93]

In February 1824 Soane costed a revised design at £23,800, and this was referred to the vestry, which, tired of the delay, proposed undertaking the building themselves. When the Commissioners pointed out that they were committed to Soane, the vestry decided to stop payments for their agreed share of the total expenditure.[94] Soane sent another set of '12 Fair Plans Elevations and Sections, and 5 Perspective Views of parts of the exterior and interior of the same design – also 20 drawings of the details of the entire Building' on 21 February 1824. He costed the building and complete finishing 'in a substantial and characteristic manner … with the strictest economy' at £23,800, but had 'no doubt Builders will be ready to contract to perform the Works for a smaller sum.'[95] Detailed drawings were made of this design for the contractors. But the vestry declined to meet Mr Soane. On 16 March 1824, with Lord Kenyon and the Bishop of Chester present, the Commissioners clearly yielded to vestry pressure and asked Soane for a Gothic design (pl. 38),[96] 'provided you should be of opinion that such a Church can be erected for the sum of £20,000, with a capability of accommodating 2,000 persons'.[97] Soane replied that as such designs would be some time in the making, he was 'extremely desirous' to explain to the Commissioners 'such parts of the Design already made as appear to have been misunderstood'. He was therefore invited to attend a Board, but also to proceed with the Gothic design.[98] None of the foregoing designs was executed.[99]

Informed on 13 July 1824 that the vestry had approved Soane's yet further amended plans, the Board instructed him to commence: however, Soane's habitual indecision produced further revisions: two designs were submitted in November, one – unbelievably, after all the previous discussion – priced at £27,200 (or by omitting columns in the north, south and east fronts, substituting Bath for Portland stone, and making the ceiling flat instead of circular, £23,340), the other at £19,860. It was, of course, the latter that the Board preferred, and forwarded to the vestry, which resolved in its favour and agreed the site on 20 November;[100] but 'the last design adopted', Soane reported in April 1825, 'made it necessary to prepare an entire new set of Working Drawings'.[101] Daniel Sharp's contract for £19,524 was agreed in August. But the east-west alignment required by the Commissioners was an extremely tight fit on the Osnaburgh Road site, and the vestry agreed unanimously that 'the whole of the expenditure for ornament would be laid out in vain unless the church is placed North and South'; the 'learned Rector' suggested that 'a trifling inclination to the East' would be sufficient.[102] In November 1825, the vestry resolved in favour of 'Plan B' at £19,860, and work was at last able to begin. In June 1826, a further vestry resolution declared that the original plan was 'extremely desirable', and the Duke of Portland headed a subscription to provide £1,280 to re-instate the balustrade and restore its amplitude to the steeple.[103]

This Classical design was in fact a revision of St Peter, Walworth, with a recessed Ionic portico to the (ritual) east as well as the very slightly advanced western Ionic portico sheltering a slightly recessed porch, the entrance from the New (Marylebone) Road, marked by its tower. The problem of handling this necessary feature, so uncomfortable when riding the traditional pitched temple roof of the conventional eighteenth-century church, Soane resolved (as at Walworth) by concealing his roof behind a balustrade, and setting the tower back slightly from the portico which he crowned with the balustrade rather than a pediment - another 'fault' condemned by Carlos. The tower is a re-working of one that in an earlier design would have been at the (ritual) east of the church,[104] but with its lower, square, element enriched, the Corinthian columns marking each corner doubled, so providing an almost Baroque elaboration seldom found in the Commissioners' churches – this thanks to the willingness of the parishioners to raise £1,280 to re-instate the steeple design rejected in January 1825;[105] the upper portion, of 'pepper-pot' character, retains recollections of the Temple of Vesta.

Despite all his efforts, Soane did not really succeed in working within the limits prescribed by the Commissioners, and he was wise to decline similar commissions. His crony, James Spicer, in fact wrote to him of the Walworth church:

> I thought the funds for this Church were more extensive and I regret exceedingly that you have coveted the Babylonish garment of the Commission and partaken of their accursed thing. The Philistines will indeed triumph when they record your acquiescence in the rules and regulations of the Commissioners which although appearing greatly amended in this exemplar ought not to be countenanced by such men as yourself and attached colleagues but certainly not by yourself.[106]

At Bethnal Green, the last of his churches, Soane was yet further constrained regarding cost; not only was the district a notoriously poor one, but by 1826 the Commissioners' funds were at a low ebb, and he was favoured to be allowed £15,999,[107] the amount of a lump-sum contract. Soane employed a more utilitarian version of his standard west front design, reducing the columns to Portland stone pilasters with grooved rectangles standing for capitals, the low square tower similarly with corner pilasters, and the crowning cupola reduced, to Soane's mortification, to a bell-turret.[108] The local boss, Joseph Merceron,[109] who had led the opposition to the rector's attempts to secure sites for new churches in the parish, had the effrontery to demand another £500 from the Board to increase the height of the tower 12 or 15 feet, referring to

> The universal sentiment prevailing both in and out of this parish, with regard to the steeple, which has really mortified and disappointed the expectations of almost every individual with whom I have conversed. ... the building in question does seem to be out of all just proportion terminating very abruptly ... the present new church approved of in every particular would be the theme of conversation among all classes and operate as a great inducement In drawing full congregations – certain it is that now I hear nothing but complaints coupled with ill-natured observations ...[110]

The Board's response was that they had spent so much on the church that they could not spend any more.

More effective than the tower was the Vanbrughian sublimity of Soane's east end, with its salient cubical robing and vestry rooms (since altered).[111] Digging out began on 12 June 1826; the first brick laid on 6 July; the first stone of the Portland plinth

set on 8 August; the roof begun on 1 December; the keystone of the tower and vane set on 28 April 1827; but the church was not consecrated until 18 October 1828.[112]

St John, Bethnal Green (John Soane, 1826-8).

★★★★★

Left: **40** The west front is an ingenious reduction of a temple front to its basic elements. Carlos thought the tower, pared down for cost's sake, a 'monstrous excrescence'.

Right:: **41** West vestibule and stairs to galleries: an unmistakably Soanic corridor.

John Nash, favourite architect of George IV, and author of the great metropolitan improvements then in progress, was a year older than Soane, but still with a stock of ingenious ideas. His Regent Street layout came to include three Commissioners' churches. He himself designed that at Langham Place to terminate the northwards vista, and his assistant George Stanley Repton (1786-1858), St Philip's chapel,[113] which like C. R. Cockerell's Hanover Chapel, formed part of the street façade.

The Commissioners had called upon Nash on 25 April 1820 for a design for 'the church proposed to be built on the bend of the new Street [Regent Street] at the entrance of Langham Place'. Some four weeks later Nash sent the plans, with a covering letter in which he stated:

> From the nature of the bend of the street the portico and spire will together form an object terminating the vista from the circus in Oxford Street. The spire (I submit) is the most beautiful of forms, is peculiarly calculated for the termination of a vista and particularly appropriate to a church. The portico I have made circular as taking up less of the passage of the street at the same time that it is most consonant to the shape of the spire.[114]

This design, based on one of his 'specimen designs' of 1818, considered above, but much more successfully composed, with the fluted cone of the spire, partially caged in its peristyle (possibly inspired by Patrington spire) rising gracefully above a circular portico, a brilliantly successful and original handling of the problem of orienting the church and at the same time closing the vista up Regent Street, is 'one of Nash's major works'.[115] It was approved by the Board, 'subject to the omission of the figures in the steeple, and the addition of one bench in width to the galleries'.[116] Nash had

All Souls, Langham Place, St Marylebone (John Nash, 1822–4).

Top: **42** View from south (in 1953). The unimpressive body was obscured by adjacent buildings, but the ingenious portico and spire closed the vista north from Regent Street and contrived the essential change of line to Portland Place.

Below: **43** Crypt. Springs, quicksands and old sewers required deep excavations, so Nash devised inverted arches to secure the superstructure. This facilitated the excavation of a crypt, seen here in the course of restoration after bomb damage, *c*.1950.

also given some attention to ensuring the permanence of his church, recommending that no timber should be used in the walls, and that 'the roof be composed of iron and brick covered with Dehl's mastic'.[117] He assured the Commissioners that the church would then never require repair. The walls should be of hardburnt bricks also covered with Dehl's mastic: 'the whole would be one entire incrustation, and susceptible only of that decay which even stone is subject to.' But mastic the Board would not tolerate; ashlar was necessary. The body of All Souls is quite plain, the windows having neither pediments nor surrounds. It is a dignified, calm building, concentrating its charming eccentricity in the portico and steeple.

Nash's lackadaisical business methods were exposed when he informed the Building Committee that he had not expected to have to provide an estimate in detail, as that would be revealed by the tenders. He came up with a sum of £20,931, exclusive of commission and incidentals – which would already exceed the Board's maximum – but explained that to cover himself he had added ten per cent to the individual trades' figures, plus a contingencies sum.

Told to deduct these, he gave an inclusive estimate of £19,514, but Robert Streather's lump-sum tender came in, to Nash's amazement, at only £15,994.[118] Work began on 18 November 1821, and completed about August, 1824. There were considerable problems in securing a sound foundation because of 'old drains, sewers, cesspools and bogs in every part', and the course of a main sewer had to be altered.[119] Nash employed an effective system of inverted arches, excavated in the later twentieth century for a crypt. The ultimate cost was £19,612, the Commissioners contributing two-thirds.

The intemperate attack on the steeple made by the Hon. Henry Grey Bennett in the House of Commons is famous: 'although he was not rich, he would give something to have it pulled down. It was a deplorable and horrible thing; … a disgrace to the metropolis. It was like a flat candlestick with an extinguisher on it.' Even the minister, Charles Arbuthnot of the Woods and Forests, was not prepared to defend it: 'The church in question certainly would be better away, but it might not be easy to remove it.' Having been compelled to disclose that Nash was the architect, he remarked that: 'If this building was not very creditable to that gentleman's taste, there were many others in its neighbourhood that were eminently so.'[120] The opinion of subsequent generations has been more favourable than Mr Bennett's, and the original architect of the B.B.C. massif carefully avoided overwhelming the church.[121] Internally, its handsome appearance always commanded respect.

Nash built only one other church for the Commissioners;[122] St Mary, Haggerston. He was desirous of again employing a classical style, partly because the mother-church, St Leonard, Shoreditch, was of 'Roman architecture'.[123] A letter of 1822,[124] setting forth for the Commissioners his ideas about the Haggerston site, which was awaiting development, shows Nash's care for the *mise-en-scène*: 'The Commissioners will observe that the plot of ground will be nearly square, and I think the church should be a square of the form of a Grecian cross, or a circle or an octagon'. He would, however, be guided by the sentiments of the Commissioners in his choice of form. With regard to the environs, he hoped they would consent to an iron railing around the churchyard instead of a brick wall. 'The whole would become ornamental to the vicinity instead of a nuisance, which dead walls always are.' As for the churchyard itself, the graves should be 'formed in straight lines, and parallel to each other, and if this is done with great accuracy and regularity [it] cannot fail to arrest the attention of the spectator, and produce in his mind that sensation of awe and respect which so solemn a record is so well-calculated to effect'. The proprietor of the land had agreed to lay out the neighbouring ground according to Nash's plan, building 'a front of handsome houses of an uniform elevation [designed by Nash] leaving a road of 25 feet between the church-yard and the front of those houses. This arrangement will place the church in the centre of a quadrangle surrounded by the church-yard and equally open to Brunswick Street and Cambridge Street.' This was desirable, as it was as yet uncertain which would be the principal road, and 'the former circumstance cannot fail of producing an ornamental effect to that part of the town'. He trusted

44 St Mary, Haggerston, Shoreditch (John Nash, 1825-7). West front, based on one of Nash's model designs of 1818. Flanking octangular turrets house gallery staircases. The west tower is crowned by a lantern in the manner of Boston parish church.

that 'as this church will be seen all round and from a considerable distance', the Commissioners would allow 'The four fronts to be faced with ashlar that it may appear throughout a stone building, as is the present one at Shoreditch'. But the Board received these proposals coldly, and some three years later work was begun on a rather meagre Gothic church (again based on one of his 1818 'specimens'), for the Commissioners had no intention of spending large sums in so inconspicuous a quarter. Nash was probably wise, with his limited funds, to concentrate all his effects in the west front, which the Rev. B. F. L. Clarke considers may justly be called 'licentious'[125] – a term not unpopular in Regency days for describing Gothic: Nazi bombs demolished it in 1941.

5

The Organization and Regulation of the Commission

Meanwhile the Bishop of Chester had fathered a line of churches by obtaining a plan from one Thomas Rickman (1776-1841), 'a very ingenious deserving man', whom he had met in 1817 when, as chairman of the Liverpool Blind Asylum, he was considering plans for that institution.[1] Bishop Law wrote to Lord Liverpool on 7 August 1818:

> In order that no time might be lost in fixing a plan, upon which the New Churches might be built in the Diocese of Chester, I have procured the accompanying design from Mr. Rickman, a very able architect in Liverpool. With some trifling alterations which I have suggested, it appears to me to be as eligible a plan as we can adopt. Churches with the appearance which churches ought to have, and capable of containing 1,500 persons may be built, upon an average for £6,000. I have therefore taken the liberty of forwarding your Lordship a copy of the design with an explanation, thinking it not improbable that you might wish to lay the plan, if approved of, before the Commissioners in Town.[2]

Many other architects were quick to realize that the Act offered great opportunities; and many applications were made to Commissioners, either directly or through distinguished intermediaries. A Mr Robertson of Greenwich[3] forwarded designs through the intermission of the Chancellor of the Exchequer; one J. Gordan enquired on behalf of a friend, 'a respectable builder', whether works would begin in the ensuing season. In April 1819 R. W. Pilkington[4] sought an introduction through the assistant secretary of the Church-Building Society, Joshua Rodber, who also sent a Mr Carr of Sheffield to the Board to explain his views on conveying sound in large churches. W. F. Pocock (1779-1849), a cottage and villa architect, published *Designs for Churches and Chapels.* Rickman meanwhile had sent the Board's Secretary a copy of his new *Essay on Architecture*, as a further step in his personal campaign for professional recognition. In September Rodber sent a Mr Smith, whose system of roofing had 'been approved by some branches of public departments'. John Walters (1782-1821)[5] sent Gothic designs, while Richard Elsam (*fl.* 1795-1825)[6] sent a selection of 23 Gothic and 14 Grecian drawings – the first instance to come before the

Commissioners of the contemporary architect's habitual ambidexterity.

A submission on a higher level than these was a lengthy paper[7] sent to Archbishop Manners-Sutton by a fashionable architect, William Wilkins (1778-1839), well-known for his scholarly Greek Revival manner, who in 1817 had won the competition for a national monument commemorating Waterloo.[8] He urged that plans for the new churches should 'obviate the inconveniences' to which churches were generally exposed.

> … A strong expression in favor of a Church, as an appropriate and useful building for the commemoration of the battle of Waterloo, having been manifested then in the Session of the last Parliament, it seemed highly probable that my design for a commemorative monument … would undergo revision; and that a building more called for by the exigencies of the period would be ultimately substituted for it.
>
> In this expectation I have for some time past given my attention to the construction of Churches, and employed myself in … studying the most favorable arrangement both of exterior and interior. In pursuing this object I have considered the various objections which have arisen to the plans usually followed and endeavoured to strike out an arrangement by which all would be more or less obviated.
>
> The principles which have guided me in the formation of that part of the building appropriated to the performance of the public service is applicable to the construction of Churches and Chapels of all dimensions. I propose illustrating them by plans, elevations and sections of such a building, which, without pretending to be incapable of improvement, I venture to offer as open to fewer objections than the generality of the best constructed places of public worship.
>
> The objections I have considered as important to be wholly obviated may be divided into three principal heads
>
> 1st. The imperfect dilation and propagation of sound; …
>
> 2nd. The means of ventilation; …
>
> 3d. The arrangement of the interior, through inattention to which the majority of the congregation is exposed to the action of constant currents.

As sound dilated in circles from the speaker, the most efficient form would, Wilkins argued, be semi-circular; but he cited his experience of ancient Greek theatres to establish that form was not the only consideration: still more important was the material used. Wood was unsatisfactory, as shown by its complete failure in modern theatres (and Wilkins was proprietor of a chain of theatres), because it destroyed distinctness. From the analogy of the human frame Wilkins proposed to use hard materials – stone and iron – wherever possible. 'A smooth or polished surface is highly efficacious in the dilation of sound'.

As to ventilation, experiment had shown that elasticity was essential for conveying sound. Therefore, for good acoustics as well as the 'safety of the audience', rarified air must be removed, by means of windows opening near the ceiling, and apertures having 'an *indirect* communication with the external air and permit at all times the escape of the respired air'. With regard to internal arrangement, the great need was to protect the 'audience' from draughts: 'The constant influx of auditors makes it difficult to prevent the admission of external air into the body of the Church; but it is possible to arrange the necessary approaches and doorways so as to break the direct rush, and expose as few as possible to its weakened influence.' The most perfect form would be that of the ancient theatres, but that would be both difficult to roof and also raised an unsuitable association of ideas. Next best would be a form where the breadth was greater than the length (such as Nash designed); which would require intermediate supports for the roof. 'If iron be used for this purpose they may be small in bulk, but the solemnity which every feature of the building should be calculated

to inspire demands the sober but more massive features of architecture – they may obstruct the view of a limited few but the sense of vision is less to be consulted in a place of public worship than that of hearing.'

Wilkins' conclusion was that these considerations suggested a plan resembling that of 'the Roman Basilica, the earliest of Christian Churches', which had been followed as examples by 'our Saxon ancestors … though not so successfully as the Gothic architects of a later period'.

It may have been Wilkins' reiterated references to the 'Antients', or perhaps his would-be scientific solutions, or even his immense self-assurance that discouraged the archbishop from laying this material before his fellow-Commissioners or referring it to the Attached Architects; or he may simply have thought the recommendations so obvious or bizarre that to do so was unnecessary: at all events, Wilkins' prolusions failed miserably to achieve their object, disappearing into the welter of primatial papers.

Although by August 1819 the Commission had been in existence a year, little seemed to have been accomplished: on vacation the indefatigable Archdeacon Wollaston had leisure to consider the Board's problem and to work out a solution. His letter to Jenner of 23 August 1819 gives a useful statement of the position at that date, and is worth quotation *in extenso*: [9]

> I cannot help wishing through you to make some representation to the other members
> who may meet during my absence, with a hope that they may be able to put our business
> in a train differing from that in which it has hitherto gone, and in which it has hitherto
> made so very little progress. Consider how we have been labouring to get Blackburn

45 St Paul, Nottingham (William Wilkins, 1820–2). One of the foremost authorities on Grecian architecture, Wilkins believed that the Roman basilican plan was best for churches, that stone surfaces diffused sound, and that acoustics as well as ventilation benefited from windows opening near the ceiling. Uniquely, he raised the side aisle floors to pew top height, so that the full height of the columns was exhibited. The minister declared that the congregation could not hear him from the pulpit in its original position, at one side, so with the archbishop's approval he moved it to the centre. Photograph *c.*1900.

'We may have either a Greek dress for the parallelogram or a Gothic dress, and we may adopt either the one or the other' (Archdeacon Wollaston, 23 Aug. 1819).

Top left: **46** St George, Leicester (William Parsons, 1823–6). The tower and spire present another imitation of St James, Louth, or perhaps of St Michael, Coventry, Parsons apparently designed parapets originally, rather than the battlements, which (the Surveyor pointed out) were most approved for this style; crockets on the spire's ribs were ordered to be omitted. Perspective drawing after spire struck by lightning, 1 Aug. 1846. Parsons supervised the repair, somewhat heightening the spire.

Top right: **47** St Mary, Somers Town, St Pancras (Henry & Henry William Inwood, 1822–4). 'Simple and unpretending' (Elmes); 'Perhaps the completest specimen of "Carpenter's Gothic" ever witnessed' (Carlos).

Bottom left: **48** St John the Baptist, Hoxton, Shoreditch (Francis Edwards, 1824–6). 'If the steeple were taken away, it would present in all its features the appearance of a large meeting-house' (E. J. Carlos, *Gentleman's Magazine*, 1827, pt 1, p. 209).

Bottom right: **49** St Peter, Regent Square, St Pancras (Henry & Henry William Inwood, 1822–4). Elmes regarded this as an inferior imitation of the same architects' outstanding Grecian Revival St Pancras parish church, but still 'a chaste and pleasing composition', though the architrave of the Ionic portico was 'incorrect', having three fascias. Soane was astonished that the Inwoods could estimate both St Mary's and St Peter's at the same price.

forward in conformity with the wish of the Archbishop, Bitton to meet the wish of Bishop Gloucester – West Bromwich, Bordesley, Erdington, proposals of long standing, which have been before us repeatedly – and where are we at this present moment in respect of them – Wakefield, Houghton and others might be added to the list. We have received plans of several of these, which we do not cordially approve, and would be glad to reject, but cannot with civility. We have received partial and hesitating certificates from the [Crown] Architects upon some of these, and upon others we are told they have not sufficient in-formation, when we had been endeavouring to get information in the very manner which had been pointed out as desirable for them. … We are by the answers from the Architects laid before us on the 12th instant totally stopped again and unable to proceed with these pressing cases. And this I apprehend will continue to be the case, while we call for separate plans from each separate place, while those plans are required without sufficiently specified instructions as to the return of those plans, and of the details which must accompany them. We get most crude devices: tasteless and unauthorized exterior; ill-arranged interior; unstable and insufficient framework; from architects connected with the parties and favoured by them, and unaccompanied by the specifications necessary for judging of the work. These we are from the circumstances disinclined to reject *in toto,* however we may see it desirable that we should do so – yet to alter the several particulars is absolutely impracticable. We meet and meet again with the same difficulty, and waste a vast deal of time without making any advance in the work. I can and do speak feelingly upon this, having … attended every meeting till the 12th …

In proof of such assertions one only need refer to the Crown Architects' reports: many designs were, as discussed in chapter 4, brought before them three or four times, to be adversely criticized in terms sometimes vague and general. The archdeacon continued:

I cannot refrain, therefore, from urging to the B[uilding] C[ommittee] to consider whether it is not highly desirable that we should endeavour to get by selection from plans, invited by advertisement, or otherwise procured if other mode can be suggested equally meeting the public expectation, such one or more forms for the different parts, as being once approved may be applied as occasion occurs. Of a form for internal arrangement we ourselves can judge entirely; and if we get one which we approve as best, adopt it and ask no farther. Of a form of framing for a roof we ourselves cannot judge entirely: but when we accept one which appears good in principle mathematically,[10] and from the approval of architects are convinced that it is good also practically, adopt that also everywhere and ask no farther; have its dimensions, scantlings, etc., specified and ready for any case which may occur. Of an exterior we also can judge, or the Board can for us, or friends may assist with their opinion – and there we may have either a Greek dress for the parallelogram or a Gothic dress, and we may adopt either the one or the other. In that which may best be approved, when offered, we may get some particulars altered to our wish, but when it is done, we adopt it and, as I said before, ask no farther – and when an application comes before us, we have to enquire as to size, and adapt the scale to it; we have to require information as to local prices, which ought to be done according to a specified form ready prepared and printed for the purpose; and then to call for tenders by competition for the quantities of work according to the specifications which will be beforehand ready, agreeing with the plans, etc.

Wollaston suggested that not only would this facilitate business; it would also save expense – for where parishes paid for plans, there was '£200 or £300 less for the building; and that sum is therefore in every case out of our pockets'. He proposed holding a competition for designs and specifications:

We may have what we want without repetition of expense or of fruitless meetings and trouble. If we frame our advertizement so as to get at first slight designs; the premium need not be large at first. If we state in the particulars the premium will not be given until it be accompanied by further detailed drawings if required; we cut off youngsters in great measure, who would be unequal to such details. If we insert that we may divide the premium according as the plan may be in whole or in part adopted, we may select what we like from each, and thus improve upon any one of the number.

He concluded with a warning:

Anxious as I am that this work and great expenditure be done economically, because we are spending the national money; but at the same time handsomely, because we are supporting the National Religion, and ought also to support the taste and the wealth of the Nation as applied to this important object, I have given it much of my thought. … I am sure that much of impediment will be thrown in the way of our proceeding thus, because it will decrease the work to be done by the trade – That, however, we must resist.[11]

Wollaston's plan, which might have silenced criticisms that the Million churches were too expensive, was not imposed, despite a number of requests from parishes for suitable plans. The rector of Gateshead, Durham, having been awarded a grant of £1,000 towards a church at Gateshead Fell to hold a thousand, in vain requested a plan. Local committees in the several parishes were entrusted with the business in the traditional way. They were directed to obtain first sites (to be approved by the diocesan) and then plans, which had to be submitted for the Commissioners' approval, which was based on liturgical as well as stylistic grounds, before reference to the the Board's own Surveyor and then to the Attached Architects for structural and technical examination. But this lengthy process often resulted in a general dissatisfaction: proposed sites might cause local disputes, plans approved by a parish might be rejected by the Board for reasons of expense, or by the Crown Architects as unsound constructionally. Although the architect was usually given an opportunity to rectify his faults, not infrequently the local committee was at length instructed to obtain other plans, as seen above for Bolton and Farnworth. Yet there were occasions when the Board yielded to requests: C. A. Busby's plans for Oldham having been rejected, the incumbent wrote despairingly: 'The [local] Committee not being acquainted with any Architect of character in this line of Building at liberty to engage in such an undertaking would feel particularly obliged to the Commissioners [if they] would have the goodness to recommend or appoint one of them'. His answer: 'The Board would prefer receiving Plans prepared by an Architect selected by the Local Committee. They therefore request that the Committee will again endeavour to find an Architect of known integrity talent and experience; but that if they should fail in obtaining one, the Board will then recommend an architect to them.'[12]

Another possibility the procedure afforded was that a rejected architect might use a friend or employee to submit alternative plans, as Goodwin did unsuccessfully at Erdington, Warwickshire, when his failure to satisfy the Building Committee about his estimate had provoked his dismissal.[13] The toing and froing between the several parties wasted time; tempers were exacerbated – it was sometimes a local committee's 'favourite son' who was thus rejected. Further trouble might arise when the rejected architect sent in his account: the Commissioners refused to be put to any expense in obtaining plans,[14] and local committees rarely had surplus funds at their disposal to meet such claims. They might consequently become involved in, or at least threatened with litigation, as happened at Leeds in 1821, when Edward Gyfford (1773-1856) was told by the local committee that his services would not be further required. The Board declined to become involved, although ultimately agreeing to pay him £150 and his costs.[15] This does not seem to have had the effect of limiting the competition among architects and that expression of local talent which the Commissioners had desired to call forth; hopes of the prospective perpetual advertisement evidently lured architects to compete despite the refusal of any remuneration for the unsuccessful.[16] Limited competitions between architects are particularly evident in the later 1820s, when the work of church extension had become widespread and the short-lived prosperity of the mid-1820s encouraged many building projects.[17]

Instead of adopting a general plan, the Commissioners attempted to reduce the number of unsatisfactory plans by demanding testimonials from would-be competitors, and by issuing their 'Instructions to Architects'. A further measure to achieve greater security and dispatch of business was the appointment of a full-time Surveyor, who was to make preliminary reports on the plans submitted, and inspect the buildings during construction. Six months after a strong warning from the Crown Architects of the need to ensure sound workmanship,[18] the Building Committee reported to the Board: 'That great delay and inconvenience had arisen from the want of immediate professional advice and assistance in regard to plans for new churches and chapels submitted to them.'[19] The Board therefore instructed them to consider a remedy, and on 11 July 1820 the Committee reported back: 'The delay and inconvenience ... may be remedied by some professional gentleman being added to the Commission.'[20] They proposed as a proper person George Dance (1741-1825), 'formerly an architect, but who has retired from his profession'.[21] Dance, who had been Soane's master, had retired as Clerk of the City Works (i.e. architect to the City of London) in 1815, and a more eminent name could hardly have been proposed. The Committee's suggestion adopted, it was ordered that application should be made to His Majesty to add Dance to the Commission. But Dance refused the burdensome honour:

> In answer to ... your letter ... in which, you inform me that His Majesty's Commissioners for Building New Churches have done me the honour to request me to furnish them with my opinion with reference to the tenders and upon the construction and durability of the Plans, I request you to inform His Majesty's said Commissioners that I find myself from old age and increasing infirmities, after having wholly declined the exercise of all professional exertion, to be unequal to the task of furnishing them with any valuable opinion upon the subjects referred and likely to occur in the course of their present and future investigations.[22]

It was yet some time after this that the decision to employ a salaried surveyor was taken, and Edward Mawley (d. 1826) was appointed to the post.[23] His first report is dated 1 May 1821. Little is known of him, apart from this work for the Board, but he had had experience of both country-house and industrial building;[24] whether he had had any previous experience of church-building is not known. An original member of the Surveyors' Club, he was president in 1799; and was also a member of the Painter-Stainers' Company. Joshua Watson probably had a hand in his appointment, as Mawley was employed on his estate by H. H. Norris, Watson's intimate friend.[25] On appointment, he was immediately attacked in Britton's *Magazine of the Fine Arts* by an anonymous but allegedly eminent architect as 'a *builder's measurer* ... who has himself been acting as a tradesman, subordinate to architects', and subsequently that periodical commented: 'As a house-painter, he is well-known to the professional architect and to the public; and as a highly respectable man, to all who have the pleasure of his acquaintance'.[26] But his functions were those that an experienced surveyor could well fulfil: to give his opinion on all plans and specifications, examine and check all building accounts referred to him, inspect and arrange all tenders, inspect and report on all sites when required, to make an annual survey and report of churches being built by the Board, and give assistance generally on all professional business referred to him, attending at the Office during working hours and at other times when required by the Secretary.[27] If the Board approved the general style and character of plans submitted, comprising drawings, specifications, estimates, and a completed copy of the Board's printed form stating details of style, size, and materials, they were then passed on to the Building Committee and the Surveyor. The Board regarded Mawley as a success: when he died unexpectedly, having been thrown out of his gig on to his head, Archdeacon Cambridge wrote of 'his punctual zealous and conscientious discharge of the duties of his office' and his 'faithful and valuable services'.[28] He was, however, as will be seen, conservative in his view of building technique, in a period when new materials were coming into use.

Mawley advised on such points as the thickness of walls, the position of doorways, and the internal arrangements of the church – particularly pointing out the several practices forbidden by the Commissioners. Thus Thomas Taylor's drawings for Attercliffe (Yorkshire), showed back boards and foot boards for the free seats, 'which the Committee usually think are not necessary'; and his inspection of Goodwin's church at Bordesley (Warwickshire) revealed aisle floors of mastic cement 'which the Committee does not usually approve'.[29] He was also able to point out omissions, such as failure to provide adequate ventilation in the ceiling, 'which the Committee have particularly directed', or provision of flues in the walls for heating should it prove to be required.[30] He checked on the number of sittings; he stated whether the estimate seemed sufficient for the specification, whether that was adequately drawn up, and whether tenders appeared satisfactory:[31] matters in which the peculiar design skill of the architect had little relevance, even though he was commonly required to deal with them.[32]

Reference was still made to the Crown Architects for a report on the constructional stability of designs,[33] though Mawley commented on this too: Taylor's roof construction for his Attercliffe church required 'further consideration'; and at Leicester, Parsons left too much space between his principal rafters.[34] Mawley identified various faults in Barry's plans for Oldham (Lancashire), which, when he had passed them, were referred to the Crown Architects.[35] From 1822, he made an annual inspection of buildings in progress, as considered below. Occasionally he intervened directly with the architect, as at Nottingham, to substitute iron for lead rain water pipes.[36] Perhaps his most important contribution was his preference for the lump-sum contract rather than tradesmen's contracting for their individual trades, as the Commissioners had originally determined: 'on every account', he declared, 'it is my advice that a Contract for the entire work should be selected as none but Surveyors can know the difficulty, the trouble and vexation of superintending a Building where a variety of Contractors are employed'.[37] He appears to have been a thoroughly competent servant of the Commission.

It is not easy to say what direct influence the Commissioners had on ecclesiastical architecture.[38] It was greatest in the Million era, about 1819 to 1829, when they were paying if not the whole, a very large part of the cost, and when church-building was a comparatively unfamiliar art. By 1830 a standard had been evolved, and there was a wider awareness of the standards the Commissioners required. Plans were nonetheless not approved without full examination. Inevitably, the Commissioners' influence waned with their funds: local committees, footing most of the bill, might not bother to refer to London alterations in the buildings, particularly alterations made after plans had been approved.

That influence might seem most immediate where the local committee asked the Commissioners themselves to select an architect or even a specific plan. As seen above, the Commissioners normally expected a parish to find both site and architect. To some local committees this labour seemed Herculean, and they requested the Commissioners to nominate an architect, provide a plan, or take over the whole business of church-building in their patch. At Chatham, the curate enquired whether the parish should obtain a plan or wait for the Commissioners to do so: architects were expensive, and parish subscriptions very limited. The Board promptly entrusted the work to Smirke.[39] At Newington, a contentious parish in London's southern suburbs, a local act had been obtained for building two churches. After the persistent failure of one of their chosen architects, S. T. Bull (1789-1847), to deliver his plans, the local committee asked the Board to furnish plans.[40] James Savage (1779-1852), having heard of the imbroglio, offered his services, pointing out the praise given his St Luke, Chelsea, as 'a revival of the Gothic principle of construction as well of design'. But the Board resolved forthwith to invite Soane to submit plans, a decision they perhaps regretted when Soane's plans came in at £1,800 more than the sum allowed – an exceeding only tolerated because the local act imposed a strict time limit for building, and the parish undertook to pay half of any excess; and doubtless regretted even more when the tenders proved higher than Soane's expectations, forcing a revision of the design, considered in chapter Four.[41]

Bermondsey was another South London instance where the local committee had difficulty in handling arrangements. They had held a competition for designs, which was won by an inexperienced relation of a committee-member, but eventually taken over by Henry Phillips, whose 'important errors and imperfections' caused the Board to reject his plans and direct the parish to obtain others. An exhausted local committee asked the Board to select a suitable plan. The Board, 'although not accustomed to obtain plans', agreed in view of the parish's 'strong wish',[42] and the work was given to Savage (pl. 157).

Confusion reigned at Netherton (Dudley), where the vicar, Dr Booker, not having seen any plans that the parish liked, had asked the Commission to furnish plans for 'a plain unostentatious edifice' to hold 1,500; whereon they applied to Smirke: but the great man was too busy to respond immediately. Left in limbo, the Nethertonians obtained preliminary drawings from Rickman, which they proposed to forward. The Board responded that was unnecessary, Smirke being instructed to go to Netherton to see whether his plans were applicable to the site, proposed to be given by Lord Dudley. Smirke reported favourably, and was told to advertise for tenders.[43] Unfortunately Lord Dudley's illness prevented the conveyance of the site, which was subsequently found to be riddled with ancient mines. When a new site was finally obtained, in mid-1827, plans by Thomas Lee (another metropolitan architect, but known to Lord Dudley) were submitted by Dr Booker, and approved.[44]

In general, the deference the Commissioners paid to the wishes of local committees was considerable, as both metropolitan and provincial cases illustrate. At Hulme, Manchester, Francis Goodwin had had to relinquish his appointment because of the Board's restriction on the number of churches any architect (especially Goodwin) might build. He had passed the work on to David Laing, who after failing to meet the cost limit threw up the commission. Goodwin's friends immediately persuaded the local committee to seek his re-appointment, as possessing much local knowledge, 'which added to his established skill and experience seems to render him peculiarly qualified for this service'. So, 'Under the very urgent recommendation of the Committee at Hulme', the Board agreed.[45]

The rich London parish of St George, Hanover Square, had agreed to pay two-thirds of the cost of two churches, one of which was provided with a site in Pimlico, where developers were creating a new suburb. Henry Hakewill's Grecian design having been chosen, he submitted an alarming estimate of £18,982, very close to the Commissioners' absolute limit of £20,000. It then proved, owing to the 'peculiar situation and the Nature of the Ground, and to bring the Floor of the Chapel to the Level of the adjoining houses' that another £1,253 were required. But so 'desirous'

50 St Peter, Eaton Square, Pimlico (Henry Hakewill, 1824-7). West front. Carlos praised the introduction of an attic (after the mother church, St George, Hanover Square) as a solution of how to place a tower on a Grecian temple body.

was the parish of having the design that the Board yielded to its 'special wish', though only because the parish was paying by far the larger part.[46]

After the several plans obtained by the Manchester committee had been rejected, the committee 'determined, as our local Architects have failed, to resort again to the suggestion of a noble member of the Board; and apply for Copies of the Plans they may have already approved; or of such part as may enable the Architects here to complete them satisfactorily'. The moving spirit of the local committee, the Rev. William Johnson, was allowed to look through the Board's collection to identify the three plans he thought most suitable.[47] His first choice was Smirke's Wyndham Place design for Salford, and Smirke duly sent down working drawings and specifications, but difficulties about the site prevented a start for several years. One of the rejected architects, Thomas Wright, had offered to superintend the plans of others if the erection of two churches was entrusted to him, at $2^{1}/_{2}$ per cent commission, but the Board preferred to have Smirke himself superintend its erection – on the same terms as Wright had proposed.[48] Meanwhile, the Board invited Johnson to send full details of the situations for the other two churches, when they would 'endeavour to select such Plans as may in their Opinion be applicable', though doubting whether plans could be selected 'without a Personal view of the Sites'.

To their annoyance they discovered that Johnson had already acquired Goodwin's Kidderminster plans. As Goodwin had been inhibited from building more than six churches, this was not merely irregular, but decidedly a non-starter.[49] One of the sites was on a summit, peculiarly suitable for the spire that Manchester lacked. The Commissioners sent Barry's Prestwich (Stand) design, asking Johnson for which site it would be most suitable. He pressed for the high site, but Barry preferred a low site, and the Board backed the architect. Barry agreed to execute the new commission at $2^{1}/_{2}$ per cent. For the third church, the Pudsey design of Thomas Taylor of Leeds was chosen (pl. 87). But Taylor died before work had started, and his successors, Atkinson & Sharp, decided to copy their own Scarborough church.

At some stage in the commissioning process the question of site was also considered, but the precise stage varied. The gifting of a site might initiate the process. When an architect had already been appointed, his views might prove decisive in choosing between alternatives, as we have seen in Manchester. Obtaining sites could prove a highly contentious matter, as will be seen.

Design was affected by a variety of factors, of which site might be one, as

51 St George, Kidderminster, Worcestershire (Francis Goodwin, 1821–4). Sited on rising ground, the elegant tower is visible over the town; the presence of galleries is indicated merely by the slight transom in the large aisle windows. In the character of the angle buttresses, the deep sills to both of the upper stages of windows – and their relative heights – and the crowning pinnacles, the tower has a close resemblance to the structure of St James, Louth (pl. 17).

examined in more detail in chapter Ten. The strong-minded vicar of Blackburn, Dr J. W. Whitaker, learning the Board had arranged with Rickman to erect three chapels on the same plan in his parish, at 2½ per cent, protested that 'the sites are totally dissimilar, insomuch that a building which would have a beautiful and graceful effect in any one of them would in my opinion be quite misplaced in either of the others'.[50] At Chatham, as in other instances, the exigencies of the site and the Commissioners' insistence on an eastward orientation for the church, determined the arrangement of the key elements. The limited area available resulted in the church's lying parallel to the road, strictly SW–NE, Smirke having to move his tower, or rather, bell-turret, from over the altar to the west end – the design acquiesced in only reluctantly 'from the principle of economy' by the local committee, the majority thinking that a larger tower 'would add essentially to the appearance and character of the Building'. An additional ten feet in height was therefore allowed.[51]

When, early in 1825, Bishop Ryder told Goodwin to reduce the cost of the

Commissioned in 1827 to build three churches in Blackburn parish, Thomas Rickman carefully discriminated his Gothic designs: he described Mellor as of about 1230, Lower Darwen about 1350, and Holy Trinity about 1460. But Rickman's classifications were based essentially on tracery rather than the comprehensive character of a building.

Left: **52** St Mary, Mellor. Requirements for entrances and gallery staircases gave Rickman the opportunity to devise an unusually interesting west end.

Right: **53** Holy Trinity, Darwen, 'of course in the Perp style' says Pevsner dismissively.

54 St John, Chatham (Robert Smirke, 1821-2). One of the first Commissioners' churches to be completed, St John's closely follows one of Smirke's model designs. The coursed Kentish rag cladding was unusual for the date.

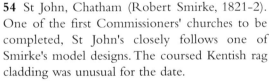

church he was designing for Derby without reducing the accommodation, Goodwin proposed that the west tower be replaced by two turrets with porches. A further saving of £800 by substituting cement for stone he expected would be rejected by the local committee – and he well knew that it was barred by the Board's regulations.[52]

Clearly, the regulations about cost and materials and the choice of site affected the appearance of the completed church. Cost was, and had to be, the governing factor. The limit of £20,000 had reference 'principally to London, on a general view of such cases as are likely to come before the Board'.[53] Similar churches in the provinces were allowed at first only four-fifths of that sum, while later even that proportion was reduced to one half.[54] According to a letter from Francis Goodwin about the proposed church at Hulme,[55] the Building Committee had stated that: 'The sum of £10,000 is the utmost they can grant for the building of a church to contain 2,000 sittings in a town at so great a distance from the Metropolis.' In the distribution of the second parliamentary grant, still cheaper churches were sought, as we consider in chapter Ten.

Faced with a demand to reduce the cost of his ultimate classical design at Holy Trinity, St Marylebone, Soane suggested that £3,860 might be saved by substituting Bath for Portland stone in the west front, entablature, balustrade, dressings around windows and doorways, the arches and piers of the nave, and the external plinth, cornice, and pediment; and by the following modifications:[56]

Steeple reduced in height and width. Columns in north, south, and east front omitted and brick arches substituted.
Stone arches and piers of nave are reduced in thickness from 2 feet to 1 foot 6 inches.
Ceiling of nave made flat instead of circular, and quantity of enrichments lessened.

Here again, the structure as well as the ornament suffers from financial restrictions. Similarly, at Spotland (Lancashire) in 1831 (pl. 209), planned to accommodate 1,500, a tower had been given up. But a review of the local situation showed that the population, though large, was dispersed over such a wide tract that a smaller church would be better; the omission of galleries, it was thought, would pay for a tower, which the inhabitants particularly desired, 'to distinguish the church from those of the Dissenters'. But the sums did not work out, particularly as the masons had exceeded their estimate at another church.[57]

But it was chiefly ornament that was the victim.[58] This was the more unfortunate as Gothic – a copied Gothic, based on antiquarian research – was in the course of being accepted as the true Church Architecture: and it is the play of light and shadow, the depth and variety of the mouldings, that provide much of the delight of Gothic. Architects had therefore to reconcile to the Gothic style not merely the Protestant auditory element, but also, as the Commissioners' funds dried up, an increasingly stringent financial control which deprived them of ornament. The result could be a box-like building with a few windows with pointed heads, and a little bell-turret, while to accommodate the necessary number of worshippers, galleries (which did have the merit of breaking the severe emptiness of the interior) were assembled along the walls and supported by plain cast-iron columns. The delight of medieval Gothic, and the charm of the slender and delicate forms of eighteenth-century rococo Gothick could alike vanish. It was at this point that Welby Pugin presented a new interpretation of Gothic, and sought to revive the old Gothic design and construction.

The Commission also exercised a certain control over materials employed in construction, an issue considered in detail below. Stucco and such artificial compositions as Coade's stone were banned.[59] This may have been basically a sound rule, preventing the concealment of bad workmanship, or the use of materials which might soon decay, but it was interpreted with extreme rigour, the only authorized exception having been the chapel at East Stonehouse (Plymouth), which was much exposed to the sea, and where the Commissioners eventually submitted rather than

55 St John, Derby (Francis Goodwin, 1826-8). West front. When instructed to reduce the cost, Goodwin replaced his tower by these twin turrets. The deeply recessed porch appears to be a Picturesque contribution to the Gothic style.

56 Holy Trinity, St Marylebone (John Soane, 1826-7). Perspective and section drawn by J. M. Gandy. The tower and the flat roof of the nave were features of the reduced version Soane offered in June 1824 in order to limit the cost, but this version retains the columns in the north and south fronts that he proposed to sacrifice.

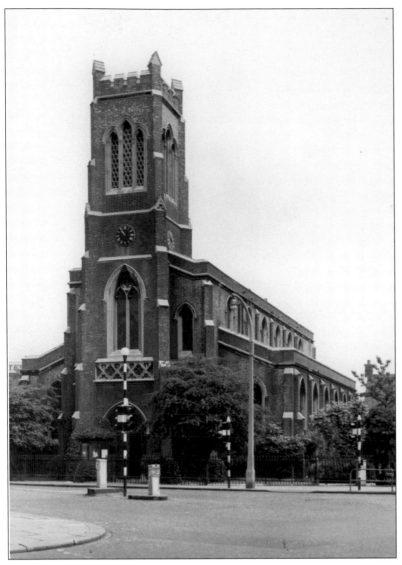

Above: **57** St John, Walham Green, Fulham (George Ledwell Taylor, 1827-8). The tower is a stylistic jumble, with an absurd quatrefoil band under a Decorated window, with triplet lancets above in the belfry. Similar bands were used by Habershon on the tower of St Peter, Belper.

Right: **58** St Paul, Cambridge (Ambrose Poynter, 1840-1). With the triumph of the archaeological approach to church design, Poynter has used such Essex churches as Tolleshunt Major and Lower Marney as his models.

consented to a coat of stucco being added over the then-completed structure.[60] In 1827 they even granted an additional £340 to provide a stone facing for the west front of St George, Claines (Worcestershire), rather than allow the local committee to case the building in Roman cement.[61]

It might have been as well to allow the use of stucco (as Nash wished) on the classical churches in London, where the mixture of stone and brickwork is not always very happy, and where that sad appearance caused by the grimy atmosphere could have been kept at bay by a periodical repainting of the stucco. However, the churches had to be faced with brick or stone. In the north plentiful local supplies of stone were available, but in the south the long distances over which it was necessary to transport stone, and the flourishing local brick-making industry resulted in the use of stone being confined to the ornamental parts of the structure, while the meaner parts were filled in with brick. But there was little of that distinguished brickwork, constructed by men glorying in the material, that may be observed in the early Georgian period before stucco had gained its ascendancy. The Commissioners' rule may be illustrative of their general conservatism, but if they had any idea of reviving fine brickwork, they had little success. Brickwork was simply the cost-effective solution.[62]

That the Commissioners did not think they were building merely for one generation or two is shown by the care they exercised in ensuring a common standard of quality. American fir was forbidden on account of its tendency to decay: only the best timber (which then came from the Baltic) was to be used in the roofing. Lead for roofing, guttering, etc., was to be of eight pounds per square foot. Adequate ventilation was to be provided in the roof. The relatively untried mastic cement[63] was objected to for flooring.

The 'lithographic paper' that architects were obliged to complete when submitting their plans contained the query: 'Whether any and what ironwork in the construction or ornamental part?'. There was in the 1820s extensive use of iron, chiefly cast iron, in roof principals, ornament on doors and pulpits, and for window tracery, as discussed in chapter Seven. With the movement for a return to Gothic forms, which came to demand a precise copying of medieval churches as the best means to that end, there arose a hostility to the use of mass-produced ornament. This hostility and the developing fashion for high-pitched, open timber roofs led to a great falling-off in the use of iron in churches.

The Commissioners' regulations on cost and materials may have contributed to the gradual abandonment of the classical style, for they made it necessary to build a portico in stone: and a stone portico was an expensive feature. Yet a portico was considered a necessary feature: so the architect in the provinces, with small funds available, was forced back on the 'alternative act' of Gothic. Similarly, a classical church called for a tower to distinguish it from a mere meeting-house; whereas Gothic, the 'characteristic' Church of England architecture, could scrape by with a bell-turret (though a tower was still desirable).[64] The Commissioners voted an additional £200 for Truro (Grecian), so that a belfry might be added, 'with a view to giving the building a more church-like appearance'.[65] Smirke expressed a prevalent opinion when he wrote that a tower or steeple had 'become by long usage the indispensable and proper characteristic of our national churches'.[66] A tower, however, was a difficult feature to unite with a Grecian temple portico, as may be seen from St John, Waterloo Road, Lambeth: there were no original models. It would also require stone, at the least for the dressings. On the other hand it was simple and relatively cheap to add a west tower to a brick Gothic church: in 1827 Chantrell of Leeds estimated that a 60ft tower with pinnacles at the angles, 'built in coarse grit wallstones or small ashlar', would add £700 to the cost of 'a plain structure in early English style'.[67] In such ways the scales were weighted against the classical mode. In addition, the mere commencing of a large church-building programme served to sharpen the antiquaries' campaign (conducted largely in the periodicals) for the adoption of the 'national and characteristic ecclesiastical architecture', as Gothic was commonly held to be.[68]

Otherwise, there does not seem to have been much in the argument from expense to favour one or the other style. Some claimed that Gothic was the cheaper,[69] others

59 St John, Waterloo Road (Francis Bedford, 1823-4). The awkwardness of this tower's riding on the pitched roof, often criticized by contemporaries, is conspicuous from this angle. Bedford repeated the lower stages of this tower, with minor modifications, on his other South London churches.

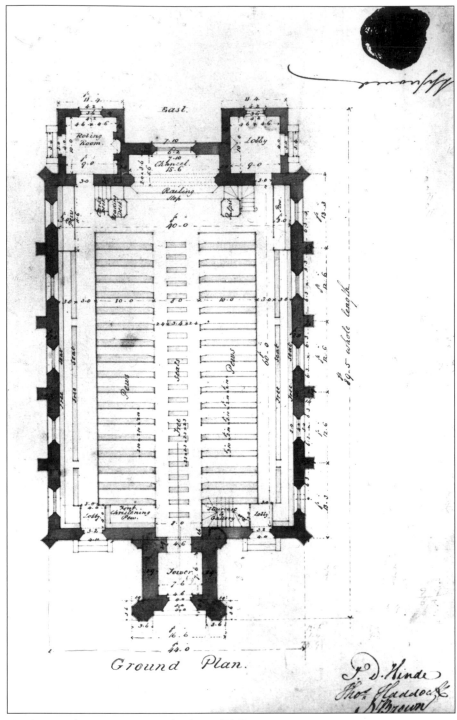

60 St Matthew, Stretton, Cheshire (Philip Hardwick, 1826-7). Plan, showing approved layout for a cheap village church: wide central aisle with free benches for the poor, who are also accommodated along the sides; pulpit and reading desk matching on either side of a shallow altar recess flanked by vestry ('lobby') and robing room, font at the west end, and separate entrance for (west) gallery stairs. Unlike Soane, Hardwick provided no w.c., which would probably have been disallowed here. This plan, signed by the building contractors, had to be returned to the Commissioners.

that Grecian was less expensive; and architects were often prepared to build in either style at the same cost. In St Pancras the Inwoods estimated the cost of a Grecian chapel for 1,800 persons at £12,042; and for variety clothed a second, similar chapel in Gothic, for £300 less.[70] A Gothic church seating 500 at Bransgore (Hampshire) cost £2,650[71] in 1821, a Grecian (without columns) of similar size at Stockingford (Warwickshire) £2,350 in 1822-3; of Rickman's Birmingham churches (pl. 117), St George (1819-22, Gothic) cost £12,750 for 1,900 persons, and St Peter (1825-7, Doric) about £13,100 for some 2,000, which, Rickman claimed, was the same as for a building in the Early English style.[72] Thus at either end of the scale, the small country church with a minimum of stylistic features, and the large town church in its full panoply of tower and pinnacles or portico, Gothic and Grecian cost about the same. It was not that one basic style was cheaper than the other, but that the cost was governed by position, size, and degree and quality of ornamentation.

The internal arrangement of the church governed its plan. And the Commissioners had a number of regulations about the arrangement. The eighteenth-century church may have given supremacy to the Word, but that meant not only the sermon but the liturgy. High Churchmen and Evangelicals alike believed in the need to ensure that the minister could be heard throughout the church, whether praying or preaching; but it was the High Churchmen who directed the Commission who ensured that due significance was given to the altar, elevated by three steps, and set apart in a shallow recess, where it should be visible by all the congregation. Above it on the wall was placed a series of panels on which were inscribed the Lord's Prayer, Commandments, and Belief, in accordance with the canon. Galleries, whether for persons or organ, were forbidden to be placed over the altar, which was always to lie due east. Side galleries, in which of necessity the seats faced north and south, were admitted because they permitted a large increase of accommodation to be effected at a low cost, and were sanctioned by custom. But otherwise all seats were to face east, i.e. towards the altar. Double or square pews were consequently forbidden, and pews were to be of a uniform low height, so that all might see. The Commissioners were also hostile to transeptal[73] or cross plans. The font was to be placed at the west end, a tradition little honoured in the eighteenth century.

The sermon not being the only part of the service in which it is requisite to hear the priest, the reading-desk for enunciating the liturgy was regarded as essential. In the eighteenth century desks had commonly been united with a pulpit above, and a

clerk's desk below, in a 'three-decker', placed in the central aisle. The Commissioners disapproved of this, because it blocked the view of the altar; and therefore insisted on separating the reading-desk and pulpit, and placing one on each side of the nave, of equal height,[74] while the clerk was relegated to a pew. Probably for economy of construction, the two were made alike: which practice became a target for criticism, though it had enjoyed the authority of George Herbert.[75] Archdeacon Wollaston writing to the Secretary, 15 July 1819, about the new church at Wakefield (Stanley), made several stipulations in accord with the Commissioners' rules, including: 'The Desk and Pulpit to stand against the East wall', i.e. either side of the chancel recess.

This placing of the pulpit was often found to be unsatisfactory, and the Commissioners had to relax their rule on a number of occasions. Bishop Blomfield of Chester, preaching the consecration sermon at Ashton-under-Lyne, complained that he found this position 'extremely unpleasant ... owing to the instantaneous reverberation of his voice'.[76] Shortly afterwards, the vicar of Sheffield reported an experiment made by the minister of St George's church (pl. 69), a man with a voice 'quite as audible as that of any Clergyman whom I ever heard'. He had spoken several sentences from the pulpit, the desk, and a platform in the middle aisle; all his auditors agreed the last position the best. The re-arrangement would determine which pews were to bear the highest rents. The Board referred the problem to the diocesan.[77] The columns of the nave in Charles Fowler's St John, Paddington (London) obstructed the view of the clergyman from the side galleries, so the Surveyor himself recommended moving the pulpit to the centre as the best solution.[78] At St Paul, Southsea (Hampshire), the minister complained that the exertions consequent upon his having to perform Divine Service from desk and pulpit 'close to the East End wall

Top left: **61** St James, Bermondsey (James Savage, 1827-9). Interior looking east, 1895. The basilican design is exceptionally fine. The twin reading desk and pulpit survived until 1901, and likewise the Commandments, reredos, and free benches in the middle aisle. The gallery is fronted by Ionic columns (of which the bases are partly exposed by means of concave gallery fronts) supporting a continuous entablature crowned by a clerestory; the ceiling is deeply coffered in a Roman fashion.

Above: **62** St Peter, Eaton Square, Pimlico (Henry Hakewill, 1824-7). Sketch of east end, c.1870, showing the shallow altar recess, flanked by the reading desk (with clerk's pew in front) and pulpit, seats for the poor in central aisle, pews on the floor and in the gallery. The Commissioners banned windows at the east end of the galleries, and here funerary monuments are substituted. The sacred monogram above the altar would have been unacceptable in the 1820s: Creed, Lord's Prayer and Commandments would have filled the reredos, but altar paintings were not rare.

63 St Matthew, Brixton, Lambeth (Charles Ferdinand Porden, 1822-4). A late survival of an 1820s interior, though the benches for the poor, as well as the reading desk balancing the pulpit, have gone. Porden placed his tower at the east end (thereby obviating the awkward relationship of tower and portico), so there was no external altar window.

of the chapel, and which are consequently very remote from the great body of the congregation' were affecting his health.[79] There arose a cry for the reunion of desk and pulpit in the central aisle, and in his general survey of completed churches in 1831 Good found this arrangement in seven of the 31 churches he inspected.[80] When the Bishop of Chester proposed the same for Spotland (Rochdale) in 1834, the Board insisted that if done, it could not be at their cost.[81] The Archbishop of York was the diocesan who most frequently assented to such requests. After a circuit of the West Riding in 1827, he declared himself in favour of smaller churches, remarking: 'In very few of the large ones, from the situation of the Reading Desk and Pulpit at the extremity of them, can the Minister, unless gifted with a very powerful voice, make himself heard, and consequently the congregation are very thin'.[82] Experiments in placing the minister were carried out in some churches, and there seems little doubt that the pulpit was often moved whether the Commission agreed or no.

There were a number of other regulations affecting drainage, guttering, external access to vestries, the needlessness of east windows in galleries, and such matters, which for the most part helped to establish a standard for architects in designing practical and weatherproof churches.

6

The Relations of the Commissioners with the Architectural Profession and the Building Trade

As it was the Commission's duty to ensure that the monies it disbursed were not wasted, it was crucial to make sure that the architects were competent and the tradesmen reliable. The choice of architect was, as we have seen, generally a matter for the local committee, though the committee at Oldham was told it should have obtained the Board's sanction before ordering Charles Barry (1795-1860) to prepare plans.[1] On the other hand, when Henry Phillips (c.1796-1851) memorialized the Commissioners about unfair treatment, his plan for Bermondsey having been rejected, the Board's reaction was that it rested with the local committee to submit further plans; and when James Elmes (1782-1862) applied for the new church expected at Hammersmith, he was told 'application to be employed as Architect must be made to the Parish'.[2] An unknown architect had, as already noted, to provide testimonials of his ability,[3] as well as presenting his plans to the several scrutinies the Board always demanded. Contemporary demands for buildings of many kinds encouraged tradesmen to turn architect, and young men to leave the office of the architect to whom they had been apprenticed in order to set up for themselves: competition was keen, and in selecting a man to design and superintend the work, care was essential. When Leeds was allotted three churches, the local committee invited designs, and selected those of two London architects, Edward Gyfford (1773-1856) and Charles Busby (1786-1834), and one man in local practice, Robert Chantrell (1793-1872). Busby's designs were rejected by the Attached Architects, to his loudly expressed indignation (as examined below); and Gyfford, despite his dozen or so testimonials, failed to produce working designs; so the local committee, after consultation with the Commissioners, dismissed him, giving rise to years of litigation.[4] George Godwin (1789-1863, father of an editor of *The Builder)* was

64 St Peter, Belper, Derbyshire (Matthew Habershon, 1822-4). East end in 1946. A shallow projection houses the altar; twin single-storey wings provide vestry and robing-room. The tower's pinnacles surmount a band of quatrefoils that recall those on John James's tower of St Margaret, Westminster. The crocketed pinnacles have now been removed. The outside walls were specified only to be done in rough ashlar, but were actually 'formed in imitation of rock work, - every stone margined and tooled - and extremely neatly set', as the Surveyor reported in January 1825.

rejected as architect of the second church at Chelsea (1821), because his testimonials showed that he had not been previously engaged as an architect, and because his estimate exceeded the appropriation.[5] This very idea of supplying an estimate in advance of receiving tradesmen's tenders surprised Nash.[6]

The effect of rejection of his design upon an architect's reputation was complained of by Henry Phillips at Bermondsey in November 1822: 'In a Neighbourhood where I have been four years practicing, this Letter, which has been read in a full and respectable Meeting, is calculated most seriously to injure my professional reputation.'[7] But once they had rejected an architect, it was seldom that the Commissioners could be persuaded to alter their determination. Phillips was told that 'the Committee having deemed it expedient to call for new Plans from another Architect, they can not again take those by Mr Phillips into consideration' – there was, of course, a potential liability towards the substitute.[8] Belper, however, is one instance in which the Board spared a rejected architect. After a design by Goodwin had been barred by the Board, the local committee employed Matthew Habershon (1789-1863), a sometime pupil and assistant of William Atkinson. When the tradesmen's tenders exceeded his estimate, the Board instructed the local committee to obtain other plans. However, Jedediah Strutt, industrialist and 'squire' of Belper, pleaded earnestly that 'Mr H has taken great pains in the affair he is a young man and may be too apt to think the World as guiltless as himself but it would be a sad blow to his future prospects if he were to lose the building of our Church'. The committee had a high opinion of his integrity, and felt themselves 'in some degree responsible' for his estimate; errors in the tenders if corrected would bring down the total. The Building Committee conceded that the tenders might be reconsidered.[9]

Reading through the minute books, one has a very clear sense of the Commission, and in particular the Building Committee that provided its executive directorship, learning on the job and making rules to answer cases as they occurred. It was not until several churches were building that they decided they must bind both contractors and architects to keep within their estimates. Architects were to be bound by a massive 15 per cent penalty should their estimates be exceeded. This innovation naturally caused some heartburning: C. R. Cockerell (1788-1863), engaged on St George (Hanover Chapel), Regent Street, resisted it 'as a duty which I owed to my profession', objecting to fill in the blank 'Estimated Costs', which had to be filled up with 'the amount within which the architect is ready to bind himself under a penalty of 15 per cent that the work shall be properly executed'.[10] He argued that while the ordinary cost of a building was that 'of erecting a certain building upon a given foundation', there might also be an 'extraordinary cost' – the result of unforeseen circumstances such as unsuspected problems in making foundations, or fire, tempest or plunder damaging the work. Though this could not be calculated, it could be made the subject of a contract, in which case the precise cost would be known, and the only effect of the architect's bond 'would be to convert him into a guarantee for … the undertaker'. Cockerell further suggested that

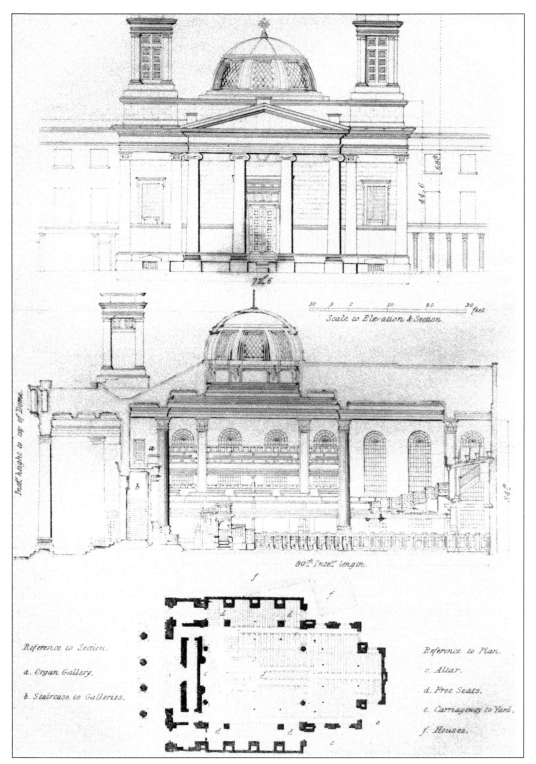

65 St George (Hanover Chapel), Regent Street, London (Charles Robert Cockerell, 1823-4). 'To the mediocrity of style observable in the new churches, the present forms a splendid exception. Its ... features are novel' (E. J. Carlos, *Gentleman's Magazine*, 1825, pt 2, p. 577). Cockerell employed Greek models he had studied at first hand: the Ionic tetrastyle portico, protected from traffic by a granite plinth, took its details from the temple of Minerva at Priene, and its proportions from that of Minerva Polias at Athens; the Doric antae of the bell-towers were based on the order of the choragic monument of Thrasyllus in Athens. Four Corinthian columns and four pairs of pilasters define respectively the lower and upper galleries. Unusually, the organ was placed over the altar. The central space was covered by a lantern and a dome pierced by windows, necessitated by contiguous buildings. From Britton and Pugin, *Public Buildings of London*.

103

the commission which the architect receives is provided as a compensation for his professional skill in the composition of the design, and for his professional attention in the superintendence of the execution of the works: and that it has no reference to an engagement of guarantee, which would in a sense convert him into a tradesman and altogether change the principle as well as the usage of the profession: ... such a change could not be more injurious to the honour of the profession, than to the interest of the Public from its tendency to induce the architect under the expectation of possible excess to sacrifice the solidity and character of the building, in diminution of expence.[11]

But he ceased opposition when he discovered that the principle had already been conceded by eminent architects.[12]

However, nothing was yet finalized. It was only in February 1822 that Nash and Smirke had met J. B. Ker of the Treasury Solicitor's Office, to discuss the general form of contracts.[13] Ker had suggested two forms – one when the whole church was contracted for by one person, the other when the several works were executed by separate tender. These, and a 'draft of bond from the Architect to the Commissioners', were drawn up according to the Crown Architects' recommendations; and the bonds from the contractor and his surety to the architect were modified at their suggestion.[14]

Smirke and Nash approved the draft contracts, but they hesitated over the bond.[15] Soane liked neither. Nash pointed out that 'the work is not to be executed by the Architect nor the materials bought or chosen by him, nor are the workmen employed chosen or paid by him'; and doubted whether 'any Architect worthy of trust could bind himself that "work shall be properly executed" over which he has no other control but to stop the work and report to his employer', when he might have thought the contract price too low, and be totally unacquainted with the contractor's character or ability; while it would also give him an interest separate from that of his employer, namely the desirability of avoiding disputes about equivocal work which as a free agent he might condemn. He further pointed out that the principles of justice required that a man's interest in an undertaking 'should be at least equal to his risque, and that therefore it cannot be meant that he should risque the forfeiture of 15 per Cent when he can gain but five [per cent commission]'. In 40 years practice he had frequently been called upon to indemnify his estimates, 'but I have always been paid 5 per Cent over and above my Commission for the risque of such indemnification and I have always chosen the Tradesmen'. But if it were merely a question of preventing the use of improper materials or workmanship by giving notice to the contractors, and, were they to persevere, informing the Commissioners, he would agree, 'though such an engagement would be hardly reasonable', because it would be in his power so to act.[16]

Soane thought the contract left the contractor no remedy 'in the event of any difficulty arising as to his payment', and doubted whether any reputable tradesmen would contract on such terms.[17] The bond he considered 'altogether improper': nothing should weaken the architect's control of the works. He quoted the opinion regarding the architect's duties that he had published in 1788, and which he now endorsed:

The business of the architect is to make the designs and estimates, to direct the works and to measure and value the different parts: he is the immediate agent between the employer whose honour and interest he is to study, and the mechanic whose rights he is to defend. His situation implies great trust. He is responsible for the mistakes, negligencies and ignorancies of those he employs: above all, he is to take care that the workman's bills do not exceed his own estimates.

In the Commission's works, the architect did not nominate the tradesmen, but even were he to do so, Soane thought the bond would be subversive of all professional custom.

One of the Commissioners, the lawyer Francis Burton, was himself doubtful about the bond, wondering if it were not so worded as 'to render the architect responsible for the default of the builder, even if it should be occasioned by death, insanity, insolvency or the like',[18] while on the other hand it did not sufficiently guard against the architect's possible default in omitting from his specification necessary articles, which might thus incur an unexpected expense. Negotiations continued through the summer of 1822. In August Smirke objected that the bond had perpetual force: 'It would be impossible for me to undertake any professional engagement upon such terms' he declared. He was only prepared to guarantee the accuracy of his estimate if the guarantee were returned and the bond cancelled upon the due completion of the work. The Commissioners replied that the bond would be cancelled as soon as they received a satisfactory certificate of the building's having been completed 'in a sufficient manner'.[19]

Despite their doubts, these architect magnificoes yielded to the Commissioners' insistence on the substance of their requirement. The Commissioners' view of architects as tradesmen who had to be bound to their estimates by financial penalties says much about the generally low status of the architect[20] at that time and his notorious failure to keep within his estimates. To protect themselves, some architects obtained preliminary estimates from tradesmen, as both Donthorn and J. P. Gandy did in respect of St Mark, North Audley Street.[21] The system they finally adopted left the architect as the agent between the tradesmen and the Commission: he was responsible for ensuring sound workmanship, and for certifying the payments due to the contractors. As a security the Commission withheld one third of the value of the works executed, until after the completion of the whole work,[22] at which time the architect's own account was normally settled. This procedure was hard on both architects and those tradesmen working on very small profit margins,[23] and occasional exceptions were allowed.[24] Greater hardship was incurred when the Board for one reason or another delayed paying the architect, as with Lewis Vulliamy who disputed about his commission accounts for more than 20 years.[25]

A lithographic form was introduced to be completed by the architect, with details of the style, materials, and dimensions of his design, together with an estimate at which he bound himself to the 15 per cent penalty should the plan not be executed within his estimate. Even when the Commissioners were making only small grants, this was enforced. Thus when tenders for Edward Welch's designs for Scholes in 1839 largely exceeded his estimate, he was dismissed, though he claimed that changes demanded by the Board, an increase in wages resulting from the great demands of railway building and the doubling of the price of stone at the quarry were responsible; his claim for £92 payment for designs was rejected.[26]

Although the Commissioners were labouring to ensure both the propriety and the firmness of their churches, Soane was contemptuous of their efforts.

It is painful to notice the different methods adopted to obtain designs and cheap estimates and how completely the Trustees for building Churches have been misled by attending to the suggestions of inexperience and a false economy. This must tend to the certain deterioration of our architecture and it will be fortunate if the deterioration extends no further than the design. Should it affect the executive construction as there is great reason to fear those who now do not feel the mistake in the first instance will if they live perhaps a few years be sure to discover it.[27]

After the Belper committee (as mentioned above) had submitted to the Board a plan by Goodwin, voracious for commissions, the Commissioners asked the Building Committee to consider whether to limit the number of churches on which one architect might simultaneously be engaged, and if so, what maximum they thought advisable.[28] The Committee reported against fixing any precise number

> as an invariable rule with respect to Architects. The security which an Architect may be able to give, the confidence which … is due to some Architects, and the peculiar claims to confidence which some may have with respect to undertaking the building of churches or chapels in particular places, especially in and near the Metropolis, appear to be circumstances important to be considered, and … no limit should be placed with respect to numbers. … Some Architects have owing to particular circumstances obtained more contracts than is desirable, which has arisen from the anxiety felt by your Committee to forward the important Work, and not to object to persons appointed by Local Committees. Your Committee have, however, felt much inconvenience from the multiplied engagements in which these architects are concerned.[29]

The Committee therefore recommended that henceforth they should not allow architects to undertake more commissions 'than they shall be able to give ample security for'; and also inhibit architects who 'have already as many engagements under the Board as they shall seem likely to be able satisfactorily to execute'. They pointed out that Goodwin was already engaged in building six churches, and had submitted plans for another five, and that Rickman was building four churches, and had offered plans for two more, one of which had been rejected. The Board approved the Committee's suggestions 'so far as the same have reference to Mr Goodwin and Mr Rickman'.[30]

The architect's remuneration was the five per cent paid on the cost of his building,[31] but where the Commission had an architect replicate his design elsewhere, it paid only two-and-a-half per cent.[32] There was some uncertainty whether commission was chargeable on clerks of works' wages and lodging, and incidental expenses such as advertising and lawyers' fees.[33] But when in May 1824 Goodwin's accounts for Southsea and Bordesley were examined, the Surveyor reported that he had charged commission on the clerk of the works' salary and incidentals, 'which on inquiry the Committee find to be contrary to the usual practice of Architects and should not therefore be allowed'.[34] Metropolitan architects also charged their costly site visits, but there was no standard practice, some charging by the day, others by so much per mile, whether 1s.6d. or 2s., so that the Commissioners had to regulate matters and limit the number of chargeable journeys to six or seven.[35] Rickman did not charge for his travelling until 1828, having been told by the Surveyor General at the outset 'that the Board would allow no travelling expences', but then discovered that his competitors had obtained them.[36]

The Board required the original plans[37] and specification[38] to be given to them. A clergyman who had borrowed plans was told that 'when the Plans have been acted upon they become the property of the Board'.[39] The Building Committee in April 1823 called for a return of those architects who had not sent in their original plans as required.[40] In 1840 the Commissioners obtained counsel's opinion that

> the Architect is paid for his plans in the commission of five per cent and they then become the entire property of the Commissioners, and the Architect has no further control over them. Consequently Her Majesty's Commissioners cannot be prevented from repeating the same design as often as they please, under the superintendence of any other person. It appears to me that an Architect can no more object to his executed Designs being

repeated by any other Architect, than a Painter, or Sculptor, to his works being copied by an other Artist.

It has been the practice of the Board to pay Architects for repeating their own design half the usual commission viz. $2^1/2$ per cent. Sir R. Smirke, who repeated his design for the Chapel in Wyndham Place, at Salford (pl. 86) near Manchester, was paid only $2^1/2$ per cent for superintending the works.[41]

The Commissioners allowed time for a new building to consolidate, at least on occasion, before paying the architect's fee. C. F. Porden, requesting payment in November 1825 of £50 on account of his church at Brixton (pl. 135), consecrated in June 1824, complained, 'It is the rule, I am informed, of H. M. Church Commissioners to withhold from the Architects employed under them, the whole of their Commission for three, four or five years; as the case may be, thereby placing them in a worse situation than any of the tradesmen employed under them'.[42] Francis Goodwin, similarly circumstanced, made frequent applications for sums on account, and Vulliamy, because of a disagreement with the Surveyor, had to wait years before obtaining his fees.[43]

★★★★★

On the architect was placed the responsibility of advertising – in the local papers and sometimes in more distant ones, even London – for tenders, each 'to contain a detail of Prices at which the same are made, care being taken so to word the Advertizement as to render it unnecessary to accept even the lowest Tender; and when the Tenders are received to send the same for the consideration of the [Building] Committee with a report as to the character and ability of the Tenderers and the sufficiency of their Sureties'.[44] The necessity for such caution is indicated by comments made by Rickman & Hutchinson on some of the lowest tenders submitted for their Fylde Road church at Preston (pl. 118). Four carpenters had put in bids - at £1,868.10s.2d., £1,868.5s.11d., £1,536.9s.8d., and £1,372.18s.2d. Of the lowest, Greaves and Gardner, the architects reported:

> we know not but that they may be responsible Men but the prices in the detailed Tender and also some of their measurement[s] are so very much below the Quantities we know are contained in the Building, and the prices which the Work can be afforded at, that we feel convinced they do not sufficiently understand the character of the Work from the Drawings. This we find often to be the case, and much inconvenience arises from it.

Reid, next lowest, said he could not comply with the condition that the tradesmen received only two-thirds of the value of work done until completion, because he was already engaged on two Commissioners' churches. So they were obliged to accept Thomas Blackburn's tender, within shillings of the highest, but at least, his work at Barnsley (to the same design) 'has been very well done'.[45]

The form of tender had to be precisely worded. Rickman & Hutchinson were rebuked for their 'highly objectionable' printed form for tradesmen at Preston, which stated: 'they engage to perform the Works for the undermentioned prices', so binding them only to a given price for materials and a given quantity. The Board wanted tenders 'at a total [given] sum without reference to "Quantities"', but the tradesmen were to supply 'the prices of the most material Articles in their Trades'.[46]

Advertising for tenders was a *sine qua non*. When the vicar of Alverthorpe (West Yorkshire) asked that the architect (Taylor) might appoint the workmen in order to

Examples of lowest tenders by trades, 1821-23, to nearest £ (Sources: CBC, MBs & SRs)

TABLE 1	Architect	Date	Mason	B'layer	Mason B'Layer	Carp'r Joiner	Plast'er	Slater	Painter	Smith	Plum'r Glazier	Tot tender / Arch's est	Lowest Tender	Final Cost incl extras	Notes
Stanley West. Yorks	Atkinson & Sharp	May 1821	6,454	–		2,929	139	211	67	232	364	10,396 / 10,500		11,989	
St George Sheffield	Woodh'd & Hurst	July 1821	–	–	8,092	3,510	446	214	461	277	807	13,807 / Unknown	–	15,181	
Stockport	Basevi	Feb 1822	6,047	1,354	–	3,028	891	222	298	429	323	12,592 / 13,802	13,202	15,613	
St George Camberwell	Bedford	Mar 1822	3,175	2,445	–	3,100	?	492★	176	249	70	9,707 / 12,136	–	18,082	★ coppersmith
Christ Church Attercliffe, Sheffield	Taylor	June 1822	–		6,119	2,897	303	287	179	429	395	10,609 / 12,812	–	12,041	
Sheffield St Philip	Taylor	June 1822	–		6,016	3,195	316	261	153	661	678	11,280 / 13,354	–	13,116	
Chorley Lancs	Rickman	June 1822	–		6,204	2,797	414	251	258	275	515	10,714 / 12,433	–	12,387	
Brixton St Matthew	Porden	June 1822	–		7,106	3,625	600	212	290	?	444	12,086 / 13,055	11,630	15,989	
Newington Holy Trinity	Bedford	Oct 1822	4,404	2,678	–	3,175	?	562★	346^	293	–	11,458 / 14,290	12,722	16,259	★coppersmith ^& glazier
Quarry Hill Leeds	Taylor	Nov 1822	–		6,344	2,090	376	260	126	230	517	9,943 / 11,386	–	10,809	
Alverthorpe	Atkinson & Sharp	Feb 1823	–		3,992	2,109	141	184	106	191	344	7,067 / 9,650	–	8,082	
Woodhouse Leeds	Atkinson & Sharp	Feb 1823	–		5,215	1,915	168	187	112	105	465	8,167 / 9,393	8,796	9,637	
St John Waterloo Road Lambeth	Bedford	Feb 1823	3,899	2,994	–	2,955	679	590★	206	393	185	11,901 / 13,515	12850	18,034	★coppersmith
Preston St Paul	Rickman	May 1823	–	2,900	–	1,796	184	133	–	120	501★	5,634 / 5,907	–	6,214	★& painter

expedite matters as the subscribers were 'extremely impatient', he was told (despite support from the Archbishop of York) that 'though advertising for Tenders may occasion some delay, the Committee cannot vary their general mode of proceeding'.[47] The minister of Attercliffe (Sheffield) reported that he had advertised in all the Sheffield and Leeds papers, and in the *Doncaster Gazette*, mostly twice, and had received 41 tenders.[48] In the first year or two, procedures were less clear-cut, or, at least, less well understood: at Ashton-under-Lyne, the local committee had obtained estimates from local tradesmen in July 1819; it was some time before Goodwin's plans were approved, and the Board ordered him to advertise for tenders in November 1820. These, received on 27 December, were opened by the chairman, but Goodwin evidently having failed to specify the need for prices and of materials, another date was set for receiving detailed bids, and they were then forwarded to the Board.[49]

The most important trades were the mason's (which almost invariably included bricklaying) and the carpenter's and joiner's (similarly tied). Table 1 gives a breakdown by trades of lowest tenders for 14 churches from the Commission's early years; Table 2, actual expenditure by trades for 43 churches completed 1822-32. Taking the approved tenders for the 13 churches in Table 1 (omitting St Paul, Preston), the masons' tenders average 53.9 per cent (range 53.1-63.8) of the total, and the carpenters' and joiners' 26.6 per cent (range, 21.0-31.4). For the actual work-costs in seven churches in Table 1, the averages are 58.9 (range 54.5 to 62.3) and 26.8 (range 24.5 to 27.8) per cent respectively. The figures for the ten churches in Table 2 completed 1830-32, for which the trades are sufficiently discriminated, are respectively 56.2 (range, 50.4-61.8) and 26.3 per cent (range, 20.5-37.3).

Actual building costs for eleven churches in Table 2 completed 1822-4 average 88.2 per cent of total cost, the remainder consisting of clerk of works' salary, advertising and legal charges respecting tenders, and architect's commission; in this, there were two obvious variables affecting the clerk of works: his rate of pay (from £1.10s. to £3.3s. a week), and the length of time the church was building. For some churches, enclosure costs were included, and some 'extras' authorized while the building was in progress may also be included. The comparable figure for the 14 churches listed completed 1830-2 (*i.e.*, omitting Winlaton for inadequate information, and assuming a distinctive smith was not employed in several churches) is 90.1 per cent. The Commissioners' rule of thumb was that commission and incidentals would add ten per cent to the bill, so that one would expect 'pure' building costs to be about 90.9 per cent of the total sum.

The Building Committee learned by experience the need for a strict rule book. In March 1820, when tenders for Southsea came in at between £11,996 and £23,780, all in excess of the architect's estimate, the matter was referred back to the local committee, with a request to investigate the two lowest tenders. The range was explained by the difficulty of pricing the specified Plymouth marble, so the local committee recommended a change to brick, with

Notes to Table 1 opposite

Architect's [Arch's] estimate includes commission.
Lowest tender is lunp sum price.

66 St Paul, Southsea, Portsea (Francis Goodwin, 1820-2). A turreted church in the fashion of King's College Chapel, Cambridge. Goodwin's characteristic prominent buttresses are here unusually constructed to form an ornamental arcade. Note the iron windows of his habitual design.

Table 2   Cost of Church Building Completions 1822-1832

broken down by trades to nearest £

Sources: CBC, MBs & SRs

	Date complete	Mason B'layer	C+J	Plast	Smith	Pb+Gl	Ptr	Slater	Total ★ Trades	Total Cost	Trades as % of Cost
Barnsley	1822	2,757	1,476	214	357	240	134	149	5,327	5,933	89.8
Birmingham, St George	1822	6,986	2,256	473	498	566	Pb+Gl	269	11,048	12,175	90.7
Wandsworth	1822	6,300	3,201	503	930	804	230	98	12,066	14,352	84.1
Blackburn	1822	6,389	2,050	300	105	300	25	175	9,344	10,513	88.9
Chatham	1822	7,765	3,201	mason	874	925	Pb+Gl	158	12,923	14,157	91.3
Erdington	1824	2,898	1,200	288	220	377	–	148	5,131	5,625	91.2
Hackney	1824	7,498	3,345	581	990	1,011	301	115	16,617★	17,887	92.9
Stanley	1824	6,716	2,967	139	281	389	72	215	10,779	11,989	89.9
Pudsey	1824	6,153	3,693	340	500	723	296	367	12,432	13,475	92.3
Brixton	1824	7,106	3,625	600	415	343+444	290	212	13,035	15,989	81.5
Kennington	1824	8,680	3,321	393	645	343+174	229	162	13,854	16,093	86.1
Chorley	1825	6,204	2,797	677	275	515	258	251	10,719	12,387	86.5
Ashton	1825	6,292	2,592	750	1,860	481	230	–	12,205	13,791	88.5
Attercliffe	1827	6,156	2,898	334	429	428	183	287	10,715	11,896	90.1
Linthwaite	1828	1,399	878	96	–	186	66	69	2,694	3,126	86.2
Sheffield, St Philip	1828	6,734	3,240	317	397	644	180	260	11,772	13,064	90.1
Derby	1828	3,516	2,000	282	733	285	79	115	7,010	7,927	88.4
Hulme	1829	8,854	2,623	910	430	515	–	204	13,536	15,025	90.1
Cloudesley Square	1829	7,132	2,610	mason	185	536	Pb+Gl	mason	10,463	11,900	87.9
Golcar	1829	1,420	810	90	–	139	54	107	2,620	2,953	88.7
Pateley Bridge	1829	2,243	1,032	126	75	251	100	165	3,992	4,612	86.6
Crosland	1829	1,110	641	88	–	159	61	86	2,145	2,480	86.6
Mellor	1829	2,300	2,085	325	–	C+J	C+J	775	4,785	5,452	87.8
Kirkstall	1829	2,514	mason	115	169	73	63	mason	2,939	3,206	91.7
Stretton	1829	1,363	766	78	51	174	13	65	2,510	2,986	84.1
Over Darwen	1829	3,070	1,700	276	–	820	Pb+Gl	102	5,968	6,741	87.6
Farnworth	1829	2,882	1,495	300	316	325	125	129	5,572	6,529	85.3
Birmingham, St Thomas	1829	7,828	3,210	586	360	915	Pb+Gl	246	13,145	14,263	92.2
Lindley	1830	1,334	670	71	–	200	26	108	2,409	2,704	89.1
Netherthong	1830	1,392	717	114	142	100	51	88	2,603	2,867	90.8
Stannington	1830	1,250	950	65	–	104	65	112	2,547	2,820	90.3
New Mill (Kirkburton)	1830	1,853	1,060	114	–	155	52	115	3,329	3,709	89.8
Paddington, St John	1831	4,736	1,616	933	175	185+130	20	100	7,895	8,772	90.0
Burslem	1831	5,126	2,925	–	399	325	–	193	9,005	10,018	89.9
Morley	1831	1,350	897	124	163	84	60	–	2,678	2,913	91.9
Sheffield, St Mary	1831	10,731	mason	488	142	1,261	Pb+Gl	190	12,812	13,927	92.0
New Mills	1831	1,560	957	125	192	90	–	mason	2,924	3,398	86.1
Winlaton	1831	993	571	–	–	177	Gl	153	1,894	2,281	83.0
Bristol, Holy Trinity	1831	5,332	2,115	mason	–	mason	mason	mason	7,447	8,321	89.5
Bedminster	1831	4,835	2,101	391	156	144+80	Plast	118	7,825	8,684	90.1
Holbeck	1832	1,955	1,044	122	81	140	mason	56	3,398	3,735	91.0
Enfield	1832	2,166	1,788	bklyr	–	C+J	C+J	C+J	3,954	4,362	90.6
Manchester, St Andrew	1832	5,628	2,149	155	–	420	100	154	8,606	9,589	89.7

★ *Includes extra work. For abbreviations to trades see opposite.*

stone dressings; subsequently Bath stone casing was allowed.[50] But soon it proved fatal to an architect if the total of lowest tenders exceeded his own estimate[51] – and a figure once given was unalterable, saving the necessity of extra foundations;[52] so the local committee would then generally be instructed to obtain new designs,[53] though an architect might, as at Belper, be rescued by a local committee's pleas and pressure on tenderers.[54]

What a lottery this was in a time of varied and perhaps rising prices is shown by Charles Barry's experience: despite laborious planning at Oldham, he was dismissed in 1824 (nor allowed to submit new plans), the excess in the tenders being almost wholly attributable to the masons' prices; but he obtained the Cloudesley Square, Islington, commission in 1826 because James Savage was similarly dismissed, the excess in tenders partly attributable to an increase in the stone price.[55] When early in 1830 the tenders for Hansom & Welch's Toxteth Park church, Liverpool, came in, at £6,500 and upwards, much higher than their estimate of £5,967, Hansom discussed it with the chairman of the local committee and discovered that 'most or all of them [the tenders] were made by one person ? a surveyor of Liverpool – whose individual mistake must have misled all those for whom he acted'. Hansom found 'a material error in quantity' in the lowest tender, as well as 'some exaggerations of price', and the contract was finally let for £6,030.[56]

When Cockerell pointed out that in making his estimates for the Hanover Chapel in Regent Street, he had not contemplated having to enter into a bond for due execution with a 15 per cent penalty, and must therefore add a further ten per cent to his figure, he was forthrightly informed that the Commissioners 'cannot allow any addition to be made to the Estimate already given, unless for unforseen Expences incurred by the necessity of Extra Foundations'.[57] Prices rose however in the North in 1822-3; the months that elapsed between an architect's delivering his estimate and obtaining tenders forcing the Commissioners to make allowances.[58] Bath stone rose by 3 1/2d. a cubic foot. At Shipley and Wilsden (Yorkshire), John Oates, who found that the tenders exceeded his estimates by £96 and £75 respectively, explained: 'both Materials and Wages have considerably advanced since the date of my Estimate. In all the West Riding of Yorkshire, Masons Wages have risen from 3s/10d to 4s/6d per day. Timber has advanced 4d per cube foot – Lead and Glass have also had an advance'.[59] But these Yorkshire rises seem odd when one reads the Office of Works' reports on prices in London: 7 February 1822, 'it appeared that a reduction had taken place in the prices of Timber and Deals'; 23 February 1822, 'a general reduction of three pence a day was to take place [in the tradesmen's charges for labour], to commence Christmas last'; 4 April 1822, no change in the past three months except for ironmongery, in which 'a considerable reduction had taken place'; and similarly in July and November 1822 and May 1823 no variation in prices of building materials was reported.[60] This shows the wisdom of the Crown Architects' refusal to pontificate on prices, and how dependent prices were on local circumstances.[61]

Particular local circumstances might also influence the Commissioners' decisions. Lambeth parish agreed to fund half the cost of four new churches. A Board order of 30 April 1822 authorized Lambeth to

Abbreviations for Table 2

B'layer	Bricklayer
C+J	Carpenter and Joiner
Plast	Plasterer
Pb+Gl	Plumber and Glazier
Ptr	Painter

67 Holy Trinity, Cloudesley Square, Islington (Charles Barry, 1826-8). For this, the third of his Islington churches, Barry, too, chose the King's College Chapel mode. Photograph *c*.1941.

111

superintend their building through its own local committee; consequently, although lump-sum tenders had come in at between £513 and £3,750 more than his estimate, David Roper, by 'the strong wish expressed by the parish', was allowed to proceed with the Kennington church, provided that the Board would 'not be answerable for any Sum exceeding £7,277.10[s.] – half of the Architects Estimate together with the 5 per Cent thereon for Commission – with a further allowance not exceeding £345.10[s.] for Incidentals if the double of that Sum shall be shewn to have been necessarily expended in Articles of that description'. Roper did find other tradesmen who were willing to contract agreeably to his estimates.[62]

The architect's estimate had furthermore to be broken down by trades;[63] if the tenders for a given trade exceeded the estimate, they were rejected, and the architect required to obtain new ones. Smirke, thus instructed at Salford regarding smith's work, took exception to such treatment:

> I beg leave however to say … I did not by any means consider myself pledged to have each seperate branch of Work in the Building contracted for within the sum at which it was estimated, for though I could place confidence in the general accuracy of my calculations I cannot presume to expect that I should never err in any particular part of them; if therefore the whole amount of the tenders did not exceed the amount of my Estimate I considered that I had done all that I engaged to do.[64]

The Committee hastened to assure him 'that the Bond required from the Architect is with reference to the gross amount not to any particular branch of the Work';[65] but nevertheless maintained their stance rejecting tradesmen who tendered higher than the estimate.

This policy, however, was not without disadvantages, as the vicar of Dewsbury pointed out forcefully when he learned from Thomas Taylor that he had been ordered to advertise a third time for tenders for Hanging Heaton church (pl. 88):

> Allow me to say, that from all I can learn, this method will not only create great dissatisfaction amongst the numerous Tradesmen, but will be also likely to prove unsuccessfull in procuring a sufficient number of Tenders. Already the Tradesmen have given in Estimates twice (the first time about two years ago …) and to be required to do so a third time prevents them from feeling confidence in the Architect, especially as making the Estimates for the large Tenders subjects them to a considerable expence and loss of time. One party has just now stated to me, that their necessary expences and time on the last occasion amounted to at least sixteen pounds, and another party has represented them at £20. And having to do this on a mere peradventure of success, and at the hazard of being required to do the same thing even a fourth time, causes them to feel hesitation in making Estimates for further Tenders.[66]

The expense of tendering was emphasized by the London builder, Robert Streather, in a note to Soane about his Bethnal Green church (pl. 40) in 1826:

> Within the last few years I have incurred expences to the amount of £2541 as the charges of my Surveyor principally for making estimates of Public Buildings, only a part of which I have erected and as the profits … will

68 St Mark, Kennington, Lambeth (David Riddall Roper, 1822-4). The Doric portico and entrance vestibule form a stone-clad unit projecting from the brick body of the church; the tower distinctly Soanic.

not enable me to pay such large sums at an uncertain risk of being the accepted Contractor, I have determined to make my own calculations in all cases where a Public Advertizement did not express that the person delivering the lowest tender should be the contractor.

He had followed that mode successfully in estimating for Mylne's church in Myddleton Square, Clerkenwell, and likewise for Bethnal Green he simply stated the amount of each trade. Soane however insisted that he 'complete the detailed account of quantities with the prices attached thereto'.[67]

At this period there was still a considerable degree of overlap in 'who did what' in the building world. Who prepared the bill of quantities on which tenders were based? About 1774, it appears 'that something closely akin to quantity surveying in the sense of making pre-building estimates from drawings, was coming into vogue', developing out of the practice of measuring executed work which was then essential for making up accounts.[68] Soane was a leader in establishing new modes of professional practice, and as his letter to Streather makes clear he had had a bill of quantities drawn up. The Commissioners' insistence on architects binding themselves to their estimates under penalty doubtless encouraged the practice; as we have seen, some church architects turned to tradesmen to prepare estimates for them,[69] which

69. St George, Sheffield (John Woodhead & William Hurst, 1821-5). An ambitious and quite scholarly effort in Perpendicular. Photograph *c*.1920.

would have required the preparation of a bill of quantities, unless it were done, in Nash's casual manner of estimating 'by the square', *i.e.,* the number of hundreds of square feet involved, essentially a calculation from experience. A bill of quantities emanating from the architect provided a sound basis for comparison of tradesmen's tenders. But this practice was not uniform in the 1820s; often the builders would appoint one of their number to prepare such a bill for common use; sometimes each seems to have made his own calculation.[70] The cost this involved had to be covered in some way, usually by adding a figure to the successful tender.[71] By 1845, however, to avoid any mistakes, it was common practice for the architect's surveyor to provide the quantities, for which he was paid a specific fee.[72]

Church-building had to compete for labour resources in a thriving economy. In London, major participating contractors, such as Richardson & Want, were also engaged in the extensive public works of the day.[73] Thomas Taylor in October 1824 in the West Riding complained of the difficulty of obtaining tenders for Earls Heaton church 'owing to the great number of Buildings now proceeding in the Manufacturing districts'.[74] At the same time Woodhead & Hurst in Sheffield had not been able to complete St George's on time 'owing to the very great demand for Workmen for the purposes connected with the Trade of the Country'.[75] Also in Sheffield, Taylor's delay in certifying the work done had forced the mason to

79 St Philip, Sheffield (Thomas Taylor, 1822-7). Of the same genre as St George's, but with Taylor's characterisict heaviness and idiosyncratic columns; nevertheless, the cheapest of Sheffield's three 'Million' churches, at £6.11s. a sitting. Photograph c.1920.

suspend operations, and his surety, announcing that the mason had now to turn off his men, remarked: 'The Workmen he has employed have been selected from the very best hands in the Country and you must be truely sensible that such Men ... are easily enticed away'.[76] Not only was labour in short supply, but quarries were exhausted: stone had to be brought from more distant places, and carriage was a heavy cost.[77] Meanwhile, incumbents and local committees were demanding new churches because of the growth of their towns, while pleading the overburdening of their parishioners by heavy poor- and church-rates.

The delay between preparation of plans and obtaining tenders in order to start the work continued to give rise to tenders exceeding the architect's estimate. In the year from April 1825 (a year of financial disturbance), a rise in the prices of materials and labour took place, which the Surveyor estimated at ten per cent.[78] James Savage in January 1826 calculated the metropolitan price increases in labour at ten per cent, in Bath stone about 6d. a cubic foot, and in iron £3 a ton, while Atkinson & Sharp in Yorkshire reckoned the advance in the price of labour at 15 per cent at least over the year.[79] In 1829, on the other hand, there was a fall in some prices, particularly that of Bath stone.[80] While, in the long run, the construction of railways reduced the costs of transporting materials, the work itself had the effect of increasing material prices. The demand for labour for railway works similarly affected church-building. In 1836 the G.W.R. works at Trowbridge caused a local advance in prices, estimated generally at ten per cent, but for metals at 35 per cent.[81] The following year James Pennethorne (1801-71) was allowed to add some five per cent to his estimate for Holy Trinity, Grays Inn Lane, London, on account of increased prices;[82] and in 1838 Edmund Sharpe (1809-77), explaining the high tenders for Stalybridge (Cheshire), stated that the cost of mason's work had advanced from 4s.6d. per foot to 6s.[83] Another increase at Scholes (Lancashire) a year later was accounted for by the great demand for railways.[84] Supply and demand seem to have balanced themselves by the 'forties – at least, there are no further records of price increases on this account.

★★★★★

The Commissioners had at first decided, probably for better security against interruption of the works by defaulting contractors, and also for ensuring that the work was done as cheaply as possible without scamping, that the old system (recommended by Wren) should be adhered to by which each trade was contracted for separately.[85] However, builders increasingly sought the contract for the whole work, a policy some architects also favoured. This was a problem much discussed at the time, with Nash as a notable advocate of the contract in gross,[86] while Soane asserted that his 'experience of the risk and hazard attending this method of erecting both public and private buildings convinces me that it is a false system of economy which ... is the certain means of entailing future expense'.[87] At Chatham, Smirke's unaccepted advice, reported by the local secretary, was that

In regard to a general Tender for the whole work, there are many facilities necessarily attending the execution of such works, by one person only, which not only lessen the aggregation of expence; but, at the same time, enable the Contractor to perform the work he has undertaken much more to the satisfaction of his Employer. In the employment of several persons, with separate Interests, many circumstances may probably occur, in which it will be very difficult for them to fix the responsibility upon any one in particular.[88]

Francis Goodwin recommended avoiding separate tenders for West Bromwich in 1820 (pl. 125), but the Board, following the generally conservative practice of the Office of Works, insisted that, while it would not object to the excavations being done by the parish poor, separate tenders for the building work were indispensable.[89] A few weeks later, however, when the Chelsea committee was unable to obtain any separate tenders for either the mason's or the carpenter's work on Savage's new church (pl. 154), the Board agreed to waive their rule, so permitting a contract in gross with the cheaper builder, provided their liability was restricted to the promised grant of one-third of £20,000.[90]

When Mawley became the Board's Surveyor he advised that it was more satisfactory to deal with a single contractor. Though this was not always accepted by the Board, it became increasingly common and their rule ceased to be effective.[91] Instead, the Commissioners adopted whatever mode was cheapest. Indeed, the Commissioners' own insistence on complete plans and specifications in advance of inviting tenders was an encouragement to lump-sum contracting, for which such unambiguity was essential for security. Tenders in gross had to be broken down by trades, and if it were possible to undercut such a tender by extracting from it only those trades in which the price was lowest, and mixing them in with the lowest bids in other trades, they did so. At Thomas Taylor's Quarry Hill, Leeds (pl. 92), where Craven, Nowell & Craven's general tender of £10,144 exceeded the £9,943 total of separate tenders, theirs was the lowest bid for the brickwork and masonry, which they secured.[92]

Of the 98 Million churches, which were mostly begun by 1825, details of contractors for 89 survive:[93] of these, 50 were built by contractors for separate trades (though sometimes with one dominant contractor for several trades), three by a single contractor for all trades save one, and 36 by contractors for the whole work. Of these 36, five were built by local committees[94] with merely a grant from the Commission, four were designed by the Crown Architects,[95] and one contract was bestowed at the special request of the parish;[96] one other, at least, was built by a firm very closely connected with the local committee.[97] By 1830 the balance was already decisively weighted the other way, except in Yorkshire: of 84 Half-million churches known to have been contracted for by mid-year, 45 were for lump-sum contracts, and two had a single contractor for all trades save smiths and founders. Of the 37 where several tradesmen were engaged, 23 were in Yorkshire. In the ensuing sixteen years, of a further 117 contracts recorded, 73 were for the whole works. After 1846 very few churches were built by the Commission itself: its 'building' activity was almost entirely confined to paying a grant upon consecration of a new church. As far as there is any indication, it would appear that those who contracted for the whole works might employ a number of sub-contractors for various trades;[98] but these did not come within the cognizance of the Commission; how often a 'firm' was formed merely to secure a contract in gross we cannot tell.[99]

In obtaining tenders, the Commission stated specifically, as noted above, that they were not bound to accept the lowest tender,[100] in order to guard against unwisely low tenders and malarkey; but in practice they generally did so, subject to their Surveyor's advice and the tradesmen's being able to provide two reliable securities,

71 St Peter, Walworth, Surrey (John Soane, 1823–4). The first of Soane's churches to be completed, with a Roman Ionic portico surmounted by a balustrade instead of a pediment, to avoid the inelegancy of the tower's riding a pitched roof.

vetted by the local committee; they had to have enough working capital to survive the Commission's two-thirds payment rule. The Board also, as a Christian body, required that tenders should allow the tradesmen a living profit,[101] and to this end required them to submit details of their base prices.[102] Just as architects' estimates might be too low, so, too, tradesmen might quote dangerously low prices, possibly through ill-judgement, possibly in the expectation that the inevitable alterations in the course of building would provide the opportunity to ensure a profit, or simply to keep a trained force at work. Mrs Elizabeth Broomfield, brickwork contractor for the Newington churches, St Peter (Walworth), and Holy Trinity (pls 34, 104), when told in December 1823 that Soane wished the work remaining to be done to stand over till the spring, complained: 'I have taken these contracts so low that I can not calculate on much profit under the most favorable circumstances, but having purchased all the bricks in the expectation that I should be allowed to finish my work before the Winter if I am obliged to wait for the balance until the Spring it will not only occasion me a severe loss but will put me to most serious inconvenience.'[103] As further precaution against fraud, the Board ruled that no tender might be amended after the closing date, and then, as a result of experience, that all tenders must be sent to them sealed.[104] That could, however, contribute to the delays that afflicted the Commission's work, as Thomas Taylor pointed out. He had been asked to explain the excess of tenders over his estimates for Dewsbury Moor without being supplied with any figures; his failure to answer caused months of delay; so before transmitting the tenders for his next church, at Earls Heaton (West Yorkshire), he opened them, thinking that 'to be prepared to answer similar questions it was necessary and permitted'.[105]

Were the hurdles of tendering successfully surmounted, the architect had then to arrange for concluding the several contracts with the successful tradesmen and securing the bonds for due execution from their sureties. A tradesman who would not sign a contract would be replaced by another willing to do the work at the lower price, a procedure that tended to bring men to heel.[106] Basevi at Stockport was pressed by the contractor, Samuel Buxton, to allow the pulpit and gallery front to be prepared in his own workshops in Manchester, though the specification required all timber to be delivered at the site unsawn. The timber, coming from Liverpool, 'could be directly discharged in the yard, and the very best chosen out and cut up to the purpose; whereas if sent to Stockport (pl. 151) it must be discharged at the Quay, and carted to the Church, and in a large quantity it must necessarily happen that many of them would not be suitable, nor could the Workmen be so closely under our inspection, as to the materials and workmanship'. The Commissioners left the decision to Basevi, remarking that the clause had been inserted in the contract 'in consequence of its having been intimated to the Board, that if the Timber was brought to the Site in the Piece it would afford the greater facilities in ascertaining the Count[r]y from whence it came'.[107]

★★★★★

All the Board's precautions could not preclude problems arising, as at Camberwell, where Francis Bedford's Grecian design had been accepted. The Board's Surveyor reported that only one tender had been received for each of the bricklayer's, mason's, and

plasterer's trades, 'which is by no means satisfactory'. He added, 'it appears there is a considerable difference in the other amounts, and some of the tenders appear so exceedingly low that your Surveyor is doubtfull if the works can be performed in a satisfactory manner for the sum specified.'[108] He therefore recommended a further advertisement for tenders. The Building Committee directed the tenders to be sent to the local committee for a report 'as to the respectability of the Parties and the sufficiency of their Sureties and that their attention be called to the small number of tenders.' The local committee's secretary replied, from Furnivals Inn, that they had advertised three times in at least eight daily journals; the bricklayers had built Guildford Gaol, but their sureties being questionable, safer ones had been obtained;

72 St Thomas, Stockport (George Basevi, 1822-5). Interior, looking east. A pupil of Soane, Basevi early veered towards antique Roman architecture. The basilican character is emphasized by fluted Corinthian columns on the galleries (corresponding to the fluted Ionic of the portico). Basevi employed here the best builder in Manchester. Chancel re-arrangement, 1890.

73 St George, Camberwell (Francis Bedford, 1822-4). West front. Bedford was keen to exhibit his first-hand knowledge of Grecian architecture, but in this Doric portico preferred cast-iron wreaths of myrtle ('a style of ornament peculiar to shop fronts', sneered Carlos) to triglyphs in the frieze, which, with its architrave and cornice, Carlos denounced as 'of a doubtful order and insignificant proportions' (*Gentleman's Magazine*, 1827, pt 1, p. 9).

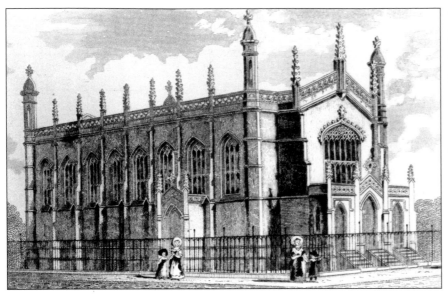

74 St Barnabas, Addison Road, Kensington (Lewis Vulliamy, 1827-9). Perspective drawing *c.*1830. Vulliamy's first plans were rejected as too grandiose, but even this towerless design in the Royal Chapel mode proved expensive (although erected by lump-sum contract) at £8.5*s.* a sitting.

the masons were respectable, as was the carpenter and joiner, Samuel Mayhew, but he had accidentally omitted £295 from his tender, which he would write down to £200. They recommended the plasterer, subject to better sureties; Fowler, Jones as smiths; and Barnard Howard as plumber, painter, glazier and coppersmith.[109] The unsuccessful candidate for carpenter and joiner, John Baker, however, protested that the Board's rule never to allow an amended estimate had been infringed by Mayhew: he had sent in his own tender on 16 March, and met Mayhew to compare prices on 20 March, when he found that they agreed in quantities, but Mayhew's prices were much lower. Summoned by the local committee on the Saturday evening to know what reduction he could make, Baker had forgotten he had calculated for £70 worth of work that was not required, and another £80 for the timber of the hoard and sheds (which could be re-sold), but heard that Mayhew had reduced his tender by £200. At the same time, Joseph Cheshire, 'the oldest Parishioner as a Plumber in the Parish', whose tender for coppersmith was lowest, complained that Howard, a 'Young Man who has served his time in my house' had been preferred because Cheshire's sureties had been objected to without his being permitted to name others, and Howard's brother 'had great influence with the [Local] Committee'. The Building Committee accordingly refused to accept Mayhew's amended tender, wanting to know if he stood by his original figure; and accepted Howard only for the trades in which he was lowest, plasterer and painter, awarding the glazier and coppersmith contracts to Cheshire.[110] It was such problems that induced the Building Committee to resolve (as noted above) that 'in future all Tenders be sent to the Board unopened'.[111]

But that was not the end of the story: Mayhew promptly declared his willingness to make affidavit that his tender had not been influenced by anyone. 'Owing to the hurried manner in which the Estimate was made, Urgent Business allowing me to take it at Intervals only (I think not more than ten hours altogether) I had not the time, agreeable to my invariable practice to go through [it]'; but subsequently found considerable omissions. The local committee was 'perfectly satisfied' about him; he had made an accidental omission; he was still much lower than his competitor; and he had 'borne for so many years' a 'very high and respectable character'. John Baker told a different tale: the local committee had considered a recommendatory letter for Mayhew, to be accompanied by his affidavit, but on his being 'closely interrogated as to the communication he had with me and the date of his application for the Two Hundred Pound advance', it was decided to send only the letter, without the affidavit: whereupon the Building Committee resolved that Baker's tender be accepted.[112] Mayhew's support at Camberwell was sufficient to launch a deputation, heard by the Building Committee on 30 April, by which time Archdeacons Wollaston and Cambridge were thoroughly sick of the affair,[113] stating that they would leave the decision to the local committee (though they by their principles felt bound to give the preference to Baker). Can they really have been 'greatly surprised' – though doubtless regretful – that the local committee, asserting 'the native independence of the true-born Englishman', appointed Mayhew? Of course, he was still the cheaper of the two.[114]

The Committee's escape route was made possible by their recommending a new rule to the Board: that where the Commissioners made only a grant towards building any church or chapel, they should leave the building arrangements, subject to approval of the general style and character, to the local committee. The Board however, on 23 April 1822, insisted that they must also approve the internal arrangements, and that necessary precautions to insure the due performance of works shall have been taken', before the Committee might leave the execution of the work to the local committee.[115] The Building Committee took the further precaution of recommending that in such cases 'that no payment be made till it has been shewn to the satisfaction of the Board that the Building can be completed for the sum which it is proposed to grant in aid[116] the Expence and when that shall have been ascertained, the Board make payments to the extent of two thirds of the Works then remaining to be performed'.[117] This was to be given immediate effect in the parishes of Lambeth, Hanover Square and Camberwell; however, the Hanover Square vestry declined the distinction.[118]

★★★★★

Although Soane stated that the architects did not choose the tradesmen for these works, and the Commission's practice was to employ whoever submitted the lowest tender, provided his references were good, it is noticeable that certain architects and certain contractors are found in association: this seems to be in fact a reflection of the efficiency of certain firms and their local pre-eminence, as it was the Commission, not the architect, that appointed the contractors.[119] Though Robert Streather of Hackney, by origin a bricklayer and carpenter, was contractor for both of Nash's churches;[120] and was employed by James Meredith at All Saints, Skinner Street (Bishopsgate), it was his unusually low prices (against which Nash warned him) that secured the jobs. Soane employed him for Bethnal Green, after he had refused to take only part of the works.[121] He also built St Mark's, Clerkenwell[122] (where he had earlier built the prison); was selected for Christ Church, Woburn Square;[123] and began St Philip's, Clerkenwell. We find a single tradesman securing the contract in several of Lewis Vulliamy's churches, but only at St Barnabas, Kensington (1827), and St Bartholomew, Sydenham (1826), was it the same man, William Woods,

75 Christ Church, Woburn Square, Bloomsbury (Lewis Vulliamy, 1831-2). A twin with St Michael, Highgate, but delayed by objections to funeral services from the Duke of Bedford, donor of the site. Erected by J. and G. A. Young on a lump-sum contract for £7,600; ultimate cost, £11,173. Photograph 1962.

76 St Michael, Highgate (Lewis Vulliamy, 1830–2). North door, under tower. The north-south alignment imposed by the site meant that the altar was on the right as one entered. The church, conspicuous from afar on Highgate Hill, was built on a lump-sum contract by William and Lewis Cubitt, at a final cost of £5.5*s* a sitting.

119

77 St George, Leicester (William Parsons, 1823-6). Interior, looking east, before a disastrous fire in 1911. An expensive church, at very nearly £9 a sitting, in the 'Ornamented' style. The Surveyor complained that the elliptical 'vaulted' ceiling (of Wyatt character) over the nave should be a gothic arch in profile. Chancel added by A. W. Blomfield, 1879.

who was also contractor for Bedford's St Mary the Less, Lambeth (1827).[124]

It was not unusual for a contractor to put forward a tender so low (as the Crown Architects suspected) that he was ruined in carrying out the work;[125] nor did the Commissioners' rule of only paying two-thirds on account of work done make things easier. At Leicester, the masons, Hull & Pollard, claimed to have lost £1,700, and the carpenter and joiner, Joseph Swain, £1,066, on their respective contracts.[126] The masons at Taylor's church at Pudsey (West Yorkshire) complained of 'the Contract not having answered our expectations but on the contrary having reduced us to a state of Pauperism'; though Taylor retorted, 'these statements without foundation I am sorry to say are not uncommon in this District'.[127] William Parsons, the Leicester architect, reported in April 1826 his fear 'that all our Contractors have made some extraordinary mistakes in their calculations, for I can ascertain by the delay in the finishing the Building that they are consuming nearly fifty per cent more in Labor than they are receiving by the amount of their contract'.[128] Messrs Broadhead, contractors for Goodwin's church at Ashton-under-Lyne (Cheshire) were bankrupted, despite their alleged skimping.[129] So too was that careful builder Robert Streather at St Philip's, Clerkenwell (Middlesex); but, obtaining his certificate, he was able to complete the church.[130]

Lump-sum contracts were most frequently sought by tradesmen practising masonry and bricklaying, the two dominant trades in church-building, which together averaged about 50 per cent of costs.[131] The three brothers Benjamin (1785-1823), Jonathan, and James (b.1793) Nowell, bricklayers and masons, variously described as of Birmingham or of Dewsbury and Liverpool, sons of Jonathan Nowell (d.1810), mason and builder of Dewsbury,[132] 'respectable men and good workmen' who had 'executed several works of magnitude', were employed by Rickman & Hutchinson at St George's, Birmingham (where their work was 'much to [the architects'] satisfaction'), and St Thomas, Birmingham, and at Erdington, and unsuccessfully recommended by them for Chorley; they also worked at Hawarden and St George's, Sheffield.[133] The vicar of Sheffield, reporting that they had completed St George's, remarked: 'They are about to sell all the working tools and tackling of every description used in the erection of this church. This is their usual practice – they don't chuse to incur the expence of carrying them from place to place.' He unsuccessfully suggested that tenders for the third Sheffield church should be advertised for immediately; Nowells would delay the sale in the hope of winning the commission, and come in the cheaper because they would have all their tackle still and at hand.[134] William Parsons, however, the Leicester architect, thought their work at St George's 'such as would not recommend the parties', and noted that one of their sureties was another brother,[135] doubtless the eldest, Joseph. He, with Hiram Craven of Keighley,[136] sought lump-sum contracts for Barry's two Manchester churches, and the Yorkshire churches at Sheffield (St Philip), Attercliffe, Alverthorpe, Woodhouse, Meadow Lane, Dewsbury Moor and Hanging Heaton, and secured the mason's and bricklayer's contracts for Quarry Hill (Leeds), and Wilsden:[137] they were said to be 'Of high Character – Industrious – Substantial – Able – trustworthy – and superior Workmen – have lately built Barracks at Leeds by Contract, also several Canal Bridges, and are now [1822] completing an extensive aqueduct in Scotland'.[138] Chantrell, however, commented in respect of their application for his church at Meadow Lane, Leeds, 'These persons have contracted for extensive rough and heavy Works and are possessed of property – they do not appear to have executed any Works of this description before, and this church should be executed in a very superior manner to the Cavalry Barracks erected by them in this Town [Leeds] in 1821.'[139] And although (or perhaps because) they had executed the bridge at York for Atkinson, he remarked on their tender for Woodhouse Church, Leeds, 'We feel it incumbent upon us to decline being concerned with them as Carpenters'.[140] John Oates, a Halifax[141] architect, however reported early in 1823 that 'they bear very good characters'. They competed against the Nowell brothers at two Leeds churches, Meadow Lane and Woodhouse, although acting as their sureties. Joseph Nowell individually obtained the lump-sum contract for Earls Heaton.[142]

That the tradesmen did not necessarily confine their operations to a particular district is apparent from the reference given for George and Samuel Johnson, who undercut Craven & Nowell for the mason's and bricklayer's work at Attercliffe: 'Samuel worked at the new Church Mary-le-bone', reported the architect, 'also at a Church lately built at Rochdale ... he has also been employed on large Buildings in America'.[143]

Another family business employed, like the Nowells, by Rickman, was John and Joseph Bennett of Birmingham, who carried out the mason's work at his two Preston churches[144] (together with a William Bennett);[145] and at St Peter, Birmingham.[146] John and James Bennett were contractors for another Rickman church, Lower Darwen;[147] while John alone contracted for Christ Church, Carlisle, and Bedford's church at Horwich (Lancashire), also performing the mason's work at Holy Trinity, Bristol, Haigh (Lancashire), and Loughborough (all by Rickman). During these last works he died, the final payments being made to his executors.[148] Two more Bennetts − Isaac and William − carried out the mason's and bricklayer's work at Houghton, near Preston.[149]

78 Holy Trinity, Bristol (Thomas Rickman & William Hutchinson, 1829-31). Having turrets instead of west tower (like Goodwin's Derby church, see p. 95), this church proved fairly cheap at £4.2s. a sitting.

Samuel Buxton, a 'substantial and responsible' Lancashire contractor, with one Bellhouse regarded as 'the principal builders of Manchester', was extensively employed by several architects in the Midlands. By 1822 he had already built non-Commissioners' churches at Marple, Newton and Radcliffe, rebuilt Stockport parish church, and additions to Manchester collegiate church, as well as the Manchester Public Exchange.[150] For the Commissioners he built St Thomas, Stockport, and Coseley and Netherton churches;[151] unsuccessfully competed for Camp Field, Manchester;[152] and completed Christ Church, West Bromwich[153] after two successive contractors had failed. St Mary, Bilston was the work of him and his son, perhaps John,[154] who had been a pupil of Soane from 1809 to 1814.

That there still existed a fluidity between architect and builder in the 1820s and '30s may be illustrated by, among others, John Ions who designed and built the church at Gateshead Fell;[155] Thomas Jones who combined both functions at Trefonnen (Oswestry);[156] Benjamin Bramble, the contractor for the churches at Alverstoke and Portsmouth (both designed by T. E. Owen),[157] who designed that at West Cowes as well as Portsmouth Guildhall;[158] and James Trubshaw, the contractor for Lane End (Potteries), designed by Thomas Johnson (his son-in-

79 All Saints, Stand, Lancashire (Charles Barry, 1822-5). Barry exploited to splendid effect the Picturesque concept of the towered porch, which he treated as a porte cochère, intending carriages to drive up to the arcade.

law),[159] and the 'architect who surveyed the building' of Brereton chapel designed by his son Thomas Trubshaw.[160] The firm of (James) Trubshaw and Johnson designed and built St Peter, Stoke and St Mary, Uttoxeter. The leading Huddersfield builder, Joseph Kaye (1780-1858), who 'referred to himself as an architect from the 1830s', executed the mason's and bricklayer's contracts at Linthwaite and St Andrew, Manchester (1827-30); and the mason's at Crosland, Golcar and Lindley (1828), and Paddock and St Paul, Huddersfield (1829); as well as the slater's at Golcar, and that for plumber and glazier at St Andrew, Manchester.[161]

How these firms handled lump-sum contracts is not entirely clear. Where their tender totals are broken down by trade, one or more of the minor trades may be omitted, and there was clearly some sub-contracting.[162] William Heap, 'Stone Mason at Manchester in a very extensive way of business'[163] had 'long been in the habit of undertaking large Contracts, and has given his Employers very great satisfaction;'[164] but for lump-sum contracts he did sub-contract minor trades.[165] Charles Barry employed him to build his two Manchester churches, but there he failed to give satisfaction, and ultimately sued the Commissioners regarding extra works, claiming nearly £6,400, much of which was 'said to have been ordered by Clerks of the Works … but it is to be feared from their present intimacy with the contractor they were executed merely for the purpose of creating a claim'; after prolonged litigation, the lord chancellor advised the Commissioners to settle at £3,000.[166] An unusual situation arose at Kennington, Lambeth, where the tenders had exceeded the architect's estimate, but thanks to the local committee's plea he had been allowed to find tradesmen who would work within the permitted sum. New tenders with separate trades were reported to the Board, but at the completion of the works, Samuel Grimsdell wrote that the contract 'was taken by Messrs Moore [mason], Grimsdell [bricklayer] and Davis [general contractor, but here carpenter], conjointly and severally', but the others as the works progressed 'had many reasons to be dissatisfied with' Davis.[167]

The carpenters and joiners were second in importance only to the masons and bricklayers, averaging about 25 per cent of total costs.[168] John Walthew contracted for the woodworking trades at Rickman's Birmingham churches, St George and St Peter, and took the lump-sum contract for his Christ Church, Coventry, having contemporaneously with St George's executed all the works save smith's for Goodwin's nearby Holy Trinity, Bordesley (Warwickshire).[169] When Marsden & Kirk of Sheffield won the woodworking contracts for Taylor's neighbouring Attercliffe (having previously been employed by him at St Philip), they were described by the vicar as 'Most respectable men … said to be remarkable for using the best seasoned wood, and for doing their Business in a Workmanlike manner, and to be entirely depended upon'.[170]

Men in minor trades are similarly to be found employed widely by the same architects or frequently in one district: John Newbold, plumber, painter, and glazier, worked at three of Rickman's Birmingham churches, St George, St Peter, and St Thomas.[171] John Holmes of Sheffield, a plasterer, was described by Taylor as 'Highly respectable and able – a very superior workman, and to be entirely depended on'; Taylor spoke from experience, having employed him at St Philip, Sheffield; he also worked on St George, Barnsley, and John Oates's Wilsden and Shipley churches.[172] John Taylor, a slater, worked at Paddock, Lindley, and Halifax for Oates[173] and another firm, the Brown family – Samuel, Charles, and James, 'Highly respectable and competent'[174] – carried out the slating at Woodhouse, Hanging Heaton, Dewsbury Moor, St Philip Sheffield, Christ Church New Mill,[175] and Stannington[176] (all in the West Riding). Smiths and founders seem to have been fewer in number than men of other trades, and not infrequently additional tenders had to be sought, as in 1822 at Chorley (Lancashire) – where no tender was made for smith and founder's work and only one for foundering – and at Attercliffe (West Yorkshire), where of the two applicants one was a working blacksmith and the other firm, 'not so well suited to undertake this work' in the vicar's view, were 'Agents or Commissioners for several different Iron Works'.[177] Weatherhead & Glover of Derby, were employed at Derby, Kidderminster, Bordesley (where their ironwork was 'universally acknowledged to be of the most superior workmanship'),[178] and Ashton (Goodwin churches), and at Leicester, Burslem, and Wordesley (the last two by Lewis Vulliamy);[179] and Fowler, Jones & Company of Lambeth at Kennington, Norwood, St John Waterloo Road, Camberwell, Holy Trinity Newington, Hoxton, Wandsworth, Regent Square, Somers Town,[180] and the three Barry churches at Islington.[181] A Yorkshire smith was John Dixon, who worked at Taylor's three churches of Pudsey, Hanging Heaton, and Dewsbury Moor, and at Kirkstall.[182]

Tradesmen thus tended to be employed frequently either in a certain district or by a certain architect (the two might coincide). Despite their caveat, the Commissioners went for the lowest practicable tenders, which suggests that men in the first category were often able to undercut their local competitors, and that those in the second were persuaded to tender sometimes outside their usual locality by the influence of architects with whom they had previously worked. A clear instance of this was at St Paul, Nottingham, that William Wilkins designed for his brother, the local rector. Wilkins explained that 'when called upon for an estimate to furnish such a one as I am prepared to pledge myself to – by producing Builders of responsibility and integrity

80 Christ Church, Coventry (Thomas Rickman & William Hutchinson, 1830–2). The body, bombed in 1940, was added to the mid 14th-century Greyfriars steeple, the architects attempting to realise an Early English east end composition in terms of the later style. Photograph 1941.

who shall execute the Work at my estimate' it was obvious that in order to do so with security, 'I must previously submit my drawings and estimate to such Builders. This is my constant mode of proceeding.' Accordingly, 'Mr Crow [sic] had long been in possession of my plans and specification, and it consequently required but little time on the spot to make the necessary revision when the plans were openly submitted to competition.' Spencer Crowe came down to Nottingham for three days with 'persons from London to assist him in making his Estimates', and secured the contract in gross, the Commissioners' Surveyor sharing Wilkins' own view that 'a variety of Contractors for the several parts was generally objectionable'.[183] At Ashton-under-Lyne, a Goodwin church, it was observed that one tendering tradesman was 'too much inclined to treat with the Architect than with the Committee.'[184]

★★★★★

A further factor in the building formula was the clerk of the works, a functionary of considerably more importance than his salary of between two and three guineas a week might suggest.[185] A specification by Charles Porden for St Matthew, Brixton, Lambeth, in 1822, sets out his duties:

> The Clerk of the Works, in the absence of the Architect, is to have full power to judge of the quality of the materials, of the manner of executing the various kinds of work, and of the proper mode of conducting them; in which particulars the Contractors will be required to follow his directions, as well as in all inferior matters, relating to the bonding of stone or bricks, mixing of the mortar, running with lead, size and number of the bond stones, cramps, joggles, plugs, screws, nails, and all other particulars affecting the proper execution of the work.
> The Clerk of the Works shall not set out any of the work but shall furnish copies of the original drawings in his possession, for the use of the Contractors; which copies, must be signed by the Architect.[186]

Whose agent was he? Was he the architect's or the client's? The Commissioners appear to have had discordant views. It was the Surveyor General who in March 1819 proposed the appointment of a professional person 'to reside upon the spot' where a building was erected by the Board's authority, to be furnished with all the working drawings and a full specification of the materials, to 'receive from His Majesty's Office of Works, the necessary instructions for the discharge of his Duty in superintending such building'; with authority to reject any unsatisfactory materials, and 'to direct alterations to be made in any parts of the building as shall be carrying on contrary to the specifications'. He would be paid two and a half guineas a week, exclusive of travelling expenses.[187] The Board's Surveyor, Mawley, told Francis Bedford in 1823 that he had no right to dismiss the clerk of works at Camberwell church, declaring, as the architect complained to the Board, 'that he was your servant and not mine'.[188] But the practice of the Commission admitted the architect's traditional power of appointment,[189] though local committees sometimes felt they had a say in the matter. Thus at Southsea, where Jacob Owen of the Ordnance was 'one of the most active of the Committee', Francis Goodwin appointed his brother, John Owen, at their request, but subsequently discharged him, whereupon he was told that 'the Committee would ... take especial care that the Architect for the second Chapel should appoint a Clerk of the Works to their order'.[190] Similar situations were not unusual: Goodwin himself met another at Ashton-under-Lyne, where his first clerk of works, a land surveyor, Hawkyard, was a member of the local committee, who executed his duties by a deputy whose own attendance was irregular. Goodwin then appointed a London man as clerk, who detected improper practices by the main contractor. But under pressure from the vicar, Rev. George Chetwode,[191] Goodwin agreed to give Hawkyard one more chance (his absence being ascribed to brain fever). When he failed immediately to reinstate him, Chetwode wrote threateningly:

> The Committee here have applied to me, as having introduced you to them, and brought you in the first instance into this Parish, and beg that you will reappoint Mr J. Hawkyard – for they say that they can put more confidence in a man who has gained professional skill amongst them, and who has consequently a character to lose than in a perfect stranger who may have nothing to lose. In fact if you persist in this appointment you will give the greatest dissatisfaction to the Committee, and cause one and all to be loud in their protest against it, and compel them to apply to the Committee in London. I assure you it is the most impolitic measure you could possibly have done, especially at this moment when it is actually necessary to gain friends and conciliate rather than lose them, and make them hostile to the new Church, and in fact every subsequent public good.

The 'Committee in London' wisely declined to do more than desire Goodwin 'to be particularly careful that a proper Clerk of the Works is in constant attendance on the Works'.[192]

The Surveyor objected to the clerk of works at Rickman's St George, Barnsley (March 1822), a sadler who kept a shop; but Rickman explained that though such by trade, by 'personal occupation' he was a surveyor of buildings who had superintended 'almost every considerable erection' in the town.[193] In the course of his 1822 tour, Mawley also commented unfavourably on the clerk of the works at Pudsey, who was a mason: a man with more general knowledge was required. In 1832, at Myton (Salop), Mawley's successor, Good, found the clerk of works was brother to the contractor. It may have been fortuitous that on a subsequent visit Good found that the tower had settled 22 inches and inclined two inches: the architects ascribed the trouble to a wet building season.[194] The proposal that Charles Child should be both architect and clerk of works at the remote Yorkshire church of St John in the Wilderness (Cragg) was condemned by Good in 1838 as depriving the Commissioners 'of that useful check upon the conduct of the Clerk of the Works (particularly with reference to his punctual daily attendance at the building) so essentially necessary to insure a sound and proper performance of the different works':[195] a very fair comment.

★★★★★

In January 1822, the Commission's then recently-appointed Surveyor, Edward Mawley, was given authority 'to enter into and inspect all the Churches and Chapels building under the direction of the Board, and in case he shall deem it necessary to stop any of the Works carrying on until he has communicated with the Board thereon'.[196] Mawley was a surveyor of long experience who clearly believed in the efficacy of traditional methods, as, for example, his insistence on the use of timber bond in brick walls;[197] he found himself dealing with young architects who were enthused by the technical developments becoming possible in architecture. In the construction of roofs, in particular, wrought iron offered possibilities of wide spans and shallow pitches not hitherto found in run-of-the-mill building construction. The Commissioners, although willing to exercise a connoisseur's opinion in architectural questions, could not risk divagating from their professional advisers, Mawley and the Crown Architects. The latter were among the technical innovators of the day,[198] but even they were necessarily cautious about roofs: admittedly most of the designs submitted were of traditional timber construction though frequently alarmingly economical in their use of principal rafters, spacing them at too wide an interval.

As well as spot inspections, Mawley made an annual inspection of the churches building. His reports give a general picture of the state of affairs. The first survey was in March 1822,[199] when at Kidderminster (pl. 51) (a Goodwin church) he found quantities of unsound bricks on the ground, which were not removed immediately as he directed: he therefore suspended the works, on which some forty men were engaged, mostly masons and sawyers and a few bricklayers and labourers. One has an impression of a martinet who expected his orders to be carried out instantly, an impression given some substance by complaints from clerks of works and architects about his actions, but he was, as we have seen, not a substantial architect in his own right and could not afford to be seen as indecisive.[200] Another view of Mawley at work is offered us, however, by Rickman in the privacy of his diary:

> This morning I found at the office waiting for me Edward Mawley Esq. the Surveyor for the Board, who was sent down to inspect the Churches. He went over the Drawings and Specification and enquired minutely after the materials went to the Church and examined everything very minutely went to the top into the roof and into every part expressing himself perfectly satisfied with everything and wondering that it could have been done for the money – he invited us to tea which we accepted, and he told us that our having no extras was a great thing and would be of great service to us.[201]

There, at Rickman's St George, Birmingham (pl. 117), the Commissioners' first church, the work was far advanced – the galleries erected, the windows glazed and most of the plastering finished. Ten masons were still at work, with eight plasterers and 23 joiners. At West Bromwich (Goodwin again), an unlucky church, only the foundations had been built, and the brickwork was so bad that most of the work had to be done again: there were 29 masons and five labourers on the site, as well as a carpenter, and two bricklayers and six labourers. The church at Bordesley had been covered in about three months, and the cast-iron windows were finished; 84 workmen were there, including 18 plasterers, four stone-carvers and 15 joiners. The works at Ashton, a fourth Goodwin church, were delayed by want of stone, and there were only 27 men there.

An unusual mode of proceeding Mawley observed at Blackburn: 'The local committee purchased all the materials and employed men to work labour only by measure at agreed prices.'[202] This church, which held nearly 2,000, was built for £11,491. A similar method was used at Bath (pl. 185) by the amateur architect John Lowder in building Holy Trinity which cost £10,000 for the same accommodation.[203] These prices compare favourably with those for similar churches erected by contracts: Kidderminster cost £19,000 or so, Chorley (near Blackburn, another Rickman church) £12,387, and St George, Birmingham, which held only 1,800, £400 more.

In several places, he found the brickwork unsatisfactory: at Barnsley it was not well built, nor the masonry well carved: about 40 men were at work. Similarly at St Paul, Nottingham, covered in about three months, the brickwork was not of the best description; the plastering was nearly finished, and there were 58 workmen. A fault Mawley noticed in London was the partial concealment of cast-iron rainwater pipes in the re-entrants.[204]

On the general inspection of September and October 1823,[205] the brickwork was frequently complained of – particularly in Lancashire, where good bricks were not made, and where for that reason there was perhaps no sound tradition of workmanship in brick. But the fault was also observed at Leicester and St Philip,

Sheffield. Work at some places was delayed by a shortage of stone (Kidderminster, Stockport, Preston, Christ Church Leeds); at Quarry Hill (Leeds) the workmen had struck, after there had been a dispute with the mason about the quality of the work, and nothing had been done for six months. At most sites 30 or 40 workmen were employed. One recommendation resulting from the tour was that graining of the woodwork in imitation of oak might well be omitted, as it was 'seldom well-performed in the country'.[206]

A year later, Mawley observed that the work was usually satisfactory, but criticized the slow progress.[207] Thomas Taylor's churches were particularly remarked on for their slow and irregular construction. Taylor had already earned a reputation for delays in planning and organization in the Dewsbury district (West Yorkshire), where he was responsible for several churches.[208] The inspection of 1825 included a number of churches that had been completed.[209] A common fault was that the plaster under the galleries cracked, because of shrinking of the timbers (Campfield, Manchester; Quarry Hill, Leeds); another, the roof admitting wet (Farnworth, Bolton, Attercliffe); while the weather drove through the west wall of St Peter, Preston, making it damp inside. This was the last inspection undertaken by Mawley who died in the following January from a carriage accident. His successor, Joseph Henry Good (1775-1857), a sometime pupil of Soane, was perhaps less critical. He highly recommended the workmanship in Soane's churches.[210] On his 1827 tour he found many roofs were admitting the wet.[211] This fault, and failure to provide ventilation in the roof or a means for the outlet of condensation (which the Commissioners had consistently demanded when vetting designs), are frequently criticized over many years.

81 St George, Chorley , Lancashire (Thomas Rickman, 1822-5). A west tower of Perpendicular character masquerades in scholarly Early English dress: but the precisely-cut and laid ashlar immediately defines this formidable erection as nineteenth century.

The inspection of 1828[212] revealed a new threat to completed churches – the presence of dry-rot, found at Ashton, St Peter Preston, Houghton, Belper, St George Birmingham, Bordesley, Erdington, and Kidderminster – fortunately to no great extent save at Ashton. Repairs, Good observed, generally had been neglected. At Quarry Hill many slates and a hundred panes of glass had been broken. The situation was rather better in the South:[213] there was no dry-rot, and the churches were mostly taken care of. In 1830, Good thought the work was satisfactory and on the whole very creditable, though the roofs of four admitted the wet.[214] The problems of repair were to exercise the Commission in the 1830s and '40s, and they often found money for such work.

In their dealings with an emerging architectural profession, the Commissioners were realistic in their attitude, however much it offended the pride of highly qualified and trained men who were leading the struggle for recognition as a defined profession. The Institute of British Architects was not founded until 1834, and until then there was no body that could pretend to establish norms for the conduct of architects; His Majesty's Board of Works might set standards, but had quite other functions from establishing a professional code. With builders, too, the Commissioners were contending with hundreds of small businesses, many of them very small, in an age of desperate competition; major contractors were few, and mostly engaged on large-scale public works.

In these conditions, the Commission's achievement was no mean one.

82 St Mary, Bramall Lane, Sheffield (Joseph Potter, 1826-9). The site, on the border of the town, near mansions with large grounds, was given by the Duke of Norfolk. Architecturally, St Mary's, with its 140ft west tower, was regarded as the finest of Sheffield's four 'Million' churches. Iron columns were used to create a traditional nave arcade. The choir-stalls and pulpit were inserted in 1888, when the ground-floor seating was changed; the gallery pews were altered in 1901. Photograph *c.*1920.

7

'Commodity, Firmness …'

The building industry in early nineteenth-century England was very much a traditional one in both its organization and its practice. New technology was coming in but slowly, like new forms of organization.[1] Durability was an essential factor in the building of new churches, because it ensured economy in the long term. The Commissioners needed to employ architects who would design and construct soundly; and workmen who would use sound materials and not scamp the work, as could so easily be done by, for example, using inferior mortar and laying it too thickly between the courses of brickwork if not closely supervised. Similarly, the bricks themselves needed to be checked carefully to ensure that inferior ones were not used. Bricks on the outsides of kilns and clamps were liable to be of poor quality, many warped in burning, as Le Neve in 1726 had pointed out, and 'some miscarry and are spoiled in every Carriage'.[2] Wood was second only to stone or brick in its constructional importance in church-building, and the Commissioners insisted that Baltic fir was to be used, rather than the cheaper American fir.[3] The architect's supervision was occasional: the churches were at least two years, often three, in the building, and six or seven journeys were all that the Commissioners would normally pay for; it was the job of the clerk of works, constantly present on site, to ensure that poor materials were excluded and that bad workmanship was condemned and re-done.

Mawley and his successor, Good, examined the designs in the first instance, proposing corrections or improvements that the Commissioners required to be incorporated before the plans were submitted to the Crown Architects, thus expediting the planning process.[4] While they did comment on major constructional elements, they also focused on points that the Attached Architects would not deal with, such as the provision of ventilation in the ceiling and roof, of flues in the walls, to be available should they subsequently prove necessary for warming the church, and placing rainwater pipes (cast iron being preferred to lead) outside the walls.[5] After the abolition of the Office of Works in 1832, the Commissioners were entirely dependent on their Surveyor.[6]

To start at the bottom: 'In so important a part of the Building as the foundation, it is the duty of the Architect to be most particularly careful in the examination of

83 Holy Trinity, Newington (Francis Bedford, 1823-4). The configuration of the site obliged Bedford to place his portico to the north, though the altar was to the east. Massive foundations proved necessary because of water logging. Carlos criticized the solecism of a Doric order used in the tower above the Corinthian portico, as well as Bedford's reproducing the lower stages of his St George, Camberwell, nearby. Bedford estimated the tower to cost £960. He wished to use artificial stone to preserve the crispness of his capitals, but that was forbidden. Photograph 1963.

the nature of the ground upon which the building is to be placed, and to satisfy himself of its sufficiency to sustain the same previously to the commencement … to see that all the works in the foundations are executed with proper materials and in the soundest manner', declared the Board's Surveyor.[7] The foundations frequently gave cause for concern, the more so as extra foundations involved extra costs. The intention of the 1818 Act had been that the recipient parishes should provide the sites for the new churches. Such sites not infrequently had unsuspected defects, for the architect could not tell unless he excavated it first; or it might be that all available sites in a given district suffered from similar disadvantages. In the low-lying riverine parish of Lambeth, London, the available sites tended to be marshy, and additional foundations were required. Mawley noticed the 'prevailing opinion' among the architects 'of introducing Yorkshire stone landings for this purpose'; but did not think it as satisfactory as 'introducing sleepers and chain plates in great lengths judiciously and properly arranged and well secured', which would not only be stronger but also 'not more than half the expence of Yorkshire landings' as used at Kennington.[8] The Board sought advice from the Crown Architects, but they declined to commit

130

themselves: the necessary measures 'depend upon many local considerations which must be referred entirely to the experience and judgment of the architect employed'.[9]

Faced with similar circumstances in the adjoining parish of Newington, Francis Bedford made 16ft borings on the site chosen for his church of Holy Trinity, Great Suffolk Street. There were quicksands of nearly the same softness everywhere; water was standing within four feet of the surface, though about four feet lower when the springs were low. He suggested that there were three possible courses: using strong plates of timber in addition to the stone landings specified in the contract - but then the plates would be alternately wet and dry, which would induce decay; the best mode was to plank and pile the whole of the foundations, the piles being cut off at depth sufficient to ensure they were always under water, but this would be expensive − £1,866; far cheaper (about £183) would be to use strong planking and sleepers (as Mawley had suggested in Lambeth), at a depth always under water. Other sites proving equally bad, the Board went for the best though most expensive mode.[10]

At much the same time, in April-May 1823,

Above: **84** St Luke, Norwood, Lambeth (Francis Bedford, 1823-5). Carlos condemned the sameness of Bedford's South London churches: the portico and tower here closely resemble those of Holy Trinity, Newington. The north and south sides, however, have a single range of arch-headed windows (probably a result of Archdeacon Wollaston's criticism of the straight heads at Camberwell: p. 117 & below), and the body of the church is of brick. Bedford was also compelled to increase the pitch of the roof to allow for slates rather than copper, and to employ bond timber in the walling.

Left: **85** St George, Camberwell (Francis Bedford, 1822-4). Carlos complained of its 'common dwelling-house rectangular windows', to which Archdeacon Wollaston had earlier objected.

Right: **86** St Philip, Salford, Lancashire (Robert Smirke, 1822-4). This was a copy of his St Mary, Wyndham Place, St Marylebone (pll. 31-2), but was more than £5,000 cheaper. Chosen by the local committee, it was supervised by Smirke for only 2¹/2% commission.

Below: **87** St Lawrence, Pudsey, West Yorkshire (Thomas Taylor, 1821-3). Woodcut of south elevation. The Surveyor complained of the great depth and extraordinary width of the foundations; the Bramley Fall stone employed he considered not suitable for carving. 'The stone work is very heavy, and the footing and plinth are of enormous blocks of gritstone' (*History of Pudsey*).

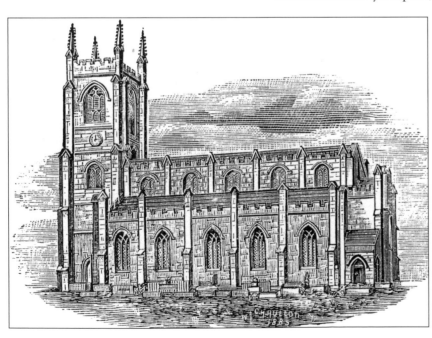

Bedford was fighting Mawley on the question of the foundations brickwork in his other London churches, where the Surveyor had found inferior bricks employed: at Norwood (Lambeth), he decided that some of the work would have to be rebuilt because of frost damage. Bedford, having already taken some down, discovered it was sound; the mortar was of a kind that would become exceedingly hard, and 'as the Walls are grouted every course the whole will become like a solid Rock.' A few days later, Bedford finding the Surveyor inspecting the work, pointed out to him some inferior bricks that had already by the architect's own orders been sorted out for removal. Mawley's report, however, implied he was permitting their use, whereas 'on all occasions' he had 'been most strict in preventing the use of bad materials ... so much so, as to have been engaged in most unpleasant altercations with some of the Contractors'.[11] Mawley's criticisms were, he asserted, 'unfair attacks upon my Professional Character and particularly calculated ... to do me serious injury in my profession'.[12]

In May 1822 Mawley noted that at Brixton (Lambeth) and neighbouring Camberwell – another Bedford church – it had been necessary to lay timber chain plates on the York stone landings.[13] On the other side of the river, in Pimlico, Henry Hakewill at work on St Peter, Eaton Square, found that he had to dig 3ft 6ins deeper than expected to reach a solid foundation, and that above it a layer of sand was flooded every spring tide. Instead of York stone landings, he proposed to execute the brickwork of the footings and a further two feet above the surface in cement. The Building Committee, presumably advised by Mawley, declared that cement 'is not necessary in case the foundations are properly executed and as cement has not been allowed in other cases, the Board is not disposed to allow such an expence unless the Parish [which was footing the greater part of the bill] especially desire it'. Hakewill responded that as the foundations 'must be built in water, and stand in water … it would be more secure as well as less expensive than using Yorkshire Stone Landings.' 'I am far from wishing to put the Parish to unnecessary expence', he continued, 'but as the responsibility rests with me I hope I may be allowed to have some opinion as to the mode of executing this part of the work.' The Committee grudgingly conceded that if Hakewill thought it 'absolutely necessary' the Board could 'not object to his doing so'.[14] In 1827, back in Lambeth, there were similar problems with Bedford's St Mary's Chapel, where the specification for extra foundations, costing £825, included 'Yorkshire Stone landings to be procured from Cromwell bottom or Ealing Edge quarries. All landings to be carefully bedded in Dorking or Mersham lime dry and when laid the trench filled with

Churches by Taylor in Dewsbury parish, West Yorkshire, where he sought to provide a variety of historic styles.

Left: **88** St Paul, Hanging Heaton (1823-5). Interior, to east. The Surveyor thought the roof timbers unnecessarily strong. Although only one-third the capacity of St Lawrence, Pudsey, St Paul was nearly one-fifth more expensive.

Below (left): **89 & 90** St John, Dewsbury Moor (1823-7). The composition recalls Bishop Skirlaw's chapel, Skirlaugh, East Yorkshire (right), published by Britton in *Architectural Antiquities*, and later drawn by Pugin for *Contrasts* (1836).

water.'[15] At Bermondsey, another riverine parish, Savage found similar problems, and tenders for foundations came in at between £2,386 and £3,930.[16]

The quality of mortar was of prime importance, and Smirke, like Bedford, had to defend the quality of that used in his Salford church. The incumbent complained in late September 1822, that a knife had punctured the mortar, but Smirke pointed out that the first brick had been laid only 16 days before; no mortar at that season would become hard in so short a time. Moreover, it had been taken from walls several feet below the internal surface, where the mortar, made of Ardwick lime, used only for work done in water, would become extremely hard. The sand used varied in fineness occasionally, being taken from freshets in the river but was generally very much the same as Thames sand – the best.[17]

In stony Yorkshire, however, Thomas Taylor was the antithesis of Bedford, being criticized for the great depth and extraordinary width of his foundations at Pudsey, where he had met a vein of small coals which he thought it necessary to pass through to a depth of 12ft. Likewise, 'walls and foundation are larger and of greater depth than is required' – and roof timbers of unnecessary strength – at Hanging Heaton and Dewsbury Moor; at Quarry Hill, with walls above the nave arcade three feet thick; and similarly, in 1824, his Earls Heaton plans, showed

91 Christ Church, Meadow Lane, Leeds (Robert Dennis Chantrell, 1823-5). Chantrell's first Leeds church was in the 'incorrect' Ornamented style of Goodwin. Such details as the frieze patterned with quatrefoils in diamonds and with small triangular pediments over the main door, and the openwork battlemented parapet, are taken from King's College Chapel, Cambridge.

foundations (and roof) unnecessarily strong.[18] Another Yorkshire church where the site proved unsatisfactory was that at Meadow Lane, Leeds, where Chantrell had to excavate to a depth of seven feet, 'there being a bed of gravel support for the body of the Church, but not for any lofty erection. It increases in hardness lower down, but not sufficient for bedding piles at 15 or 16 feet.'[19] Chantrell proposed foundation walling of wallstones partly from Bramley Fall stone, but chiefly from Woodhouse, 'which being a self faced or bedded stone, will be most advantageous, for the Counter Arches described in the Drawings and is worked at less expense.' These footings of Woodhouse rag stones six inches to one foot broader than the walls would be 'bedded solid in lime and to have the joints well crossed'. For the steeple Chantrell required

large Bramley fall stones, the footing course 16 inches thick, bedded upon memel fir timber spiked down to the pile heads ... dovetailed stone dowels at every joint of this course, as described. This course will form a perfect square of 34ft. The second course which takes the form of the buttresses, is one foot thick of large stones similar to the first, the joints well crossed. A third course one foot thick will take the form of the walls above, but two inches broader, the courses gradually diminishing up to the Plinth course. Four arches to support walls described in the Section, upon which rough flags will be laid for bedding the faced flags, on the general floor level.[20]

Sound foundations secured sound walls. From the Surveyor's remarks, we learn that walls were required to be not be less than 1ft 10ins or two and a half bricks thick, unless there were buttresses.[21] Even clerestory walls at Blackburn were to be 1ft 10^1/2ins.[22] By 1842 many new churches were obtaining grants both from the Commissioners and the Society, so when the ICBS altered its regulations, henceforward requiring a minimum of 2ft 3ins, this became effectively an official requirement.[23] Hollow-built walls should be not less than 2ft 6ins thick.[24] As late as 1838 even experienced architects were proposing walls that were too thin, as was Chantrell at Batley Carr (Yorkshire), and Edward Blore (1787-1879), who proposed using Ranger's stone, at Barkingside, Essex (his roof construction was also rejected).[25] A. F. Livesay (c.1807-79) wanted flint walls for a small chapel at Milton, Hants, but was told that stone string courses were necessary to provide stability.[26] In 1851 Thomas Shaw (fl. 1840-68) was told that the east and west walls of his Embsay chapel (Yorkshire) should be not less than 2ft thick; while a west wall supporting a belfry should be not less than 3ft thick.[27]

★★★★★

A further issue on which Bedford had contended with Mawley, justifiably but in vain, was the use of bond timbers in the walls of St Luke, Norwood (pl. 84). The Surveyor had commented on their omission; the Committee had directed their inclusion. Bedford replied that 'Chain Bond, Scaffolding Pieces, and wood Plates to support the Galleries … I considered them as highly detrimental … The mode of supporting the timbers of the Galleries is the same by which the immense Timber framing of the dome of St Paul's Cathedral is supported'. Oak lintels over the windows, too, became superfluous when the Committee decided they should be round-headed.[28] However, Mawley's further report caused the Committee to reiterate its instructions, whereupon Bedford, with 'utmost deference' to the Commissioners' instructions, declared passionately that

With respect to Chain Plates and Bond Timbers in the Walls, I have so strong an objection to them, that I think it my duty to urge it and to call the attention of His Majestys Commissioners to the subject they are not to be found in any of those works which the Ancients have left as Models of perfect Masonry nor in the better Buildings of Modern times and cannot with propriety be introduced in any but common slight works. It is evident that that [sic] Timbers laid into a Mass of Wet Masonry must inevitably decay in a few years leaving Channels in the Walls, which must materially take from their Strength.[29]

The Committee having, prior to sending their previous letter, 'fully considered their objections', directed that Bedford 'be desired to comply with the directions therein contained'. He subsequently reported that he had obeyed, inserting timber in the walls, 'a practice which I consider so contrary to the first principles of sound construction, that only the repeated directions of His Majestys Commissioners could induce me to comply with it'.[30] In 1838, Richard Carver (c.1792-1862), reporting a settlement in the wall of his Bridgwater church, suggested using bond-timber to

92 St Mary, Quarry Hill, Leeds (Thomas Taylor, 1823-5). The local committee insisted on the use of the somewhat coarse Bramley Fall stone, for its durability. The Surveyor again commented on the unusually strong appearance of Taylor's work.

stop it: but Good blamed unsatisfactory foundations, the architect's responsibility.[31] As late as 1849, Edward Dobson in *Rudiments of the Art of Building* commented that bond timber was 'usually provided for brick walls' as security against irregular settlement, despite the 'great objection' to its use, as 'often endanger[ing] its stability by rotting'.[32] Nevertheless, one can understand the reluctance of the Commissioners to differ on a technical issue from their professional advisor.[33]

An associated constructional question of some importance respecting durability was the very choice of walling material. Nash at this time was, as the doggerel had it, turning London into a city of plaster, i.e., brick covered with stucco or cement, jointed in imitation of stone. Some durable forms of stucco or cement had been devised, but the Commissioners were consistently hostile to their use, whether because of doubts about durability, or because of a belief that such an imitative material was unworthy of a church, we cannot tell.[34] Stone had been the preferred material for the Queen Anne churches. But in much of southern England, stone, which had to be transported long distances, was expensive,[35] so that the Commissioners tended to prefer brick, unless the parish were willing to pay the difference in order to have stone, as in Southsea and some of the Lambeth churches.[36] Bricks were widely variable in quality, and of the white brick preferred for churches there were differing sources, those from Ipswich being generally preferred to those from Southampton. But bricks had to be made, as stone had to be quarried, and there were problems sometimes with supply, whichever was chosen. Bedford, for example, applied to use Portland instead of Bath stone at Norwood, because of the difficulty of obtaining Bath in large enough scantlings.[37]

It was clearly important that the brick, at least for the external walling, should be of good quality. At Ashton-under-Lyne (Lancashire), the incumbent admitted that the local brick was not of the first quality, and furthermore that incessant rain at the end of 1821 had damaged the brickmakers. The architect, Goodwin, argued however that the bricks were from the best local kilns, but weathered on the surface, so that they appeared very unfavourable; he agreed that bad weather had resulted in their being exposed before being burnt. 'Any person who really understands what constitutes a good brick will look to the quality of the Earth; the proportions of Argil, or Alumina and Silex, and the union they have formed in the fire, and the comparative specific gravity according to their component proportions.' Common Lancashire bricks were, he asserted, stronger than the best London stock ones.

An architectural firm that was, on the contrary, decidedly unhappy about the local brick, was Rickman & Hutchinson of Birmingham. Pressed by the local committee to suggest possible savings on their nearly £15,000 estimate for St Thomas, Dale End (pl. 114), in 1826, they mentioned the possibility of reducing it by some £700 were the ashlar facing to be replaced by brick. The Commissioners seized on this to Rickman's dismay. In a series of notes and letters he urged (eventually with success) that stone be preferred, mainly because of the poor quality of the brick, but also on aesthetic grounds:

in Birmingham the use of brick for the exterior of a public building is very objectionable — ... on account of the glaring red colour of this material, when contrasted with the stone dressings, destroying all harmony of effect and appearance; — but more especially on account of the great difficulty — approaching almost impossibility — of procuring bricks the durability of which could be at all insured for <u>exterior</u> work, where they are exposed to the influence of frost; — at least such as have been made the last few years in this town and neighbourhood are only fit for interior work — the backing of stone walls — or in buildings where great durability is not an object.[38]

As important as the quality of the bricks was the quality of the medium employed to unite them: the lime mortar generally employed needed the lime to be mixed with a sharp sand, free of salt, and to be well mixed. Saunders and Ware, inspecting works at West Bromwich in 1822, found that the sand had not been sharp enough for the proportion of lime in the mortar, nor adequately mixed.[39] Its mode of application was also to be considered: in 1838 Good found the brickwork at Tipton (Staffordshire) 'finished in a very unworkmanlike manner ... extremely rough and unsightly'. The architect, Robert Ebbels (d.1860), asserted that the walls were 'specimens of the very best and soundest brickwork that ever was executed', but Good retorted that the objection was to the exterior finishing, the mortar being left rough, 'quite contrary to usual practice and by no means calculated for any Building where external appearance is an object'. Exposed brickwork should be built in Flemish bond, not in English bond.[40]

The ban on stucco had been lifted at Stonehouse (Devon) because of its exposed position, but was enforced at George Wightwick's Trinity chapel, in more sheltered neighbouring Plymouth. Wightwick (1802-72) then sought ashlar and granite at an additional £1,000; Good responded that 'wall stone laid in parallel courses' should replace ashlar, and limestone the granite, at a considerable saving.[41] G. L. Taylor (1788-1873) of the Navy Board proposed another innovation at Sheerness in 1835: the use of Ranger's patent stone for the nave columns, of which Good remarked 'although much recommended and getting into general use, has not been sufficiently tested by time to enable me to give a decided opinion upon as to its stability.'[42]

In northern England, stone was much more accessible than in the south, but was again of variable quality. The distance of the quarry from the site, too, was a factor that could not be ignored, because of the high cost of carriage.[43] Thomas Taylor of Leeds, one of the more experienced of the church architects of the early 1820s, who went into considerable detail explaining why he preferred one stone to another, pointed out that a new road from Sheffield to Manchester through the quarries had brought down the price of ashlar for his St Philip, Sheffield, to 6$\frac{1}{2}$d. per cu.ft delivered.[44] And the large quantities of stone required made a small difference in unit costs a serious matter: in March 1822, Mawley found 1,200 tons of Beverley stone on site for the foundations alone of St George's, Sheffield (pl. 69).[45] Taylor, with three churches in Dewsbury building simultaneously, had specified Stancliffe stone, but the quarry was 'nearly run out' by work on the first two, so that he substituted Morley Quarry stone for the third, at Earls Heaton, a mile further from the site than Stancliffe, but freer to work, 'which makes up for the extra carriage'. It was not quite as durable as Stancliffe, 'but its appearance is far superior and is sent to very distant parts for the most superior Masonry', he reported, enclosing samples.[46] Charles Barry, in his specifications for his Manchester churches, to prevent a run on one quarry, named three different stones for which masons were invited to give prices, and he similarly supplied the Board with samples (as did other architects), so that they might judge the quality and aesthetic effect.[47]

Taylor was canny with his contractors; he 'almost invariably named two Quarries for the different descriptions of Stone required - thereby forming a Competition in the supply of Stone'. Bramley Fall stone[48] was that with the best local reputation, but the three churches under construction at Leeds would require about half a million cubic feet, which would have given the quarrymen control of prices, so Taylor for his Quarry Hill church (pl. 92) specified Burrows, also called Scot Hall, as an alternative: 'the general charge for this Stone exceeds Bramley Fall, but its being nearer to the Site by two miles enabled me to place it in competition, the result was that both Quarries agreed with the Masons to deliver at ten pence per foot Cube on the Site'.[49] The local committee having raised some doubts about the durability of Burrows stone, Taylor explained at length that, Bramley Fall apart, it was 'the most superior close gritstone in use in any part of the Kingdom', with great quantities sent to London and elsewhere, including Arundel Castle; he had himself used it in part of the front of the Union Bank at Leeds in 1812, which was 'in a most perfect state'. Sending a collection of samples to London, and discoursing on their geological composition, Taylor added that Hare Hills stone, similar in appearance to Burrows, but much softer, was sometimes illicitly used by masons when Scot Hall was specified.[50]

The local committee's demand that Bramley Fall be used for the new church led the contractor to claim an extra three-halfpence per foot cube on the grounds that Bramley Fall was more expensive, whereas Taylor had settled at the outset that all the three quarries in question would charge the same price; he therefore asked the Commissioners to direct the use of Bramley Fall, when he thought the contractor would submit. The Committee, however, asked what difference in price the use of Bramley Fall would involve. As the specification required that the contractor was 'liable to furnish the Stone from either of the three Quarries mentioned … the price being the same', Taylor replied that 'it is my opinion, that if His Majesty's Commissioners determine to use the Stone from Bramley Fall, their order to me … will be complied with without any additional expence'. He added that to allow the contractor's claim would be a dangerous precedent: 'every Workman may say he can not procure his Materials as cheap as he expected', and that would be an injury to all competition. The Committee then ordered him to insist on the use of Bramley Fall 'according to the Contracts'.[51]

This temporising had resulted in two months' delay. It was the more curious because a similar request for Bramley Fall in another of the Leeds churches, Woodhead & Hurst's Woodhouse (pl. 169), had been rejected initially. But at Woodhouse, the architects had specified another local stone, Park Spring, where the quarrymen, on this being known, had upped their price; so the mason-contractors were willing to change to Bramley Fall for an additional £300 which the Commissioners naturally would not agree to. Their refusal, however, roused the local committee: 'Having most decidedly expressed our opinion with respect to the Church at Quarry Hill that Bramley Fall Stone is best suited for the building of Churches of any Stone in this Neighbourhood we feel it a duty incumbent upon us to make the same Statement with regard to the Church at Woodhouse – the situation of which is more exposed to the violence of weather than either that at Quarry Hill or the one in Meadow Lane'. The Committee responded that the change at Quarry Hill had cost nothing: if the same could be achieved at Woodhouse, the Board would permit the change.[52]

Where stone was readily available, it was commonly used for backing the ashlar facing; but whether stone or brick were used for that purpose, it was essential to bond the inner and outer work effectively.

At Walcot (Somerset) in 1829 Good found that the ashlar walling was being

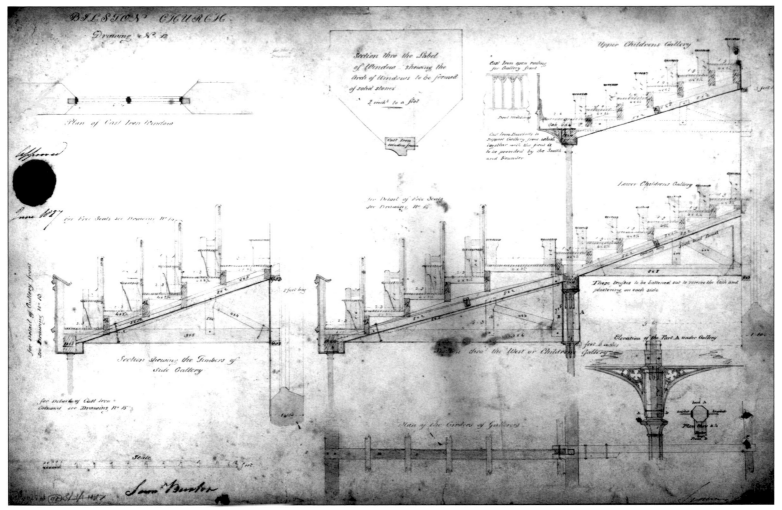

backed with 'random masonry in the manner often practised by the Bath masons', so that he called for increased vigilance.[53] Similar problems were discovered at Hansom & Welch's Toxteth Park (Liverpool) and Myton (Hull) churches, and at the latter there was considerable settlement by June 1832, which Good ascribed to the architects' injudicious construction, so that they were directed to pay £50 towards rectification costing £60; their defence was that the building season had been wet.[54] Good told Richard Carver, county surveyor for Somerset, that he should have avoided irregular settlement of backing and ashlar in Holy Trinity, Bridgwater, in 1838, by 'laying the backing stones in parallel courses on horizontal beds, by performing the works with very close joints and bonding the same to the ashlar by means of through or bond stones at proper intervals'.[55]

93 St Mary, Bilston, Staffs (Francis Goodwin, 1827-9). Contract drawing, signed by the contractor, for west galleries: four rows of pews, backed by seven rows of children's seats, with another children's gallery above; also cast-iron window plan.

★★★★★

However good the materials, faults in execution might entail unpleasant consequences. In 1828, the Surveyor's annual inspection of the north and Midlands revealed the presence of dry rot in eight churches, but only seriously at Ashton-under-Lyne where it had destroyed the greater part of the north wall wainscoting and part of the pew framing and floor; the Surveyor blamed the fixing of wainscoting before the walls were thoroughly dried out. Another cause was insufficient excavation of the ground under the floor joists.[56] Chantrell's remedy, recommended by Good as 'a very effectual mode of preventing a recurrence', was to take up the floor and pews,

Right: **94** St George, Newcastle-under-Lyme (Francis Bedford, 1827-8). West front. In 1834, two of the 20 pinnacles were blown off: few survive today. At £6.4s. a sitting, this was not one of Bedford's cheap provincial churches.

Below: **95** St Clement, Spotland, Rochdale (Lewis Vulliamy, 1832-4). Iron columns and girders support the gallery.

excavate the ground to a depth of two feet, and cover 'the surface with engine ashes and lime, incorporated with a solution of copperas, and preparing the new woodwork required with Kyan's patent remedy for the dry-rot'.[57] Good himself prescribed a very similar remedy at Horwich and Farnworth (Lancashire) in November 1836.[58] Another suggested cause for dry rot in timbers inserted in the walls identified at Norwood (Lambeth) was that the water used in making mortar, taken from a well in the yard, was strongly saline.[59]

Galleries were sometimes a constructional problem. The Board required a secure construction, as in Goodwin's working drawing for Bilston (Staffordshire), and an interval of 10ft between the floor and the underside of the gallery. Rickman in his early churches allowed only 8ft 6ins.[60] When the Commissioners required an additional foot's headroom in his Preston chapel designs, he pointed out that it would add 'very considerably' to the cost: every part must be raised one foot in height, the staircases must be enlarged to get up the additional height, and the gallery stepping raised because of the changed angle of view of the pulpit.[61] The Attached Architects required horizontal ties for galleries, which even architects as experienced as John Dobson (1787-1865) and J. A. Picton (1805-89) had omitted. At Paddington the Architects had insisted on their provision, despite Fowler's expressed reluctance, but the local committee applied for their omission.[62] Some plans proposed excessively wide side galleries, like Goodwin's at Hulme, at 18ft instead of the usual 15ft.[63]

The strength of an architect's work might be tested by hurricanes that struck the country occasionally. In February 1822, Rickman's St George, Birmingham, was hit, where the newly-set tower pinnacles had been constructed with a 16in copper pin, run in with lead in a dovetail from both ways, about $2^1/2$ins square at the extremities and $1^1/2$ins at the middle. One falling pinnacle damaged the north aisle turret and battlements, while another fell on the nave, breaking through the ceiling and part of the west gallery. To avoid further trouble, Rickman reset all four pinnacles with iron bars, completely covered from any action of the air and run with lead, 'so as to fix every part of the Pinnacles together'.[64] High winds in May 1829 brought down the four pinnacles on each of Savage's turrets at Sloane Street, though they had been fixed with iron pins nine inches long ('of the length and strength usually adopted for Pinnacles of this description') at each joint, inserted equally in the bed and upper stones, 'secured with roman cement', a mode preferred to lead by many architects, 'and the joint set with cement mixed with a small portion of Dorking lime mortar'. Unfortunately they had not had time for a complete adhesion to have taken place.[65]

A similar occurrence at St George, Newcastle-under-Lyme, exposed a difference of views between Henry Ward, the architect employed to report by the local committee, and the Surveyor. Ward thought that the chief cause of the fall had been a cutting away of the bases for guttering, which Good thought 'quite incorrect': there were only two damaged pinnacles out of twenty, and it was the tops that had been blown off. Ward wanted to refix with 12in dowels, which Good believed excessive, six inches being enough if the work were well done; and to narrow the gutters so as to leave the bases entire, which Good declared objectionable and unnecessary.[66] At All Saints, Beulah Hill, Norwood (Surrey), unusually violent winds in December 1834 brought down the south-east turret: 'In such exposed situations it would be almost impossible to guard entirely against mischief during such tempestuous weather'.[67]

★★★★★

So we arrive at the roof. Trussed roofs, in which the pair of principals running from wall to ridge (which carry the horizontal purlins and the common rafters on which the roof covering is laid) and the tie-beam from wall to wall which joins them are united and strengthened by a vertical post (king-post) itself enhanced by diagonal struts to the principals, had come into general use for large buildings in England by the early nineteenth century, influenced by the lower roof pitch called for in the Classical style.[68] Further strengthening on wide spans was provided by additional vertical posts (queen-posts), which also would be strutted diagonally. The roof was the most problematical feature of the new churches, where the span was commonly about 60ft, unusual in ordinary building, and was the element most frequently criticized in the Crown Architects' reports. These do not, however, set out positive criteria, and one has to ascertain minimum requirements from comments made by the Surveyors. The commonest faults appear to have been spacing the trusses too

widely, and employing timber of too slight dimensions or scantlings. The Attached Architects regarded ten feet as the desirable interval between trusses,[69] but in 1839 Surveyor Good allowed 12ft as the maximum.[70] Scantlings were more complex, depending upon the span and on the timber's function: tie-beams, principals, purlins, common rafters, and on the span. Good however remarks that roof rafters (principals) should not be less than 8ins by 5 or 6ins; tie-beams to aisles trusses, $11^1/2$ins by 6ins, and those of the side galleries 10ins by 6ins. At St Philip, Bristol, he required the roof purlins should not be less than 9ins by 6ins, nor the common rafters less than $4^1/2$ins by $2^1/2$ins.[71]

Increasing the scantlings, however, was not entirely a straightforward matter, as Thomas Taylor pointed out, in altering his plans for his Sheffield church to shorten the bearing of the purlins and avoiding weight on the crown of the arches: he offered alternative designs, with trusses at 6ft 4ins from centre to centre, or at 9ft 6ins, commenting that the cost would be much the same, as 'the general strength of the heavy Timbers will be reduced in proportion to the bearing of the purlins'.[72] His neighbours Atkinson & Sharp likewise were told that the tiebeams at Woodhouse must not sit on the crowns of the arches.[73] Even architects as experienced as Thomas Hardwick were criticized for injudicious roof design. In Rickman's large St Thomas, Dale End, Birmingham, where economy was the first consideration, he proposed 'the tie beams to be in two

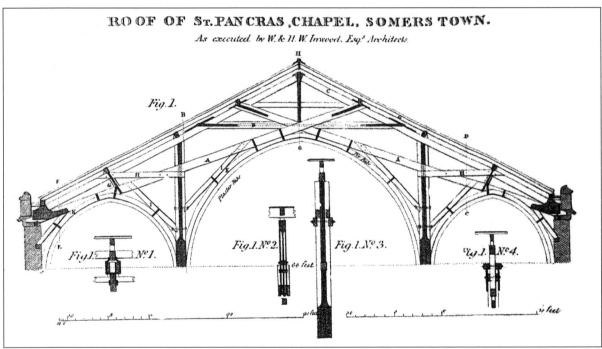

ROOF OF St. PANCRAS, CHAPEL, SOMERS TOWN.

As executed by W. & H.W. Inwood, Esqs. Architects.

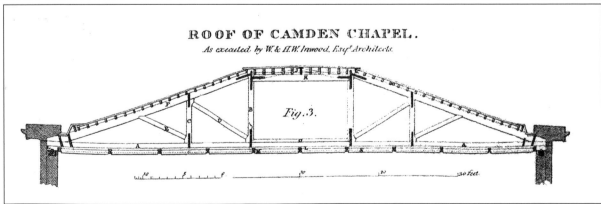

ROOF OF CAMDEN CHAPEL.

As executed by W. & H.W. Inwood, Esqs. Architects.

142

Opposite: **96, 97, 98** St Mary, Somers Town, St Pancras (William & Henry William Inwood, 1822-4).

The roof of this Gothic church with plaster vaulting (top: photograph looking east 1960) required a more complex construction (centre) than the architects' neighbouring Classical Camden Chapel (bottom). Diagrams from P. Nicholson, *New and Improved practical Builder*, 1837 edn.

Left: **99** The nave of the Temple Church is a likely model (cp. also Pl. 14b). Francis Bedford designed similar plaster vaults in the late 1820s, but executed them much more cheaply. The galleries were removed and a new apse formed in 1888. From Britton and Pugin, *Illustrations of the Public Buildings of London*, I (1823).

Below: **100** Christ Church, Leeds (Robert Dennis Chantrell, 1823-5). Interior looking east. Chantrell had proposed a roof based on local models, but was compelled to employ a London mode of construction, with a plaster vault of remarkably low pitch.

pieces and grafted which is', said Mawley, 'highly improper and decidedly bad Carpenters Work' – despite its similarity to Wren's ceiling construction in the Sheldonian Theatre at Oxford.[74]

When Chantrell's first design for Meadow Lane, Leeds (pl. 100), was criticized by Mawley, he replied that 'The Roof I had composed from various designs that I had seen and had executed in the course of my practice and which I am aware differs widely from those generally used in London, but I shall be obliged to you if you can give me any idea of those most approved of by the Board'. But the Commissioners declined to be drawn: 'the Committee cannot give any instructions with reference to the construction of the Building'.[75] So in May 1822 Chantrell fell back 'on the principle of those [roofs] to which I was accustomed when residing in London'.[76] Henry Phillips at Bermondsey was another whose roof 'from the novelty of its construction may not have been sufficiently comprehended by the Section' drawing submitted.[77] Rickman & Hutchinson proposed for their Carlisle churches 'to construct their roofs in three compartments in the manner adopted by the late Mr Gibbs in his church of St Martin-in-the-Fields, to which in all material points the construction appears similar, by this means the Architects are enabled by keeping down the sides and raising the center, to give a more architectural character to the Building and very much to improve the effect'.[78]

The most alarming proposal to be laid before the Commissioners was Savage's, for St Luke, Chelsea (pl. 155), 'to have a groined ceiling built with stone ... of great weight and expence', 'the first which has been executed since the revival of Gothic architecture'.[79] Mawley therefore 'thought it most advisable to direct Mr Savage ... to prepare Drawings and Estimate for a groined ceiling to be formed in wood and plastering instead of stone as first intended. And also an Estimate of the stone groined ceiling as included in the Contract in order to point out the difference of expence between the two modes'. But the walls were rising,

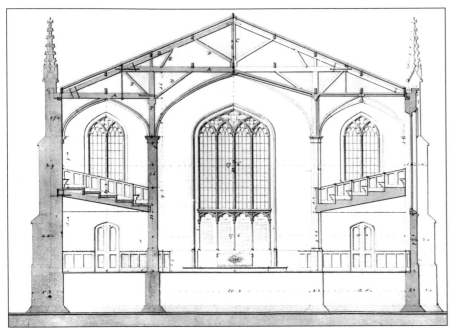

St Mary the Less, Lambeth (Francis Bedford, 1827-8).

Top: **101** Architect's cross section drawing, looking east, 1826. The roofs of Bedford's Grecian churches were much criticized by the Office of Works and by Mawley, but the Gothic form adopted here was essentially similar to the Inwoods' at Somers Town (Pl. 7.12b).

Bottom: **102** Interior, looking west (cp. p. 239) in 1964. Bedford's success in building this capacious London church (1,950 sittings) for less than £4 a sitting resulted in his being employed for Holy Trinity, Holborn, and several provincial churches.

and a strong local committee had matters well in hand. About the same time, 1821-2, C. A. Busby's proposed iron roofs for churches at Leeds and Oldham were under consideration, but the agitation that Busby raised on their rejection is treated in another chapter.[80]

Another architect with his own ideas about roofs was Francis Bedford. In 1811-13 he had spent two years in Greece and Asia Minor as a young architectural draughtsman to Sir William Gell's expedition. Filled with enthusiasm for, and first-hand knowledge of, Greek temple architecture, Bedford was keen to re-create it in the new churches, and speedily obtained four commissions in his home territory of south London: St George, Camberwell; St John, Waterloo Road, and St Luke, West Norwood, both in Lambeth; and Holy Trinity, Newington. To preserve the crispness of Corinthian capitals, which executed in Farley Down (Bath) stone 'very soon begin to moulder away', he proposed using artificial stone, which was high on the Commissioners' list of bans. It was, he argued, far more durable than Bath, or any other natural stone.[81] To permit the low Grecian roof-pitch he required, he proposed to use at Newington a truss 'a close Copy from the celebrated Roof of the late Drury Lane Theatre, which was … universally considered as one of the boldest and strongest Roofs ever constructed', but with improvements including cast iron abutments to the queen-posts 'by which the Jagging of the Roof, occasioned by the shrinking of the Queen Posts is altogether prevented',[82] with a covering of copper, a light[83] and hard, but expensive, material hitherto little-used for that purpose, and for which there appears to have been but a single experienced contractor.[84] Mawley recorded his disapproval:

From many years experience which your Surveyor has had … he does not recollect any substantial building where this mode of covering has been adopted but it has happened in several cases that copper coverings have been taken away and lead introduced … he has made diligent enquiry among experienced and respectable Architects Surveyors, and Builders and he does not find any one who will venture to recommend roofs to be covered with copper for any large or substantial buildings … the roof of the Six Clerks Office in Chancery Lane which was covered some time back with copper was blown off in a high winds … a part of the roof of the Speakers House is also covered with copper and … it will not keep out the weather. … I have likewise examined Lambeth Church the covering of which [is] copper, and although no complaints are at present made I am of opinion in a few years it is likely some defects will appear.[85]

Mawley's opinion was in some degree justified. Cracks in the ceiling at St John, Waterloo Road, in 1827 alarmed the parishioners, and the Board asked 'doctor' Smirke to inspect, and then to mend. He found that the roof had sunk 'very much in many parts', but thought there was no immediate danger:

The principle of the design for the roof, adopted apparently from a desire to obtain its object at the smallest possible expense, required for its successful execution great perfection in the quality both of the materials and workmanship, and its security was rendered on this account liable to injury from imperfections against which the utmost care will not always guarantee a work, but which under other circumstances might have been unimportant or easily remedied.

It is to some imperfections in these respects that the present condition of this roof is to be ascribed, and I think chiefly to the shrinking of the timber in drying since it has been fixed, for the different parts composing the frames which support the roof are not connected in a manner well calculated to obviate the effects of this shrinking, nor has the timber in some essential parts of the roof proved to be of the perfect quality that was necessary. ... For the permanent safety of the roof ... means should be

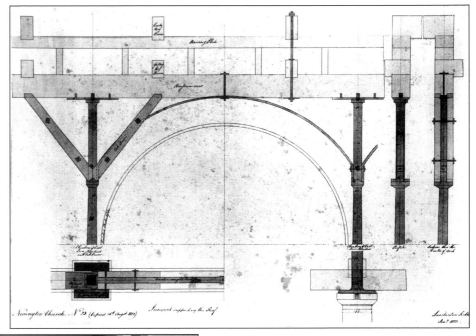

St Peter, Walworth, Newington (John Soane, 1823-4).

Top: **103** Contract drawing showing construction of roof and arches of arcade. Soane employed cast iron in compression and wrought iron in tension, but his roof was constructed essentially of timber.

Left: **104** Interior, looking east. Soane's gallery arcades create something of a traditional parish church interior.

Left: **105** St George, Tyldesley (Robert Smirke, 1821-4). Design for iron framing of roof, with span of 30ft 1¹/2ins. A conventional timber roof was actually executed.

taken to counteract the effects of the partial failure that has taken place, giving at the same time some additional strength to the framed principals and purlins …[86]

Smirke's further report was more disconcerting: had the measures now necessary been adopted originally, they 'would have made but a small addition to its cost'; now they would incur 'great expence', £700 at least, as the ceiling would have to be re-plastered. He insisted on using tradesmen on whom he could rely: 'it is obvious that no contract would be made for a work of this nature'. With the final bill £937, Smirke reiterated his criticism of Bedford and, implicitly, of the Commissioners. The failure had been 'wholly occasioned by the extreme anxiety of the Architect to construct his work at the smallest possible expence', requiring 'great perfection in every thing connected with the work'. The copper roof was so thin that the heat of the sun would occasionally cause defects.[87]

In 1832 Mawley's successor, Good, found that at Camberwell the roof had been affected by water, the trusses had sunk, being too far apart, though the workmanship was excellent and the timber of the best quality; and at Newington in November 1832 shrinking of the timbers had caused the tie beams to sink between half an inch

106 St George, Chorley (Thomas Rickman, 1822-5). Detail of unique iron hammerbeam style roof.

and two and a half inches. There was however no cause for alarm.[88] The problem was nonetheless referred to Smirke, whose repairs were completed at a cost of £1,382.[89] In 1834, further defects were remarked in the Newington roof near the ridge and on the south side. Good found that the roof was continually cracking and admitting the wet because the copper was too light. He therefore recommended stripping the roof and recovering with stronger copper. Iron ties attached to the principal rafters would secure the poll plate that had been forced a little out of its original situation, and make the roof safe. The more drastic proposals by Savage and Cottingham (called in to advise) for inserting iron columns proved unnecessary.[90] Smirke was again employed to doctor the roof, which was re-covered, the trusses braced with iron straps, and corbels placed under the ends of the tie beams.[91]

At West Norwood (pl. 84), Bedford had intended to use the same type of roof as in his other London churches, but the parish objected to copper; so he remodelled it for slate, with no parapets and a pitch two-elevenths of the span. The Crown Architects objected to this as too low for slate, so Bedford revised it to two-ninths, at an additional cost of £424, pointing out that copper would have been more economical: the aisles at Hackney and Wandsworth new churches (by Smirke) were covered with lead flats costing more than the whole roof he had designed in copper. The Committee persisted in rejecting copper, and resolved 'that the lowest pitch of roof which has been approved … for a Slate Roof be adopted'.[92] In 1838 the truss nearest the altar (one of only four trusses the whole length of the church) had failed, the king-post was rent, and the tie-beam, having lost its support, had sunk seven inches; other

king-posts were shaky. Repairs were estimated at £500. A further examination revealed that the other three trusses would require more additional iron straps than at first thought, raising the estimate to £566.[93]

Back at Camberwell (pl. 85) in 1823, Bedford had run into trouble with his sub-structure: with his penchant for daringly economical construction, he had designed groined vaults under the church (the sale of which was expected to provide a considerable income as the old churchyard was nearly full) of the wide span of 18ft 3ins, but low elevation, rising only 2ft 6ins from the springing to the underside of the head of the arch. When one of them failed, probably because Bedford had struck the centering too soon, a long-gathering storm broke over his head. He had been in dispute with the contractors, Want & Richardson, a major firm, on several questions, and had replaced the clerk of works. Bedford was convinced of the efficacy of his designs – 'I did not venture upon a bold and unusual Construction, either in the Groins, or in the roof of the Church, without having well considered and perfectly satisfied myself of its goodness'. He blamed bad workmanship, but Mawley, he alleged, fomented the differences that had arisen in the parish by stating in the presence of the contractors and their workmen that the arches were bad in principle, and 'would never stand however well executed'; a criticism which, Bedford felt, appeared, 'together with the rest of his conduct towards me for sometime past, more like the result of personal hostility, than the conscientious discharge of his duty'.[94] Archdeacon Wollaston himself went down to Camberwell and Newington to inspect the works.[95] George Saunders, FRS (1762-1839), expert on construction, especially vaulting and brickwork, was called in and recommended taking down the arches and rebuilding with a greater elevation. Bedford disputing, Samuel Ware (1781-1860) was asked to make a joint report with Saunders, which favoured reconstruction, leading the Commissioners to insist on Bedford's redesigning – 'with deep regret' – all the crypt vaults in his London churches.[96]

107-9 Thomas Rickman, cast-iron window tracery: repeated use of the same mould.

Left: St George, Birmingham (1819-22).
Centre: St George, Barnsley (1821-2).
Right: St Barnabas, Erdington, Birmingham (1822-3).

110-12 Francis Goodwin, cast-iron window tracery: repeated use of moulds.

Left: St George, Kidderminster, window in west front (1821-4).
Centre: Christ Church, West Bromwich, Staffs (1821-8).
Right: St Peter, Ashton-under-Lyne (1821-4).

113 St Peter, Ashton-under-Lyne (Francis Goodwin, 1821-4). Gothic cast-iron ornaments to door panels.

The conventional slate roof was specified by Chantrell at Meadow Lane, Leeds, with 'best light blue Westmorland Slates to have three inch lap at the lower end and to decrease to two inches or one and three-quarters on the top, fastened with copper nails and fir laths not less than two inches and a half or three-quarters of an inch in thickness, and well pointed in lime and hair.'[97]

Dripping eaves without gutters were objectionable, as James Lucy (d.1829) was told at Claines (Worcestershire) in 1829, and Edward Haycock (1790-1870) at Abersychan (Monmouthshire) in 1830.[98] Ebbels similarly was again in trouble in October 1839 when revising his designs for Upper Gornal (Staffordshire) to reduce expense: his substituting dripping eaves for raised parapets on the side walls Good considered injurious to the Church-like and architectural character of the building; Ebbels argued pointlessly that although parapets were shown on his drawings, they were never intended to be executed.[99] In Cragg's exposed position on the Yorkshire moors Good thought the use of heavy blue rag slate might save damage. Tockholes suffered from a similar exposure: rival builders disputed in 1839 whether the placing of iron bars across the slates had deranged the slating or preserved the building from serious mischief.[100] Lapidge's roof at Hampton Wick, a small Middlesex church, was considered by Good 'ingenious and tolerably safe', although 'not such as has generally been admitted'; and likewise Barry's for Saffron Hill, London – though the trusses were to be at 16ft intervals, 'the scantlings of the timbers are strong and the purlins well supported, and [as] there appears to be some difficulty in placing them nearer together it might be … probably, be admitted'.[101] To reduce the expense at Abersychan, Haycock was permitted to omit one roof truss, which would not, Good reported, affect the building's stability[102] Another alteration allowed, to cut costs, was the substitution of iron eaves gutters for a parapet and lead gutters at the small chapel of Hetton-le-Hole (Durham). Good also found that in exposed situations, the lapping given to slates had been insufficient, and the wet was getting in. At Oxenhope (West Yorkshire), the lap was not to be less than $2^1/2$ins.[103] At Bolton in 1829 he decided that because of the exposed position it was necessary to bed the slates in mortar.[104]

Writing in the *Gentleman's Magazine* in December 1818 'WFW' urged the merits of iron for 'Gothic (or, as it has perhaps more properly been termed, the British style of Architecture)' as providing 'a more light, elegant and finished character, than can be produced by any other material: to this may be added indestructibility and economy'.[105] In his early work, Rickman had used iron constructionally in his Liverpool churches for the ironmaster, John Cragg, but for the Commissioners he generally adopted the more conventional construction, though at Chorley (Lancashire) he employed cast-iron roof principals with ornamental spandrels of a hammer beam design.

He also followed up his recommendation of cast iron window tracery, which he advocated for its cheapness, one pattern being easily replicated. It is not, however, clear how far costs of re-casting made it practicable to re-use the same moulds from church to church. Rickman certainly used the same design of cast iron tracery in windows at St George, Birmingham (1819-22) and Erdington (1822-3). Goodwin however stated that the contractors for his Southsea church (Hants) had calculated 'the Cast Iron windows and models at the sum of £500 more than I knew that similar Cast Iron windows at [*sic*] cost at Walsall Church', so that he turned to

Weatherhead & Glover of Derby (Weatherhead being 'a particular friend of Mr Goodwin'), who had done his Bordesley work, and were prepared to do the windows at Southsea more cheaply.[106] This 'very respectable' Derby firm were probably the leaders in this business.[107] Goodwin used the same window design at West Bromwich, Ashton-under-Lyne, Kidderminster, Bordesley and Southsea; the east rose windows, too, at Kidderminster, Ashton and West Bromwich are identical. But in the later 1820s, iron tracery seems to have been abandoned in favour of stone, for reasons that do not emerge, though possibly aesthetic, as a change at Goodwin's Southsea church suggests: 'The Spires were altered from Cast Iron to Cast Iron Skeleton Spires with the External surface slated, and the whole proposed to be painted to imitate Stone.'[108] Such a practice was to be roundly denounced by Ruskin in 1849; in 'The Lamp of Truth' he allowed metal to be used only as a cement, not as a support.

Increasingly in the early 1820s iron was used to strengthen the roof construction. Both Nash and Smirke were early advocates of iron construction, and both made extensive use of iron for their own practices.[109] But an entirely iron roof structure was viewed with suspicion.[110] Smirke proposed an iron roof for his church at Tyldesley (Lancashire)[111] (and in his abandoned Netherton design), but in the building substituted wood. Soane more conservatively merely reinforced his arches with wrought iron bands, as at Walworth. Taylor, unusually for the 1820s, eschewed iron in his Dewsbury churches, except for straps and bolts in the roof.[112]

In his abortive Erdington design, Goodwin placed iron 'Gothic Brackets ... under the principal rafters with a view of diverting the pressure of the roof ... connected with the Iron plate placed against the face of the principal rafters', and appears to have employed a similar arrangement at Ashton-under-Lyne, where he refers to 'Cast iron Bracketts and Buttresses to support the roof'.[113] Goodwin also used iron in the roof at Bordesley, but complained that 'I was perfectly astonished at the difference between what was intended by the Contract and what was actually charged', the clerk of works having allowed 'broader and thicker Iron work to be used and applied to the building without my knowledge'. He had therefore obtained pieces of iron 12 inches long, 'hammered to the form described in the Drawings, and ascertained the weight per foot of every description of Iron that was intended to have been used by the Contract', making a difference of £448.[114]

Iron columns to support the galleries were extensively employed,[115] and at St Paul, Nottingham (pl. 45), Wilkins used iron cores in his stone nave piers; but for piers to support the roof, Soane and Smirke expressed a decided preference for stone rather than iron coated with plaster.[116] Nevertheless, iron piers, as well as iron roof principals, were used by Chantrell at Christ Church, Leeds; and by E. B. Lamb at St Philip, Clerkenwell.[117] At Portsea, Livesay proposed to replace two iron columns by stone. Later he suggested columns of fir of six inches diameter, in place of oak, to support the gallery; Surveyor Good wanted at least 6^1/2ins. But they finally agreed to strengthening the fir with iron.[118]

Iron was also used ornamentally, for instance on pulpits, doors and capitals.[119] Goodwin had specified iron and wood for the altarpieces in several of his churches, but obtained permission to change this to plaster without making a detailed estimate 'which is difficult to be valued in Gothic ornament', merely judging that by the comparative value of the materials he would save at least 30 per cent, whereas on the contrary the plaster proved more expensive.[120] Oak was sometimes specified for such internal fittings as the pulpit and reading desk, but deal was usually employed for the seating because it was cheaper.

8

Rickman, Goodwin & Busby

Thomas Rickman

The Commissioners wanted cheap churches, and the man whose name is most associated with the era of Commissioners' churches was jogging their elbow – fat little Thomas Rickman (1776-1841), a Quaker from Liverpool. The career of this sometime medical practitioner and clerk, who in 1817 had published an *Attempt to discriminate the styles of English Architecture from the Conquest to the Reformation,* and some six months later had commenced in practice as an architect, illustrates the degree to which it was yet possible for the gifted, though untrained, amateur to engage in the architectural profession. With great energy and single-mindedness he built up the largest practice in ecclesiastical architecture known from the days of Wren to those of G. G. Scott. Until 1831 he was assisted by Henry William Hutchinson (*c.*1800-31), as his pupil from 1818, then from 1821 as his partner in Birmingham. It is impossible to distinguish the work of the two[1] but Rickman bears witness to Hutchinson's ability, a better draughtsman than he.[2]

Opposite: **114** St Thomas, Holloway Head, Birmingham (Thomas Rickman & William Hutchinson, 1827-9). Intended from the outset to be the church of a new parish, St Thomas was designed in Grecian Ionic to give variety from the town's other new churches, and shows the competence of these architects, regarded as Gothic protagonists, in a Classical style. The building cost over £14,000, for some 2,000 sittings. Only the west front survived war-time bombing.

Left: **115** St George, Chorley (Thomas Rickman, 1822-5). Interior, looking east. A large church for a cotton-manufacturing town. The ironwork 'hammer beam' roof is unique.

While still an insurance clerk, in 1813 Rickman designed the church of St George, Everton, for John Cragg, a rich iron-master. To reduce the cost, Cragg had the whole interior cast in iron. The external walls were of local stone, but 'slender cast-iron columns bordered the nave and carried the galleries above the side aisles; from simple capitals sprung cast-iron traceried arches for the support of the iron and slate roof'.[3] The window-tracery, too, was of cast iron. A second church built with Cragg's aid, St Michael, Toxteth Park (1813-15), used many of the wooden casting-patterns already at hand from the earlier building; and iron was used in the external construction also. A third church, St Philip, Hardman Street (1816) (pl. 14), was similar, though externally of brick. Rickman was not satisfied with these churches, for he wrote: '[Cragg's] iron-work is too stiff in his head to bend to any beauty';[4] but he employed iron extensively in the churches he designed for the Commission. Yet where funds were available (as at Hampton Lucy, 1822-6) he evidently preferred stone, even for window-tracery; nor did he seek to develop any new principles of construction by the use of iron.

Like most architects of his day, he was prepared to build in either Gothic or Grecian style, according to the taste of his client, and even prefixed his *Attempt*, avowedly 'a text-book for the architectural student' as well as a guide for 'the guardians of our ecclesiastical edifices',[5] with a sketch of the Grecian and Roman orders. But his predilection was unquestionably for the Gothic or 'English' style, (so termed because he distinguished 'a very different character' in Continental Gothic from the 'pure simplicity and boldness of composition which marks the English building'),[6] which he used for the great majority of his churches.[7] Yet it was a Gothic stemming from that of the eighteenth century; and if his 'descriptions are more precise than any before',[8] and his detail more correct, his assembling of features was often hardly more correct than his contemporaries': though, given large funds, he could rise well above them; the leader, as Summerson comments, of the more archaeological school of church architects of the day.[9] Rickman 'can, as a practising architect never have considered it ... a moral duty to design according to his principles of accuracy.'[10] The architects of the 1820s were not cabined by the rules of pointed architecture as revealed by A. W. N. Pugin or the Cambridge Camden Society; they were free to dress a fundamental form as their imagination chose, subject to the tastes and pocket of the client. While the details in Rickman's *Attempt* are usually taken from real buildings, the compositions – 'A Perpendicular porch set against the aisles of a building', 'A Norman composition which may be considered as a view of one side of a nave'– are not, as he confesses, 'of any particular building, but composed to introduce as many parts as it was expedient to describe'.[11]

The auspicious year 1818 opened with Rickman's preparing his entries for two important competitions: those for a palace for the Duke of Wellington, and for a new church for the large metropolitan parish of St Pancras, neither of which was to yield success.[12] He was then encouraged to propose a design for the new Church Building Society, and worked on an essay on economy in building churches. Bishop Law of Chester, already an admirer of Rickman's work, wanted a design for a church to accommodate a thousand persons, which he was able to discuss with the bishop and two of his clergy: 'it is possible I may have some considerable work from them', he noted.[13] He managed to get his estimate down to 'a trifle under £5 per sitting',[14] and the bishop, who 'suggested a few alterations', proposed to send the designs (as he did) to the prime minister; he also wanted another set 'to take round the Diocese with him'.[15] The upshot was a summons to the Office of Works on 27 August 1818, where the Crown Architects conducted 'a long minute (and I fear reversing) examination of near 4 hours'. A few days later, he was interviewed by the Commissioners, 'asked a few questions and directed to prepare figured drawings and detailed estimates'.[16]

Rickman had submitted 'a few explanatory notes'[17] with his design: 'The principle on which this design has been constructed is an endeavour to combine three primary considerations – extent of accommodation, durability and capability of being easily repaired, and an appearance analogous to ancient ecclesiastical edifices – with as little expense as the nature of the case would admit supposing the outside of the building to be of stone.' He found that what he considered the most economical size accommodated a greater number than he expected, but 'by a judicious curtailment the principles of the arrangement may be preserved for the same cost per sitting, down as low as 1,000 persons', though he doubted whether it would be possible, or even advisable, to go lower. That 'characteristic' feature, the tower, 'which from the necessary thickness of walling is a source of considerable expense', he had used to furnish a gallery and portions of the staircases, thereby, as Soane noted, detracting from its strength;[18] 'although ... its cost is considerable it might not be easy to substitute any arrangement which would so clearly and properly designate the building as a church, at any important diminution of expense'. The great economy of his design, compared with others of a similar style, Rickman claimed, lay in 'the lowness of the aisles and the mode of roofing, which allows the clerestory windows to be but low, and that also keeps down the nave' (so sacrificing the analogy to 'ancient ecclesiastical edifices'). He had banished all ornament which did not 'materially contribute to the general effect'.

The estimate[19] had been prepared on the basis of not only his own work, but others' also; moreover, parts of the detail had been checked by builders who had contracted for similar works. The amount was £6,087 for 1,313 persons. but this did not include commission, furnishings, or such special items as levelling the ground. To this, Rickman added an interesting note: 'I must notice the cost of patterns for the windows and other cast-iron work. These, if only one church was to be erected and the patterns then become useless might perhaps cost £150; but as many churches are to be built, the windows and other things being carefully prepared to be generally useful, the cost of patterns might be reduced to a trifle for each church',[20] – though he ignored the cost of re-casting. A further economy might be achieved, he suggested, by 'contracting for various parts for several churches together', Rickman hoping that his plan might be generally adopted for the new churches, at least in the Chester diocese.

Optional extras included raising the height of the tower (£6 per foot for ten or 15 feet, more thereafter), making it strong enough for a peal of bells, or groining the nave (about £60 for each division, or £300 for the whole – the aisles could not be groined without great additional height). Finally, before entering upon details of the construction, he commented: 'It is possible that the adoption of cast-iron roofs might save something in some situations, but I was desirous to construct everything as much as possible in the common way that it might be executed by common workmen on the spot.' This suggestion in particular[21] roused the ire of Soane's advisor, James Spiller, who condemned Rickman's report as 'entirely made up of assertion and vague descriptions', neither the report itself nor the appended 'details of construction' giving 'any thing like what an Architect would call detail ... his struggles to erect his building for the present, and the lowest possible sum are extreme ... he is willing to that end to make sacrifices of a kind such as an Architect is the least inclined to make. … every thing appears to bend to cheapness which is his first and leading principle'.[22]

All three Attached Architects signed their devastatingly critical report on this assemblage of shams (as Pugin or Ruskin would have thought it):

> Upon a minute personal examination, and after receiving from Mr Rickman all the explanation which he was prepared to give us, we beg leave to state our opinion that in respect of the first-mentioned object, extent of accommodation, a building of the proposed form cannot under any circumstances be made to provide the greatest accommodation at the least expense; and that we consider the proposed construction of the building in many of its parts by no means calculated to provide for a proper degree of durability.

Having told Rickman this, they had asked for 'some detailed drawings exhibiting the intended construction of the building' (none being then ready), which they had since received with a corrected set of designs. Rickman had made many alterations, but the report remained unfavourable:

> The number of persons to be contained in the church is reduced in consequence of the alterations, while at the same time the estimated expense is increased; and although several of the defects have been remedied, we cannot see any reason to alter our opinion expressed upon the first design, as they are founded upon objections applicable to the general principle of both the designs with reference to the three primary objects by which they are professed to be regulated.[23]

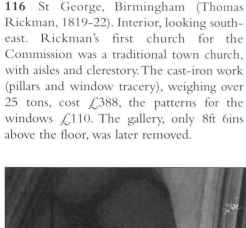

116 St George, Birmingham (Thomas Rickman, 1819-22). Interior, looking south-east. Rickman's first church for the Commission was a traditional town church, with aisles and clerestory. The cast-iron work (pillars and window tracery), weighing over 25 tons, cost £388, the patterns for the windows £110. The gallery, only 8ft 6ins above the floor, was later removed.

After this bad start, it may seem surprising that Rickman (with his partners, William Hutchinson, 1800-31, and R. C. Hussey, 1802-87) eventually built 22 churches for the Commission – more than any other firm of architects. But he was a man of pertinacity and unusual powers of endurance;[24] his rivals were no more meritorious; and he had the useful patronage of a Commissioner, Bishop Law of Chester, who informed him in March 1819 that, although the Commissioners did not intend to appoint a general architect, '*he* should be glad to avail himself' of Rickman's services in his diocese.[25] Meanwhile, he had chased commissions at Bordesley and West Bromwich (respectively in and near Birmingham) without success, but was invited by the High Church rector of St Martin, Birmingham, the Rev. J. H. Spry, key of the local committee, to draw plans for a new church there.[26] Though these won unanimous approval from the local men, London was less enthusiastic. Rickman attended the Building Committee on 8 June 1819: Lord

Kenyon and the Surveyor-General were present, but it was evidently Archdeacon Wollaston who took the lead.[27] Rickman was told to make a new design and estimate for the Birmingham church. Later that month he was examined by the whole Board; many objections were made, apparently of a vague character, as he remarked, 'But at length I got some data to go upon'; the criticisms were chiefly of the ornamental parts, which the vicar was sorry to lose.[28]

Rickman had also in the previous April been invited to design a church for Barnsley, and at a subsequent Board, after 'much examination' he received the Board's final orders about both the Birmingham and Barnsley churches. 'The meeting was pleasant, and their intentions thoroughly explained.'[29] The Crown Architects reported on the former that they did not 'perceive any particular defects in the proposed construction. … the depth and breadth of the foundations are not properly described; … the lead proposed to be used for the gutters is of insufficient thickness. In reference to the enquiry made in the letter which accompanies the specification, respecting the use of iron with plaster or stone for the material with which the piers are to be constructed, we have to state our decided opinion that preference should be given in all similar cases to the use of stone.'[30] Rickman was therefore directed to start operations immediately – 'after expecting from the length of time which has elapsed, that the Commissioners would reject my plan'.[31] 'It will not make so good a thing as the first design', he had thought, 'but still it may do'; and the Commissioners even thought of using the design elsewhere.[32]

The Board's Surveyor visited St George's, Birmingham, in March 1822, and after a minute examination 'expressed himself perfectly satisfied'.[33] He told Rickman that his 'having no extras was a great thing, and would be of great service to us' – for he had now taken into partnership his clerk, William Hutchinson, 'an able designer in his own right', whose 'contribution to [their] success was probably considerable'.[34]

Eastlake's somewhat carping description of Rickman's earliest Million church, St George's, Birmingham,[35] the first completed of those of which the Commission paid the whole cost, throws an incidental light on mid-Victorian opinion, shaped in the late 1830s, and codified in the '40s by the Cambridge Camden (Ecclesiological) Society:

> Its style may be described as late Middle Pointed. It consists of a lofty nave, with clerestory, nave and side aisles, a square tower at the west, and flanked by porches, and a sort of parvise at the east, connected with the main body of the church by flying buttresses. The window tracery is remarkably good in motive, but, sad to say, is all executed in cast iron. For this unfortunate solecism various reasons might be assigned, the most probable one being that it was a cheap means of obtaining an effective fenestration. Yet it is remarkable that no other structural meanness is observable in other parts of the building. The walls are of fair thickness, stouter indeed than those in some of Pugin's churches. The tower, especially in its upper part, is well-designed; and but for the rigidly formal arrangement of its subordinate features, the west end would have been an effective composition. Internally,

117 St George, Barnsley (Thomas Rickman, 1821-2). East end, with vestry and robing room. A low-cost church at just under £5 a sitting (thereby securing commissions for Rickman at Preston), so there was no tower, though it was aisled. The gallery, as at Birmingham, was lower than the approved 9ft above the floor.

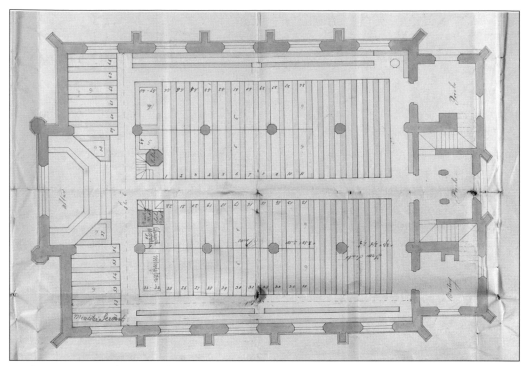

the nave arches have a bolder span, and the aisle windows are splayed more deeply than was usual in contemporary work.[36] The roofs of both nave and aisles are flat, and divided by ribs into square panels. It was only in later years that the high pitched and open timber roof was recognized as an essential feature both for internal and external effect.

The reredos, though of a design we should now call commonplace, is unobjectionable in proportion, and really refined in detail. The introduction of galleries in the aisles was an inevitable concession to the utilitarian spirit of the age. In dealing with them it is, however, only fair to state that Rickman left them independent of the nave arcade, and not as now intruding on it.

St George's took 124 weeks to build, and cost, according to Rickman's accounts, £12,735, inclusive of commission and incidentals, as well as some £300 of repairs to hurricane damage, which was £1,168 less than his estimate.[37] He himself in 1823 noted some faults in St George's: a want of chancel room; passages too narrow; porches too small for the entrances of so large a congregation.[38]

Coeval with the Birmingham church was St George's, Barnsley, a much cheaper church (roughly £6,000 for 1,250 persons, as against £12,700 for 1,900), which lacked a west tower, but was a picturesque composition, with cast-iron window tracery of the same attractive design. Inside, the impression was one of height: from slender piers sprang arches which seemed to rise only to half the height of the nave. An expanse of blank wall intervened between the heads of the arches and the small, square-headed clerestory windows. The architect had difficulty in wedding the internal and external aspects produced by aisles and a clerestoried nave. The ceiling was similar to that at Birmingham.

By early 1822 Rickman and Hutchinson had plenty on their hands. During 1820 Rickman had been in vigorous pursuit of commissions. The Bishop of Chester had sent him the important information that eleven churches had been decided upon in his diocese.[39] Preoccupied with the competition for Kidderminster, Rickman nonetheless on 5 February wrote to his patron, presumably to try to obtain some of the commissions; the reply sent him hurrying to Manchester, where he thought he had 'made some impression as to Prestwich',[40] a large parish for which he was in fact

shortly afterwards asked to design a church. During the rest of February he was interviewing clergy at Stockport, Oldham, Chorley, and Blackburn. In March he was in pursuit of Sheffield,[41] and in May (on the advice of Bishop Law) he wrote for the proposed small church at Hawarden;[42] next he answered an advertisement for Leicester.[43] But then the axe fell: the Board decided he was to be restricted to the four commissions already before them.[44] This felled his hopes at Manchester (where his design had been approved by the local committee)[45] as well as at Liverpool, Preston (whose vicar had been attracted by his 'well-known Architectural talents')[46] and the several places with which he was negotiating. Nor were his trials with the Crown Architects concluded: they had declared his Chorley design to be 'ill-constructed, both as to strength and stability',[47] and had, at the second time of asking, rejected outright that for Prestwich (Stand) as 'so unskillful that we cannot recommend its being carried into erection'.[48]

This seems a curious judgment upon an architect now experienced in church-building. As the construction of this church was, Rickman claimed, exactly that which had been passed for Birmingham, he felt confirmed in his belief that a sinister hostile influence was at work.[49] Although Rickman submitted new designs, the Architects adhered to their objections:[50] so that he undertook another visit to London, where Jenner assured him that the Board had no prejudice against him. Bishop Law advised him to 'bring the matter of the Architects before the Board'. But the Board declined to see him, though allowing him to send a written statement; so the following day he called on Joshua Watson, who soothed him; 'the result is that it will be best to let things take their course'.[51] Part of the trouble was that the Commissioners feared he was 'going to work too cheap', not building substantially enough.[52]

Things did improve for Rickman after this. In March 1821 he was invited to offer a new design for Chorley; and in May the Rev. J. H. Spry, now a personal friend (a factor of material benefit to Rickman), attended the Board and obtained sanction for him to offer plans for further churches at Birmingham.[53] A month later, when

121 St Mary, Mellor (Thomas Rickman & William Hutchinson, 1827-9). Interior, looking east. 'Gothic of about 1230.' One of three churches for Blackburn parish, each of a different stage of Gothic (characterised for Rickman essentially by window tracery), St Mary, adorned externally with a spire, was proportionately the most expensive of the three, at nearly £5.16s. a sitting.

Rickman was again in London, Jenner told him that his rival Goodwin had been discharged from Erdington (near Birmingham):[54] so he promptly visited the township in hopes of that commission, which he eventually obtained, though not until he had had to draw up a more detailed specification and revise his estimate upwards; he declared he had kept economy in view, consistent with the requirements for accommodation and solidity and church-like appearance; to dispense with the tower would give little saving because it contained the principal stair, and to ensure its church-like character, 'some Corner Turrets or other erection containing the same Quantity of work or nearly so' would be necessary. 'The great weight of cost … is the extent of Walling and Timber in the Roof', he argued, and 'a little ornament more or less will not make any difference of importance'.[55] The Crown Architects passed his plans for both Chorley and Erdington in February 1822: 'We see nothing objectionable in the proposed construction of these churches.'[56]

Preston then came into view. In July 1820, the Commissioners had granted £12,243 for a church to a design by Palmer of Manchester, but the gift of two sites at opposite ends of the town induced the local committee to apply for two smaller churches. The Board had no objection if that could be done for the same cost. When, after negotiations, Palmer withdrew, 'the only Architect in this part of the Country to whom we could turn with any confidence in his Ecclesiastical skill, was Mr Thos Rickman of Liverpool'; but he too thought two could not be built for the price of one, and doubted whether he was himself permitted to build any more.[57] The Commissioners, however, having found their stand-by, Smirke, of the same opinion, enquired of Rickman whether a church could be built at Preston for the same amount as that at Barnsley, which Rickman was unable to promise: he had reduced his Barnsley estimate 'once if not twice' thanks to an excellent new quarry and several large iron works nearby, whereas Preston involved higher costs amounting to an extra thousand pounds; but given that, he would replicate his design at 2½ per cent.[58] The Commissioners then invited him to erect a copy of Barnsley on one site, and another on a different plan, for the £12,200 originally allotted for one larger church. Rickman suggested that he should copy his Barnsley drawings (with less ornament) and obtain tenders to establish the exact cost and prices; he would then know how much would be available for the second, which might be of an earlier style and pared of 'every ornament not absolutely necessary', and possibly a little smaller. By building both simultaneously, one clerk of works would serve. But if the Commissioners insisted on 9ft 6ins headroom under the galleries, instead of the 8ft 6ins of Barnsley, that would add very considerably to the cost, as the chapel would have to be raised one foot in height throughout, and the staircases would have to be enlarged.[59]

The pressure Rickman was under at this time is indicated by a letter to the Commissioners' Secretary, 4 April 1822, explaining that the Preston drawings were preparing in his Liverpool office and were 'so dependent on each other, that it would delay the whole of them for the whole time if they were absent if however when finished, thee wish to see them before they are sent to Preston for Tenders, I shall be happy to do it'. At that moment he was in his Birmingham office, about to set off for Preston, Chorley (where the drawings were exhibiting for tradesmen to draw up their tenders) and Barnsley, but he would be back in a week. Three weeks later, he wrote that he was in such a hurry to get the Preston drawings off that evening, to be available on the date advertised for inspection by tradesmen, that he was unable to get any copies taken 'that would be intelligible to thee'. But as they would be returned with the tenders, he would send them up 'for thy inspection' while the tenders were being arranged by the Surveyor for the Board. In a post-script, he asked for blank forms for contracts and bonds; 'we are not properly informed as to our Duties or Powers'.[60] Before anything as to the second chapel was decided, Rickman was ordered to obtain tenders for the first, which in June 1822 came in at £6,761 inclusive.[61]

All, however, was not plain sailing thereafter. Mawley condemned the printed form Rickman had used for obtaining tenders (presumably not having received from the Board those he had applied for) because it engaged tradesmen 'to perform the Works for the undermentioned prices', so that they were bound only to prices and a given quantity, instead of a given total sum. The tradesmen, the Committee decided, must also give the prices of their chief materials, and the architects supply their own calculations of the building's cost, and explain the excess of the tenders over the cost of Barnsley – a remarkable instruction in view of Rickman's earlier letter, as he did not fail to point out. As proof of how carefully the work had been gone into by everyone, he commented that the three stone masons, 'who we are sure have no concert with each other, are very near each other, and two of them only differ 10/-[ten shillings]'; the carpenters ranged from £1,373 to £1,869, but the upper two differed by less than five shillings, and the lowest was unreliable. The Committee authorized building on contracts of £6,263, which with incidentals and 2¹/2 per cent commission totalled £6,728, compared with Rickman's estimate of £6,989, leaving about £5,500 for the second church.[62] The inclusive estimate for the second chapel proved to be very nearly £6,000 for about 1,200 sittings, which the Committee approved with the proviso that Rickman keep down the expense as much as possible, but referring the designs to the Surveyor, who again expressed disapproval.[63]

It is remarkable that in this, his sixth church for the Commission (not counting rejected designs), Rickman should still have spaced his principal roof rafters too widely, at 13ft, run the lead in his gutters only 4ins under the slates instead of 9ins, made the battens for slates insufficiently thick, and miscalculated the accommodation by about eight per cent. One supposes that the need to keep his estimates down was the cause. The next three months were occupied by correcting these faults and others, and passing the scrutiny of the Surveyor and the Crown Architects, who reported – again, rather surprisingly – that 'the drawings do not explain clearly in many parts the intended construction of this Building but as far as we are able to judge from those before us, we do not observe anything objectionable in what is proposed'.[64]

By this time Rickman was thoroughly established in

122 Holy Trinity, Over Darwen, Lancashire (Thomas Rickman & William Hutchinson, 1827-9). Interior, looking west. Described by Rickman as 'Gothic of about 1460.' Second of the three churches for Blackburn parish. This was the largest, with the highest proportion of rentable pews (36 per cent), but proportionately the least expensive at under £4.9s. a sitting.

the profession; he secured the three chapels for Darwen (Lancashire) parish (carefully designing each in a different period of Gothic), as well as the two for Carlisle, one at Bristol, and several more in the Birmingham area. In claiming travelling expenses, for the first time, in the Lower Darwen accounts, December 1828–6 journeys out of 14 made – as he had discovered London architects were allowed to do, he commented 'that in no case have we ever incurred extras beyond the approved estimate and in most cases there has been a considerable saving'; a claim that comparatively few of his rivals could make justly. Until his death he and his successive partners (R. C. Hussey after Hutchinson's early death in 1831) continued to build churches in most parts of the country;[65] churches which, architecturally, as Eastlake says, 'served … as beacons to many'.[66]

Although we may not go so far as Eastlake in giving the priority to Rickman in reproducing 'with accuracy of form' 'the details of old work',[67] for Taylor and Chantrell of Leeds, Savage and Goodwin and Blore of London, were similarly and contemporaneously 'amateurs of English Architecture', yet because of his writings and the national scope of his activity, Rickman was indeed the most outstanding in that respect. As Sir Howard Colvin remarks, 'the detailing of his buildings was unusually scholarly',[68] and his preference for Perpendicular, even if achieving a somewhat brittle effect, did him no harm with contemporaries. Where private patrons provided ample funding, as at Ombersley (Worcestershire), 1825-9, for the Marchioness of Downshire, 'one of the richest of her sex in the empire',[69] he and Hutchinson produced deeply impressive results.

Rickman and Hutchinson also produced two handsome Grecian churches for Birmingham, St Peter, Dale End, and St Thomas, Holloway Head. Variety's sake and expense induced this change from their usual style. To provide variation from St George's, they had supplied plans for St Thomas, intended from the outset to be a parish church, in the Grecian style;[70] and for the Dale End chapel in Early English,[71] 'the principal exterior feature of which style is the simple, long, lancet window'.[72] Rickman attended the Board on 8 July 1823 in connexion with Dale End, and was examined by the Building Committee (Watson, Cambridge and Stephenson, with the Secretary, Jenner), and afterwards saw Watson on his own. He jotted in his workbook the instructions he received: to keep within the area of St George's, to accommodate not fewer than 1,903 persons; the centre aisle to be 10ft 6ins wide, and 5ft benches in the area. The vestry might be on the side of the church if reasons were given. The

123 All Saints, Handsworth, Birmingham (Thomas Rickman & William Hutchinson, 1832-3). A very cheap church, at £3.5s. a sitting.

designs were to be accompanied by reasons why the church would be more expensive because of the nature of its situation – but, seemingly inconsistently, the expenditure was to be limited to that for St George's with the addition of a foot in height, in consequence of the Board's insisting on more head-room below the galleries, only 8ft 6ins at St George's.[73] But then the Building Committee wanted the height of its nave reduced, and larger windows inserted. The architects thereupon commented that if 'any appearance of this style' were to be preserved, a large additional outlay would be necessary; and suggested trying Grecian (plain Doric), 'which so far as it may regard the purpose for which it is designed, would perhaps be better adapted ... as neither piers nor arches would be required, and therefore in the interior there would not be anything to interfere either with the speaking, seeing, or hearing. The expense in either case might be the same.' In sum, a Grecian church would prove 'better adapted for this particular site than a Gothic one deprived as it must be of its characteristic tower or spire'.[74] All these are very significant admissions, coming from the leading propounder of ecclesiastical Gothic.

A fourth Birmingham church, All Saints, Handsworth, 1831-2, was a much smaller brick structure in lancet style, costing a mere £3.5s. a sitting, as against the £6.14s. for St George's.

Francis Goodwin

An architect who had more flair for selling himself to local committees than even Rickman was Francis Goodwin (1784-1835), a handsome, broad-browed man, with a large aquiline nose and evidently a persuasive manner.[75] 'Rickman and Goodwin, in fact,' comments Summerson, 'are the representative architects of the Gothic provincial church-building of the period [after Waterloo], Goodwin tending to be "incorrect" and harking back to the Wyatt school and Rickman "correct" and tending forwards to the orthodoxy of *The Ecclesiologist*.'[76] Nevertheless, both, in their early churches made much use of iron, notably cast-iron window tracery and wrought iron in the roof construction, as has been described above. Goodwin was even praised by the *Gentleman Magazine*'s captious critic, E. J. Carlos, for luxuriating 'in the tasteful ornaments of the windows, by employing the material in which they are formed, cast-iron answering very well in such situations for the construction of ornaments, while the expence of working in stone is frequently the cause of their omission'.[77]

As with most of his compeers, the known facts of Goodwin's early life are few. Born at King's Lynn, son of a carpenter and 40-shilling freeholder, he claimed to have entered the profession about 1803; at some point he became a pupil of an otherwise unknown Coxedge of Kensington; but his first recorded work was a minor rebuilding of Trinity Chapel, St Margaret's church, King's Lynn, in 1809. About the same time, he repaired St Faith's, Gaywood (Norfolk), devising a remarkable plaster groined vault.[78] In 1818 he was assistant to John Walters (1782-1821), for he wrote to Soane soliciting recommendation to 'those Gentlemen who may be concerned in the building of the new churches': 'Although Mr Walters was the appointed architect to the Stepney new church, I had the honour to make the design and to superintend the building hitherto'. Soane had been making extensive

124 St Philip, Stepney (Francis Goodwin, 1819-20). Although John Walters was the nominal architect, Goodwin told Soane that he had designed and supervised it. St Philip's certainly resembles the showy, 'incorrect' Perpendicular churches that were Goodwin's hallmark. King's College Chapel, Cambridge, was an obvious source, with which Goodwin, as a native of King's Lynn, was likely to be familiar. The ornamental features were made of 'compo', having been built before the Commissioners' ruling against this material.

125 Christ Church, West Bromwich (Francis Goodwin, 1821-8). Interior, to west in 1979. Beset by under-capitalized contractors, Christ Church eventually emerged as one of Goodwin's most admired works. Pews largely occupied the ground floor, free seats the galleries, despite the Commissioners' desire for a mix.

enquiries about this church, the first grant-aided church to be completed under the Commissioners' aegis, and Goodwin took the opportunity to press himself on Soane's notice. [79]

In December 1818, Goodwin competed against Rickman and others for the proposed Commissioners' church at West Bromwich. His designs, evidently attractively drawn, showy, and such as might appeal to amateur local committees,[80] were selected and approved, though he altered them in January and again in March 1819. Rickman thought him a dangerous rival, and recorded allegations that Goodwin obtained a sight of his own estimate, and then merely gave the committee a lower figure without calculating it.[81] At any rate it was in June 1819 that Goodwin made, by the Commissioners' order, a 'full detailed estimate of quantity and price with full description, amounting to £11,089 7s.', for which he charged one-half per cent commission.[82] Because of successive contractors' bankruptcies, this church was not completed until 1828, long after Holy Trinity, Bordesley, which was of similar construction.[83] Goodwin's practices with tradesmen were also not above suspicion: his relationship with a master-mason at Ashton-under-Lyne was commented on by the incumbent, and at Derby he unsuccessfully urged the contractors to buy materials from 'parties recommended by him'.[84]

The years 1819 and 1820 must have been a time of intense activity for Goodwin. Plans for Erdington, Southsea, Bordesley, West Bromwich were repeatedly under the Attached Architects' consideration in 1819, joined in 1820 by Ashton-under-Lyne and Kidderminster. In general they pronounced favourably on construction, noting, for example of West Bromwich and Bordesley that 'the proposed construction will be substantial provided the several works are executed conformably to these designs and specifications'; but expressing reluctance to pronounce on prices, though they thought Goodwin's Bordesley estimate 'very large' in comparison with others.[85] A subsequent account of local prices did 'not appear to have been made with reference to these buildings – in order to enable us to give an opinion upon the accuracy of calculations it is necessary we should see the details of the estimates and be informed of the prices at which materials and labour are supplied at those respective places'.[86] From their comments it seems that Goodwin's characteristic weakness lay in drawing up his specifications and estimate. Thus, of Southsea, the Architects commented:[87]

Not being called upon to comment upon the taste of that design we have confined our examination to the constructive part ... and to the specification of the materials and manner of executing the work – to those we see no material objection ... if executed in a workmanlike manner [it] will be substantial. But with regard to the estimate ... and specification we apprehend there are several contradictions. For instance under the head of Bricklayers Work ... several articles are stated to be of brick yet there is not a single article of brickwork in the estimate – and under the head of Masons Work ... the whole of the walls are stated to be of hammered Plymouth Stone laid in courses ... yet there is in the estimate an article of rubble work amounting to one-fifth part of the whole estimate though the term 'rubble work' does not occur throughout the whole of the specification. But as rubble work is not set forth in the specification or described by the drawings, and as we presume that those drawings and that specification will be the basis of the contract,

we shall take no further notice of the estimate than that we see great occasion to advise that very ample security indeed be taken for the performance of every part of the whole according to the drawings and specification.

When submitting new designs, Goodwin took to remarking that the construction was according to principles sanctioned by the Attached Architects in earlier designs. This led them to comment: 'that though we have thought it our duty to point out material defects in construction we have by no means intended to convey our approbation of the whole of the constructive part of any one of the designs laid before us'.[88] A few weeks earlier, Goodwin had called on Soane at Lincoln's Inn Fields to obtain from him a certificate of the adequacy of iron columns under the gallery at Ashton-under-Lyne, about which the Building Committee had qualms.[89]

A characteristic delay was caused at St Paul's, Southsea, by a difference of opinion between the Commissioners and the local committee. Widely differing tenders had been received for the works, which the Building Committee ascribed to the difficulty of 'estimating the price of obtaining and working Plymouth stone', recommending that brick with stone dressings should be substituted.[90] The local committee did not like this idea, and induced the Commissioners to agree to a facing of Bath stone.[91] Goodwin in his turn had difficulty with the local body, arising from his discharging the clerk of the works, John Owen, who was related to members of the committee. This appears to have cost him the commission for the second chapel in Portsea parish, for which he had originally been chosen, but in which he was superseded by Jacob Owen of the local Ordnance Office.[92]

Holy Trinity, Bordesley, Birmingham (Francis Goodwin, 1820-2).

Left: **126** West front. Another example of Goodwin's 'royal chapel' mode.

Right: **127** Interior, looking east. 'Eminent for its simplicity chasteness and beauty ..Will long remain a monument of the correct taste of the period', remarked a correspondent in the *Gentleman's Magazine* (1827, pt 2, p. 201). The vestry, as with many of Goodwin's churches, lay behind the altar.

St George's, Kidderminster, dates from 1820. As in several Goodwin churches, a single room behind the altar served for both vestry and robing room. But here the planning was uncomfortably economical, the approach to reading desk and pulpit being from behind the altar, instead of from the body of the church, as the Commissioners required.[93] The design was to accommodate 1,500, but the Commissioners considered increasing that number to 1,800 or 2,000; Goodwin estimated the cost of enlargement at £6 per additional sitting.[94] His estimate of £16,401 for 2,000 was thought large, and the Board referred it to the eminent architect, George Dance.[95] Goodwin achieved an impressive west front with conspicuous west tower visible from afar, rising over a striking arched porch; deep buttresses (as at Southsea) flank the nave, with its large 'Perp' windows of cast-iron tracery. In the Commissioners' Second Report it was announced that contracts had been concluded for £16,131 4s. 2d. for a church to hold 2,000. Work had started at churches in Ashton-under-Lyne and Bordesley in the summer of 1820, while Goodwin was also rebuilding old parish churches at Walsall and Bilston.

Holy Trinity, Bordesley, has always been regarded as one of Goodwin's finest churches. Goodwin recorded his satisfaction 'to find that the Public unanimously approve and admire this Building particularly the West front (without the Tower) beyond any other of the Churches erected by [the Commissioners'] direction in this style of Architecture'. The committee of subscribers, who had raised £3,000 for the site and enclosure works, 'exclusive of £400 for the vaults cast iron sashs ornamental windows and pinnacles [that] have been added to adorn, and as long as possible to prevent the necessity of repairing the Building', informed the Board that they were delighted with 'the simple beauties of its Architure [sic] … We feel it but justice to state that the Building from its beginning to the end has been conducted by the Architect in a manner that does honor to the confidence you have reposed in him, and highly deserving of your future patronage, and it is the general opinion that the solidity of the monument he has raised will mark for many centuries the good taste of the present age.'[96] But Bishop Ryder, surveying his new diocese in the late summer of 1824 thought it too expensive and too small: 'I should strongly recommend more attention to economy and less to decoration'.[97]

Goodwin acknowledged he had added crockets 'on the lable of the great Portal Arch' and some extra ribs and bosses to the groining of the portal ceiling, but 'It is now only chastely decorated.'[98] Despite the Crown Architects' having examined the plans, drawings and specification for the church in May and June 1819, Goodwin claimed in June 1823 that they had never been submitted to the Office of Works, and that after modelling the original roof he had considered extra ironwork (47cwt of cast and 117cwt of wrought iron), to correspond with roofs subsequently approved, 'absolutely necessary', at a cost of some £300.[99] The explanation doubtless lies in the three stages of alterations required after tenders for the original design came in at near £20,000, bringing it down to £14,000, and then the Board's demand further to reduce the cost 'by taking away the Tower and substituting a something in lieu of it, for the requisite Bells', in Goodwin's words. The church tendered for in April 1823 was quite different from that viewed by the Office of Works. But in March 1824 Goodwin had a different story: the weight of ironwork in the roof had been much increased by the clerk of works allowing 'broader and thicker ironwork' to be used without Goodwin's knowledge.[100] Yet Goodwin had made six journeys there in 1820, and five again in 1821, and a further nine to completion – 14 more than Mawley considered necessary.[101]

Despite all these visits, Goodwin was clearly careless about his paper work. Although on 27 February 1820 he had set out the site of the church and taken levels;

and although tenders were not received by the Board until 4 April, Goodwin appears not to have provided for facing the lower part of the east end with stone, requisite because it was 11ft lower than the west end, since the local committee referred to this as 'a considerable expence beyond the original estimate'. More explicable was his spending £17.11s. in altering five interior doorways from square heads to pointed, 'being the only part of the building the Antiquary and Visitor complained of'.[102] Accounting for more than £100 extra in stone work to the arch of the portal and the west front, Goodwin admitted that working drawings had not been made out at the time of the contracts being settled, 'small drawings one-sixth inch to one foot being unequal to shew the great details required in execution. It is a matter of great regret to the Architect', he continued, 'that the Board does not order that the Architect shall have the Plans after they have been approved by the Board, and the Architects to complete the necessary Working Drawings prior to a contract being made upon them.' But if that had been true in 1820, it was no longer true in 1823, as the Board was constantly calling for working drawings.

As a group, Goodwin's churches are distinctive for boldness of ornament and detail. Mr Whiffen's view is less than fair to Goodwin: 'A busy man, he worked out his own formula for a Commissioners' church and then proceeded to repeat it, with such modifications as his fancy or the money at his disposal dictated, until he — or was it his clients ? — grew tired of it.'[103] These churches 'formed a group which so far as their interiors were concerned differed only in dimensions and detail'.[104] Externally, Goodwin liked 'fat pinnacles and lean towers'. But Goodwin was busy only because he had established his reputation with his Commissioners' churches; which were designed primarily as auditoria, and hence rectangular in plan. Gothic forms (as distinct from Gothic details) were then neither required nor welcomed. The time was not propitious for an architect of great originality, as Soane discovered. The classical desire for symmetry still survived as a standard for public buildings, and shone through the Gothic decoration. Nor was there the money (whether or not there was the talent) to produce something equal to Wren's kaleidoscopic variations in his City churches. Far from Goodwin's 'liking' lean towers, the leanness was enforced on him: at Oldham he had to scale down his original design for the upper stages to a mere bell turret: entirely on account of the lack of money; there was nothing else he could scale down, for the Commissioners insisted on maintaining the original accommodation, and only the minimum of ornament could have been allowed for in the first instance. But his towers do not have the positively starved look of many of those built around London by his contemporaries, and his buttresses as well as his pinnacles are fat. His

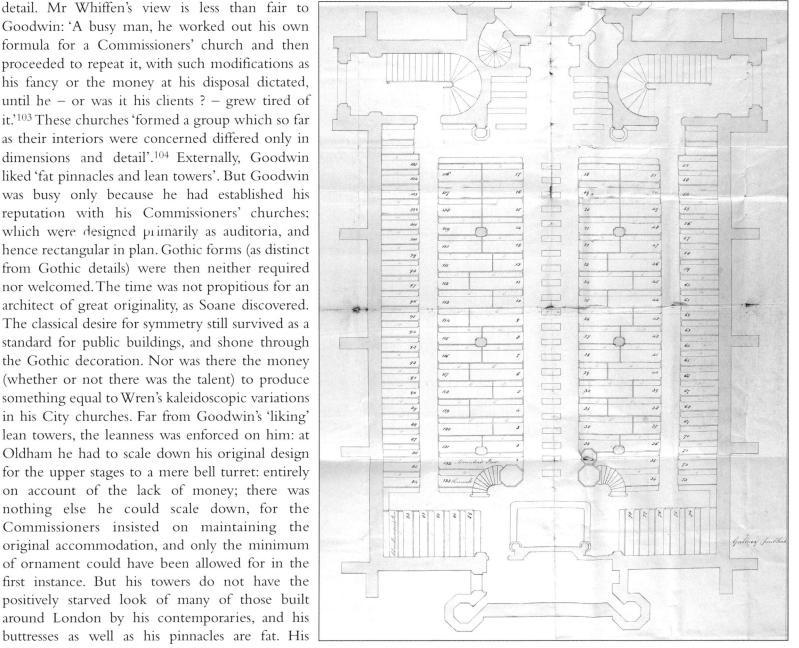

128 St John, Derby (Francis Goodwin, 1826-8). Pew-rent plan, showing Goodwin's characteristic siting of the single-storey vestry behind the altar.

Francis Goodwin: east ends - economical repetitions. The rose windows at Ashton-under-Lyme and Kidderminster employ the same cast-iron tracery as Bordesley:

Top: **129** St George, Kidderminster, 1821-4.

Bottom: **130** St Peter, Ashton-under-Lyne, 1821-4.

designs are no less varied than those of other architects; and are more distinctive than those of most other architects. And Goodwin was original in employing the device of a deeply-recessed western portal (as at Bordesley), on the model possibly of Peterborough, when a tower was not permitted him. Without a tower, western turrets at either side provide stairs to galleries; but he clearly delighted in the opportunity of designing an impressive tower with tall pinnacles, as at Kidderminster and Hulme. In plan he often places a single-storey vestry behind the altar (as at Ashton-under-Lyne, Derby and Kidderminster), rather than the vestry and robeing-room on either side of the altar that is the common form of the day.

That outstanding contemporary, C. R. Cockerell, an architect both learned and fastidious, in the privacy of his diary encapsulated Goodwin's qualities: 'truly a man of genius seizing the characteristics of a style and applying them in the most powerful manner [He] is sometimes almost over-charged and caricatured but with a bold and striking manner'. And again, 'Goodwin for raciness invention recource [*sic*] and sometimes for grandeur beats anything but he is certainly not a gentleman in his works'.[105]

Indeed, Goodwin was 'not a gentleman' in his way of working: his rival, Rickman, in his diary, calls him 'shuffling', 'pushing' and 'impudent'; complains he 'behaved ill', and played 'a strange game'; but admitted that his designs were 'very rich' and 'very imposing'.[106] Keenly ambitious, with a gift for richly ornamented drawing, and having to support a large and sickly family, Goodwin was avid for work. Based in London, but constantly travelling the turnpikes by the new mail-coaches, Goodwin (in Rickman's words), inundated the local committees with pictures and promises.[107]

Their first encounter was over the competition for one of the earliest Commissioners' churches, at West Bromwich, which attracted a considerable number of architects: Goodwin had come down from London, bringing plans with him; 'from what I hear of Goodwin's plans I can't but fear he may get it', Rickman confided to his diary that evening. Next morning the local committee met at the Bull's Head, and reduced the competition to four, 'so near alike that they wished to send them to the Commissioners to decide'; but three of the four wanted an immediate decision, 'so it was decided in about 1 1/2 hours in favor of Goodwin', Rickman noted, but not without hopes: 'I apprehend after all the designs must go before the Commissioners and I think it seems impossible for Goodwin to finish a very rich piece of work as his is for the money he has contracted for and they will I believe tye him tight.'[108] He later noted that another of the competitors had told him about 'various matters connected with Goodwin, some of which are very curious', but unfortunately he failed to record them.[109] Then in January 1820 some of the West Bromwich candidates reassembled at nearby Kidderminster: 'Goodwin came by the London mail'. The next day, Rickman 'drunk tea with Goodwin and he has shewn me most of his designs - they are all perpendicular with various poornesses but much of very imposing character and appear to me to have all of them much more ornament than can possibly be admitted in Execution.' Nonetheless, he feared that 'Goodwin's inundation of pictures and promises' would carry it - as they did. Two days later Rickman, on the Bishop of Chester's advice, was at Manchester, where he learned that 'Goodwin has been invited to Hulme and has that and has made some impression at Manchester'; he feared, falsely, that he might have Stockport too.[110]

Goodwin was the very pattern of that new swarm of professional architects, roving about the country after commissions, to whom the Million Act came as an act of grace which created the opportunity to set up in independent practice – such as R. D. Chantrell, following commissions to the industrial towns of the north or midlands, and settling there: Goodwin however elected to stay in London, the centre of things, though establishing a strong influence in Manchester,[111] where he designed, not the new churches (save Hulme), but the town hall and assembly rooms.

Nevertheless, Mr Whiffen was not the first to suppose that an architect might be too busy: a practice as extensive as G. G. Scott's was not in the reign of George IV automatically a sign of grace. When Goodwin's plans for Belper (Derbyshire) came up for consideration, the question whether the number of commissions awarded to any one architect should be limited was raised.[112] Goodwin was 'already engaged in building six new churches or chapels under the Board, and has offered plans to the consideration of the Committee for five others; ... Mr Rickman ... is engaged in building four new churches or chapels and has offered plans for two others, one of which has been returned as disapproved by the Board'. It was decided that these two men should be limited to six apiece. But Rickman, stricken by the news, was later informed by the Secretary in conversation that the resolution was directed against Goodwin, not himself.[113]

Rickman was to be fully re-established in the enjoyment of the Board's confidence. But certainly this marks the end of Goodwin's triumphal period; thereafter he was frequently in financial difficulties, writing, for instance, on 20 October 1821 that he would be very grateful for an advance of £300 on account 'as I am very much pressed for Money'; if the Board were to refuse, 'I shall be forced to sell an Estate by doing which at this time I must sacrifice at least Five hundred pounds'.[114] Finally, in May 1832, Goodwin memorialized the Commissioners: 'that from a long series of reverses in his professional pursuits', he had been 'compelled to surrender all his effects for the benefit of his creditors', a situation he blamed on the Commissioners' decision in 1820 to deprive him of the building of 12 of the 18 churches to which he had been appointed architect by the local committees, a loss of more than £2,000. These commissions had involved him in a 'vast expense'. He had had to erect additional offices for his clerks, much space being required to make out the drawings for such extensive works; drawing out the plans preparatory to their submission to local committees likewise incurred 'vast expenses'; and travelling to the parishes was costly, as was furnishing estimates, 'for no part of which has he received the least compensation'. He hoped the Board might vote him a sum in reparation.[115] He hoped in vain.

Goodwin, with twelve more plans approved (he claimed) by local committees, and unwilling to see such opportunities slip entirely from his grasp, may, when the Board limited the number of his commissions, have induced his clerks and other architects to offer his designs as their own; they would then superintend the works but pay Goodwin half the commission or more, in return for his having supplied the drawings, 'Mr Goodwin absurdly boasting in bacchanalian revelry [a hostile witness claimed], that "in this way he should make £3000, which was less troublesome than to gain an equal sum by building Churches".'[116] Rickman records a story that 'there was a scheme laid for Tutin [a Birmingham architect] to execute Kidderminster church from Goodwin's drawings';[117] but the Busby case, confused though it may be, presents much more evidence.[118] The arrangement was explicit in one case: Goodwin admitted he disposed of his plans for Hulme to David Laing (1774-1856): 'I considered that the arrangement that Mr Laing was to execute my plans was by the order and concurrence of your Hon. Board, and that you would conclude that either Mr Laing or the local committee would have to reimburse me for my designs and expenses.'[119] (In the end, the plans submitted by Laing were rejected as too expensive.)

Although Goodwin specifically denied any further such arrangements,[120] it is interesting to observe that Gyfford, whose designs were accepted in the first instance for one of the three Leeds churches, was writing from Goodwin's office, and that when Goodwin's plans for Erdington were rejected, the local committee forwarded others from Charles Squarhill (or Squirhill), who was in Goodwin's office, and then his clerk of works at St Paul, Southsea.[121] And his temporary clerk, C. A. Busby, another whose designs were initially accepted for one of the Leeds churches, claimed that Goodwin had made him all sorts of promises.

The Busby Episode

It was in November 1821 that the name of Charles Augustin Busby (1786-1834)[122] first came before the Board, when the Building Committee, reporting on plans he had submitted for churches at Oldham and Leeds, stated that the Crown Architects had twice rejected them for an unsafe roof construction, despite Busby's having 'given particular attention', as he claimed, 'to the Design ... both as regards its ... effect as a work of art, and its practical construction in a more scientific point of view'.[123] Busby had been absent from the British scene for some years: financial disaster resulting, it was claimed by Goodwin, from the failure of a roof he had built on a new principle,[124] and similar problems, had driven him across the Atlantic in 1817. Busby declared that this was a false allegation. Late in 1819 he had returned to London, and had soon been engaged by Goodwin as a clerk. Whether the suggestion came first from him or from Goodwin, it was agreed (Busby alleged), after the Commission's six-churches ruling that the plans preparing for Newington, Camberwell, Birmingham, and Leeds churches should be offered in Busby's name: if they were chosen, he was to pay Goodwin half the commission. He also drew a bill for £325 in Goodwin's name, held by a common friend, which would be handed over if he secured the commission for Belper.[125]

According to Busby, Goodwin failed to implement his promises, and eventually, when pressed, deliberately deceived him at Belper, by rigging a false interview with local committee members.[126] Goodwin explained the circumstances, pointing out that he had subsequently assisted Busby to set up an office of his own, where plans should be prepared at Goodwin's expense; but ultimately, he asserted, having learned something disadvantageous about Busby's history before his withdrawal to America, he decided to end the connection. Busby, on the other hand, claimed that it was he who made the final break because of Goodwin's duplicity.

By declining to intervene, the Commissioners decided virtually in favour of Goodwin. As for the matter from which all this had sprung, Busby's architectural ability, that was again weighed and found wanting. On the Crown Architects' advice, the Board refused to accept new designs from Busby which had a conventional roof construction. Leeds and Oldham committees were instructed to obtain other plans. Busby then wrote to the Archbishop of Canterbury (the Board having refused to hear him further), declaring his intention of publishing his case, and threatening to expose transactions involving servants of the Board. Thus forced to open communication with him again, the Commissioners called on him to elucidate. But he could name only one servant – the clerk, Richardson, who (Busby claimed) 'pursued at one time the practice of communicating (perhaps unguardedly) to him [Goodwin] premature information of your proceedings and of the various provisional applications to the Board'.[127] Aware of this intimacy, he was alarmed by Goodwin's threat, 'that he could work my dismissal without being at all suspected by anyone, and that then instead of having two churches to build I should certainly have none'. How an assistant clerk

could accomplish such a feat he did not suggest, even if he had been giving Goodwin information. The Commissioners continued to employ Richardson after hearing the allegations, and did 'not see any occasion to trouble Mr Busby further on the subject', so Richardson evidently cleared himself on that - though not on a future - occasion.

To set against the tacit acquittal of Goodwin, there is the evidence from rival architects that he was a person of doubtful integrity. Employing several clerks at an annual expense of at least £500, his principal employer, the Commission, notoriously slow to pay architects, his family sickly, he might therefore be none too scrupulous about means of augmenting his income. He certainly did learn very early of proposed new churches. It will be remembered that Rickman thought his practice at West Bromwich unethical. The Rev. J. H. Spry, of the Birmingham committee, who had had considerable experience of Goodwin, and who knew Busby also, 'was glad' Busby published his case,[128] which he did in a folio-sized broadsheet.[129] In this, a copy of which he claimed to have sent to every architect and member of parliament, Busby implied that Nash and Smirke (who alone had signed the Architects' reports),[130] with Wollaston and Stephenson, were the villains, using their censorial office to benefit themselves. He quoted eight testimonials in support of his iron roofs, but these fluctuate wildly in their estimates of the strength of the construction. The Goodwin issue is relegated to a footnote, and he not even named.

While Goodwin's own account appears to be corroborated at several points by witnesses, Busby produced some telling ripostes. The paper signed by his clerks relating to Busby's employment was written by Goodwin, which lends credence to Busby's claim that Goodwin 'obtained the unguarded sanction of those youths, and of Mr Gandy, over a bottle of wine'.[131] But in seeking redress, Busby employed a technique of hints and threats. He succeeded in keeping the affair before the Board for nearly half a year, and his attempts to cause the Board to restore his lost appointments amounted to blackmail. There appears to be little to choose between these two professional gentlemen: Goodwin always out for gain, Busby burning with resentment and seeking the downfall of his largely imagined enemies.

The affair seems to have made little stir in the country. Rickman, who earlier had found Busby a 'very civil and intelligent person who talked much of Goodwin – but

I know not how much of his information may be correct',[132] merely observed that Busby's churches 'have been rejected and in a strange way, by the Crown Architects for insufficiency of roof'.[133] The *Monthly Magazine,* a Radical paper, seizing the opportunity to attack an official body, suggested that Busby's 'indisposition to yield, in silence' (how mild the phrase!), had aroused the hostility of Wollaston and Stephenson; and echoing Busby, stressed the significance of the Crown Architects' being both 'censorial and co-acting architects' under the direction of the Board.[134]

The dispute with Busby has the merit of throwing light on Goodwin's practice arrangements.[135] In 1820, he had four permanent assistants, Henry Berry, John King,[136] George Simmonds and Thomas Allom, supervised by Michael Gandy.[137] He also had assistance on a temporary basis from Thomas H. Blake (d.1821). Busby, according to a paper signed by the clerks (but, according to Busby, written by Goodwin) 'was never employed in any other Office but the supernumerary office where all assistants employed as the urgency of Business may require are placed … Mr Busby was solely employed … in making copies of Drawings for the Clerks of the Works and office duplicates and correcting them to the original drawings.'[138] Gandy, however, subsequently wrote of Busby's 'presiding' over the third office, and considered him as his own professional equal.[139]

Goodwin's Ill-Luck

Though he escaped censure over the Busby episode, Goodwin does seem to have been an unlucky architect. Despite his skills of self-promotion, he was always short of money, and time and again progress on his churches was held up by some untoward incident. Was he autocratic? quarrelsome? or simply, as the Commissioners implied, too busy to give due attention to any one building? We cannot say – even on the last point, the evidence is equivocal. He charged for numerous journeys to his sites: to Bordesley between February 1820 and March 1824, twenty, whereas the Surveyor considered six enough, as that was all that Smirke had needed for supervising his church at Bristol. Similarly at his other sites: four journeys to Southsea in 1822 were two too many, and 13 over the whole course of building seven too many, in the Surveyor's view. The invariable trip for the laying of the first stone was 'not necessary', significant though such celebration was for each locality to stir up enthusiasm - and subscriptions.[140]

When the Surveyor inspected the works at Ashton-under-Lyne in March 1822, he found that the architect had allowed a large quantity of unsatisfactory materials to stay on the ground, and although he had been nearby at Manchester all week he had not visited Ashton. Goodwin retorted that he had spent three days there a week later (though he had not been there since the previous November), and explained the difficulty he had had about the absentee clerk of works, a member of the local committee, that he had tried to resolve by sending down a man from London,[141] thereby offending the local committee; the mason contractor had proved unreliable and was eventually made bankrupt; the church not completed until December 1824.[142] At Southsea, a similar story regarding clerk of works and local committee - 'The truth is … that the strictness with which I exact the performance of the contract has rendered me obnoxious to the Builders and their friends on the Committee',[143] - and delays allegedly caused by the architect's want of attention.[144] At Kidderminster, troubles with contractors; work stopped by the Surveyor because unsound bricks were being used; resort to arbitration over charges for extra foundations.[145] Worst of all, West Bromwich, where John Hedge, 'Builder Dealer and

Chapman' of Starr Court, Little Compton Street, Soho, London,[146] the lump-sum contractor, 'proved that all the Commissioners' defences against slippery contractors were of limited avail – so much so that the case deserves fuller consideration.

Why did it take eight years to build Christ Church, West Bromwich (pl. 125)? It is one of the worst cases in the Commission's history, but extreme though it is, it presents vividly the problems that could hit a church in the building. West Bromwich was intertwined with nearby Kidderminster, because Hedge was a principal contractor there also;[147] but for clarity, we will leave Kidderminster (equally chaotic) out of the story. We have seen that Goodwin secured the commission against Rickman and others in the earliest days of the Commission's building activity. All three Attached Architects had signed the report on Goodwin's West Bromwich and Bordesley designs on 6 May 1819: 'the proposed constructions will be substantial provided the several works are executed conformably to these designs and specifications'.[148] Subsequently they twice declared that as to prices they could not judge for want of local information.[149] In November 1819, an acquaintance alerted Rickman to 'dissensions at … West Bromwich and that Goodwin was likely to be discharged'.[150] What happened in the next eighteen months we do not know. Mawley's earliest written report as Surveyor, 1 May 1821, included a list of objections to various features of Goodwin's designs, including the roof construction.[151] Goodwin recorded his first journey to the building works as 6 August 1821; the foundations were completed by 25 September, when Goodwin made his third visit, for the laying of the first stone.[152]

Thereafter it soon became 'very evident that Mr Hedge has neither sufficient money nor Credit to manage the Works he has engaged … or he is acting from a worse Motive'.[153] He 'did for some time totally neglect to proceed with the Works … pleading that he was endeavouring to procure the Tixal Stone at a Cheaper rate by procuring a Quarry to work himself from Sir T. Constable alias Sir T. Clifford'. Goodwin therefore gave him notice of terminating the contract unless immediate progress were made. This had had some effect but a 'great proportion of the Work which has been prepared and is preparing is not satisfactory'. The reliable clerk of the works had reported that a considerable quantity of bad stone had been delivered which the masons continued to work though he had given them notice that he would not allow it to be used.[154]

The Building Committee, with all the deliberation of contemporary Chancery proceedings, summoned Hedge to attend the Board's next meeting, when Goodwin's reports were read to him, and he was desired to reply.[155] Hedge now attempted to alter the contract by substituting stone window tracery for the iron specified, and Goodwin at first agreed, as the contractor had not procured the cast-iron windows nor even prepared the requisite models, and to do so would cause great delay – but as Hedge was displaying 'almost total neglect', the architect decided that it would be 'very improper' to alter so material a part of the contract.[156] Hedge had sent his foreman in November 1821 to contract for Tixal stone, agreeing to pay cash every 15 boatloads; but when the quarryman sent in his bill, Hedge told him to draw a bill on him at three months.[157] At this time there were 80 tons of Tixal stone on site (of which about two-thirds were prepared) and another 17 tons at the wharf.[158]

The Surveyor's inspection early in March 1822 condemned the works at West Bromwich: much of the brickwork must be rebuilt, and the 'Mortar cannot be worse'; he had suspended the works. The Committee confirmed his action while waiting for a report from the local committee,[159] that defended their brickwork, asserting that it was only a few surface courses exposed to the winter (which Goodwin had already ordered to be replaced) that were bad; the Surveyor should have dug deeper. Hedge himself appealed for a payment, as rumours about the church had destroyed his credit-worthiness. The Commissioners, however, called for a survey by two architects 'of known talent and respectability': George Saunders[160] and Samuel Ware on 9 April reported that many unsatisfactory bricks had been used, though the majority were hard; the lime was good, but the sand unsatisfactory, and not well-mixed with the lime. The brickwork should be taken down to the surface of the ground and rebuilt with better bricks and better mortar. It was so ordered, Goodwin assenting.[161]

Although the quarryman had heard nothing more from Hedge, he had, as the workmen were at a standstill, sent another boat load. The Committee required an explanation, but Hedge failed to appear, so that again his matter was postponed.[162] Hedge was claiming entitlement to a stage payment, without which he could not continue – although he was putting in a low general tender for Brixton church, Lambeth.[163] He was also threatening action against Mawley for circulating a story that he was bankrupt, but, wrote Goodwin, his credit was 'thoroughly injured before Mr Mawley circulated such report'. A few days later, Goodwin reported that there were only five masons, two labourers and a carpenter at work at the church, and often the workmen were unpaid. The merchants would not send any more materials, and it was a 'miserable sacrifice of time' to attend to any more of Hedge's promises. The clerk of works disclosed that the stone work he had ordered to be taken down 'has a large hole in it which was concealed by Cement. The pugging Mill is put up for the purpose of incorporating the Mortar, but is such as I am sure you would not approve.' Both Goodwin and Hedge attended the Board on 4 June, to little purpose; payment would be made to Hedge on the architect's certificate being produced.[164]

The Committee resumed deliberations on 9 July 1822, learning from Goodwin that the works proceeded 'in a very lingering manner'; he had waited three days in Birmingham for Hedge's arrival: only six masons and two carpenters were at work. Hedge now claimed another 13 masons and carpenters were in his employ.[165] At their next meeting, on 18 July, the Committee at last, after six months' procrastination, again warned by the architect that they were deluded week by week by promises that were never fulfilled, instructed him to take effectual steps to compel Hedge to execute his contract forthwith. Goodwin duly issued legal notices to him and his sureties, James Biggs, bookseller, and Benjamin Hatchard, stone merchant, that in 14 days' time he would employ another contractor. Hedge, for his part, threatened legal proceedings unless given the certificate for his £500 second instalment. Goodwin insisting that Hedge had not done work enough, the Committee directed him to enforce the contract.[166]

By August 1822, however, Hedge was bankrupt, so that work stopped on 4 September. Then began a tussle between his assignees, determined to extract as much as utterly possible from his estate, and his sureties, who in the first instance could not continue the work until his assignees had been chosen; and then would not continue it unless the Commissioners would guarantee that they only, not the assignees, would be paid for the work and for the value of the materials on site. Hedge was as uncooperative as ever, refusing to give up his books and contract to the assignees, and then petitioning the lord chancellor, 'alledging that he was not a trader and had not committed an Act of Bankruptcy, and praying that the Commission against him might be superseeded'. These legal tussles continuing, the Committee referred the matter to the Law Officers.[167] The local committee were petitioning for work to be

resumed, Hedge having told them that if his petition were granted, his debts should be paid in full.[168] On 25 February 1823 the Committee directed Goodwin to take the steps pointed out by the contract, and sought counsel's opinion whether any further notice need be given to contractor and sureties. The Committee sought further legal advice, the lawyers further information, and the sureties battled on with the assignees.[169] Hedge's bankruptcy was established by a special jury at Kingston assizes in April 1824.[170] Goodwin urged the Committee to order tenders to be obtained for completing the works, but the Committee urged the sureties to settle with the assignees,[171] the difference between them reduced to £300. The Committee concluded that it was a bargain expedient to accept, and in September 1824 were able to approve the assignees' release and indemnity, enabling the sureties to discharge their obligation of completing the church.[172]

After 15 months' delay, work resumed. In January 1826 the Board instructed the Building Committee to obtain a valuation of the work done and recommend the best mode of completion.[173] The estimate was no less than £13,278. The sureties' contractors then quarrelled with only some £600 worth of work done, work was again suspended for 14 weeks in 1827, and the contract cancelled.[174] Finally the reliable Samuel Buxton of Manchester contracted for the completion at some £12,667. On his September 1827 inspection Surveyor Good noted: 'carving is particularly well executed'; though there was a delay again in 1828 caused by the difficulty in getting stone of large enough dimensions.[175] Goodwin's accounts were finally approved on 9 June 1829, the bill totalling £17,105 (allowing him 12 journeys, twice the usual number), as against his original estimate of £11,662 and Hedge's contract of £11,290.[176] But misfortune still dogged the church: the gales of May 1829 blew down its pinnacles.[177]

From 1822 Goodwin was employed on a number of major public buildings in Manchester, Leeds, Derby and neighbouring towns; in 1825 he recovered the major

133 St John, Derby (Francis Goodwin, 1826–8). Elevation from the south-west. In the 'Ornamented' style, but deprived of a tower for economy's sake, and costing a moderate £5 a sitting.

commission for Hulme (Manchester) church, which at over £15,000 was to be one of the more expensive provincial churches,[178] and obtained that for a Commissioners' church at Derby, as well as those for rebuilding parish churches at Walsall and Bilston (Staffordshire). The Evangelical Bishop Ryder, who was translated in 1824 from Gloucester to Lichfield, was keen to have more churches, but more economical and less ornamental than those already built. So Goodwin found himself cutting down his handsome Derby designs (priced at £10,500 exclusive of commission, etc.) to meet the bishop's requirements: 'I have only to suggest that the Tower be replaced by two Turrets with small portals, to ground entrance, by which a saving of seven hundred pounds may be made.' Cement in lieu of stone would save another £800, but the local committee 'consider themselves entitled to a handsome Building in consequence of the liberal subscription [of £4,500] they have made in opposition to the dissenting party'. The Board decided to accept the subscription for church and site, and themselves build such a church as they thought fit.[179] Goodwin however did secure the commission; St John's cost £7,927 for about 1,500 persons, against his estimate of £8,203.[180]

The wheel turned full circle at Oldham after Harrison's resignation, and Barry's dismissal for the tenders' exceeding his estimate. On learning that Barry would not be permitted to revise his plans, an ally of Goodwin's, Henry Barlow, immediately recommended him to the local committee, which promptly invited him to become their architect.[181] Goodwin's design, estimated at £10,648 for over 2,000 sittings, was approved by the Board.[182] Applying in January 1829 for the second new church for St Luke's parish, Old Street, London, he pointed out that he no longer was engaged on six churches simultaneously, and begged the Commissioners 'to take into consideration the injury which I have sustained by that limitation [to six] in the heavy expences of journies to attend the Local Commissioners and in the preparation of at least twelve sets of complete plans, working drawings and estimates which I completed by the order of the respective Local Commissioners which were rejected by the Board on account of the order of limitation'.[183] He was allowed to submit a design, but it met no success.

Goodwin also built two churches similar to Derby, St Mary's, at Bilston (Staffordshire) in 1827–30 on an estimate of £6,012, and St Thomas, Pendleton (Lancashire), the latter in partnership with Richard Lane, the leading Manchester architect of the period.[184] These churches gave Goodwin less opportunity to exercise his talent for display, and those approved in the years immediately following still less so. But he found attractive country-house commissions in Ireland, and in 1833 was one of 17 architects invited by a parliamentary committee to design a new House of Commons:[185] his submission, principally in the Perpendicular style, was much praised,[186] and it was in the course of designing new Houses of Parliament after the fire of 16 October 1834 that he suffered a fatal stroke.

176

9

Styles and Local Schools

In considering the church building of the era, the stylistic division between Classical and Gothic suggests one line of enquiry. To what extent did the Commissioners exercise a choice? Was the style influenced primarily by geography or architect? The choice of architect usually depended on the local committee, so that a local man, a newly-established architect hunting the country for commissions, or some famous London practitioner, any of these might become the architect for an obscure country parish or the deprived quarter of some industrial town. Did this system of itself have any important stylistic consequences?

First, however, one has to establish whether the Commissioners themselves favoured any particular style, or whether they indirectly fostered the adoption of any special sort of church design. Their having decided against adopting a general plan, and preferring to rely on local committees promoting talent by competition, would suggest that they had no strong predilection. They were concerned to elicit the truth about the costs of the rival styles, commissioning Smirke in April 1820 to 'prepare two designs for a Church fit for a considerable provincial town, giving to one of these the characteristic Style of a Gothic Building', with detailed estimates and specifications, so that they might 'judge of the comparative expence'.[1] Insofar as they were thought to have any predilection, it was said to be for the classical style. The critic W. H. Leeds, writing 'On the Architecture of the New Churches' (seen in the four churches proposed in Lambeth parish) in May 1821 referred to the Commissioners' 'attachment to Greek and Roman designs', while arguing that the Gothic was 'more applicable and appropriate to the purposes and convenience of our worship than any other' - though admitting the merits of the Palladian style.[2] During 1822 there was a rumour current that they had decided to pass no more plans in the Gothic style. An article in the *Quarterly Review* stated: 'The Commissioners have now determined to adopt nothing but pure Grecian architecture.'[3] A clear-cut expression of preference for a Grecian rather than a Gothic church on the prominent Eaton Square site, Pimlico, may have ignited this rumour. The Hanover Square vestry had declared that it favoured a design by Hakewill imitating St Mary's church at Oxford, but threw away that option by remarking that if the Commissioners 'still entertain

Opposite: **134** St Mark, Kennington, Lambeth (David Riddall Roper, 1822-4). Doric portico and west tower with Ionic cupola. Roper was well-known in Lambeth as a surveyor, and the local committee pressed to retain him as architect at Kennington even when the tenders exceeded his estimates. Decades later, it was claimed that the church was designed by his assistant, A. B. Clayton.

135 St Matthew, Brixton, Lambeth (Charles Ferdinand Porden, 1822-4). West front. Well-versed in Grecian architecture, having supervised the building of new St Pancras church, 1819-22, Porden solved the problem of uniting a temple portico with a tower by placing the tower at the east end, with the portico at the west. Doric appears to have been favoured for porticos by the Lambeth local committees.

any strong objections to the ... Gothic plan, the Committee submit to them the accompanying Grecian plan'.[4] But Eaton Square was being built in a classical manner, so it was essentially a decision determined by site. Rickman records a letter from Jenner denying the truth of the rumour.[5] Although Rickman, the outstanding exponent of the use of Gothic, designed Grecian churches at Birmingham, St Peter's, at this period, it was (as we have seen) for particular reasons of situation and cost, though he stated that in general the cost of a simple church in either style would be the same;[6] a view supported by the Inwoods' identical estimates – to Soane's incredulity – for their two chapels in St Pancras, one Grecian, the other Gothic.[7] The Bishop of London told one enquirer that 'the question of Gothic or Grecian' was one 'which the local committee was fully at liberty to decide for itself'.[8] It is clear from their records that the Commissioners had, as a body, no predilections for either of the dominant styles, Classical or Gothic.

By the mid-1790s Gothic had become again an acceptable style for churches. The rococo Gothick of Shobdon (1746-56) yielded to the 'archaeologically perfectly convincing' St Mary Magdalen, Croome d'Abitot (Worcestershire, 1763), or the restrained late Gothic of St Mary Magdalen, Stapleford (Leicestershire, 1783), and a quiverful of comparable churches, with a tendency to what Rickman was to define as Perpendicular[9] – churches more archaeological in character than the Rococo, but composed rather than copied, characterised by a lightness and a spaciousness well-adapted to a form of worship dominated by the Word; a type that needs to be considered on its own merits, a reflexion of its times, and not as an inadequate precursor of Pugin and the ecclesiological movement. These churches were familiarizing clerics and laymen alike with the attractions of Gothic, the more acceptable in that day for its supposed Englishness. John Carter's drawings from the late 1770s, and his influential articles in *The Gentleman's Magazine* from 1798 'marked the start of a new attitude towards Gothic'.[10] Although for accurate drawings architects had to await the publication of A. C. Pugin's and E. J. Willson's *Examples of Gothic Architecture* (1828-30),[11] there was enough in print to supply general charac-teristics and establish the capabilities of the style in the public mind. John Britton's *Architectural Antiquities of Great Britain* (1807-14), followed by his *Cathedral Antiquities of England,* 'made gothic available as never before';[12] and Rickman's 'Attempt to Discriminate the Styles of English Architecture' appeared, if obscurely, in 1815 – and appeared as a book in 1817. E. J. Carlos throughout the 1820s used *The Gentleman's Magazine* as his pulpit for preaching the merits of the Gothic style, especially that of the thirteenth century, for English churches,[13] despite a moment of disillusion in 1820, when he declared that as the adoption of the Pointed Style 'depends so much upon parish committees, guided by professional men [*i.e.,* architects], who by education are prejudiced in favor of *modern* architecture, and generally ignorant of the principles of the "Gothic style" as they call it, the present age is likely to be as far from perfection as Wren, Hawksmoor or Batty Langley, ever were'.[14]

So successful was this flow of literature that the clergy, who often dominated the local committees, developed, as the Leeds-based architect R. D. Chantrell remarked to Soane, a 'mania for plain Gothic work'; he and his contemporaries, grounded in Classical architecture, had accordingly to contrive designs 'utterly at variance with [Classical] principles', which they had 'no time to study or collect data'; instead having to 'adapt fragments of the various medieval styles' to the 'utilitarian masses' of the new churches.[15]

It does seem that the Commissioners, whose most active members included the two architecturally-informed archdeacons, Wollaston and Cambridge, followed the prevalent formula, 'Classical for town, Gothic for country';[16] but 'town' is a term itself requiring definition. Carlos in 1827 complained that St Luke, West Norwood, Lambeth, being a country church, ought not to have been Classical but Gothic in style.[17] At Bristol in 1828 they at first approved a Gothic design, despite the alternative (by C. R. Cockerell) being Grecian, but subsequently they informed the local chairman that they would accept whichever his committee preferred. In Sheffield, John Rawstorne (1761-1832) understood in mid-1820 that 'all the Plans likely to be adopted are not Gothic', but his Grecian composition was not approved by the Board.[18] Certainly, suburban churches were not necessarily Classical. Indeed, in responding to the New River Company's request that its surveyor, W. C. Mylne, design the church for the site it was giving in suburban Clerkenwell, the Board, while not guaranteeing that Mylne would be the architect, insisted that his plans 'must be of a plain Gothic Design'.[19] Even in Marylebone, the Commissioners were, as we have seen above, prepared to concur in the vestry's wish that Soane's design should be Gothic.

Topography was certainly a factor: they were advised that the site recommended in Lower Darwen (Lancashire) was 'in so wild a country very little traversed by great high roads that a very handsome church would be lost there'.[20] Similarly, at Netherton (Dudley), the vicar asserted that 'In a District of simple habitation, full of Mines and Furnaces, we desire only a plain, unostentatious Edifice ... One of any other kind would be totally out of character.'[21] 'The particular nature of the site' was also a factor in choosing the cheaper of Basevi's designs for the termination of the tower of St Mary's, Greenwich, as recommended by the vicar,[22] – 'a far from happy design', thought Carlos.[23] Time and again, the views of the local committee carry great weight with the Board.

The Commission itself, however, avoided generic decisions about style. It was in London that well-known architects, firmly based in the the Classical tradition of Wren and Gibbs, were commonly employed, partly because metropolitan parishes deemed it appropriate to have the leading men; or, like other parishes, favoured local sons. When a young man was employed it was usually one who had local connexions, and it was chance that Camberwell-based Francis Bedford (1784-1858) was an enthusiastic 'Grecian', who had drawn Grecian ruins for the Society of Dilettanti. Basevi's St Mary, Greenwich, was designed with an eye to its situation between

136 St Mark, Clerkenwell (William Chadwell Mylne, 1825-7). West front. Mylne was surveyor to the New River Company, donor of the church site, and was employed at the company's request. The Commissioners insisted on Gothic for this suburban church. Although it is insulated in a square, Mylne, like Roper, concentrated his effects in the west front.

Wren's Royal Hospital and Hawksmoor's St Alphege.[24] Even architects with a flair for Gothic designed Grecian churches for London – like James Savage's Bermondsey St James. In London it was locality and public opinion that determined that Grecian (or, occasionally, Roman, as in Thomas Hardwick's) was the fit mode for the churches of the early 'twenties, a view that was strongly held by C. R. Cockerell, who considered that the Maison Carrée at Nimes and similar buildings, 'ever admirable and pleasing to the eye, seem to offer the best example of imitation', and their style 'the best suited to a durable and sacred edifice, because it is that which has received the sanction of all ages since its origin, and is therefore the most likely to withstand the vicissitudes of taste and fashion which may hereafter occur'.[25]

137 St James, Bermondsey (James Savage, 1827-9). Deep Ionic portico, with full Classical Roman treatment.

How deep lay the Commissioners' interest in architecture is difficult to determine from their records, since minute books are records of decisions and not of discussions; however, the occasional phrase supports the evidence of Archdeacon Wollaston's letter, that among the Commissioners were men with a lively interest in and an educated layman's knowledge of architecture, and in the case of Wollaston himself and his colleague Cambridge, something deeper. The Rev. Richard Mant, who before his elevation to the Irish episcopate was regular in attendance at the Board, was another enthusiast.[26] The function of a committee reviewing architectural designs, however, is not itself to provide designs (arrogating the architect's function), but to judge. That few criticisms of stylistic detail or design proposals for specific features are recorded in the Commissioners' books indicates neither an indifference to nor an ignorance of architecture as understood in the 1820s, which is the

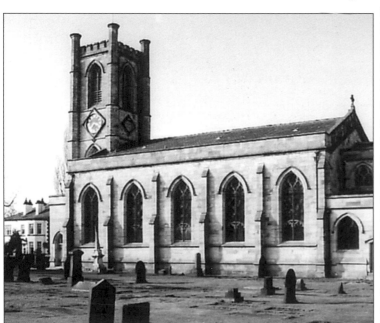

138 St John, Farnworth, Lancashire (Thomas Hardwick, 1824-6). Hardwick was instructed to differentiate his two Lancashire churches from that he was building at Workington, Cumberland.

standpoint from which it has to be assessed. No doubt it was for liturgical and economical reasons that they wanted the altar brought forward four or five feet at Bolton,[27] but the instruction to Hardwick to vary his designs for Farnworth (Dean parish) and Bolton (both Lancashire) from that for Workington (Cumberland) suggests an architectural interest, as does that to Palmer at Preston to give the tower and roof greater elevation.[28] The Building Committee in 1820 wanted the deep portal under the tower of Goodwin's St George, Kidderminster, to be closed (but Goodwin kept it open).[29] In 1825 they suggested that an alteration 'in the character of the Windows' at Soane's St John, Bethnal Green, might improve 'the general appearance of the Building', and the Board agreed.[30] In Atkinson's Woodhouse, Leeds, design they called for the lower part of the tower to be 'more ornamented', and for Nash's Haggerston design to be 'less ornamental'.[31] But in administering a parliamentary grant controlled by clearly-stated criteria, the Commissioners' scope for connoisseurship was severely limited.

Christ Church, Cosway Street, St Marylebone (Thomas Hardwick, 1822-4).

Left: **139** West front from north-west. Hardwick as architect of the parish church was chosen by the St Marylebone vestry for one of their four new churches, to which they contributed £20,000.

Right: **140** Nave, looking west. Carlos praised Hardwick for following Wren's style.

Nevertheless, it was exercised to a certain degree. Archdeacon Wollaston, a pillar of the Building Committee, objected, for instance, to the tops of the windows in Bedford's Camberwell church being straight instead of rounded, because it much injured the appearance; he also found serious objections to the groining of the vaults, though 'It may be thought presumptuous in me to offer an opinion contrary to that of a professed Architect ...'. His detailed criticism of the groins exhibits a considerable knowledge of the subject, and was endorsed by the expert constructional architect, George Saunders.[32] Archdeacon Cambridge, with the cool confidence of a man of taste, wrote to the Secretary of 'a correction that occurred to me in reading over the minute respecting the proposed church at Wakefield – the battlements of which should rather be of the *fourteenth* than the thirteenth century, as the buildings on which they are found are chiefly of the reign of Edward the 3rd'.[33]

Below left: **141** St John, Workington, Cumberland (Thomas Hardwick, 1822-3). West front. Hardwick sustained the Palladian tradition of Inigo Jones.

Below right: **142** St George, Kidderminster (Francis Goodwin, 1821-4). West tower. Goodwin was instructed to close up his western portal, for which it is difficult to find a medieval precedent. But the Commissioners' orders were not enforced.

A significant Commissioners' influence in the Battle of the Styles may therefore be discounted: largely they accepted the fitness of Grecian for the town and Gothic for the country. Other styles did not appear until the late 1820s, and did not enjoy a vogue until about 1840. Grecian and Gothic alike had plaster ceilings, apart from St Luke, Chelsea.[34] Nor was the chancel an exclusive, or necessary, appurtenance of Gothic: but this was not the long chancel of late medieval times, which later captured the imagination of the Camdenians. During the Million era the battle was one affecting merely the grammar of the superstructure; there was little dispute over the plan of a church, which was primarily an auditorium,[35] with two liturgical centres,[36] one, the font, at the west end near the entrance to the church, and the other, principal

143 Holy Trinity, Little Queen Street, Holborn (Francis Bedford, 1829-31). This photograph of *c*.1870 shows an interior little changed since it was built, complete with free benches in the centre aisle. Bedford stated that the form of his columns was copied from Winchester, and the knobs or bosses in the window tracery from Westminster, Salisbury, and elsewhere. The angled triple chancel arch was a novel feature, demarcating Bedford's first chancel.

centre, composed of altar, pulpit and reading desk, at the east. The altar was ministerial,[37] and the altar recess, occasionally termed 'chancel' was usually no more than four or five feet in depth, flanked by a vestry and a robing room; pulpit and reading desk balancing each other on either side immediately to the west of the recess. Worship was conceived of as 'a taking part in the liturgy'; prayer and preaching 'being equally useful', in George Herbert's words, should have 'an equal honour and estimation'[38] – though frequently congregations demanded a combined pulpit and desk in the central aisle. Choirs and several clergy participated only in cathedral services; congregational singing was Methodistical, and hence there was no call for a choir to lead it. Since long chancels were not in consideration, the Commissioners' ban on seats facing north or south did not influence the architect's choice between styles, though it hindered a departure from the parallelogram plan.

★★★★★

The leading architects who assisted the Commissioners include Nash, Soane, and Smirke, Thomas Hardwick, William Wilkins (1778-1839), and Charles Robert

144 St George, Brandon Hill, Bristol (Robert Smirke, 1821-3). A reduced version of St James, West Hackney (pl. 30), and proportionately much cheaper (£7.2*s*. a sitting against £9.16*s*.). Photograph 1978.

Cockerell (1788-1863). Cockerell 'never designed a Gothic building by choice':[39] for the Commissioners he built only one church, the Grecian Hanover Chapel, Regent Street, hailed by Carlos as a splendid exception to the general mediocrity of the new churches.[40] He also made a design for Bristol, but there the local committee at length chose Gothic. Wilkins, who likewise worked chiefly in the Grecian Revival manner, designed St Paul, Nottingham, an idiosyncratic Roman basilica, for his brother,

145 St Paul, Nottingham (William Wilkins, 1820-2). A singular design by the arch priest of the pure Grecian, with exceptionally wide central intercolumniation closely resembling the woodcut of a tetra-style Doric temple in Martin & Goujon's first French edition of *Vitruvius' Architecture*, (Paris, 1567), f. 59r.

the vicar. His recommendations for church design having been ignored by the Commission, he did not otherwise participate in the building programme.

Soane refused to build churches in the provinces; nor did Nash build any. Smirke, however, who was highly regarded by the Commission (despite his ordering extra works without obtaining clearance first), built four, by the Board's recommendation to applicants.[41] These have been considered in Chapter 4: three in large towns – Manchester (a copy of his Marylebone church), Bristol, Chatham – were in his characteristic Grecian; the fourth, Tyldesley (Lancashire), was in an area of coal-mining and industrial villages, for which he used Gothic. Smirke also supplied plans for Netherton (Dudley), where the vicar requested the Commisssion to supply a

St Paul, Balls Pond Road, Islington (Charles Barry, 1826-8).
Below left: **146** Exterior from the south. The tower was at the east (entrance) end. Carlos thought Barry 'almost rivals' the work of ancient architects in his two North Islington churches.

Below right: **147** Nave, looking east. The entrance lay behind the altar, with the tower above. The reredos, 'in the style of the altar tombs of the 15th century', impressed Carlos; the outer divisions were inscribed with the Decalogue, and the next inmost held seats for the clergy, as in St Margaret, Westminster, Barry's parish church.

148 St John, Upper Holloway, Islington (Charles Barry, 1826-8). Designed in a later style than St Paul, for variety's sake. The nave is almost identical to St Paul's, but the short chancel, unimpeded by entrances, has a large east window, and is vaulted in imitation of stone.

St Peter, Brighton (Charles Barry, 1824-8).

Right: **149** West front. Barry's Perpendicular essay won in competition. Pevsner calls it 'entirely pre archaeological', in his view a 'fault', but one remedied 'by remarkable inventiveness and boldness' (*BoE, Sussex*, p. 135). The tower is a development of that of Stand, not an open porch, but with deeply-recessed doorways on all three external sides.

Opposite top: **150** The frieze above the lowest stage is derived from King's College Chapel, south porch, illustrated in Britton's *Architectural Antiquities*, I (1807).

Opposite below: **151** St Thomas, Stockport (George Basevi, 1822-5). View from south-east. The entrance was originally at the east, because that lay nearest the road.

design, but after years' delay over the site they were not used.[42] Hardwick, the sustainer of Sir William Chambers' Palladianism, was commissioned in 1821 to build churches in Workington and at Farnworth (pls 138, 141) and Bolton where designs by others had been thrice rejected by the Attached Architects; he was specifically asked to vary the design (as remarked above) from that for Workington (in Roman), so for the two Lancashire churches he turned to Gothic.[43]

The other London architects working in the provinces were young men who, with the exception of Basevi, habitually used Gothic for their churches: Francis Goodwin (considered in Chapter 8) and Charles Barry (1795-1860) above all. Although Barry himself subsequently deprecated his work in the London suburb of Islington, where he built three churches, varying the styles between successive periods of Gothic, they were archaeologically advanced for the 1820s, and are works of some distinction, praised by Carlos as standing 'in the highest rank' of modern churches.[44] His two Manchester churches, at Camp Field and Stand ((pls 187,197) only the latter survives) are highly successful essays in Perpendicular, Stand's fine

tower rising from a porch open on three sides (an adaptation of the secular Gothic porte cochère then admired in Picturesque architecture). His St Peter, Brighton (1826-8), largely resourced locally, was even more inventive, a bravura re-interpretation of the Boston stump, (pl. 15) in which the richly pinnacled upper stage of the west tower is connected by flying buttresses to the large corner pinnacles of the lower stage, in which a giant ogival arch embraces both door and window.

George Basevi (1794-1845), a pupil of Soane, who favoured the Classical tradition, built the handsome St Thomas, Stockport, where he solved the problem of tower and portico by separating them, placing the tower at the west, the portico at the east end. Rickman's two Classical churches were in Birmingham – again, a large town, and again the style was chosen in one for the sake of variety, his first Birmingham church, St George, being Gothic, and in the other to stay within cost limits. The only other Classical provincial church built from the Million was St Paul, Stockingford (Warwickshire), seating 600 and described as 'Grecian, without columns; tower'.[45] This was the work of one John Russell, an architect-builder from Leamington Spa, the only provincial architect, save Rickman, to use Grecian for a Million church. Hardly any of the Half-million churches were Grecian, or even Classical. When Walker Rawstorne submitted Grecian drawings for one of the new Sheffield churches in 1820, the local committee 'made some objection to their being in the Grecian style' and declined sending them to London with the other architects' plans. The Archbishop

of York having told him that there was still a vacancy for the Sheffield church, he himself despatched the plans, but the Building Committee submitted them 'without comment' to the Board, which did not approve them, the local committee's lack of enthusiasm doubtless a factor.[46]

On the other hand, the London Million churches include several in Gothic, partly because of long delays caused by powerful and hostile vestries, and the difficulty of obtaining sites, so that the Commissioners were looking for economies; the others were built in the suburbs, some of which were still distinct townships. Nash eventually chose Gothic for St Mary, Haggerston (pl. 44), having been

Above: **152** Holy Trinity, Brompton, Kensington (Thomas Leverton Donaldson, 1826-9). View from south-east. It is difficult to believe that this church cost nearly £7 a sitting. Carlos asserted that few churches offered 'so complete a specimen' of 'Carpenter's Gothic', the south flank displaying 'all the faults of the modern Gothic school; in the pilaster-formed buttresses … in the windows, more acutely pointed than any genuine specimen, and which are too wide for lancet windows, at the same time that they are too narrow to admit of tracery, and in the paltry coping … only to be met with in the most ordinary of dwelling houses' (*Gentleman's Magazine*, 1830, pt 1, p. 579). A plea from the churchwardens in November 1829 for 'some Architectural ornament' was refused by the Commissioners.

Right: **153** St Michael, Burleigh Street, Westminster (James Savage, 1832-4). View from south-west. Savage spent only £5.9s. per sitting here, and that is reflected in his architecture. The asymmetrically-placed tower is remarkable for the date.

confined to a reduced grant; at Somers Town the Inwoods used it to give variety – the nearby chapel in Regent Square (pls 47, 49), though Grecian, was closely similar in plan and specification. Goodwin, whose bent was for the flamboyance of Gothic, claimed to have been author of the 'exceedingly beautiful'[47] St Philip, Stepney (pl. 124). William Chadwell Mylne (1781-1863) was selected for St Mark, Clerkenwell, at the request of the New River Company, donors of the site, whose engineer he was: this was his only church, condemned by Carlos for its 'clumsiness and utter want of taste', a jumble of different periods.[48] Thomas Leverton Donaldson (1795-1885) author of Holy Trinity, Brompton, was a young man keen to establish himself, given a brief for 'the plainest possible design' for economy's sake, when the Board's resources were stretched to the uttermost[49] – Carlos denounced it as epitomising the faults of contemporary Gothic.[50]

Of these Gothic churches, St Luke, Chelsea,[51] 'was the most important and the most expensive'. James Savage (1779-1852), its architect, had already acquired a reputation as a bridge-builder. Savage was to prove capable of dull Gothic in cheap churches (e.g., St Michael, Burleigh Street, Strand), but for the work at Chelsea large funds were raised (and even more spent). Savage's antiquarian and constructional interests united to present the first serious large-scale attempt to reproduce Gothic methods of construction. He gave his Perpendicular-styled church a stone-vaulted roof, above an unusually high clerestory, supported by flying buttresses. There are resemblances to Bath Abbey, in the fan-vaulting of the sanctuary bay (as Britton pointed out), and also in the high clerestory and slender flying buttresses. The church has been criticized for its disproportionate height, but it exhibits a French, rather than an English, profile. This resemblance is strengthened by its remarkable internal similarity to Notre Dame, Alençon (*c*.1480), in the tierceron vault (which Carlos accurately criticized[52] as of the wrong date, in English terms, for the rest of the church), the high and wide clerestory, the amount of bare wall between openings and vault shafts, and the remarkable triforium with its accompanying quatrefoil band (above, rather than as at Alençon, below); and possibly even the panelled gable and arch of the projecting western porch.[53] This similarity is unique for any English Gothic church of the period. The high clerestory does however have a functional reason, to compensate for lack of light on the ground floor, the aisle windows

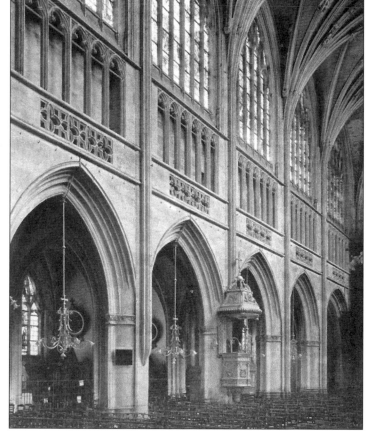

154-6 St Luke, Chelsea (James Savage, 1820-4).

Above: Carlos, versed in Gothic, disapproved of the 'fantastic order' of the western portico, Picturesque rather than archaeological. Unique in its day for its stone-vaulted roof, high clerestory and flying buttresses, St Luke resembled the choir of Bath Abbey (though that lacked its flying buttresses before 1833), but those features, like the crocketed gabling, are found also at Alençon.

Right: The exceptionally large clerestory windows, required because there were no ground-floor windows to the aisles under the gallery, the arcade, with continuous responds from base to impost, the Perpendicular vaulting over the sanctuary bay, and the great east window itself resemble Bath Abbey as Savage knew it; but Christopher Wilson points out the similarity of the clerestory and tierceron vault, as well as the triforium (absent at Bath) to that of Nôtre Dame, Alençon (below: begun *c.*1477) though Savage transposed the triforium arcade and its perforated panelling. Carlos, torn between admiration for Savage's 'boldness which designed and the talent that executed' the noble stone vault, and despair at his choice of a style for the church two centuries later than that of the vault – Perpendicular at the point when it was 'hastening to its decline' (*Gentleman's Magazine*, 1826, pt 1, p. 201) – would not have realized that Savage was adopting the proportions of a French church.

lighting only the galleries. The vaulting scheme was adversely criticized by the Crown Architects, but successfully persisted in, evidently because the parish was paying most of the cost. A projected spire to crown the 142ft tower was abandoned, however, as too expensive.

As a church-architect Savage also showed himself highly accomplished and sensitive in the Grecian idiom: in the splendid St James, Bermondsey,[54] he resolved the old problem of the steeple's riding on the portico by interposing an attic block between pediment and nave, where the clerestory conceals the roof. The tower, 'an intelligent adaptation of ... the Baroque to the rectilinear ... Grecian', is composed of six recessive stages topped by spire and dragon. The east end, a blind arch linking wings, has a Soanean character. The interior (pl. 61), too, was accomplished: square piers support the gallery fronts, from which rise Ionic columns supporting in their turn an entablature and attic, which contains the clerestory. The deeply coffered ceiling is articulated by incised beams marking the bays.[55]

In the early 1820s, then, the Classical style, usually in a Grecian Revival version, was favoured for churches in London and some of the major provincial cities, or fashionable spas like Cheltenham; but Gothic was generally accepted as the appropriate style for a country church, and was also well-established in the urban scene. Most older architects preferred to work in the more immediately traditional Classical style, but were prepared to employ Gothic in unimportant or picturesque situations. The younger generation for the most part preferred

Above: **157** St James, Bermondsey (James Savage, 1827-9). From the north-west. Widely regarded as one of the finest of the Classical churches of the 1820s. Ably designed, it was large and expensive (about £11.10s. a sitting). The massive attic provides a good base for the tower, with Wren-like upper stages. The clerestory is an exceptional feature in Classical churches of the period, one that Soane had hoped to include in Holy Trinity, St Marylebone. The Grecian-style windows, however, give no indication of the galleries within.

Gothic, though they were prepared to use Grecian in a city if required. The *Quarterly Review* article already referred to urged the merits of Gothic, created in Northern Europe, adapted to our climate: 'In a Gothic church no idea can possibly come, save that of Christianity and of the rites of Christianity. ... All things fairly considered, the Gothic style appears to be the most reasonable order for an English church. It is consecrated by its associations, and the most ordinary architect may easily learn to avoid any marked impropriety.' The church-building programme served to focus popular interest on the 'national' style, and as the younger architects came to the fore, public taste became more and more addicted to Gothic.

Stylistically, the Gothic churches may be divided into two main classes: the Plain and the Ornamented. Architects now had Rickman's *Attempt to discriminate the styles*

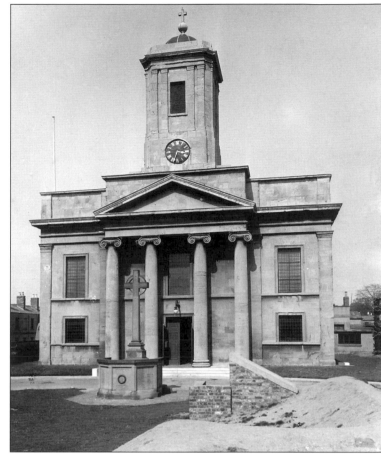

of English Architecture to guide them,[56] and the historic styles cut across these two classes. Although the Plain style usually employs Early English lancet windows, as at Taylor's Hanging Heaton and Earls Heaton (Yorkshire), Early English may also be employed, as by Thomas Taylor at Dewsbury Moor and Chantrell at Kirkstall (Yorkshire) (pl. 163) in a quite elaborated manner; while the later styles may be employed with some severity, as in several of Oates's Yorkshire churches (pls 170-1). The lack of chancels, transepts and north and south porches left little opportunity for that articulation of the several members of which Pugin was to be so notable an illuminer. The Plain lancet style lent itself to inexpensive churches; as Rickman remarked of the Early English, 'in small buildings, the windows are generally plain, with the slope of the opening considerable',[57] but for the sake of light the windows might be wider than their thirteenth-century models, and sometimes employ Y-tracery. Buttresses (often mere pilasters), if they rise above the parapet, have a simple triangular-faced cap. It is a style which gives an impression of having been designed in only two dimensions. The Ornamental style is characterized by large windows, often of three lights, with a transom which is sometimes so deep as to form a stone panel across the window – a convenient device if there were galleries. Buttresses are splayed, and crowned with crocketed pinnacles and finials. The model might be either Rickman's Decorated or his Perpendicular. This style was generally employed for the urban churches seating 1,500 or 2,000 persons. It died with the exhaustion of the Million, while the simpler and cheaper style lingered on into the 'forties, sometimes in a Norman dress.

★★★★★

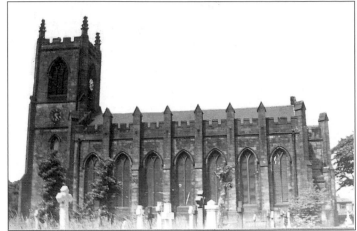

Left: **162** St Stephen, Kirkstall, Leeds (Robert Dennis Chantrell, 1828-9). Despite a greater degree of elaboration than Taylor's Early English or 'Plain' style, Chantrell some three years later was able to build for less than half Taylor's price, at £3.4s. a sitting.

Above:**163** St John, Dewsbury Moor (Thomas Taylor, 1823-7). Taylor's 'Ornamental' style here for his third Dewsbury church cost £1 a sitting more than Earls Heaton.

Below: **164** Christ Church, Liversedge (Thomas Taylor, 1812-16). Taylor's first church, built by subscription, and without galleries, was of different proportions from his churches for the Commission. This was claimed to be the first modern church to revive the open timber roof, a feature Taylor later employed at Hanging Heaton.

Another line of inquiry is whether local schools existed. Several factors militated against this: improved communications, the Commissioners' requirements, the influence of metropolitan models. Thomas Harrison (1744-1829) was the outstanding provincial architect of the day, his practice limited to the north-west, but from his innate diffidence he failed to produce any of the designs he prepared for the new churches, Oldham in particular, which he resigned in February 1823.[58] Nor did he establish any school of followers. In the 1820s Rickman was the leading ecclesiastical architect in the provinces, but his work was of uneven quality and did not in general fulfil the promise of his writings; though having bases in both Liverpool and Birmingham, his practice can hardly be regarded as a provincial school.

In Yorkshire, the church architects of the 1820s appear to form a self-contained group of a size convenient for analysis. The growth of new towns and expansion of old ones had set up a demand for public buildings answered by an invasion of architects from the South. The church-building programme attracted more. Some hurried from London by mail-coach,[59] but it was the residents (whether old or new) who proved successful. Thomas Taylor (*c.*1778-1826) had come to Yorkshire as early as 1805 from London, where he had for eight years been employed in James Wyatt's office. In 1812 Taylor was

Yorkshire doors:

Top left: **165** St Paul, Huddersfield (John Oates, 1828-30). South aisle west doorway, with crocketted hood-mould.

Top right: **166** St George, Sheffield (John Woodhead & William Hurst, 1821-5). Battlemented south porch doorway, with minimal carving.

Economical windows:

Below left: **167** St John, Farnsworth, Lancashire (Thomas Hardwick, 1824-6). Ornamental iron tracery of original pattern in plain wide lancet. The church cost £6.11s. a sitting.

Below right: **168** St John, Bollington, Cheshire (William Hayley & Thomas Brown, 1832-4). More deeply splayed, Y-tracery lancet, in a church costing under £4 a sitting.

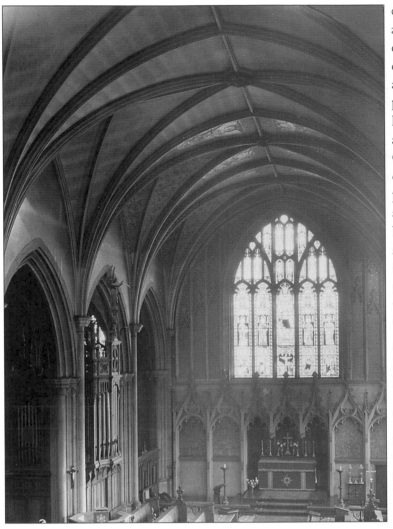

employed by the Rev. Hammond Roberson to design a church at Liversedge. He recommended Gothic as more suitable and even cheaper than Classical, commenting: 'Our ancient, and certainly original architecture was a style of which every English amateur must be proud, and consequently wish to see adopted in preference to the total want of character with which structures have of late years been erected as places of worship.'[60] The antiquarian and topographer, the Rev. T. D. Whitaker (the local Commissioner), noted its having 'every constituent part of a church of the fifteenth century', and praised Taylor, 'who, with a perfect conception of old English models, has the modesty to adhere to them, and by that means has the merit of producing beautiful copies instead of monsters.'[61] It did not have galleries, and its proportions differed accordingly from those of the Commissioners' churches. Liversedge was also praised in print in the late 1840s by Robert Dennis Chantrell[62] and by Andrew Trimen.[63] Chantrell (1793-1872) was an architect rival of Taylor's, who had come to Leeds to exploit its potential:[64] a pupil of Soane until 1814, living at Walworth (Surrey), he moved to Leeds (already in the market for new churches) in 1819, where he soon established a high reputation.

The scene was dominated, however, until his death in 1826, by Thomas Taylor, who, his work much admired by the archbishop and local clergy,[65] executed seven of the 16 'Million' Commissioners' churches in the West Riding, against Chantrell's singleton. But the settlers did not sweep all competition aside: Peter Atkinson (c.1776-1843) of York (assisted by R. H. Sharp, 1793-1853) carried on his father's practice, which had derived

Above: **169** St Mark, Woodhouse, Leeds (Peter Atkinson & Richard Hey Sharp, 1823-5). Churches in the Leeds suburbs were treated more ornamentally than those in outlying villages. Here we have a mixture of historic styles, with the east window tracery modelled on windows in York Minster.

170 John Oates of Halifax (1793-1831): picturesque composition and careful detailing. Right: St Paul, Shipley (1823-5). A fairly large church, seating 1,500, for a manufacturing township near Bradford, tending to the 'Ornamented'.
Far right: **171** St Stephen, Lindley (1828-9). This small church, for 867, in a woollen manufacturing township near Huddersfield cost proportionately less than two-thirds of that of Shipley.

Left: **172** St Mary, Quarry Hill, Leeds (Thomas Taylor, 1823-5). Plaster vaulting of nave. One of the more expensive West Riding churches of the early 1820s at nearly £9 a sitting.

Peter Atkinson of York (c.1776-1843). West towers of two neighbouring Huddersfield out-village small, cheap churches of the late 1820s, at under £4 a sitting.
Below left: **173** Holy Trinity, South Crosland (1827-9).
Below right: **174** Christ Church, Linthwaite (1827-8). The Rev. Hammond Roberson, a local church-building parson (Taylor's patron), complained in 1829 that it would be 'abhorrent' if Linthwaite were to be copied at other proposed sites because they were very prominent, and objected to Atkinson's having a hand in the designs (CBC, MB 35).

Robert Dennis Chantrell of Leeds (1793-1872). Still cheaper churches of 1829.

Above: **175** Emmanuel, Lockwood, near Huddersfield (1828-9), cost only £3.8s. a sitting.

Right: **176** St Peter, Morley, near Leeds (1829-30), cost less than £3 a sitting. The tower's pilaster buttresses are derived from the west towers of Ripon Minster, as are the ideas of the triple lancets, and of the quatrefoil in the gable.

Opposite: Robert Dennis Chantrell. Churches of the 1840s with a more archaeological character, having absorbed influences of Pugin and the Camdenians − and more expensive:

Top left: **177** (with John Boham Chantrell and Thomas Shaw) St Paul, Denholme (1843-6). View from south-west. There are similarities in tower and massing to A. W. Pugin's St Wilfrid, Old Swan, Liverpool (1840-2). Cost £5.15s. a sitting.

Top right: **178** St Paul, King Cross, Halifax (1844-6). View from south, contemporary engraving. Almost a copy of Denholme (£6.2s.).

Bottom left: **179** (with Thomas Shaw) All Saints, Robertown (1844-5). South front. Perhaps inspired by Skelton or Adel (Yorkshire) (£4.3s.).

Bottom right: **180** St Philip, Bean Ing, Leeds (1845-7). An asymmetric tower had become a fashion (£5.15s.).

from that of John Carr (1723-1807), himself a son of a mason, securing three 'Million' churches. John Woodhead (d. *c.*1835) and William Hurst (1787-1844), who obtained one, worked from Doncaster, where the firm had originally been Lindley and Woodhead, again with a Carr connexion. John Oates of an old Halifax family, won two: Shipley and Wilsden. In the later 1820s and up to Oates' death in 1831, Chantrell could claim a further five, but Oates won six, Atkinson & Sharp (or Atkinson alone) seven, and Woodhead & Hurst three more. But no clear stylistic distinction can be discerned between architects, like Taylor and Chantrell, trained in the metropolis, and those raised in Carr's Yorkshire tradition: natives or immigrants, their churches for the Commissioners − all built other churches − exhibit close similarities. Most have embattled parapets with pinnacles, handsome west towers, and some a spire, achieving a picturesque silhouette that made a significant contribution to the townscape. In plan the parallelogram is the rule. There is only one with transepts (Taylor's Earls Heaton), which the Commissioners disliked, as transeptal sittings did not face the altar. Chancels would have been a useless expense: the east wall may break into an apse which houses the altar; or there may be a vestry and robing-room; but structurally-distinct chancels are later additions. A western tower is characteristic, and was omitted only for economy's sake, when a shrunken version,

194

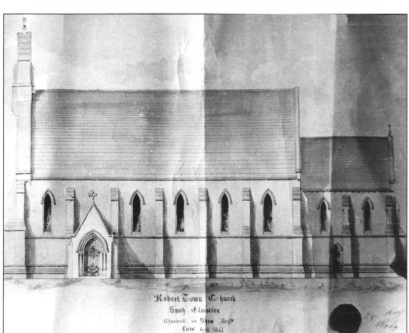

Robert Cown Church
South Elevation
Chantrell & Shaw Arch'ts
Leeds Aug 1842

the bell-turret, might be substituted. The big town churches
sometimes have a clerestory, but this feature is invariably omitted in
the village church. Roofs, low in pitch, rose behind battlements or
parapets, and internally were concealed by a plaster ceiling,
sometimes groined or ribbed in imitation of a stone vault, but
more often flat, gently curved, or a repetition of the low external

pitch. But then a similar description could be given of many of the Million churches throughout England.

A distinguishing feature that contributes a local character to the Yorkshire churches is their use of local stone, always used for the facing, whether as ashlar or merely hammered. The availablity of stone also promoted the design of sturdy west towers. And architects who had been working in the region for several years seem to have acquired a thorough knowledge of the capabilities of the local quarries. Oates was himself the son of a quarry owner.[66] Taylor's correspondence with the Commissioners goes into close and lengthy detail about the relative merits of the available quarries.[67]

These men were eager antiquaries, and the local colour in their work is derived from their imitation of the details of local churches. Atkinson & Sharp's St Peter, Stanley, has a west front, not with a tower, but with turrets, 'closely modelled on the lantern of All Saints', Pavement in York'.[68] But although details were copied, architects in the 1820s tended to compose the whole: Chantrell reported in 1828, 'I have in progress a design in the Early English style ... partly on the model as far as respects the west front, of Ripon Minster, and the east part a composition from buildings of the same date which abound in this county'.[69] He had had earlier, however, in 1821, for his Christ Church, Meadow Lane, Leeds, the first of his major ecclesistical commissions,[70] to adopt a metropolitan, rather than a local, form of roof construction to satisfy the Board's advisors.[71] Submitting drawings for New Mills (Glossop), he remarked that the style was 'collected from some specimens of the 13th century'.[72] His churches have a picturesque quality; even where there is no tower, his substitute turrets and battlements form an attractive grouping, as at Lockwood. 'His contribution to West Yorkshire architecture had been underrated. ... Both Chantrell and Oates detailed their churches from a closer observation of medieval originals than Taylor.' But Oates's later churches were, in Professor Linstrum's view, 'more conventional than Chantrell's, but little inferior in quality'.[73] Apart from Christ Church, Chantrell's Commissioners' churches were from the Half-Million grant. Mr Webster divides them into two groups, the small Lockwood and Netherthong, for 920 and 700 respectively, merely turreted, but in the character of Christ Church, dating from 1826; and the larger four, New Mills (Glossop), Holbeck, Morley, and Kirkstall, of 1827-8, designed with towers and spires , in which he sees Chantrell 'trying to capture the spirit of medieval architecture ... a total mass and contour ... made up of units as big as a whole elevation, discriminatingly taken from a specific medieval structure'. Morley's tower, he points out, shares details with the west towers of Ripon Minster, and its broach spire is similar to that of All Saints, Glossop, its east end is derived from the north transept of Rievaulx, and the sides from Kirkstall or Fountains.[74]

This taking of selected features from models was no new thing; the change that came a few years later was the production of a convincing imitation of a medieval church as a whole, something that Chantrell himself perhaps accomplished in his more expensive churches of the 1840s. In a group designed in 1842-5, including All Saints, Robertown, St Paul, Denholme; St Philip, Bean Ing, and St Paul, King Cross, he employed a geometric system that he believed medieval architects had applied to the proportions of their churches; a system that offered a 'capacity for variety within the principle'.[75]

Thus local influences merged with London training: but the result was no characteristic local school; instead, it served rather to emphasize the uniform characteristics observable among the churches of this period. There was no style peculiar to Yorkshire, merely details. Rickman, for instance, was using very similar designs in Lancashire and the Midlands. In the late 1820s the Yorkshire architects themselves overflowed into other northern counties, but their works do not stand out in such foreign areas. Architects based in London were able, thanks to improved roads, and mail-coach services travelling at eleven miles an hour to traverse the kingdom (and in the 1840s even faster by rail), with their portfolios. The chief distinctions that can be drawn, after that between Classical and Gothic, are chronological and geological: in the early 1820s a richer character was afforded architecturally; in the north and west where stone was plentiful the Million churches were faced with stone; in the south-east, on the other hand, the material usually employed was brick, stone being confined to the ornamental portions – though the more conspicuous churches in the Metropolis were usually to be faced with costly ashlar – from Bath rather than from Yorkshire.

More generally, we may conclude that the Commissioners' unwillingness either to adopt a model design or to impose a particular stylistic character on their churches fostered the *Zeitgeist*, the prevalent tendency to revive and develop the Gothic style.

182 St Paul, Bedminster (Charles Dyer, 1829–31).

Bedminster, a suburb of Bristol, was a large, poor parish, which nevertheless in the late 1820s raised a subscription of a thousand pounds, on the basis of a design by Rickman, to qualify for a substantial grant from the Half-Million. The Commission, however, looking for a one-third subscription, commissioned cheaper plans from Dyer, a native of Bristol. The parishioners then threatened to withdraw their subscription, and there was, furthermore, a prolonged dispute about a proper site for the new church, ultimately determined by the Commission.

Dyer's church, for 622 in pews and 933 in free seats, ultimately cost £8,684, or about £5.11s.8d. a sitting.

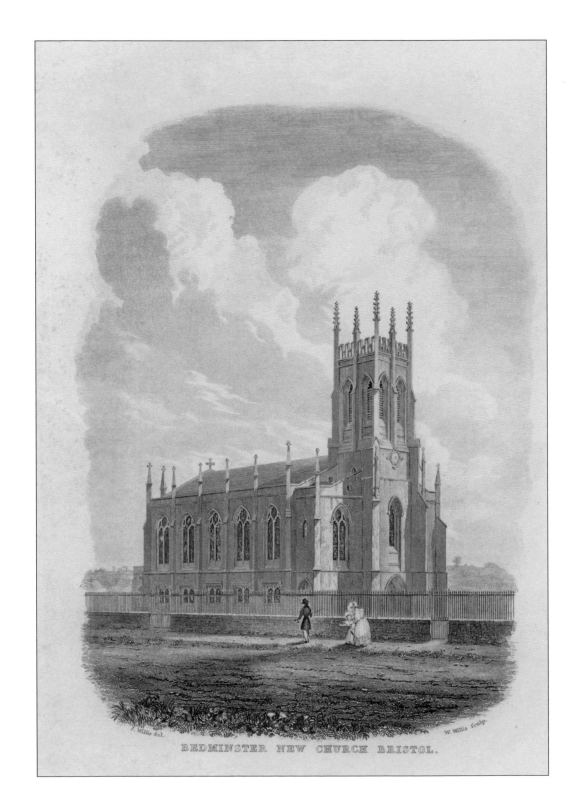

BEDMINSTER NEW CHURCH BRISTOL.

10

Sites and Cognate Powers

The Commissioners were empowered by the Church Building Acts to secure sites for the new churches; to recover the customs and excise duties paid on materials used in church-building in general (not merely Commissioners' churches); to establish scales of pew rents to pay stipends and other expenses; to determine the status of the new churches and divide parishes, subject to certain consents; and to establish select vestries. This last power was not used very extensively, disused after 1845,[1] and rescinded by the Act of 1851 (14 & 15 Vic. c.97, s.23) that abolished select vestries altogether. The problems of parish division are so complex as to require a monograph on their own, and there will be no attempt to deal with them here. The other matters, integral to the design and cost of the new churches, will now be explored.

1. SITES

One of the principal problems with which the Commissioners had to contend was the selection of sites for the new churches. A site needed to be well-situated for the population that it was intended to serve: hence it must be accessible by a considerable population of poorer inhabitants, and at the same time attractive to a sufficient number of wealthier inhabitants who could afford the pew-rents that were a vital part of the proposition, providing a stipend for the minister and, it was hoped, an accumulating fund to pay for a parsonage house. Some sites, satisfactory in many respects, were in the centre of a purely poor district, others too middle-class. Landowners might be willing to give sites, but often with a view to the profitable development of their own estates - as at Plymouth in 1827, where a developer advocated a particular site to finish a street of new houses he was building.[2] The distance from other churches, particularly the mother church, had to be considered. Cost was an important factor: prices differed widely. Naturally, it was in London that they tended to be most expensive;[3] and although some landowners donated sites, others held out for full value.[4] In a provincial town, alternative sites might vary widely in cost;[5] and in different towns and townships they tended to range between £500 and £2,000.[6]

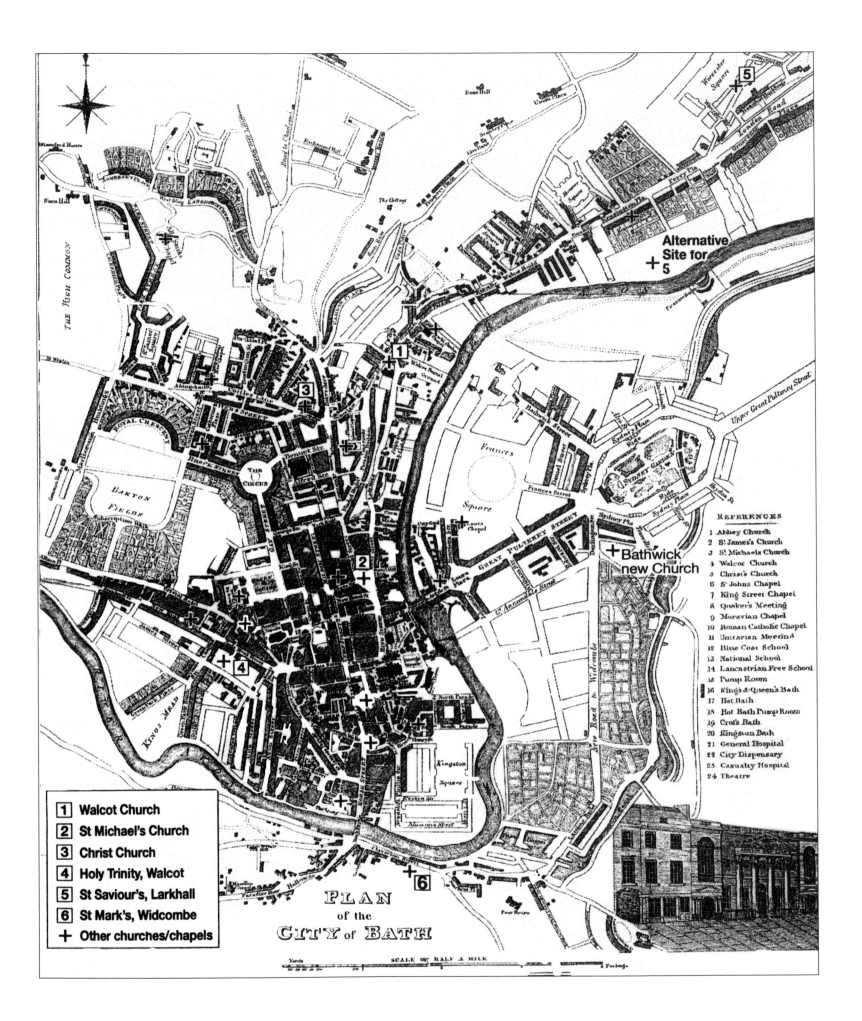

REFERENCES

1 Abbey Church
2 St James's Church
3 St Michaels Church
4 Walcot Church
5 Christ's Church
6 St Johns Chapel
7 King Street Chapel
8 Quaker's Meeting
9 Moravian Chapel
10 Roman Catholic Chapel
11 Unitarian Meeting
12 Blue Coat School
13 National School
14 Lancastrian Free School
15 Pump Room
16 King's & Queen's Bath
17 Hot Bath
18 Hot Bath Pump Room
19 Cross Bath
20 Kingston Bath
21 General Hospital
22 City Dispensary
23 Casualty Hospital
24 Theatre

Alternative Site for 5

Bathwick new Church

1 Walcot Church
2 St Michael's Church
3 Christ Church
4 Holy Trinity, Walcot
5 St Saviour's, Larkhall
6 St Mark's, Widcombe
+ Other churches/chapels

PLAN
of the
CITY of BATH

SCALE OF HALF A MILE

200

It was the responsibility of the parish to provide the site, which often caused difficulties with open vestries. Although the Commissioners possessed powers of compulsion, these involved drawn-out legal processes, including having site value assessed by a jury, often sympathetic to the owner. Under the 1818 Act, they could not require a parish to provide a site for a district parish church (as distinct from a chapel of ease) before obtaining an order-in-council dividing the original parish; nor could they call on a vestry to provide more than one site at a time.[7] To avoid difficulties, the Commissioners occasionally paid for a site out of their own funds. Up to mid-1837, the Commission paid some £46,000 for sites.[8] Once a site had been chosen, it sometimes proved unsatisfactory from geological or topographical reasons, or from popular prejudice, and another had to be selected.[9]

A closer consideration of some of the more contentious cases will illustrate the practical effect of such factors. Two districts that came persistently before the Commissioners were Bath, with nearby Bedminster, and Lewisham.

Bath: Walcot

Although enjoying many proprietary chapels, as well as several parish churches, Bath was inadequately provided with churches open to anyone. Joshua Watson's wife's uncle, Archdeacon Daubeny, had raised funds in the mid-1790s to build a free place of worship for the poor, consecrated in 1798 as Christ Church, on a site given by Lord Rivers, a large landowner, to the north of John Wood's King's Circus in Montpelier Row. Bath's largest parish was Walcot, with a population in 1811 of 20,560, and church room for 2,900. The rector, the Rev. Charles Abel Moysey, who had raised a subscription for another church to provide for the poor, applied to the Commissioners on 22 January 1819 for the necessary forms to secure a grant, which he returned promptly with a description of the proposed design, an estimate for £9,000, and an explanation of the local situation:[10]

> The situation which was most desirable is in the lower part of the Town as near as possible to Avon Street which is the sink of Bath, for it is the seat of every kind of vice. The houses therein are let by rooms, so that the population of that one street probably exceeds that of any three or even four streets in the town, and is of the very worst description. The value of land in Bath and the knowledge that we were seeking a site in that neighbourhood made it very difficult to procure one. … We have now secured the site … in Lower James Street.

That was a nearby new development, and the Commissioners promptly voted £4,000. The church, Holy Trinity, designed by John Lowder, was reported completed at the Commissioners' meeting on 26 November 1822. However, when G. H. Law, on his translation in April 1824 to the bishopric of Bath and Wells, investigated his new diocese he found that three new churches were 'much wanted': one at Bedminster (Bristol), and two 'at the extremities' of Bath; 'few can present stronger claims'.[11]

The 1821 census enumerated a population of 24,050 in Walcot, and Dr Moysey had already raised the possibility of dividing the parish into four districts.[12] He now proposed a site behind Worcester Terrace (probably that belonging to a Miss Tanner, and close to the London Road turnpike, on the north-east) that could be obtained for £500, but the Commissioners, besieged with requests for grants, felt unable to authorize the purchase.[13] On 28 February 1826, however, after a

Opposite: **183** Plan of Bath from Meyler's *Bath Guide*, 1817, with the sites of new churches added.

184 Christ Church, Bath (John Palmer, 1798). Interior, looking east. This was the first church of the church extension movement to have entirely free seating. The apse was added in 1886.

Holy Trinity, Walcot, Bath (John Lowder, 1819-22).

Right: **185** Exterior, south side. A perspective drawing supplied by the architect to the Church Building Society, 1818.

Below: **186** Interior, looking east. Lithograph from painting by J. C. Moggs. Archdeacon Moyscy drove forward the building of this church, in which nine-tenths of the seats were free. Unusually, because the north side adjoined other buildings, the galleries were double-stacked on that side. The position of the three-decker pulpit was irregular.

general consideration of how to dispense the additional half-million, the Commissioners agreed to grant two-thirds of the cost of a second new church at Walcot, provided that the parish provided a site and the remaining one-third of the cost.[14]

It was then that the situation grew complicated, with regard to both site and architect. In accordance with their usual practice, the Commissioners left it to the local committee to obtain plans, who appear to have advertised, and received several sets. Those supplied by Charles Dyer (1794-1848), an architect practising in London, but a native of Bristol, who was at this period keenly pursuing church commissions, were described by Moysey as 'very beautiful, but I should fear too expensive'. He had also failed to incorporate catacombs, important because the parish vault was full. G. P. Manners (1789-1866), a local architect, sent in two Grecian designs, which had 'the merit of cheapness but are I think [reported Moysey] essentially deficient in ecclesiastical character'. H. E. Goodridge, a young man 'constantly employed' by the rich William Beckford, late of Fonthill, provided both Gothic and Grecian designs, Moysey preferring either to the others' plans, and a local architect to a London man. The Commissioners, however, preferred Dyer's, provided the parish would meet the difference between the grant and Dyer's estimate; otherwise, they would accept Goodridge's Gothic design.[15]

John Pinch jun. (d. 1849), another local man, son of the surveyor[16] to the important Pulteney and Darlington (Bathwick) estates, then came forward with an attractive Grecian design, which Moysey favoured because they had no Grecian church in Bath, but Pinch then withdrew. Moysey believed that all would turn on the question of cost.[17] The vestry consisted of two or three hundred persons, 'many of them very tumultuous on such occasions … and there will be violent opposition and hostility'. The architects, including Pinch, were canvassing

> as for an election, and the whole lower part of the parish will be in a ferment, and the decision will be made not according to merit, but to interest.
> If the Commissioners will be kind enough to say whether they prefer the Grecian or the Gothic, that will bring the matter to an issue at once, and save much indecent behaviour and violence. This parish is I regret to say, scarcely better than a mere Democracy where the higher orders cannot be persuaded to take their part except in very few instances; but the ignorant and turbulent among the lower orders do nearly what they will. I am almost tired out with the plague which I have had for three years on account of this chapel, and nothing but my conviction of its infinite importance should induce me to persevere.[18]

The Commissioners declared that if the parish rejected Dyer's design because of expense, they preferred Goodridge's Gothic to Pinch's Grecian. And, casting another apple of discord, they suggested that as the parish would not provide an acre for a burial ground, a smaller site should be obtained in the populous area of King's Field.

The bishop then entered the fray. There was a proprietary chapel almost opposite King's Field, so a site at Dyers Field was agreed on to end faction.[19] If the parish would not contribute one-third of the cost of the new chapel, he recommended that the grant be withdrawn.[20] Far from Dyers Field ending faction, however, 'very great dissatisfaction generally [was] expressed' about it, so that a vestry was held on 15 December, which resolved in favour of King's Field as 'infinitely the best calculated for diminishing the expence of the building … and for the accommodation of the parishioners'.[21] But the bishop saw things differently from the rector. Complaining of violence, underhand dealing and unfairness shown by persons of whom he expected better things, he stated that 46 householders had voted for Dyers Field, and only 32 for King's Field, though on the basis of property owned, the latter had won. He intended making a house-to-house canvass, because in the matter of a church, the opinion of the small householders was so important. The churchwardens meanwhile explained that King's Field had been proposed originally, but because the bishop preferred Dyers Field – 'the worst in the parish' – they had recommended that site. If the church were not built on low ground, the parish would not vote the money. The bishop retorted that since he had had a letter from the churchwardens strongly recommending Dyers Field, he could not take much notice of their current views.[22]

This dispute grew sharper in the new year. The bishop persuaded Lady Rivers to give an acre in the best, higher part of Edward's Garden, in the midst of the population, where the foundation would be better than lower down, and the church would be 'an ornament to the city of Bath', removed from other churches. Dr Moysey insisted that King's Field was to be preferred because of the increasing population in the eastern district. The churchwarden stated that the bishop had been expected to declare in favour of Dyers Field, which would have satisfied all parties, but that Edward's Garden was too close to other churches, and a very unpopular choice; King's Field was, he claimed, unobtainable. Archdeacon Daubeny weighed in, declaring that Edward's Garden was too near Christ Church (the free church he had

187 St Saviour, Larkhall, Walcot, Bath (John Pinch jun., 1829-31). From the south-west. Similar to his father's St Mary, Bathwick (1814-20), inspired by Somerset Gothic.

sponsored in 1798). To resolve the dilemma the Commissioners proposed building two churches, one in Edward's Garden and the other in the eastern district.[23]

Moysey having requested the Commissioners to fix the exact sites to prevent disputes in vestry, the Board's Surveyor was instructed to investigate. He reported that Miss Tanner's ground, at the back of Beaufort Gardens and not far from King's Field, was the most eligible situation in the east, explaining that 'From the great extent of the parish and the situations of the present places of worship public and private, belonging to the Establishment it appears impossible to find a spot for a central chapel which would afford convenient accommodation to every part of this extensive district which would not interfere materially with the places of worship already erected.'[24] The Board accepted his advice. Moysey then asked if the eastern site could be considered as having been voted, or whether a vestry book must be opened for votes on the question of both churches; and whether new plans were required, or whether they would take Goodridge's 'for whom the Public Voice was decidedly given on a former occasion, though in an irregular and tumultuous way, when no question could be fairly and properly tried on account of the riot made by a party'. But circumstances having changed, new votes and new plans were the Commissioners' demand.[25]

The owner of the proprietary Kensington Chapel,[26] near King's Field, the Rev. Mr Godfrey, then offered to sell it to the Commissioners, who declined to alter their arrangements.[27] Godfrey vainly persisted, declaring that two new churches were not needed, there was church room for well over a quarter of the population, that his interest would be injured, that Goodridge was a dissenter and had accompanied the Board's Surveyor on his inspection.[28]

By September 1827, Dr Moysey had obtained plans from six architects, but still lacked sites. Prospective site donors, Miss Tanner and Lady Rivers, argued strongly in favour of those by Pinch and Manners respectively. Moysey himself dithered, stating a liking for four designs, but he feared that Dyer as a stranger would be too unpopular 'when so many Bath architects are candidates'. He dared not establish a local committee, because it would have to be named in vestry, where 'they would put in some of those wretched economists who would spoil all to save a very few pounds.' The Board now most approved of Pinch's design and one of Manners', but remitted the question to its Building Committee.[29]

Given so contentious a matter in such a prominent city, Archdeacon Cambridge, as a leading member of the Building Committee, himself made a 'minute investigation'. He found no difference of opinion respecting the eastern church, to be erected on Miss Tanner's ground:

an increased population is growing on every side of it, and the houses are chiefly of a description to ensure a sufficient income by the letting of the pews for the support of one or two respectable clergymen, for it is evident that none but superior preachers will fill the churches in Bath.
This however is not the case in respect to the other church to be placed in Edward's Garden in the neighbourhood of which the population is of so inferior a description that I can hardly discover a single house likely to furnish pew renters, except the row in which the proprietary chapel stands, whose inhabitants will naturally adhere to that chapel. ... this inferior population may be equally well provided for elsewhere.
The other objection arises from the nature of the surrounding ground, and the extreme steepness of the hill on the face of which it is proposed to place the church.

He suggested that by postponing the western church, the eastern could be enlarged to seat 1,500 persons, and a chapel provided for an isolated population of retired traders and poor on Beacon Hill and Lansdowne, to the north. The Board referred the question to Archdeacon Cambridge and the bishop.[30] The bishop's views appear to have triumphed, and on 17 June 1828 the Commissioners considered revised plans from G. P. Manners for the Edward's Garden site, reducing the cost of the tower by omitting the pinnacles in order to allow for increased scantlings of some of the timbers, and an increase in the size of the pillars, as had been required in his plans for another church (neighbouring Widcombe) by the Crown architects.[31] The tenders obtained by Pinch for the eastern church came before the Commissioners on 30 September, but progress was stopped by correspondence from the bishop, the rector, and the Rev. Mr Fenwick, new proprietor of the Kensington Chapel, considered by the Board on 11 November.

The bishop (supported by the self-interested Mr Fenwick) persisted in his view that if only one church were built, it should be in the west. The vestry refused to raise its promised third of the cost because only one church was to be built.[32] Dr Moysey attended the Board in person at its next meeting, on 25 November, and himself offered to pay one-third of the cost of the eastern chapel, but a decision was postponed. Miss Tanner then added to the confusion by reserving the water coming from her site, with the right of laying pipes there, to which the Board strongly objected.[33] With this finally arranged to the Commissioners' satisfaction, Pinch was able to begin work on the eastern church, known as St Saviour's, Larkhall, of which the foundation stone was laid on 2 April 1829.[34] It accommodated about 1,100, in almost equal proportions of pew-renters and free, at a cost of £6,386, of which the Commissioners paid the promised two-thirds.

The Walcot vestry's recalcitrance ensured that the Commissioners' second church was not built: the Board on 4 August 1829 cancelled its grant, which had been made for a specific object and on certain conditions that had not been complied with.[35] To the south-east of the city, however, in the growing parish of Lyncombe and Widcombe, on the opposite side of the Avon, the Commissioners approved a design by Manners for a church to seat some 1,200 at a cost of £5,587.

Bedminster

At nearby Bedminster, a suburb of Bristol, the parish had missed the first allocation of funds, but applied again on 5 December 1823, in the hope that further funds would become available. The curate stressed the political importance of the Church's role, referring to 'multitudes who are losing all attachment to the constitution and authorities in Church and State, and becoming an easy prey to the fanatic and the demagogue, in consequence of not enjoying the benefits of religious instruction in early youth'.[36] Bedminster, as mentioned above, was one of the three places in his new diocese, along with Bath, in which Bishop Beadon declared a new church was 'much wanted … few can present stronger claims'. But, as at Bath, it was not until 28 February 1826 that the Board resolved to pay two-thirds of the cost of a church at Bedminster, provided that the parish provided a site and the rest of the cost. Further negotiations persuaded the Commissioners to offer to pay for building a chapel to hold 1,600, if the parish subscribed £2,000, and provided the site and furnishings.[37]

Several architects then offered plans: the entrepreneurial Thomas Rickman; Charles Dyer, a friend of one of the churchwardens, keen to build a church in or near his native Bristol; and Edward Brigden (fl. 1810-35), who had worked for Smirke for 12 years, and was now engaged on two other churches in the Bath and Wells

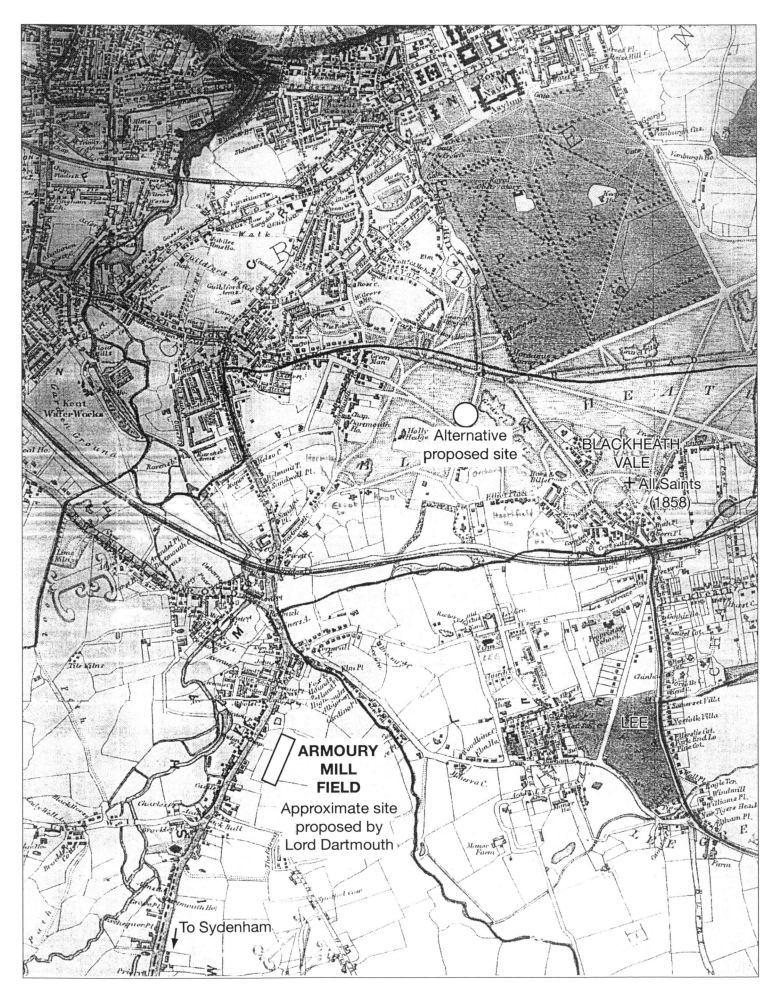

Alternative proposed site

BLACKHEATH VALE

+ All Saints (1858)

LEE

ARMOURY MILL FIELD

Approximate site proposed by Lord Dartmouth

To Sydenham

Kent Water Works

diocese.[38] The minister, however, preferred Rickman, sent his plans to the bishop, and collected subscriptions on the basis of Rickman's designs, estimated at £9,796. The Commissioners replied that the parish having stated its inability to raise the remaining third, they had themselves obtained plans (by Dyer) on an estimate of £6,503, exclusive of commission, etc. [39]

There was then an argument about the site, which led the churchwarden to request the return of the subscription of £1,002, the subscribers having demanded their money back because of the change of site. 'The situation of a churchwarden', he declared, 'in a large poor parish, where the greater part of the people are dissenters or profess no religion is not in these revelling times a very enviable situation, but when to the burthen of such an office is added that of providing for the religious instruction of the people the place becomes intolerable.'[40] Negotiations were resumed, but the minister declared that he would not take the responsibility of deciding on the site proposed at a meeting of subscribers attended by the bishop. He requested that the Board's Surveyor be sent down, and agreed to abide by his decision. The Commissioners agreed, provided that all parties would accept their Surveyor's opinion.[41] The matter was also referred to the bishop, who replied that he had visited the two sites at Easter: one was in the midst of the population, and free; the other, in fields, and to be bought. All had seemed to agree with his choice of the first, but since then there had been 'changing and jobbing', which so disgusted him that he had no current communication with the parish.[42] The churchwardens reported that there was no unanimity in the parish, but that the difficulties were now better understood, so that all would accept the site chosen by the Board.[43]

On his return from inspections in the North, Good, the Commissioners' Surveyor, duly made his visit and recommended a suitable site. The churchwardens then forwarded Rickman's plans, only to be told that the Board had long since selected those by Dyer.[44] How little the protestations of accepting the Board's decision meant was shown in June 1829, when a petition from some of the inhabitants for a change of site was read and rejected.[45] Work then began on Dyer's Perpendicular design, where by October 1830 the slater was at work on the roof. The final accounts for St Paul's church were approved at the end of 1831, the cost of building totalling £7,867, with commission and incidentals (including £140 for Dyer's travelling expenses from London) bringing the whole amount to £8,684.[46]

Lewisham

Lewisham was a parish that applied for aid only from the Half Million grant. Developments paralleled those in Bath: the Board tried to compromise with local interests, but kept its primary objectives in view. Lewisham church, rebuilt in 1777, held about 1,200, but 5,785 inhabitants living in Sydenham and Blackheath were 16–30 furlongs (2–3¾ miles) distant. The parish was taking steps to obtain two sites, and offered to raise £6,000 by loan, repayable by a rate. The Board agreed that a new church and chapel at the north and south ends of the parish were expedient, to accommodate 2,000 in all, including 1,250 free seats. It would grant £8,500, half the cost of the buildings and sites.[47] The parish lost no time in rejecting this offer, calling for a larger grant, which the Board refused, consistently with the basis of its current proposals to other parishes.[48] Further discussions led to a revised offer from the Board: if the parish would raise £8,000 and provide sites, the Board would build a church and a chapel.[49]

The point at issue was essentially one of viability. The dominant party in the vestry wanted sites with good carriage-access, convenient for the better-off, whose pew-

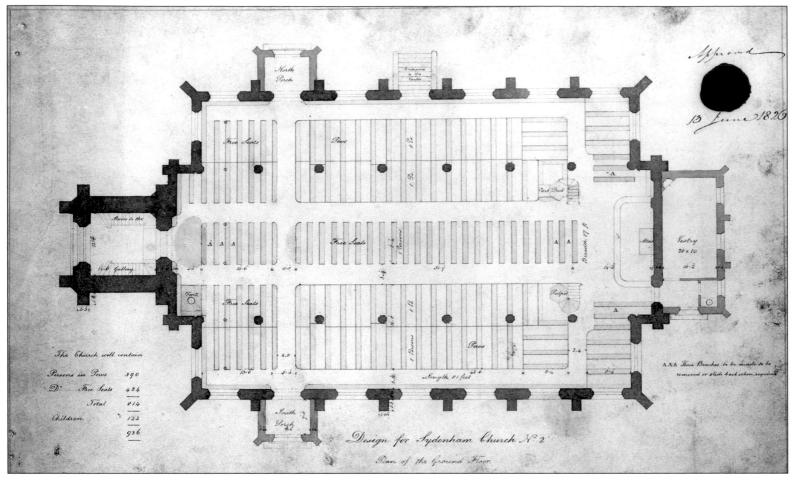

The Church will contain

Persons in Pews	390
D° Free Seats	424
Total	814
Children	122
	936

Design for Sydenham Church N° 2

Plan of the Ground Floor.

189 St Bartholomew, West Hill, Sydenham, Lewisham (Lewis Vulliamy, 1826-31). Contract drawing.

A regular Commissioners' plan, with desk and pulpit corresponding on either side and just in front of the slightly raised altar, with vestry (and w.c.) behind; free benches in middle aisle and under west gallery; font at west end. Signed by the contractor, W. Woods. The tower is used to house stairs to the galleries.

rents would ensure that a new church would not be a burden on the rates. Such a site they believed the south-west corner of Blackheath to offer the northern sector. The parish could acquire it for nothing under the Commons Act of 1818, and it was close to a district with 212 of its 339 houses rated at more than £10 p.a., and paying nearly a third of the entire parish rate assessment.[50]

The obstacle was William Legge, fourth earl of Dartmouth (1784-1853), lord of the manor, principal landowner, and patron of the parish, head of a highly clerically-oriented family.[51] The vestry's site adjoined Legge family residences. Dartmouth first offered to sell a site in his Armoury Mill Field, downhill from Blackheath, a projected housing development, recommending 'the Tuscan order of Architecture' as 'best adapted to the situation' close to modern houses. It offered, he suggested, an inducement to attend church 'for the poorer classes in those parts of the Parish which for a number of years furnished a regular supply for the house of correction and the gallows and transportation'.[52] But that was what the vestry feared: it would not attract those who could rent pews, particularly as it was exposed to 'Volumes of Smoke issuing from a neighbouring Steam Engine'.[53]

Whether from a disposition to please Lord Dartmouth, who attended the Board on several occasions, or from a fear of legal obstacles to a title to the common land (the assent of the lord of the manor was requisite), the Commissioners rejected the Blackheath site, preferring Dartmouth's Armoury Mill Field. The local committee appointed by the vestry to manage the business, led by another local landowner, John Forster, then suggested a site owned by Morden College, the lease of which Lord Dartmouth held. Negotiations over that broke down partly because of Lord Dartmouth's insistence that a road regarded as necessary by the promoters should not be built. On 22 November 1825 the Board resolved to adhere to its choice of site. The local committee with great reluctance then acquiesced in the Armoury Mill Field, marking out 170ft by 256ft. Dartmouth, only under guidance from the Board, now offered to give a site with a 90ft frontage on the Lewisham-Deptford road, and a depth of 130ft, remarking there could be no objection to eastern entrances to the building, which he had observed in several of the new London churches. The Board, though usually unenthusiastic about eastern entrances, merely expressed the hope that they would be able to make a satisfactory arrangement with the parish.[54]

Forster reported that the parish did not like the proposed northern site, that it made it difficult to raise the intended £3,000 subscription, but that they would raise £8,000 by rate. The Board agreed to meet this with a similar sum, for a church and a chapel.[55] About the South End, or Sydenham, site there was no difficulty, Forster himself offering two acres for £600. The Board then commissioned plans for both northern and southern buildings from Lewis Vulliamy. His designs for the north end, a chapel to hold 1,328 (904 free) for £9,929, and Sydenham, to the south, a church with tower, for 936 (546 free) at £10,722, both inclusive of commission and incidentals, were approved by the Building Committee on 9 May 1826, and suitable tenders obtained in October.[56]

But the vestry rejected its committee's report on 22 June, which Forster ascribed to general dissatisfaction with Armoury Mill Field. A proposal a month later to raise £1,000 for immediate expenses was negatived by a large majority. Forster then offered his Sydenham site as a gift in order to expedite matters; and Dartmouth, having quibbled about the precise area on Armoury Mill Field, – remarking that in the plan 'marked no. 3 the width of the piece of ground on either side of the Chapel appears to me to be more than sufficient and unquestionably would be so if the unnecessary projections on the sides of the edifice were omitted or reduced', – instructed his solicitor to prepare his conveyance.

When Dartmouth's comment was referred to the architect, Vulliamy replied robustly: 'In a neighbourhood not yet formed it is always more necessary to take precautions for preserving a building from the too near approach of future buildings than in one where the adjacent buildings being already erected their height, extent and destination are known.' Although there might be no current intention to erect mills, factories or workshops there, 'yet from the change in the times as regards the building of dwelling houses on speculation and from the vicinity of the stream of water, and other advantages which the situation presents', such buildings might later be erected. Furthermore, to make the chapel appropriate and worthy of its purpose, 'considerable expense will be bestowed in the decoration of all the several fronts'. So not less than the quantity of ground originally intended would do, 250ft by 170ft in front with a 30ft road at the side, 200ft in all.[57]

The Board's Surveyor recommended a frontage of only 124ft; with a road all the way round, the architect's object would be achieved. The Board so informed Lord Dartmouth, adding that their main objects were to ensure the security of the church and 'the convenience of light and access thereto ... the general effect of the Building to the eye, although a secondary consideration, being still one which neither His Lordship nor the Board can wholly overlook'.[58] Lord Dartmouth then agreed to grant 90ft by 140ft in addition to 32ft on the north, south and west for roads.[59] Meanwhile, Vulliamy had advertised for tenders, and that of Benjamin Smith had been accepted for the northern site. When in December 1826 he asked that if prices rose, he might be allowed to increase his tender, the Board directed Vulliamy to begin the works.[60]

St Bartholomew, West Hill, Sydenham, Lewisham (Lewis Vulliamy, 1826–31). Contract drawings:

Right: **190** South front, in Vulliamy's preferred Perpendicular.

Opposite: **191** East End. Section, showing the king-post roof construction and reredos with the Decalogue. Elevation, with single-storey vestry. The gable cross proved uncontroversial, though at that period it was by no means universal.

But no work was started there, in contrast to Sydenham, and the local committee complained in March 1827 that a contracted site was being taken, different from that marked out by the committee. After further discussions, the Board minuted on 1 May 1827 that after the decision to build in Armoury Mill Field, the Surveyor had met the parish's architect (presumably Vulliamy) to fix the exact site (approved by Lord Dartmouth); they conceived that there was now no objection to an immediate start, regretted unpleasant feelings had been raised in the parish, and hoped that all difficulty was now removed.[61] Alas for the vanity of human wishes: the Lewisham vestry passed a resolution against the current Armoury Field site, to the Board's surprise and regret.

The vestry's attitude seemed to threaten the entire Lewisham scheme. The Board reverted to what had been agreed earlier, but the vestry hardened its opposition to any site in Armoury Mill Field. After meeting local committee members on 17 July, the Board called on the vestry to honour their original undertaking; meanwhile work at Sydenham was to be suspended. The vestry retorted that their preferred Gravel Pit site on Blackheath was both convenient for the inhabitants of the lower district and had residents 'able and willing to rent pews and sittings within the new Chapel and thereby provide a suitable stipend for the Minister and the several expences of such Church or Chapel'.[62] They considered that they had found a suitable site and the Board should go ahead with it.

The Commissioners in a spirit of compromise agreed to consider any site the parish might point out.[63] To the local committee's enquiry whether the Blackheath site would be acceptable if it could be obtained without compulsion, the Board replied that they could not promise in advance of an offer 'in a legal manner', but saw no decided objection to any of the sites indicated on the committee's map.[64] But the Gravel Pit site was stymied by Dartmouth's refusing assent to an application under the 1818 Commons Act.[65] Forster, for the local committee, explained why the parish would not vote a rate for one chapel only.

Section shewing the East End.

Approved

13 June 1826

Reluctant to see its work at Sydenham wasted, the Board then asked what voluntary subscription might do. The good spirit of 1825, however, had 'subsided, in consequence of the subsequent delays, and the untoward discussions respecting the intended [northern] Chapel'. A licensed but unconsecrated chapel at Sydenham[66] (built by John Forster) was being enlarged, affording the locality enough accommodation – but some local committee members would subscribe £50 each.[67]

Forster having withdrawn his offer to give the Sydenham site, the Board negotiated to buy part of it for a total of £331.[68] Arrangements were then made to cut costs: Vulliamy was told to revise his plans, the contractor was persuaded to relinquish his contract, and the Board approved the new designs in general character.[69] Thomas Smith undertook a lump-sum contract to finish the church on the old foundations but in a less expensive manner, for £4,194, though the simplicity of the design was subsequently alleviated by a subscription of £50 raised to pay for battlements on the north side.[70]

The books had to be closed, too, for the unstarted northern site: the contractor, Benjamin Smith, claimed not only for wharfage and cranage, and men's time in loading and unloading 135 tons of stone, but also for having had to sell 1,900 consols at $80^{1}/_{2}$ on 1 February 1827, thus sustaining a loss in consequence of a seven per cent advance in the funds.[71] But the person who really suffered (apart from the unredeemed criminous classes of Lewisham) was the architect, whose claim for commission was disputed by the Board, and did not receive anything until 1856.[72]

London

In London, the cost of sites was a serious consideration. A site in Mecklenburgh Square, St Pancras, was valued at between £6,850 and £7,450, subject to a depreciation of one-third if the plan of the square were changed.[73] In Brunswick Street, Shoreditch, the land developer William Rhodes was willing to sell an acre and a half for £900; while in neighbouring if more salubrious Hoxton, the Haberdashers' Company wanted £2,400 for a suitable site; and a jury empanelled to fix the compensation for compulsory purchase of a two-acre site at Poplar awarded £3,620 to the owners.[74]

St Leonard, Shoreditch (1811 population, 43,488), and St Matthew, Bethnal Green (33,000), were identified at the outset as two of the London parishes in the worst state of spiritual destitution. Both were governed at this time by open vestries, that at Bethnal Green controlled by a local 'boss', Joseph Merceron.[75] The Bishop of London, Howley, reported his apprehension 'that in the places where the wants are the greatest very little can be done to meet the Parliamentary Grant by voluntary contribution, and still less by rates. … In the parish of St Matthew Bethnal Green where the number of houses exceeds 7,000, forty-two only are assessed at a rent of more than £50 per annum and upwards of 5000 under £10.' He pointed out the burden of the ordinary rates on householders 'whose means of subsistence are hardly more abundant than those of the paupers whom they are taxed to support', and the difficulties of collecting them; there was little hope of obtaining the vote of a rate for building new churches. He requested the Commissioners immediately to build churches in five East London parishes, and they responded by resolving that Bethnal Green, Shoreditch, and St George-in-the-East were fit parishes for erecting a church entirely from their funds, save for the provision of a site.[76] Accordingly, notice was given to the churchwardens that the Commissioners intended to build two new churches in Shoreditch, at New Hoxton and Haggerston, and required one and a half acres for each; and in Bethnal Green churches in the north-west of the parish, and east of the parish church, requiring one acre for each.[77]

Called upon to provide two sites, the Shoreditch vestry resolved that they could not comply with the Commissioners' request because of their incapacity to support any new rate. The Bethnal Green vestry similarly refused to comply, 'having at all times a great proportion of Poor to maintain, added to the difficulties resulting from the increasing stagnation of trade', though the churchwarden suggested that a compromise might be possible if the Commission abandoned the idea of providing churchyards as well as the new churches.[78] Action to enforce provision was deferred because of legal doubts, confirmed by the opinion of the law officers of the Crown that notice could not be given to a parish to provide sites for more than one church or chapel at the same time.[79] The prospect of even a single new church was too much for the Shoreditch vestry, which on 24 May 1820 appointed a committee to represent the parish's inability to meet the expenses which must accrue were a new church to be built, 'and to adopt such measures as [they] may think proper for the preventing of, or procrastinating the building of any new church or chapel'. In face of such resolute intransigence the Commissioners decided to invoke one of their new powers under the 1819 Church Building Act, and themselves defray the cost of a site or sites in Shoreditch.[80] They secured two sites, in Haggerston and Hoxton, not yet laid out for building, at the moderate expense of £750 and £1,050 respectively.[81]

It was not until April 1822 that the Commissioners made significant progress in Bethnal Green, when they agreed a compromise with the curators of the poor, to buy a site south of the green, rather than on the green itself. The vicar, supported by a memorial from parishioners, then claimed that the majority of the curators were dissenters, led by Merceron, who wished to push the new church to an obscure corner. A site on the green would be at a greater distance from the lunatic asylum 'where much vociferations would greatly disturb Divine Service'. Further correspondence made it clear that it was impossible, as the senior curator of the poor remarked, to suit all, and the Commissioners invited the Crown architect John Soane to design a church 'suited to the situation and within the limits of the grant proposed to be made'.[82]

Similar problems hindered, even blocked, the Commissioners' endeavours in several of the most densely-inhabited urban parishes, and particularly in London. The parish of St Luke, Old Street (population, 36,000), one of the Queen Anne churches, was an early beneficiary, St Barnabas, King Square (pl. 18), having been completed early in 1824 at a cost of about £14,100. The parish then proved signally resistant to the proposal to build a second church. After much negotiation, a built-up site in Golden Lane, a 'low district', with confined entrances, approved by the Dean of St Paul's as the Ordinary, was purchased at a cost of £3,000. The prospect of obtaining a 'more eligible' site caused the Board to decide to sell the Golden Lane site, but that hope fading, the Dean advised that it was 'inexpedient, from the great hostility evinced by the Parish, to build a Chapel on the present Site', which, now cleared of buildings, had to be sold, after a jury valuation, for a mere £1,050.[83] Thereafter, Old Street vanished from the Commissioners' map.

Nor was it only in London that sites could be extraordinarily expensive. In the developing industrial and commercial cities demand for good sites was keen. Searching for a site for the second new church for St Philip's parish, Birmingham, the Rev. J. H. Spry reported: 'I have reason to believe, that the terms on which the [three] Proprietors are willing to sell are not exorbitant, and I really despair of being able to accomplish a purchase for less Money. ... We have not been able to find any person willing to sell at all, until the negotiation was entered into for the site in question.' The price? £5,700. The Commissioners agreed to pay it.[84]

Given the difficulties with recalcitrant parishes, and the risks of popular disturbances, as well as costly and prolonged legal proceedings if the Commissioners used their powers to compel parishes to pay, and the probable inefficacy of the only penalties available to them through the spiritual courts, the Board paid the entire costs, including the site, of fourteen churches, of which six were in London, three in Manchester and two in Birmingham, at an average cost of £2,116. The six London sites cost an average of £2,821, the most expensive of all being St Peter, Saffron Hill (1830-2), in St Andrew, Holborn parish, at £6,695.[85]

2. DRAWBACKS

Duties of Customs and Excise on building materials contributed significantly to building costs in the early nineteenth century. Excise duties were charged on bricks and glass. Bricks measuring $8^1/2$ins x 4ins x $2^1/2$ins paid 5s.10d. a thousand, while those measuring 10ins x 5ins x 3ins or larger paid 10s. The duty of 4s.10d. on plain tiles was repealed in 1833, but the brick duty was not abolished until May 1850, though from 1839 it was calculated on volume rather than linear measurements. That on glass was reduced from 6d. to 2d. per *lb* in 1835 and abolished ten years later. Customs duties on sea-borne stone brought into the Port of London[86] were generally repealed in July 1823 (though Caen stone had to wait till March 1845), followed by those on slates, charged according to size and quality, in 1831; but those on wood imports endured. Fixed at 55s. per load of 50 cu. ft on Northern European timber (large trees squared) in 1820, in 1842 it was reduced to 25s., though deals (planks more than seven inches wide) and battens (less than seven inches) paid 32s. Further reductions came in 1847, 1848 and 1851, bringing the duties down to 7s. 6d. on timber and 10s. on deals.[87] Canadian timber paid a smaller duty.

Section 21 of the second Church Building Act, 59 Geo.III, c.134, created a means for useful additional funding for church-building in general, not only those built under the Commissioners. It was to have a role in prolonging the life of the Commission, through which the duties on building materials could be reclaimed, and either – where the Commissioners had made no grant – repaid to the parish, or used to purchase Exchequer bonds for augmenting the Commission's own resources. A Treasury letter[88] prescribed the procedure to be followed:

> It appears to … be very desirable that all contracts or agreements entered into by the Commissioners should be upon the Terms of the Timber, Bricks and other Materials having paid the Duty – that whenever the Building shall be completed, the Commissioners shall transmit to this Board [the Treasury] separate Certificates sworn to by the Builders containing the particulars of the quantities of Customable and Exciseable Articles used in such Building, and for which a drawback is claimed by the Commissioners which Certificates are to be Certified as correct by the Surveyors employed in superintending the same and approved by the Commissioners when their Lordships [the Commissioners of the Treasury] in those cases where they shall have no reason to doubt the accuracy of the Claim will in each case grant their Warrants to the Commissioners of Customs and to the Commissioners of Excise respectively directing the repayment to the Commissioners for building Churches of the amount of the Drawback of the Duties on the Articles comprised in such Certificates.

Someone, however, realised very quickly that the Act was unclear whether duties were to be allowed on the rebuilding or enlarging of churches as well as upon the building of new churches,[89] and this was provided for in a second clarificatory Act,

214

not in fact obtained until 1822, when it was specified that the work had to provide an increase in accommodation. Accordingly, an application from Littlehampton in May 1821 for the drawback of duties had to be postponed.[90] In February 1824 the lord provost of Edinburgh applied to the Treasury for drawbacks on a new church erecting in Bellvue Crescent (St Mary, by Thomas Brown, 1823-6): his application was referred to the Church Building Commissioners, who did 'not feel themselves competent to give an opinion whether Churches and Chapels built in Scotland come within the meaning of the Act', but should the Treasury think they did, the Commissioners would not withhold their certificate. The Treasury did think so, and authorized the granting of the requisite certificates.[91] An application from a church in Ireland, however, that had slipped through as far as the Excise Board in 1837, caused the Treasury to seek the opinion of the Law Officers of the Crown, which was adverse to Irish claims.[92] Likewise an attempt in 1838 by the minister of the Scotch church in Manchester to recover the duties paid on Church of Scotland churches built in Lancashire proved fruitless.[93]

The amounts of drawback in the early years were significant. The very expensive, non-Commissioners' new parish church of St Pancras, London, recovered £3,654; the rebuilt parish church at Walsall (Staffordshire), £831; and the Commissioners' churches of St George, Birmingham, and St George, Barnsley (pls 116-17), £657 and £241 respectively. The excise (bricks and glass) on Soane's Walworth church was £307, the customs duty on timber alone for his Holy Trinity, St Marylebone (pls 34, 39), £596. Even in the 1830s, when duties had been reduced, the amounts were a valuable aid, a new chapel at Stockton-on-Tees obtaining £401, and the rebuilt chapel at Brentwood, Essex, £203.[94] By April, 1838, when a return was made to the House of Commons, repayments had been received for 596 churches or chapels, including those of the established (non-episcopal) church in Scotland.[95] At this period the individual amounts tended to be much smaller than at first, partly because of reductions or abolition of duties, partly because many of the claims were for quite inexpensive repairs. The Commissioners began to have scruples about the work entailed on the Revenue departments for very small returns, and after consultation with the Treasury in 1840 fixed on works to the value of £400 as the minimum below which drawback could not be claimed.[96] At the same time, because of the great increase in church building and repair, the total drawbacks remained considerable: in 1840, 1841 and 1842, sums of £16,615, £23,521 and £26,484 respectively were reclaimed.[97]

Printed forms were issued by the Commission, specifying the detail to be supplied:[98]

State the Articles and quantity used, the number of pieces of Timber, content in cubical feet, whether Fir, Oak, or any other sort, and of eight inches square and upwards when imported, the number of Deals and Battens, weight of Mahogany with their length, breadth, and thickness; the Value of Laths (imported) upon which the duty was paid, but if made in this Country from Lathwood imported, the number of fathoms, and the length of the pieces must be stated.

Some of the early applications are recorded in detail in the Minute Books: thus the material that had paid £1,028 in duties for building G. S. Repton's chapel of St Philip, Regent Street, consisted of:[99]

849,00 bricks
149 loads of Memel and Riga timber
1300 of 3in. Christiana and other deals, average 14ft lengths

600 of 2^{1}/2in. do. do. do.
418ft cube Portland stone
319ft cube Aberdeen granite
2877ft supl. Yorkshire stone paving
49 do. 3ins thick
1284 Yorkshire stone landings 4ins thick
76 do. 5ins thick
16 tons of slates
1442ft supl. Crown Glass.

We also have details of two churches by Smirke: at Wyndham Place, 1,295,000 bricks were used, 1,700 cu. ft of Portland stone, 3,900 sq. ft of York paving of various thicknesses, 198 loads of Memel and Danzig timber, 2,600 loads of 12ft 3ins Christiana deals, 6 fathoms of lath wood, and 1,950 sq. ft of glass. Similarly St Anne, Wandsworth, absorbed 1,035,000 bricks, 750 cu. ft of Portland stone, 3,850 sq. ft of York paving, 127 loads of Baltic timber, 2,000 loads of deals, 5^{1}/2 fathoms of laths, and 1,400 sq. ft of glass.[100] Excise on bricks at Wyndham Place amounted to £377.14s.4d., on glass, £39.19s.3d., customs duty on timber, £1,064, and on slates, £62.2s.3d. The equivalent sums for Wandsworth were £301.12s.6d., £28.4s.3d., £752.12s.6d. and £47.9s.[101]

The amounts repaid on Heworth chapel in 1823 were £277.2s.6d. for timber, £27.13s.5d. for glass, and £14.15s.1^{1}/2d. for slates, on a total cost of £2,176.[102] Barry's two churches stone-built near Manchester, at Stand (Prestwich) and Camp Field, recovered £152.19s.1d. and £299.15s.2d. respectively on the excise on bricks and glass, and each £499.15s.7d. customs on stone, slates and timber; while Bedford's brick-walled Norwood church benefited more from the excise with amounts of £406.16s.2d. and £271.19s.[103]

The Commissioners were surprised to find in July 1824 that David Laing, surveyor to the Board of Customs, was charging commission on duties remitted on St George, Birmingham, never having previously been called upon for such payments. Laing replied that having in 1821 been consulted by them on 'the mode of ascertaining and preparing lists of materials' used in church building, he had acted in his private capacity as a surveyor. He had also had directions from the local trustees in Chelsea, St Pancras and elsewhere to survey the said churches at different periods and to ascertain the quantities and qualities of the materials and to assist in the computation of Duties and in the formation of schedules during which I have had many interviews with the respective Architects and Builders ... I have made a charge of 2 ¹/2 per cent where the amount of duties remitted have been small and which I do not consider more than equivalent for the trouble and contingent expences.[104]

Where the Commissioners had made only a grant towards a new church, they shared the drawbacks with the parish in the proportions that each had contributed to the cost.[105] Applications from contractors had to be accompanied by a declaration from the parochial authorities that when the contracts were made, it had been expressly stipulated that the contractors, having made an equivalent deduction from the amount of the contracts, were to have the benefit of the drawbacks. The Bishop of Exeter refused in 1828 to endorse an application for drawbacks for improving Okehampton parish church on the ground that they would only benefit the builder, who had already been paid in full.[106] A similar application about Cluny church, Perthshire, in 1841, drew a query from the Board of Customs whether this did not infringe the conditions of the Treasury letter of 1820. The Church Commissioners pointed out that the Act of 1822 had extended the drawback provisions to churches 'built or enlarged with the approbation of the Board', but conceded that contractors' applications might 'have a tendency to encourage fraud', so that they would not in future certify such cases; but it was clearly impractible for the Commission to superintend the building or enlargement of all the churches in England and Scotland in respect to which applications might legally be made for drawbacks.[107]

One prospective church builder enquired in 1841 whether

it may be anticipated that the drawback would be allowed on blocks of lava made of refuse cinder from the furnaces [of the Old Oak Iron Works, Staffordshire] in the same manner as upon bricks used in building churches? And whether it would be so allowed in case the blocks thus employed should be of larger dimensions than the bricks which are commonly used for such purposes?

The Rt Hon. W. E. Gladstone was informed that as the coals had paid no tax, it was apprehended that no drawback might be claimed.[108]

However, a problem occurred when the tradesmen for Bedford's Camberwell church refused to swear affidavits as to quantities of materials used.[109] An inability to obtain sworn affidavits from the various contractors occurred in several other instances, so in 1828 a list of all such cases was referred to the Treasury with a request that the architects' affidavits might suffice, coupled with an assurance that procedures had been tightened to obviate such occurrences. The Treasury was merciful.[110]

The drawback accounts were to occasion great alarm to the Commission in 1834. When the Secretary, George Jenner fell fatally ill in 1829, the Treasury had at the Commissioners' request authorized the Customs and Excise Boards to accept receipts signed by the chief clerk, Richardson (he whose relationship with Goodwin had been attacked by Busby in 1822).[111] He did not inform George Jelf, the new Secretary, of this power. Jelf's laborious duties included acting as the Commission's treasurer, but the drawback accounts he left to Richardson, who had made them very much his own province, keeping the books in his own closet, 'with a view of mystifying them'. Jelf had 'never interfered in the previous matters of obtaining affidavits &c &c', and Richardson 'did not enter up from the letter Book his correspondence for affidavits &c which', Jelf recorded, 'was by my desire begun upon

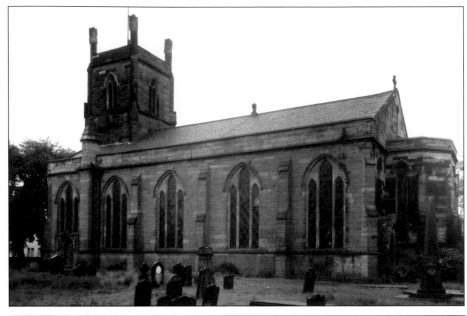

St Paul, Warrington (Edward Blore, 1829-30). Blore was an exquisite antiquarian draughtsman and became a leading exponent of the Old English style of country house, but his churches were mediocre.

Top: **193** Exterior in 1976. The triple lancets give no indication of the gallery within.

Lower: **194** Interior, looking east, in 1976. The chancel is made distinct, albeit very shallow; but there is no attempt to suggest a nave and aisles, merely an auditorium. The chancel screen and pulpit are of course later.

Opposite: **195** Pattern Pew Plan. The Commissioners published a lithographic seating plan, on which proposed rents for pews were to be indicated. It shows clearly their preferred arrangement.

by Mr Waples and Mr Beachcroft not long after the latter came to the Office together with the accounts appearing to be received which upon the face of them betrayed no fraud.'[112] But Richardson was a prudent fraudster.

When Jelf was absent from the Office on holiday or official duty elsewhere in the years 1832-4, Richardson had signed receipts for drawbacks received from the Customs, but had not paid the whole amount into the Commissioners' account with Drummonds Bank. The drawbacks on Goodwin's Bordesley and Kidderminster churches (£536.5s. and £683.19s. respectively) and that on Atkinson's Scarborough church (£290.6s.1d.) he had retained. How the fraud came to light we do not know, but presumably as a result of Richardson's disappearance in September 1834. Jelf then asked the Board of Customs for a full account of their drawback payments. Richardson was thought to be in Calais, refusing to supply any account unless the Commissioners promised him immunity. At this period of the year it was impossible to raise a Board: the Rev. John Lonsdale was the only member then in London. Jelf wrote a hasty account of his discoveries to Watson, and the matter appears to have been hushed up.[113] There is no relevant entry in the Minute Books, and *Jupiter* was silent.

The total sums recovered from duties made a significant contribution to the Commission's finances. In mid-1837, with 219 churches completed, the drawbacks on their building materials amounted to nearly £90,000, excluding drawbacks for churches not built by the Commission; and the interest and profit on Exchequer bills (the means by which the Treasury paid the drawbacks to the Commission) provided another £11,000, so adding just over £100,000 to the Commission's coffers – enough to build another 18 churches similar to St Paul, Warrington, which held 1,200.[114] By the end of 1856, when the Church Building Commission was superseded, 2,520 applications from churches for drawbacks on materials used in building, re-building and enlargement had been certified. The total amount of drawbacks is uncertain, but already by 1843 some £277,000 had been reclaimed (enough to build at least fifty respectable churches), on about half the eventual number of applications.[115] By February 1853 the Commission had received in drawbacks from its own church-building and interest and profits on related Exchequer bills a total of £146,076.[116]

3. PEW RENTS

Pew rents have been called 'the sheet-anchor of the Church Building Acts'.[117] Without pew rents there would have been no means of financing clergy to minister in the new churches. Pew rents also attracted the 'middling sort' as well as the upper

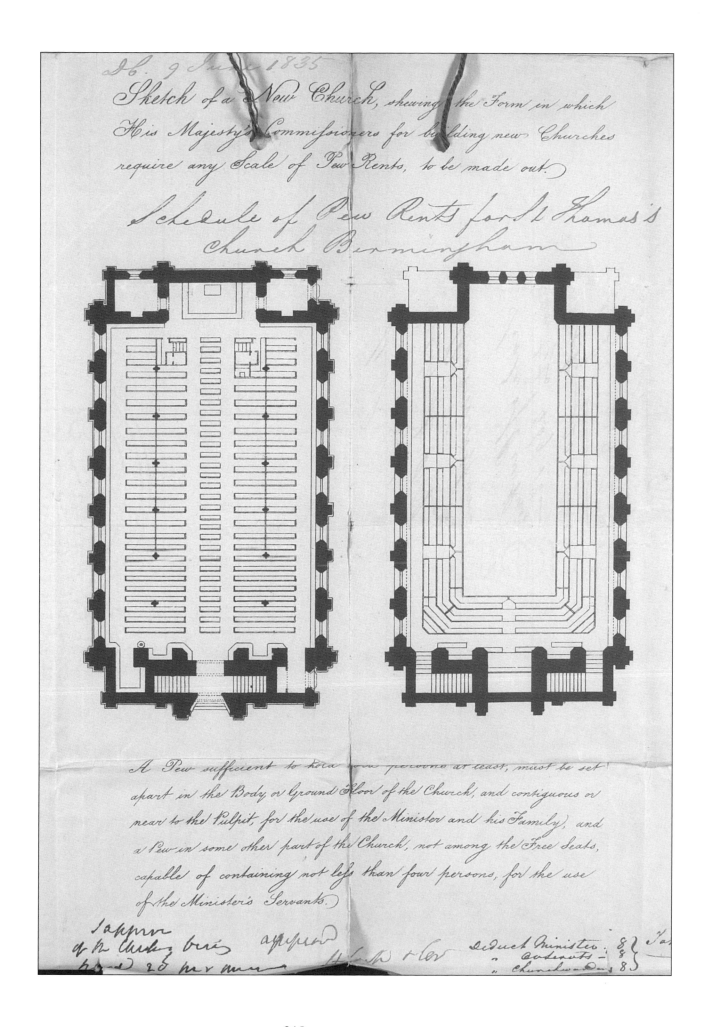

No. 9 June 1835

Sketch of a New Church, shewing the Form in which
His Majesty's Commissioners for building new Churches
require any Scale of Pew Rents, to be made out.

Schedule of Pew Rents for St Thomas's
Church Birmingham

A Pew sufficient to hold four persons at least, must be set
apart in the Body or Ground Floor of the Church, and contiguous or
near to the Pulpit, for the use of the Minister and his Family, and
a Pew in some other part of the Church, not among the Free Seats,
capable of containing not less than four persons, for the use
of the Minister's Servants.

I approve
of the Architecture being   approved
fixed at 20 per annum   Deduct Minister . 8
                                                      " Servants . 8
                                                      " Churchwardens 8

219

orders. The renting of pews was an old-established custom in many places, though of doubtful legality.[118] Often it not only provided a fund for the minister's stipend but also for other church expenses. Particularly in the cities, as noted above, it had become general, and was also the rule in Anglican proprietary chapels and Dissenting meeting-houses alike. Under the 1818 Act, the Commissioners were empowered to establish a scale of pew rents to provide salaries for the minister and the clerk of a new church. The Commissioners' aim being to bring all classes into the church, St Mary's parish, Nottingham, was told that it was 'inexpedient' for the Commission 'to grant aid towards the building of a church in which all the seats are proposed to be allotted to the use of the poor to the exclusion of the other classes: it being further the opinion of the Board that the joint attendance of the different classes of society in the same place of Divine Worship is specially desirable.'[119] A pew to hold six persons at least 'must be set apart in the Body ... of the Church, and contiguous or near to the Pulpit, for the use of the Minister and his Family, and a Pew in some other part of the Church, not among the Free Seats, capable of containing not less than four persons, for the use of the Minister's servants'.[120] At least one-fifth of the seats must be free (allowing 18 inches a sitting), but a decent proportion of sittings (at 20 inches) must be reserved for the paying classes.

For pew rents were a necessary means of attracting the middle classes, as well as of providing a stipend for the minister. As early as December 1818 resolutions by a meeting of inhabitants of Camberwell parish in favour of building a new church, in which the pews should be rented at no more than £1 per sitting, came before the Board.[121] The Commissioners' practice, however, was to require the local committee to submit a scale of pew rents when a church was consecrated, and to obtain the diocesan's approval before sealing the schedule. Smirke's church at Chatham was one of the first: a rate of 10s. per annum a sitting, with a charge of £2 for a five-person pew was proposed at the outset, but the total income of £200 was thought insufficient to maintain a minister, so a revised scale rated front seats at 15s. and others at 12s., to produce £336, which the bishop thought to be only what was sufficient.[122] Some pew-holders, however, were forced to resign their sittings (to the diminution of the minister's stipend) because of the draught, so that inner doors were demanded.[123] At St George, Bristol, the dean asked Smirke for more pews, but the Board did 'not deem it expedient to permit any alteration', an attitude they consistently maintained, in view of the figures for pews and free seats having been reported to parliament in their annual reports.[124]

Generally, the pew rents were sufficient only to provide a salary for the minister, with a sum, usually £10, for the clerk, in poor parishes £5. In wealthy parishes the clerk might be allotted £40, including any fees received, and any further surplus was directed to form a fund for the purchase of a parsonage house. Such were the provisions respecting Charles Barry's three large Islington churches (pls 146, 148), where St John, Upper Holloway, and St Paul, Balls Pond, with pew rents potentially over £500 allowed the minister £400, and Holy Trinity, rented at £585, promised a £500 stipend. But in the early 1840s, the last had a balance of only £46, and St Paul only £22; that at St John's had not reached £5 after 20 years. These small sums were accordingly awarded to the respective incumbents.[125] There were 14 parishes in 1837 where the pew rents were reckoned at more than £600 yearly, of which 11 were in London or its inner suburbs; at Wyndham Place, Langham Place, and Pimlico (pl. 62) the proceeds expected were over £1,000, with 528, 1,430, and 1,016 pew sittings respectively. Criticism that the Commissioners had been over-generous to wealthy parishes[126] received support from such statistics, particularly as there were at Langham

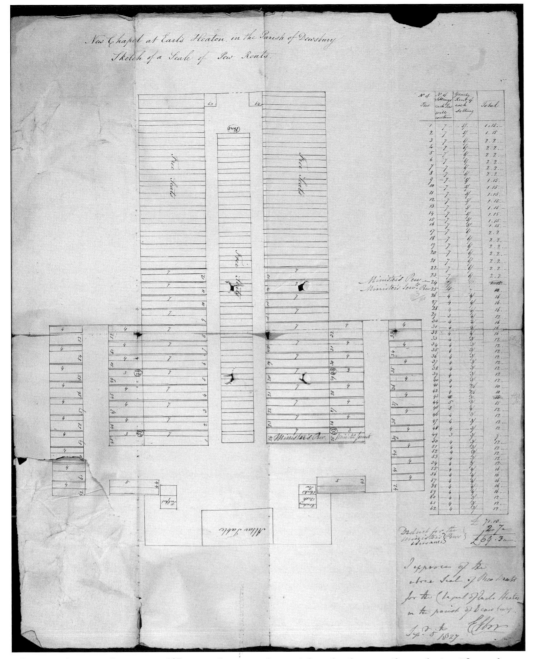

196 St Peter, Earls Heaton, Dewsbury (Thomas Taylor, 1825-7). Pew rental plan and schedule, 1827. Unusual in having transepts, though all seats faced east, as the Commissioners required. The accommodation provided a potential income of £69.3s., approved by the Archbishop of York.

Place only 322 free seats.[127] But then such parishes had contributed significantly to the cost of building their churches.

By the 1845 Act (8 & 9 Vic. c.70) the Commissioners' powers to fix pew rent scales were extended to consolidated chapelries to which they had made a grant; and by that of 1848 (11 & 12 Vic. c.71) they were empowered to establish moderate charges for some free seats, and alter pew rent scales (s.1), and to establish scales for churches built since 1800 (s.4). In 1851 the Act 14 &15 Vic. c.97 enabled them to extinguish pew rents where a satisfactory endowment was provided, an indication of the growing strength of the anti-pew movement.[128]

Several scales were discussed by the Board on 8 October 1822, when the vicar of Nottingham reported hostility in the parish, and declared that 12s. per sitting was the highest rate feasible; he had previously reported that he had had only two applications for pews, and two for single sittings: the minister was allotted £200. At St Paul, Southsea, Portsea, where pews and free sittings were nearly equal in number, all the gallery seats being free, a scale was proposed for 76 sittings at 6s., 192 at 8s., 176 at

10s. and 342 at 12s. per annum, to bring £394 (£15 for the clerk). Walcot, Bath, presented a different picture: although generally poor, with 1,800 free sittings out of 2,000, there were also wealthy inhabitants, and a top rate of 25s. was proposed for front-row lower gallery seats, down to 15s. in the third and fourth rows; the upper west gallery provided sittings at between 5s. and 10s., the total £275.[129] A parliamentary return in 1824 of the 13 churches in which scales and stipends had been fixed shows a range of stipends from a miserable £17.16s. (Kingswood, Bitton, Gloucestershire) and the little-better £32.10s. at Buckley (Hawarden, Flintshire) to £379 at Southsea; while for Barnsley, where the proposed schedule had ranged from 4s. to 7s., to produce £164, the stipend was stated at only £89.4s.[130]

Other West Riding churches' scales indicate a similar absence of wealthy inhabitants: the three churches built by Thomas Taylor in Dewsbury parish , with between 348 and 380 rentable sittings, would only produce between £64 and £74 annually for the minister's stipend, less an allowance of £10-£15 for the clerk.[131] Similarly among the least productive of the new churches were those in neighbouring Huddersfield and Almondbury parishes: six of the West Riding churches in 1837 were among the 18 in the whole country with rents calculated at less than £70. Allowing the clerk his portion, the ministers were probably little if at all better off than the nine, nation-wide, whose pew-rents were calculated to produce less than the £50 p.a. which was the minimum endowment (secured in land or the funds) that the Commissioners required from would-be patrons.[132] Across the Pennines, another five were under £70; and St Peter, Preston (pl. 119), Mellor and Lower Darwen only slightly higher, though the larger church at Over Darwen (pls 121-2), with 544 rentable sittings was calculated to produce £150.[133] Bishop Blomfield indeed thought the St Peter's scale 'considerably too low'; and the incumbent reported that though there was 'a fair attendance of the poor' not all the free sittings were occupied, and it was desirable to let some of the 361 free seats at a low rent.[134]

This idea became a crucial issue. In a Birmingham suburb, Bordesley (pls 126-7), that could reckon as high as 14s. a sitting, the district board was invited to consider whether letting 200 of the free seats at 3s. a sitting 'might not be the means of bringing a more decent class of the people to the chapel, but with the understanding that unless they occupied the seats before the beginning of the Psalms, other persons should have the right of using them'. The district board reported adversely, fearing that such a move would create difficulty in letting the cheaper pews.[135] Similar proposals, however, were made from a number of churches. As early as 1819, the rector of Walcot (pl. 185), Bath had asserted that the local tradesmen 'will neither pay the high rent usual here nor will they sit free'.[136] When the Board itself proposed in 1824 that 300 seats in the aisles at Christ Church, Marylebone, should be rented at 5s., 'for the accommodation of small Shopkeepers who might be unwilling to occupy the Free seats and yet unable to afford the expence of taking the higher rated seats', the vestry acquiesced.[137] St Thomas, Birmingham, contained 2,200 sittings, of which only 711 were enclosed as pews, letting at between 12s. and 17s. to produce £470. Bishop Ryder enquired in 1829 whether seats in the front row of the gallery might not be let at 5s. in lieu of 15 pews below that 'are not likely to be let on account of the Situation. … The Middling Class i.e. respectable Mechanics – are meant to prefer rented to Free Sittings.' The rector of the mother church, St Martin's, reported however that the local committee thought this impracticable, the consecration deed stating that '1033 sittings in the Galleries have been set apart and appropriated as and for free and open sittings for ever hereafter for the use of the poor.' He himself was unwilling to see the rentals made much lower: the majority of the pews had been taken at the designated rates; and reductions would prevent the minister's employing a curate, the number of poor making the duties 'far more than any one person will be able to discharge'.[138] 'The forms [for the poor] in the [centre] aisle are not liked because the sittings are so cold.'

Several years later, the rector and churchwardens reported that

> The Free Sittings are occupied by various classes of persons; from the poorer classes to those who occupy comfortable stations in Society. Many of the latter it is well known would gladly occupy seats let at a moderate Rent; and it is therefore suggested that a sufficient number of Sittings in the Galleries might be enclosed as Pews and let at low Rates to meet the ordinary expences of Public Worship. ... Another advantage ... might be stated viz. that it would ensure in the Galleries (which are at present wholly free) the presence of a Body of respectable Persons who might serve as a Check upon those who so often frequent the Galleries in an Evening for purposes very foreign to the proper object.[139]

At Chorley (Lancashire), with 1,590 free seats and 422 sittings in pews calculated to produce £276, the minister found himself in a quandary: 'although the free sittings ... are much better occupied than the pews, especially those in the Gallery, they are seldom entirely filled', and some former renters had gone to the free seats, while some persons were willing to rent single sittings in the pews, if that were allowable. His income was insufficient, and he thought that it would be possible to let some of the free sittings at between 2s. and 5s. But that might give general dissatisfaction to those occupying the free seats, so that his inclination was against so doing.[140] A later scale of rents between 6s. and 12s. a sitting, dated 12 December 1844, provided a total of only £132 a year.[141] At St John, Derby, a different approach was suggested to the same end in 1828, that of lowering rentals from 4s. and 5s. to 2s. and 2s.6d., but Bishop Ryder thought it would sadly diminish the minister's income. Four months after consecration 'not one half of the pews' were yet let, and a scale between 4s. and 15s, to produce £237 was approved.[142]

In view of the widespread feedback from the localities, the Commissioners in mid-1828 ordered that the incumbents of all parishes in which a new church had been built should be asked whether all the free seats were occupied, and whether any, and what number of them, beyond one-fifth of the capacity should be let at a very low rent.[143] Unfortunately the responses are not extant.

In some measure, the receipts from pew rents were 'payment by results': an energetic preacher could often attract a more considerable congregation than an indifferent one. (The disputes about the position of the pulpit, considered above, lend weight to this.) The example of St Matthew, Camp Field, Manchester, illustrates the importance of the minister. The church, a fine building by Barry, in a poor district, opened in 1825, with 860 pew sittings, rented at £457, and 978 free sittings. About 1835 a new incumbent 'found the district in an almost heathen state – the church nearly deserted and in such debt, and the school still more deeply involved . ... On coming to the church three years ago', the minister reported, 'I found 108 pews [usually of 5 or 6 sittings] of which only 32 were let. At the present time there are

197 St Matthew, Camp Field, Manchester (Charles Barry, 1822-5). The local committee urged the aesthetic need for a spire in Manchester; other Barry churches were denied one. Serving a poor district, this church required a vigorous minister.

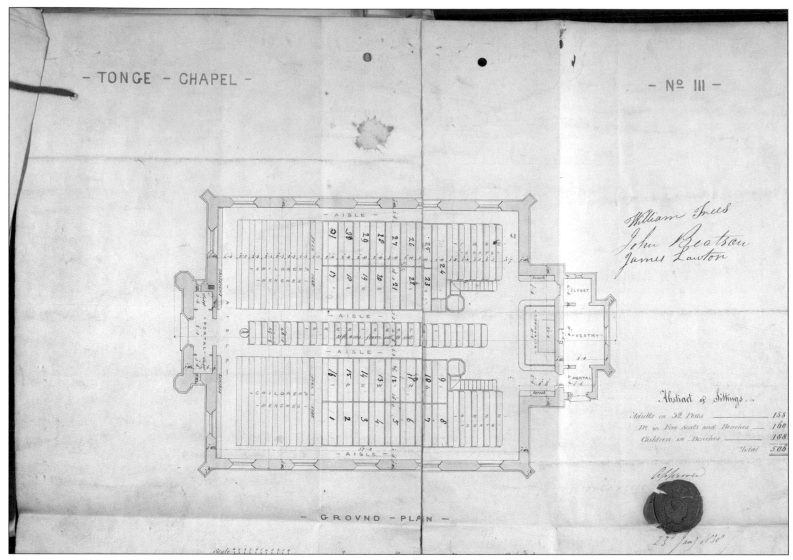

- GROVND - PLAN -

198 St Michael, Tong(e), Lancashire, (William Hayley & Thomas Brown, 1838-9). Pew rental plan, sealed by the CBC. A small, cheap church (£3.8s. a sitting), with a very high proportion of children's seats. Free seats for adults are unusually at the front, as well as in the central aisle.

137 pews, whereof 102 are tenanted … the pews which still remain unoccupied are the largest and highest-rented; the demand for small and low-rented pews being far beyond supply.'[144] On Manchester in general Professor Ward comments: 'By 1850 there was a very ready market among the middle or pew-holding classes, but among the working classes, there was, particularly for protestants, a vast deal of sales resistance'.[145]

There was considerable diversity in the siting of free seats. The Commission insisted on a wide central aisle to provide space for free benches, and also objected to benches along the north and south sides as provided in some plans, as such seats did not face the altar. Generally they required some free seats to be provided on the ground floor, as at St Thomas, Birmingham, with 396 free sittings in the area, and 816 in the galleries. But some churches largely segregated the poor in the galleries – cases cited above refer to wholly free galleries; in others, however, the front gallery seats were among the more expensive sittings. At Walcot, Bath, the free seats were in the area, on benches with a back rail; sittings at 5s. and 3s.6d. for tradesmen were in upper galleries; and 25s. sittings in the lower gallery for the 'Higher Orders', whose servants were to sit on an open bench round the back of the gallery.[146] Longton and Shelton churches, in the Staffordshire Potteries, proposed letting 492 and 558 gallery seats respectively at rates between 4s. and 12s., as on the ground floor – though at Shelton, where the 1152 seats in pews were reckoned to produce £592, the 206 second-class

Right: **199** Holy Trinity, Newington, Surrey (Francis Bedford, 1823-4). West gallery with free seats, probably intended for children, behind the pews on either side of the organ. Photograph 1962.

Below: **200** Christ Church, Woburn Square, Bloomsbury (Lewis Vulliamy, 1831-2). Interior looking east in 1966. A large church in a mixed district, with some 500 free seats and 1,000 in pews, letting at £812 a year. The galleries are an essential feature aesthetically as well as financially, and provided the necessary seating at moderate cost (£5.14*s*. a sitting).

201 St Paul, Huddersfield (John Oates, 1828-30), is a fine example of the somewhat smaller town church financed by the Half-Million grant. It seated about 1,250, about two-thirds in pews, and cost £5,700. An engraving of the 1850s shows it before the addition of a chancel in 1883.

seats, at 9*s.*, were entirely in the gallery.[147]

Another consideration was adequate provision for children: the founders of the church-building movement believed it to be essential that the children filling the new week-day schools should come to church for religious instruction on Sundays. At Christ Church, Leeds, Chantrell provided for 306 adults and 143 children in pews, and 640 adults and 240 children in open seats. Such precision was required because only 14 or 15ins were allowed for children, against 20ins in pews and 18ins in free seats for adults.[148] St Thomas, Birmingham, managed squeeze in more children than the nominal 312 'by letting them fill up the space about the Organ'.[149]

Despite the growing hostility to pew-renting in the 1850s, rents remained an essential factor in providing ministers' stipends. When the Church Building Commission was merged into the Ecclesiastical Commissioners on 1 January 1857, there was a small sum[150] in the former's account that was maintained by the latter (paying three per cent on it annually) in order to make nominal (and apparently sometimes fictitious) grants to new churches to bring churches within the benefits of the Church-Building Acts and enable the establishing of pew rents. In 1886 a parliamentary question elicited that about £8,000 were so retained, 'not solely, but partly, for making in aid of the erection of churches small grants which the persons building and promoting these churches desire to obtain for the purpose specified', that is, bringing them within the pew-rent provisions.[151] Although rentable pews were in increased demand in some places with a considerable middle-class element till late in the century,[152] dissatisfaction with the system which so clearly divided the wealthy from the poor continued to grow. At a general meeting of the Ecclesiastical Commissioners on 15 July 1897, the Bishop of London proposed the discontinuance of making £5 grants towards the erection of churches with a view to legalizing pew-rent scales, and the motion was carried unanimously.[153] In 1907 it was stated the account had been closed, grants having been made since 1857 to 281 churches and 181 pew rent scales established.[154]

11

The Half-Million Grant

The second parliamentary grant for building churches was the result of a windfall: the repayment by Austria in 1823-4 of some £2,500,000, part of a wartime loan that had been written off as lost. But despite the flourishing state of the national finances, in 1824 the Opposition were more vociferous, and not prepared to allow such a grant to pass again almost without comment. Joseph Hume, the radical M.P. for Preston, had attacked the Commission in the previous session,[1] and he continued a bitter critic. At the beginning of the 1824 session, F. J. Robinson as Chancellor of the Exchequer indicated that further support for church-building was planned, but when on 5 April he moved that the House go into committee on granting £500,000 for church-building, he ran into strong opposition, led by Hume, and agreed to postpone the motion for several days.[2]

When the House did go into committee on the grant,[3] Robinson presented a strong case, asserting that 'no established church could be maintained otherwise than at the public expense'; that dissenters even paid tithe and church-rate; and that the principle involved was 'the general advantage of the community'. He quoted parochial statistics to show that in 179 places there were still some three and a half million people to be provided for: 'it was utterly impossible, and the house would find it so, to leave matters in such a situation.' It had been supposed, he remarked, that the Million would build 85 churches to hold 145,000 worshippers; it had built 98, for 153,000, and 'excited the zeal and emulation of the professors of the established church', who had already raised £200,000 more for building places of worship. He then illustrated how effective the new churches were; for instance, the report from Birmingham, among others, was 'gratifying in the highest degree'; while at Nottingham, the new church 'had absolutely been taken by storm; it was very much attended by females in the evening. ... no sum of money ever granted by the house had been bestowed with more advantage.'

The opposition employed three modes of attack against the grant. The first was to deny the need for more churches. In the cities particularly, seats might indeed be available because of the prevalence of pew-renting; but the poorer classes were excluded by their inability to pay. Thus John Cam Hobhouse, supporting Hume's onslaught on 'a most profligate way of laying out the public money', could accurately claim that there were plenty of empty seats in Westminster churches and chapels. He had, he declared, personally examined the situation in those six of Westminster's eight parishes in which the ministerial statistics showed serious deficiencies of church-room. He admitted that some of the churches were full, even 'thronged', – with a seven-year waiting list for seats at St James's – and that the new chapel, St Philip's, in Regent Street, was nearly full. But there were plenty of chapels of ease (in fact, mostly proprietary chapels, i.e., chapels built by private subscribers, often as an investment, outside the parochial framework of the Church), and he had found that sittings were readily available in most of them. This could not be because people stayed away: 'There was hardly a respectable shopkeeper or other householder who did not go to a place of worship every Sunday morning.' It was Peel who inquired whether the poor were admitted to the half-empty chapels: Hobhouse had 'confined his remarks to the accommodation required by the rich, and those who were able to pay'. The Commissioners, in any case, had not found the circumstances of Westminster as pressing as elsewhere.

The second mode of attack, accepting the official statistics, was to claim that the situation was irremediable. Hobhouse was not averse to employing this argument also: to supply the whole deficiency would cost twenty millions, or even sixty – was that the government's intention? The country's inability to afford the grant was stressed, while some members insisted that it should be spent on some form or other of education. For the government, Lord Palmerston pointed out that a million had been voted without dispute when the country was in a worse financial situation. Peel estimated that provision was required for one person in six; but the likelihood of dissenters' returning to the Church should not be ignored; church-room should therefore be provided for a quarter of the population. The situation was far from hopeless: 'Let them do as much good as they could.'

The third mode was to admit a deficiency in some areas, and to use this as a lever for securing a reform of the Church. More services should be held; church funds should be devoted to church-extension; and, above all, subscribers to new chapels should be allowed to elect their own ministers, which would show the churchmen as zealous as the dissenters. This last argument was one that appealed to the Evangelicals, and the 1819 Act had made a step in that direction. Hobhouse, now leading the charge, made much of this idea: more services were the answer; or if a community were too large to find room in the parish church, they should be allowed to build themselves a chapel and to appoint a pastor.[4] He himself thought that the pastor chosen should be subject to the approbation of the bishop, 'though it might appear to some too illiberal and too favourable to Church of England doctrine'. Proprietary chapels were very profitable. 'The more genteel the neighbourhood, of course, the more lucrative such a speculation became.' The condition of the poor did not appear in the least to disturb him. Peel responded that there were already five services in some parishes, and that the choice of pastors by the people would lead to party contests. Dr Stephen Lushington, a leading ecclesiastical lawyer, soon himself to be appointed a Commissioner, insisted that the need was to provide church-room for the poor, who then often had to choose between worshipping in a dissenting chapel or not at all. He wished the Church of England 'to have fair play and that the dissenters should not have their doors open, while those of the former were shut'. He objected to the election of ministers because the canvass would be degrading to the dignity of the Establishment, and it favoured 'popular preachers'. But he did criticize the Commissioners for building too expensively: they should at least furnish one free sitting for every five pounds expended. He also called for an increase in the stipends of stipendiary curates, and an end to the need for the incumbent's consent to increased church-room in his parish. Hume seized the opportunity to renew an attack he had earlier launched against the Church of Ireland, extending his condemnation of pluralism and non-residence to England, and claiming that the Church's own resources were adequate for its needs.[5]

It was not only the Opposition who were aware of the stimulus to church-building that allowing subscribers to nominate a minister might give. Joshua Watson had regretted Sir William Scott's deleting an empowering clause from the 1818 Bill. The Act of 1824 did provide that subscribers of over £50 might elect three life trustees, who could nominate the minister for the first two turns, or during forty years; the right would lapse if the trustees failed to nominate. But there was strong opposition from the High Church party to this new principle that threatened the entrenched parochial system.

In this contentious debate, light relief was unintentionally provided by the young connoisseur, Henry Bankes jun. Insisting that every state had to provide for the decent performance of the religious rites that it chose to uphold, he asserted:

> As for the general principle of building new churches, it certainly ought to be a main object with Government to provide for the union of sexes (sects [notes the reporter]). (Much laughter.) That union had been an object much attended to in Ireland. (Continued laughter.) It was an union that it was of the greatest consequence to keep up. (Renewed laughter.) He apprehended from the laughter in which hon. Gentlemen indulged that he had inadvertently committed some verbal inaccuracy.

Palmerston summed up the general conservative attitude to the new grant; voluntary contribution was very well, but 'with respect to the Church of England, it was the poor alone who felt the want of church accommodation'. 'Nothing … could tend more to the general tranquillity and happiness of a people, than a community of sentiment, as far as it could be obtained without intolerance to any party, in matters of religious doctrine.' It was greatly for the country's advantage that dissenting numbers should not increase. As for devoting the money to education, reading and writing were not the true objects of education; moral and religious instruction were. The bill's committal at a later stage was carried by 148 votes to 59.

Subsequently, William James, a Whig claiming to be not hostile to the Church, complained of inflexible ecclesiastical regulations, impeding 'the exertions of the Protestants'. Ralph Leycester, another landed Whig, clearly hostile, asserted, 'It was pastors and priests that the people wanted and not edifices of brick and mortar. The people sought for spiritual bread and the Chancellor of the Exchequer gave them a stone.' Hudson Gurney, an independent brewer and banker, thought it unfair to tax the country for building churches in the towns. Irish members aired Irish grievances, and J. B. Monck, representing Reading, complained large sums had been advanced to parishes where the inhabitants were rich, like St Marylebone, and nothing had been done for equally populous parishes where they were poor, a circumstance he blamed on the faulty regulations of the Act. If the Methodists were allowed to build churches and retain the patronage, 'a numerous and respectable class of dissenters' would return to 'the pale of the church'.[6] At this point the House began to tire, and Sir Isaac Coffin cried: 'I say, Sir, let us go on, and have the churches.' The hostile motion to defer the bill was lost by 9 to 42. On the night of 14–15 June, the Chancellor moved the third reading, which despite the efforts of Hume, Brougham and their friends to delay it, was carried by 85 to 15. It then passed rapidly through the Lords.[7]

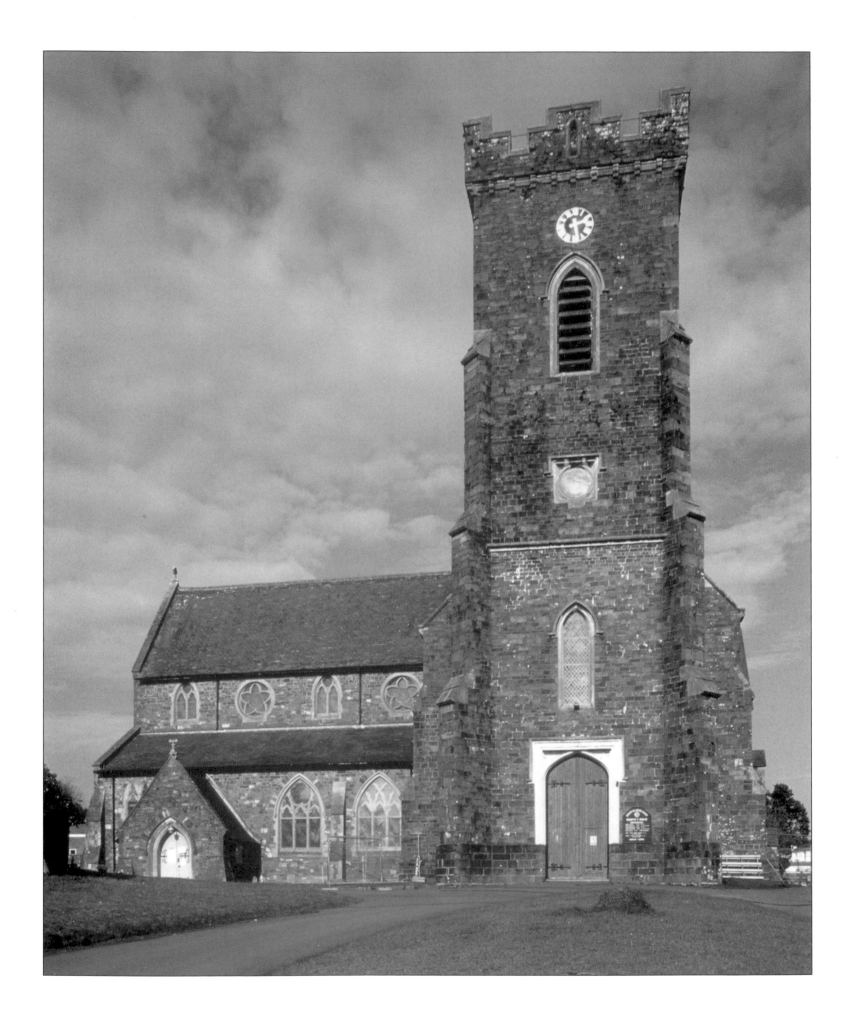

12

Handling the Half-Million

Changes in Emphasis

The remainder of the Commission's life may be conveniently divided into two periods, marked by the issue of new Letters Patent in 1845. The chief characteristic of the middle period, from 1825 to 1845, is a shift of emphasis: turning from building churches themselves, the Commissioners assimilated their methods to those of the Church Building Society; so that ultimately the Commission was distinguished from the many other bodies founded to aid church-extension only by the new functions it had accumulated in the course of its life.

When the second Parliamentary grant was confirmed, various steps were taken to strengthen the Commission and improve its efficiency; to meet the criticisms of extravagance that had been made against it; and to do what it had been doing, both more cheaply and on an extended scale. After about 1830 the Commission was compelled to struggle to eke out its resources merely to survive, in the hope that the political climate might grow more favourable and another government grant at length be forthcoming. But it was a day of anticlericalism and the dissenters had come of age.

First, a select committee, composed of Howley, Pott, Cambridge and Watson, was appointed to decide how the new grant should be applied.[1] Their report regretted the 'vast disproportion' between church-room and population that still existed in many of those towns for which churches had already been provided. But as the new grant was clearly inadequate for the completion of the whole work, they thought that attention should be given to great towns 'with very inadequate provision of church-room which have received nothing from the first grant'.[2] They listed twenty-four places most in need,[3] but pointed out the difficulties occasioned by the form of the population returns, as local clergy had been stressing for years past: some of the largest parishes were made up of 'several townships and villages scattered over a great extent of country at considerable distances from each other, and in some instances containing a population so small that places of worship erected in them would contribute comparatively little to the general accommodation of the parish'. The only way of overcoming this difficulty they could suggest was for the ministers of

Opposite: **202** St David, Carmarthen (Edward Haycock, 1835-6). It took this parish nearly a decade to meet the conditions for the Commissioners' grant of £3,000.

231

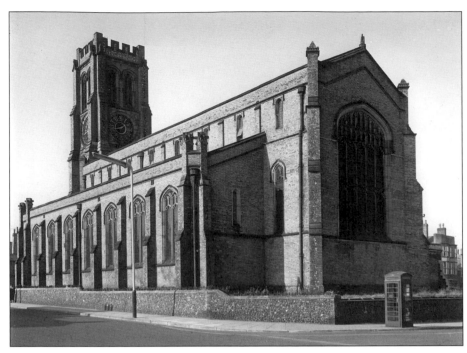

203 St Peter, Great Yarmouth (Joseph John Scoles, 1831–3). A Roman Catholic, Scoles was widely employed after Catholic emancipation in 1829 in building for his co-religionists. His wife came from a Great Yarmouth family. Sturdy in white Suffolk brick banding with faced flint squares and Bramley Fall stone dressings, St Peter's was not expensive for its date at £4.6s. a sitting. Photograph 1962.

parishes concerned to be asked to inform their diocesans of the actual church accommodation, the number of divisions within the parish and their population, their relative distances, and the most convenient situations for new churches. This would form but a rough guide, yet was probably the best that could have been obtained without a special survey of a wide range of counties that the Commission had no means of carrying out, and would be supplemented by the advice of the several bishops.[4]

A requirement for the incumbent to state 'the amount of contribution which may be obtained by rate or subscription' indicates a factor that was strongly to influence distribution of the Half Million. As a preliminary economy it was decided to revert to the plan of 1818, that the parish should always be required to provide the site.[5] The motive of economy produced a change of approach: no longer were churches to be planted in those places most badly provided, but hostile; instead it would be for the parish to make out a case for a new church and show what they could offer to call forth the Commissioners' bounty.

In line with this was the committee's second recommendation. It was desirable to assist parishes less in need, but which came forward with offers of money or sites, 'as these offers if not met with encouragement may be withdrawn, and the loss of a site in some instances be irreparable'.[6] To such parishes a limited sum should be offered on condition that they should raise all other funds necessary. A nation-wide plan was not possible, and the best means to provide the maximum number of churches must be adopted. That tens of thousands would be left unprovided for was no valid reason for not seizing the chance to provide for thousands. Such encouragement may also have inspired subscriptions in other places.

Their report approved, the committee were then directed to consider what further steps might be taken with regard to the distribution of the new grant along such lines. It was not until January 1825 that this work was completed. They had the assistance of a very detailed survey of the needs of the Lichfield diocese from Bishop Ryder, who had succeeded the octogenarian Cornwallis early in 1824. He referred to the industrialization of much of his extensive diocese (Stafford and Derby shires, and parts of Salop and Warwickshire), the great increase of population in the previous 50 years, 'and the total transformation of little valleys into populous towns'. In most of the existing churches there was 'scarcely one free and unappropriated sitting for the Poor', who in consequence resorted, some to meeting houses, and far more 'to haunts of idleness and vice and to the Public House'. Little could be expected by way of subscriptions, he warned, and in view of the inadequacy of the new grant he listed the needs of his diocese, so that an equitable distribution might be made, until parliament supplied aid on the necessary scale.[7] He therefore stressed that new churches should be built economically: churches for 1,200 in the smaller towns, but for 2,000 in Birmingham – with less attention to decoration: 'Bordesley appears to me to be too expensive and to contain too few' – just over 1,800. Another of Goodwin's churches, however, Holy Trinity, Burton-on-Trent (1823–4, not a Commissioners' church), was 'almost a model of moderately ornamented Gothic and most commodious', presenting a model for a 'greatly wanted' church at neighbouring Derby, where 'Socinians peculiarly prevail ... [and] Radicalism is not unknown'. At Wolverhampton 'the prevalence of immorality on the one hand, and dissent on the other is great indeed': there was church-room for only one in seven; a potential site could be paid for by rate. Sedgley (Staffs), with 14 blast-furnaces, was an extensive parish divided into nine villages: 'It is not easy to imagine a more deplorable case'. The 'immensely rich' Lord Dudley was chief proprietor and might be expected to help; a church for 2,000 costing £10,000 was needed. A similar plain church for 1,200 or 2,000 at Bilston should be a chapel-of-ease 'to avoid another election of the People [i.e., inhabitants] who are the Patrons'. At Tipton, 'immense National and Sunday Schools ... containing 1300 children' offered 'a peculiarly

Above: **204** St George, Wolverhampton (James Morgan, 1828-30). A provincial classical church was unusual at this date, but Morgan (Nash's erstwhile assistant) built at average cost for this date (£5.6s. a sitting), for a parish riddled with immorality and Dissent. The Surveyor complained that 'the stone used in the South front ... above the Arches of the lower windows is of a red order, and the whole below the arches of a light grey ... a very unsightly appearance' (CBC, SR 3, f. 62). Photograph 1976.

Left: **205** St Mark, Shelton, Hanley, Stoke-on-Trent (John Oates, 1831-3). View from south-west: an 'Ornamented' version of the Lancet style. Average costs had fallen to about, as here, £4.12s. a sitting; a church for 2,100 persons, in a district dominated by Dissent. Photograph 2003.

favorable prospect of large congregations', but 'strange doubts were hinted about the patron's consent'. At Darlaston a 'new church could not be attempted with any prospect of letting sittings'. But it was the Potteries to which Bishop Ryder had devoted the greatest attention: a 'case of extraordinary pressure of a population above 30,000 – three churches holding less than 3000, and 20 Meeting Houses holding 15,000 (where opulent inhabitants are peculiarly deficient …)', and where 'very liberal' efforts had been made to enlarge the mother church: Hanley (Shelton) and Lane End (Longton), Burslem (with 12 Dissenting meeting-houses), Newcastle and Tunstall were cases there that he pressed 'with a warmth and a strength to be excused'.[8]

The committee concluded that the several components of vast parishes ought to be considered independently, 'without regard, on the one side to their connection with parishes of enormous population, or on the other, to the accommodation existing in other parts of the parish from which they reap no advantage'. The standard for judging the various claims should be 'their real wants, and the number of persons who will be actually benefited by the erection of new chapels'.[9] They therefore had divided the applications into three classes: those with a population greater than 20,000; those with between 8,000 and 20,000 inhabitants; and those with less than 8,000. They proposed that to the first class £100,000 should be immediately appropriated, and that 'a selection be made therefrom … of

206 St James, Lane End, Longton, Stoke-on-Trent (Thomas Johnson, 1832-4). View from south-west. Another 2,000-seater for the Potteries – with some archaeological character: a clerestory and Y-tracery. In 1836 a wooden screen was proposed to divide this over-large church (ICBS). Photograph 2003.

Right: **207** Christ Church, Tunstall, Stoke-on-Trent (Francis Bedford, 1830-1). Bedford was able to meet the Commissioners' demand for a cheap church, even including a steeple, at a cost of £3,146 for 1,000 sittings. The transepts and chancel date from 1885-6.

the most urgent cases offering sites, or contributions to an equal amount, and presenting … a large mass of population which can be accommodated in the same place of worship'. To the second class a similar sum should be appropriated under the same provisions. A third £100,000 was to be set aside for places in any class, where the urgency was less, but which had 'a claim to favorable consideration from the amount of their contributions'. The sum remaining might be held in reserve with a view of assisting either places which had not yet made any application, or those which, 'after every exertion', should be unable to raise the contributions demanded in the first instance by the Board.

The final and significant recommendation referred again to the possibility of calling forth public subscriptions – the hope that had been with the Commission from pre-natal days; £25,000 was already available, but the committee had hopes of raising much more, 'if applicants were informed that a subscription in a certain proportion would be met by a grant which would enable them to effect their object'. This idea was adopted, and the 'certain proportion' fixed at one-half. A circular was then sent to those parishes that had offered sites or money; and consequent upon the replies received, the committee recommended six grants.[10] Another circular announced the Commission's offer of a pound for pound grant; but if parishes were unable to raise enough, the Board desired to know what they could offer, as any sums left over would be distributed among the most deserving parishes.

Above: **208** Holy Trinity, St Day, Gwennap, Cornwall (Charles Hutchens, 1826-8). At the height of the Cornish mining boom, churches were essential to compete with Methodism. At £2.11s. a sitting, this was one of the cheapest churches: 'Even the granite appears like paper' (Pevsner). Photograph 2005.

Left: **209** Christ Church, Watney Street, St George in the East, London (John Shaw, 1840). Difficulties in obtaining a site delayed implementation of a 'Million' grant for nearly two decades. Shaw's twin towers do little to relieve the dreariness of this example of 'Norman Revival', costing just under £5 a sitting.

210 St Clement, Spotland (Lewis Vulliamy, 1832-4). East end. A Picturesque composition, although one of the cheap churches provided to meet neglected Rochdale's needs, at about £2.13s. a sitting. With nearly two-thirds of the seats free, the potential pew-rental was £158.

Meanwhile, further to increase the Commission's efficiency, the Board had obtained new Letters Patent appointing additional members in the place of five who had died. The most important was the new Bishop of Chester, Charles James Blomfield (1786-1857), a protégé of Howley, with an 'ungovernable passion for business', who became the leading ecclesiastical administrator of the Reform era. A friend of Watson, the two worked closely together[11] until Watson's age and provincial retirement curtailed his activities, when Blomfield took his place. Other new members of importance were the new Bishop of Lichfield and Coventry, Henry Ryder (1777-1836), Lord Harrowby's brother, who has already been quoted extensively; the new Dean of St Paul's and Bishop of Llandaff, Charles Richard Sumner (1790-1874); and two of the archbishop's acolytes: George D'Oyly (1778-1846), who had succeeded Wordsworth as rector of Lambeth, and John Lonsdale (1788-1867), rector of St George's, Bloomsbury, 1828-36, and from 1843 Bishop of Lichfield, 'the best bishop the diocese ever had'.[12] These two were immediately called in to lighten the labours of the executive members, and were included in the very important standing committee appointed in May 1825 to examine and report on pew-rent schedules, 'the character to be given to the new churches and the duties to be performed therein, the division of parishes, and assignment of stipends and fees'. This committee, which included Pott, Cambridge, and Watson, and which a year later the Bishops of Chester and Llandaff joined, was moreover entrusted with the work of appropriation, and dislodged the Building Committee from its role as the primary if unofficial executive body of the Commission, though largely composed of the same persons. The Commission's Sixth Report listed 66 grants-in-aid from the Half-Million;[13] the Seventh added a further 34.[14]

The urban parishes continued to be the Commission's gravest anxiety; early in 1827 the committee recommended that the sum remaining should be applied in the first instance in parishes of great population where nothing had yet been done[15] – which implied falling back on the earlier method of paying most if not all of the cost; grants should be confined to these places, 'where the population in each parish exceeds 20,000, and the church accommodation does not extend to the proportion of one-eighth and where no grant has yet been made out of the parliamentary fund – namely, Eccles, Halifax, Rochdale, Whitechapel, Merthyr Tydfil, and Spitalfields – and that the Board take immediate steps for erecting new churches or chapels therein'. They advised next aiding Stockport (Hyde), Leeds (Holbeck and Kirkstall), and Oldham-cum-Prestwich (Tong), where also the population was more than 20,000, and where although new churches had been provided, there was still room for fewer than an eighth of the inhabitants; and that the church in St George in the East (London), for which £16,000 had been allocated from the Million (Christ Church, Watney Street), should be begun as quickly as possible.[16] A rider was added to this resolution on 1 May, ensuring that it would not preclude the Board's making grants 'under special circumstances, to such parishes as may be willing to advance one-half of the expence of building'.[17]

The Seventh Report, dated three months later, shows that Rochdale (1821 population: 37,229; church-room 4,620), alone of the first six, had yet been allotted grants (Spotland and Wuerdle), though the four in the second group (as named above) each had an allocation of funds. Most of the 'proposed grants' in the Eighth Report, 1827-8, had been announced previously; only six new grants were proposed, but plans under consideration included places from the list of applications postponed for want of funds (Fourth Report, 1824) not listed in the one hundred 'proposed grants' of the Sixth and Seventh Reports: Alverstoke (Hampshire), and two for Wigan (Lancashire). For all their detail the annual reports lack precision: only two of the 15 'proposed grants' listed in 1829 were actually new, which shows the extent to which funds had been exhausted. Merthyr Tydfil had in some measure been provided for by the consecration of a building erected by the Iron Company. Though the possibility of building three chapels at Halifax (St James Halifax, Hebden Bridge, and Brighouse) had earlier been considered, it was not until the Ninth Report that the parish appears in the list – and then already under 'plans approved'.[18]

How, then, were things in the field? The Rev. J. C. Franks of Huddersfield, offering £370 subscription and one site, was allocated four chapels at a total cost of not more than £12,000; by May 1826 he had obtained 'pretty sketches' for chapels at Lindley and Paddock, from John Oates, 'something like Stanley, though with lancet windows, but he almost despairs of bringing the estimate much within £3,000'. Franks had had many interviews with Thomas Taylor before his death, and he likewise had thought £3,000 'the very least sum' for 1,000 sittings. The Board agreed to increase Huddersfield's grant to £15,000, provided the accommodation were increased to 1,200.[19] When Franks withdrew the Lindley and Paddock plans because Oates had been unable to bring the estimate within the grant, Oates suggested leaving out the galleries ('they will be sufficiently large for the present population'). That would bring down the figure to £2,822 inclusive, for 408 in pews and 459 free (about £3.5s. a sitting), at which they were approved.[20] For Golcar, Franks had at first had

Churches of the late 1820s for villages around Huddersfield, by Peter Atkinson's York practice.

Top left: 211 St John, Golcar (1828-9). Another 'Plain' style church, at £3.6s. a sitting. Rather less than half the seats were free but the pew-rental was only £95.

Top right: 212 Christ Church, Linthwaite (1827-8). Interior: timber nave arcade and gallery, open roof; for 800, only one-quarter free, pew-rental £111. Parson Roberson, the local incumbent, wanted no more Atkinson churches.

Bottom: 213 Holy Trinity, South Crosland (1827-9). Interior, looking west: open roof; for 700, nearly half free, pew-rental only £77.

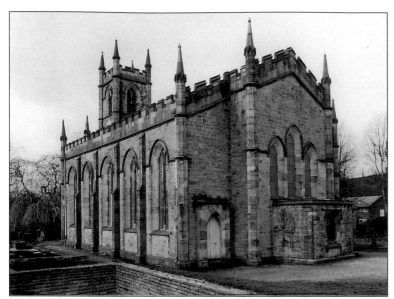

214 St John, Bollington, Cheshire (William Hayley & Thomas Brown, 1832–4). Similar to Hammerton's contemporary Brighouse, but more expensive at £4 a sitting; more than half the seats were free.

designs from Clark Rampling (1797–1875), 'an Architect not altogether to my mind', but it was Peter Atkinson's plans that the Surveyor passed in May 1827, at £2,950, exclusive of commission, etc. Both his and Oates's plans were among those the Surveyor selected as suitable for Rochdale in January 1828, as providing accommodation for 1,000 at less than £4 per head.[21] The architects, however, were not working quite within the guidelines, Franks reporting in February 1828 that Oates had completed his plans for Huddersfield town to hold nearly 1,500, only to find that Atkinson had exceeded his allocation by several hundred pounds, so that the total for the four churches had overrun the specified £15,000. He argued that it was the general opinion that 1,200 was the largest congregation a clergyman could address 'with success and for a continuance', so that smaller churches 'will be more beneficial than larger ones … I cannot but conclude that the accommodation need not be extended'. The Board approved; and Oates's designs for Huddersfield (pl. 201) were altered in June.[22] Lindley and Paddock were built to hold 867 each, Golcar 950, and St Paul, Huddersfield, 1,243, at a total expenditure of £14,253.

Only on learning that two miles of 'high bleak moor' separated sites at Linthwaite and Crosland in neighbouring Almondbury did the Board abandon the idea of making Linthwaite serve both townships.[23] Plans for Glossop (Derbyshire), at £3,667 for 1,000 sittings, were rejected as £250 over the appropriation.[24] Wigan parish, granted chapels at Pemberton for 1,600 and Aspull for 800 on the ground floor (galleries to be added later if needed) was instructed to obtain plans '<u>without towers</u>'.[25]

Rickman & Hutchinson were told to reduce the cost of their Wigan churches by omitting ornament, their estimates having exceeded the funds available because the subscription was less than expected and partly spent on site and enclosure.[26] They submitted plans for that at Pemberton

> prepared on a principal [*sic*] totally different from the former designs, hoping thereby to have reduced the amount more considerably than on making a very careful Estimate (at prices which are quite as low as we can venture to insert) we find is the case. The cost now proposed is we are fully convinced, as small as in the locality of the chapel it can be performed for, without either materially lessening the solidity of Workmanship which the Board are so properly requiring in their Works, or introducing Brick as the essential walling which would spoil the appearance.

The Board demanding of the vicar whether cheaper plans might not be obtained from other architects,[27] were told there was no such likelihood, and that if other architects were applied to, Rickman & Hutchinson would have to be paid. The Board returned revised plans with an instruction to reduce the cost of the two buildings to £9,000. The architects' only solution was to turn to brick walls with stone dressings: to which the Board had 'no objection' if that would keep within the appropriation.[28] In 1828, for a church at Clerkenwell, London, where a site was given, the Board made a grant on the basis of £4 per sitting; but for a chapel for a thousand at Bollington, Cheshire, where two acres and £500 were given, the whole expense was not to exceed £3,500.[29] At the same period, Thomas Hardwick sent in his plans for Horwich, in Dean parish, Lancashire, where he had already built St John's, Farnworth (pl. 138), to a similar design at a contract price of about £5.11s. per sitting; the new

St Mary the Less, Lambeth (Francis Bedford, 1827-8). Cost £7,800 for 1,960 sittings (£3.16s. each), setting a new standard for cheapness in metropolitan churches and securing Bedford's continued employment.

Above: **215** Interior, to east. Iron columns and plaster vaults. As at St Mary, Somers Town, the nave of the Temple Church was probably a source. Photograph *c*.1910.

Left: **216** West front, from Bedford's drawing.

church to cost £6,000 for 1,500 sittings. In achieving this reduced rate he had omitted a tower. The Board wanted a tower, but at no greater cost.[30]

> I regret to state [Hardwick responded] that the contractor for [Farnworth church] is now totally ruined, which is attributed to the loss he sustained upon that contract. ... I should not feel that I was doing justice to the Board were I to lay before them an estimate of £6000 to include the architect's commission, the clerk of the works etc for a chapel to be built in the same parish upon a site not so convenient for stone similar in all respects as to its design, its dimensions to be increased to hold 1500 persons, and with a tower proportionate to the size of the building [which would cost £800] ... Although I have prepared four sets of plans for this chapel and have bestowed much pains upon it, I would rather decline it altogether than pledge myself at a lower estimate.[31]

Hardwick's plans were therefore rejected as too expensive: as the Commissioners remarked, 'Plans which the Board have approved have been carried into effect at the rate of £4 per sitting.'[32]

The Surveyor was instructed to see if there were any suitable plan in the office by R. D. Chantrell, by this time the leading Yorkshire church architect,[33] but reported: 'There appears to be no design of Mr Chantrell's in the office for a church calculated to accommodate more than 1000 persons, nor does there appear to be any plan in the office of a church with a tower capable of accommodating 1500 persons which can be built for so small a sum as £6000.'[34] So keen were the Commissioners for a tower at Horwich that they then turned to the London architect, Francis Bedford,

217 St Peter, Hoyland, West Yorkshire (Watson, Pritchett & Watson, 1829-30). Architect's drawing of the south elevation. To keep the cost under £2,000, the architects proposed economies, including omission of a weathercock, and Countess instead of Westmorland slates. It appears, however, that the threatened buttresses were retained.

whose St Mary-the-Less, Lambeth, was within a few weeks of consecration, having cost £7,801 for 1960 sittings, i.e. just under £4 a sitting.[35] Bedford was 'most happy to prepare a design', having no doubt that the brief could be executed for £6,000, if without vaults and extraordinary foundation expenses.[36] And he did it.

Yet Warminster (Wiltshire), 'a plain, church-like edifice' by T. E. Owen (1804-62),[37] whose plans had been chosen from 12 sets received, secured an additional £500 because of the rise in the cost of local stone ('certainly the most durable that can be procured'),[38] and kept its tower: sited on so conspicuous a spot that 'the absence of a tower would have been a striking defect'. But the Warminster design cost some £3.15s. per sitting, and Hardwick's Horwich £5. So apparently inconsistent decisions may be reconciled on closer inspection.

For a church at Hyde (Cheshire), than which 'no part of the Empire is more in want of a new church and the discipline that belongs to it',[39] the local squire in January 1828 recommended Thomas & Charles Atkinson of London;[40] their plans provided 1,610 sittings for £4,500 inclusive of commission, etc.[41] Then in July the squire announced that a subscription had been given for a tower, and suggested that the accommodation be reduced. The Atkinsons presented a revised estimate of £5,582, but thought that the tenders would come in at a lower price. The Board's reaction was to seek a plan with the same accommodation at a lower cost, for which

240

they again turned to Chantrell. He duly sent plans in November 1828, remarking: 'In the several churches I have in progress I find that these plain Early English buildings will cost in this part of the country where the free and enclosed sittings are equally divided from £3 to 3 guineas per sitting and where only one third are free about £3.10s. per sitting.' However, to bring their estimate within the sum allowed, Atkinsons omitted their buttresses and reduced the thickness of walls on which it had been hoped that the tower might subsequently be raised. Thanks to their then proving cheaper than Chantrell, and possibly to the squire's patronage, their revision was approved.[42]

Similarly, Watson, Pritchett, and Watson presented a more detailed list of the omissions which might be made to reduce the estimate for Hoyland (West Yorkshire) church to £2,000, or £4 per sitting:[43]

1. Buttresses of the church.
2. The mouldings in the ceiling.
3. Part of the framing against the walls of the church.
4. The flue for heating the church.
5. Substituting a plain instead of an ornamented pulpit and desk.
6. Omitting the Gothic mouldings in the communion rails.
7. Omitting the painting of the pews.
8. Covering the roof with Countess instead of Westmorland slating.
9. Omitting the ornamented ends to the free benches.
10. The weathercock.

It may be seen that buttresses were sometimes regarded as part of the ornament, to be dispensed with if necessary, and not as a structural necessity. That might also be deduced from the flimsiness of many of the buttresses of the period, though this is by no means true of them all. The Commissioners always endeavoured to ensure that the structure should be strong and durable, but where large funds were available, a stouter as well as more ornamented structure would probably be designed; where they were not, quality suffered: the substitution of inferior slates at Hoyland is an

Left: **218** St John, Burscough Bridge, Ormskirk (Daniel Stewart, 1829-31). The cost was £3,440 or £4.12s. a sitting. The average pew cost 11s. a year here, a total of £177.

Right: **219** St Thomas, Brampton, New Belper, Derbyshire (John Woodhead & William Hurst, 1830-1). The local vicar insisted that a tower was essential in a district of meeting-houses, and raised nearly one third of the total cost.

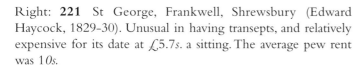

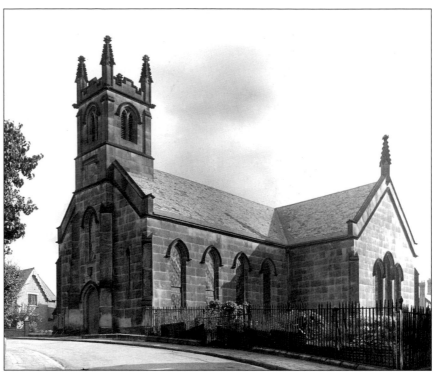

Above: **220** St James, Riddings, Derbyshire (Francis Bedford, 1830-1). South front of another of Bedford's later, cheap churches (under £3.8*s*. a sitting); the buttresses have lost their pinnacles. Pevsner thought it 'handsome for its date'.

Right: **221** St George, Frankwell, Shrewsbury (Edward Haycock, 1829-30). Unusual in having transepts, and relatively expensive for its date at £5.7*s*. a sitting. The average pew rent was 10*s*.

illustration. A local subscription of £400, however, won approval for Daniel Stewart's design for a chapel for Burscough Bridge, Ormskirk (Lancashire), at nearly £4.12*s*. a sitting.

There were always occasions when the Commissioners breached their general rule. At Brampton (Derbyshire) the vicar squeezed an extra £150 from them, sending two designs by Woodhead & Hurst, one with, the other without, a tower: 'the putting of a tower … in the place of the deformed and unmeaning bell-turret becomes an object of more importance … to make the protestant church (surrounded by Sectarian chapels …) as respectable as possible - and placed as it will be to front ... the much frequented road between Chesterfield and … Manchester'. If given the extra £150, he offered to find the balance.[44] Episcopal pressure could be influential, as on 12 February 1828, when the Bishop of Bristol secured a two-thirds grant for the parish of St Philip and St Jacob, Bristol, the petition urging that 'The close connection which subsists between religious instruction and immoral conduct, between a devout observance of the Sabbath Day and industrious orderly behaviour throughout the week is too obvious to need any comment'.[45] The inconsistencies that one may observe in the Commissioners' decisions may have been influenced by their personal knowledge of the needs of individual parishes or representations made to them. Such factors might embrace topographical considerations. For instance, as at Brampton or Warminster, the siting of one church might seem to demand a tower, which might be less necessary in a different situation. A study of the contemporary topography would be required in order to make a just assessment. Here, one can only record some of the apparent inconsistencies.

Thus, at the same meeting, 6 May 1828, the Board both instructed Owen and Son to omit the tower and substitute a bell-turret in their revised design for Forton (Alverstoke, Hampshire) 'which is of a plainer character and consequently less expensive than the former plan, and in this design are embodied the several improvements suggested by the Board'; and also rejected the Building Committee's suggestion that £220 might be saved on Bedford's cheaper chapel at Riddings

(Derbyshire), precisely by replacing the tower by a bell-turret.[46] A week later, at Shrewsbury, where there was increasing hostility to the new church, the town 'in an absolute ferment', Edward Haycock's plans for St George, Frankwell, were referred to the Building Committee with an instruction to consider substituting bell-turret for tower (but a tower was saved). Yet when Edward Lapidge (1779-1860) declared that he could not bring the cost of a church at Hampton Wick (Middlesex), below £4,000, or £5 a sitting, the Board increased its grant.[47]

The demand for cheaper churches did not stop at the point marked by Hoyland, or even Stannington (West Yorkshire), at £3.18s. a sitting, or Bonomi's amazing St Patrick, Winlaton (Durham, 1827-8), at as little as £2.17s. In July 1834 the Board decided in favour of one Tattersall of Manchester to design a church at Habergham Eaves (Lancashire), instead of Lewis Vulliamy (who had been proposed by the incumbent), because it was desirable to employ local rather than London architects in order to save the cost of journeys, which was considerable on a small church.[48] Tattersall was to design a church seating 1,100 at an expense of not more than £2,750 – an average of £2.10s. per sitting. Cheap as Hoyland had been, it was now regarded as expensive, for in December 1841 the Board complained of plans for Wednesbury that the estimated cost (£4,000 for 1,000 sittings) 'appeared large'.[49] In January 1845, they refused even a grant for a chapel at Armitage Bridge (West Yorkshire), because the cost was too high at £2,500 for 430, or slightly over £5.16s. a sitting.[50] It may be concluded that the Commission was a potent influence in reducing the costs of church-building between 1825 and about 1845. Thereafter such newly-popularized ideas as that expressed in Ruskin's 'Lamp of Sacrifice' became increasingly influential, and as private donors sprang up, the Commission's influence was waning.

Left: **222** Christ Church, Stannington, West Yorkshire (John Woodhead & William Hurst, 1828-9). Even at under £4 a sitting, it was possible for an able practice to design an attractive church. With the average pew rent at 4s., the total rental was only £77.

Right: **223** St Patrick, Winlaton, Durham (Ignatius Bonomi, 1827-8). A simple but sturdy church by a highly competent architect, for the amazing cost of £2.17s. a sitting.

★★★★★

The committee's plan was strategically inadequate because of the difficulty of obtaining an accurate and detailed picture of the situation over the country as a whole. There were for instance, no Ordnance Survey maps for the northern counties

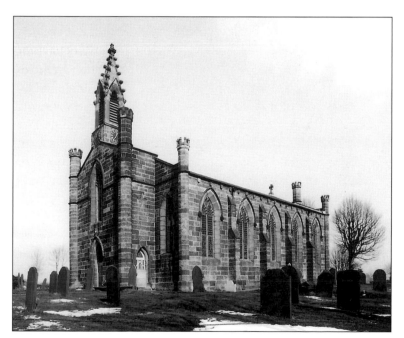

before 1840,[51] and one notices the neglect of the north-east in particular in the grants handed out in the 1820s. Then although the Commission had benefited Birmingham from the Million, it had provided little to the Black Country and the Potteries – though the omission of Stoke-on-Trent was the consequence of apparently insoluble difficulties regarding patronage. Given the intractable nature of their task, the committee's proposals were probably as useful as any that could have been devised; had they concentrated purely on the cities, little progress might have been achieved. As it was, the Half-Million plan broke down because of lack of funds, the impossibility in some places of letting enough pews to provide a stipend, the difficulty of finding sites, and the hostility of vestries. The Commission was able to continue making grants, but much smaller ones: the average grant to the six churches completed in 1836-7 was £2,009, compared with £10,340 in 1823-6; and to the 18 churches of 1838-9, only £1,116.[52]

This did not, however, result in less work for the Board: the grants were smaller, but there was still the work of assessing the applications, vetting the designs, establishing pew-rent schedules (363 in all), administering drawbacks, signing certificates for payments to building contractors, checking architects' accounts, querying extra works, and – perhaps most burdensome of all, evaluating proposals for creating new parishes or chapelries of one form or another. Under the 1818 Act, the Commissioners, the diocesan consenting, might establish ecclesiastical districts, or, subject also to the patron's consent, create new ecclesiastical parishes; the 1819 Act added the power to unite contiguous parts of separate parishes into chapelries, and assign districts to chapels-of-ease, which might, by the Act of 1822 be subsequently converted into district parishes. In all, the Commissioners created 671 district chapelries, 118 consolidated chapelries (taken from contiguous parishes), 81 district parishes, and 39 distinct and separate parishes. The low figures for the latter categories suggest how difficult it was, and how reluctant the Commissioners might be, to interfere with existing ecclesiastical rights of patronage, glebe, and fees. The mere administrative arrangements were laborious: even when all the necessary agreements and approvals had been obtained, the description and map had to be enrolled, returned to the Board for sealing, and submitted to the Privy Council for publication as an order-in-council. Of all these parochial arrangements, 332 related to Commissioners' churches. Their powers to simplify the acquisition of sites were the more in demand as church-building became a national passion, used in 1,159 cases. Similarly, they were called upon to assist in the acquisition of sites for parsonage houses (326) and new burial grounds (875), as well as authorizing the purchase of 115 additional burial grounds, which, as Dickens was to emphasize, was becoming a gruesomely pressing matter in many old parishes.[53]

In the late 1820s the Board was as busy as ever, meeting between 25 times (1826) and 35 times (1827) a year, most active in the first half of the year, when parliament was in session, and more or less in recess in August through to October. Activity was hardly less in 1830 and 1831, with 25 and 26 Board meetings, with those of the two main committees, Building and Pew Rents, &c. in addition. For 1832 we have the record only to 17 April but it certainly started busily, with 14 meetings; in the following five years, however, the average was only 18, though the pattern was more regular, with two meetings almost every month, apart from August and September, when any Commissioners in Town would meet to sign certificates for payments. But they did not regard their work as by any means nearly finished after 1832, or lose hope of another government grant, delusive as that might be. The repeal of the Test and Corporation Acts in 1828 (so removing the civil disabilities formerly imposed on dissenters), and still more perhaps, the Catholic emancipation measure of 1829, weakened the claims of the Church, but while a Tory ministry remained in office, the situation was by no means lost. When the Whigs came to power at the end of 1830, supporters of the Establishment were certainly scared, fearing a total disruption of the order ecclesiastical. But by the middle 'thirties, the feeling was rather that the government might demand reforms in the Church, but would not overturn it; and the view was still expressed in the highest quarters that parliament should do something more for the Church.[54] Hopes rose again when Peel came briefly to office in 1834, but he could not assist, except by establishing a commission to investigate the Church's own revenues.[55] Indeed the Church might still be established as far as the dignified element was concerned, but for financial grants – were there not dissenters and papists in parliament to resist such unjust taxation of their co-religionists?

Although in 1828 a list was made of applications, 'to be taken into consideration in the event of any further grant being made', Blomfield had already penetrated to the truth when he remarked in his First Charge to the Diocese of London, in 1830, that the recent legislation would compel the Church 'for the future to depend more entirely upon our internal resources and will be a test of their sufficiency'.[56]

The financial organization of the Commission's work was discussed in a report made in April 1829[57] during the fatal illness of the Secretary, George Jenner, who had also acted as Treasurer. Subscriptions had been paid into an account at Messrs Drummonds, bankers of Charing Cross (who continued as the Commission's bankers until its determination). With regard to the payment of contractors and architects, the committee considering how the work of the Board should be carried on suggested drawing a certificate on the Exchequer for the total amount authorized at each meeting of the Board. This would be deposited with Drummonds. The various specific payments would then be made by drafts on Drummonds signed by three Commissioners and the Secretary, whereon Drummonds would sell sufficient Exchequer bills to meet the total. A separate account had been kept of all sums received for the return of duties on the materials used in building and enlarging churches – the 'drawback account'. The committee suggested that this also should be transferred to Drummonds, and payments from it made in the foregoing manner. This was the mode adopted, and maintained even when, after the death of Jenner, George Jelf (1796-1859), a connexion of Archdeacon Cambridge,[58] of an orthodox High Church family, was appointed Secretary, a post he retained until 1854. Jelf, a practising barrister-at-law, was extremely useful in drafting legislation; and eventually the task of preparing the annual Report to Parliament, hitherto done by a committee, was entrusted to him.[59]

In response to Treasury pressure for staff cuts in 1837, Jelf commented that, judging from their correspondence alone, the business of the office had increased over the previous four years; yet the mere number of letters did not afford

> any true criterion as to the amount of the labor required in the proper conduct and dispatch of the business, the details and preparation of which, before it is ready for the consideration and decision at the general and Committee meetings of the Board ... necessarily occupy much time and attention on the part of the respective officers of the Establishment. ... the minutes of the proceedings of each general meeting are generally very long and are not diminishing: at the last general meeting sixty three cases were brought before the Board for their decision.[60]

The general Board met 20 times in 1835, 16 in 1836, and 17 in 1837, less often than in 1825-32, but still regularly. Its leading clerical members were likely also to be members of the Ecclesiastical Commission. Because of the pressure of business, the Board no longer granted interviews.[61] The establishment of the Commission at this date consisted of the Secretary (£700), the Surveyor (£700), a chief clerk (£300), three assistant clerks (£250, £125, and £75), and an office-keeper (£160, including two servants). There were also two assistant clerks paid by the week, and a messenger, also paid weekly.[62] In 1842 Jelf complained of the deficient means of carrying on the greatly increased business, and was instructed to engage a clerk for two years at £2 a week (subject to Treasury approval); and in February 1843 to employ a copying clerk at £1 a week, as required.[63]

There were attempts to make economies. Rickman and Hutchinson noted that: 'The Board would not in future allow us a commission on the small expenses [costs of printing, advertisements, contracts] paid by us for the different churches.'[64] They were also refused travelling expenses for their church at Lower Darwen, since they had already obtained them for the adjacent Mellor and Over Darwen sites.[65] There were ingenious attempts to site a single church so as to serve several places; one of which induced the Bishop of Chester to point out that the two chapels proposed in Rochdale parish would not alleviate the condition of Todmorden, as one was ten, and the other seven miles from that township: whereupon the Commissioners decided to try to squeeze three churches out of £12,000 instead of two from £11,000.[66]

Various grants, the conditions not having been complied with, were cancelled,[67] and this action was followed in 1834-5 by attempts to recover outstanding debts, culminating in legal proceedings against some recalcitrant parishes. A certain accrual of funds, partly arising from the foregoing causes, partly from the interest from Exchequer bills, partly from the drawbacks, then enabled the Board to undertake a re-examination of applications before it. In November 1835 a circular was sent to the applicants most in need of aid stating that the Board was 'disposed to consider those cases the best entitled to a grant where the subscriptions are the largest, and an eligible site placed at their disposal'.[68] The parishes now had to outbid one another for the small sums still left in the parliamentary fund.

Assessments were carried out by the usual committee of Cambridge, D'Oyly, Lonsdale and Watson, and in April 1836 grants were offered to 21 parishes on certain conditions[69] – conditions varied slightly from place to place, but were in sum that the chapels should be erected under the superintendence of the Board, on plans and estimates approved by them, on sites placed at their disposal, and that sums sufficient for completion should be paid to them before the work was begun: the new factor was this last condition. Grants were calculated roughly on a basis of £1 per sitting, up to a maximum of 1,200. A further series of grants was voted in February 1837,[70] and others not infrequently thereafter.

One of the crucial arguments of this period, closely linked with the planning and cost of churches, was that of their optimum size. An application suggesting that one for 1,200 would be sufficient, instead of for 1,500 as originally proposed, was endorsed by the Archbishop of York: 'A thousand would answer the purpose.'[71] He added,

I recommend to the consideration of the Commissioners the suggestion of a smaller church. I have lately made a circuit of the West Riding, and reports which I have received from my clergy at different places convince me that smaller churches would here succeed better. In very few of the large ones, from the situation of the reading desk and pulpit at the extremity of them, can the minister, unless gifted with a very powerful voice, make himself heard, and consequently the congregation are very thin.

Table 3 **Size and Cost of Completed Churches Year by Year**

Year	No. built	Ave in pews	Average Free	Average Total	Average building cost	Average grant	Average per sittings
1819–22	10	408	990	1,403	£10,665	£6,397	£7.12.0
1822–3	5	607	890	1,497	£11,119	£11,376	£7.8.7
1823–4	11	587	776	1,363	£11,487	£9,855	£8.8.7
1824–5	20	931	839	1,770	£15,081	£10,894	£8.10.5
1825–6	18	616	793	1,409	£9,745	£9,452	£6.18.5
1826–7	5	720	824	1,544	£12,844	£13,034	£8.6.5
1827–8	15	643	713	1,356	£13,152	£7,424	£9.14.0
1828–9	25	638	842	1,480	£9,808	£7,654	£6.12.5
1829–30	25	547	591	1,138	£6,098	£5,477	£5.7.2
1830–1	34	516	638	1,154	£5296	£4,104	£4.11.9
1831–2	20	616	702	1,318	£6,106	£5,543	£4.12.7
1832–3	10	412	489	902	£3,633	£2,394	£4.0.8
1833–4	10	626	655	1,281	£5,584	£4,901	£4.7.2
1834–6*	6	546	666	1,212	£3,898	£2,992	£3.4.5
1836–7	6	495	627	1,122	£4,023	£2,009	£3.11.7
1837–8	5	329	641	970	£3,602	£849	£3.14.2
1838–9	18	373	543	916	**£3,186	**£1,166	£3.9.7
1839–40	15	373	551	923	£3,298	£759	£3.11.5
1840–1	22	472	490	962	£3,306	***£1,215	£3.8.9
1841–2	15	311	509	820	£2,744	£453	£3.7.0
1842–3	19	424	414	838	£3,407	£550	£4.1.4
1843–4	10	271	682	953	£4,104	£628	£4.6.1
1844–5	17	247	481	728	£3,430	£550	£4.14.2
1845–6	27	296	472	768	£3,650	£603	£4.15.0
1846–7	19	182	598	779	£3,960	£635	£5.1.7
1847–8	30	215	528	753	£3,684	£471	£4.17.9
1848–9	29	221	474	695	£3,317	£243	£4.15.5
1849–50	20	230	463	694	£3,331	£367	£4.16.0
1850–1	27	217	535	752	£3,571	£363	£4.15.0
1851–2	22	196	425	621	£3,698	£194	£5.19.0

★ Two years (few completions).
★★ Deduct Holy Trinity, Grays Inn Road (grant £6,169), and the average grant falls to £875.
★★★ Deduct Christ Church, Watney Street (grant £7450), and the average grant falls to £876.

This view was widespread. The vicar of Huddersfield declared: '1,200 is, generally speaking, as large a number as one clergyman can address with success and for a continuance. ... Indeed, extended observation confirms the remark that more and smaller churches will be more beneficial than larger ones.'[72] The need for two priests to serve a large congregation was stressed by the rector of St Andrew, Holborn: 'If the chapel proposed to be built on Saffron Hill be made to accommodate 1,600 persons it will be preferable to one of a larger size, where the income will not allow of two persons to perform the duty.'[73] A Lancashire correspondent of the Incorporated Church Building Society keen to make his point suggested that the deficiencies of church-room might have been supplied by the parliamentary grant, 'at least in the great manufacturing towns of the kingdom';[74] the object being achieved by 'buildings of about one-half the dimensions of those erected, and a proportionate multiplication of the number of them'. That experienced church-builder, the Rev. Hammond Roberson, writing about the churches proposed for Birstall, hoped they would not be like that at Linthwaite; and suggested smaller churches which the inhabitants might enlarge with galleries when necessary.[75]

The Commission nonetheless continued to favour large churches. Experience at Preston, for instance, had shown that it was cheaper to build one church for 2,000 than two churches for 1,000; and in London and the cities particularly, the obtaining of sites could be a further drain on finances. At Saffron Hill it required one for 1,800; and Roberson at Birstall was informed that while new plans would be considered, the accommodation was not to be reduced. The tendency was, nevertheless, towards smaller churches generally. Whereas the average capacity of the 48 churches reported completed in the three years 1823-6 was 1,578, that of the 16 churches completed in 1833-6 was 1,256. The average capacity of churches completed from mid-1829 to mid-1837 fell to 1,132. Thereafter, the fall was marked: 1836-7 was the last year in which the average capacity of the churches built in any one year exceeded one thousand; the average for 1837-52 was only 811 sittings.[76]

Costs, also, were down, and to a greater extent, the average per church in 1823-6 being £12,570, against £4,951 and £4,185 respectively in 1833-4 and 1834-6 (two years). As we have seen, the Board held to a cost-cutting policy in the late 1820s. Thus the average cost per sitting fell from £8.10s. in 1824-5 to £3.4s. in 1834-6, the lowest average in the Commission's history.[77] The average remained in the range £3.7s. to £3.14s. between 1836 and 1842, rising gradually again to nearly £5.2s. in 1846-7, but otherwise remaining under £5 until 1851 (Table 3). The Board decided in 1843 that if their grant 'does not amount to £1000 they do not take on themselves the erection of a new church'; and in 1848 they refused a request to build St James, Stoke Damerel (Plymouth), because, among other reasons, 'of their being obliged as trustees of the Public money to require that the whole of the funds necessary beyond their grant to build the new church should be paid to them before they advertised for tenders, which regulation was complained of as an obstruction and a hindrance to the erection of the church'.[78]

How was this reduction in costs achieved? Partly by a slight reduction in the space allowed per sitting; partly by an insistence on churches of 'the plainest possible character' – a requirement expressed as often by the recipient parish as by the Board itself. Chiefly, however, by building smaller churches: a sort of self-perpetuating spiral: the grant smaller, so the church smaller; the church smaller, so the grant smaller. The reduction and gradual disappearance of most duties of customs and excise also helped to cut costs (the figures given above do not take account of the drawback of duties). Wholesale commodity prices seem to have fallen from 1825 to 1830, risen in the later '30s, and fallen back from 1841, but building costs varied from place to place, so generalizations are unhelpful. Competition in the building industry tended to keep prices down, as we have seen, while very slowly technical improvements, such as Spurgin's 'endless ladder' for raising materials, increased efficiency,[79] as did the increasing familiarity of workmen with Gothic design. Very occasionally, in small churches, the Board's Surveyor relaxed his standards, but there is no evidence of the Commissioners relaxing their stringent code in general, as expressed in their 'Instruction to Architects', revised by the Board in April 1843 in collaboration with the Incorporated Church Building Society – requiring, among other things, roofs of a higher pitch than previously.[80] Another change, disclosed in response to a request from the ICBS to select from plans in the Board's possession such 'as may appear desirable to have copied', was that, after an opinion from the Institute of British Architects that it was 'contrary to the practice of the Profession' for plans to be copied by other architects, the Board would no longer loan plans in their possession.[81]

Public or Private Aid
Church rates

There were two matters of special complexity which engaged much of the Commissioners' attention during these years: church-rates[82] and patronage. The latter was dealt with in a series of Acts; the former was found too hot a subject for them to meddle with, and the problem remained until church-rates after much contention were abolished in 1868. They had originated in the common-law obligation for every parish to keep the body of its church in repair,[83] and to provide the prerequisites for divine service. The parishioners might be compelled to perform their obligations by an action in the courts ecclesiastical. This liability was a primary reason for the hostility to any new churches expressed in some parishes – a hostility which might come as strongly from those having pews in existing churches as from dissenters, expressed both before work commenced, and also subsequent to the completion of a church, manifested in a refusal to vote the necessary rate for its maintenance. The former was of concern to the Commissioners chiefly in the Million era when they were trying to force churches on unwilling parishes – though in the late 1820s incumbents were often confiding difficulties with hostile vestries to the Commission. At Tunbridge Wells the local committee complained that the parish would not provide even a site, unless under notice served by the Commissioners.[84] Holborn presented a similar problem, complicated by the difficulty of finding a vacant site; although the select vestry was favourable, the parish at large – which alone could vote rates – was not. The Law Officers assured the Board that they might buy sites already built on, and charge the expense on the parish rates: if the parish officers refused to make a rate, they thought the Court of King's Bench would compel them upon an application for a Mandamus.[85] A characteristic complaint came from Cheshunt (Hertfordshire), that there were seven dissenting meeting-houses maintained in the parish by their worshippers, and that it was a hardship for them to have to pay for a doctrine from which they conscientiously dissented.[86]

Opposition to paying the expenses of the new churches naturally came to a head when the churches had begun to be used, and is the more apparent and vigorous form of hostility at this time; though such struggles had occurred as early as 1822. The churchwardens of St Luke, Old Street (London), declined to furnish the chapel in King Square. The rector had inquired in June 1822 about the parish's liability to provide the communion plate, altar cloths, service books, etc. Two and a half years later, after much wrangling, the vestry formally resolved to refuse to provide the necessary articles, trumpeting their reasons:

> The vestry ... apprehend that any admission of the chapel to be a parochial chapel will lessen the fees and regular receipts of the parish, may demand a large immediate expenditure, will occasion great further trouble, and will impose an uncertain but increasing annual burden and distressing rate, and that such evils are most to be now deprecated, when an expenditure of several thousand pounds will be soon required for the needful repair of their parish church.[87]

The Law Officers advised that the 'proper ecclesiastical authority' should call upon the churchwardens to perform their duty, and then if they failed to do so, an action would lie in the ecclesiastical courts.[88] Accordingly the Commissioners called upon the Dean and Chapter of St Paul's (the ordinary) so to act. Not until a year later was the rector able to announce that the parishioners had agreed to provide the requisite furnishings.[89]

In 1827-8 there seems to have been a concerted attack against rates for the new churches in the West Riding;[90] Manchester was exhorted to follow suit, and the Tory stronghold of Rochdale was assailed violently in 1831-4, and again, this time successfully, in 1838-40.[91] At Leeds the vestry refused to allow that part of the accounts for 1826 relating to the outfitting and repairs of the new churches; but as the church-wardens had sufficient money in hand they nevertheless paid those expenses. In July 1827 the churchwardens convened a vestry for levying the annual rate for repairs to the parish church (in which they comprised all expenses for the new churches also): some 1,500 inhabitants attended, and voted an order to the wardens not to make any payment on account of the new churches; as well as voting such a rate that they would be unable to do so.

> The leading persons at the meeting admitted the liability of the parish to provide the necessary funds for the repairs of the new churches; but they said ... the only redress of the churchwardens was by suit in the spiritual court, and that that court could not compel the parishioners to obey its mandate further than by pronouncing against them ecclesiastical censures for which they cared little.[92]

The vicar obtained counsels' opinions:[93] Dr Phillimore advised an action in the ecclesiastical court; Dr Herbert Jenner thought this unwise, but the churchwardens might of themselves proceed to make a rate. He did not see how ecclesiastical censures were to be inflicted upon such a body as the parishioners of Leeds. But as conflicting opinions made it a case of great difficulty, and as it was one which might eventually come before the Common Law courts, he recommended its reference to counsel practising in those courts. This being done, counsel hesitatingly pronounced in favour of the churchwardens alone making a rate, to be enforced by the spiritual court; but he recommended that the case should be referred to the Commissioners for legislative rectification. The Leeds committee therefore sent a draft of clauses proposed for incorporation in the bill contemplated for the 1827 session, clauses which were promptly referred to the committee on the new bill. The Act 7 & 8 Geo. IV c.72 did include a clause authorizing the churchwardens of district churches to make rates.

In the following January the Sheffield vestry refused a rate. The vicar of Sheffield inquired of the Commissioners, 'When will the Church of England be practically, as well as professedly, protected by the law?'[94] He suggested that vestry meetings for church-rates should be superseded, as had been done for highway and poor rates.

A similar hostility was shortly manifested at Dewsbury, where the vestry took the budget item by item, reduced its total, extinguished the bell-ringer's wages, and negatived the votes for the new churches: 'It was enough to have one church to maintain.' Over a thousand persons had attended, mostly of the labouring classes whose church-rates would 'scarcely amount to one penny per annum each'; and 'such a hostile spirit was evinced towards the church that it was afterwards remarked ... that if a proposal had been made to pull down the church it would have been agreed to'.[95] The churchwardens of Dewsbury, bolder than their fellows at Leeds, intended to lay a rate themselves, and cite the inhabitants before the ecclesiastical court. But they too suggested amending the law. The Commissioners replied that they were 'extremely anxious to provide a remedy', that a bill was in progress which was intended to overcome such difficulties, but that its passing was very doubtful. Opposition did cause its withdrawal in July 1828.

In October 1828 suggestions made to the chancellor of the Exchequer with regard to the problem were referred to the bill committee, as were the views of Dr Wilkins, Archdeacon of Nottingham, on the difficulties of obtaining church-rates from 'rabble vestries'.[96] In March following, when the vicar of Bradford announced that rates for the new churches at Shipley and Wilsden had been resisted, advice was again sought from the Law Officers.[97] The Ecclesiastical Law Commissioners' report of February 1832 remarked: 'The whole subject of church-rates demands *immediate* attention; for the mischiefs resulting from the present state of the law are rapidly spreading.' Numerous pamphlets and sermons were fired off: but no bill was forthcoming until 1834, when the Whigs, having set up the Ecclesiastical Commission to enquire into Church revenues,[98] proposed to abolish church-rates. But as there was no other source of funds for repairing the vast majority of churches, a sum equal to the annual average cost of repairs (to be certified by the district surveyor), £250,000, was to be appropriated for this purpose on the Land Tax. The bill, however, was abandoned, because 'it had the whole force of the dissenters against it', according to the vicar of Halifax, or because the government 'petered out absurdly as a government' in Professor Owen Chadwick's view.[99]

No remedy was found during the Commission's lifetime, although in Peel's brief administration of 1834-5, Lord Ellenborough at the Privy Council was entrusted with a bill on the lines of Althorp's abandoned measure, on which Jelf, Howley, Blomfield. and D'Oyly commented.[100] The Whigs took up abolition again in 1837, but failed to secure enough support.[101] In 1845 the Commissioners still 'lament the unsatisfactory state of the law respecting church-rates,[102] but they do not feel themselves competent to suggest any remedy'.[103] After 1832 the hostile sects were in a position to block any legislation favouring the enforcement of church-rates, but not yet strong enough to achieve their abolition. The Board's own opinion was that 'nothing short of a comprehensive measure, including the whole subject of church rates, brought forward under the sanction of Government, will be effectual';[104] and not even Peel felt himself strong enough to propose such a measure. Of 638 contested church rates laid in 1831-51, only 148 were successful; and this statistic conceals the abandonment of rates in great cities, such as Birmingham and Leeds.[105] At last, after several abortive bills, church-rates were abolished, without compensation, in 1868 by Gladstone's endeavours.[106]

Patronage

The problem of patronage was more restricted, but quite as complicated. Every benefice was in a sense the property of a patron – Crown, Bishop, Dean and Chapter, or private individual. But the nomination of ministers to chapels-of-ease belonged to

224 Holy Trinity, Ulverston, Lancashire (Anthony Salvin, 1829-31). Despite its severity, a forerunner of design developments a decade later, with more steeply sloping roofs than most contemporary 'Lancets', and an asymmetrical tower, though the mean buttresses are typical of its period, and the nave has a flat ceiling. It cost nearly £4.12s. a sitting, but one-third of the cost was subscribed.

the incumbent of the parish church. This position was not touched by the first Church Building Acts. But these did envisage the division of parishes in one mode or another. To maintain the 'rights of property', it was enacted that when a parish was divided into distinct parishes, the patronage of each should vest in the patron of the original parish; but when division was merely into districts, the incumbent of the parish church should have the nomination, as if to a chapel-of-ease.

To encourage subscriptions it was found necessary to make some provision for granting patronage to subscribers, similar to that clause rejected in 1818.[107] A clause was tacked on to an Act of 1827 which allowed the Commissioners to declare the right of nomination to vest in persons building and endowing chapels, without compensation to the incumbent. This hastily-passed statute left the Commissioners with powers so vague that they were unable to exercise them: in August 1829 they called for an Act to define and explain their powers.[108] But bills brought forward to rectify the situation were abortive, so that in May 1830 they agreed reluctantly to execute an instrument granting the perpetual patronage of one chapel, because further delay would have caused serious inconvenience.[109]

At last a statute emerged in October 1831 which repealed the earlier clause and replaced it by 28 others.[110] In certain circumstances the bishop might declare the right of nomination to be in the person building and endowing a chapel (s.2); in all other cases where a chapel was built and endowed to the Commissioners' satisfaction, they might, with the bishop's consent, declare the patronage to vest in the person responsible (s.5). But the patron of the parish was to be given due notice of the intended work, and had the option of undertaking it himself (s.7). This Act was modified in 1840,[111] when subscribers were allowed to nominate a patron after making application to build (ss.9, 10): and further conditions for the exercise of the bishop's or Commissioners' jurisdiction were laid down (ss.12-16). Either might also make a disposition of the fees (s.18).

In addition to the statutes, the Commissioners made certain regulations: they required for an endowment not less than £50 per annum from either land or government securities;[112] and also that, save in very special circumstances, districts should be assigned to such chapels within their jurisdiction.[113]

Subscription

Patronage was only one means of promoting subscriptions. Another occasionally resorted to was to free subscribers of a certain sum (usually £50 or more) from the payment of pew-rents for a limited term. Yet another means was the encouragement of diocesan societies and the Church-Building Society, to which the Commission allowed a proportion of the drawback on duties commensurate with their grants. The importance of the C.B.S. was recognized by the government in 1828, when it was incorporated by statute. During the 'twenties the Society had given its aid, for the most part, to those parishes which the Commission was legally inhibited from assisting. This was a very valuable extension of the Commission's work, and as its funds became exhausted it adopted for itself the Society's methods. The Society was, in truth, the Commission in the guise of a Church, as distinct from a State, society. The leading Commissioners usually sat also on the Society's committee; and some of the Commissioners appointed in 1825 had been acquiring experience on that committee beforehand, like D'Oyly and Lonsdale.

By 1828, the funds of the Society, derived from voluntary subscriptions, had been almost used up. Bishop Blomfield wrote to one inquirer: 'I am sorry to say that you have no chance of obtaining £2,000 from either the Commissioners or the Society, or from both, for the simple reason that they have no funds, the former having granted away all their money except a small part reserved for unforeseen emergencies, and the latter not having more than four or five hundred pounds in hand.'[114]

At this point an old means of raising money was seized upon and modified in the interests of church extension. The ancient system of briefs, long under critical fire, was abolished: in its place was set the Royal Letter, to be read from every pulpit, and calling upon the faithful to give generously for some specified national Church society. By the same Act[115] the Society was incorporated, its constitution laid down, and the administration of sums raised by Royal Letter entrusted to it.[116] Thus the Commission's *alter ego* was saved and perpetuated, and the great work able to go forward vigorously in the very years when the Commission's own activity was restricted.

The abolition of briefs was a work in which a number of Commissioners were closely concerned. Several efforts to improve the system had been made since Waterloo. A bill proposed in 1821 would have provided for an annual collection for church-building.[117] The following year Lord Kenyon became chairman of a Lords' committee on the subject, but nothing more was done until June 1826 when Peel moved for a return of briefs laid since May 1819. This return showed that up to 1 June 1827 60 briefs had been laid for repairing or rebuilding 48 churches.[118] Costs of collection averaged two-thirds of the sums subscribed. The system lasted only a few months longer.

Joshua Watson and Christopher Wordsworth were responsible for the introduction of the Royal Letter[119] (which was granted to the I.C.B.S., S.P.G., and S.P.C.K. in turn yearly). Wordsworth thought this preferable to parliamentary grants, partly to avoid the unseemliness of party conflicts on such questions, but chiefly because he thought

That the raising of money by an appeal through the clergy, and afterwards the laying out and superintendence of money so raised, would both of them conduce much better to the

225 Broadsheet to mark Bishop Blomfield's campaign to build ten churches in Bethnal Green, 1836-47. Only eight of the ten received grants from the Commission. They exhibit the range of styles employed at that time; St Simon Zelotes (second from bottom on right), by Benjamin Ferrey, Pugin's friend, is the one that has best assimilated Pugin's influence.

introduction of the system generally throughout the kingdom, and to the maintenance of it when so introduced. If you employ the clergy to raise money, we are laid in some degree under an obligation to understand what it is for, and to show that the object is a good one. And afterwards also we are laid under another obligation of responsibility, that the money shall be well disposed of. In short, the getting at the gold is but a small part of the business.[120]

The 1828 Act is indicative of two trends: the replacing official support of the Establishment by private; and the entailing of statutory duties on bodies not, or incompletely, responsible to parliament, induced by the desire to keep certain questions out of the field of current politics and of political patronage. The desire to limit government patronage also found expression in hostility to some church-building enactments regarded as tending to concentrate ecclesiastical patronage in the hands of the bishops.

There were two directions in which to look for financial aid: government and people. Governmental aid had proved inadequate; and now it dried up. Many leaders of the Church thought that it was the State's duty to provide churches, and still hoped for a further grant. Others recognized that changing conditions made it unrealistic to hope for one – at least, one open and avowed, on the necessary scale.[121] They were therefore driven, like the Bishop of London in 1836, to appeal to the generosity of individual churchmen. The first great appeal to the public (apart from that of the I.C.B.S.) had been launched a little earlier by the Chester diocesan society to build churches in the manufacturing districts,[122] which raised some £12,000. Now Bishop Blomfield called for subscriptions on 'a scale of unusual magnitude' in order to build 50 new churches in London – 'a work of prudence, not less than of charity'.[123] He desired to provide church-room for one-third of the population, and one church and minister for every 3,000 persons. The response, though less than hoped for, had aroused much attention, and was followed by the setting up of similar local funds, as in Bethnal

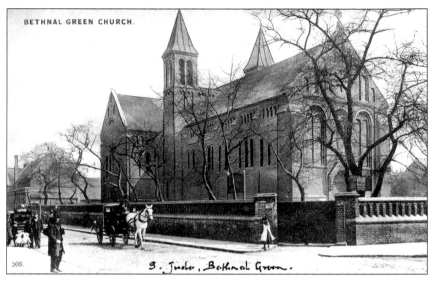

Green in 1839, where ten churches were built during the next eleven years.[124] The bishop still hoped for some sort of parliamentary aid, and fell back on the old resource of a tax on coals coming into London: an additional 2*d.* per ton, while hardly felt by consumers, would yield £18,000 a year: if mortgaged for a period, this would provide funds sufficient for 30 or 40 churches. But the coal tax had already been attacked as a heavy burden on the poor, and no increase was acceptable.[125] Sir Robert Inglis was hopeful of state aid: his motion calling on government to 'relieve the spiritual destitution of large masses of the people' failed by only 17 votes in a House of over 300.[126] When Peel came to power in 1841, Inglis was talking in terms of two or three million, but Peel and his colleagues regarded him as a loose cannon. Peel's unwillingness to provide cash is discussed below.

226 St Jude, Bethnal Green (Henry Clutton, 1845-6), for 1,000 entirely free sittings, cost £5,149. In Lombardic style, then briefly popular. It was unusual, however, for its twin towers in the angles of the transepts; the detail was very suitable for execution in stock-brick.

Further Legislation

There was a considerable amount of church-building legislation during this period, in addition to that already referred to. From about 1827 the Commissioners were hoping for a comprehensive Act, which would have dealt with the difficulties already mentioned, and overhauled the complicated series of existing Acts – which Dr Stephen Lushington called 'a most complicated mass of confusion'.[127] A committee (Blomfield, D'Oyly, Lonsdale, Watson) appointed in June 1827 to consider the draft of such a bill, recommended that because of the importance of the clauses and the advanced state of the session, legislation should be confined for the time being to two points of urgency: the renewal of the Commission for a further term of years, and authorizing the burial in the parish cemetery of those who died in a new ecclesiastical district without a burial ground of its own. To these was added the vexed patronage clause already mentioned, repealed by the Act of 1831 that extended and clarified it. A bill of 1828 did not pass.[128]

In 1837 the Secretary, Jelf, drew up a statement of the case for a continuation of the Commission.[129] He summarized the position regarding the Board's funds: 219 churches had already been built out of the parliamentary grants; five were building, and grants had been made towards a further 55, which would be commenced when suitable sites and funds sufficient for their completion were placed at the Commission's disposal. There was £17,000 left from which to make grants, and £75,000 was due on account of loans to parishes, secured chiefly by charges on their church-rates. The average annual rate of repayment over the previous three years had been £4,000, at which it was expected to continue for three or four years more.

Subscriptions promised for particular churches, but still unpaid, amounted to £7,800; but the collection of £2,700 of this was considered hopeless. Because of the difficulty of obtaining eligible sites and raising the requisite funds, often several years would elapse between making a grant and the work's starting. It might therefore be some time before the 55 proposed churches were completed.

But this was by no means the only reason for prolonging the Commission's life, Jelf argued. It had certain duties to perform consequent upon its erection of new churches: to establish scales of pew-rents, out of which stipends had to be assigned to the ministers; the division of the parish or the creation of an ecclesiastical district for the new church had to be considered – 'matters so necessary to insure all the benefits of increased church accommodation'. All these were questions of detail requiring much time and attention, and similar powers were exercised with respect also to churches not built by the Board. Districts or parishes had already been assigned to 74 of the new churches; clearly there was still much to be done before the ideal was realized, as laid down in the Second Report of the Ecclesiastical Commissioners: the assignment of a district to every church – 'necessary to the ends of pastoral in-struction and for carrying into full effect the parochial economy of the Established Church'.

The Commission also possessed powers to facilitate obtaining additional burial grounds for parishes, and of sites for churches and parsonage houses which they were only just beginning to exercise to any degree.[130] They had the duty of examining all applications for a remission of the duties on customable and excisable articles used in building or enlarging churches of any of the Establishments in the United Kingdom, and of transmitting the monies so recovered to the applicants.[131] They could further encourage private liberality by their power of declaring the perpetual patronage of churches to be vested in the persons building and endowing them.

Jelf concluded his report by remarking:

> There are many other powers vested in this Board which are practically valuable to the Church Establishment, but of which it is perhaps unnecessary to enter into a detail, as this outline will be sufficient to show that the amount of business still to be done, as respects even the special objects of the Commission, requires a considerable extension of the period of its present existence. … The general business of the Board is increasing.

This report was transmitted to the Home Secretary by the Archbishop of Canterbury. Lord John Russell approved of an application to parliament to continue the Commission for ten years more, but warned that the Chancellor of the Exchequer thought that the Secretary might be shared, presumably with the Ecclesiastical Commission.[132] The Act of 1837[133] duly continued the Commission until 1848, but a Treasury letter, approving the issue of the usual £3,000 for the annual charges, stated that before any further issue was made, My Lords would consider 'whether some more economical arrangement may not be made for con-ducting this service', 'no Public Funds being now administered' by the Board.[134] It was therefore necessary to follow up the broadside of the report with a further salvo.

A committee (inevitably Cambridge, D'Oyly, Lonsdale, Watson) discovered a surprisingly large amount of public funds being still administered by the Board – as much as £267,603.2s.1d., made up of sums 'such as remain unexpended out of the Parliamentary grants, or have arisen out of Parliamentary provisions, or from resources produced by the application of the Parliamentary grants by the Board'. When analysed, this sum does not appear so impressive: £60,000 in subscriptions was yet to be received, and £71,000 was on loan – part of which it was notorious that there was little hope of recovering.[135] But the Commissioners reminded the Treasury that they had many duties to perform, and remarked that their present expenses were 'as low as ... is practicable consistently with the proper discharge of their duties'.[136]

Then followed a spate of legislation affecting the Commission. The long delay in bringing forward much of this was undoubtedly due to the pressure on parliamentary time caused by the struggles over the Reform Bills of 1831-2, and the subsequent legislation embodying the Whig reforms. The Act of 1838[137] clarified the conditions on which bishop and Commissioners might declare the right of patronage (ss.1-7). It also extended the powers for conveying lands to cover those (to a maximum of five acres) acquired as a site for a parsonage house (s.9), and declared that any parish or extra-parochial place might be divided in the several ways possible at the same or at different times (s.12); while the security of tenure of stipendiary curates was protected (s.13). The next year saw a measure[138] which allowed the new districts to benefit from Queen Anne's Bounty, the restrictive clause of the 1819 Act being repealed. The Commissioners also received wider powers to assign districts (s.3). The exclusive cure of souls was secured to ministers of district churches, whether they were built from public or private funds (ss.8, 10). The object of the Act was to assure the independence and security of the ecclesiastical districts, and to provide an income where the yield from pew-rents was insufficient.

An Act of 1840[139] asserted the Commission's power to form new districts out of those already formed – provision forgotten in framing s.12 of the 1838 Act. The nomination was to vest in the incumbent of the original parish (s.1), unless legally vested in others (i.e. subscribers). Endowments under the Church Building Acts of less than £300 per annum were freed from the Mortmain statutes (ss.2, 4). The work of the previous Act was carried on by allowing the augmentation of stipends from surplus pew-rents (s.5). That Act was the last spurt of this flood, which derived from the increasing extent of church-building activities, both public and private, and the almost inevitable failure of earlier legislation to foresee all contingencies. And though the Whig ministers of the 1830s refused a further parliamentary grant, they were prepared to ease the process of building churches by private liberality: the Church, as Blomfield had foreseen in 1830, had to rely on its own resources, but it was given the opportunity to make use of them.

Jelf himself was employed in drafting and revising legislation, and attending its progress through parliament; and Stephen Lushington worked on an abortive consolidating measure in 1845,[140] for which a limited, but useful, clarificatory Act (8 & 9 Vic. c.70), discussed below, was substituted.

227 As a result of the work of the Church Building Commission, Richard Tress, architect, in 1841 produced a booklet, *Modern Churches. Designs, Estimates and Essays; also plans, elevations, working drawings, and specifications of modern churches already executed.* For his frontispiece Tress displayed St Luke, Cheetham Hill, Manchester (T. W. Atkinson, 1836-9) [right], which, although erected by subscription, displayed the characteristics of a Commissioners' church of the more scholarly class, the tower closely modelled on that of Louth (p. 51), in a district that Atkinson had studied closely.

A few years later, in 1849, Andrew Trimen published an historical sketch of church architecture containing more than a thousand sections of Gothic mouldings, remarking that the Church Building Act of 1818 had given an impulse 'to the study of architectural science, which promises to make this century celebrated'.

13

The Commission's Last Years

The Commission's labours seemed as necessary in 1847 as in 1837. The great and continuing increase in the population of England made church extension a Sisyphean task. Church building societies set up in most dioceses seemed unequal to the unceasing demands. In June 1832 the Whigs had instituted a royal commission to inquire into ecclesiastical revenues, renewed in 1833 and 1834; Blomfield, a member, contemplated the possibility of a commission of clergy and laymen to consider the reform of the Church; and Peel, during his brief ministry of 1834-5, had established a permanent commission on those lines, which included among its functions consideration of the 'best mode of providing for the Cure of Souls' and redistribution of Church revenues.[1] Hope of state aid had not died among the friends of the Church, particularly if it could be shown that the Church was managing its revenues more efficiently and rationally. Sir Robert Harry Inglis's motion for government aid for church extension failed in the Commons on 30 June 1840 by only 17 votes. When a Tory government came to power in 1841 hopes of a grant rose again. The anonymous author of *Church Extension in relation to the present national crisis*,[2] hailing the new administration of Sir Robert Peel, insisted that 'the demand for Church Extension which now exists cannot be met by individual benefactions'; the national religion ought not to rely on voluntary subscriptions. The government should compel parliament to vote some two or three millions annually (!) for Church extension and endowment. But it was the Rev. William Palmer who had his feet on the ground: effective state aid was improbable: 2,500 new churches were needed; but there were 3,000 existing parishes with fewer than 300 inhabitants. Parochial re-arrangement, Sunday collections, deacons in place of parish clerks, and additional bishops were the needs.[3] Inglis, a blinkered High Tory, unheedingly memorialized the prime minister for a really substantial grant of two or three millions.

Yet Peel had made his position plain as early as April 1840, in a Commons debate on the Ecclesiastical Duties and Revenue Bill; 'the most likely way to induce the Legislature and assist the Church' would be for the Church to set an example in providing a remedy. 'But I am convinced', he declared, 'that the Legislature will never consent to come forward without the Church make the sacrifice'.[4] Now, as prime minister, Peel discussed with his Home Secretary, Sir James Graham, the need for local inquiries about lack of churches, and the problem in general terms with W. E. Gladstone, the leading churchman in the government.[5] But, ever the pragmatist, Peel's discussions were designed only to find a way of helping the cause of church extension. He never favoured a public grant – a course that he thought would only unite those hostile to the Establishment and create difficulties for all concerned.

Graham agreed. Even a committee of enquiry would generate a spirit of resistance: even when the need for more churches had been shown, there would be no hope of parliamentary aid. Religious differences would prevent any drain on the public revenue for extending the doctrines of the Church of England. The only hope, he thought, was (as critics had been saying for years past) gradually to render church property 'more available for the sacred use of the Church; and less subservient to the temporal interests of its ministers'; then from time to time public aid might be obtained – presumably for specific limited purposes.[6] Even church-coloured education clauses in Graham's Factory Bill had to be withdrawn.[7]

By the end of 1842 Peel had come to the consideration of ways and means. It had become very clear that the provision of stipends for ministers of the new churches was a fundamental obstacle retarding extension: pew rents were all too often inadequate. Goulburn, at the Exchequer, favoured a tax on clerical incomes to provide stipends for additional ministers. The idea of some sort of financial assistance was discussed in Cabinet during 1842, and Goulburn supported a small grant, but Peel would not agree. He thought that if an endowment could be provided, considerable voluntary contributions for building could be raised in some districts; they would be greatly stimulated by the promise of an advance from public funds. But all he dared suggest was an interest-free loan: and even of the expediency of that he was doubtful. As he put it to Graham:[8]

> I recommend, therefore, that we should exhaust in our consideration every plan by which we can unite voluntary contribution and contribution from the revenues of the Church before we make a demand on the public purse. We cannot go further, I think, in that direction, than loan without interest. Can we go so far?

Endowment would, he thought, stimulate subscriptions for building churches. His great concern was to avoid raising a storm.

> It is very well for clergymen and for Sir Robert Inglis to argue that it is the duty of the State to provide religious edifices wherever they are wanted, and that Dissenters are bound to build and repair and endow their own churches, and those of the Establishment also . . . but you and I know that the Church and religion would suffer, and peace and charity would be sacrificed, were we to push these arguments to their just logical conclusion.

For fear of the consequences, he was not willing to compel dissenters to pay for the churches of the Establishment. 'I dread, for the sake of the Church and its best interests, stirring up that storm, which large demands on the public purse would immediately excite. Ireland, Scotland, Dissent and religious indifference might be brought by skilful management to combine against a vote for Church Extension in England.' In other words, it might prove fatal to the ministry.

A month later Peel outlined a practical scheme. He differed totally from Inglis, whose scheme would provoke the question whether the application of the Church's property to *bona fide* spiritual purposes would not be enough: there would be demands for an inquiry, which would be most hostile in spirit. Instead, he suggested 'the measures which I believe would be best for the general welfare':[9]

First – The charge of maintaining the fabric should be borne either as at present by a levy on property, or by public funds assigned in lieu of that levy.

Secondly – I would propose a grant of public money, probably an annual one, to be applied forthwith to the *endowment* of new churches in the districts most requiring them. I would trust much to voluntary contributions for the building of new churches.

Thirdly – I would undertake maturely to consider the whole state of the remaining Church property with a view to the administration of it on trust principles for purely religious purposes.

Shall we, in order to avoid the consideration of these matters, leave untouched the much greater matters connected with Church Extension? Or shall we, touching those greater matters, content ourselves with proposing – in the present state of the Revenue – a large grant from the public funds, trusting that the question of Church property, and the means of making it more productive and available, will escape notice in Parliament?

Such a trust on our part would be in my opinion thoroughly delusive. If you are to consider Church Extension at all, the inquiry into Church property will infallibly come. Whether it come in a friendly shape or a hostile one will depend upon the nature of the proposal made by the Government …

Peel's arguments against 'a large Parliamentary grant, two or three millions',[10] were purely political, and the difficulties he opposed to it partly the making of his own policy in 1829. Of his personal attachment to the Church there was no doubt, and he made liberal private gifts for church extension.[11]

But in the long run no public aid was forthcoming: partly perhaps because of the expense of colonial wars, and ministers' desire to reduce tariffs; partly, the reluctance of the Church to abandon the administration of her own revenues, but primarily because of the political situation. Peel's discussions led to the Populous Parishes Act of 1843 (6 & 7 Vic., c.37) which enabled the Ecclesiastical Commissioners to create districts (which became known as 'Peel districts') wherever necessary, under the pastoral care of a priest, provided an endowment of £1,000 were provided. Building a church, not a function of the Ecclesiastical Commissioners, was to be left to the subsequent exertions of the minister and his flock. Up to £600,000 might be borrowed from Queen Anne's Bounty for endowing the new districts. These 'Peel districts' were established without consultation with the Church Building Commission, which however made many grants towards the erection of churches in them, after an initial period of uncertainty regarding their power to do so.[12] Many of these grants were small, averaging in 1848-9, for example, £243 each to 29 churches, and in 1851-2 £176 to 22 churches,[13] and then shrank to the purely nominal - £10 or even £5 - but had the effect of bringing the churches within the provisions of the Church Building Acts. Thus the Commissioners were able to establish for them scales of pew-rents, which usefully augmented the minister's stipend; and the parish was able to borrow money on the credit of its church-rates.

There was also a body of opinion – ultra High Church, and closely connected with the Oxford Movement of the 1830s[14] – which was opposed to Erastianism, and hence to the notion of state grants for building churches. Here they were on common ground with their most extreme opponents; but their views, expressed through such organs as the *British Critic* (after Newman became editor in 1838), were based not on the needlessness of new churches, but on the desire to see the people themselves building them, in a manner they imagined churches were built 'in truly Catholic days'. 'Parliamentary money has not done the Church much good; it has

St Paul, Wilton Place, Westminster (Thomas Cundy, 1840-2).

Above: **228** Interior, looking west in 1967. An expensive but essentially old-fashioned church, despite its hammerbeam roof. It cost nearly £6.12s. a sitting, but received only £1,000 grant.

Below: **229** Chancel as seen *c.*1850. Cundy, however, followed the Ecclesiologists in providing a true, elevated chancel, with sedilia for the ministers.

proved like that kind of food which puffs up more than it nourishes; it has been blessed neither in the giver nor in the receiver.'[15] A few years later Ruskin, putting the 'Lamp of Sacrifice' first among his lamps of architecture, wrote: 'It is not the church we want, but the sacrifice; ... not the gift, but the giving.'[16]

*****

During the last period of its life the Commission acted chiefly as an administrative body, superintending the work of church extension, but always deeply involved, as mentioned above, in detailed questions about forming parishes, establishing scales of pew rents, and obtaining sites not only for churches, but also for burial grounds (320 between 1838 and 1848, 'taking care that the sites are well selected and the purchase money and cost of enclosure reasonable'), and parsonage houses, work that required a proper investigation of titles and 'the removal of legal difficulties in many instances, which but for the assistance of the Board would have been insurmountable'.[17] The Board, faced in February 1850 with the Manchester Rectory Division Bill, with its medley of Peel districts formed by the Ecclesiastical Commissioners, district parishes and chapelries formed by the Board itself, and others by the bishop under an 1831 act, declared, ineffectively, that ecclesiastical division should be under its exclusive jurisdiction.[18]

At the close of 1845 the Secretary was directed to inform applicants that: 'The exhausted state of their finances will not admit of their making any grant,' though (hope not yet dead) details would be kept lest 'future circumstances ... admit of H.M.'s Commissioners making fresh grants'.[19] There were, indeed, few expensive churches applying for grants throughout the 1840s and 1850s: in 1842-3, St James, Paddington, designed to replace St Mary, Paddington Green, as the parish church, costing £11,500 for 1,616 sittings, was granted £2,000; and St Paul, Wilton Place, in Belgravia, its 540 free sittings perhaps intended to accommodate the poor of neighbouring Pimlico or the service ranks of the immediate locality, obtained £1,000 towards its £10,000 estimate and £3,200 site. An hugely expensive church, Holy Trinity, Bishop's Bridge Road, also in Paddington, but just north of the Park, received £1,000 in 1845-6 towards a cost of £18,459.[20] H. H. Norris's promotion of St John, South Hackney (£11,841) for 572 in pews and 935 free seats, received £1,000 in 1847-8; and in 1850-1, Holy Trinity, Haverstock Hill, St Pancras (promoted by a wealthy City rector), received £400 towards a cost of £10,054 for 1,426 sittings (851 free).[21] After mid-1848, of churches completed, only four received grants of more than £500.[22] But all these grants, except Haverstock Hill, were actually awarded before April 1846. After that date, there were only eleven grants of more than £300 awarded.[23] The Board's grant at this time was usually calculated on the basis of ten shillings per free sitting, down from one pound.[24] For lack of funds, the Commission had not been able to pay until the following year legal costs incurred in 1848-9 of £559.[25]

Although the Surveyor kept a critical eye on the new churches, irregularities were allowed to pass, such as there being no middle aisle in Holy Trinity, Oxford, where a reluctant approval was given, although the Board had earlier declared their entertaining 'so strong an objection … that they would be disposed to make an additional grant, provided such a centre passage could be obtained without diminishing the Accommodation and without adding side galleries'.[26] Similarly allowed, as all the sittings in the middle of the church were free, were no middle aisle, and a

Above: **230** St Thomas, Kimberworth, Rotherham (Matthew Habershon, 1841-2). Architect's drawing, showing substitution of bell-turret for tower, to bring cost below £3 a sitting (approved by both CBC & ICBS).

Left: **231** St John, Charlotte Street, St Pancras (Hugh Smith, c.1845). A neo-Norman church in a densely-populated London parish. It was allowed a grant despite the church's having been built before approval of the design. It lost the upper part of the south-west tower and the crossing spire.

Below: **232** All Saints, Ennismore Gardens, Westminster (Lewis Vulliamy, 1848-9). Interior, looking east, c.1944. The design may date from the mid-1830s; the columns are iron. The sgrafitto work was begun in the 1890s.

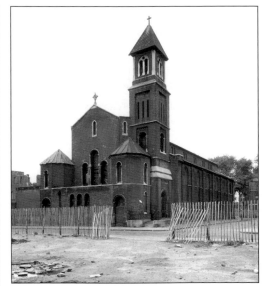

Neo-Romanesque churches of the late 1830s and early '40s in London.

Top left: **233** Holy Trinity, Gough Square, St Bride's parish (John Shaw, 1837-8). At £3.15*s*. a sitting, seating 1,100 in a hexagon 47ft 6ins in diameter; with an octagonal recess for chancel; double galleries on all sides save the east, on which there was only one; faced with yellow stock-bricks. This commission prompted Shaw to publish a pamphlet recommending Romanesque for new churches.

Top centre: **234** St James the Less, Bethnal Green (Lewis Vulliamy, 1840-2). South-west view, drawn by the architect. The church seated 1,133 at £4.6*s*. a sitting. The west front had some similarity to Vulliamy's All Saints, Ennismore Gardens, but the features were differently proportioned.

Top right: **235** St Andrew, Bethnal Green (Thomas Henry Wyatt & David Brandon, 1840-1). The asymmetrical tower was becoming a cliché, but the narthex was an unusual feature. The size and cost were very similar to St James the Less; each received £500 from the Commission.

Right **236** Holy Trinity, Blackheath Hill (James Wild, 1838-9). From north-east, *c.*1920. Twin towers for this style were not infrequent; it is surprising that they could be achieved for £3.14*s*. a sitting, but the church was built in yellow stock brick. Wild exhibited the design in the Royal Academy in 1836, and it was published in the *Companion to the Almanac*, 1840. Its plastic richness anticipates Pugin.

united pulpit and reading desk in front of the chancel, in St Alban, Bevington (Lancashire). All Saints, Burnley (Lancashire), was to have its grant, despite having been completed before its plans were approved[27] – though building at St John, Pendeen (Cornwall) was only authorized before the plans had been supplied, on condition that the walls were of dimensions and mode of construction stated by the architect, 'solely in consequence of the excellent feeling shewn by the Miners and population generally'.[28] Although the plans had not been submitted, the grant of £300 to St John, Charlotte Street, St Pancras, was similarly allowed to stand.[29]

Nevertheless, the Board continued to supervise design. In 1838, Habershon was obliged to forego his tower at Kimberworth (West Yorkshire) (pl. 230), in order to bring down the cost to under £2.12*s*.[30] At St John, Woolwich, Francis E. H. Fowler was told to enlarge the chancel arch.[31] Lewis Vulliamy was told to prepare a fresh elevation, 'particularly for the North side' of his proposed church in Ennismore Gardens, Westminster, 'as the general style and character of the Building as shewn in the reduced plans [to cost not more than £5,000] now laid before them does not possess that church-like Character and appearance which is so desirable particularly in a neighborhood like that for which the church is intended'. When additional funding permitted a return to the original, more expensive design, the Board stated its preference for the campanile shown in Vulliamy's perspective to that shewn in a geometrical elevation of the west end.[32]

Vulliamy's choice of a 14th-15th century Italian style is symptomatic of a period

264

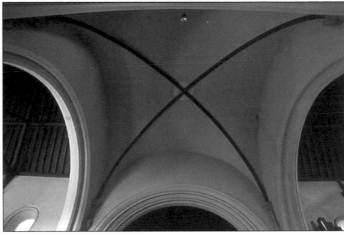

Neo-Romanesque in the Provinces.

Top left: **237** St Mary, Cardiff (Thomas Foster, 1841–3). Interior, looking east; photograph of 1895. A big church, for nearly 1,800, nearly two-thirds free, at £3.4s. a sitting. It is said to have been built at the expense of the 2nd Marquess of Bute, but the Commission granted £1,663. Note the massive three-decker pulpit in front of the altar.

Top right: **238** Dilton Marsh. Interior: rib-vault under crossing tower. 'Wyatt was a scholarly worker, with a good knowledge of various styles' (*DNB*).

Left: **239** Holy Trinity, Dilton Marsh, Wiltshire (Thomas Henry Wyatt, 1844). From southeast. Like some of Pugin's Irish churches: cruciform, with apse and crossing tower.

Left: **240** Christ Church, Watney Street, St George in the East (John Shaw, 1840). Interior looking east in 1907. The treatment of the gallery problem, with superimposed arcades, 'upon the system of the ancient triforium', is that advocated by Shaw in his *Letter on Ecclesiastical Architecture, as applicable to Modern Churches* (1839). The apse and raised choir are of 1870; originally, more than half the seats had been pews, with a potential rental of £634. Free seats may be discerned at the back of the gallery.

241 St Thomas, Charlton, Kent (Joseph Gwilt, 1849-50). A late example of the neo-Romanesque. Gwilt had praised the German Rundbogenstil ('round-arch style') in his *Elements of Architectural Criticism* (1837). Photograph of 1965.

that saw a wider range of stylistic models appear, under the varying influences of Pugin, the Ecclesiologists, and architects' growing familiarity with Continental church architecture, whether by means of the railway or the periodical press. The Ecclesiologists promoted the idea of spending money on churches, and their advocacy of the long chancel was unwelcome to the Commissioners. At St Paul, West Leigh (Lancashire), it was the 'great depth of the Chancel, and the position of the Tower' that concerned the Board, the tower standing Puginwise outside the south aisle.[33] Likewise, a chancel one-third of the length of the building in S. B. Gabriel's St Jude, Bristol, was only reluctantly approved: 'if the plans had been differently arranged, a larger accommodation might have been provided without detriment to the internal appearance of the church'.[34] Perkin & Backhouse were told to shorten the chancel at Cullingworth (West Yorkshire).[35] A general problem, familiar to today's planning committees, was the substitution of less expensive designs for some already approved, as with C. & J. Trubshaw's St Peter, Macclesfield (Cheshire), where a 'less decorative' design had been built.[36]

One mode of securing a 'less decorative' design was to apply a severe Norman (or in Continental terms 'Romanesque') style. The odd church had been built in 'Norman' in England in the early nineteenth century, and there was a measure of literary discussion of Romanesque in the 1820s. The perceptive architectural writer W. H. Leeds praised Ludwig I of Bavaria's patronage of the style in periodical articles of 1831 and 1834. But before the late 1830s there were few neo-Norman churches, although in 1827 Atkinson & Sharp, who had been awarded the commission for Travis Street, Manchester, after Taylor's untimely death, reported that

> We have adopted the Saxon or Norman stile of Architecture which we consider appropriate to the situation of the intended Chapel which will be environed by large and massive buildings employed in the manufactories of the place, and remote from the more decorated part of the town.
> This stile of building offers the advantages of great durability and economy, the more so

266

as it allows with great propriety of the employment of the coarse sandstone which is unfit for the more delicate ornaments of the Gothic.

They were, however, uncertain whether the 'general stile and character of the Designs' would meet the Board's views. At £15,000 for 2,000 sittings, they did not.[37]

The decade from the mid-1830s, in contrast, saw a brief flowering of the style.[38] Thomas Henry Wyatt (1807-80) was an early three-dimensional exponent, with St Paul, Newport (Monmouthshire), in 1835-6, followed by Glyntaff (Glamorgan) in 1838, and Dilton Marsh (Wiltshire), 1844. John Shaw, jun. (1803-70) found it to answer his requirements, contriving to seat 1,100 in a hexagon of less than 50ft diameter on an exiguous site in the parish of St Bride, Fleet Street, London, which prompted him to indite *A Letter on Ecclesiastical Architecture, as applicable to Modern Churches* (1839), to the Bishop of London, advocating the utility of the 'Lombardic' style. His most important church was Christ Church, Watney Street, Stepney (1840), with a twin-towered façade, to seat 1,250 at a cost of some £6,000. James Barr in 1842 advocated Norman for 'small rural churches' from its 'great simplicity';[39] witness Richard Carver's tiny St Paul, Easton (Somerset), 1842-3, which cost only £1,035 for 220 sittings (though that was £4.14s. a sitting: small churches were not necessarily proportionately cheap); more distinguished was St Mary, Oxenhope (West Yorkshire),[40] by Bonomi & Cory, 1844, £1,200 for 437 (all free). Romanesque was

242 St Michael, Stockwell, Lambeth (William Rogers, 1840-1). West front, much in the manner of Bedford's neighbouring St Mary-the-Less, the style termed 'Macaronic' by the *British Critic*.

St Jude, Mildmay Park, Islington (Alexander Dick Gough, 1854-5).

Above: **243** Woodcut, south-eastern view. With its highly-articulated exterior, cruciform plan, chancel and asymmetrical tower, one might take this for an exemplary post-Puginian church.

Opposite top: **244** The interior, however, pictured *c.*1870, suggests an unreconstructed pre-archaeological hand at work.

Opposite lower: **245** St Paul, Paddington, Salford (Edwin Hugh Shellard, 1855-6). Plan, showing compromise between ecclesiological and Commissioners' requirements: a distinct, elevated chancel, asymmetrical features at east and west, pulpit and reading desk of differing heights but placed at either side of and immediately to front of chancel, font at main entrance towards the west, western gallery only (for children), free seats corresponding precisely to rented pews.

a style judged appropriate for congested Bethnal Green, used for six of Blomfield's ten new churches. A late specimen was St Thomas, Charlton (Kent), 1849-50, by Joseph Gwilt (1784-1863), the encyclopaedist of architecture, who praised German Romanesque in his *Elements of Criticism* (1837); a round-arched church costing £5,000, built in red and white brick, with pilaster buttresses, the brick galleries supporting wooden columns crowned by a hammerbeam roof.

*****

Though there is little evidence of the use of new constructional techniques, such as iron-framing, in church-building during the 1830s and '40s, there had grown up a new and wider interest in church architecture. The ideas of those antiquaries who had been for twenty years past crying out from the pages of the *Gentleman's Magazine* for a 'correct' Gothic, were exploited by the brilliant young Augustus Welby Northmore Pugin (1812-1852); the Cambridge Camden Society was born, and for a brief year or two terrorized ecclesiastical architects into building 'Catholic' (i.e. quasi-medieval Gothic) churches; and Ruskin's great influence popularized these views. Such influences are observable in certain pronouncements of the Commissioners, but because of the change in the nature of their activities, the subject no longer occupied that central position which it had held in their deliberations in the twenties. We have noted above instances of plans including long chancels as drawing the Board's opprobrium, but by the 1850s chancels were undoubtedly a normal feature of church design. The new style spread rapidly: the 'lithographic papers' record an increasing number of long chancels and open roofs; in the accounts, the much diminished charges for plasterer's work reflect the increased popularity of these timber roofs and of exposed brickwork. Transepts and asymmetrically-placed towers become common. But these churches have a heaviness of detail, a certain grossness, far removed from the best work of the Million era.

Building costs continued to be reduced by the progressive repeal of various duties on the materials used, beginning with the reduction of the duty on slates in 1831; but this also reduced the Board's income from drawbacks. There was also, as referred to above, a slow adoption of industrial techniques, as in wood-working: powered saw mills from the 1820s; then wood-working machines, and in the 1840s carving machines.[41] New materials, however, were not encouraged: when G. L. Taylor suggested using Ranger's patent stone for the columns of the nave arcade at Sheerness, the Surveyor objected.[42] Iron, instead of being used more freely, almost disappeared from use. This was probably due in some measure to the influence of the Ecclesiologists (the Cambridge Camden Society and its allies), and especially Ruskin, who called it 'perhaps the most fruitful source of these kinds of corruption which we have to guard against in recent times'.[43] The Ecclesiologists carried their theory that medieval churches should be precisely imitated, to the length of excluding materials in common use, as well as new ones. Churches were buildings apart; 'Vulgar associations should be as much as possible excluded in their plan, materials, ornaments, etc.'[44] They wanted churches to be built of stone (chiefly for symbolic reasons) and would gladly have left brick to secular uses had not cost been a compelling factor. But they preferred even brick to stucco, 'as being a genuine material not needing constant renewal'. Long chancels separated the sacred altar from the congregation, and focused attention on it. The pulpit was not to be near the altar, which was to lie due east, with a middle aisle forming the chief approach to it. The sittings should so be spaced that the people might kneel. Such rules had, for the most part, been long observed by the Commissioners, but the Ecclesiologists based them on symbolism. These usages referred to 'certain divine realities'. Wide slate roofs and plaster ceilings were abhorrent to the Ecclesiologists: roofs should be open and high-pitched, 'after the ancient English model'. The Board's amended 'Instructions to Architects' of 1843, indicates Ecclesiological influence. More space was allowed for sittings to facilitate kneeling, and the pitch of the roof was required to be higher.

From about 1840 the question of consolidating the various and complex Church Building Acts had often been discussed, and schemes considered. Stephen Lushington, leading ecclesiastical lawyer, judge of the London Consistory Court and a Commissioner, declared that he knew the Acts 'to be a most complicated mass of confusion. ... every one conversant with those Acts must

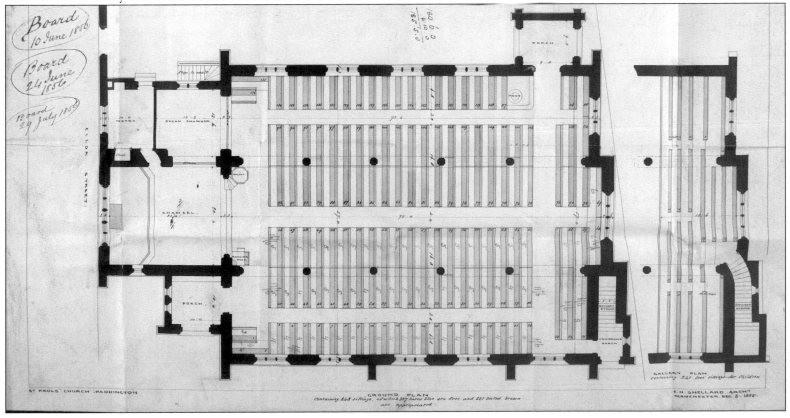

269

246 St Thomas, Coventry (Edmund Sharpe & Edward Graham Paley, 1848-9). North porch and bell-turret, by a practice that had thoroughly assimilated Ecclesiological doctrines. Photograph 1972.

know that scarcely a single provision can be considered alone, but reference must be had to prior or subsequent enactments'.[45] Yet such was the burden of legislation within the limited Victorian parliamentary sessions that time was not to be found for so complex and probably controversial a measure until members were more disciplined. Jelf wrote to the Treasury Solicitor on 18 April 1840, asking him to consider a consolidating measure because of their 'number and intricacy ... and the variety of matters introduced into them at different periods, as well as the vagueness and conflicting nature of many important provisions contained in them.'[46] But the Act of 1840 (3 & 4 Vic., c.60) was a mere tinkering. In 1842 a Bill was 'prepared and left at the Secretary of State's Office',[47] where it stayed. Dr Lushington worked on drafting that of 1845 (8 & 9 Vic., c.70), much amended in its passage,[48] which provided for the appointment of churchwardens for new districts (ss.6-8); provisions relating to consolidated chapelries were clarified (ss.9, 10). The Commissioners' power to fix pew-rent scales for any church to which they had made a grant was declared (s.11),[49] thus clarifying the 1818 Act; and the speed with which apportionment of fees, etc., might come into effect was increased by permitting an incumbent to resign the church of a district parish, which would count as an avoidance of the original parish (s.15); and a large number of miscellaneous points were modified or settled.

New Letters Patent were also issued during 1845, appointing additional Commissioners: a necessary step, as many of those of twenty years before were dead, or full of years. The metropolitan archdeacons were again called to fill some vacancies, and proved to be among the most active members for the final eleven years. William Hale Hale (1795-1870), Pott's successor as Archdeacon of London from 1842, was a protégé of Bishop Blomfield, having been closely connected with him since 1821, when he had been his curate at St Botolph, Bishopsgate, subsequently following him to Chester as domestic chaplain. John Sinclair, Archdeacon of Middlesex from 1843 (died 1875), also owed his advancement in some measure to Blomfield, whose examining chaplain he had become in 1839; three years later he had succeeded Archdeacon Pott as Vicar of Kensington. Benjamin Harrison (1808-87) was one of Archbishop Howley's chaplains, and a great Hebraist. Richard William Jelf (1798-1871) of the old High Church school, a brother of the Commission's Secretary, had succeeded Lonsdale as principal of King's College, London, in 1844.

Sir Robert Harry Inglis (1786-1855), the outstanding layman among the new Commissioners, was one of the old school of High Church Tories who believed, as we have seen, in the duty of the State to support the Established Church. He had started in public life as private secretary to Lord Sidmouth, and had ousted Peel as

Burgess for the University at Oxford after the minister's change of front on Catholic emancipation in 1829.

Further minor church-building legislation of the period dealt with assignments of patronage (9 & 10 Vic., c.88), and of ecclesiastical districts (11 & 12 Vic., c.37) – giving the Commissioners greater powers to modify boundaries.

The Commission was due to expire in 1848; and to present to the Government the case for its renewal the Secretary prepared a report[50] similar to that of 1837. The position on 1 April 1848 was that 411 churches had been built, 30 were building, and grants had been promised for 91 others, a total of 532 aided from the parliamentary fund. £12,700 was available for further grants, and £19,600 was still due in repayment of loans. After referring to the Board's duties of establishing pew-rent scales, forming districts,[51] etc., the report pointed out that there were now 15 Church Building Acts under which the Commission exercised various general powers in ecclesiastical matters; they were 'extending and improving the parochial system contemporaneously with the exertions which are making for the diffusion of education through the country'. The erection of a new church and creation of a district were closely connected with the institution of the National school. 'Without a church, the main objects of education cannot be attained and without an incumbent and a district belonging to such a church the daily instruction and super-intendence of the school cannot be safely reckoned on.' The continuity with the views of 1818 is very strong.

247 St Matthew, Great Peter Street, Westminster (George Gilbert Scott, 1849-50). Looking south-east in 1967. Ecclesiology was not a cheap option, and here it cost nearly £6.4s. a sitting; but three-quarters of the seats were free.

248 Christ Church, Trafalgar Road, Greenwich (John Brown, 1847-9). Looking east in 1967. Aisleless, but originally galleried nave, shallow apse, plastered ceiling; a late example of the auditory church.

249 St Saviour, Warwick Avenue, Paddington (Thomas Little, 1855-6). Looking east in 1967. A very late and expensive (at £7.5s. a sitting) galleried auditorium, a style 'we innocently thought had died out of London ... ten years back' (*Ecclesiologist*, 17 (1856), p. 425). Chancel of 1884.

The report recited other duties and powers of the Commission, and commented somewhat ingenuously: 'Even if Parliament should not immediately make a fresh grant of money, a useful and important branch of labour will with others connected with it survive to the Board after the exhaustion of their funds, in carrying on with care and impartiality and a due regard to the interests of the clergy and spiritual wants of the people the task thus specially entrusted to them by Parliament.' The Secretary concluded: 'The objects and duties of this Commission are easily distinguishable from those of the Ecclesiastical Commissioners and, except in the case of districts *(without new churches)* constructed under the 6 & 7 Vic., c.37,[52] and endowed out of the funds of that Corporation, bear no close resemblance to each other.'

The Archbishop of Canterbury transmitted this to the Home Secretary in the form of a memorial for the continuation of the Commission for a further ten years. Sir George Grey replied that, while intending to introduce a bill for the renewal of the Commission, 'under present circumstances' he did not 'think it expedient to do so for the same period as before'.[53] The Board expressed an anxious hope that he would reconsider his decision, but the 11 & 12 Vic., c.71, renewed the Commission for only five years.

The Treasury again inquired about the Commission's expenses, then running at about £3,500 annually. A select committee of the Board, considering the matter, pondered a reduction in the Surveyor's salary, but he, 'with feelings of much pain', responded that the labours of his office related to 'the number of plans examined and perfected and buildings surveyed by him' – since 1839, ranging from 40 to 58 a year. The Attached Architects had been abolished in 1832, along with the Office of Works: Good's labours were greater than when first appointed; 'all plans undergo the same critical examination and pass the same ordeal, whether the Board's grant be £5,000 or only £50 in aid of the building'. With rare exceptions (chiefly from being engaged elsewhere on the Commission's business) he attended the office daily. His salary was less than that of comparable official architects, and the usual charge of an architect paid by the day was from five to ten guineas.[54] The committee therefore reported that no saving was practicable except by reducing the Surveyor's travelling expenses to 1s. per mile (from 1s.6d.); and by accepting the report of the local surveyor to the Ecclesiastical Commissioners as to the proper construction of new churches in 'Peel districts'[55] in aid of which they had made a grant, instead of sending their own Surveyor – 'The amount now of the Board's grants is small and ... they are not responsible for the stability of the building'.[56] This suggestion was put into practice forthwith. Thus the two Church Commissions were brought more closely together. As with the I.C.B.S. (whose grants were now paid over to the Board, and with whom it was agreed in 1851 that both should examine plans before either affixed its seal),[57] these two bodies were to a large extent composed of the same personnel. The way was being prepared for their merging.

A Bill was printed in 1850, dealing with church rates and repairs, among other questions,[58] but it was not until the following year that a major measure was carried, though the church-rate question was again deferred. The 1851 Act (14 & 15 Vic., c.97) enabled the Commissioners to extinguish pew-rents where a satisfactory endowment had been provided: a significant move in the reverse direction to the earlier Act, and a reflection of the growing agitation against such distinctions in church. The apportionment of fees was arranged (ss.2-6) and provision for compensation made for their loss. Patronage again was the subject of further regulations (ss.7-15). The bishop's sole jurisdiction in certain cases was abolished; and the Commissioners given a universal power, subject to the bishop's consent, and the serving of due notice on incumbent and patron (who preserved his option to build), to declare the right of perpetual patronage to vest in persons building and endowing a church. Their power of dividing parishes, etc., was extended to those formed by the Ecclesiastical Commissioners (s.16) and those regulated by local Acts (5.2.1). The policy of refusing to form any more select vestries[59] culminated in the abolition of those already formed (5.23) – a step practicable now that churchwardens could be appointed for districts.

One has a sense of business being tidied up for conclusion in the proceedings of 1851, when the Board cancelled 20 outstanding grants made between 1839 and November 1848, unless the church were shown within a short time to have been started on the approved plans.[60] Co-operation between the Commission and the ICBS became closer; in February 1852 the two bodies agreed that neither would accept plans unsatisfactory to the other; and in March 1853 it was arranged that whichever received the plans in the first instance should have them made to its satisfaction before transmitting them to the other body: by this means time would be saved and mistakes avoided.[61]

In 1853 a measure was under consideration which would have allowed the sale of Crown livings. By this and other means it would have put '£6 or 700,000 into the chest of the Church building Commissrs. for Church extension, beside £9,000 a year for incomes'.[62] In 1854 a brief Act continued the Commission for a further two years (17 & 18 Vic., c.14).

Finally came the Act of 1856 (19 & 20 Vic. C.55), which extended the Commission for the last time – for a further six months to 1 January 1857, declaring that: 'It is expedient that the said Church Building Commission should be continued for a Time hereinafter limited, and that thenceforth the powers of the said Commission should be vested in the Ecclesiastical Commissioners for England.'

A few gleams of light are all that are thrown on the final five years of the Commission, which for want of the records cannot be studied in detail. In 1854 Archdeacon John Allen of Salop complained loud and long about the excessive legal charges made by the Commission's solicitor (the Treasury Solicitor) for investigating conveyances and titles to sites, charges that by Treasury order had to be borne by the local interests concerned. As a better model he cited the practice of the Privy Council Office in regard to sites for schools, a rather simpler matter. He then criticized the Commissioners for failing to do all in their power to promote church building. Jelf (whom he had found 'sitting without a written paper of any sort before [him], or (so far as [he] could see, any within reach') 'referred to the complexities of the Church Building Acts'. Allen retorted that as he supposed Jelf's office 'was consulted as to their framing, the country might charge part of that perplexity to your account'.

The Board defended its position, denying any analogy between conveyances for schools and those for churches, a much more complex business. After discussion with the Treasury, they found that the effect of Allen's proposed simplification of procedure would increase rather than save expense and delay.[63]

Allen persisted in his criticism, writing to *The Times*[64] and then to the prime minister, Palmerston. He also charged Jelf with incompetence and failing to give his whole time to the Commission's work (the terms of his appointment allowing him to undertake other duties). But after investigation by a Committee of the Board (the Bishops of Lichfield and Ripon, Archdeacon Sinclair and Sir R. H. Inglis), Jelf was completely exonerated: 'during a very able and faithful service of twenty-three years, Mr Jelf has shewn himself perfectly master of the business of his office; that he has constantly given to it the full measure of attention which it required; and has thereby conferred great benefit upon the Church'. When ill-health persuaded Jelf to resign towards the close of 1854, the Board again recorded 'their sense of his faithful and able services'.[65] To succeed him, Thomas Beachcroft was appointed, who had 'zealously and efficiently discharged the duties' of Chief Clerk since Richardson's exit in August 1834, and whom Allen had mentioned to Palmerston as 'highly spoken of by all who have had dealings with him'. William George Kent, appointed a clerical assistant at £1 a week in 1836, was promoted to Chief Clerk at £250 p.a., having displayed his assiduity by compiling, in his own time, a list of 651 churches to which districts had been assigned. The result of these and other promotions was a saving of £251 p.a., 'while a graduated increase in the Salaries of the majority of those employed recognizes their past services and encourages future exertions'.[66] But the axe fell on 1 January 1857. Beachcroft was retired on £200 and Good on £466.13s.4d. p.a. The Church Building Commission was absorbed into the Ecclesiastical Commission.

Although the Commissioners' work was not completed – the Royal Commission on the sub-division of parishes was told in 1853 of the immediate need for 600 new churches,[67] – yet its funds were largely exhausted, and such grants as were being made were for the most part purely nominal in order to permit the establishment of pew-rent scales. The creation of new districts was to a large extent carried out by the Ecclesiastical Commissioners, and there would be an obvious saving of administrative costs, and perhaps a gain in efficiency and convenience in merging the two bodies whose functions were so complementary. At the same time a consolidating bill was again considered, but it was 1863 before it was printed. Presumably time was lacking to consider its four hundred clauses, and it was dropped. Not until the Statute Law Revision Acts of 1873 and 1875 were the Church Building Acts tidied up.

14

The Church Building Commission: Some General Conclusions

'Of late years an abundant shower of curates has fallen upon the North of England.'[1] Church extension schemes had evidently had some effect there, in Charlotte Brontë's view. In concluding, one may try to estimate how far the Church Building Commissioners had succeeded in the task on which they had been at work for thirty-eight years. The original purpose of the Commission had been to make better provision for public worship according to the rites of the Church of England: this implied building and furnishing a church and providing for a minister. Fundamental in this was the preservation of the traditional parochial system. One of the Commission's functions was to decide the status of a new church: chapel-of-ease, district parish, or separate and distinct parish. The division of a parish into distinct parishes entailed a division of any endowments, of glebe, tithes, surplice fees; and a decision about patronage. In Birmingham it was possible, thanks to a co-operative rector and patron, to divide the extensive glebe among new parishes.[2] Elsewhere, interested parties might block similar proposals.[3] And in the great northern parishes, with ten or fifteen townships each to be provided for, the financial sources were inadequate: Leeds, for example, with a population in 1841 of 152,000, embraced 11 townships, and 21 Anglican chapels of which 18 lacked 'cure of souls' (i.e., could not receive surplice fees).[4] Many of the new towns exhibited similar problems. Recourse to pew rents was the only practicable solution. But, as we have seen, pew rents were often barely adequate as a nominal provision for a minister. They proved an uncertain one: middle-class renters in the industrial towns tended to move to the suburbs; Andrew Saint has written of small but fashionable London parishes 'beginning by the end of the [nineteenth] century to rely for their congregations on non-parishioners'.[5] The result was, as early as 1840, the creation of what Professor Ward terms 'a clerical proletariat, who 'saw their income restricted, their usefulness circumscribed, their new churches already decaying'.[6] The ever-increasing complexity and scope of the Commission's activities are in some measure an indication of its success in building of new churches, but at the same time its failure to resolve the sequential problems.

The funds at the disposal of the Commission were the two parliamentary grants totalling one and a half million pounds, the drawbacks of duty paid on customable and excisable materials used in building churches,[7] the interest on these monies and on loans made from them, and some insignificant sums derived from legacies. By 1838 some two millions had been spent on 225 Commissioners' churches. By 1856, the total sum derived from public funds paid out by the Commission in aid of church-building was about £1,675,000. A further £14,864 remained in their hands, to be transferred to the Ecclesiastical Commissioners; of this sum £10,240 had already been promised in grants to fifty churches.[8] These grants had been met by subscriptions, or parish rates totalling, up to February 1853, £1,356,000, and by the end of 1856 another £200,000 had probably been raised. This total of over three million pounds had provided 612 churches.[9]

Overton estimated that between 1818 and 1833 six millions sterling were spent on building and enlarging churches.[10] The Customs and Excise 'drawback account' published in 1838 shows that duty had been recovered on 512 churches in England and Wales of which 44 per cent (costing some £2,000,000) were Commissioners' churches.[11] As it was the Commissioners' rule from 1840 only to allow an application for the drawback of duty where more than £400 had been spent in the work, this suggests a considerable total expenditure, though perhaps not quite as much as Overton estimated. In his survey based on the 1851 census, Mann calculated that 2,020 new churches had been built in the twenty years since 1831, at a cost of some six millions, only half a million of which derived from public funds. During the Commission's life, 1818-56, clearly at least eleven millions were spent on church-building, including enlarging churches.[12]

In the Commissioners' churches accommodation had been provided for nearly 600,000 worshippers, including some 358,000 free places, at an average cost of roughly £5 per sitting. But while this was being accomplished, the population of England had increased by seven millions: for every new seat there were twelve new inhabitants. Thus the Commissioners' efforts alone had not succeeded in keeping pace with the increased population. But Mann found that the Church of England in 1851 provided accommodation for about five millions, or well over a quarter of the population. This was only half what was considered desirable, but in many industrial regions the situation had much improved within twenty years. In 1831 there had been one church for every 4,578 persons in Lancashire: in 1851 one for every 3,899. Similarly in the West Riding, there was now one church for every 2,384 instead of 3,431. On the other hand, in the archdeaconry of Durham, where population increase had been exceptional, despite an increase of 22,820 sittings between 1801 and 1851, the proportion of the population provided for had sunk from 37 per cent to 18 per cent. The religious census showed the proportion of the Durham archdeaconry population attending Anglican services to be only 26 per cent: the national average was 48 per cent.[13] Over the country as a whole, the distribution was more satisfactory than at the earlier period, and the Church was in a much stronger position generally in the industrial towns, though the proportion of church-room to population nationally had slightly fallen (one church for every 1,296 instead of 1,175).[14] In general terms, the Church had retained its leading position. But to maintain that, let alone increase its lead, it would have to run faster than ever. As the

Sub-division of Parishes Commission discovered in 1853, six hundred new churches were needed immediately.[15]

Although the brave hopes of 1818 had not been realized, without the impetus given to voluntary efforts by the work of the Commission, the Church of England would surely have declined to a numerically insignificant position, and become a church of rank and wealth disassociated from the mass of the people. Mann shows that church-building roughly doubled itself in each successive decade from 1811 to 1851;[16] for this progression the Commission may fairly claim a large part of the credit. Not only did it supply a stimulus financially, but by its experience it was able to formulate legislation enabling private beneficence to have the fullest rein within as without the Church.

How far the work of the Commission affected the morals of the industrial classes, in an age noted for its philanthropic effort, is almost impossible to say. In 1823 a squire had described in glowing terms the transformation wrought in one corner of Hampshire by the building of the church at Bransgore (Bransgrove), and the consequent presence of a minister.

> Our numerous population heretofore consisted, in a very great degree, of smugglers, poachers, etc. ... The Sabbath which heretofore was really a carnival - spent in boxing, riot, and debauchery, is now a day of order, repose, and solemnity; the public worship of the Church is regularly attended, morning and evening, by multitudes ... a cleanliness of person succeeds to filth and neglect, and an exhibition of perfect respect to superiors is never wanting.[17]

Many of the incumbents of the new churches announced that they had gratifyingly large congregations; but a note of disappointment was sometimes heard. The Archdeacon of Nottingham complained that although he had, at St Paul's (pl. 45), congregations of more than 1,200 every Sunday, the pews were not all occupied, and it was difficult to collect the pew-rents: in consequence he was compelled to pay his curate more than he received from the rents. Finding it impossible so to continue, he announced his intention of closing the church.[18]

Elsewhere, congregations sometimes fell off because the position of the pulpit made it difficult to hear the preacher throughout the church: preaching was still a great attraction. Sometimes the complaint was the converse to that from Nottingham: that the poor did not attend. 'A church by itself was a weak lure for the urban masses'.[19] A reviewer declared in 1840: 'The vast Ionic and Corinthian temples built twenty years ago, though inviting the multitude with all the eloquence of porticos, cupolas, and handsome iron palisades, are, after all, frequented almost exclusively by persons who could well have afforded to build the churches out of their own pockets.'[20]

To some extent, subsequent building in less salubrious districts may have contributed to this result, as in Bethnal Green in the 1840s; but that eleven-year enterprise appears not to have been altogether successful, several of the clergy, finding themselves 'operating in impecunious isolation', taking to odd behaviour.[21] A similar criticism was made in 1851 that local action was aroused chiefly to meet the needs of the middle classes. 'The considerable addition made ... to the religious edifices of large towns has been in very near proportion to the rapid growth, in the same interval, of the prosperous middle classes.'[22] The Commissioners, however, were anxious that their churches should cater for all classes, and in order to foster the harmony of the community had opposed wholly-free seating; while wholly-rented seating was forbidden by the Church Building Act. The erection of churches, each with its minister, and the extension of the National schools system which went hand-in-hand with it cannot have been without influence on the life of many of the poor. It is, however, arguable that too many churches were built, or the wrong sort of church. The 2,000-seater battleships of the 1820s were soon obsolescent, the middle-class pew-renters migrating, as remarked above, to the suburbs; while a great part of the still-resident population was irredeemably secular in its outlook, and indifferent to religion.

The Commission was in its day both a guiding and a liberating influence. It canalized the liberality of individuals within the bounds of the parochial system of the Established Church; and at the same time lifted restraints, so enabling churchmen to aid their holy Mother: previously a matter of extreme difficulty. 'The progress of the Church of England has, in recent times, been very rapid, and conspicuously so within the twenty years just terminated [1851]. Latterly, a sentiment appears to have been strongly prevalent, that the relief of spiritual destitution must not be exclusively devolved upon the state.'[23] The Commissioners had done much to foster this sentiment and the 'spirit of benevolence' which was being diffused. Perhaps the parochial system was not the best that might have been devised for the evangelization of the industrial areas. Fewer churches, each served by a staff of priests, might have proved more efficient in the long run: since the early twentieth century considerable numbers of these churches have been demolished: the population has been removed and the church must follow suit.

Yet among the multiplicity of interests permeating the early nineteenth-century Church, and the confusion of laws governing its several aspects, it would surely have been impossible to set up official non-parochial churches and difficult to provide for several priests in a single parish. The progressive sub-division of the old parishes was the most effective practicable way of promoting the doctrines of the Church in the great towns at that time.[24] Professor Ward suggests that the huge ancient parish of Manchester 'might have made an excellent missionary diocese', but points out that 'any concerted attempt to tackle its problems was deferred indefinitely by the triumph of Anglican parish mythology in the Manchester Rectory Division Act' (1850).[25] James Fraser, Manchester's second bishop (1870) would probably have agreed: he was an early advocate of team ministries. Dr Mole has remarked that despite the division of Leeds parish and endowment of 17 new parishes there between 1844 and 1851, the problem remained of making the parish an effective unit of pastoral oversight: 'the rural ideal for the urban parish had broken under the strain'.[26]

The Commissioners' operations were clearly facilitated at the start by their being in the main a group of men already long accustomed to working together in Church affairs. A preview of the problem had already been obtained from their work in the Church Building Society. The close connection between these two bodies, their similar composition, was of great value in, first, ensuring that they did not duplicate one another's work; and then as the Commission assimilated, of necessity, its methods to those of the Society, in harmonizing their operations. Similarly, in 1856 the transfer of functions to the Ecclesiastical Commissioners will have been facilitated by the presence of many members on both Commissions.

The anonymity of a Board's proceedings make it difficult to trace the influence of individual members; and their policy was ultimately controlled by the ministers of the Crown. But during the 1820s Joshua Watson was the key figure, employed by bishops as their channel of communications with the Board, and sought out for advice by petitioners. The most active Commissioners were his close friends, who had the utmost respect for his judgement. In the 1840s his place was yielded to his friend, Bishop Blomfield, who by his energy and willingness to work with forces of reform, secured the dominant position in all affairs of Church administration during the 1830s, when others had given up the Church's cause for lost.

So far as the new churches architecturally were concerned, the influence of the three architects of the Office of Works was significant in questions of construction rather than design. Archdeacons Wollaston and Cambridge pontificated on design issues, and Benjamin Stephenson, the Surveyor-General of Public Works, who was a regular member of the Building Committee, may well have contributed comments; while Joshua Watson was ever at hand with practical advice. From 1821 the creation of the office of Surveyor to the Commission introduces a new factor, chiefly, again, in constructional matters, but also reporting on design features. Initially, however, local interests, frequently dominated by the clergy, had a crucial role in selecting designs from lively competition from work-hungry architects whose skills, whether of design or construction, varied vastly. In the later period when the Board was making only small grants, it left a lot to the Surveyor and the local interests. But throughout its life, the Commission was closely concerned to ensure the stability and durability of the churches for which it was, in some measure at least, paying. It was similarly concerned to ensure that the buildings had a church-like character, both externally and internally. Generally speaking, a tower was an essential indicator, though penury forced an acceptance of bell-turrets in lieu, and internally a particular arrangement was specified, though, again, local circumstances might impose modifications: the visibility to all the congregation of the ministerial altar, placed at the east, and the audibility of the minister were the key elements, together with a large capacity.

Although there was a variety of styles from which to choose, these requirements, together with price controls, imposed a measure of uniformity on the Commissioners' churches, of which the most obvious are the height required for side galleries and the absence of a distinct chancel. That feature, coupled with the habit of architects either to employ a Classical style, or to compose their Gothic churches from a collection of design items (instead of copying an old church more or less as a whole), brought down on the Commissioners' churches the obloquy of the Victorian Ecclesiologists, who have proved among the most successful of propagandists. Their views are still prevalent today, despite the increasing regard for Georgian ecclesiastical architecture. Indicative of the continuing force of that restrictive mind-set is the exclusion from a selection of 'England's thousand best churches' of any church by Barry, Goodwin, Hardwick, Nash, Oates, Smirke, Soane, or Thomas Taylor; with only a private commission by Rickman, – and by Chantrell only Leeds parish church, apparently for the liturgical significance of the Rev. W. F. Hook, its Victorian decoration and surviving features from the old church.[27]

Summerson, who once wrote that the Commission's architects concerned themselves with only two problems: how to accommodate 2,000 people, and how 'to make a great show at the west end' and yet keep within the appropriation,[28] came round to acknowledge their ingenuity, good workmanship, and graceful, even brilliant composition of steeples and porticos.[29] But it was often the siting as much as the financial limitations that forced architects to concentrate their effects; and given the standard plan, the west end was the obvious place and efficient place for this, with entrances to the gallery stairs inviting a picturesque composition. If closely circumscribed, as Rickman found himself at St Thomas, Birmingham, there was no alternative; if an insulated site on a hill, as Goodwin's St George, Kidderminster, or Thomas Taylor's St Mary, Quarry Hill, Leeds, it was a Stendhalian *devoir de situation*.[30]

A less blinkered vision than the later Victorian (accepted undiscriminatingly by most in the twentieth century) cannot but admit that the Million churches in particular have notable qualities of effective siting, form and proportion, picturesque grouping of architectural elements, effective and lively features in the townscape (though many sadly need cleaning). A Goodwin tower in an industrial town lifts the spirit, as does Nash's playful steeple in Langham Place; large windows with slender cast-iron tracery make for light-filled interiors; the altar recess (if not replaced by a Victorian chancel) suits the current liturgical fashion; galleries take off from any barn-like character in spacious naves. One contemporary referred to Barry's St Matthew, Camp Field, as, after the Collegiate Church, 'one of the most beautiful buildings in Manchester'.[31] Marcus Whiffen writes of the manifest sensibility of Barry's design, commenting 'correctness is not everything – or for that matter as much as ... Victorian critics believed'.[32] A recent historian while criticising the 'stiffness and rigidity ... [and] enslavement to symmetry', perceptively praises the 'architectural experimentation which characterizes the Commissioners' Million Fund churches', the 'ingenuity in the plaster vaulting', and their 'measure of power and impressiveness'.[33]

These features need to be studied, the churches looked at with a seeing eye, as alert and informed an eye as that focused on a medieval church. Where did a Savage or a Goodwin gather his ideas? Nor should we ignore the innovative handling of iron displayed by several of the Commission's architects in the 1820s, as in Rickman's remarkable roof in St George, Chorley. The churches must be seen in the terms of their own day, as well as in the terms of the present day, with regard to both architecture and patterns of church use.

The Commissioners' care to ensure high standards of workmanship was a significant factor in the nineteenth-century building industry, and the erection of a hundred churches in the 1820s a valuable contribution to the domestic economy, giving employment to thousands of craftsmen and labourers in a period of instability. On the debit side must be set the Commissioners' contribution to the utilitarianism which overtook church-building at the end of the 1820s and through the '30s, – from which it was the merit of Pugin, the Ecclesiologists, and Ruskin to rescue it. But nonetheless the importance of obtaining a sound construction before laying out money on lavish ornament had been impressed upon architects. The insecurity which Kenneth Clark attributed to early nineteenth-century churches[34] was not a failing of those built by the Commission. If the churches of the 'thirties were dreary 'god-boxes', they at least avoided the perilous insecurity of Fonthill. And it was the great revival of church-building by the 1830s which paved the way for the flowering of the Ecclesiological school. Their plea and Ruskin's was to stress the necessity of providing funds for ornament as well as basic construction; and for the further development of ecclesiastical architecture in the direction of that Catholic revival which was the main Anglican contribution to Christianity in that century. The importance of the Commission in church-building is not merely, as Kenneth Clark would have it, that it provoked the Ecclesiological reaction, but that it alone rendered development possible.

Abbreviations & Notes

BL	British Library
CBC	Church Building Commission
CC	Church Commissioners
Cmns Jnls	*Journals of the House of Commons*
Comm.	Committee
DBA	Howard Colvin, *A Biographical Dictionary of British Architects 1600-1840* (3rd edn)
Dec.	Decorated
Dem.	Demolished
DNB	*Dictionary of National Biography*
E.Eng.	Early English
GR	Goodhart-Rendel card-index of nineteenth-century churches and architects in the RIBA Library
ICBS	Incorporated Church Building Society
LPL	Lambeth Palace Library
MB	Minute Book
PP	*Parliamentary Papers (House of Commons)*
PP (HL)	*Parliamentary Papers (House of Lords)*
ODNB	*Oxford Dictionary of National Biography*
Parl. Deb.	*Parliamentary Debates*
Perp.	Perpendicular
PRO	Public Record Office, Kew (now National Archives)
RIBAD	Royal Institute of British Architects Drawings Collection (now at Victoria and Albert Museum)
S.M.	Sir John Soane's Museum
SR	Surveyor's Reports

Chapter 1

1 Archdeacon John Law in his charge to his Rochester clergy, 1811, stressed their role in discouraging 'the restless spirit of innovation' that led to insubordination. Cited by R. Hole, *Pulpits, Politics and Public Order in England 1760-1832* (Cambridge, 1989), p. 184.

2 This was essentially a Church response to a 'British and Foreign Schools Society' founded three years earlier, in 1808, largely by dissenters, and seen by Anglicans as promoting deism, Hole, *Pulpits*, pp. 193-5.

Notes to page 15.

3 Cf. P. Gay, *The Geography of Religion in England* (Worcester, 1971), p. 72: 'There were virtually no churches built from the beginning of the eighteenth century to the time of the Million Act in 1818.'

4 A. D. Gilbert, *Religion and Society in Industrial England. Church, Chapel and Social Change, 1740-1914* (1976), p. 7. But G. Best, *Temporal Pillars. Queen Anne's Bounty, the Ecclesiastical Commissioners, and the Church of England* (Cambridge, 1964), p. 202, n. 8, sees this as illustrating the Parliamentary return's 'incompleteness as a description of how non-resident incumbents saw to the serving of their churches'.

5 Archbishop Howley in 1835 stressed 'the great evils occasioned by impropriations … absolutely the revenues which should go to the support of parochial clergy. Next to the accumulated population of large Towns … this misappropriation of property originally destined for the spiritual improvement of the people is the greatest misfortune to the Church'. Howley to Sir R. Peel, 30 Jan. 1835, BL, Add. MS 40412, ff. 207-8.

6 *PP* 1809, IX, 37; Gilbert, *Religion and Society,* p. 5; Best, *Temporal Pillars,* pp. 29, 204. About one-fifth of the impropriations were owned by the higher clergy, Gilbert, ibid. Best refers to the lack of respect experienced by poor clergy, *Temporal Pillars,* p. 14.

7 Best, *Temporal Pillars,* pp. 152-3. Increasingly the clergy were taking a role as J.Ps in the counties; see A. Russell, *The Clerical Profession.*

8 Best, *Temporal Pillars,* pp. 166-8; Gilbert, *Religion and Society,* p. 72. See C. Brooks, 'Building the rural church', in C. Brooks and A. Saint (eds), *The Victorian Church. Architecture and Society* (Manchester, 1995), for its partial survival in Devon: 'more church-building and restoration were undertaken, and sustained more consistently over a longer period, in parishes where the squire was resident than in squireless parishes', p. 56; also p. 63 for Leicestershire. A similar situation could prevail where a dominant manufacturer, not necessarily Anglican, was a squire-substitute (a situation that needs further exploration), as with Jedediah Strutt at Belper about 1820.

9 Gilbert, *Religion and Society,* pp. 98-9, referring to J. Thirsk, *Agrarian History of England, IV, 1500-1640* (Cambridge, 1967), pp. 2-14, for character of 'highland' and 'lowland' areas; Best, *Temporal Pillars,* p. 153.

10 Gilbert, *Religion and Society,* p. 100. Based on *PP,* 1812, XI, p. xxix. This gives an average population per parish in the two counties of about 6,400 in 1811, which is just ten times the population traditionally considered appropriate for an average parish (ibid., p. 117, citing Rev. R. Yates, *The Basis of National Welfare* (1817), p. 122; though the average here misleads, as some were much more heavily populated towns, and others had huge areas hardly populated save in occasional industrial villages.

11 Figures vary: S. Lewis, *Topographical Dictionary of England* (1831), sub Blackburn, and W. A. Abram, *History of Blackburn* (Blackburn, 1887), p. 587, give 22 townships/chapelries; *VCH, Lancashire,* VI (1911), names 24 (and map, p. 236), and CC 15217, pt 1, petition, states the number as 26; *VCH, Lancashire,* V (1911), measures Rochdale as 41,828 acres; CC 18219, petition, states the area of Warrington as 'about 16,000 acres', but *VCH, Lancashire,* III (1907), as 12,954 acres; CC file 20536, petition.

12 R. A. Soloway, *Prelates and People. Ecclesiastical Social Thought in England 1783-1852* (1969), p. 281.

13 Notably that of Dr Terry Friedman, e.g., *Church Architecture in Leeds 1700-1799* (Leeds, 1997), showing that between 1708 and 1793 there were seven Anglican churches built in Leeds and its suburbs, and one more purchased. Already in 1963, Rev. B. F. L. Clarke (who mentions three Leeds churches) listed 114 eighteenth-century statutes for building or re-building churches, *The Building of the Eighteenth-Century Church* (1963). National statistics are disputatious: the *Convocation of Canterbury Report* (1876), pp.22-7, states that 28 new churches were built, 1801-10, and 70 in 1811-20, whereas Gilbert, *Religion and Society,* p. 28, table 2.1, numbers of churches and chapels, based on *Parliamentary Papers,* shows an increase of 65 in the first decade and 114 in the second.

14 Cp. N. Yates, R. Hume and P. Hastings, *Religion and Society in Kent 1640-1914* (Woodbridge, 1994), pp. 25-6.

15 On which see W. B. Maynard, 'The Response of the Church of England to Economic and Demographic Change: the Archdeaconry of Durham, 1800-1851', *Journal of Ecclesiastical History,* 42 (1991), pp. 437-62. Kelloe, for instance, was a purely agricultural parish in 1831, with a population of not more than 700; in 1834 a colliery opened at Thornley, followed by four more in other townships of the parish, which in 1841 had a population of more than 11,200.

16 As Archbishop Howley admitted to Peel in 1835, writing of 'the accumulated population of large Towns, which from its denseness and the peculiarity of its Character, can never enjoy the full benefits of religious instruction'. BL, Add. MS 40412, ff. 207-8.

17 P. Virgin, *The Church in an Age of Negligence. Ecclesiastical Structure and Problems of Church Reform 1700-1840* (Cambridge, 1989), pp. 112-25; D. McClatchey, *Oxfordshire Clergy 1777-1869* (Oxford, 1960), chap. XII.

18 See W. R. Ward, *Religion and Society in England 1790-1850* (1972), pp. 51-62; Gilbert, *Religion and Society*, pp. 78-9.

19 E.g., Bishop Horsley of Rochester's denunciation of Methodism as a Jacobinical tool, *Gentleman's Mag.*, vol. 70 (1800), pt 2, p. 1077.

20 BL, Liverpool Pps, Add MS 38328, f. 23v, 3 Jul. 1812; for examples proving Liverpool's assertion, see J. Walsh, 'Methodism at the End of the Eighteenth Century', in R. Davies and G. Rupp, eds, *A History of the Methodist Church in Great Britain* (1965), vol. 1, p. 288.

21 W. R. Ward, *Religion and Society in England*, pp. 29ff.

22 D. Hempton, *Methodism and Politics in British Society 1750-1850* (1984), 15-16. In his *Religion and Political Culture in Britain and Ireland* (Cambridge, 1996), p. 34, Professor Hempton has remarked on the ambivalence displayed towards the Methodists by Anglican sympathisers at this time.

23 Gilbert, *Religion and Society*, pp. 7, 9-12, 106, 113-15.

24 CC file 18112, Wilson to George Jenner, 23 May 1825.

25 O. J. Brose, *Church and Parliament. The Reshaping of the Church of England 1828-1860* (Stanford, 1959), p. 17.

26 CC file 18158, 31 Jul. 1819.

27 J. B. Sumner, *A Charge Delivered to the Clergy of the Diocese of Chester* (1832), pp. 9-13, cited by R. A. Soloway, *Prelates and People*, pp. 309-10.

28 Virgin, *The Church in an Age of Negligence*, pp. 20-3.

29 For a broad summary of High Church views in this period, see P. B. Nockles, *The Oxford Movement in Context. Anglican High Churchmanship, 1760-1857* (Cambridge, 1994), pp. 25-6.

30 G. F. A. Best, *Temporal Pillars*, pp. 60-1.

31 A counterblast to the Evangelicals' manifesto proclaimed by William Wilberforce, *A Practical View of the Prevailing Religious System of Professed Christians in the Higher and Middle Classes ... contrasted with Real Christianity* (1797).

32 *DNB*.

33 G. I. Huntingford, *A Sermon Preached ... June 2, 1796, Being the Time of the Yearly Meeting of the Children Educated in the Charity Schools ...* (1796), pp. 23-4; cited by Soloway, *Prelates and People*, pp. 285-6. Huntingford became Bishop of Gloucester in 1802, and was translated to Hereford in 1815.

34 1732-1807. A City hosiery-merchant, ecclesiastical pamphlet writer, and treasurer of Queen Anne's Bounty 1782-1807.

35 1771-1855. His life and work are described by A. R. Webster, *Joshua Watson* (1954), where an account is also given of the Hackney Phalanx. See also E. Churton, *Memoir of Joshua Watson* (2 vols, Oxford, 1861), and P. B. Nockles' article in *ODNB*.

36 On which, see also P. B. Nockles, *The Oxford Movement in Context*, and E. A. Varley, *The Last of the Prince Bishops* (Cambridge, 1992), chapter 3.

37 1767-1839. Vicar (later Rector) of Hackney from 1799; Rector of Digswell (Hertfordshire) from 1811; Archdeacon of St Albans from 1816; and a prebendary of St Paul's from 1825. A contemporary of Lord Liverpool at Charterhouse and Oxford. See *ODNB*.

38 1771-1850. Curate of Hackney 1810; Rector of South Hackney 1845; prebendary of Llandaff 1816, of St Paul's 1825. 'Generally thought to be Lord Liverpool's confidential adviser on ecclesiastical patronage.' (Webster, *Joshua Watson*, p. 25).

39 1763-1838. Justice of the Common Pleas, and knighted, 1816. Author of *A Layman's Earnest Exhortation to a Frequent Reception of the Lord's Supper* (1804), and Stevens' biographer.

40 1771-1841. Justice of the Common Pleas 1818-24; knighted 1819.

41 1745-1823. A writer of religious pamphlets, of independent means, who supported Daubeny's doctrines. See *DNB* and *Memoir of the late John Bowdler Esq.* (1825), by his son Thomas, Secretary of the ICBS.

42 It was founded in 1800. A biographical list of members from 1800 to 1885, prepared by G. E. Cockayne, was printed for private circulation 1920.

43 Died 1819. Commissioner of Bankrupts. Wrote numerous pamphlets.

44 1767-1844. City merchant; High Sheriff of Kent 1831.

45 1776-1855. A Church Building Commissioner 1818.

46 Rev. William Jones (1726-1800), vicar of Nayland 1777. See *DNB* and Churton, *Memoir of Joshua Watson,* I, p. 104.

47 His last recorded attendance at a Board meeting was 24 Jun. 1851.

48 Best, *Temporal Pillars*, p. 123.

49 See below, p. 34.

50 Charles Manners-Sutton: see below, pp. 32.

51 Webster, *Joshua Watson*, p. 26.

52 See *ODNB*.

53 See Varley, *Last of the Prince Bishops*.

54 See below, pp. 32.

55 William Waldegrave, 1753-1825; third son of 3rd Earl Waldegrave; naval officer; created Baron Radstock, 1800; member of Nobody's Friends from 1806.

56 See below, p. 35.

57 Ibid.

58 City banker; friend of the Cottons (see below p. 285, n.102).

59 Churton, *Watson*, I, p. 7.

60 Ibid., p. 169.

61 Webster, *Joshua Watson*, p. 117. For Howley, see below, p. 31.

62 An anonymous correspondent told Howley, 28 Jun. 1817, that in five years in a parish the only accommodation he had been offered for his family was in a chapel of ease: half a pew at floor level, behind the pulpit, at an annual rent of ten guineas, LPL, Howley Papers, vol. 10, f. 221.

63 As in Buckerell church, Devon, for which see A. Warne, *Church and Society in Eighteenth-Century Devon* (Newton Abbott, 1969), pp. 60-1.

64 Soloway, *Prelates and People*, p. 285.

65 R. Watson, *Anecdotes of the Life of Richard Watson, Bishop of Llandaff* (1817), II, pp. 111-13.

66 R. Watson, *A Sermon Preached before the Society for the Suppression of Vice* (1804), quoted by Soloway, *Prelates and People*, p. 287.

67 J. Fisher *Sermon Preached before the Lords Spiritual and Temporal ... February 25, 1807*, quoted by Soloway, *Prelates and People*, p. 287.

68 Soloway, *Prelates and People*, p. 288. Randolph was concerned in 1811, however, with an abortive bill to encourage church-building, LPL, Randolph Pps, 15, f. 1.

69 Best, *Temporal Pillars,* p. 257. Marsh, the foremost English biblical scholar of his day, became Bishop of Llandaff in 1816 and was translated to Peterborough in 1819. See *DNB*.

70 *PP (HL)*, 1816 (116 and 118) LXXIX; 1818 XCIII.

71 *PP,* 1818 (5) XVIII.

72 See P. C. Hammond, *The Parson and the Victorian Church* (1977), chap. 1.

73 'In any change that altered the legal status of the benefice (erection of chapels-of-ease, daughter churches, parish division, exchange of lands or buildings) he had a right to be consulted and a power to prevent any change he disliked.' Private patrons owned 6,000 benefices. G. F. A. Best, *Temporal Pillars*, pp. 189, 235.

74 Best, *Temporal Pillars*, pp. 192-3. See also W. R. Ward, *Religion and Society*, pp. 110-11, 178.

75 W. A. Bewes, *Church Briefs, (*1896), p. 6.

76 Some parishes voted a fixed sum to be paid on each brief, sometimes as little as 2*d*. (Bewes, p. 49).

77 'From 1805, the annual average of briefs laid for rebuilding or repairs to churches was 6 to 7' (*PP*, 1819, XVII).

78 *C J, 74* (1819), app., pp. 1158-66.

79 Lord Sidmouth complained in 1811 that licences were being taken out by unsuitable people, *Parl. Deb.,* XIX, 1130 (9 May 1811).

80 An instance is quoted in *Parl. Deb. N.S.,* XI, 1080.

81 *C J, 58*, pp. 600, 602, 605, 612, 616, 619, 628, 637, Jul. 1803. It facilitated to a very limited degree the making of donations for these purposes.

82 See D. Gray, *Spencer Perceval, 1762-1812, the Evangelical Prime Minister* (Manchester, 1963).

83 *Parl. Deb.,* XIV, 831 (1 Jun. 1809); it was thought that of some 11,700 Church of England livings, 3,291 had an income of less than £150 p.a., of which 800 received less than £50.

84 Dudley Ryder, 2nd Baron and 1st Earl of Harrowby (1762-1847).

85 *Parl. Deb.*, XIV, 857 (2 Jun. 1809).

86 *Parl. Deb.*, XVII, 765, et seq.

87 Ibid., 770.

88 A scheme of church-extension was proposed to Lord Sidmouth in 1809 by Dr Booker, Vicar of Dudley (CBC, MB. 28, p. 78).

89 *Parl. Deb.*, XVII, 770. Lord Liverpool admitted (27 May 1811) the importance of 'some measure being adopted to facilitate the building of additional churches'. B.M, Add. MS 38323 f. 145. For the returns resulting from Sidmouth's Address, see *PP (HL)*, 1811 (48 & 75) XLVI.

90 *Parl. Deb.*, XXXVIII, 718.

91 LPL, Howley Papers, 10, ff. 215-19v; printed in T. Bowdler, *John Bowdler,* pp. 237-43.

92 G. Pellew, *Life of Lord Sidmouth* (1847), vol. 3, p. 138.

93 Henry Ryder (1777-1836), Bishop of Gloucester 1815, of Lichfield 1824.

94 Nicholas Vansittart (1766-1851), Chancellor of the Exchequer 1812-23, created Lord Bexley 1823.

95 Harrowby MSS., 3rd series, LVIII, p. 74 (dated 23 Nov. 1814).

96 T. Bowdler, *John Bowdler*, pp. 244-5.

97 As noted above, 'The church's main function was social control.' Best, *Temporal Pillars*, p. 152.

98 Cp. the remarks of the Dewsbury and Islington incumbents quoted above, pp. 17, 18.

99 ICBS, MB (Prior to foundation).

100 Sir Robert Harry Inglis, 2nd Bart. (1786-1855), M.P. 1824-6 and 1828-9; then displaced Peel as M.P. for Oxford University in 1829 (to 1854); a strong opponent of Roman Catholic relief.

101 1783-1869. An independent-minded M.P. for Ripon, 1807-23, and John Bowdler's son-in-law.

102 Joseph Cotton (1745-1825), Deputy Master of Trinity House, a director of the East India Co. His son, William (1786-1866), a director of the Bank of England from 1821, had been employed by C. H. Turner. An obituary (*Gentleman's Magazine,* 1867, I, p. iii*)* states: 'In a letter to John Bowdler, dated 1813, he suggested the formation of the Church Building Society.' His daughter married John Bowdler's son, Thomas. See *ODNB.*

103 See T. Falconer, M.A., *Outlines of a Plan for Building 25 Churches or Chapels at an Expence of £100,000 to Government, or, at no Expence to Government, should it be thought advisable to have Recourse to the Fund called Queen Anne's Bounty for this Purpose,* 2nd edn, revised and enlarged, 1818, in LPL, Howley Papers, vol. 10, ff. 225-6; Richard Watson, *Anecdotes*, II, 111-13.

104 1769-1834; a chaplain of Chelsea Hospital and Rector of Ashen, Essex; a popular preacher in the fashionable London chapels. See Best, *Temporal Pillars*, p. 147, and *DNB*, 'which [Best remarks] most deplorably under estimates the ability of Yates's writings on church reform'.

105 Best, *Temporal Pillars*, p. 148.

106 ICBS, MB (Prior to foundation).

107 Pellew, *Sidmouth*, III, p. 139. This sounds like a scheme similar to the annual grant of £100,000 to Queen Anne's Bounty made from 1809 to 1820.

108 Ibid., p. 140.

109 ICBS, MB (Prior to foundation).

110 As is indicated by two highly important returns made to the House of Lords in 1816: *PP (HL)* 1816 (116 and 118) LXXIX, 'Account of the Population, and Capacity of Churches and Chapels, in all Benefices or Parishes wherein the Population consists of 2,000 and upwards, and the Churches will not contain One Half': and 'Comparative Statement of the Population, and Capacity of Churches and Chapels, in all Parishes in which the Populations exceeds 4,000, and the Churches or Chapels will not contain One Fourth'. These papers were basic material with which the propagandists worked, but inaccuracies and omissions limited their value. Further inquires produced the returns of Feb. 1818, *PP* 1818 (5) XVIII, pp. 137ff., Account of benefices and population, &c.; and *PP* 1818 (4) XVIII, pp. 93ff., Accounts of Benefices or Parishes and Capacity of Churches &c.

111 Harrowby MSS, 1st series, V, p. 106.

112 BL, Liverpool Pps, Add. MS 38265, f. 119, 18 Mar. 1817 (see also f. 46, 8 Mar. 1817).

113 T. Bowdler, *John Bowdler*, p. 246.

114 *Hist.MSS.Comm. Kenyon,* pp. 464-5. C. Wordsworth to Lord Kenyon, 5 Dec. 1816.

115 ICBS, MB (prior to foundation).

116 1787-1871. An independent-minded M.P. for Devon 1812-18 and 1820-31, highly-

respected. Associated by marriage with the Clapham Sect of evangelicals. In 1828 Sir Walter Scott referred to him as 'the head of the religious party in the House of Commons'. See *DNB*.

117 Cf. BL, Liverpool Pps, Add. MS 38267, f. 211, Sir Thomas Acland and Mr Gipps to Liverpool, 30 Jun. 1817.

118 Also Lord Kenyon and F. Burton, but neither attended the decisive meeting (ICBS, MB Prior to foundation).

119 Another rule – to be strongly echoed in the Church Building Act and the Commissioners' regulations – was that in churches to which grants were made, 'no expense shall be incurred for ornamental architecture, beyond what shall ... be deemed essential to give ... the character of churches ... of the Established Religion'.

120 Webster, *Joshua Watson*, p. 63.

121 Watson, Nicholl, Burton, Cambridge, Pott, Van Mildert, Wordsworth, and Inglis. D'Oyly and Lonsdale were added later (ICBS, MB).

122 BL, Liverpool Pps, Add. MS 38271, Harrowby to Liverpool, 22 Mar. 1818, cited by Best, *Temporal Pillars*, p. 269n.

123 *Parl. Deb.*, XXXVII, 1116.

124 *Parl. Deb.*, XXXVIII, 709.

125 *PP* 1818, (5) XVIII (Feb. 1818), Account of benefices and population &c.

126 *Times*, 26 Mar. 1818.

127 With the important exception of Yates. In Dr Varley's view, Bishop Samuel Horsley (d.1806) would have provided a clerical lead: *The Last of the Prince Bishops*, p. 63.

128 Referring to the clergy. Harrowby MSS, 3rd series, LVIII, p. 74 (23 Nov. 1814).

129 C. R. Sumner, an Evangelical favourite of George IV, was put forward for a canonry by that king, in 1821; but Liverpool refused, on the grounds that his appointment would have offended the High Churchmen (v. Webster, *Watson*, p. 25, n. 2).

130 Instances include CC file 21744, pt 4 (21 May, 14 Sep., 1 Oct. 1822); CBC, MBs 3 (29 Feb. 1820); 6 (12 Feb. 1822); 19 (17 Nov. 1825); 25 (5 Jun. 1827); CC file 21745 (Jelf to Watson 8 Oct. 1834); S.M. X.H., 22 Jun. 1824 (Watson to Soane).

131 See M. H. Port, ed., *The Commissions for Building Fifty New Churches*, London Record Society, 23 (1986), pp. xxxiv-vi.

132 BL, Liverpool Pps, Add. MS 38272, f. 180, 24 Jun. 1818.

133 Ibid., ff. 181-2.

134 See J. R. Garrard's article in *ODNB*.

135 For sympathetic views of Howley, see O. Chadwick, *The Victorian Church*, I (1966), pp. 11-12, 133, 453, and Best, *Temporal Pillars*, p. 346; Soloway, *Prelates and People*, pp. 88, 227-8, 235, is more critical. He is the subject of an Oxford D.Phil. thesis (1992) by Garrard that I have not seen, doubtless summarized in his *ODNB* article.

136 LPL, Howley Pps, vol. 10, ff. 221-2; Howley, *Charge* (1818), pp. 17-19.

137 O. Chadwick, *The Victorian Church*, I (1966), pp. 11-12, 133. Cp. H. Reeve, ed., *The Greville Memoirs*, pt. I, ii, (1874), pp. 250, 263.

138 LPL, Howley Pps, vol. 10, ff. 245-8, 255.

139 Ibid., ff. 195-214, 259-64.

140 Ibid., ff. 245-306; CBC, MB 1, 10 Nov. 1818; MB 3, 16 May 1820; MB 12, 17 Feb. 1824.

141 He wrote to Lord Liverpool, 2 Jul. 1824, suggesting that Edward Davison (incumbent of St Nicholas, Durham) whom Liverpool had suggested for a vacancy at Kensington, 'might hold one of the new Churches in Marybone [*sic*] *with* his northern Living – residing eight months in London and passing the summer months in the Country. The only object is the distance. In other respects it is desirable that the Incumbent of a populous Parish in London should have a place of retirement in the hot weather.' BL, Liverpool Pps, Add. MS 38299, f. 34.

142 Harrowby MSS, 3rd series, LVIII, p. 74.

143 A grandson of the 3rd Duke of Rutland, and great-grandson of Robert Sutton, 2nd Lord Lexington.

144 Sixth son of the 1st Lord Vernon. In 1831 he assumed the surname of Harcourt, having succeeded to the estates of that family.

145 Soloway, *Prelates and People*, p. 250, n.

146 Soloway, p. 293; CC file 20812, pt 1, Bp Cornwallis to Jenner, 20 Aug. [1826]; see also CBC, MB 1 (8 Dec. 1818); MB 3 (6, 13 Jun. 1820). Mr Tomlinson, the patron of Stoke, who was avid for the new churches, agreed with Cornwallis's specific objections that, one imagines, so disturbed Professor Soloway, ibid., 13 Jun. 1820.

147 BL. Liverpool Pps, Add. MS 38272, f. 111, 10 Jun. 1818.

148 CBC, MB *I*, 23 Sep. 1818. He had recommended two new churches at Stoke, ibid., 8 Dec. 1818.

149 He had climbed through a deanery and three bishoprics before he was forty. When his brother, Frederick Lord North, the Prime Minister, was criticized for the rapid promotion of so young a man, he remarked that 'he might not have a Prime Minister as his brother when he was older'.

150 CC file 21744, part 1.

151 See Soloway, *Prelates and People*, pp. 50-1.

152 CC file 21744, part 1. On 7 Apr. 1820 he wrote to Lord Liverpool: 'As the building of the new churches at Manchester and its neighbourhood proceeded slowly, I thought it advisable to expedite the business, by looking after it on the spot.' (BL, Add. MS 38284, f. 48.)

153 For a list of the Commissioners, see Appendix 2.

154 They were appointed for this purpose on the diocesan's recommendation. (BL, Add. MS 38272, ff. 110-12.)

155 He had served on the Committee of the National Society from 1811.

156 This involved him in difficulties in his diocese when the Society fell from grace through accusations of Romanism, and he resigned his connection.

157 LPL, Howley Papers, vol. 10, p. 255, 21 May 1818. Unfortunately the letter is badly faded.

158 Churton, *Memoir of Watson,* I, p. 237.

159 Ibid., I, p. 200.

160 *DNB.*

161 Harrowby MSS, main series, V, 15 Apr. 1812.

162 He was instrumental in obtaining the second parliamentary grant, see Harrowby MSS, 1st series, XIV, p. 184.

163 *Farington Diary*, VIII (ed. K. Cave, New Haven and London, 1982), p. 3079, 3 Jul. 1807. Kenyon had been a pupil of the Rev. William Jones (1726-1800), Vicar of Nayland, a leader of the high-church party, whose intimate friend and biographer, Rev. William Stevens, was a close friend of Joshua Watson, see Webster, *Joshua Watson*, pp. 24-5. Kenyon was also a friend of Rev. Christopher Wordsworth (*Hist. MSS Comm., 14th Report,* App., pt 4, p. 563).

164 See Best, *Temporal Pillars*, pp. 192n., 200.

165 *DNB.*

166 This timid Act, which in its preamble notes the insufficiency of churches, allowed an individual or corporation to make a single gift of up to five acres or £500 for church building or parsonage house work, *PP (HL)*, 1802-03, V, p. 515.

167 R. G. Thorne, ed., *The House of Commons 1790-1820* (1986).

Chapter 2

1 *Times*, 16 May 1818, p. 2, a.

2 *Parl. Deb.*, XXXVII, 1116 et seq.

3 The Commons authorised government to issue half a million pounds worth of Exchequer bills for completing public works for the encouragement of fisheries and the employment of the poor; repayment was to be in small instalments. *Parl. Deb.,* XXXVI, 27.

4 1775-1855, Regius Professor of Civil Law at Oxford.

5 *Times*, 30 Apr. 1818, p. 3, b.

6 *Cmns Jnls, 73* (1818), pp. 217, 295, 304, 314, 321, 325, 359, 395-6 (Lords' amendments in detail), 402.

7 *Parl. Deb.,* XXXVII, 1162, 16 Mar. 1818.

8 *Times*, 1 May 1818, p. 2, d.

9 *Parl. Deb.*, XXXVIII, 426; *Times*, 1 May 1818.

10 The Simeon Trust, founded in 1817 by the wealthy Rev. Charles Simeon (1759-1836), bought advowsons and installed Evangelical clergymen on vacancies arising; see O. Chadwick, *The Victorian Church*, I (1966), p. 449.

11 Van Mildert, metropolitan incumbent and Regius Professor of Divinity at Oxford, who wrote to Peel, 30 Apr. 1818, warning him of the danger from Evangelicals possessed of considerable funds; cited, Soloway, *Prelates and People,* pp. 293-4.

12 *Times*, 1 May 1818, p. 2, d.

13 LPL, Howley Papers, vol. 10, p. 245-8.

14 On which, see Ward, *Religion and Society in England,* p. 113; P. Virgin, *The Church in an Age of Negligence,* pp. 36-40, 47-59.

15 LPL, Howley Pps, vol. 10, pp. 259-60, undated.

16 Ibid., p. 261.

17 Ibid., pp. 262-4.

18 *Parl. Deb.,* XXXVIII, 709.

19 Evidently the government envisaged churches at £10,000 each, which was the estimate suggested by Nash, although the other government architects had made much higher estimates. (See below, pp. 61-5).

20 *Parl. Deb.,* XXXVII, 830.

21 C. D. Yonge, *Life and Administration of … 2nd E. of Liverpool,* II, p. 362.

22 58 Geo. III, c.45.

23 59 Geo. III, c.134.

24 See M. H. Port, *The Commissions for Building Fifty New Churches,* (London Record Society, 23 (1986).

25 See below, p. 321, n. 49, note.

26 For example, Sheffield, in 1847, was worth only about £300 per annum (CBC, MB.63, p. 107).

27 See Best, *Temporal Pillars,* pp. 192-4, and below, pp.. 249-51 et seq.

28 For example, Lord Fitzwilliam, who gave a site at Sheffield, and contributed largely to building the new church at Greasborough.

29 *Times,* 26 Mar. 1818.

30 *Times,* 27 Mar., p. 2, d; 8 Apr. p. 3, b; 25 Apr. 1818, p. 3, e.

31 *Quarterly Review,* vol. 23, no. 46 (1820), pp. 549ff.

32 *New Annual Register,* 1818, p. 326.

33 A view shared by some High Churchmen in the 1840s. See below, pp. 261-2.

34 As it had been trying to do since 1803.

35 The term is sometimes applied only to the four churches built in the old parish of Lambeth (St John, Waterloo Road; St Luke, West Norwood; St Mark, Kennington; St Matthew, Brixton). This may originate from St John's having been commonly termed (even in the Minute Books of the Commission) 'Waterloo Church', which refers, of course, to its site. None of the Commissioners' churches was built as a war memorial.

Chapter 3

1 Member of a High-Church dynasty of ecclesiastical lawyers, a proctor in Doctors' Commons (and deputy registrar of the Province of Canterbury from 1820; registrar of the Arches Court from 1824), younger brother of (Sir) Herbert Jenner (later Jenner-Fust, 1778-1852), on whom see *ODNB.*

2 LPL, Howley Pps, vol. 10, ff. 210-14, undated.

3 *PP (HL),* 1816 (116 & 118) LXXIX.

4 There were five with want of room for from 78,000 to 59,000; three, where the deficiency was from 48,000 to 41,000; nine, with deficiency from 39,000 to 31,000; and 14 from 29,000 to 20,000 – a total of 31, rather than 32 - and Harrowby did not name them, as they were in the parliamentary lists.

5 Halifax and Rochdale, being divided into townships, were omitted from list A; the precise grounds for including the other six are not given.

6 *PP* 1818 (5) XVIII, pp. 137-214.

7 Consisting of the Archbishop of Canterbury, the Speaker, Archdeacons Pott, Wollaston, and Mant, Dr Wordsworth, Lord Grenville, Colonel Stephenson and Watson (CBC, MB. 1, p. 3).

8 Churton, *Joshua Watson,* I, p. 200.

9 CBC, MB 1, p. 6.

10 CBC, MB 1, 4 Aug. 1818; CC file 21744, pt. 1, 26 Aug.-8 Oct. 1818. The Archbishop of York replied that he had appointed a district board in each of four archdeaconries, selecting 'such of the Clergy as he judged to be most competent to collect the Information required'; they were to report to him as the channel of communication with the Commission. (CBC, MB 1, 2 Sep. 1818).

11 CBC, MB 1, p. 60ff.

12 A lease was obtained of this dilapidated house (13 Aug.) for 7 or 14 years at £105 p.a. Repairs cost £475, and it was several months before the Commission could move in, CC file 21507. Meanwhile they met at Bartlett's Buildings, Holborn, home of the SPCK.

13 (*London*): St Marylebone, St Pancras, Shoreditch, Stepney, St Giles-in-the-Fields, St Luke Old Street, Bethnal Green, St George Hanover Square, St Andrew Holborn, St George-in-the-East, St James Westminster, St Martin-in-the-Fields, Whitechapel, Clerkenwell. (*Winchester*): Lambeth, St George Southwark, Portsea. (*Chester*): Liverpool, Manchester, Stockport, Blackburn. (*Exeter*): Plymouth. (*Lichfield*): St Martin Birmingham. (*York*): Sheffield, Leeds. Harrowby did not name his 32 parishes, but the difference in the two lists illustrates the difficulties that faced the Commissioners.

14 CBC, MB 1, 2 Sep. 1818.

15 To take one example, at the Commissioners' meeting on 23 Sep. 1818 (two weeks after their previous meeting), they received replies about district boards from York, Rochester, and Lichfield & Coventry; and applications from the parishes of West Bromwich, Aston, Barnsley, Belper, Deino, Shadwell, South Mimms and Bedwelty, CBC, MB 1.

16 CBC, MB 1, 2, 7, and 23 Oct. 1818.

17 CBC, MB 1, 13 Aug. 1818. See below, chapters 5 and 8.

18 CC file 21744, pt. 1 (7 Aug. 1818). For Rickman, see below, p. 64ff. Ibid. (20 Oct. 1818).

19 CBC, MB 1, p. 94 et seq.

20 *PP*, 1821 (29), X.

21 The Chancellor of the Exchequer (Vansittart), the Bishop of London (Howley), Archdeacon Cambridge, Colonel Stephenson (Surveyor-general), and Watson were appointed, 10 Nov. 1818.

22 See below, pp. 61-5.

23 Howley, Vansittart, Lord Grenville, Watson, Wollaston, Cambridge and Stephenson, CBC, MB 1, 23 Oct. 1818.

24 CBC, MB 1, 4 Nov. 1818.

25 For example, St Marylebone church, 1813-18, cost about £60,000.

26 Printed as appendix D to CBC First Report to parliament, *PP* 1821 (29) X, pp. 13-15.

27 CBC, Rules and Regulations, etc. (MS).

28 Specimen forms are appendices B and C to the CBC First Report, *PP* 1821 (29) X, pp. 10-13.

29 These forms generally survive in the Church Commissioners' parochial files.

30 Some examples are considered below, pp. 90-2.

31 CBC, First Report (*PP, 1821, (29) X*, p. 1 et seq.). There does not appear a specific resolution to this effect, but when a correspondent inquired whether the Commissioners had 'fixed or intend to fix on any Plan to be uniformly acted upon throughout the Kingdom', the answer was no, CBC, MB 1, 8 Dec. 1818.

32 *History of the King's Works, VI, 1782-1851* (1973), p. 431; *Parl. Deb., N.S.* XL, 234 and 1437.

33 See chapter 6 below.

34 CBC, First Report (*PP*, 1821 (29) X), pp. 1 ff.

35 CBC, Rules and Regulations, etc. (MS.). Dean Ireland was also nominated, but resigned.

36 *PP* 1821 (29) X.

37 See below, p. 89.

38 For example, at Leeds in 1821. See F. Beckwith, *Thomas Taylor, Regency Architect, Leeds* (1949), p. 56.

39 CBC, MB 5, 8 May 1821.

40 For example, St Luke Old Street, and Bethnal Green.

41 CBC, MB 1, 24 Nov. 1818.

42 Ibid., 20 Dec. 1818, 19 Jan. 1819.

43 Ibid., 26 Jan., 2 and 16 Feb. 1819.

44 CBC, MB 3, 18 Apr. 1820.

45 As late as 1846 the Commissioners declined to use their compulsory powers (59 Geo. III, c.134, s.36) for compelling churchwardens to provide additional burying-space, because of 'the expense, delay and difficulties' in so proceeding (CBC, MB 61, p. 201).

46 CBC, MB 1, 9 Feb. 1819.

47 CBC, MB 3, 13 Jun., 11 Jul. 1820.

48 Ibid., 28 Mar. 1820.

49 Ibid., 13 Jun. 1820.

50 Ibid., 2 May 1820.

51 Ibid., 29 Feb., 2 May 1820.

52 LPL, Howley Pps, vol. 10, f. 210.

53 *PP*, 1821 (29) X.

54 CC file 21744, pt 3, Watson to Jenner, 20 Jan. 1821; pt 4, same to same, no date (misplaced in Sep. 1823).

55 The Commissioners received two per cent interest on the exchequer bonds that were issued to them.

56 Harrowby MSS, 1st Series, V, pp. 132-40.

57 Bishop Ryder's handwriting is far from clear.

58 *Cmns Jnls*, 74 (1819), pp. 578, 626.

59 The passage of the Act left no impact on the published *Parliamentary Debates*, but may be followed in *Cmns Jnls*, LXXIV, pp. 529, 542, 547, 565, 578, 592, 598, 604, 626, 627, and 639, 12 Jun.-13 Jul. 1819.

60 See below, chap. 6.

61 St Pancras, Poplar, and St Clement Worcester.

62 For example, signatures to the 19th Report include Lords Melbourne, Lincoln, and Duncannon, Lord John Russell, and T. Spring Rice – members of the government who had never attended a meeting of the Commission.

63 The increase in business may be judged by the rise in charges for stationery and postage, porterage, etc., from £30.1s.10d. and £45.18s.1d. respectively in 1819-20, to £89.8s.6d. and £75.5s.2d. in 1820-1, *Cmns Jnls* 76 (1821), app., p. 1254. Jenner also managed the CBC's receipts and payments – 'no part of the proper business of his situation as Secretary' – and for this and his 'zealous and laborious Services' in general, was awarded a £1,000 bonus in 1825, CBC, MB 16, 11 Jan. 1825.

64 He attended the Board for the first time on 19 Jan. 1819, and subsequently every meeting until 9 Mar. 1819. As CBC, MB 2 is missing, we know nothing of his further attendance until 29 Feb. 1820. From then until 18 Jul. 1820, he missed only one meeting. Again, a missing Minute Book deprives us of immediately subsequent information.

65 Bishop of Chester to Secretary of CBC, 20 Sep. 1820 (CC file 15097, pt. I).

66 *Cmns Jnls* 76 (1821), pp. 294, 314, 324, 435, 446, 453, 459; *Lords Jnls* 1821, p. 540 (25 Jun.).

67 *Cmns Jnls* 77 (1822), pp. 323, 335, 392, 408, 442, 446. Its committee stage was deferred six times, and the third reading twice; it passed the Lords without amendment.

Chapter 4

1 See J. M. Crook and M. H. Port, *History of the King's Works, VI, 1782-1851* (1973), ch. V.

2 PRO, Work 6/183/ 1, no. 5; Work 4/23, p. 61.

3 The elevations were published by R. Liscombe, 'Economy, Character and Durability: Specimen Designs for the Church Commissioners, 1818', *Architectural History*, 13 (1970), pp. 43-57. The article's opening statement is inaccurate. Nash's elevations are again reproduced in M. Mansbridge, *John Nash: A Complete Catalogue* (1991), pp. 214-15.

4 Those in London are exhaustively studied in G. L. Carr, 'The Commissioners' Churches of London, 1818-1837: A Study of Religious Art, Architecture and Patronage in Britain from the Formation of the Commission to the Accession of Queen Victoria', University of Michigan Ph.D. thesis, 1976; copy in RIBA Library.

5 *Monthly Magazine,* LIV, p. 211 (Oct. 1822).

6 S.M., X.E.4, 1-8, Apr.-May, 1821: J.H.G Archer, *Manchester*, pp. 47-9.

7 S.M., X. B. 3.

8 CC file 21744, pt 1, 14 Mar. 1818; PRO, Work 6/183/1, pp. 7-8; RIBA, Shide Ledger, 14 Mar. 1818.

9 CC file 21744, pt 1.

10 CC file 21744, pt 2.

11 Ibid.

12 PRO, Work 6/183/ 1, no. 2.

13 Ibid., nos 7-8. Eleven of Smirke's model plans and elevations are in RIBAD, PB 474/1.

14 S.M., X. B. 1.

15 Ibid., 7, 27 Mar. 1818.

16 S.M., X. B. 6. Printed in A. Bolton's *The Works of Sir John Soane*, p. 91, note; CC file 12131, pt 1.

17 S.M., X. B., 8.

18 Soane was aware of the cost of some of the country churches then being built, as notes of the estimates for such buildings occur among his papers: e.g. the whole expense at Frome had been £3,627, ibid., f. 10.

19 See below, pp. 45-7. NB pp. 73-8.

20 S.M., X. B. 11, Charles Bacon to Soane, 14 Apr. 1818.

21 PRO, Work 6/183/1, no. 3.

22 Ibid., no. 9.

23 J. Summerson, *The Life and Work of John Nash Architect* (1980), p. 111; R. Liscombe, *Architectural History*, 13 (1970), p. 49.

24 T. M. Parry, 'The Incorporated Church Building Society 1818-1851', Oxford D.Phil thesis, 1984, includes the entire 'Suggestions' in an appendix.

25 *Times,* 30 Jul. 1818, p. 3b.

26 S.M., X. B. 14.

27 Ibid., 13, 15, 16, 18-20.

28 Ibid., 17.

29 Ibid., 17, 22, 23.

30 CC file 21744, 10 and 16 Nov. 1818.

31 Lecture XI (written on paper watermarked 1829-31), D. Watkin, *Sir John Soane. Enlightenment Thought and the Royal Academy Lectures* (Cambridge, 1996), pp. 637; 290, n.12.

32 PRO, Work 6/183, 18-25; report 5 Dec.1818.

33 See Colvin, *DBA.*

34 PRO, Work 1/9, p. 386, 26 Apr. 1819.

35 Ibid., p. 389, 14 Jun. 1819.

36 Ibid., p. 418.

37 Ibid., p. 468, 4 Oct. 1819.

38 PRO, Work 1/10, pp. 45, 99.

39 PRO, Work 1/9, pp. 387, 418 (26 Apr., 5 Aug. 1819). D. Verey and A. Brooks, *BoE, Gloucestershire 2: The Vale and the Forest of Dean* (3rd edn, New Haven and London, 2002), p. 555, describe Holy Trinity as 'Quite an attractive Gothic exterior, of Bath ashlar. Sturdy three-stage W tower, embattled, with big cornice and pinnacles, and diagonal buttresses; round quatrefoil windows on the lowest stage, cusped Y-tracery above. Simple three-light Dec-style nave windows'. How Fosters did it on some £3,300 is difficult to understand.

40 PRO, Work1/10, pp. 45, 72, 102, 153, 250 (6, 27 Mar., 15 May, 5 Jun., 22 Nov. 1820).

41 PRO, Work 1/10, pp. 100, 153, 171, 250 (15 May, 5 Jun., 26 Jun., 22 Nov.1820).

42 CBC, MBs 3 (27 Jun. 1820), 5 (22 May 1821).

43 See below, p. 163-4.

44 PRO, Work 1/9, p. 388.

45 Ibid., p. 418.

46 PRO, Work 1/10, p. 216.

47 See below, pp. 186-7.

48 PRO, Work 1/9, p. 510.

49 Ibid., 1/10, p. 163, 27 Mar. 1820.

50 Ibid., 1/11 (23 Feb. 1822).

51 Ibid. (28 Jun. 1822).

52 See chap. 6.

53 See Appendix 3.

54 CBC, MB 1, 9 Feb.1819; CC file 15452; CBC, MB 3, 29 Feb. 1820.

55 CBC, MB 1, 9 Feb., 2 Mar. 1819. The church was closed in 2002.

56 Ibid., 3, 29 Feb. 1820.

57 Ibid.

58 Britton and Pugin, *Public Buildings of London*, I (1825), pp. 167-79.

59 CBC, MB 3, 7 and 14 Mar.1820. The vestry asked the Commissioners not to act in the parish without consulting them, CBC, MB 1, 9 Mar. 1819.

60 For these and other London churches, see Carr, thesis.

61 Perhaps derived from St Paul's Cathedral, or St Paul, Deptford.

62 CBC, MB 3, 18 Jul. 1820.

63 *Gentleman's Magazine,* 97, pt II., p. 9.

64 CBC, MB 5, 8 May, 10 Jul. 1821.

65 *Gentleman's Magazine,* 99, pt II., p. 577.

66 In 1822 from his designs there were building six churches; and he was about to embark on a series of important public buildings in London, as well as his provincial and domestic commissions. Cf. Colvin, *DBA.*

67 Cf. also Rickman, who at Chorley (Lancashire) 'settled to have the Birmingham church exactly'. (MS Diary, 25 Feb. 1820).

68 CC file 21744, pt. 1.

69 Pevsner praised it as 'archaeologically much more careful than most'; though he then criticised the chamfers of the nave arches as 'too slight for the Perp period' and the capitals as 'wrong' *BoE, South Lancashire* (Harmondsworth, 1969). But as only the clerestory appears 'Perp', and the aisle windows have 13th-century 'Y' tracery, Pevsner's criticism appears off-point.

70 CBC, MB 5, 8 May 1821. Smirke reported to the Commissioners that he proposed to construct the roof of iron.

71 CBC, MB 6, 22 Jan., 12 Feb. 1822.

72 CBC, MB 3, 25 Apr. 1820.

73 CBC, MBs 25 (22 May, 12, 19 Jun., 3 Jul.) and 27 (11 Dec. 1827).

74 CBC, MBs 40, p. 449 (Apr. 1832), 42 (5 Mar. 1833); SR 3, ff. 159, 163, 183, 198v-9.

75 Draft reply, S.M. X. E.4.

76 CBC, MB 8, p.120.

77 *Gentleman's Magazine*, 1829, pt 1, p. 290.

78 CBC, MBs 6 (9 Apr.), 7 (9 & 16 Jul.), 8 (20 Aug. 1822).

79 S.M., X.C. 2, 1 (Jenner to Soane 20 Aug. 1822), 10 (Soane to Jenner, 11 Nov. 1822).

80 Ibid., 29, n.d., but about 16 Mar. 1823.

81 Ibid., 39, 39a-c; CBC, MB 10, 29 Apr., 6 May 1823.

82 S.M., X. C.2, 77, 1 Sep. 1823.

83 Dorothy Stroud, *The Architecture of Sir John Soane* (1961), p. 132; du Prey, *Sir John Soane*, p. 77; S.M., drawer 54, set 6, for working drawings.

84 *PP*, 1837 (437) XLI, Return of sums expended … The Commissioners had to pay more than they had intended, because the Vestry refused to meet the cost of extra foundations. The church, for many years until 2004 the headquarters of the S.P.C.K., is now (Jun. 2004) at risk of significant changes.

85 CBC, MB 3, 18 Apr. 1820; S.M., X. H. 1, 2 (Jenner to Soane, 25 Apr., 6 Jul. 1820).

86 P. de la R. du Prey, *Sir John Soane (Catalogues of Architectural Drawings in the Victoria and Albert Museum)* (1985), no. 226; S.M., Drawer 54, set 3, item 11.

87 G. Darley, *John Soane. An Accidental Romantic* (New Haven and London, 1999), p. 264.

88 S.M., X. H. 3 (Soane to Jenner, 9 Jan. 1821), 4, 6 (Jenner to Soane, 24 Feb., 3 May 1821).

89 S.M., Drawer 54, set 1; du Prey, pp. 74-5, nos 227, 229, 230.

90 CBC, MB 10, 22 Apr. 1823.

91 This model has a vaulted ceiling cut into by windows, see A. T. Bolton, *The Works of Sir John Soane*, p. 88.

92 S.M., X., H. 21, 22, 24.

93 CBC, MB 10, 27 May 1823; Jenner to Soane, 30 May 1823, S.M., X. B. 49.

94 CBC, MB 12, 17 Feb., 16 Mar. 1824.

95 S.M., X. H. 26.

96 See du Prey, *Sir John Soane*, pll. 37, 38, and cat. nos 222-8, 231-7.

97 CBC, MB 12, 16 Mar.1824.

98 Du Prey, *Sir John Soane*, pll. 32-4; S.M., Drawer 54, set 3, nos 16-18, varieties of a Gothic design, May 1824.

99 A. T. Bolton, *The Works of Sir John Soane* (n.d.), 93, reproducing Soane's account presented to the Commissioners in Apr. 1829 and Sep.1832.

100 CBC, MB 15, 9 and 23 Nov. 1824.

101 S.M., X., H. 50, Soane to Jenner, 7 Apr. 1825.

102 S.M., X., H. 53; 57a, Sir Peter Laurie to Soane, 31 Oct. 1825.

103 Ibid., 58, 61 (circular for subscriptions), 62; CBC, MB 22, 24 Oct. 1826, acquiescing if the parish pay the £1,280.

104 See du Prey, p. 139.

105 CBC, MB 22, 24 Oct. 1826.

106 S.M., X. C. 2. 31, 19 Mar. 1823.

107 This was the amount of Robert Streather's tender for the whole work including vaults and boundary wall, S.M., X. F. 1, Jenner to Soane, 14 Apr., and 6, Streather to Soane, 8 May 1826. Streather's prices in detail are in item 4.

108 S.M., X. F. 11, copy, Soane to J. Merceron, 5 Jul. 1827. Soane would have given £100 towards a subscription for implementing the original design. An anonymous correspondent told him that the steeple was being compared with 'that ridiculous pile of rubbish', Nash's steeple at Haggerston, ibid., 10.

109 See F. Sheppard, *London 1808-1870: The Infernal Wen* (1971), pp. 26-7.

110 CBC, MB 26, 12 Jul, 1827.

111 Du Prey, *Sir John Soane*, p. 76; D. Stroud, *Sir John Soane, Architect* (1984), p. 233.

112 S.M., X. F, 8.

113 His brother, the Rev. Edward Repton, was the minister there.

114 CBC, MB 5, pp. 70, 71.

115 J. Summerson, *Life and Work of John Nash*, p. 112.

116 CBC, MB 5, p. 76 (22 May 1821).

117 Ibid., pp. 70, 71.

118 CBC, Building Comm. MB 4, pp. 16, 88 (27 Oct., 27 Nov. 1821), 219-20, 255 (29 Jan., 12 Feb. 1822).

119 CBC, Building Comm., MBs 6, p. 159 (14 Sep. 1822), 9, pp. 127, 192-4.

120 *Parl. Deb. N.S.,* XI, 35.

121 But the 1950s B.B.C. extension has marred the vista, and 2004-5 work yet more so.

122 He designed a church for Carmarthen, but when work was started several years later, other plans were employed.

123 CBC, MB 8, p. 316.

124 CBC, MB 8, p. 314 et seq.

125 B. F. L. Clarke, *Nineteenth Century Church Builders*, p. 41.

Chapter 5

1 RIBA Lib., Rickman, MS Diary.

2 CC file 21744, pt. 1.

3 Probably Daniel Robertson: see Colvin, *DBA*.

4 Redmond William Pilkington (1789-1844), who also wrote to Soane about the CBS recommendations to architects.

5 See Appendix 2.

6 Richard Elsam, b. *c*.1775. Author of works on rural architecture.

7 LPL, Manners-Sutton Pps, I, ff. 164-6.

8 *Gentleman's Magazine,* 1817 (i), p. 624; *Farington Diary*, XIV, pp. 5022-3, 5030.

9 CC file 21744, part 2.

10 Here speaks the Senior Wrangler.

11 Wollaston's contemptuous attitude towards the architectural profession in general was no doubt justified by his experience. But it was conduct such as he proposed for handling architectural competitions that brought those into disrepute, so that good, established architects often declined to compete. His reference to 'the trade' was repeated by A. W. N. Pugin in his title-page to *Contrasts* (1836).

12 CBC, MB 6, 8 Jan. 1822.

13 CBC, MB 5, 8 May, 10 Jul. 1821. The local committee having been instructed to obtain plans from another architect, a set by Charles Squarhill (*sic*) was submitted. Squirhill was a clerk of Goodwin's.

14 E.g. although the Commissioners had granted £2,800 for a new church at Bransgrove, Christ Church (Hants), and the whole expenditure was only £2,591.2s. 1d., the architect Hannaford's claims for 10 guineas for 'preparing Plans Elevations, Sections, Specifications, estimate and detailed bill'; and 15 guineas for 'three other additional sets of drawings, revising and reducing estimates, altering Specifications corresponding therewith, under the express directions of the Commissioners', were rejected, 'that charge being always included in the £5 per cent allowed for Commission', CBC, MB 9, 26 Nov. 1822.

15 CBC, MB 6, 8 Jan. 1822; MB 28, 12 Feb. 1828.

16 At Richmond in 1828, six asked leave to submit plans: Charles Dyer, Thomas Taylor, Robert Wallace, J. B. Watson, Lewis Vulliamy, and Ambrose Poynter (CBC, MB 32, pp. 297-8; 33, p. 42).

17 See below, chap. 10.

18 PRO, Work 1/10, 10 Jan. 1820.

19 CBC, MB 3, p. 377.

20 Ibid., p. 392.

21 See Colvin, *DBA*.

22 CC file 21744, pt. 3.

23 The actual date cannot be ascertained, as the relevant Minute Book is missing.

24 CC files 21744, pt. 5; 21819.

25 CC file 21819, H. H. Norris to Henry Mawley, 6 Feb. 1826.

26 *Magazine of the Fine Arts*, 16 Apr. 1821; Britton and Pugin, *Public Buildings of London* II (1828), p. xiv. Cited by Carr, thesis, p. 215. Soane's friend, James Spiller, also attacked Mawley in his *Second Letter* to Soane as demonstrating the Commissioners' contempt for architects.

27 CC file 21819, Surveyor's duties.

28 CC file 21819, 31 Jan. 1826. He was assisted, unofficially, by his son, Henry (ibid., James Bailey to H. Mawley, 11 Feb. 1826).

29 CBC, Building Comm. MB 5, 29 Mar. 1822 (pp. 33, 9).

30 CBC, Building Comm. MB 5, p. 13.

31 E.g. Bedford's Camberwell church, 26 Mar. 1822: there was only one tender each for bricklayer, mason and plasterer. 'Upon further examination it appears there is considerable difference in amounts, and some of the Tenders appear so exceedingly low that your Surveyor is doubtfull if the work can be performed in a satisfactory manners for the sum specified.' CBC, Building Comm. MB 5, p. 21.

32 His bound reports, 1821-6, which survive in entirety, help to fill the gaps left by missing Minute Books.

33 PRO, Work 1/9-12.

34 CBC, Building Comm. MB 5, pp. 33, 58.

35 CBC, Building Comm. MB 7, 3 and 17 Jun. 1824.

36 CBC, Building Comm. MB 5, p. 114.

37 Ibid., p. 115; SR 1, p. 4, 8 May 1821.

38 Designs were also modified by incumbents, patrons, and other local interests.

39 CC file 15452, 30 Dec. 1818.

40 CBC, Building Comm. MB 5, p. 330 (24 Jun. 1822); CBC, MB 8, 20 Aug. 1822.

41 Ibid., 20 Aug., 29 Oct. 1822; MB 10, 29 Apr., 6 May 1823; S.M., Drawer 54, set 6.

42 CBC, MBs 8, 29 Oct. 1822; 9, 7 Jan. 1823.

43 CC file 18124 (16 Jun. 1821); CBC, Building Comm. MBs 5, p. 348 (Jun. 1822); 6, pp. 149-50.

44 CC file 18124, 15 Apr. 1823, 4 May 1824, Lee's lithographic paper; CBC, MB 26, 10 Jul. 1827.

45 CBC, MB 8, 29 Oct. 1822.

46 CBC, MB 9, 26 Nov. 1822.

47 The following account is derived principally from CBC, Building Comm. MB 4, pp. 101, 146, 167-8, 362-3, Sep. 1821-Feb. 1822.

48 CBC, MB 5, 8 May, 10 Jul. 1821.

49 CBC, MB 6, 22 Jan. 1822.

50 CBC, MB 17, 17 May 1825.

51 CC file 15452, local secretary to Jenner, 15 Jul. 1819; Rev. G. Harker to Jenner, 11 Aug. 1819; CBC, MB 8, pp. 97-9. One observes that Smirke's lithographic form, stating the estimate which he binds himself not to exceed, under a 15 per cent penalty, is dated 28 Jul. 1821 (approximately when the church was finished). The tower is given as 87ft high (ibid.).

52 CC file 18484, Goodwin to CBC, 30 Apr. 1825.

53 CBC, MB 1, p. 89.

54 CBC, MB 28, 12 Feb. 1828, respecting Cheltenham.

55 1 Jul. 1824 (CBC, MB 14, p. 34).

56 CBC, MB, 15, pp. 161-2.

57 CBC, MB 40, 20 Dec. 1831, 10 Jan. 1832.

58 Rickman & Hutchinson were instructed to reduce their estimate for Wigan by 'the omission of ornaments' (CBC, MB 25, p. 333); and presented a design for Whittle-le-Woods (Lancs) 'of the simplest possible character' (CBC., MB. 26, p. 233). This was in 1827.

59 CBC, Rules (MS).

60 CBC, MB 44, pp. 197, 198; 45, p. 347.

61 CBC, MB 26, p. 22.

62 E.g. brickwork instead of stone facing at the west end of Hetton-le-Hole (Durham) kept within the estimate, CBC, SR 3, f. 119 (6 Jul. 1831).

63 'much more difficult to use than the other cements', J. Gwilt, *An Encyclopaedia of Architecture* (1899 edn), p. 543.

64 CBC, MB. 30, p. 214.

65 CBC, MB 21, p. 101.

66 CC file 21744, pt. 2.

67 CBC, MB 25, 12 Jun. 1827.

68 Notably by the *Gentleman's Magazine*.

69 T. Taylor compared the cost of windows in either style, to show that Gothic was the cheaper, in a letter printed in F. Beckwith, *Thomas Taylor, Regency Architect, Leeds*, pp. 91-2.

70 CBC, SR I, 11-13.

71 These figures are taken from the return made to Parliament in 1837, *PP* 1837 (437) XLI.

72 CBC, MB 12, 9 Mar. 1824; nonetheless, Rickman came up with an estimate of £21,046.16*s.* for a plan obviating inconveniences found at his earlier Birmingham church, St George's, Building Comm. MB 7, 10 Jun. 1824.

73 Cp. Good's comment on a transeptal plan for Toxteth Park, 15 Dec. 1828, CBC, SR 3, f. 29v.

74 So that the minister might be seen from the galleries; see CBC, SR 3, f. 27.

75 A minority maintained this tradition through the eighteenth century; for an examination of Anglican practice, see N. Yates, *Buildings, Faith and Worship. The Liturgical Arrangement of Anglican Churches 1600-1900* (Oxford, 1991), pp.69-123.

76 CBC, MB 16, 11 Jan. 1825.

77 CBC, MB 16, 8 Feb.1825.

78 CBC, SR 3, f. 154 (Feb. 1832).

79 CBC, MB 17, 7 Jun. 1825.

80 CBC, SR 3, ff. 142ff.

81 CBC, SR 4, f. 49v.

82 CBC, MB 26, 25 Sep. 1827.

Chapter 6

1 CBC, Building Comm. MB 7, p. 38.

2 CBC, MB 7, 14 May 1822; Building Comm. MB 9, pp. 340-2.

3 E.g. Matthew Habershon at Belper (Derbys), in 1822, CBC, Building Comm. MB 4, pp. 239-42; Jacob Owen for All Saints, Mile End, Portsea (Hants), ibid., 5, pp. 212-13; Edward Gyfford at Leeds, ibid., 4, pp. 115ff.; and Francis Edwards at Hoxton, CBC, MB 10, 18 Mar., 8 Apr. 1823.

4 CBC, Building Comm. MB 4, pp. 113-16, 136-9; 9, pp. 218-28, 265-9; CBC, MB 28, 12 Feb.1828.

5 CC file 15455/1.

6 CBC, Building Comm. MB 4, p. 88 (27 Nov. 1821); when he had to supply an estimate for Langham Place church, Marylebone, he added ten per cent on each trade as a precaution.

7 CBC, Building Comm. MB 6, pp. 275-6.

8 Ibid., pp. 282-3.

9 CBC, Building Comm. MB 5, pp. 299, 343-7.

10 CC file 21744, pt 4 (25 Mar. 1822).

11 CBC, MB 6, 12 Mar. 1822.

12 CBC, MB 6, 26 Mar. 1822.

13 CC file 21744, pt 3 (15 Feb. 1822).

14 Ibid., pt 4 (18 Apr. 1822).

15 Ibid. (30 Apr. 1822). Some of their suggestions were accepted by the Commission's lawyers, CBC, Building Comm., MB 5, pp. 157-8, 18 Apr. 1822.

16 CBC, Building Comm., MB 4, pp. 256-9 (12 Feb. 1822).

17 S.M., X.B. 44 (29 Apr. 1822). The form of contract is reproduced in *Architectural Magazine*, IV (1837), pp. 341-8.

18 CC file 21744, pt 4 (11 May 1822).

19 Ibid. (13 Aug. 1822); CBC, Building Comm. MB 6, pp. 97-9. There is a blank bond form in

S.M., X.C.2. 16.

20 When Archdeacon Wollaston wrote to the Secretary, 23 Aug. 1819, about the possibility of adopting a general design, he commented that such a mode would be much impeded 'because it will decrease the work to be done by the trade', CC file 21744, pt 2. One recalls A. W. N. Pugin's satirical title-page to *Contrasts* (1836), dedicated to 'The Trade'. The vicar of Dewsbury on 23 Mar. 1823 wrote indignantly to the architect Thomas Taylor (trained under James Wyatt), who had failed to send the Commissioners the tenders the vicar had passed to him at the turn of the year, of his 'unaccountable and *untradesmanlike* [my italics] delay', CBC, Building Comm. MB 7, p. 171.

21 CBC, Building Comm. MB 9, pp. 90, 96.

22 This practice was derived from the Office of Works and Public Buildings. A Devon correspondent in 1838 claimed that it was not strictly maintained, CBC, SR 4, f. 211.

23 Atkinson & Sharp, architects, applied in March 1823 for Verity & Dickinson, the selected masons for their church at Woodhouse, Leeds, to be allowed three-fourths payments, because as also contractors for Stanley church, 'they will have occasion for an outlaying capital to an extent that may prove inconvenient'. They were informed 'that the Committee cannot alter the rule which they have deemed it necessary to make', CBC, Building Comm. MB 7, pp. 66-7. Does one hear the Secretary's unrecorded voice?

24 Goodwin in particular applied several times for commission payments on account, see below, Chap. 9.

25 CC file 21819. Vulliamy claimed for items that the Board disputed. As his churches at Richmond and Sydenham had both experienced changes of builder, the matter was somewhat complex, and appears not to have been resolved until 1856, by which time he was owed £855 (simple) or £2101 (compound) interest.

26 CBC, SR 5, ff. 47, 51, 52, Apr.-Jul. 1839.

27 S.M., X.E.4. 6, Draft, Soane [to W. Weston, Manchester, May 1821]; Soane's actual reply to Weston was considerably toned down, ibid., 8.

28 CBC, MB 3, p. 246.

29 Ibid., p. 271 et seq. , 6 Jun. 1820.

30 Ibid.

31 The Board's Surveyor reported, 11 Aug. 1840, on an application from Richard Carver for commission on his estimate for Bridgwater church (Somerset): 'It appears to be the invariable rule of the Board (and it is also the custom in private practice) to regulate the amount of the Commission by the amount of the works executed <u>only</u>, and never, in any case, by the amount of the Architect's estimate.' (CBC, SR 5, f. 131).

32 As intended at Travis Street, Manchester, where Taylor was to repeat his Pudsey design, but he died before the second church was begun, CBC, Building Comm. MB 9, pp. 192-4. There are a number of such cases; *e.g.* Smirke received 2½ per cent for Salford, a copy of St Mary, Wyndham Place, London; and Blore agreed to adapt his Plaistow plan for Waltham Cross 'upon the terms usual in such cases, viz. 2½ per cent commission', SR 3, f. 88v.

33 Thomas Taylor, Rickman and Smirke were charging commission on incidentals in 1822-3, cf CBC, Building Comm. MBs 6, pp. 9-11, 151, 286, 314; 7, pp. 54-61.

34 CBC, Building Comm. MB 9, p. 125. Rickman did likewise at St George's, Birmingham, CBC, MB 8, pp. 107-11, but Smirke did not at Wandsworth, ibid., pp. 284ff., Aug.-Oct. 1822.

35 CBC, Building Comm. MB 4, p. 5 (6 Nov. 1821); SR 4, f. 79 1s.6d. was the sum allowed per mile in the 1820s; it was later increased to 3s. for a period.

36 CBC, MB 33, 23 Dec. 1828.

37 CBC, Building Comm. MB 5, p. 63 (29 Mar. 1822). The ownership of architects' drawings was a vexed question in the nineteenth century, but the case Landless *v.* Wilson (1880), 8 Ct of Session 4th series, 289, decided that, when paid for, they became the property of the employer; the copyright normally remained with the architect.

38 Chantrell complained that he had 'suffered much inconvenience in consequence of the original Specification being returned [to the CBC] having been obliged to copy out another set from the rough documents of the first, which were much interlined and imperfect', CBC, Building Comm. MB 6, p. 233 (9 Nov. 1823).

39 CBC, Building Comm. MB 4, pp.146-7 (8 Jan.1822). The drawings that Rickman sent with his specification and estimate for St Paul, Preston, on 31 Dec.1822, consisted of ground and gallery plans, east, west and south elevations, transverse and longitudinal sections, details of roof framing and gallery framing, and shaded drawings of the west and south elevations, CBC, Building Comm.

40 CBC, Building Comm. MB 7, 29 Apr. 1823.

41 CBC, SR 5, f. 116. This archive was unfortunately dispersed after the amalgamation of the Church Building Commissioners with the Ecclesiastical Commissioners in 1857: some remnants of it were given to the RIBA Drawings Collection by the Church Commissioners in recent years. The re-use of plans was abandoned after protests from the IBA, see below, p. 248.

42 CBC, MB 19, 22 Nov. 1825.

43 See below, chap. 8 for Goodwin and chap. 10 for Vulliamy.

44 CBC, Building Comm. MB 5, p. 62. Charles Barry performed this last duty remarkably thoroughly for his Manchester churches (ibid., pp. 236-43), but sometimes it was discharged by the incumbent as chairman of the local committee, as at Thomas Taylor's church at Attercliffe (Yorks), CBC, Building Comm. MB 6, pp. 123-33.

45 CBC, Building Comm. MB 6, pp. 120-2. Taylor experienced similar problems at Sheffield, St Philip, ibid., p. 9.

46 Ibid., p. 17 (16 Jul. 1822).

47 Ibid., pp. 210-11.

48 CBC, Building Comm. MB 6, p. 123.

49 CC file 15017, Rev. E. France to CBC, 6 Mar. 1821.

50 CBC, MB 3, 14 Mar., 18 Apr., and 2 May 1820.

51 Even Nash had a narrow escape at Haggerston; a complex story. Streather's tender exceeded Nash's estimate by £5.18s. 2d., and Nash was told: 'that as the lowest Tender exceeds his Estimate the Committee cannot consistent with their general rule accept it'; the case was suspended pending the passage of a Bill then before Parliament (Jun. 1824). Meanwhile, Streather agreed to execute the contract at Nash's estimate. CBC, Building Comm. MB 9, pp. 129-31, 162-6, 193-5.

52 CBC, Building Comm. MB 5, p. 191 (23 Apr. 1822).

53 Rickman was warned in respect of his Erdington, Birmingham, church that 'if any but the lowest Tenders had been selected, they would have exceeded the amount of his Estimate and … the smallest excess of the Smith and Founders work [on a prices for quantities basis] beyond the sum named will carry them beyond the amount of his Estimate which the Committee cannot permit' (CBC, Building Comm. MB 5, p. 125).

54 As at Belper (Derbys) in 1822, where the tenders exceeded Habershon's estimate, but the dominant local figure, Jedediah Strutt, mill-owner, pleaded for Habershon, and pointed out that one contractor had estimated stone 'higher than it can be obtained for': in such a large quantity, a small addition in price swelled the cost 'prodigiously'. Nevertheless the Commissioners insisted that, unless one of the general contractors could bring down his prices for minor trades, new tenders must be obtained; CBC, Building Comm. MB 5, pp. 299, 343-7.

55 CBC, SR 2, f. 30; Building Comm. MB 9, pp. 172-4, 182, 274; CBC, MB 19, 17 Jan. 1826.

56 CC file 21744, pt 5, Hansom to Jenner, 30 Mar. 1830; CBC, SR 4, p. 290; MB 40, pp. 356-7.

57 CBC, Building Comm. MB 5, pp. 140-1.

58 As for Cockerell's Hanover Chapel, Regent Street, where he was allowed to add £430 for increased prices, CBC, Building Comm. MB 6, p. 267.

59 CBC, Building Comm. MB 7, pp. 119-21, 184, 187, 235.

60 PRO, Work 4/25, pp. 201, 215, 248, 318, 413; 4/26, p. 53.

61 Most of the national price indexes that have been compiled are concerned with real wages; they show a steady improvement through the first three decades of the century; cp. M. Daunton, *Progress and Poverty* (Oxford, 1995), p. 436 for real wages rates of bricklayers. For some of the problems regarding price indexes, cp. Linda Clarke, *Building Capitalism* (1992), pp. 62-8.

62 CBC, SR 1, p. 102; Building Comm. MB 5, pp. 199-200. This offers no basis for the claim that this church was ghosted by A. B. Clayton, see Colvin, *DBA*, *sub* Roper, David Riddall.

63 CBC, Building Comm. MB 6, pp. 72, 269: Soane provided a total estimate for Walworth, and was told to furnish the detail 'as required in all cases'.

64 CBC, Building Comm. MB 6, p. 228.

65 Ibid., p. 230.

66 CBC, Building Comm. MB 7, p. 108 (19 Apr. 1823). Benjamin Smith, who won the contract for a new church in North Lewisham, subsequently abandoned because of arguments over the site, claimed £87 for making his estimate (reduced by the Surveyor to £50) as well as £35 in loss of interest on 1900 consols sold at $80^{7}/_{8}$ in order to carry on his works, CBC, MB 35, 11 Aug. 1829.

67 S.M., X. F. 6-7, 8 and 10 May 1826. Streather was bankrupted during the building of St Philip,

Clerkenwell in 1831-2, but quickly re-established himself to complete the church.

68 F. M. L. Thompson, *Chartered Surveyors the Growth of a Profession* (1968), p. 81, referring to T. Skaife, *A Key to Civil Architecture. The Universal British Builder* (1774).

69 As did Wilkins with Spencer Crowe; and J. P. Gandy and W. J. Donthorn for St Mark, North Audley Street, see n. 21 above.

70 Parsons complained of a general miscalculation by all the tradesmen engaged at St George, Leicester, obviously emanating from a common source, CBC, MB 20, 11 Apr. 1826; and likewise Hanson at Liverpool, where the error is specifically ascribed to the tradesmen's common surveyor, see n. 56 above. For individual tradesmen's estimating, cp Dewsbury (n. 66 above) and Camberwell (pp. 117-18).

71 See n. 66 above.

72 Dr Timothy Brittain-Catlin has kindly brought to my notice 'Minutes of Evidence taken before the Ecclesiastical Commissioners 30th July 1845' (CC 3421/45 inside file 8129, pt 1), in which William Railton explains the system then used. See also E. Dobson, *Rudiments of the Art of Building* (1849), pp. 151-2, who refers to the building surveyor preparing 'from the drawings and specifications of the architect ... bills of quantities ... for the use of the builder on which to frame his estimates'; and to 'A meeting of builders proposing to tender ... at which a surveyor is appointed in their behalf to take out the quantities'.

73 Richardson & Want were contractors for the Royal Mews at Pimlico, a £49,000 job (*King's Works VI*, p. 303); they also worked on Smirke's churches at Wandsworth, Hackney and Bristol, among others.

74 CBC, Building Comm. MB 9, pp. 361-2.

75 Ibid., p. 359 (14 Oct. 1824).

76 Ibid., 7, pp. 103-5.

77 Ibid., 9, pp. 362-3; see also ibid., p. 39: Lower Darwen (Lancs) – 'Owing to the distance from which the stone must be brought, [the architect] has been unable to afford a Tower and Steeple.'

78 CBC, SR 2, f. 84v.

79 CBC, MB 19, 17 Jan., 7 Feb. 1826.

80 CBC, SR 3, f. 73.

81 CBC, SR 4, ff. 131, 159.

82 Ibid., f. 162.

83 Ibid., f. 200.

84 CBC, SR 5, f. 51.

85 CBC, MS 'Rules'.

86 See M. H. Port, 'The Office of Works and Early Nineteenth-century Building Contracts', *Econ. Hist. Review*, New Series XX (1967), pp. 94-110. The development of the lump-sum contract is discussed in A. Satoh, *Building in Britain. The Origins of a Modern Industry* (Aldershot, 1995), pt 1.

87 S.M., X.C.1. 27 (in Spiller's hand).

88 CC file 15452, 21 Jun. 1819.

89 CBC, MB 3, 11 Apr. 1820.

90 Ibid., 23 May 1820.

91 Mawley recommended it for St George, Sheffield; Bransgrove (Hants); Kennington, King Square, Brixton, and Camberwell (London); and Stockport in 1821-2, CBC, SR 1, ff. 25, 28, 47, 48, 58, 59, 97v. At King Square the lowest general tender was actually about £600 more than the sum of lowest bids for individual trades.

92 CBC, SR 1, f. 130; Building Comm. MB 6, p. 308. Although the total was well inside Taylor's estimate of £11,356, he was told that because the lowest plasterer's tender exceeded his estimate, it could not be accepted.

93 CBC: MBs and SRs, *passim*.

94 Chelsea, St Luke; Greenwich, St Mary; St Philip, Regent Street; St George, Regent Street; St Peter, Eaton Square.

95 All Souls, and Holy Trinity, Marylebone; St John, Bethnal Green; Haggerston.

96 Lambeth, Brixton. J. & H. Lee had previously done work for the parish.

97 St Paul, Southsea (Hants), where Jacob Owen, a leading member of the local committee was related to the contractor Ellis.

98 See E. W. Cooney, 'The origins of the Victorian Master Builders', *Econ. Hist. Review*, 2nd series, VIII, no. 2 (Dec. 1955), pp. 167ff.

99 As seems to have happened at St Mark, Kennington, Lambeth, 1822-4, see p. 122 below.

100 E.g. when the Board, having approved the 'general style and character' of Barry's design for Stand (Prestwich, Lancashire), remitted it to the Building Committee to proceed as usual, the Committee ordered the architect to advertise for tenders, each 'to contain a detail of the prices at which the same is made, care being taken so to word the Advertizement as to render it unnecessary to accept even the lowest tender; and when the tenders are received to send the same for the consideration of the Committee with a report as to the character and ability of the Tenderers and the sufficiency of their Sureties.' CBC, Building Comm. MB 5, p. 62 (29 Mar. 1822).

101 The Building Committee on 16 May 1820 asked the Board for instructions 'as to the enquiry they are expected to make with respect to Prices in the consideration of Tenders and especially whether previous to acceptance of any offer of contract, the Committee are to ascertain that the Prices proposed by the Contractor will afford him a living Profit on the work'. They were directed to obtain the opinion of the Crown Architects on the proposed prices as well as on the plans, CBC, MB3, 16 May 1820.

102 Thus Charles Barry, in calling for tenders for his churches at Stand (Prestwich, Lancs) and Camp Field (Manchester), required 'Prices to be given as follows, according to Specification

Brickwork in Ardwick lime at pr Rod	Inch deal rough at pr foot Supl
Ditto in Roman Cement Do	Floated render, set in rough stucco on groins at per Yard
Rough wallstone backings at pr foot Cube	Circular moulded ribs to Do at p foot supl girted
Stone in dressings at pr foot Cube	Slating at pr Square
Rough tooling to face of walls at pr foot Supl	Milled lead at pr Cwt
Plain work do	Cast lead at pr Cwt
Moulded work do	Glazing in lead lights at pr foot supl
Fir without labor at per foot Cube	Ornamental cast iron &c at pr Cwt
Oak do do	
Elm do do	

Masons to estimate difference between Lomoswood, Horroxfold, and the summit [stone] (Prestwich Church); and Huddersfield, Horroxfold, and Summit in Manchester [Camp Field] Church ', CBC, Building Comm. MB 5, pp. 239-41.

103 S.M., X.C.1. 83a, 13 Dec. 1823. Broomfield's brickwork tender included 'reduced stock Brickwork at per rod £14'; her contract for Walworth was £3,812, ibid., 49, 53. She later claimed to have lost £1,400 on the two churches, but Soane was not satisfied with her accounts, ibid., 199.

104 CBC, Building Comm. MB 5, p. 301 (11 Jun. 1822).

105 CBC, Building Comm. MB 9, pp. 363, 400.

106 Cp Day, an ironfounder, at Hackney, CBC, Building Comm. MB 6, pp. 99-101, 118.

107 CBC, Building Comm. MB 6, pp. 376-7. Buxton remarked: 'As respectable men we wish to fulfil the duties due to our employers to their entire satisfaction; but as Tradesmen, we do not wish our profits to be dissipated in matters from which no benefit can be derived to either of the parties', ibid.

108 CBC, Building Comm. MB 5, p. 21 (26 Mar. 1822). The various tenders were:
Bricklayer: Wells & Berriman, £2,445. *Mason:* Sharp & Day, £3,175; (Wells & Co., and D. Sharp already making foundations). *Carpenter & joiner:* John Baker, £3,100. Sam. Mayhew, £2,446.11 (excl. hoard & sheds). *Smith & founder:* Jas Bradley, £446. J. & W. Kelk, £346. Fowler, Jones & Co., £249.9. *Plasterer:* S. Bellamy, £461. *Plumber:* Wells & Berriman, £144.15. Thos Castle, £79. Josh. Cheshire, £81.10. J.Bond, £84.10. Barnard Howard, £70. *Coppersmith:* B. Howard, £540. J. Bond, £539.10. Josh.Cheshire, £492. *Glazier:* Wells & Berriman, £82.4. B.Howard, £90. J. Bond, £78.10. J. Cheshire, £67. T. Castle, £55.5.4. *Painter:* T. Castle, £268.3.10. J. Cheshire, £215.8. Jas Goody, £195. J. Bond, £180.18. B. Howard, £180. Wells & Berriman, £175.10.

109 CBC, Building Comm. MB 5, p. 88ff. (13 Apr. 1822).

110 Ibid.

111 Ibid., p. 301 (11 Jun. 1822).

112 Ibid., pp. 148-53.

113 One or the other had been at each meeting at which Camberwell tenders had been considered, and both were present on 30 April, together with Lord Kenyon.

114 CBC, Building Comm. MB 5, pp. 189, 197.

115 CBC, Building Comm. MB 5, pp. 187-8; CBC, MB 6, 23 Apr. 1822.

116 The clerk, not infrequently careless, wrote 'and'.

117 CBC, Building Comm. MB 5, p. 205.

118 Ibid., pp. 204, 233.

119 But they might be able to veto contractors: at Alverthorpe (Yorks), Atkinson & Sharp 'decline[d] being concerned with' Craven & Nowell as carpenters, and the Commissioners accepted the next lowest tender, CBC, Building Comm. MB 7, p. 68.

120 CBC, MB 10, p. 231; MB 21, p. 230; Building Comm. MB 4, pp. 219-21, 231-2, 255. Nash had doubted whether Streather could execute the Langham Place church for the price he quoted, but he agreed to contract for the works by measurement at the prices stated in his tender. Nash's concern over Streather's Haggerston prices is recorded in CBC, Building Comm. MB 9, pp. 162-4, 194-5.

121 CBC, MB 21, p. 430; SR 2, p. 89.

122 CBC, MB 21, p. 228.

123 CBC, SR 3, p. 115 (26 Mar. 1831).

124 CBC, MBs 36 (10 Nov. 1829), 39 (12 Apr. 1830); SR 3, f. 197.

125 The aim of the contractor at Bordesley was 'to obtain credit', CBC, MB 10. Nash reported that he was anxious to do Streather justice for his fine work at Langham Place, Marylebone, 'because the Commissioners must recollect how much I strove to prevent them entering into this Contract knowing that the Man must inevitably be a great loser, and seeing that he was himself ignorant of the result', CBC, Building Comm. MB 9, p. 127.

126 CBC, MB 25, 3 Jul. 1827.

127 CBC, Building Comm. MB 9, pp. 295, 335-7.

128 CBC, MB 20, 11 Apr. 1826.

129 CBC, SR 2, f. 212.

130 CBC, MB 42, 12 Feb. 1833.

131 Calculated on building accounts of 39 Commissioners' churches, 1822-31.

132 Info. *ex* Mr Frank Smith, who has explained to me some of the Nowell and Craven connexions. Hiram Craven's son John married Joseph Nowell's sister in 1819, and his son Edward married Nowell's daughter. James Nowell's son was born in Liverpool in 1820.

133 CBC, Building Comm. MB 6, p. 239; MB 7, pp. 205-6; SR, 1, ff. 25, 31. They also competed for Alverthorpe (Yorks), and Woodhouse, Leeds (Atkinson & Sharp churches), SR 1, ff. 135, 137; Rickman's St Peter, Preston, SR 1, f. 114, and his Chorley (Lancs), ibid., f. 108 and Building Comm. MB 5, pp. 225-6, 304-5; Chantrell's Meadow Lane, Leeds, SR 1, f. 131; and Hardwick's Farnworth, Dean (Lancs), ibid., f. 160. Craven & Nowell, their competitors at Meadow Lane, Leeds, were also their sureties, Building Comm. MB 6, p. 239. James Nowell was so short of cash to pay his Birmingham workmen that he had to borrow from Rickman, RIBA, Rickman MS Diary, 26 Aug. 1820.

134 CBC, Building Comm. MB 9, pp. 299-301, Rev. T. Sutton, 9 Sep. 1824.

135 CBC, Building Comm. MB 7, pp. 204-6.

136 Rickman records a Hiram Craven as a surety of James Nowell, Diary: note at front of 1820 volume.

137 They are variously described as 'of Leeds' or 'of Dewsbury', and were joined by John Craven: CBC, Building Comm. MB 5, pp. 246, 250 (Manchester); SR 1, ff. 106, 135, 137, 131, 144, 145; Building Comm. MB 6, p. 308; MB 7, pp. 124, 238-9.

138 CBC, MB 6, pp. 127 (vicar of Attercliffe), 360. There may be some confusion or collaboration between the two branches, Nowell Brothers being reported as unable to sign the mason's contract for Sheffield St George on 6 Dec. 1821 because they were unexpectedly detained in Scotland, Building Comm. MB 4, p. 326. Joseph Nowell gave as references Messrs Atkinson & Sharp, architects, of York (for whom he had built a bridge at York), and Rev. Hammond Robinson (*recte* Roberson) of Healds Hall, Leeds, who was active in church-building in the Dewsbury district and associated with Thomas Taylor, the Leeds architect (ibid.).

139 CBC, Building Comm. MB 6, pp. 237-8.

140 Ibid., p. 360; MB 7, p. 68.

141 Ibid., pp. 119ff.

142 CBC, MB 19, p. 4; SR 2, f. 58.

143 CBC, Building Comm. MB 6, p. 128.

144 CBC, MB 12, p. 122.

145 CBC, MB 9, p. 420.

146 CBC, MB 19, p. 120.

147 CBC, MB 24, p. 218.

148 CBC, MBs 35, p. 54; 38, p. 32; 36, p. 328; 42, p. 21; 45, p. 422; 46, p. 358.

149 CBC, MB 9, p. 321.

150 CBC, Building Comm. MB 5, pp. 142, 250.

151 CBC, MBs 9, p. 39; 26, p. 288; 28, p. 22.

152 CBC, Building Comm. MB 5, pp. 237, 250.

153 CBC, MB 25, p. 210.

154 CBC, MB 27, p. 134; see Colvin, *DBA*.

155 CBC, SR1, p. 129.

156 CBC, MB 10, p. 111.

157 CBC, MB 36, p. 442.

158 Colvin, *DBA*.

159 CBC, MB 42, p. 1.

160 CBC, MB 50, p. 239; Stoke, Uttoxeter and Brereton were not Commissioners' churches. See A. Bayliss, *Life and Works of James Trubshaw* (Stockport, 1978).

161 CBC, MBs 26 (24 May 1827), 32 (14 Oct. 1828), 34 (10 Feb. 1829), 35 (2 Jun. 1829), 36 (22 Dec. 1829). See D. Linstrum, *West Yorkshire Architects and Architecture* (1978), p. 379, referring to an obituary in *Huddersfield Examiner*, 27 Mar. 1858.

162 See Nash's evidence, *PP* 1828 (446), IV, 'Report from the Select Committee on the Office of Works', p. 59: 'some builders ... do every branch of business themselves, but more frequently they make their estimates in conjunction with each other ... and one of them sends in an estimate of the whole'.

163 CBC, Building Comm. MB5, p. 237; he built Knutsford Gaol, several bridges and restored part of the north side of Manchester Collegiate Church (ibid.).

164 According to Halifax architect John Oates, CBC, Building Comm. MB 7, pp. 119ff.

165 Ibid., 5, p. 238. In tendering for Oates's two churches at Shipley and Wilsden (Yorks), he tendered also separately for each trade, and won the smith's and founder's for Shipley, ibid., 7, pp. 119-25, 236.

166 CBC, MBs 22, 28 Nov. 1826; 23, 9 Jan. 1827; 28, 12 Feb. 1828; 40, 13 Sep., 11 Oct. 1831.

167 CBC, Building Comm. MBs5, pp. 23ff, 199; 9, pp. 370-1.

168 Calculated on building accounts figures for 29 Commissioners' churches, 1822-31, see Table 1.

169 CBC, MBs 8, 20 Aug. 1822; 21, 27 Jun. 1826; 38, 10 Aug. 1830; SR 2, f. 8.

170 CBC, Building Comm. MB 6, p. 130.

171 CBC, MBs 8, p. 107; 22, p. 132; 27, p. 132.

172 CBC, Building Comm. MB 6, p. 132; CBC, SR 2, f. 166; CBC, MBs 9 (28 Jan. 1823) and 19 (27 Dec. 1825).

173 CBC, MBs 36, pp. 122-4; 39, p. 210.

174 CBC, Building Comm. MB 6, p. 131.

175 CBC, MBs 15, p. 360; 17, p. 386; 21, p. 134; 22, p. 130; 36, p. 364.

176 By Charles alone, CBC, MB 36, p. 330.

177 CBC, Building Comm. MBs 5, p. 303; 6, p. 133. Yet there were 58,000 blacksmiths numbered in the 1831 Census (*PP* 1833, xxvii, pp. 1044ff), though Clapham reckons that at least 45,000 would have been handicraftsmen, J. H. Clapham, *Economic History of Modern Britain. The Early Railway Age 1820-1850* (Cambridge, 1939), p. 169.

178 CBC, MB 10, 6 May 1823, report by committee of subscribers.

179 CBC, MBs 8, p. 182; 10, p. 285; 16, p. 244; 26, p. 76; 36, p. 188; 38, p. 250 (twice).

180 CBC, SR 1, ff. 102, 124, 140, 92, 126, 139; MBs 8, p. 285; 15, p. 4.

181 CBC, MBs 26, p. 86; 32, p. 200.

182 CBC, MBs 9, p. 157; 16, p. 326; 35, p. 428.

183 CBC, Building Comm. MB 5, pp. 113-15. According to the disappointed Nottingham tradesmen, Crowe had only 'spent a few hours on pretence of viewing the drawings, and examining the specifications, then returned [to London]' (CBC, Building Comm. MB 4, p. 406).

184 CC file 15097, Rev. E. France to Jenner, 6 Mar. 1821.

185 Rickman allowed his clerks at Erdington and Barnsley 2 guineas, as did Taylor at Pudsey; Nash

2¹/₂gns to W. J. Browne at Langham Place; but 3 gns was general.

186 S.M., New Churches Folder, AL SC/D (R).

187 CBC, MB 1, 9 Mar. 1819.

188 CBC, Building Comm. MB 7, pp. 215-19.

189 There is no record of the Commission's having appointed a specific clerk of works.

190 CBC, MB 7, 21 May 1822.

191 Grandson of Lord Stamford, who owned the town.

192 CBC, Building Comm. MBs 5, pp. 361-3; 6, pp. 40-1, 148-9.

193 Ibid., 5, pp. 3-5, 103.

194 CBC, SR 3, ff. 96, 127, 169.

195 Ibid., 4, f. 203v.

196 Ibid., 4, p. 339.

197 Notably in Holy Trinity, Great Suffolk Street, Newington, and St Luke's, Norwood, Lambeth, where Francis Bedford fought doggedly against 'Chain Plates and Bond Timbers in the Walls, I have so strong an objection to them, that I think it my duty to urge it … It is evident that Timbers laid into a Mass of Wet Masonry must inevitably decay in a few years leaving Channels in the Walls, which must materially take from their strength.' The Commissioners insisted that Bedford adhere to their (i.e. Mawley's) instructions, and despite Bedford's pleas and the Crown Architects' silence on this point when Bedford's designs were referred to them, were immovable, CBC, Building Comm. MB 7, pp. 214-16, 261; also pp. 26, 68, 225, 295.

198 Smirke proposed an iron roof for his church at Tyldesley (Lancs), CBC, MB 5, 8 May 1821; Smirke's estimate had to be reduced £1,500 and the iron roof appears to have been part of the reduction. More generally, see J. M. Crook and M. H. Port, *History of the King's Works, VI, 1782-1851* (1973), p. 415 and the references there given; and (for Nash), ibid., pp. 276, 303.

199 CBC, SR 1, pp. 79-91.

200 Ibid., p. 80; Building Comm. MB 4, pp. 371ff.

201 RIBA Lib., Rickman MS Diary, 8 Mar. 1822.

202 CBC, SR 1, p. 85.

203 CBC, MB 12, p. 237.

204 CBC, SR 1, f. 146.

205 Ibid., ff. 165-7.

206 CBC, SR 2, f. 12.

207 Ibid., ff. 32-46.

208 Partly because of his frequent attendance in Rochdale, where he was surveyor to the improvements commission, see CBC, Building Comm. MB 7, pp. 72, 108-9, 169-71.

209 CBC, SR2, ff. 60-70.

210 Ibid., f. 89v. Good had been a pupil of Soane.

211 Ibid., ff. 119-32.

212 CBC, SR 3, ff. 12-19.

213 Ibid., f. 25.

214 Ibid., f. 107.

Chapter 7

1 A. Satoh, *Building in Britain* (Aldershot, 1995).

2 R. Neve, *The City and Country Purchaser and Builder's Dictionary* (2nd edn, 1726), p. 51.

3 Rickman had proposed American fir at Chorley, CBC, SR 1, f. 27; and despite written warning Philip Sambell, the deaf and dumb architect, had used it at Truro, though not in constructional parts, ibid., 3, ff. 23v., 28v.

4 Occasionally, some of Mawley's corrigenda were ignored by the architect, and sometimes the Crown Architects did not endorse all his requirements.

5 E.g., rainwater pipes should be of 3¹/₂ins diameter, and preferably of cast iron. Four flues, 14ins by 10ins, should be inserted in the walls to be available if needed (SR5, ff. 211, 213v. Jan.-Feb. 1842, Pelsall, Staffs).

6 Good was decidedly unhappy about Welch's designs for St Philip, Bristol, in 1841: the walls of the parapet and of the upper spire were too thin; the lead gutters should be at least a foot wide, with a fall of 1¹/₂ins in ten feet and the lead 8lbs to the foot. (SR 5, f. 181).

7 CBC, SR 5, p. 8 (22 Nov. 1838).

8 CBC, SR 1, f. 73 (9 Feb. 1822).

9 PRO, Work 4/25, p. 208 (16 Feb. 1822); CBC, Building Comm. MB 4, pp. 235, 284.

10 CBC, Building Comm. MB 6, pp. 320-5; SR 1, f. 140v; CC file 17706, pt 2.

11 A retired architect of our own era has recalled the hostile attitude of men on site, treating an architect as dirt, 'to be put in his place as quickly as possible' in a letter in *RIBA Journal*, Feb. 2004, p. 18.

12 CBC, SR 1, ff. 146, 149; Building Comm. MB 7, pp. 150-4.

13 CBC, SR 1, f. 103.

14 CBC, Building Comm. MB 9, pp. 71, 138, 167, 188-91, 245-7, 249.

15 CC file 18135, pt 4.

16 CBC, SR 1, f. 194, 9 Dec. 1823.

17 CBC, Building Comm. MB 6, pp.225-7. The Committee also obtained mortar from Barry's work at Camp Field, Manchester, 2 Oct. 1822, ibid., pp. 331-2.

18 SR 1, ff.86 (16 Mar.), 99 (22 Apr.), 113 (1 Jul. 1822); 2, f. 20v. 30 Mar. 1824.

19 CC file 20548.

20 Ibid.

21 SR 4, ff. 115, 167, 5 Mar., 1 Jul. 1836; 5, f. 19, 5 Feb. 1839.

22 SR 5, f. 228v, 22 Jun. 1842.

23 As Griffin discovered at Willenhall (Staffs) (SR 7, f. 104, 22 Mar. 1851). See SR 5, f. 233v, 23 Jul. 1842.

24 SR 7, first f. (unnumb.), v. 11 Apr. 1848.

25 SR 5 , f. 86v, 7 Feb. 1840; SR 4, ff. 220, 224, 225v, 226v.

26 SR 5, f. 98, 6 Mar. 1840.

27 SR 7, ff. 88v, 130, 11 Apr. 1853; see also ff. 134v (23 Jun. 1853), 173, (22 Jan. 1856).

28 CBC, Building Comm., MB 4, p. 26.

29 Ibid., pp. 215-16.

30 Ibid., pp. 216, 261.

31 CBC, SR5, f. 8.

32 Op. cit., p. 42.

33 Nash, however, a few months earlier, in submitting his plans for All Souls, Langham Place, St Marylebone, recommended 'that no timber be inserted in the walls of this Church', and the Board had registered no objection, CBC, MB 5, 22 May 1821.

34 'When we look at a building we are gratified by considering the labour and skill in its construction … but when the materials pretend to perform a part which does not belong to their nature, then we are offended by the deception.' *Quarterly Review* (Apr., Jul. 1822), p. 333.

35 Carriage over short distances was a considerable item of expense, as Messrs Burnley & Farrar, masonry contractors for Pudsey church (Yorks), found in 1823-4: having to get wallstones from a quarry 3¹/₂miles distant instead of the 'Half Mile Quarry' in Pudsey cost them 'upwards of £180', CBC, Building Comm. MB 9, p. 295.

36 When the vicar of Dean (Lancs) requested ashlar cladding in place of hammered stone for the new church at Farnworth in 1824, he was told that while the Commissioners had 'no wish to restrain the Parish from adding to the Church the … Ornaments mentioned', they could not defray the bill, CBC, Building Comm. MB 9, p. 234.

37 CBC, MB 10, 22 Apr. 1823.

38 CC file 15225, pt 1, Rickman & Hutchinson to Jenner, 4 Mar. 1826. For Godwin's assertions, see CBC, MB 6, 9 Apr. 1822.

39 CBC, MB 6, 9 Apr. 1822.

40 CBC, SR 4, ff. 2v., 14; SR 5, ff. 28, 16v.

41 Ibid., ff. 29,32, 38, 42v, 44v (23 Apr., 14 May, 10 Jun., 24 Jun., 8 Jul. 1839).

42 Ibid., f. 75, 23 Mar. 1835.

43 Cp. Samuel Buxton's claim for an extra 3*d.* a ton carriage for 2,110 tons of stone because they had to be brought 200 yards further than contracted for, and up a hill, CC file 18124 (Netherton, Worcs, 1831); and Francis Goodwin's note on his Lithographic Form for Oldham, St James, that despite its 'plain and simple character' the cost would be greater than his contemporaneous Manchester church (Hulme) 'owing to the distance from which the Materials are to be conveyed by Land Carriage', CC file 20536 (1 Feb. 1825).

44 CBC, Building Comm. MB 5, pp. 228-30.

45 Ibid., p. 11. 14¹/₄ cu. ft of Yorkshire stone weigh a ton (Dobson, *Art of Building*, p. 116).

46 CBC, Building Comm. MB 9, pp. 361-3.

47 Ibid., 5, p. 145.

48 Described by A. Clifton-Taylor as one of the two classic Millstone Grit sandstones, 'in steady demand, largely for engineering enterprises,' because of its great strength; used in constructing some of the London docks, and in Hardwick's Euston Arch, *The Pattern of English Building* (2nd edn, 1965), p. 144.

49 CBC, Building Comm. MB 7, p. 96.

50 Ibid., pp. 71-2, 89-92.

51 Ibid., pp. 69-72, 89-95, 172-5.

52 Ibid., pp. 96, 241-2.

53 CBC, SR 3, f. 56.

54 Ibid., ff. 96 (14 Sep. 1830), 169.

55 CBC, SR 5, f. 11.

56 SR 3, f. 214, 16 Dec. 1830.

57 SR 4, f. 70, 9 Mar. 1835 (Birkenshaw).

58 Ibid., f. 135.

59 CBC, SR 5, f. 148, 9 Nov. 1840.

60 SR 1, ff. 65, 66, 127; Building Comm., MB 4, p. 203. But in 1853, in the small church for Brampton (Yorks) Good stipulated a minimum height of only 8ft (SR 7, f. 137v.).

61 CBC, Building Comm. MB 4, pp. 359-60.

62 CBC, SR 3, ff. 129, 153, 217 (26 Apr. 1831).

63 SR 2, f. 56, 16 Feb. 1825.

64 CBC, Building Comm. MB 4, pp. 248-52, 307-9.

65 CBC, SR 3, f. 43.

66 SR 4, ff. 19ff., 21 Feb. 1834.

67 Ibid., f. 76.

68 See D. T. Yeomans, *The Trussed Roof: Its History and Development* (Aldershot, 1992). The truss is clearly depicted in Fig. 53, p. 50, of E. Dobson's *Rudiments of the Art of Building* (1849).

69 The view also expressed in Joseph Gwilt's *Encyclopaedia of Architecture* (2nd edn, revised by Wyatt Papworth, 1899), p. 627.

70 CBC, SR 5, ff. 39v., 41.

71 Ibid., f. 181.

72 SR 4, ff. 74-5.

73 CBC, Building Comm. MB 6, p. 139 (Attached Architects' report, 27 Sep. 1822).

74 CBC, SR 7, p. 279; K. Downes, *The Architecture of Wren* (1982), p. 34.

75 SR 1, f. 45; Building Comm. MB 4, pp. 90-2.

76 CBC, Building Comm. MB 5, p.201. Chantrell constructed models for the workmen: his ten guinea charge was queried by the Surveyor as unusual, SR 2, f. 100.

77 CBC, Building Comm. MB 6, p. 278. Phillips' designs were ultimately rejected.

78 CBC, SR 3, f. 207, 4 Feb. 1828.

79 SR 1, f. 33v.; *Quarterly Review*, XXVII (Apr., Jul., 1822), p. 324.

80 See pp. 168-70.

81 CBC, MB 10, 22 Apr. 1823; Building Comm. MB 4, p. 214.

82 CBC, Building Comm. MB 4, pp. 23-5.

83 Roofing sheets weighed about 16 oz. per square foot, compared with lead, at 7 lbs, or as the Commissioners required, 8lbs, to the sq.ft, E. Dobson, *Art of Building*, p. 65.

84 This was R. & C. Kepp, Chandos Street, Covent Garden, London, whose father, John Kepp, had constructed at least 14 copper roofs, 1789-94, including St Botolph, Aldersgate; St Peter le Poer, Broad Street; and Dorchester, Chelmsford and Monmouth Gaols, CBC, Building Comm. MB 4, p. 357.

85 CBC, SR 1, f. 39 (16 Sep. 1821); Building Comm. MB 4, p. 204. In Dec. 1822 Mawley commented: 'No other architect has *ventured* to recommend such a covering for the roof [of] a Church', SR 1, f. 66.

86 CC file 18135, pt 3, Smirke to Jenner, 28 Apr.1827; also CBC, MB 24, 15 May 1827.

87 CBC, MBs 25, 19 Jun.; 27, 11 Dec. 1827.

88 CBC, SR 3, ff. 159, 161, 163, 183; CBC, MB 40, p. 361.

89 CBC, MB 40, p. 441 (10 Apr. 1832); SR 3, f. 199 (2 Mar. 1833).

90 SR 4, ff. 30, 41.

91 Ibid., f. 62, 6 Dec. 1834.

92 CBC, Building Comm. MBs 4, pp. 214, 366-7; 5, pp. 143, 206-7, 209. Mawley had inspected roofs of two types in houses in Camberwell and Denmark Hill that Bedford had built, and condemned them as having an insufficient pitch, CBC, SR 1. f. 30 (30 Jul. 1821).

93 CBC, SR 4, ff. 227-8.

94 CBC, Building Comm. MB 7, pp. 115-19, 144-50, 215-26, 252-4.

95 CBC, MB 10, 22 Apr. 1823; Building Comm. MB 7, pp. 115-18.

96 CBC, MB 10, 29 Apr., 6 May 1823; Building Comm. MB 7, pp. 157, 211, 252-4, 273-4, 300, 325-7, 331, 337. The report was precautionary rather than condemnatory: '… knowing how difficult it is always to detect defective workmanship; and the propriety in such Works of making allowances for accidents, We are of opinion that although these Arches by the use of Roman Cement round the springing Stones, and in the Groins, and by great care in the construction of them, may at present stand, yet we do not think they can be relied upon with perfect security nor be held to be permanently stable', ibid., pp. 253-4.

97 CC file 20548.

98 CBC, SR 3, ff. 68v., 89, 91.

99 SR 5, ff. 58,62.

100 SR 4, f. 5v; SR 5 ff. 49, 55.

101 SR 3, ff. 35 (4 Feb. 1829), 75 (9 Jan. 1830).

102 SR 3, ff. 110v., 119, 125v.

103 SR 7, f. 20v., 10 Nov. 1848.

104 Ibid., f. 41, 16 Apr. 1829.

105 *Gentleman's Magazine,* 1818, pt 2.

106 CBC, Building Comm. MB 9, p. 24.

107 They supplied the window frames as well as iron columns for St George, Leicester, ibid., pp. 353-4.

108 Ibid., p. 24.

109 *History of the King's Works, VI, 1782-1851*, pp. 154, 275, 416. There appears to have been no familiarity with the French use of iron roofs from as early as 1785, described by J. Ondelet, *Traité théoretique et pratique de l'art de bâtir* (5 vols, Paris, 1802-17). Rickman recorded the breaking of an iron beam, killing one man and injuring others, at the Birmingham Theatre, in his diary, 22 May 1820, stating (wrongly) 'Iron is in consequence to be banished', MS Diary, RIBA.

110 The collapse of the iron roof of the Brunswick Theatre in Goodman's Fields, London, in 1828, cannot have helped. See *Companion to the Almanac*, 1828, p. 174.

111 CBC, MB 5, 8 May 1821. See also RIBAD.

112 CC file 18158, pt 2, architect's lithographic papers.

113 PRO, Work 1/9, p. 386; CC file 15097, architect's lithographic paper.

114 CBC, Building Comm. MB 9, pp. 29-30.

115 E.g., by Rickman extensively, Oates at Shelton, Smirke at Chatham, and Lee at Netherton.

116 PRO, Work 1/9, p. 468.

117 CC files 20548, 18196, architect's lithographic paper.

118 CBC, SR5, ff. 40v, 25 Jun.; 67, 72v, 77v., 8 Nov., 28 Nov., 24 Dec. 1839.

119 As by Chantrell at Christ Church, Leeds.

120 CBC, Building Comm. MB 9, p. 26.

Chapter 8 (pages 151-175)

1 RIBA Lib., Ann James, 'Thomas Rickman', R.I.B.A. prize thesis.

2 RIBA Lib., Rickman's MS Diary.

3 T. C. Bannister, *Architectural Review*, 127 (1950), pp. 231-46.

4 Quoted by Bannister, loc. cit.

5 T. Rickman, *An Attempt to Discriminate the Styles of English Architecture* [1817], p. iii.

6 Ibid., p. 37.

7 This is not the place to discuss either the origins of Gothic, or the arguments about what style best represented our national consciousness.

8 N. Pevsner, *Some Architectural Writers of the Nineteenth Century* (Oxford, 1972), p. 30.

9 J. Summerson, *Architecture in Britain 1530-1830* (rev. edn, Harmondsworth, 1955), p. 299.

10 N. Pevsner, *Some Architectural Writers*, p. 32.

11 Op. cit., 1st edition.

12 RIBA Lib., Rickman's MS diary, 9, 22 Jan., 8 Jun. 1818. Rickman was third for St Pancras

church.

13 Ibid., 27, 30 Apr., 2, 3 July 1818.

14 Rickman's 'general amounts of Estimates for Free Church', dated 8 Aug. 1818, in the Office of Works papers, total £6,087.0s.8d. for 1,313 persons (PRO, Work 6/183, f. 18).

15 Ibid., 27 July, 4, 6 Aug. 1818.

16 Diary, 27 Aug., 2 Sep. 1818; PRO, Work 6/183. 1, no. 13 (14 Aug. 1818).

17 Ibid., no. 17.

18 S.M., X.E.2. 3.

19 PRO, Work 6/183. 1, no. 18.

20 Rickman informed the Surveyor-General that in order that the cast-iron work might 'rest as to its weight on a sure foundation I have had some panel heads carved and intend to have them cast', S.M., X.E.2. 1, 19 Sep. 1818.

21 'What wrecks do many of our fine old churches … present under the … incongruous repairs of incompetent workmen'; and iron roofs 'ought not to be hazarded upon churches'. Ibid., 9.

22 Ibid.

23 PRO, Work 6/183. 1, no. 25 (5 Dec. 1818).

24 According to his partner R. C. Hussey, 'he could, without material inconvenience, pass two nights of three in travelling', quoted Colvin, *DBA*, p. 813.

25 RIBA Lib., Rickman's MS Diary, 5 Mar. 1819.

26 Ibid., 31 Oct., 13 Nov., 7, 8, 14 Dec. 1818.

27 Ibid., 8 Jun. 1819.

28 Ibid., 22, 25 Jun. 1819.

29 Ibid., 27 Jul. 1819.

30 PRO, Work 1/9, p. 468.

31 Rickman's MS Diary, 17 Nov. 1819.

32 Ibid., 2 July, 4 Dec. 1819.

33 Ibid., 8 Mar. 1822.

34 Colvin, *DBA*, p. 524.

35 C. L. Eastlake, *The Gothic Revival*, (1872), pp. 123-4.

36. This is not wholly true: many strictly contemporary works exhibit a similar boldness.

37 CBC, MB 8, p. 106.

38 CBC, Building Comm. MB 7, pp. 258-63.

39 RIBA Lib., Rickman's MS Diary, 15 Jan. 1820.

40 Ibid., 11 Feb. 1820.

41 Ibid., 22 Mar. 1820. Rickman's designs at £14,229 were rejected by the Building Committee, 23 May 1820, CBC, MB 3. The local committee had complained that 'the side passages to the Gallery are too contracted'.

42 Ibid., 21 May 1820.

43 Ibid., 5 Jun. 1820.

44 Ibid., 18 Jun. 1820.

45 Ibid., 5 May 1820.

46 CC file 17887, Rev. R. Carus Wilson to Jenner, 3 Mar. 1821.

47 PRO, Work 1/10, p. 99.

48 Ibid., 1/10, pp. 82 (6 Apr.), 171 (26 Jun. 1820).

49 Diary, 2 Jul. 1820.

50 PRO, Work 1/10, p. 272.

51 Diary, 10 to 13 Feb. 1821.

52 Ibid., 28 Mar. 1820.

53 Ibid., 19 May 1821.

54. Ibid., 9 Jun. 1821.

55 CBC, SR 1, f. 60, 17 Dec. 1821; Building Comm. MB 4, pp. 15-16, 233 (approved by the Attached Architects on estimate of £5,633 inclusive, 12 Feb. 1822).

56 PRO, Work 1/11 (7 Feb. 1822).

57 CC 17887, Statement from Sir James Allan Park (site donor); Rev. R. Carus Wilson to Jenner, n.d., and 31 Jul. 1820.

58 Diary, 21 Feb. 1822; CBC, Building Comm. MB 4, pp. 312-14.

59 CBC, Building Comm. MB 4, pp. 315, 359-60.

60 CC file 17887, Rickman to Jenner, 25 Apr., 18 May 1822.

61 CBC, Building Comm. MB 5, pp. 358-61.

62 Ibid., 6, pp. 17, 93-5, 120-2, 151.

63 Ibid., 6, pp. 374, 403; 7, pp. 17-18, 33-5.

64 Ibid., 7, pp. 85-6, 176-7, 188, 248-9.

65 Earning the firm some £7,300 in CBC commission fees.

66 C. L. Eastlake, *The Gothic Revival* (1872), p. 123.

67 Ibid., p. 122.

68 Colvin, *DBA*, p. 813.

69 *Annual Register*, 1806, cited, G.E.C., *Complete Peerage,* XI, p. 451.

70 RIBAD, *Catalogue, O-R,* plan and west elevation (reproduced , fig. 87), p. 41.

71 Ibid., west elevation 'Romanesque – Early English', p. 143.

72 CBC, MB 12, 9 Mar. 1824.

73 BL, Add. MS 37794, f.80.

74 CBC, MB 12, p. 394 et seq. See also CBC, Building Comm. MB 7, pp. 258-63, 292, 302, 352-6 (Jun.-Aug. 1823); and CC file 15225, pt 1; and chapter 9, n.6 below.

75 A portrait in chalks of Goodwin by Agostino Aglio, *c.*1825, reproduced in National Art-Collection Fund *2002 Review*, p. 99, is now in RIBAD.

76 J. Summerson, *Architecture in Britain 1530 to 1830* (rev. edn, Harmondsworth, 1955), p. 303. A. Trimen's historical sketch, *Church and Chapel Architecture* (1849), placed Goodwin 'high in rank among the architects of the present century', selecting particularly St George, Kidderminster (pp. 85-6).

77 *Gentleman's Magazine*, 1827, pt 2, p. 201.

78 Info. *ex* Mrs Elizabeth James.

79 S.M., X.E. 3. 1 (29 Sep. 1819), 2 (22 Oct. 1818), 3 (n.d.).

80 Rickman, too, could be guilty of this trick: C. R. Cockerell in competing for a church at Bristol in 1828 remarked that he had 'understood a general design in Indian ink' would be sufficient for the Commissioners to judge of the fitness of a design; whereas Rickman was sending 'very beautiful tinted elevations', CBC, MB 30, 27 May 1828.

81 RIBA Lib., Rickman's MS Diary, 8 Feb. 1820.

82 S.M., X. E. 3. 5.

83 Ibid., X. B. 27.

84 CC file 18484, Newton to Jenner, Apr. 1826.

85 PRO, Work 1/9, p. 388, 6 May, 4 Jun. 1819.

86 Ibid., p. 418, 5 Aug. 1819.

87 Ibid., p. 482, 4 Nov. 1819.

88 Ibid., 1/10, p. 216, 11 Sep. 1820.

89 S.M., X.E. 4.

90 CBC, MB 3, p. 119.

91 Ibid., p. 172.

92 CBC, MB 7, p. 52.

93 CBC, MB 3, p. 138.

94 Ibid., pp. 431-2.

95 See above. The loss of CBC, MB 4 prevents our knowing what Dance's reply was.

96 CBC, MB 10, 6 May 1823, letter dated 28 Apr. 1823.

97 CBC, MB 15, 23 Nov. 1824.

98 CBC, Building Comm. MB 9, p. 29.

99 CBC, MB 10, 3 Jun. 1823.

100 CBC, Building Comm. MB 9, pp. 28-9.

101 CBC, Building Comm. MBs 4, pp. 43,63; 9, pp. 121; 9, pp. 121, 125. Smirke had charged only six journeys for his Bristol church, about as far from London as was Bordesley (ibid., p. 125).

102 CBC, MB 10, pp. 285, 435.

103 Marcus Whiffen, *Stuart and Georgian Churches* (1947-8), pp. 83-4.

104 Equally true of nearly all the churches of the period.

105 RIBA Lib., Rickman's MS diary, 26 Aug. 1825; and quotation by D. Watkin, *Life and Work of C. R. Cockerell* (1974), pp. 66-7.

106 RIBA Lib., Rickman's MS diary, 11 Jan. 1819, 2 and 14 Mar. 1820, 18 Sep.1820, 8 Dec. 1818,

26 Jan. 1820.

107 Ibid., 9 Feb. 1820.

108 Ibid., 7, 8 Dec. 1818.

109 Ibid., 27 Mar. 1819.

110 Ibid., 25, 26 Jan., 9, 11 Feb. 1820.

111 The chairman of the local committee at Hulme, a Manchester suburb, asked that Goodwin might submit plans for their new church, as 'He possesses much local knowledge', CBC, Building Comm. MB 6, pp. 101-2.

112 CBC, MB 3, 30 May 1820.

113 RIBA Library, Rickman's MS diary, 10 Feb. 1821.

114 CBC, Building Comm. MB 4, pp. 5-6.

115 CC file 21819.

116 CC file 21819, C. A. Busby to Abp of Canterbury, 16 Mar. 1822. Busby alleged that four bills (equivalent to cheques), each for £250, had been made out by Goodwin's clients, and that Laing, on his appointment to build Hulme church, handed over one such bill.

117 RIBA Lib., Rickman's MS diary, 8 Feb. 1820.

118 A fuller account may be found in the author's 'Francis Goodwin, 1784-1835', *Architectural History*, 1 (1958), pp. 60-72, though further light is shed by CC file 21819, only seen subsequently.

119 CBC, MB 6, p. 136 (26 Feb.), Goodwin's letter dated 22 Feb. 1822.

120 Ibid.

121 CC file 20548 (Leeds), E. Gyfford, 24 Feb. 1821, from 29 Francis Street, Bedford Square (Goodwin's office); CBC, MBs 5 (10 Jul. 1821), 6 (12 Feb. 1822); Rickman's MS diary, 15 May 1821.

122 The following account is based on letters from and statements by the several parties to the Board, which are given at length in CBC, MBs. 5 and 6, supplemented by N. Bingham's biography, *C. A. Busby. The Regency Architect of Brighton and Hove* (1991), and CC file 21819.

123 CBC, MB 5, p. 291 et seq.; CC file 20548, lithographic paper.

124 One such is illustrated in Bingham, *C. A. Busby*, p. 44. Busby declared that the roof failure story referred to 'an unsuccessful experiment of a Roof of French Arches, formed of bricks and cement, which I made in the year 1809, in a building (my own property) at Tooting', and the 'untoward scheme' alleged by Goodwin was 'a water-saving canal-dock', recommended by the late Earl Stanhope. CC file 21819, Busby to Abp of Canterbury, 16 Mar. 1822.

125 Cp. n. 111 above.

126 A letter from Jedediah Strutt, the dominant figure at Belper, to Busby, 26 Jan.1822, lends some colour to this allegation, CC file 21819.

127 CBC, MB 6, p. 245.

128 RIBA Lib., Rickman's MS Diary, 18 Feb. 1822.

129 There is a copy among the Cockerell drawings in the Victoria and Albert Museum (Print Room).

130 But this was a common occurrence.

131 CC 21819, Busby to Abp of Canterbury, 16 Mar. 1822.

132 RIBA Lib., Rickman's MS Diary, 16 Apr. 1821.

133 Ibid., 17 Feb. 1822. Rickman had earlier thought Busby's designs 'much frittered' (16 Apr. 1821).

134 *Monthly Magazine,* LIV, pp. 211-12 (Oct. 1822).

135 CBC, MB 6, 26 Feb. 1822, annexes to Goodwin's defence, 4 Feb. 1822.

136 Exhibited at Royal Academy, 1817-29, including Goodwin's Kidderminster church, 1822.

137 1778-1862, younger brother of Joseph, architect of St Mark, North Audley Street, London. A pupil and later assistant of James Wyatt from 1793, in 1800 he was serving in the East India Company's naval service; later he assisted Wyatville for many years. See Colvin, *DBA*.

138 CBC, MB 6, 26 Feb. 1822.

139 CC file 21819, M. Gandy to CBC, 8 Mar. 1822.

140 CBC, Building Comm. MBs 4, pp. 43-7; 9, pp. 121-5. Contemporary newspaper reports highlight the significance of this ceremony.

141 CBC, Building Comm. MB 4, pp. 387-9, 400.

142 Ibid., 6, pp. 37-9, 41, 148-9; CBC, MB 16, 11 Jan. 1825.

143 CBC, MB 7, 21 May 1822.

144 CBC, Building Comm. MB 5, pp. 214, 288, 314.

145 CBC, Building Comm. MBs 4, pp. 371-2, 395; 5, p. 355; 7, p. 318.

146 Ibid., 9, p. 306-7.

147 Unfortunately the Kidderminster and West Bromwich tenders were apparently received at dates not covered by the CBC's extant records. Hedge had the carpenter's and joiner's contract at Kidderminster, neglected it totally, and had to be dismissed, CBC, Building Comm. MBs 4, pp. 371-2, 395; 5, pp. 48-54.

148 PRO, Work 1/9, p. 388.

149 Ibid., pp. 389 (14 Jun.), 418 (5 Aug. 1819).

150 RIBA Lib., Rickman's MS diary, 12 Nov. 1819.

151 CBC, SR 1, f. 3.

152 CBC, Building Comm. MB 4, pp. 46-7.

153 Ibid., pp. 144-5, Goodwin to Jenner, 7 Jan. 1822.

154. Ibid., p. 145.

155 Ibid., p. 165 (19 Jan. 1822).

156 Ibid., pp. 320-1, 24 and 25 Feb. 1822; 6, pp. 103-7 (13 Aug. 1822).

157 Ibid., 7, pp. 216-17.

158 CBC, Building Comm. MB 4, pp. 44-5, 336.

159 CBC, SR 1, ff. 80, 82; MB 6, 19 Mar. 1822.

160 CBC, MB 6, 26 Mar. 1822.

161 Ibid., 9 Apr. 1822.

162 CBC, Building Comm. MB 5, pp. 216-17, 322.

163 CBC, MB 6, 9 Apr.1822. The local committee preferred a firm that had worked for the parish, though at a higher tender.

164 CBC, Building Comm. MB 5, pp. 270-5.

165 Ibid., 6, p. 15.

166 Ibid., pp. 41-8, 103-10.

167 Ibid., pp. 167, 187-9, 244-8, 264, 309.

168 Ibid., p. 363, 28 Jan. 1823.

169 Ibid., 7, pp. 25-8, 77, 195-7, 250-1.

170 Ibid., 9, 195.

171 CBC, MB 10, 27 May 1823.

172 CBC, Building Comm. MB 9, pp. 37, 83, 99, 178, 195, 205, 231, 306-7; CBC, MB 14, 13 Jul. 1824.

173 CBC, MB 19, 24 Jan. 1826.

174 CBC, SR 2, f. 133v, 13 Nov. 1826; MB 27, 18 Dec. 1827.

175 CBC, SR 2, f. 186; 3, ff. 12-18.

176 CBC, SR 3, f. 50; MB 35, 9 Jun. 1829.

177 CBC, SR 3, f. 45.

178 St George, Hulme, is described in J. S. Leatherbarrow, *Victorian Period Piece* (1954), pp. 140-2, quoting a contemporary description from S. Hibbert's *History of the Foundations in Manchester*, 3 vols (1830) as 'the most attractive object at the entrance to the town from Chester, ... remarkable for its simplicity and the beauty of its proportions'. 'The tower is of a most ornamental character ... and may perhaps be reckoned the most beautiful of [Goodwin's] many beautiful works ... it bears the appearance of much greater elevation than in reality it possesses'.

179 CBC, MB 17, 3 May 1825.

180 CBC, MB 33, 25 Nov. 1828.

181 CC file 20536, Barker to Goodwin, 23 Sep. 1824.

182 CBC, SR 2, f. 109v., 8 Jul. 1826.

183 CBC, MB 34, 6 Jan.1829.

184 CBC, SR 2, f. 162v.

185 *PP,* 1833 (269) XII.

186 See M. H. Port (ed.), *The Houses of Parliament* (New Haven and London, 1976), p. 111.

Chapter 9

1 CBC, MB 3, 2 May 1820. Smirke reported that he had calculated the additional expense of the portico of St Anne, Wandsworth, at £1,600, and the tower at about £2,000.

2 ΩΦ [W. H. Leeds], 'On the Architecture of the New Churches', *Magazine of the Fine Arts*, 16 May 1821, pp. 130-8.

3 *Quarterly Review* (1822), no. 27, p. 323.

4 CBC, MB 7, 7 May 1822.

5 RIBA Lib., Rickman's MS Diary, 18 Nov. 1822.

6 For their second Birmingham church, St Peter at Dale End, Rickman and Hutchinson had, 'in order to vary the appearance adopted the earliest style of the Gothic … the principal exterior feature of which style is the simple, long lancet window; should this feature be altered by enlarging the windows, either a considerable extra expence must be incurred to preserve any appearance of plain style, or another must be adopted'. As the Board wanted the height of the nave reduced, 'we are fearful', wrote Rickman, ' that the consequent diminution of the clerestory windows would prevent the body of the church being sufficiently lighted, and more particularly from the height of the surrounding buildings'. He therefore suggested abandoning the Gothic design for 'a simple Grecian plan', which might be better adapted for its purpose 'inasmuch as neither piers nor Arches would be required, and therefore in the interior there would not be anything to interfere either with the speaking seeing or hearing the expence in either case might be the same', i.e. as the original plain Gothic. The local committee 'would not object to a Grecian church', which might be 'better adapted for this particular situation than a Gothic one, deprived as it must be of its characteristic tower or spire', CBC, MB 12, 9 Mar. 1824.

7 S.M., X.B. 38.

8 CBC, MB 31 (10 Jun. 1828).

9 See M. Whiffen, *Stuart and Georgian Churches* (1947-8), pp. 71, 73 and chap. V generally; N. Pevsner, *BoE, Worcestershire* (1968), p. 125.

10 T. Friedman, *The Georgian Parish Church* (Reading, 2004), p. 22. See also J. M. Crook, *John Carter and the Mind of the Gothic Revival* (1995).

11 Reviewing A. C. Pugin's, *Specimens of the Architectural Antiquities of Normandy* (1828), *The Athenaeum* hailed Pugin as 'the Stuart and Revett of the [Gothic] style', inspiring 'our artists' and developing 'the principles and science' of the style; and subsequently called *Examples* the pre-eminent publication, whether in England or on the Continent, 'in all that appertains to practice and execution', *Athenaeum* (1828), pp. 47, 822. I am grateful to the late Professor Phoebe Stanton for these references.

12 C. Brooks, *The Gothic Revival* (1999), p. 134.

13 E.g., *Gentleman's Magazine*, 92 (1822), pt 1, p. 601.

14 Ibid., 90 (1820), pt 2, p. 127.

15 S.M., XV. A. 32 (6 Jan.1821), cited by C. Webster, *R. D. Chantrell, Architect: His Life and Work in Leeds 1818-1847* (Leeds, 1992), p. 82; *Builder*, 5 (1847), p. 300.

16 Cp. *Gentleman's Magazine*, 97 (1827), pt 1, p. 393 et seq.

17 Ibid., p. 394.

18 CBC MBs 30 (27 May, 3 Jun.), 31 (10 Jun. 1828); MB 3, 20 Jun. 1820.

19 CBC, MB 9, 26 Nov.1822.

20 Ibid., 7 Jan.1823, Rev. J. W. Whittaker.

21 CC file 18124, Dr Booker to Jenner, 16 Jun. 1821.

22 CBC, MB 9, 16 Dec. 1822.

23 *Gentleman's Magazine*, 99 (1829), pt 2, p. 397.

24 CBC, MB 9, Rev. Mr Matthew, 16 Dec. 1822.

25 Cockerell to Lord Middleton, 10 Jul. 1822, V&A Mus. Print Room, DD3, E3008A 1909.

26 Mant published *Church Architecture considered* in 1843, and was associated with the Cambridge Camden Society.

27 CBC, MB 3, 14 Mar. (complaining of waste of room at the east end) and 9 May 1820.

28 CBC, MB 5, 22 May, 25 Sep. 1821.

29 CBC, MB 3, 25 Apr.1820.

30 CBC, MB 19, 27 Dec. 1825.

31 CBC, MB 6, 26 Mar., 25 Jun. 1822.

32 CBC, MB 10, 29 Apr., 6 May 1823. Saunders (1762-1839) made 'an important contribution to the study of vaulting', Colvin, *DBA*.

33 CC file 21744, pt 2 (15 Jul. 1819).

34 Though the Surveyor thought that for 'the ceiling to be quite flat … for a Gothic design appears objectionable', CBC, SR 1, f.241 (11 Mar. 1823).

35 In general, transepts were disapproved of, CBC, SR 3, f. 29v.

36 See G. W. O. Addleshaw and F. Etchells, *The Architectural Setting of Anglican Worship* (1948), p. 63.

37 Ibid., p. 200.

38 Ibid., p. 76.

39 Colvin, *DEA* (1st ed., 1954), p. 145.

40 *Gentleman's Magazine*, 95 (1825), pt 2, p. 577.

41 The Board appears to have suggested him to Chatham (CC file 15452, incumbent's letter, 30 Dec. 1818); and his Wyndham Place plan was one selected by the leading Manchester incumbent from the Board's stock (CBC, MB 5, 8 May, 10 Jul. 1821).

42 CBC, MB 5, 10 Jul. 1821.

43 Ibid., 22 May 1821.

44 *Gentleman's Magazine*, 99 (1829), pt 1, p. 13.

45 *PP*, 1823 (573) VII. (3rd Report, CBC).

46 CBC, MB 3, 20 Jun. 1820.

47 *Gentleman's Magazine*, 99 (1829), pt 2, p. 579.

48 Ibid., pt 1, p. 580.

49 CBC, MB 9, 25 Feb. 1823.

50 *Gentleman's Magazine*, 100 (1830), pt 1, p. 579 et seq.

51 Described by Eastlake, *Gothic Revival*, pp. 141-4, where the cost is given as £40,000.

52 *Gentleman's Magazine*, 96 (1826), pt 1, p. 201: 'To the architect the highest praise is due for the boldness which designed and the talent that executed this noble piece of masonry ... The style of vaulting is, however, full two centuries earlier than the building.'

53 I am most grateful to Professor Christopher Wilson for pointing out to me the resemblances to Notre Dame, Alençon, and Bath Abbey.

54 'One of the handsomest' of Commissioners' churches (*Gentleman's Magazine*, 100 (1830), pt 2, p. 297); 'where every peculiar architectural difficulty of the type is solved in a design of great dignity and good sense', H. S. Goodhart-Rendel, *English Architecture since the Regency* (1953), pp. 50, 52.

55 E. and W. Young, *Old London Churches* (1956), p. 166 and pl. 56B. The Youngs note that the model 'is as much the Roman basilica as the Greek temple'.

56 First published as an essay in James Smith's *Panorama of Science and Art* (Liverpool, 1817), and re-published as a book 'at a price which shall not present an obstacle to extensive circulation', as Rickman put it in his preface, in 1817, avowedly as a 'text-book for the architectural student', and a guide for the judgment of 'the guardians of our ecclesiastical edifices'.

57 Rickman, *An Attempt* ..., p. 59.

58 CBC, Building Comm. MBs 6, pp. 112-16 (Sep. 1822), 7, pp. 37-8 (Feb. 1823).

59 See pp. 166-7.

60 F. Beckwith, *Thomas Taylor, Regency Architect, Leeds* (Leeds, 1949), p. 91. Taylor argued that the cost of Gothic mouldings was 'trifling', as against Classical features.

61 T. D. Whitaker, *Loidis and Elmete* (Leeds, 1816), pp. 249-50, quoted by Beckwith, p. 30.

62 R. D. Chantrell, *Builder*, 5 (1846), pp. 300-3, cited by Beckwith, p. 29.

63 *Church and Chapel Architecture* (1849), p. 83, cited by Beckwith, p. 29, praised Taylor as 'the first to reintroduce open roofs and benches, instead of pews, into the churches of this country' (ie, at Liversedge), p. 83.

64. C. Webster, *R. D. Chantrell*, pp. 36-45.

65. S.M., XV. A. 32, cited by Webster, *Chantrell*, p. 83.

66. Colvin, *DBA*.

67. See p. 137-8.

68. D. Linstrum, *West Yorkshire Architects and Architecture* (1978), p. 213.

69. CBC, MB 32, p. 382.

70. Mr Webster has suggested that this design is so much more sophisticated than that of his contemporary minor work that perhaps it was by Goodwin, an example of his 'lending' designs for execution by others, when he was limited to six churches by the Board, *Chantrell*, p. 86. Although the tower of Christ Church has some resemblance to Goodwin's work, there is no documentary evidence that even hints at such an arrangement. It would be highly surprising if Busby, with his intimate knowledge of Goodwin's office and his uncontrollable urge to get every aspect of the Leeds Affair (see Chapter 8) on paper, had not commented on a Goodwin–Chantrell link.

71. CBC, Building Comm. MBs 4, pp. 90-2; 5, p. 201. See p. 143 above.

72. CBC, MB 26, 4 Sep. 1827.

73 Linstrum, *West Yorkshire*, p. 213.

74 Webster, *Chantrell*, pp. 88-9.

75 Ibid., pp.114-17; R. D. Chantrell, 'On the Geometric System', *Builder*, 5 (1847), pp. 300-2; J. Gwilt, *Encyclopaedia of Architecture* (ed. Wyatt Papworth, 1899), pp. 1014-15.

Chapter 10

1 From a 'sense of their being inconvenient and useless', CBC, MBs 56 (24 Jan. 1843), 59, p. 394 (25 Feb. 1845).

2 CBC, MB 24, 24 Apr. 1827.

3 The CBC negotiated for a site in Mecklenburg Square, St Pancras, valued at £6,850-£7,450, CBC, MB 1, 22 Dec. 1818.

4 Thus, while the governors of St Bartholomew's Hospital were happy to give a site in the parish of St Luke, Old Street (though in fact legally a consideration proved necessary, so that they sold it for £100), the Haberdashers' Company wanted £2,400 for a suburban site at Hoxton, and Mr Rhodes, a land developer, in neighbouring Shoreditch was willing to sell at £600 an acre. CBC, MB3 21 Mar., 25 Apr., 11 Jul., 18 Apr. 1820.

5 As at Derby, where in the early 1820s a thousand houses were built in four years, one back street site was offered in 1825 at 8s. a sq. yard (about £2,000 an acre, usually the minimum area required), another at 4s., while some were only 3s, CC file 18484.

6 In 1820, proprietors at West Bromwich refused an offer based on the prices that building land was fetching of 2s.6d. and 1s.9d. a sq. yard (about £420-£605 an acre); a jury awarded 2s.8d. and 2s. a yard, amounting in all to £1,168, which was £93 more than the CBC had offered. CBC, MB 3, 14 Mar., 25 Apr. 1820. In 1827, the landowner sold one acre in Travis Street, Manchester, for £1,000; and a site for Christ Church, Coventry, cost £1,780; CBC, MBs 25, 5 Jun., 26, 25 Sep. 1827.

7 CBC, MB 1, 16 Feb. 1819, opinion of Law Officers.

8 *PP* 1837 (437) XLI. Thereafter, the parliamentary returns do not sufficiently distinguish law charges and public subscriptions from sites expenditure to identify CBC payments for sites.

9 E.g., a site chosen at Netherton (Dudley), proved to be riddled by ancient mine workings, CC file 18124.

10 CBC, MB 1, 26 Jan., 16 Feb. 1819.

11 CBC, MB 14, 14 Sep. 1824.

12 CBC, MB 9, 28 Jan. 1823. The Commissioners' committee on Walcot finally recommended forming two parishes, Upper and Lower Walcot, dividing the latter into two districts, Christ Church (as the parish church) and Trinity. Ibid., MB 10, 18 Mar. 1823.

13 CBC, MB 15, 9 Nov. 1824.

14 CBC, MB 19, 28 Feb. 1826. A similar offer was made simultaneously to neighbouring Lyncombe.

15 CBC, MB 22, 14 Nov. 1826.

16 John Pinch, sen. (d. 1827), author of St Mary, Bathwick, 1814-17, in Somerset Perpendicular.

17 CBC, MB 22, 21 Nov. 1826.

18 Ibid., 28 Nov. 1826.

19 It has not proved possible to pinpoint these sites on contemporary plans, nor Edward's Garden, referred to subsequently, but King's Field was to the north-east of the city, near Kensington Place

20 CBC, MB 23, 12 Dec. 1826.

21 Ibid.,19 Dec. 1826.

22 Ibid., 9 Jan. 1827.

23 ibid., 13 Feb. 1827.

24 CBC, MB 24, 13 Mar.1827.

25 Ibid., 27 Mar. 1827.

26 See W. Ison, *The Georgian Buildings of Bath* (1948), pp. 78-9.

27 CBC, MB 25, 5 Jun. 1827.

28 Ibid., 3 Jul. 1827.

29 CBC, MB 27, 6 Nov. 1827.

30 CBC, MB 28, 12 Feb. 1828.

31 CBC, MB 31, 17 Jun. 1828.

32 CBC, MB 33, 11 Nov. 1828.

33 CBC, MB 33, 23 Dec. 1828; 34, 6 Jan. 1829.

34 Ison, *The Georgian Buildings of Bath*, p. 83.

35 CBC, MB 36, 4 Aug. 1829.

36 CBC, MB 12, 23 Dec. 1823.

37 CBC, MBs 19 (28 Feb. 1826), 24, (8 May 1827).

38 CBC, MB 25, 22 May 1827. Brigden rebuilt Easton-in-Gordano church, Somerset, in 1827 (Colvin, *DBA*, p. 162).

39 CBC, MB 27, 11 Dec. 1827.

40 CBC, MB 30, 29 Apr. 1828. The loss of MB 29 leaves the argument about the site obscure.

41 CBC, MB 31, 17 Jun. 1828.

42 Ibid,, 22 Jul. 1828.

43 CBC, MB 32, 16 Sep. 1828.

44 CBC, MB 33, 28 Oct. 1828.

45 CBC, MB 35, 9 Jun. 1829.

46 CBC, MB 38, 26 Oct. 1830; MB 40, 13 Dec. 1831.

47 CBC, MB 16, 8 Mar. 1825.

48 Ibid., 15 Mar. 1825.

49 Ibid., 10 May 1825.

50 CC file 18132, comparative view of sites. The following account is based on the original letters and memoranda sent to the Commissioners in CC file 18132 (partly copied in CBC MBs).

51 Two of his father's brothers were clerics, one, Edward Legge, vicar of Lewisham and Bishop of Oxford (d. 1827); his son Henry was vicar of Lewisham, 1831-79.

52 CC file 21819, Lewisham memorandum.

53 CC file 18132, J. Forster, 'Observations', 18 Jul. 1825.

54 CBC, MB 19, 21 Feb. 1826.

55 Ibid., 28 Feb. 1826.

56 CBC, MB 20; CC file 21819; architect's lithographic forms in CC file 18132.

57 CC file 18132, Vullliamy to Jenner, 14 Nov. 1826.

58 Ibid., 21 Nov. 1826.

59 Ibid., 27 Feb. 1827.

60 CBC, MB 23, 19 Dec. 1826.

61 Ibid., 3 and 24 Apr., 1 May 1827.

62 CC file 18132, vestry resolution, 9 Aug. 1827.

63 CBC, MB 27, 23 Oct. 1827.

64 Ibid., 27 Nov. 1827; MB 28, 15 Jan. 1828.

65 CC file 18132, Vestry clerks to Jenner, 21 Feb. 1828.

66 St John, Bromley, built and endowed by John Forster, 1824.

67 CBC, MB 30, 1 and 22 Jul. 1828.

68 CBC, MBs 32, 19 Aug., 30 Sep.; 33, 25 Nov. 1828; 34, 27 Jan. 1829.

69 CBC, MBs 35, 2 Jun.; 36, 27 Oct., 10 Nov., 8 Dec. 1829.

70 CBC, MBs 38, 10 Aug.1829; 40, 11 Oct. 1831, 17 Apr. 1832.

71 CBC, MB 36, 11 Aug. 1829.

72 CC file 21819.

73 CBC, MB 1, 12 Jan. 1819. The St Pancras parish trustees then offered £6,500, one-third to be paid into Chancery until the square was completed. But according to a modern historian, the vestry agreed to the purchase for £1,600 on 27 Sep. 1820 (C. E. Lee, *St Pancras Church and Parish* (1955), p. 46.

74 CBC, MB 3, 18 Apr., 11 and 18 Jul., 1820; the Poplar site was for All Saints, not a Commissioners' church, but the site bought under their power of compulsory purchase, see *Survey of London, XLII: Poplar, Blackwall and the Isle of Dogs* (1994), p. 177.

75 S. and B. Webb, *English Local Government: The Parish and the County* (1906), pp. 79-90, 228.

76 CBC, MB 1, 24 Nov. 1818.

77 Ibid., 22 Dec. 1818.

78 Ibid., 19 and 26 Jan. 1819.

79 Ibid., 26 Jan., 16 Feb. 1819.

80 Ibid., MB 3, 23 May 1820.

81 *PP,* 1837 (437) XLI, pp. 6, 8.

82 Ibid, MB 6, 9 Apr., MB 7, 4 and 25 Jun. 1820.

83 CBC, SR 2, f. 209v. (19 Jan.1828), 229 3, ff. 126v., 138v., Sept., 21 Nov. 1831; CBC, MBs 30, (3 June, 22 July 1828), 32 (9 Dec.1828), 39 (5 Jul. 1831), 40 (11 Oct. 1831, 10 Jan., 6 Mar. 1832).

84 CBC, MB 7, 21 May 1822. Eventually the site was secured for £4,980, *PP* 1837 (437) XLI.

85 *PP,* 1837 (437) XLI, 1840 (262) XXXIX, 1852-3 (125) LXXVIII, Accounts of sums expended under the direction of the Commissioners for Building Churches.

86 E.g., On 3in. Yorkshire paving, valued at 45*s.* per 100sq. ft, the duty was 11*s.*10^1/2*d*; on 4in. Yorkshire landings at 55*s.* per 100sq. ft., 14*s.* 6^1/4*d.*; and on Portland stone (16 cu.ft to the ton), at 25*s.* per ton, 6*s.*7^1/4*d.* – CC file 12107, 'Account of Valuation and Duties on Stone entered Inwards Coastways in Port of London'.

87 S. Dowell, *A History of Taxation and Taxes in England*, IV (2nd edn, 1888), pp. 380-4, 409-14; CC file 12107, Board of Customs to Jelf, 26 Oct. 1848.

88 CC file 12107, Drawback of Duties, C. A. Arbuthnot to CBC, 21 Apr. 1820; CBC, MB 3, 25 Apr. 1820.

89 CBC, MB 3, 16 May 1820.

90. CBC, MB 5, 22 May 1821.

91 CC file 12107, correspondence Feb. to May 1824.

92 Ibid., 13 Nov. 1837.

93 CC file 21744, pt 7, 25, 30 May, 19 Jun. 1838.

94 *PP,* 1837-38 (325) XXXVIII.

95 Ibid. In Scotland, St Enoch, Glasgow, for example, recovered £390.

96 CC file 12107, C. E. Trevelyan to CBC, 17 Feb. and 13 Mar. 1840.

97 CC file 12107, Drawback cash account.

98 CC file 12107.

99 CBC, MBs 7 (4 Jun. 1822), 10 (13 May 1823); *PP* 1837-38 (325) XXXVIII.

100 CBC, MB 10, 13 May 1823.

101 CBC, MB 40, pp. 16-18 (27 Sep. 1831), 104-7 (7 Nov. 1834).

102 CBC, MB 10, pp. 302-3.

103 CBC, MB 21, 27 Jun. 1826.

104 CBC, Building Comm. MB 9, pp. 254-5; CC file 21744, pt 5, 14 Sep. 1824.

105 CC file 21744, pt 8, 22 Apr. 1840.

106 CBC, MB 30, 13 May 1828.

107 CC file 12107, Scovell, Board of Customs to CBC, 11 Mar. 1841, Minutes of CBC, 23 Mar., 8 Jun. 1841.

108 CC file 21744, pt 8, 1 May 1841.

109 CBC, MB 22, 26 Sep. 1826.

110 CBC. MB 33, 11 Nov. 1828; MB 34, 27 Jan. 1829.

111 CC file 12107, 18 Apr. 1829, Mr W. Richardson, 'who acts as temporary Secretary', to sign receipts made out to Jenner.

112 CC file 21745, Jelf to Secretary of Board of Customs, 30 Sep., and Jelf to Watson, 8 Oct. 1834.

113 Ibid.

114 *PP,* 1837 (437) XLI, pp. 429-45, 'Accounts of the Sums expended under the Direction of the Commissioners for Building Churches …'.

115 CC file 12058, pt 1, statement of totals of CBC cases, 1818-31 Dec. 1855. An account of drawbacks recovered on each church up to Mar. 1838 is given in *PP* 1837-8 (325) XXXVIII, pp. 141ff.

116 *PP,* 1837 XLI, 1840 XXXIX, 1852-53 LXXVIII.

117 W. R. Ward, 'The Cost of Establishment: Some Reflections on Church Building in Manchester', *Studies In Church History*, 3 (Leiden, 1966), p. 286.

118 See G. W. O. Addleshaw and F. Etchells, *The Architectural Setting of Anglican Worship* (1948), pp. 86-98; C. J. Abbey and J. H. Overton, *The English Church in the Eighteenth Century* (1878), II, pp. 21-5, 422-4; H. S. English, *The Laws Respecting Pews or Seats in Churches* (1826); O. Chadwick, *The Victorian Church*, I (1966), pp. 520-2.

119 CBC, MB 1, 9 Mar. 1819.

120 Lithographed form for pew rent schedule, CC file 15225, pt 2.

121 CBC, MB 1, p. 236.

122 CBC, MB 5, 10 and 31 Jul. 1821.

123 CBC, MB 9, 28 Jan. 1823.

124 CBC, MB 9, 11 Feb. 1823.

125 CC file 18112, pt 2.

126 *Parl. Deb. N.S.*, XI, 1093 (4 Jun. 1824).

127 *PP*, 1837 (437) XLI, pp. 432 ff. 'An account of the sums expended under the Direction of the Commissioners for Building Churches …'.

128 See Chadwick, *Victorian Church*, I, pp. 520-2.

129 CBC, MB 8, 23 Jul., 8 Oct. 1822.

130 Ibid., 29 Oct. 1822; *PP* 1824 XVIII, p. 55.

131 CC file 18158, pt 2.

132 *PP*, 1837 (437) XLI, pp. 432ff. 'An account of the sums expended …'; CBC, MB 35, 26 May 1829. The lowest rentals, apart from the special case of Tockholes (Lancs), substituted for an old chapel with proprietary pews, were Bitton (Glos), £22.16s., and Cross-Stone (Yorks), £22.5s., with 131 and 604 pew sittings respectively.

133 CC files 17887, pt 2; 15217.

134 CC file 17887, pt 2, 21 Jun. 1825.

135 CBC, MB 10, 18 Mar., 22 Apr. 1823.

136 CBC, MB 1, p. 347, 9 Feb. 1819.

137 CBC, MB 14, 27 Jul. 1824.

138 CC file 15225, pt 1, 21 Dec. 1829 and 8 Jan. 1830.

139 CC file 15225, pt 2, 10 Mar. 1835; pew rent plan; and rector, etc to CBC, n.d., but marked 'Ansd 15 Feby 1839'.

140 CC file 18206, 26 Dec. 1828.

141 Ibid.

142 CC file 18484, 11 Aug. 1828 and 6 Jan. 1829.

143 CBC, MB 31, 17 Jun. 1828.

144 Ward, 'The Cost of Establishment', *Studies in Church History*, 3 (1966), p. 287, quoting Archdeacon Rushton's MS Visitation, vol. 39, Manchester Central Library.

145 Ibid., p. 282.

146 CBC, MB 1, 9 Feb. 1819.

147 CC files 15225, 20812, pt 1.

148 CC file 20548.

149 CC file 15225, 10 Mar. 1835.

150 Stated as £1,229 in CC file 12131, Statement of the Assets and Liabilities of the Church Building Commissioners on 31 Dec. 1856; but in 1877 reported to the House of Lords as standing at £7,704, *PP, HL* (71, 71A) XII, possibly because some of the 64 grants outstanding in 1856 had not been taken up.

151 *Times,* 18 Jun. 1886.

152 At St Mark, Kennington, a South London suburb with a strong middle-class element, the pew rent scale gave a total rental of £868. In 1877, the actual product was £405, which increased to £463 in 1892, after which there was an unbroken fall, *Free and Open Church Advocate, 42nd Annual Report, 1907-8*, p. 7. See also *PP, HL*, 1877 (71) XII.

153 Ecclesiastical Commissioners, general meeting 15 Jul. 1897, minute in CC file 23735.

154 *PP, HL* 1908 (183).

Chapter 11

1 *Times*, 13 Feb. 1823, p. 2e.

2 *Parl. Deb. N.S.*, XI, 171, 5 Apr. 1824.

3 *Times*, 10 Apr. 1824, p. 2. The following paragraphs are based upon the reports in *The Times* and in *Parl. Deb. N.S.,* XI, 332ff.

4 This was a popular notion that had been urged during the preliminary discussion on 5 Apr. by Sir John Newport and the City magnate John Smith.

5 Hume's hostility had an unintended effect in persuading one Whig M.P., R. Gordon, to support

the grant, he never having heard in the House 'a speech with which he was more dissatisfied', *Times*, loc. cit.

6 *Parl. Deb. N.S.*, XI, 1080, 1093–5.

7 Ibid.; *Cmns Jnls*, 1824.

Chapter 12

1 CBC, MB 14, p. 145.

2 Ibid., p. 158.

3 Halifax, St Giles-in-the-Fields and Bloomsbury, Rochdale, Wolverhampton, Wigan, St George Southwark, Stoke Damerel, Whitechapel, Stoke-on-Trent, Hull, Tynemouth, Huddersfield, Jarrow, Almondbury, Islington, St Margaret Westminster, Birstall, Newcastle-on-Tyne, Bristol SS Philip & Jacob, Spitalfields, Sedgley, Yarmouth, Merthyr Tydfil, St John Westminster. In each, the population exceeded church-room by 15,000 or more.

4 The one-inch-to-a-mile Ordnance Survey had only reached the southern borders of Yorkshire and Lancashire by 1824, when it was suspended until 1840. Only in 1844 was the Hull-Preston line reached. Not till 1851 was the survey of these counties completed. See H. S. Palmer, *The Ordnance Survey of the Kingdom* (1873).

5 The only distinct breaches of this rule were for sites for All Saints, Skinner Street (St Botolph, Bishopsgate, London), £4,702; Christ Church, Montpelier Row, Brighton, £930; and Christ Church, Barnwell, Cambridge, £1,040, *PP* 1837 (437) XLI; 1840 (262) XXXIX; 1852–53 (125) LXXVIII.

6 Delays at Hebden Bridge (Halifax) enabled the Methodists to buy the best site, and build on it (CBC, MB 12, p. 425).

7 CBC, MB 15, 23 Nov. 1824.

8 Other parishes for which Ryder pleaded were Wellington and Dawley (Salop); Coventry and Foleshill (Warks); Alfreton, Chesterfield, Duffield and Glossop (Derbys); Walsall, Tipton, Kingswinford and Stone (Staffs).

9 CBC, MB 15, p. 24, et seq.

10 Redruth, Kenwyn, Gwennap (Corn); Ripon, Almondbury, Scarborough (Yorks). CBC, MB. 16, pp. 469–73.

11 He was added to the Building Committee on 26 Apr. 1825, CBC, MB 17.

12 *DNB*.

13 The name of the recipient parish is given, followed (where necessary) by the location, in parentheses, of church for which a grant was awarded: *Cumberland:* Carlisle (St Cuthbert, St Mary parishes). *Cheshire:* Great Budworth, Prestbury (Macclesfield). *Cornwall:* Gwennap, Kenwyn (Chasewater, Truro), Redruth. *Derbyshire:* Alfreton (Riddings), Derby St Werburgh, Glossop. *Devon:* Kenton (Starcross). *Gloucestershire:* Cheltenham. *Kent:* Maidstone, Margate, Tunbridge. *Lancashire:* Leyland (Whittle-le-Woods), Middleton (Birch), Ormskirk, Wigan (Aspull, Pemberton). *London:* Fulham (Hammersmith, Walham Green), Holborn, Islington (Balls Pond, Cloudesley Sq., Holloway), Kensington (Edward Sq.), Lambeth (St Mary), Paddington, St Giles-in-the-Fields (2 chapels), Tottenham, Westminster (St Margaret). *Norfolk:* Great Yarmouth. *Salop:* Dawley, Wellington (Ketley). *Somerset:* Bath (Walcot), Bedminster, Lydcombe & Widcombe. *Staffordshire:* Bilston, Burslem, Newcastle under Lyme, Sedgley, Stoke-on-Trent (Fenton, Shelton). *Surrey:* Croydon (Croydon Common, Norwood), Lewisham (Lewisham, Sydenham). *Sussex:* Brighton. *Warwickshire:* Coventry St Michael. *Worcestershire:* Claines, Halesowen (Oldbury). *Yorkshire:* Almondbury (Linthwaite, Lockwood, Netherthong), Huddersfield (Golcar, Huddersfield, Paddock, Linley), Rotherham (Gresborough), Ripon (Pately Bridge), Scarborough. *Wales:* Carmarthen, Newtown [*Montgomerys*].

14. *Cheshire:* Stockport (Hyde). *Derbyshire:* Brampton. *Devon:* Plymouth (Stonehouse). *Durham:* Ryton (Winlaton). *Essex:* Barking, West Ham (Plaistow, Stratford). *Hertfordshire:* Cheshunt (Waltham Cross). *Lancashire:* Dean (Horwich), Prestwich (Tonge), Rochdale (Spotland, Wuerdle), Walton-on-the-Hill (Toxteth Park), Ulverston, Warrington. *London:* Battersea, St Botolph Bishopsgate. *Middlesex:* Hampton (Hampton Wick), Isleworth & Heston (Hounslow). *Northumberland:* Tynemouth. *Somerset:* Bath (Walcot East). *Staffordshire:* Kingswinford, Wolverhampton. *Surrey:* Richmond. *Yorkshire:* Almondbury (Crossland), Birstall (Birkenshaw, Cleckheaton, Heckmondwike), Calverley (Idle), Ecclesfield (Stannington), Kingston-on-Hull (Myton), Kirkburton, Leeds (Kirkstall, Holbeck).

15 CBC, MB 24, pp. 248-50 (10 Apr. 1824).

16 Christ Church, Watney Street, was not built until 1840, but the grant had been held over from the 'Million'.

17 CBC, MB 24, 1 May 1824.

18 *PP*, Annual Reports of CBC, 1824 (430) IX, 1826 (533) XI, 1827 (566) VII, 1828 (826) IX, 1829 (677) V.

19 CBC, MBs 19 (24 Jan.), 21 (30 May, 13 Jun. 1826).

20 CBC, MB 25, 3 Jul. 1827.

21 CBC, MB 21 (30 May 1826); SR 2, ff. 172v, 173 (6 Aug.); f. 164 (17 May 1827); f. 210 (14 Jan. 1828).

22 CBC, MB (5 Feb. 1828); SR 2, ff. 223, 235 (10 May, 24 Jun. 1828).

23 CBC, MB 21, 25 Jul. 1826.

24 CBC, MB 22, 28 Nov. 1826.

25 CBC, MB 19, 14 Feb. 1826.

26 CBC, MB 26, 19 Jun. 1827.

27 CBC, MB 27, 6 Nov. 1827.

28 CBC, MBs 27 (27 Nov. 1827), 30 (22 Apr. 1828). In the event Haigh cost £3,433 for 796 sittings (£4.6s. a sitting) and Pemberton £4,913 for 1,586 (£3.2s.).

29 CBC, MB 30, 22 and 29 Apr. 1828.

30 Ibid., 22 Apr. 1828.

31 Ibid., 3 Jun. 1828.

32 CBC, MB 27, pp. 433-4.

33 C. Webster, *R. D. Chantrell, Architect: His Life and Work in Leeds* (Leeds, 1991).

34 CBC, MBs 30 (3 Jun.), 31 (17 Jun. 1828).

35 This church was also recommended by the Board to the Building Committtee's consideration for replication at Little Queen Street, St Giles-in-the-Fields, London, an exceptional case where the parish was paying poor relief to an average of 1,325 persons, had 200 infants at nurse, and a 15 per cent defalcation in payment of the poor rate; the Treasury provided the site, and the Commission offered to pay the whole cost up to £8,000 if the parish would provide a site and contribute the cost of a second church. CBC, MB 27, 11 Dec. 1827.

36 CBC, MB 31, 8 Jul. 1828.

37 Though ultimately plans by J. Leachman were adopted.

38 CBC, MB 27, p. 419.

39 Capt. Clarke, donor of the site, Hyde Hall, 1 Jan. 1828, CBC, MB 28, 22 Jan. 1828.

40 Thomas Witlam Atkinson (1799-1861), formerly clerk of works at St Thomas, Stockport (Ches) and St George, Ramsgate (Kent), and Charles Atkinson, probably his brother, of Stamford Street, London. See Colvin, *DBA*.

41 CBC, MB 28, 22 Jan. 1828.

42 CBC, MBs 31 (22 Jul.), 33 (11 Nov. 1828).

43 CBC, MB 33, p. 411 (23 Dec. 1828).

44 CBC, MB 30, 29 Apr. 1828.

45 CBC, MB 28, 12 Feb. 1828.

46 CBC, MB 30, 6 May 1828.

47 CBC, MBs 30 (13 May 1828), 34, (6 Jan. 1829).

48 CBC, MB 44, p. 39. But Vulliamy, backed by the local committee, secured the job by agreeing to compound for his journeys.

49 CBC, MB 54, p. 304.

50 CBC, MB 59, pp. 253-4.

51 See n.4 above.

52 Calculated (to nearest pound) from figures given in *PP* 1837 (437) XLI and 1840 (262) XXXIX, 'Amount ... expended by H.M. Commissioners ... '.

53 CC file 12058, totals of CBC cases to 31 Dec. 1855.

54 E.g., Blomfield's suggestion for a tax on coals; see his *Proposals for a Fund to be applied to the Building and Endowment of additional Churches in the Metropolis* (1836), p. 13.

55 See below, pp. 259.

56 Charles James, Bishop of London, *Charge at his Primary Visitation, 1830,* quoted by the *British Critic,* IX (1831), p. 210.

57 CBC, MB 35, p. 249 et seq.

58 *The Letters of King George IV, 1812-1830*, ed. A. Aspinall (3 vols, Cambridge, 1938), III, p. 128. George Jelf was the elder brother of orthodox High-Churchman Richard William Jelf, Principal of King's College London, 1844-68, preceptor to Prince George of Cumberland 1826-39.

59 After 1840 (CBC MBs).

60 CC file 21745, Jelf to Spearman, 28 Sep. 1837.

61 CBC, MB 59, 11 Mar. 1845.

62 CC file 21745.

63 CBC, MB 56, 13 Dec. 1842, 14 Feb. 1843.

64 CBC, MB 27, pp. 78-9.

65 CBC, MB 40, p. 218, 10 Jan. 1832.

66 CBC, MB 27, p. 285.

67 CBC, MB 42, pp. 392-3.

68 CBC, MB 45, p. 279. A list of 31 such parishes is given.

69 CBC, MB 46, pp. 90-104.

70 CBC, MB 47, pp. 66-70.

71 CBC, MB 26, pp. 378-9.

72 CBC, MB 28, pp. 271-2.

73 CBC, MB 32, p. 225.

74 CBC, MB 34, p. 156.

75 CBC, MB 35, p. 18.

76 Calculated from *PP,* 1837 (437) XLI, 1840 (262) XXXIX, and 1852-53 (125) LXXVIII.

77 *PP,* 1837 (437) XLI, pp. 433-40.

78 CBC, MBs 56 (9 May 1843), 64 (13 Jun. 1848).

79 See A. Satoh, *Building in Britain* (1995), *passim*.

80 CBC, MB 56, 11 Apr. 1843. On 14 March the Board had received a memorandum from Rev. Benjamin Webb, secretary of the Cambridge Camden Society, on the subject.

81 CBC, MB 59, 14 Jan. 1845.

82 See O. Chadwick, *The Victorian Church, I* (1966), pp. 146-58; B. F. L. Clarke, *The Building of the Eighteenth-Century Church* (1963), chap. 6.

83 'The imposition of rates for the reparation of churches has been sanctioned by the immemorial usage of ages.' Dr Dealtry, Chancellor of Winchester, quoted in *British Critic,* XI (1832), p. 325. See also Burn's *Ecclesiastical Law* (3rd edn, 1775), pp. 323, 329, 330.

84 CBC, MB 19 (21 Feb. 1826).

85 CBC, MB 22 (24 Oct. 1826).

86 As the *British Critic* pointed out (XIV, 497): 'The principle of a Church Establishment does involve the principle, that all the inhabitants of a country shall *bear a part of the expense* of a state religion, whether they attach themselves to its communion or not.' But it was anxious lest the church-rate question should drag down the whole Establishment. For Cheshunt, see CBC, MB 24, p. 290.

87 CBC, MB 15, pp. 446-7. The vestry had opposed the church since 1819.

88 CBC, MB. 15, p. 449.

89 CBC, MB. 19, p. 101. The proposal to build a second new church in this parish caused a further outcry. The radical M.P., Joseph Hume, presented a petition from the parish to the Commons (8 June 1830), and moved for a select committee to investigate the Commission (17 Jun. 1830). Among the critics John Wood was conspicuous, charging the Commission with a 'grasping and overreaching disposition', and 'prodigality and extravagance'; and alleging that churches had often been built in order to raise the value of adjacent land. Lushington defended his colleagues and claimed they 'had had to encounter greater difficulties than any man could originally have conceived'. Hume's motion was negatived by 64 votes to 14. *(Parl. Deb. N.S.,* XXV, 92, 430.)

90 See *British Critic,* 14 (1834), p. 445, where the view is expressed that the refusal to pay church-rates had spread from Ireland; and 'in more parishes than one' the usual rates had been refused by large majorities.

91 W. R. Ward, *Religion and Society in England,* pp. 178-92.

92 CBC, MB 28, p. 286.

93 The legal opinions are recorded in full: CBC, MB 28, p. 284 et seq.

94 CC file 21744, pt. 6.

95 CBC, MB 31, p. 168 et seq.

96 CBC, MB 34, p. 270.

97 Ibid., p. 477.

98 See O. Brose, *Church and Parliament*, pp. 122-3.

99 BL, Add. MS 40412, ff. 235-8, Rev. C. Musgrave to Sir R. Peel, 30 Jan. 1835; O. Chadwick, *The Victorian Church I,* p. 89.

100 BL, Add. MS 40412, ff. 169-85, 235-8, 303-6, 312-15.

101 Brose, *Church and Parliament*, pp. 56-7.

102 The two Braintree cases, that dragged on through the courts from 1837 to 1853, gave a succession of contending judgments on the power of churchwardens to lay a rate without parochial consent. See O. Chadwick, *The Victorian Church I,* p. 157 n.

103 CBC, MB 60, p. 362.

104 CBC, MB 61, p. 391.

105 Chadwick, *The Victorian Church I,* p. 152.

106 See W. F. Monypenny and G. E. Buckle, *The Life of Benjamin Disraeli, Earl of Beaconsfield* (1929 edn, 2 vols), II, pp. 87-8; R. Shannon, *Gladstone: Heroic Minister 1865-1898* (1999 edn); O. Chadwick, *The Victorian Church II* (2nd edn, 1972)p. 53.

107 See above p. 38.

108 CBC, MB 36, p. 148.

109 CBC, MB 39, p. 196: Sennicoats chapel (Sussex).

110 1 & 2 Wm. IV, c.38.

111 By 3 & 4 Vic., c.60.

112 CBC, MB 35, p. 388.

113 CBC, MB 45, p. 407.

114 BL, Add. MS. 34587, f. 20 (17 Apr. 1828).

115 9 Geo. IV, c.42.

116 Until 1851, when Royal Letters were discontinued, the Society received about £250,000 by this means (F. W. Cornish, *The English Church in the Nineteenth Century,* pt. 1, p. 81).

117 *PP*, 1821, I, 73. The CBS. appointed Kenyon, Cambridge, and Watson to consider the Bill (ICBS, MB, 21 and 28 May 1821).

118 *PP*, 1826-7, XX, p. 487.

119 Churton, *Watson*, I, pp. 191-2.

120 Ibid.

121 The Rev. B. W. Noel, in *The State of the Metropolis considered in a Letter to the Rt Hon. and Rt Rev. the Lord Bishop of London* (3rd cdn enlarged, 1835), recognising that the parliamentary aid necessary was such 'as we cannot venture to look for', urged more services each Sunday, division of parishes, and the multiplication of chapels in parishes, using licensed rooms and even open-air preachings.

122 See advertisement in BL, Peel Papers, Add. MS 40412, ff. 231-2.

123 C. J. Blomfield, *Proposals for a Fund* (1836).

124 Chadwick, *The Victorian Church I,* p. 337n.; 'wasted effort', according to Charles Booth (cited by B. F. L. Clarke, *The Parish Churches of London*, p. 160.

125 See M. H. Port, *Imperial London* (New Haven & London, 1995), pp. 10-11, 282 nn. 67, 71.

126 *3 Parl. Deb.,* LV, 272-354.

127 CBC, MB 52, p. 179.

128 *Parl. Deb. N.S.,* XIX. 1555: *Times*, 9 Jul.

129 CBC, MB 47, pp. 303 et seq.

130 About 800 sites for burial grounds, 1,200 for churches, and 340 for parsonage houses were obtained under the Commission's powers.

131 A return to an order of the House of Commons, made on 10 April 1838, lists 596 remissions (512 for England and Wales). After "Free Trade" Budgets, this matter became of little importance – see above, p. 214.

132 CC file 12058, Russell to Abp, 15 Jun., 11 Jul. 1837.

133 7 Wm. IV & 1 Vic., c.75.

134 CBC, MB 48, pp. 157-8.

135 Parishes which received loans from Church Building Commissioners, not repaid by February 1853.

Parish	Amount due, 26 March 1840			Amount since repaid		
	£	s.	d.	£	s.	d.
Newington	9767	2	2	6250	0	0

Walsall	2000	0	0			
Barnsley	1408	0	1			
Southampton	983	4	0			
Frimley Ash	1000	0	0			
Ramsgate	7650	18	10	6840	16	2
Oldland, Bitton	535	3	6			
Stoke-on-Trent	1500	0	0	1327	13	3
Margate	4781	16	1			
Burslem	340	0	0			
	Balance due		£15484.15s.3d.			

(*PP*, 1852-3 (125) LXXVIII.)

136 CBC, MB 48, p. 162.

137 1 & 2 Vic., c.107.

138 2 & 3 Vic., c.49.

139 3 & 4 Vic., c.60.

140 CBC, MBs 59 (17 Nov. 1844), 60 (22 Jul., 11 Nov.1845). The relevant Acts were 3 & 4 Vic. c.70; 7 & 8 Vic. c.56; 8 & 9 Vic. c.70; and 11 & 12 Vic. c.37 and c.71.

Chapter 13

1 See Brose, *Church and Parliament*, chap. VI; Best, *Temporal Pillars*, chap. VII.

2 Reprinted from *Church of England Quarterly Review*.

3 *An Enquiry into the possibility of obtaining means for Church Extension without Parliamentary Grants* (1841).

4 3 *Parl. Deb.*, LIII, 602.

5 C. S. Parker, *Sir Robert Peel from his Private Papers* (3 vols, 1891-9), II, p. 547 (9 Sep. 1842); pp. 516-17 (19 Oct. 1841).

6 Ibid., pp. 548-9 (17 Sep. 1842).

7 Brose, *Church and Parliament*, pp. 195-8.

8 Parker, *Peel*, pp. 550-1, 22 Dec. 1842.

9 Ibid., pp. 563ff.

10 Ibid., p. 563.

11 N. Gash, *Sir Robert Peel. The Life of Sir Robert Peel after 1830* (1972), p. 383.

12 CBC, MBs 64, 11 Apr. 1848; 67, 13 May 1851.

13 *PP*, 1852-53 (125) LXXVIII.

14. See P. Nockles, *The Oxford Movement in Context* (Cambridge, 1994).

15. *British Critic,* XXXVIII, pp. 481-2.

16. J. Ruskin. *The Seven Lamps of Architecture* (Library edn 1903), pp. 39-40.

17 CBC, MB 64, 11 Apr. 1848.

18 CBC, MB 66, 12 Feb. 1850.

19 CBC, MB 60, p. 416.

20 The Rev. John Miles had offered £4,000 on condition that the church cost more than £10,000, and the Ecclesiastical Commissioners gave £2,000 and the site, formerly part of the lands of the bishopric of London.

21 Rev. Dr David Laing, rector of St Olave, Hart Street.

22 All Saints, Ennismore Gardens, Westminster, £2,000; St John, Whitby (Yorks), £750; St John, Clayton, Bradford, £1,031; St Matthew, Great Peter Street, Westminster, £2,000 – all cases of long standing. *PP*, 1852-3, LXXVIII. The first grants of less than £100 were made to Byley church (Lancs), £75, and Antrobus (Ches.), £50, on 3 Apr. 1847; the £10 era began on 24 Feb. 1852 (Trinity, Woolwich).

23 *PP*, 1856 (387) XLVI, p.129, 'Sums … Granted … within the last Ten Years …'

24 CBC, MB 66, 12 Mar. 1850.

25 Ibid., 23 Apr. 1850.

26 CBC, MB 58, 25 Jun., 9 Jul. 1844.

27 As also at St Peter, Blackley (Lancs) and Dilton Marsh (Wilts), where payment of the grant was at first refused, but afterwards allowed on explanations having been submitted, CBC, MB 59, 26 Nov., 10 Dec. 1844, 14 and 28 Jan. 1845, but specifically not as a precedent.

28 CBC, MB 66, 15 Jan., 12 Mar., 11 Jun. 1850.

29 CBC, MB 61, 26 May 1846.

30 CBC, MB 48, 13 Feb. 1838.

31 CBC, MB 58, 23 Apr. 1844.

32 CBC, MB 64, 9 and 23 May 1848. Vulliamy's design was in the Lombardic style. See *Survey of London, XLV, Knightsbridge* (2000), pp. 186-7 and frontispiece.

33 CBC, MB 61, 10 Mar. 1846. Pevsner remarks of the church, 'Surprisingly post-Commissioners in style … Dec. style, i.e. in cognisance of the Pugin-Scott revolution.' *Buildings of England: Lancashire I, South* (Harmondsworth, 1969), p. 136.

34 CBC, MB 63, 14 Dec. 1847.

35 CBC, MB 67, 10 Dec. 1850.

36 CBC, MB 63, 13 Jul. 1847: but the grant was only £257.

37 CBC, MB 23, 27 Feb. 1827.

38 See H.-R. Hitchcock, *Early Victorian Architecture in Britain* (1954), 1, pp. 116-17; R. Fedden, 'Thomas Hopper and the Norman Revival', *Studies in Architectural History*, 2 (ed. W. A. Singleton, 1956); N. Pevsner, *Some Architectural Writers of the Nineteenth Century* (Oxford, 1972), ch. 9; T. Mowl, 'The Norman Revival', in *Influences in Victorian Architecture*, ed. S. Macready and F. H. Thompson, 1985, pp. 45-7; and J. B. Bullen, 'The Romanesque Revival in Britain, 1800-1840', *Architectural History*, 47 (2004), pp. 139-58.

39 B. F. L. Clarke, *Church Builders of the Nineteenth Century* (1938), p. 42, citing J. Barr, *Anglican Church Architecture* (1842), p. 77.

40 I have not seen it, but Pevsner declares: 'The church has undeniably a true ring' *Buildings of England: Yorkshire, The West Riding* (Harmondsworth, 1959), p. 389.

41 See A. E. Musson, 'Industrial Motive Power in the United Kingdom, 1800-70' *Economic History Review*, 2nd ser., 29 (1976); E. W. Cooney, 'Eighteenth Century Britain's Missing Sawmills: A Blessing in Disguise', *Construction History*, 7 (1991), pp. 34, 42; H. Louw, 'The Mechanisation of Architectural Woodwork in Britain … Part I: The Period c.1790 to c.1860', *Construction History*, 8 (1992), pp. 21-54.

42 CBC, SR 4, f. 75.

43 *The Seven Lamps*, chap. II, 'The Lamp of Truth', IX.

44 *British Critic*, XXVI., p. 466 et seq.

45 CBC, MB 52, 14 Jul. 1840.

46 CC file 9881, pt. 1.

47 *Church Chronicle*, 5 Feb. 1858.

48 *PP*, 1845 (441) (512) (572) I, pp. 295, 311, 327.

49 This provision resulted in the Ecclesiastical Commissioners (after 1856) keeping alive the parliamentary fund by allowing 3% interest, and making purely nominal grants, until 1898 (*PP*, *(HL)*, 1877, XII, p. 71; and CC MS. Register of Pew Rents).

50 CBC, MB 64, p. 266 et seq.

51 The Commission's power to assign districts to churches, extensively employed in the early 'forties, was less used after the Act of 1843 (see above, p. 261). They formed some 450 districts, consolidated chapelries, and new parishes up to July 1844 (24th Report); and thereafter a further 450.

52 Under this Act, the Ecclesiastical Commissioners endowed about 250 'Peel' districts in the next few years, and so encouraged the demand for new churches.

53 CBC, MB 64, p. 427.

54 CC file 21819, memo, Good to CBC, 9 May 1850.

55 Districts created under the Act of 1843.

56 CBC, MB 66, p. 345, 14 May 1850.

57 CBC, MBs 59, 26 Nov. 1844; 67, 11 Mar. 1851.

58 *PP*, 1850 (702), I, p.291.

59 'From a sense of their being inconvenient and useless' (CBC, MB 59, p. 394, 25 Feb. 1845).

60 CBC, MB 67, 24 Jun., 11 Nov. 1851.

61 CC file 15964. Letter from J. H. Good to Secretary, ICBS.

62 CC file 9881, pt. 1. Letter from Charles Hume, 3 Feb. 1854.

63 The history of this affair is set out in *PP*, 1854 (51) L, pp. 131-45, which contains the correspondence in full.

64 *Times*, 14 Mar. 1854. This letter is not in the parliamentary paper.

65 CC file 21745, draft report [Feb. 1854], resolution, 28 Nov. 1854. The published version of the Board's report and minute of 13 June 1854 is slightly different from the draft report, recording that Jelf 'has shown himself perfectly master of the business of the office, that he has constantly given to it *the full measure of attention that was required of him by the conditions of his appointment* [my italics], and that he has promoted to the utmost of his power the cause of church building' (*PP* 1854 (399) L, pp. 12-13. Jelf had continued to practice at the Bar after his appointment.

66 Ibid., Kent to Jelf, 4 Mar. 1847; committee report, 6 Dec. 1854.

67 *PP,* 1852-53 (51) LXXVIII, p. 23.

Chapter 14

1 Charlotte Bronte, *Shirley* (1849), p. 1.

2 D. E. H. Mole, 'Challenge to the Church. Birmingham, 1815-65', in H. J. Dyos and M. Wolff, *The Victorian City. Images and Realities* (1973), vol. 2, p. 828.

3 Bishop Maltby of Durham proposed in 1835 to endow the new church at Stockton-on-Tees with demesne lands worth £150 p.a., subsequent on division of the parish. But dissenters 'prevailed' at the parish meeting to block this, for fear that any division would increase church rates; they wanted the new church to remain a chapel-of-ease; but the vicarage was worth less than £300 p.a., and the vicar paid £50 p.a. for a resident curate. Likewise the proposal of the rector of Bishopwearmouth in 1848 to endow two new churches out of his emoluments of £3,800 p.a. was blocked by the Sunderland vestry, which as part of Bishopwearmouth until 1719 claimed an equal share. W. B. Maynard, 'The Response of the Church of England to Economic and Demographic Change: the Archdeaconry of Durham, 1800-1851', *Journal of Ecclesiastical History*, 42 (1991), pp. 452-4.

4 D. E. H. Mole, 'The Victorian Town Parish: Rural Vision and Urban Mission', *Studies in Church History*, 17 (Oxford, 1979), p. 361 et seq.

5 A. Saint, 'Anglican church-building in London, 1790-1890: from state subsidy to the free market', in C. Brooks and A. Saint (eds), *The Victorian Church. Architecture and Society* (Manchester and New York, 1995), p. 44.

6 W. R. Ward, *Religion and Society in England*, p. 227.

7 The Commissioners ceased to benefit much from this after about 1840; their own grants becoming so small, they allowed the whole sum to the subscribers; after 1850, there was only the duty on imported timber.

8 *PP, (HL),* 1877, XII, pp. 71 ff.

9 *PP,* 1852-52, LXXVIII, p.61 et seq. Kenneth Clark incorrectly states the number of Commissioners' churches as 214 *(The Gothic Revival,* 2nd edn, 1949, p. 128). This is the number reported as provided in the Commission's Ninth Report (1829). The Commission's 36th Report (1856) states that 615 churches had been completed, but this includes several for which the grants were not paid before the determination of the Commission. Up to 1876, the Ecclesiastical Commission paid another 50 grants that had been promised by the Church Building Commission.

10 J. H. Overton, *The English Church in the Nineteenth Century* (1894), p. 153.

11 *PP,* 1837-38 (325) XXXVIII, p. 141 et seq.

12 *PP,* 1876 (125 – I) LXVIII, pp. 657-8, states that £25,548,703 were spent in 36 years, in building 1,727 churches and 'restoring' 7,144. But the returns (pp. 553-656) were made on a diocesan basis, and the calculations differ so widely from diocese to diocese that the total is unreliable. Some 'restored' figures include new churches (e.g., Chichester, 'including 7 new churches, cost not known'; some appear to include schools or parsonage houses, and others are avowedly unreliable; e.g., York's return of £1,291,336 is annotated 'believed to be far below the sum actually expended in the restoration and building of churches in the diocese of York for the period stated'; and Lichfield had no returns from 134 churches.

13 Maynard, 'Response of the Church of England … Durham', pp. 456-7.

14 H. Mann, *Sketches of the Religious Denominations abridged from the Official Report,* 1851.

15 *PP,* 1852-3, LXXVIII, p. 23.

16 Mann, *Sketches,* Table 5.

17 CBC, MB 10, p. 277.

18 CBC, MB 16, pp. 151-8.

19 Saint, 'Anglican church-building in London', p. 47.

20 *British Critic*, XXXVIII (1840), p. 481.

21 Saint, 'Anglican church-building in London', p. 37.

22 Mann, *Sketches*, p. 13.

23 Ibid.

24 See *The Times*, 13 Dec. 1856, p. 9, for Blomfield's defence of his policy.

25 W. R. Ward, *Religion and Society in England*, p. 232.

26 Mole, 'The Victorian Town Parish', p. 361ff.

27 S. Jenkins, *England's Thousand Best Churches* (1999).

28 J. Summerson, *Architecture in Britain, 1530-1830* (2nd edn 1955), p. 302.

29 See 'Foreword' to first edition of this book.

30 CBC, Building Comm., MBs; 5, pp. 328-30; 7, p. 256.

31 S. Hibbert, *History of the Foundations in Manchester* (3 vols, Manchester, 1830), cited by J. S. Leatherbarrow, *Victorian Period Piece* (1954), p. 139.

32 Whiffen, *Stuart & Georgian Churches*, p. 85.

33 Leatherbarrow, *Victorian Period Piece*, pp. 139-40.

34 K. Clark, *The Gothic Revival* (2nd edn, 1950), p. 129.

APPENDIX 1

Grants made by the Church Building Commission, 1818-1856

This list is divided into two sections: those churches aided under the first parliamentary grant, and those assisted under the second. It does not include churches to which grants were promised, but not paid before the determination of the Commission on 31 December 1856. It has been compiled from the Annual Reports of the Commission, the Returns of sums spent on church-building made to Parliament in 1837, 1840, 1853, and 1856, and the Church Commissioners' files relating to particular parishes.

Counties: as at time of building except for (Greater) London.

Cost: the amount given in this column is that of the actual building. Where the cost of the site, legal charges, etc., were paid by the Commission, the grant exceeds the cost.

★ indicates the architect's estimate, not the actual cost.

Remarks: details of style and the features of the churches are taken principally from the Annual Reports of the Commission. Churches were sometimes reported as having a spire or tower, which was not built at the time because of shortage of funds. Details of the subsequent changes to and the present condition of the churches are given where they have come to my notice and are not intended to be exhaustive (Neil Burton has kindly informed me of many changes). 'Replaced' implies that an entirely new church has been built; 'rebuilt' that parts of the old work remain.

Abbreviations:

Directions are given by N, S, E, W

Add	Addition(s)	Conv	Converted	Reb	Rebuilt
Alt	Alteration(s)	cup	cupola	Repl	Replaced
Bom	Bombed	Dec	Decorated style	Rest	Restored
b-c	bell-cote	Dem	demolished	Rednt	Redundant
b-g	bell gable	E.Eng	Early English style	sp	spire
b-t	bell-turret	Enlgd	Enlarged	stpl	steeple
brk	brick	op rf	open roof	tr	transept
chl	chancel	Perp	Perpendicular style	turr	turret
clery	clerestory	pinns	pinnacles	twr	tower
clsd	closed	port	portico		

CHURCHES BUILT WITH THE AID OF THE FIRST PARLIAMENTARY GRANT

Church	Architect	Contractor	Cost £	Grant £	Date	Accommodation		Style & Remarks
						Pews	Free	
CHESHIRE								
Stockport, St Thomas	G. Basevi	Samuel Buxton	15,611	15,636	1822-5	1,020	932	Ionic: E port, W twr. Chl 1890
CUMBERLAND								
Workington, St John	T. Hardwick	Paul Nixon[1]	10,488	Whole	1822-3	500	970	Roman (Tuscan): port, wooden cup.Twr 1847; chl 1881
DERBYSHIRE								
Belper, St Peter	M. Habershon	Spicer Crowe	11,922	Whole	1822-4	600	1,204	Gothic: W twr, pinns
DEVON								
Lower Brixham, All Saints	T. Lidstone		2,995	1,522	c.1819-24	800	300	Gothic. Reb 1894-1906
DURHAM								
Bishopwearmouth, St Thomas	P.W. Wyatt		5,576	4,570	1827-9	472	681	Gothic. Bom, dem
Gateshead Fell, St John	J. Ions[2]	J. Ions	2,580	1,000	1824-5	300	700	Gothic. Rest 1885
West Rainton, St Mary	J. Anderson		1,012	550	1824	100	400	Mixed Gothic: belfry. Reb 1864
GLOUCESTERSHIRE								
Bristol, St George, Brandon Hill	R. Smirke	Separate trades	10,042	9,263	1821-3	494	920	Doric: port, cup
Kingswood (Bitton), Holy Trinity	J. Foster & Sons	Foster & Aust	3,291	2,457	c.1820-1	131	888	Gothic: twr. Chl 1889
HAMPSHIRE								
Bransgrove (Bransgore)	J. Hannaford	Separate trades	2,649	Whole	1822	46	461	Gothic: twr, sp. Chl 1873
Portsea, All Saints, Mile End	J. Owen	Ellis & Absalom	13,682	13,023	1825-7	633	1,106	Gothic: b-t. Bom; rest
Southsea, St Paul	F. Goodwin	Ellis & Absalom	17,451	16,869	1820-2	918	903	Gothic: 4 turrs. Bom c.1941; dem.
KENT								
Chatham, St John	R. Smirke	Separate trades[3]	14,157	13,797	1821-2	534	1,090	Doric: twr. Alt 1869; clsd 2004
Ramsgate, St George	H. Hemsley[4]	D. M. Jarman & Thomas Grundy	23,034	9,000	1824-7	806	1,208	Perp: W twr. Rest 1884, 1946
LANCASHIRE								
Ashton-under-Lyne, St Peter	F. Goodwin	Separate trades	14,080	13,191	1821-4	918	903	Dec: W twr, pinns
Blackburn, St Peter	J. Palmer	Local committee hired labour	11,491	8,000	1819-22	805	1,160	Gothic: twr, sp
Bolton, Holy Trinity	T. Hardwick	Separate trades[5]	13,924	Whole	1823-5	632	1,274	Gothic: twr
Chorley, St George	T. Rickman	Separate trades	12,387	Whole	1822-5	422	1,590	Gothic: twr. Chl 1891
Farnworth, St John	T. Hardwick	Thomas Heaton	6,604	6,704	1824-6	304	704	Gothic: twr. Chl 1871

CHURCHES BUILT WITH THE AID OF THE FIRST PARLIAMENTARY GRANT

Church	Architect	Contractor	Cost £	Grant £	Date	Accommodation		Style & Remarks
						Pews	Free	
Houghton, Holy Trinity	R. Roper	Separate trades	2,269	2,037	1822-3	240	207	Gothic: 4 turrs. Reb 1891
Liverpool, St Martin	J. Foster jun.		19,948	Whole	1825-8	1,082	828	Gothic: twr, sp. Dem.
Lower Darwen, St James	Rickman & Hutchinson	John & Jas Bennett	5,491	5,501	1827-8	246	723	Gothic: twr. Reb 1969
Manchester:								
St Andrew, Travis St[6]	Atkinson & Sharp	Separate trades	9,588	10,591	1829-31	1,251	749	Gothic: twr, clerestory. Dem
St George, Hulme	F. Goodwin	Separate trades	15,010	15,025	1826-8	831	1,171	Perp: twr. Conv to flats 2000
St Matthew, Camp Field[7]	C. Barry	William Heap	14,937	16,733	1822-5	860	978	Gothic: twr, arcade, sp. Dem 1952
Salford, St Philip[8]	R. Smirke	Separate trades	14,670	16,804	1822-4	528	1,300	Ionic: S port, twr
Mellor, St Mary	Rickman & Hutchinson	Separate trades	5,496	5,534	1827-9	273	678	Gothic: twr, sp. Chl enlgd 1897
Oldham, St James	F. Goodwin[9]	James Patteson	9,652	Whole	1827-8	796	1,285	Gothic: turr on low twr
Over Darwen, Trinity	Rickman & Hutchinson	Separate trades	6,786	6,799	1827-9	545	985	Gothic: twr
Preston, St Paul	Rickman & Hutchinson	Separate trades	6,214	6,221	1823-5	446	813	Gothic: corner turrs. Chl 1882
St Peter, Fylde Road	Rickman & Hutchinson	Separate trades	6,765	Whole	1822-4	389	861	Gothic: b-g, cler. E twr & sp 1852
Stand, All Saints	C. Barry[10]	William Heap	13,728	13,812	1822-5	860	978	Gothic: twr, arcade
Tyldesley, St George	R. Smirke	Separate trades	9,646	9,706	1821-4	305	1,132	Gothic: twr, steeple. Chl 1886
LEICESTERSHIRE								
Leicester, St George	W. Parsons	Separate trades	16,130	Whole	1823-6	801	999	Gothic: twr, sp. Burned 1911; reb
LONDON								
Bermondsey, St James	J. Savage	Separate trades	22,990	17,666	1827-9	800	1,200	Grecian, twr
Bethnal Green, St John	J. Soane	Robert Streather	17,346	18,226	1826-8	800	1,200	Grecian, twr. Fire 1870; add 1888
Brompton, Holy Trinity	T. L. Donaldson	Archibald Ritchie	10,407	7,407	1826-9	899	606	Gothic: twr. Chl 1878
Camberwell, St George	F. O. Bedford	Separate trades	16,700	5,000[11]	1822-4	976	758	Doric: port, twr. Alt 1893, 1909; clsd 1970
Chelsea, Holy Trinity	J. Savage	Separate trades[12]	6,136	6,729	1828-9	752	650	C15 Gothic: 2 W twrs & sps. Dem 1890
St Luke	J. Savage	John Wilson	28,109[13]	8,333	1820-4	1,078	927	Perp: twr, W arcade
Clerkenwell, St Mark	W. C. Mylne	Robert Streather	15,850	15,893	1825-7	775	847	Gothic: twr. Rest 1957,conv
Greenwich, St Mary	G. Basevi	Thos & Geo. Martyr	15,000	11,285	1823-4	1,068	645	Ionic: twr, port. Dem 1935
Hackney (West), St James	R. Smirke	Separate trades	17,910	Whole	1821-3	636	1,192	Doric: port, cup. Bom 1940-1
Haggerston, St Mary	J. Nash	Robert Streather	15,153	15,803	1825-7	700	1,000	Gothic: twr. Bom 1940-1
Highgate, St Michael	L. Vulliamy	Wm & Lewis Cubitt	8,171	4,811	1830-2	1,002	555	Gothic: twr, sp. Chl 1881, 1903
Hoxton, St John Baptist	F. Edwards[14]	Separate trades	15,394	16,444	1824-6	666	1,066	Ionic: twr
King Square, St Barnabas	T. Hardwick	Separate trades	14,092	14,200	1822-3	691	917	Roman: Ionic port, steeple. Alt 1870; bom; rest
Lambeth:								
St John, Waterloo Road	F. Bedford	Separate trades	18,034	9,976	1823-4	1,181	851	Doric: port, twr, sp. Bom, rest
St Luke, Norwood	F. Bedford	Elizabeth Broomfield	12,347	6,449	1823-5	724	688	Corinthian: port, stple. Alt 1870

CHURCHES BUILT WITH THE AID OF THE FIRST PARLIAMENTARY GRANT

Appendix 1

Church	Architect	Contractor	Cost £	Grant £	Date	Accommodation		Style & Remarks
						Pews	Free	
St Mark, Kennington	D.R. Roper[15]		16,093	7,651	1822-4	1,082	934	Doric: port, stple. Bom; rest 1949
St Matthew, Brixton	C.F. Porden	John & Henry Lee[16]	16,089	7,917	1822-4	904	1,022	Doric: W port, E twr. Rest
Newington, Holy Trinity	F. Bedford	Separate trades	16,259	8,960	1823-4	1,277	771	Corinthian: N port, twr. Conv 1975
St Peter, Walworth	J. Soane	Separate trades	18,592	9,354	1823-4	1,500	500	Grecian: twr
Saffron Hill, St Peter	C. Barry	Messrs Souter	9,524	16,219	1830-2	994	798	Tudor Gothic: 2 W turrs. Dem 1955
St Marylebone:								
All Souls, Langham Place	J. Nash	Robert Streather	19,612	12,819	1822-4	1,439	322	Grecian: port, sp. Rest 1950s
Christ Church, Cosway St	T. Hardwick	Separate trades	18,804	13,804	1822-4	914	930	Ionic: port, twr. Conv offices 1980s
Holy Trinity, Portland Rd (now Marylebone Rd)	J. Soane	Daniel Sharp	24,709	19,041	1826-7	1,269	743	Grecian: twr. Chl 1878; int'l reconstruction 1956
St Mary, Wyndham Place	R. Smirke	Separate trades[17]	19,955	14,955	1821-3	528	1,300	Ionic: S port, twr
St Pancras:								
St Mary, Somers Town	W. & H.W. Inwood	Isaac Thomas Seabrook	13,629	Whole	1822-4	1,030	885	Gothic: twr. Chl 1878
St Peter, Regent Square	W. & H.W. Inwood	Isaac Thos Seabrook[18]	16,450	Whole	1822-4	1,058	774	Ionic: port, twr. Bom
Westminster:								
Stepney, St Philip	J. Walters[19]	John Trenchard[20]	12,660	3,500	1818-19	408	930	Gothic, pinns. Dem
Wandsworth, St Anne	R. Smirke	Separate trades	14,511	Whole	1820-2	426	1,332	Ionic: port, twr. Chl 1896
St George (Hanover Chapel), Regent St	C.R. Cockerell	William Herbert	16,628	5,556	1823-4	854	726	Ionic: port, 2 W twrs. Dem 1896
St Mark, N Audley St	J.P. Gandy-Deering		13,299	5,556	1825-7	726	784	Ionic: port, turrs. Alt 1878, 2005
St Michael, Burleigh St	J. Savage		5,290	7,478	1832-4	485	449	Gothic: sp, clere. Dem c.1909
St Peter, Eaton Sq.	H. Hakewill	William Herbert	22,427	5,556	1824-7	1,016	641	Ionic: port, twr. Gutted 1834; reb
St Philip, Regent St	G. Repton	Archibald Reid	19,272	2,000	1819-22	1,000	500	Grecian: port, cup. Dem c.1875
MIDDLESEX								
Winchmore Hill, St Paul	J. Davies	Separate trades	4,250	3,250	1827-8	274	286	Gothic: b-t. Chl 1873
NOTTINGHAMSHIRE								
Nottingham, St Paul	W. Wilkins	Spicer Crowe	13,946	15,748	1821-3	488	1,365	Doric: port, twr, cup. Dem
SHROPSHIRE								
Trefonnen, Holy Trinity	T. Jones	T. Jones	700[21]	300	1820		400	Gothic: porch, belfry. Chl 1876
SOMERSET								
Bath, Holy Trinity Walcot	J. Lowder	Architect engaged workmen	10,000	4,000	1819-22	206	1,810	Gothic: SW twr, sp. Bom 1942; dem 1957
STAFFORDSHIRE								
West Bromwich, Christ Ch.	F. Goodwin	Samuel Buxton[22]	17,431	17,273	1821-8	671	737	Gothic: twr. Alt c.1880

Church	Architect	Contractor	Cost £	Grant £	Date	Accommodation		Style & Remarks
						Pews	Free	
WARWICKSHIRE								
Birmingham, St George	T. Rickman	Separate trades	12,752	Whole	1819-22	525	1,378	Gothic: twr, clere. Dem 1960
St Peter, Dale End	Rickman & Hutchinson	Separate trades	13,086	18,066	1825-7	540	1,431	Doric: cup. Dem 1899
St Thomas, Holloway Head	Rickman & Hutchinson	Separate trades	14,263	15,915	1826-9	626	1,423	Grecian: twr. Bom 1941
Bordesley, Holy Trinity	F. Goodwin	John Walthew[23]	14,235	14,246	1820-2	918	903	Gothic: 2 W turrs. Rednt 1971
Erdington, St Barnabas	T. Rickman	Separate trades	5,621	5,348	1822-3	318	357	Gothic: twr. Add 1883
Stockingford, St Paul	J. Russell	J. Russell	2,340	2,354	1822-3	108	506	Classical: twr. Chl 1897
WORCESTERSHIRE								
Kidderminster, St George	F. Goodwin	Separate trades	19,015	17,047	1821-4	714	1,289	Gothic: twr. Rest 1924 after fire
Netherton, St Andrew	T. Lee jun.[24]	Samuel Buxton	8,661	Whole	1827-9	515	992	E.Eng: twr. Add
YORKSHIRE, WEST RIDING								
Alverthorpe, St Paul	Atkinson & Sharp	Separate trades	8,082	Whole	1823-5	758	832	Gothic: twr
Attercliffe, Christ Church	T. Taylor[25]	Separate trades	11,896	12,041	1822-6	976	1,024	Gothic: twr. Bom 1940; dem save twr
Barnsley, St George	T. Rickman	Separate trades	5,963	Whole	1821-2	389	861	Gothic: b-t, clere. Dem 1992
Dewsbury Moor, St John	T. Taylor	Separate trades	5,918	Whole	1823-7	352	248	Gothic: twr
Earlsheaton, St Peter	T. Taylor	Joseph Nowell	5,301	Whole	1825-7	348	252	Gothic: tr, twr, sp. Dem 1971
Hanging Heaton, St Paul	T. Taylor	Separate trades	4,811	Whole	1823-5	380	220	Gothic: twr. Alt 1894
Leeds:								
Christ Church, Meadow Lane	R. D. Chantrell	Separate trades	10,555	Whole	1823-5	449	880	Gothic: twr. Dem by 1983
St Mary, Quarry Hill	T. Taylor	Separate trades	10,809	11,029	1823-5	406	801	Gothic: twr. Dem late 1970s
St Mark, Woodhouse	Atkinson & Sharp	Separate trades	9,637	Whole	1823-5	400	800	Gothic: twr. Rednt
Pudsey, St Lawrence	T. Taylor	Separate trades	13,475	Whole	1821-3	1,244	756	Gothic: twr. Rest 1907
Sheffield, St George	Woodhead & Hurst	Separate trades	15,181	Whole	1821-5	922	1,011	Gothic: twr
St Mary	J. Potter	Separate trades[26]	13,927	13,941	1826-9	1,252	740	Gothic: twr. Bom; reb 1957
St Philip[27]	T. Taylor	Separate trades	13,116	Whole	1822-7	1,245	755	Gothic: twr. Dem 1952
Shipley, St Paul	J. Oates	Aspinall[28]	7,961	7,992	1823-5	1,156	332	Gothic: twr. Rest 1876
Stanley (Wakefield), St Peter	Atkinson & Sharp	Separate trades	11,989	Whole	1821-4	773	724	Gothic: turrs. Burned 1911; reb 1913
Wilsden, St Matthew	J. Oates	Separate trades[29]	8,146	8,174	1823-5	1,156	332	Gothic: twr. Clsd 1954; dem
WALES								
FLINTSHIRE								
Buckley	J. Oates	Separate trades	4,000	4,052	1821-2	322	418	Gothic: twr, sp. Reb 1897-1902

Notes

1 All works save smith's and founder's.

2 Design improved by I. Bonomi: CBC, MB 16.

3 But S. Siddons & Sons were mason, carpenter and joiner.

4 Succeeded by H. E. Kendall (who modified the design) after his death in 1825.

5 Bateman, mason & carpenter.

6 T. Taylor prepared designs for this church, but after his death Atkinson & Sharp were appointed in his stead, and made new plans.

7 Built to the same design as Stand (q.v.), but Stand lacks a spire.

8 To same design as at St Marylebone, St Mary, Wyndham Place.

9 Foundations were dug on plans by C. Barry, but the tenders greatly exceeded his estimate, and he was replaced. This was one of the two churches for which C. A. Busby made plans unsuccessfully in 1821.

10 Plans by Rickman were rejected by the Crown Architects. Soane had then been invited to supply plans, but had declined. See Manchester, St Matthew regarding design.

11 An additional £1,382 was granted for repairs soon after the building's completion.

12 But principally T. Grissell, except mason and plumber.

13 Contract price, said to have been much exceeded.

14 H. H. Seward resigned, March 1823, on appointment to Office of Works.

15 Design perhaps by A. B. Clayton (Summerson, *Georgian London* (1945), p. 208).

16 At the special request of the parish; but additional foundations by Want & Richardson.

17 Principally Baker & Son.

18 All works save plumber's.

19 F. Goodwin stated that he made the design and superintended the work (S.M.).

20 Francis Meid, builder, was also concerned.

21 Built at a loss.

22 After two other contractors had successively become bankrupt.

23 All works save smith's.

24 R. Smirke prepared designs in 1824, but they were not used.

25 T. Taylor's churches were completed after his death in 1826 mostly by his assistant L. Hammerton.

26 Principally Webster.

27 Completed after Taylor's death in 1826 by Woodhead & Hurst.

28 W. Cudworth, *Round about Bradford* (Bradford 1876).

29 Only Hiram Craven, according to Cudworth.

Church	Architect	Contractor	Cost £	Grant £	Date	Accommodation		Style & Remarks
						Pews	Free	
CAMBRIDGESHIRE								
Cambridge, Christ Church	A. Poynter		5,439	500	1837–9	708	700	Tudor: W turrs; brk
St Paul	A. Poynter		5,766	300	1840–1	450	450	Tudor: W twr; brk. Chl 1864, trs 1893
Coates, Holy Trinity	J.W. Wild		1,563	250	1841		450	Norman: NE twr; brk. Aisles 1874, 1890
CHESHIRE								
Antrobus, St Mark	G.G. Scott		1,550	80	1847	84	166	E.Eng: b-t; stone
Bollington, St John	Hayley & Brown	Jas & Samuel Patteson	3,873	3,475	1832–4	396	575	E.Eng: twr; nave aisles. Gallery 1854
Bredbury, St Mark	E. H. Shellard		3,063	250	1847–8	350	512	E.Eng: W twr; stone
Byley, St John Ev.	J. Matthews		1,000	75	1847	58	133	Norman: op rf; brk. Twr added
Congleton, St James	J. Trubshaw		3,800	350	1847–8		610	E.Eng: b-t, chl
Danebridge, St Paul	J. Clarke		2,070	150	c.1849	200	402	Dem 1904
Dukinfield, St John	E. Sharpe	Separate trades	3,299	2,599	1838–40	802	432	E.Eng: W twr & Galilee
St Mark	J. Clarke		3,108	250	1847–8	100	815	E.Eng: NW twr. Twr 1881; alt 1887
Elworth, St Peter	J. Matthews		1,600	150	1845–6	42	246	E.Eng: b-c; rock-faced
Godley-cum-Newton St John	E. H. Shellard		2,244	400	1849	386	417	c.1300 Gothic. W twr 1878
Hyde, St George	T. & C. Atkinson	Separate trades	4,781	4,788	1831–2	596	1,004	Gothic: twr
Kingsley, St John Ev.	G.G. Scott		2,000	150	1849–50	60	294	Late C13 Gothic: W twr
Macclesfield, St Paul	W. Hayley		5,000	1,000	1843–4	326	506	Gothic: twr, sp
St Peter	C. & J.Trubshaw		2,224	257	1849	514		
Minshull Vernon, St Peter	J. Matthews	John Matthews	1,450	150	c.1847–8	10	206	E.Eng: b-t; rock-faced. Enlgd 1902
Newton, St Mary	Hayley & Brown	Separate trades	2,193	1,018	1838	374	250	Norman: turrs, Chl 1876–7
Norbury, St Thomas	Hayley & Brown	Henry Wallington	2,793	2,000	1833–4	502	503	E.Eng: W twr
Portwood, St Paul	Bowman & Crowther		3,830	300	1849–50	206	402	Perp: twr, sp, chl. Sp dem
Rainow, Holy Trinity	S. Howard		1,744	400	1845–6	258	249	E.Eng: twr; stone
Staleybridge, St George	E. Sharpe	Separate trades	4,012	2,712	1838–40	501	521	Gothic: W twr
Stretton, St Matthew	P. Hardwick	Separate trades	2,986	2,121	1826–7	250	250	Gothic: twr. Repl 1870
CORNWALL								
Baldhu, St Michael	W. White		2,260	200	1847–8		530	Dem 1991
Carnmenellis, Holy Trinity	J. Hayward		c.45	150	1848–51		346	E.Eng: b-t, op rf. Dem
Charlestown, St Paul	C. Eales		1,478	250	1849–50	24	536	E.Eng: trs. Dem
Chacewater, St Paul	C.Hutchins	John Liscombe Rickard	3,730	2,976	1826–8	302	1,202	Gothic: twr. Reblt save twr 1892
Godolphin, St John B.	J. P. St Aubyn		1,320	220	1849–51		467	C13 Gothic. Rednt 2002
Pendeen, St John	Rev. R. Aitken			200	1850–2		595	E.Eng: twr
Penponds, Holy Trinity	J. P. St Aubyn		1,223	150	1850–4		303	E.Eng
Redruth, St Mary	C. Hutchins	John Liscombe Rickard	2,392	1,523	1827–8	360	647	E.Eng: W turr; granite. Dem
St Day, Holy Trinity		John Liscombe Rickard	3,852	3,178	1826–8	300	1,207	Gothic: W twr; granite. Ruin
Treverbyn, St Peter	G. E. Street		1,129	150	1849–51		308	Early Dec: W b-g, op rf
Truro, St John	P. Sambell	Philip Sambell	1,342	1,407	1827–8	208	800	Grecian: b-t. Alt 1893–1900

CHURCHES BUILT WITH THE AID OF THE SECOND PARLIAMENTARY GRANT

Church	Architect	Contractor	Cost £	Grant £	Date	Accommodation		Style & Remarks
						Pews	Free	
Truro, St George	Rev. W. Haslam		1,850	100	1848-55	120	340	E.Eng:trs, twr, sp. Sp unbuilt
CUMBERLAND								
Carlisle, Christ Church	Rickman & Hutchinson	John Bennett	6,629 }	} 9,697[1]	1828-30	605	399	Gothic: twr. Fire 1938; dem 1952
Holy Trinity	Rickman & Hutchinson	Nixon & Denton	6,894 }	}	1828-30	605	399	Gothic C13: twr. Dem 1981
DERBYSHIRE								
Brampton, St Thomas	Woodhead & Hurst	Separate trades	3,013	2,063	1830-1	344	380	E.Eng: W twr. Chl 1891
Bridgehill, Christ Church	H. I. Stevens		2,579	200	1849-50	152	448	E.Eng: b-c, no aisles
Charlesworth, St John	J. Mitchell		2,333	250	1848-9	250	250	E.Eng: N twr
Cotmanhay, Christ Church	H. I. Stevens		2,550	300	1847		660	E.Eng: polygonal b-t. Dem 1987
Derby, St John	F. Goodwin	Separate trades	7,926	4,619	1826-8	543	929	Dec: 4 angle-turrs. Chl 1871
Hazelwood, St John Ev.	H. I. Stevens		2,206	200	1844-6	91	202	E. Eng: b-g. Restd 1903 after fire
Idrigehay, St James	H. I. Stevens		?	50	1853-6	65	138	
Milford, Holy Trinity	W. B. Moffatt		2,000	250	1847-8		516	E.Eng: SW b-t. Vestry 1910
New Mills, St George	R. D. Chantrell	Separate trades	3,398	2,691	1829-30	500	500	E.Eng: twr, sp. Chl 1897-8
Riddings, St James	F. O. Bedford	Thomas Cooper	3,140	2,140	1830-1	306	622	E.Eng: twr, sp, no aisles
Somercotes, St Thomas	E. Christian		?	10	c.1853			Dissenting chapel converted. Nave 1902
Whitfield, St James Gt	E. H. Shellard		3,692	1,000	1844-6	500	500	Gothic: twr, sp, Chl enlgd 1897
DEVON								
Barnstaple, St Mary Mag.	B. Ferrey		3,100	500	1845-6		802	Late C13: twr. Dem c.1977
Devonport, St James	J. P. St Aubyn		6,580	400	1849-51		1,093	C14: SW stpl. Bom 1942; dem
St Mary	J. P. St Aubyn		6,450	350	1850-1		809	C14: twr, sp. Bom 1942; conv
St Michael	B. Ferrey		4,453	1,000	1843-5	576	624	E.Eng: b-g turr. Bom 1942; dem
St Paul	J. P. St Aubyn		3,210	350	1849-50		741	Dec: sp. Bom 1942; dem
East Stonehouse, St Paul	J. Foulston	Isaac Benvy & Wm Ambrose	3,160	3,180	1830-1	464	531	E.Eng: low W twr. Chl 1891; dem
Plymouth, Christ Church	G. Wightwick	T. Mitchell	3,786	1,000	1844-5	512	544	Tudor: b-ts. Alt 1876; dem
Holy Trinity	G. Wightwick	William Burgoyne	2,588	1,000	1840-2	446	636	Italian: pediment, b-t. Dem
Starcross, St Paul		C. Hedgeland	1,933	1,491	1826-7	250	350	Grecian: cup. Reblt 1854
Sutton-on-Plym, St John Ev	B. Ferrey		3,086*	300	1851-5		563	E.Eng: twr, sp, op rf. Add 1883
DURHAM								
Ayres Quay (Deptford), St Andrew	T. Moore		2,700	500	1840-1	338	882	E.Eng: sp.
Benfieldside, St Cuthbert	John Dobson		2,547	200	1849-50	113	281	E.Eng. Enlgd 1881-6
Bensham, St Cuthbert	John Dobson		1,800	200	1846-7	274	284	Norman: SW twr, sp. Enlgd; rednt
Birtley, St John	G. Pickering		1,986	200	1848	35	324	Norman, apse. Enlgd 1887-9
Darlington, St John	J. Middleton		2,520*	150	1847-8	240	382	E.Eng: W twr, aisles
Hartlepool, Holy Trinity	J. Middleton		2,887	250	1850-1	256	514	Dec: no twr. Alt 1864, 1891
Hendon, St Paul	John Dobson		2,980*	150	1851-2	242	318	Gothic. Enlgd 1857; dem

CHURCHES BUILT WITH THE AID OF THE SECOND PARLIAMENTARY GRANT

Church	Architect	Contractor	Cost £	Grant £	Date	Accommodation		Style & Remarks
						Pews	Free	
Hetton-le-Hole, St Nicholas	J. Anderson		1,650	650	1831-2	160	340	Gothic: cup. Repl 1898
Heworth, St Alban	T. Liddell[1]	Thomas Liddell	777	200	1841-2		300	Gothic: belfry, op rf. Enlgd 1888
Monkwearmouth, All Saints	John Dobson		1,592*	150	1846-9	364	184	E.Eng: SW b-t
Pelton, Holy Trinity	G. Jackson		1,500	300	1841-2	150	250	Gothic: twr, sp, stone
Thornley, St Bartholomew	R. Dunlop		887*	250	1842	158	316	E.Eng: belfry, stone. Chl late C19
Winlaton, St Patrick	I. Bonomi	Separate trades	2,281	1,531	1827-8	163	637	Gothic: twr. Chl added
ESSEX								
Barkingside, Holy Trinity	E. Blore		2,339	355	1839-40	170	296	Norman: belfry. Chl 1875
Forest Gate, Emmanuel	G. G. Scott		3,500	125	1850-1	187	253	C14. Now mixed use
Halstead, Holy Trinity	Scott & Moffatt		3,000	500	1843-4	199	504	C13: SW twr, sp
Ilford, St Mary	J. Savage	Thos Curtis & Son	3,717	3,117	1829-31	366	485	Gothic: twr, sp. Chl 1920
Noak Hill, St Thomas	G. Smith		1,883	150	1841	76	230	Tudor: twr, sp, trs
Plaistow, St Mary	E. Blore	Thos Curtis & Son	3,239	3,100	1828-9	252	332	Gothic: turrs, belfry. Repl 1889-94
Stratford, St John	E. Blore	Jas & Jos. Butler	7,194	6,200	1832-3	486	364	Gothic: W twr, sp. Chl 1882
Stratford Marsh, Christ Ch	J.Johnson		2,337	350	1851		691	C13: twr. Repl c.1974
GLOUCESTERSHIRE								
Bristol, Holy Trinity	Rickman & Hutchinson	J. Bennett, save woodwork	8,231	6,031	1829-31	517	1,490	Gothic: 2 turrs, clerestory. Enlgd 1889
St Clement	Gabriel & Hurst		2,000*	100	1854-5	299	402	C13: b-t. Reb
St Jude	S. B. Gabriel		2,600	275	c.1849		549	Gothic
St Luke	S. T. Welch		2,886	500	1842-3	45	979	Gothic: twr, cup, sp
St Michael	S. B. Gabriel		2,033	250	1847-8	100	411	Gothic. Alt 1897
St Simon	Gabriel & Hicks	William Robertson	3,165	300	1846-7	208	495	E.Eng: twr, sp. Alt 1876
Cheltenham, St Luke	F.W. Ordish		4,150*	250	1853-4	514	526	Dec: W twr, sp, trs. Alt 1866
St Paul	J. B. Forbes	Edward Cope	6,871	3,626	1829-31	630	1,230	Ionic: port, twr. Add 1917
Lydbrook, Holy Jesus	H. Woodyer		3,388	100	1850-1		405	C14: twr, op rf. Alt 1913
Stroudshill, Holy Trinity	T. Foster		3,188	1,142	1838-40	300	701	E.Eng: b-t.
Whiteshill, St Paul	T. Foster		1,540	400	1839-41	104	396	Norman: twr. Trs 1882
HAMPSHIRE								
Forton, St John	J. Owen & son	Benjamin Bramble	4,214	3,731	1829-30	305	864	Gothic: b-t. Repl 1890
Milton, St James	A. F. Livesay		849	150	1840-1	158	165	Norman: b-t. Repl 1913
Portsea, Holy Trinity	A. F. Livesay	Hendy & son	3,093	1,086	1839-40	489	719	Gothic: b-t. Ruins
Portsmouth, St Mary	T. E. Owen	Benjamin Bramble	3,051	1,003	1838	498	715	Gothic: twr. Dem c.1888
Southampton:								
Northam, Christ Church	Lock & Duckett		2,052	175	1855-6	92	364	C15: brk, rubble facings. Dem. c.1890
St Peter	O. B. Carter		3,472	350	1843-4	230	332	Norman: twr, sp. Rednt 1981
Newton, St Luke	J.Elliott		3,200	250	1853	350	504	E.Eng: turr, rubble. Sikh temple
Winchester, Holy Trinity	H. Woodyer		4,780	300	1853	180	600	C14: turr, chalk
HERTFORDSHIRE								
Hockerill, All Saints	G. E. Pritchett		2,738	160	1850-1	112	394	E.Eng. Repl 1937

CHURCHES BUILT WITH THE AID OF THE SECOND PARLIAMENTARY GRANT

Church	Architect	Contractor	Cost £	Grant £	Date	Accommodation		Style & Remarks
						Pews	Free	
Leavesden, All Saints	G. G. Scott		2,600	125	1852-3	66	250	Gothic. Add 1920
Waltham Cross (Cheshunt), Holy Trinity	E. Blore	Augustine Wyatt	3,283	1,783	1831-2	226	346	Gothic: belfry (copies Plaistow, Essex) Chl 1913
West Hyde, St Thomas	T. Smith		1,742	300	1844		314	Norman: turr, flint
KENT								
Chatham, St Paul	A. D. Gough		4,174	300	1853-4	662	343	Late Norman: twr. Rest 1890; dem
Dover, Holy Trinity	W. Edmunds	Separate trades	6,398	3,556	1833-5	969	583	Gothic: 2 turrs, sps. Dem
Gravesend, St James	S. W. Daukes		3,400	200	1848-52	300	527	Gothic: trs. Dem 1968
Lee Park, Christ Church	G. G. Scott	Piper & Son	6,000★	5	1853-4	700	300	Gothic. Stple 1877; dem
Maidstone, Holy Trinity	J.Whichcord	John Allen	11,900	7,373	1826-8	707	1,133	Doric: twr, stple. Conv
Margate, Holy Trinity	W. Edmunds	White, Jenkins & Mercer	24,983	10,000	1825-8	800	1,200	Dec: twr. Bom; dem
Milton, Christ Church	R. C. Carpenter[2]		2,670	125	1854-6	227	146	C14 Gothic: central twr. Enlgd 1870; repl 1934
Holy Trinity	J. Wilson		4,200	600	1844-5	400	600	Gothic
Sheerness, Holy Trinity	G. L. Taylor	William Ranger	4,128	2,595	1835-6	347	738	E.Eng: twr, brk
Tunbridge Wells, Holy Trinity	D. Burton	Henry & Aaron Barrett	10,591	8,059	1827-9	561	939	Dec: W twr, stone. Rednt 1974
LANCASHIRE								
Adlington, Christ Church	E. Welch		1,560	400	1838	298	331	Norman
Ashton-under-Lyne, Christ Church	Dickson & Brakspear		2,800	300	1846-7	112	708	Gothic: E b-g, brk
Audenshaw, St Stephen	E. H. Shellard		2,900	500	1845-7	300	400	E.Eng: twr. Chl 1900
Bevington, St Alban	A. H. Holme		5,350	300	c.1848	359	650	Gothic
Birch, St Mary	C. Rampling	Joseph Petty	4,102	3,881	1827-8	496	504	Gothic: Dem
Birtle, St John Baptist	G. Shaw		1,350	200	1845-6	400	400	Gothic: b-g
Blackburn, Holy Trinity	E. Sharpe	Separate trades	5,019	1,519	1843-5	792	834	Gothic: twr
Blackley, St Peter	E. H. Shellard		3,162	700	1844-5	415	450	Gothic. Enlgd 1880
Bretherton, St John B.	E. Sharpe		1,058	250	1839-40	176	224	Gothic: b-t
Burscough Bridge, St John	D. Stewart	John Frost or Twist	3,440	3,040	1829-31	324	425	Gothic: belfry
Burnley, St James	H. P. Horner		2,556	250	1846-9	150	377	Gothic: twr, sp. Dem save later twr
St Paul	W. Rawstorne		5,150	150	1852-3	420	305	Norman: twr, stpl. Dem
Chorley, St Peter	C. Reed		1,981	250	1849-50	168	648	E.Eng. Trs 1911
Coldhurst, Holy Trinity	E. H. Shellard		1,541	250	1847-8	201	300	E.Eng: b-t. Enlgd 1887-91
Croft, Christ Church	E. Blore	James Pierpoint	2,667	1,457	1832-3	226	292	Gothic: twr, sp
Denton, Christ Church	G. G. Scott		4,500★	250	1848-53	360	501	C14
Droylesden, St Mary	E. H. Shellard		3,549	500	1846-8	200	532	E.Eng: twr, sp
East Crompton, St James	J. Clarke		3,196	250	1845-9	246	340	Gothic: SW twr. Rest 1876
Edgehill, St Stephen	G.G. Scott		4,085	300	1850-1	429	572	C13 Gothic
Failsworth, St John	E. H. Shellard		3,200	500	1845-6	206	601	C13 Gothic: W stpl. Twr 1878, rest C20
Farrington, St Paul	E. Sharpe		1,700	500	1839-41	204	275	Romanesque. Chl 1909

CHURCHES BUILT WITH THE AID OF THE SECOND PARLIAMENTARY GRANT

Church	Architect	Contractor	Cost £	Grant £	Date	Accommodation		Style & Remarks
						Pews	Free	
Glodwick, Christ Church	A. D. Cuffley		2,520	500	1844	373	427	E.Eng: W twr. Rest 1894; dem save twr
Habergham Eaves, Holy Trinity	L. Vulliamy	Separate trades	2,918	1,168	1835-6	476	580	Gothic: twr. Conv 1993
Haigh, St David	Rickman & Hutchinson		3,433	Whole	1831-3	298	498	Gothic: b-t. Chl 1886
Healey, Christ Church	G. Shaw		2,543	150	1849-50	150	450	Dec
Heaton Mersey (Didsbury), St John Baptist	P. Walker		3,950	150	1846-50	536	268	E. Eng: W twr, sp. Chl 1891
Heaton Norris, Christ Ch.	W. Hayley		6,889	500	1843-9	595	625	E.Eng: W stpl. Chl 1882; dem save twr
Hulme, St Mark	E. H. Shellard		4,144	250	1851-2	502	508	Gothic: Dem
Horwich, Holy Trinity	F. Bedford	John Bennett	5,999	5,621	1830-1	511	1,061	Gothic: twr
Hurst, St John Ev.	E. H. Shellard		2,400	250	1848	150	495	E.Eng: b-t. Enlgd 1862; dem
Leesfield, St Thomas	E. H. Shellard		3,815	850	1844-8	196	500	Gothic: twr. Twr 1865; enlgd 1885
Lumb, St Michael	J. Clarke		2,060	300	1847-9	155	448	Gothic: twr
Liverpool, St Matthias[3]	Stewart & Picton	T. & J. Lloyd	3,318	1,000	1832-3	314	736	Ionic: brk, stone. Repl and burnt down 1848
All Souls, Vauxhall	A. Holme		5,598	200	1856	304	646	Dec. Dem
Manchester, All Souls, Ancoats	W. Hayley		4,818	1,000	1839-40	700	697	Norman: 2 W turrs, brk. Rest
Musbury, St Thomas	E. H. Shellard		2,500	200	1850-1	101	399	Dec: W twr. Repl 1975-6
Paddington (Salford), St Paul	E. H. Shellard		4,856	220	1855-6	320	568	Dec: b-t
Pemberton (Wigan), St John	Rickman & Hutchinson	Separate trades	4,913	Whole	1830-2	548	1,038	E.Eng: turrs
Pendleton, St Thomas	Goodwin & Lane	James Patteson	7,673	6,673	1829-31	852	752	Gothic: twr. Rest 1887
Pinfold (Rochdale), St Alban	J. Clarke		4,000*	100	1854-6	300	370	C14: twr, sp. Dem c.1971
Ramsbottom, St Paul	I. & J. P. Holden		3,270	350	1844-50	102	426	Gothic: sp. Enlgd 1866
Ringley, St Saviour	Sharpe & Paley		2,500*	200	1850-4	180	482	C13
Rooden Lane (Prestwich), St Margaret	Travis & Mangnall		2,000*	200	1849-51	50	454	C14: gabled aisles. C19 add; part reblt 1985
Salford, St Simon	R. Lane		4,658	500	1845-6		850	Gothic: twr, sp. Part dem
Scholes, St Catherine	E. Sharpe	Separate trades	3,130	962	1840-1	654	459	Gothic: twr, sp
Shuttleworth, St John	E. H. Shellard		1,912	200	1847	129	284	Dec: b-ts
Spotland, St Clement	L. Vulliamy	Separate trades	4,006	4,056	1832-4	590	920	E.Eng: b-t
Stretford, St Matthew	W. Hayley		2,700	300	1841-2	566	351	E.Eng: twr. Enlgd 1861, chl 1906
Tockholes, St Stephen	Rickman & Hutchinson	Thomas Walsh	2,804	1,604	1831-3	439	424	Gothic. Dem 1965
Todmorden, Christ Church	L. Vulliamy	Separate trades	3,913	3,379	1830-1	250	1,005	Gothic: twr. Chl 1885
Tong, St Michael	Hayley & Brown	Separate trades	1,731	1,200	1838-9	158	348	Gothic. Repl 1902
Tonge (Brightmet), St James	J. E Gregan (compl. by W. R. Corson)	T. Isherwood	3,195	75	1855-6	196	251	E.Eng: twr, sp
Toxteth Park, St John B	Hansom & Welch	Wm Thomas & W. Kendall	6,612	5,262	1830-1	862	938	E.Eng: twr. Bom

CHURCHES BUILT WITH THE AID OF THE SECOND PARLIAMENTARY GRANT

Church	Architect	Contractor	Cost £	Grant £	Date	Accommodation		Style & Remarks
						Pews	Free	
Trawdon, St Mary	T. Chaffer		1,400	350	1844-5	154	346	E.Eng; twr
Ulverston, Holy Trinity	A. Salvin	Separate trades	4,978	3,423	1829-31	606	613	E.Eng; NW turr, sp. Chl 1870; dem save twr
Walsden, St Peter	C. Child		3,910	250	1846-8	387	246	E.Eng; twr, sp
Warrington, St Paul	E. Blore	Thomas Haddock	5,489	4,239	1829-30	611	587	Gothic; twr
Waterhead, Holy Trinity	E. H. Shellard		2,900	500	1846-7	300	500	E.Eng; b-t. Rest 1884
Werneth, St John	E. H. Shellard		3,026	1,000	1844-5	453	458	Dec: twr, sp, Chl & trs 1883
St Thomas	Trimen & G. Shaw	Smith & Appleford	3,600	125	1853-5	250	348	C12-C13. Enlgd; twr 1885
West Leigh, St Paul	W. Young		3,100	400	1846-7		441	Dec: SE twr, sp
Whittle-le-Woods, St John	Rickman & Hutchinson	Robinson & Harrison	2,960	Whole	1828-30	204	557	Gothic: Dem 1880
Wuerdle (Smallbridge), St John	L. Vulliamy	Separate trades	3,253	Whole	1831-3	422	590	Gothic: b-t
LEICESTERSHIRE								
Ashby-de-la-Zouch,	H. I. Stevens		3,404	400	1838-40	442	452	Gothic: twr. Chl 1866
Leicester, St John	G. G. Scott	Broadbent & Hawley	6,619	1,000	1853-4	460	540	C13. Conv to flats
Loughborough, Emmanuel	T. Rickman	Separate trades	5,533	2,143	1835-7	308	865	Gothic: twr. Adds 1909, 1990
LINCOLNSHIRE								
East Stockwith, St Peter	T. Johnson		1,313	100	1845-6	41	182	E.Eng: b-t. Rest 1899
Gainsborough, Holy Trinity	T. Johnson		4,061	600	1841-2	360	540	Gothic: stple. Chl 1864
Morton, St Paul	T. Johnson		1,996	150	1845-6	43	264	Gothic: twr. Repl 1891 save twr
LONDON:								
Balham, St Mary V.	Lee & Bury		2,500 [4]	10	c.1807-13	597	426	Classical. Consec. 1855
Battersea, Christ Church	E. Blore		7,300	200	1848-9	460	461	Dec. Dem 1944
St George	W. B. Hays	Fcs Richman	3,111	Whole	1827-8	212	384	E.Eng; b-t. Dem
Bermondsey, Christ Church	S. S. Teulon	George Allen	5,000	300	1847-8	103	1,097	Late Norman. Dem
St Paul	Wyatt & Brandon		5,420	400	1846-8	103	1,107	Gothic. Chl 1901; dem
Bethnal Green, St Andrew	W. Railton		4,733	500	1840-1	554	537	Lombard: NE twr. Dem 1960
St Bartholomew	L. Vulliamy		4,324	800	1842-3		1,058	C13. Conv to flats 1983
St James the Less	H. Clutton		4,885	500	1840-2	488	645	Norman: twr, sp. Bom; rest 1961
St Jude	T. H. Wyatt		5,149	500	1845-6		1,000	Lombard: transeptal twrs. Bom; dem
St Matthias	L. Vulliamy		5,600	1,200	1846-7		893	Italianate; SW twr, sp. Dem 1957
St Peter	T. L. Walker		5,252	500	1840-1	472	658	Norman: W stpl, flint
St Philip	B. Ferrey		5,040	500	1841-2		1,112	Norman: 2 W twrs, brk. Conv
St Simon Zelotes			4,733	500	c.1846		933	E.Eng; b-c. Dem
Bloomsbury, Christ Church, Woburn Square	L. Vulliamy	J. & G. A. Young	11,173	5,097	1831-2	1,016	510	Gothic: twr, sp. Dem
Camberwell:								
St Paul, Herne Hill	G. Alexander		5,000	700	1843-4	453	247	Perp: W twr, sp. Reblt after 1858 fire
Emmanuel	T. Bellamy		4,899	992	1841-2	500	511	Norman; 2 stunted W twrs. Dem c.1957
St Mary Magdalene	R.P. Brown		4,309	1,000	1839-40	770	332	Gothic: twr, sp. Bom; dem

CHURCHES BUILT WITH THE AID OF THE SECOND PARLIAMENTARY GRANT

Church	Architect	Contractor	Cost £	Grant £	Date	Accommodation		Style & Remarks
						Pews	Free	
Charlton, St Thomas	J. Gwilt		5,169	500	1849-50	308	530	Romanesque. Apse 1893
Chelsea, St Jude	G. Basevi		3,940	400	1842-4	250	600	Gothic: SW twr. Dem 1934
St Saviour	G. Basevi		5,411	500	1839-40	610	587	Norman: turrs.[5] Enlgd 1878, chl 1890
City:								
All SS, Skinner St	M. Meredith	Robert Streather	5,984	10,686	1828-30	446	754	Gothic. Dem c.1869
Holy Trinity, Gough Sq.	J. Shaw		4,152	1,000	1837	360	740	Gothic: twr. Dem 1913
Clapton, St James	E.C. Hakewill		5,249	912	c.1840	624	549	Gothic: Chl 1902
Clerkenwell, St Philip, Sharp Sq.	E. B. Lamb	Robert Streather	4,805	4,893	1831-2	680	426	Gothic: belfry. Dem
Dalston, St Philip	H. Duesbury		4,612	1,000	c.1840	738	396	Gothic. Alt
St George-in-the-East								
Stepney, Christ Church, Watney Street	J. Shaw	G. & J.W. Bridger	6,042	7,450★	1840	702	547	★ Grant reserved from the Million. Norman: 2 twrs. Apse 1870; dem
St Giles-in-the-Fields								
Christ Church, Endell Sq.	B. Ferrey	Winsland	4,460	1,000	1844	303	697	Gothic: sp. Dem c.1931
H. Trinity, Little Queen St	F. Bedford	J. & P. Bedall	8,521	Whole	1829-31	809	1,171	Gothic: turr, sp. Repl 1910
Greenwich:								
H. Trinity, Blackheath Hill	J. Wild		4,610	1,000	1838-9	620	620	Gothic: 2 E turrs, sps. Bom; dem
St John, Blackheath	A. Ashpitel		6,500★	5	c.1854	626	200	Perp
Christ Church	J. Brown		7,741	450	1847-9	580	753	Gothic: twr. Bom; conv
Hackney, South, St John of Jerusalem	E.C. Hakewill		11,841	1,000	1845-7	572	935	Gothic: W stpl, trs
Hammersmith, St Peter	E. Lapidge		12,059	9,099	1827-9	1,001	600	Doric: W twr
St Stephen, Shepherd's Bush	A. Salvin	Messrs Bird	5,800	370	1849-50	294	338	C14: twr
Hampstead, South, St Saviour	E. M. Barry		5,000	5	1849-56	588	122	E.Eng
Hatcham, St James	W. L. B. Granville		4,695★	400	1853-4	404	412	Dec. Dance centre
Holborn:								
H. Trinity, Gray's Inn La.	J. Pennethorne	P. Pearse & J. Guerrier	7,609	6,109	1837-8	720	804	Grecian: twr. dem
Homerton, St Barnabas	A. Ashpitel	James Gerry[6]	4,836	1,050	1845-7		607	Perp: W twr. Bom; rest 1956
Islington:								
Christ Ch., Highbury	T. Allom		7,000	50	1847-8	503	229	Gothic: central octagon. Alt 1872, 1911
H. Trinity, Cloudesley Sq	C. Barry	Separate trades	11,900	9,231	1826-8	1,151	858	King's Coll Cp type. Restd
St Andrew, Thornhill Sq	Newman & Johnson		7,000★	350	c.1852-4	762	758	Gothic, SW twr, trs
St John , Upper Holloway	C. Barry	Ward (save smith)	12,658	9,958	1826-8	1,029	753	Gothic: W twr, brk
St Jude, Mildmay Park	A. D Gough		4,725★	250	1854-5	592	480	C14: S twr, sp. Chl & clerest 1871
St Mark, Tollington Park	A. D Gough		4,500★	210	c.1853	642	433	Gothic: New aisles 1884
St Matthew, Essex Road	A. D Gough		4,115	50	c.1850	638	412	Gothic: Bom; dem
St Paul, Balls Pond	C. Barry	R. Dean (save smith)	11,222	8,654	1826-8	976	817	Gothic: E twr, brk (like St John). Conv 2004
Kensal Green, St John Ev.	H. E. Kendall		3,435	650	1843-4	287	293	Norman: 2 W twrs. Chl later
Kensington, St Barnabas	L. Vulliamy	William Woods	10,983	7,983	1827-9	818	512	Perp: corner turrs. Chl 1861 & 1909
St James	L. Vulliamy		4,941	500	1844-5	378	381	E.Eng: twr. Chl 1876

CHURCHES BUILT WITH THE AID OF THE SECOND PARLIAMENTARY GRANT

Church	Architect	Contractor	Cost £	Grant £	Date	Accommodation		Style & Remarks
						Pews	Free	
St Mary, the Boltons	G. Godwin		6,000	85	1849-50	473	205	C14: Greek cross plan. Bom, rest
Lambeth:								
All SS, York Rd	W. Rogers	John Wilson	6,513	2,350	1844-5	800	680	Anglo-Norman: twr. Dem c.1899
Christ Ch., Kennington, Brixton Road	V. Arnold		6,500	5	1855	862	543	Independent chapel bought and consec in 1856. Italian. Dem 1899; reblt
Holy Trinity, Carlisle Street	E. Blore	Geo Locke & Thos Nesham	3,809	1,000	1838-9	498	501	Norman: twr. Bom; dem
St Andrew, Coin St	S. S. Teulon		6,400*	230	c.1855	602	405	Gothic: NW stpl, polychrome. Dem 1955
St Barnabas, Guildford Rd	Clarke & Humphreys		5,760	200	c.1849	900	526	E.Eng
St John, Angell Town	B. Ferrey	H. & R. Holland	5,302[7]	10	1852-3	705	400	Dec: W Twr. N tr 1876; fire 1947
St Mary the Less	F. Bedford	William Woods	7,801	5,801	1827-8	613	1,347	Gothic: b-t, sp. Dem c.1960
St Michael, Stockwell	W. Rogers	John Jay	4,126	1,200	1840-1	658	572	Gothic: E twr, sp. Rest
Limehouse, St John Ev	H. Clutton		5,000*	400	1852-3		800	C13: turr. Dem
St Marylebone:								
St Andrew, Wells Street	S.W. Daukes	G. Myers	8,095	800	1846		1,200	Perp: twr, sp. Re-erected at Kingsbury, 1933
St Luke, Nutford Place	E. Christian	G.Myers	8,650	10	c.1854		820 [8]	Gothic: S twr. Dem save twr
St Stephen, Portland Town (St John's Wood)	S.W. Daukes		5,700	500	c.1848	479	556	Gothic: SE twr. Dem
Paddington:								
All SS, Cambridge Pl.	H. Clutton	G. Myers	7,011	100	1846-7	856	454	Gothic: b-t. Burnt down 1895
Christ Ch., Craven Hill (Lancaster Gate)	F. & H. Francis		14,500	10	1854-5			Dec. Conv
H Trinity, Bishop's Rd	T. Cundy		18,459	1,000	1844-6	1,007	610	Perp: twr, sp. Dem
St James, Sussex Gdns	Goldicutt & Gutch		11,500	2,000	1841-3	1,001	616	Gothic: twr, sp. Reblt 1881
St John Ev.	C. Fowler	T. Grissell	8,735	6,275	1830-1	984	455	Perp: belfry. Alt 1888
St Saviour, Warwick Ave	T. Little		12,140	5	c.1855-6	1,108	567	Dec. Chl 1883; dem
St Stephen, Westbourne Park	F. & H. Francis		10,200	10	c.1855-6	1,057	500	Early Dec: twr, sp. Apse 1900
St Pancras:								
Holy Trinity, Haverstock Hill	Wyatt & Brandon		10,055	400	1849-50	575	851	Gothic: twr, sp
St John Ev, Charlotte St	H. Smith		6,250	300	c.1845	615	415	Romanesque: SW twr. Bom; dem
St Mark, Albert Road	T. Little		8000*	250	1851-3	785	456	C13: twr, sp. Enlgd 1890; rest 1957
St Paul, Camden Square	Ordish & Johnson		8,598	500	1847-9	519	670	Dec: twr, sp. Dem
Rotherhithe, All Saints	S. Kempthorne	Piper & son	4,117	949	c.1839	434	576	E.Eng. Dem
Holy Trinity	S. Kempthorne	Thomas Sneezum	4,149	1,161	1837-8	351	652	Gothic: twr. Bom; dem
St Paul	W. Beatson		1,950	150	c.1849		320	Dem
Shoreditch,								
All Saints, Kingsland	P. C. Hardwick		7,296	200	1856	550	400	E.Eng
Southwark, St Mary Magdalene	B. Ferrey	Cobham & Wright	4,696	1,696	1841-2	600	600	Gothic: turr, trs
Stoke Newington, St Matthias	W. Butterfield		4,900*	250	1851-3		552	Gothic: central twr. Bom; rest

CHURCHES BUILT WITH THE AID OF THE SECOND PARLIAMENTARY GRANT

Church	Architect	Contractor	Cost £	Grant £	Date	Accommodation		Style & Remarks
						Pews	Free	
Streatham, Christ Ch.	J.W. Wild		7,591	300	1840-1	650	550	Byzantine: SW campanile. Bom; rest
Sydenham:								
St Bartholomew, W Hill	L. Vulliamy[9]	William Woods[9]	9,357	9,325	1826-31	390	546	Gothic: twr. Chl 1857, add 1883
Ch. Ch., Forest Hill	E. Christian		3,850*	140	1851-6	267	277	Gothic: W stpl. Conv 2004
Walham Green, St John	G. L. Taylor	Samuel Baker & sons	9,539	6,957	1827-8	826	544	Gothic: W twr, lancets
Westminster:								
All SS, Ennismore Gdns	L. Vulliamy	Geo Baker & son	7,454	2,000	1848-9	828	480	Italian C14-15: twr. Russian Orthodox from 1955
Ch. Ch., Broadway	A. Poynter	Joshua Higgs	6,058	1,441	1842-3	268	1,232	C13. Dem 1954
Holy Trinity, Bessborough Gardens	J. L. Pearson		?	10	1849-52			Late C13. Dem 1954
St Luke, Berwick Street	E. Blore	George Brookes	6,221	2,500	1837-9	608	937	Gothic: belfry. Dem
St Andrew, Ashley Pl.[10]	G.G. Scott	George Myers	7,158	2,000	1853-5	500	600	C14: turr. Dem c.1955
St Mary the Virgin, Vincent Square	E. Blore	T. H. Hartley & Jane Grundy	4,898	2,898	1835-6	413	806	Gothic: stpl. Dem
St Matthew, Gr Peter St	G.G. Scott	George Myers	7,347	2,000	1849-50	300	909	C14. Rest after fire 1984
St Paul, Wilton Place	T. Cundy jun.		10,000	1,000	1840-2	980	540	Gothic: twr. Alt 1870, 1891
Whitechapel, St Jude	F.J. Francis	Hugh Walsh Cooper	5,353	2,103	1845-6	782	1,006	E.Eng: SW twr. Dem 1927
Woolwich, Holy Trinity	Hopkins		3,425	10	1833		258	Georgian: W twr, stuccoed. Former proprietory chapel; dem
St John	F. E. H. Fowler	Charles Kirk	5,478	2,012	1845-6	597	653	E.Eng. Rest 1912
MIDDLESEX								
Chiswick, Christ Church, Turnham Green	Scott & Moffatt		6,900	500	1841-3	425	505	E.Eng. Chl 1889
Edmonton, St James	E. Ellis	Separate trades	3,800	100	1849	310	310	E.Eng. Rednt
Enfield, St James	C. Lochner		4,361	2,146	1830	496	516	Gothic. Chl1864
Hampton Wick, St John	E. Lapidge	F. Richman & son	4,558	Whole	1829-31	402	398	Gothic: b-t. Chl 1888
Hounslow, Holy Trinity	H. Mawley	J. Taylor	5,782	3,730	1828-9	617	418	Gothic: turrs, dwarf sps. Enlgd 1857; fire 1943, repl 1961
Isleworth, St John Baptist	J. Deason		5,742	10	1855-6	263	381	Perp
Tottenham Green, Holy Trinity	J. Savage	Separate trades	5,205	3,205	1828-9	415	386	Gothic: 2 E & 2 W turrs
NORFOLK								
Great Yarmouth, St Peter	J.J. Scoles	Pigg, Wright et al	7,735	5,755	1831-3	704	1,096	Gothic: twr, brk. Greek Orthodox 1964
King's Lynn, St John Ev.	A. Salvin	Bennett & son	6,164	500	1845-6		897	E.Eng. twr. Bom, dem
NORTHAMPTONSHIRE								
Daventry, St James	H. Smith		2,239	200	1839	244	244	Dem 1962
Northampton, St Edmund	C. Vickers		3,636	250	1841	266	534	Gothic. Enlgd 1891; dem
NORTHUMBERLAND								
Benwell, St James	J. Dobson		1,700	250	1831-2	186	414	Gothic: twr. Chl etc 1895

CHURCHES BUILT WITH THE AID OF THE SECOND PARLIAMENTARY GRANT

Church	Architect	Contractor	Cost £	Grant £	Date	Accommodation		Style & Remarks
						Pews	Free	
Morpeth, St James the Gt	B. Ferrey		5,435	400	1844-6		1,042	Norman: central twr
Newcastle-on-Tyne, St Peter	J. Dobson		5,858	700	1840-2	742	369	Gothic: Dem
North Shields, H. Trinity	J. Green	Separate trades	3,594	2,276	1835-6	604	616	Gothic: twr. Dem
Seghill, Holy Trinity	J. Green		1,624	200	1848	80	426	E.Eng
Walker, Christ Church	A. B. Higham		1,222	150	1847		412	Gothic: SE twr, sp.Twr 1871
NOTTINGHAMSHIRE								
Hyson (Ison) Green, St Paul	H. I. Stevens		2,067	325	1843		500	Enlgd 1889-95
Leenside, St John Baptist	Scott & Moffatt		3,607	800	1843-4		802	E.Eng: b-t. Bom; dem
Mansfield, St John	H. I. Stevens	Lilley & John Elliott	7,358	100	1854-6	360	634	C14
New Radford, Christ Ch.	H. I. Stevens		4,125	500	1844-5	200	790	Gothic: b-g. Dem c.1948
Sneinton, St Stephen	Rickman & Hussey	William Surplice	4,511	1,303	1837-9	402	830	Gothic: twr. Repl 1912
OXFORDSHIRE								
Oxford, Holy Trinity	H.J. Underwood		3,300	300	1844-5	373	430	E.Eng: b-t. Dem 1957
South Banbury, Christ Ch.	B. Ferrey		2,820★	350	1851-2	218	710	C14: twr, sp. Stpl 1880; dem
SHROPSHIRE								
Coalbrookedale, H. Trinity	Reeves & Butcher		7,500	10	1853-4	309	243	Dec
Ironbridge, St Luke	T. Smith		3,176	200	1836-7	396	666	E. Eng (similar to Wellington)
Little Dawley, St Luke	R.Griffiths		1,350	300	1845		515	Norman: b-t
Shrewsbury, St George, Frankwell	E. Haycock	Joseph & Benjamin Birch	3,752	2,551	1829-31	290	460	E.Eng: twr trs, ashlar
Wellington, Christ Church	T. Smith		2,887	400	1838-9	400	744	E.Eng
Wrockwardine Wood	J. Baddeley[11]		1,550	300	1832-3	170	430	Grecian: twr, brk. Enlgd
SOMERSET								
Bath, St Mark, Lyncombe	G.P. Manners	James Chappell	5,587	4,840	1830-1	552	631	Dec: W twr. Chl 1883; rednt 1972
St Saviour, Larkhall	J. Pinch		6,386	4,263	1829-31	562	534	Perp: W twr. Chl 1882
Bedminster, St Paul	C. Dyer	Separate trades	8,684	6,607	1829-31	622	933	Perp: twr. Chl 1892; bom, reblt
Coxley, Christ Church	R. Carver		1,104	250	1838-9	77	187	Gothic
Easton, St Paul	R. Carver		1,035	150	1842-3	44	176	Norman: trs
Selwood Frome, H. Trin	H. E. Goodridge		2,454	300	1836-9	63	730	E. Eng: NE tr, spirelets. Rest 1890s
Hampshire Hamlet (Bridg-water), Holy Trinity	R. Carver	Thomas Hutchins	3,413	962	1838-9	518	575	Gothic: porches. Rest 1876; dem
Tatworth, St John Ev.	C. Pinch		1,450	300	1850-1	55	251	E.Eng
STAFFORDSHIRE								
Bilston, St Luke	T. Johnson		3,075	300	1851-2	200	600	E.Eng: SE twr
St Mary	F. Goodwin	Samuel Buxton & son	7,749	Whole	1827-9	538	956	Gothic: twr
Brockmoor, St John	T. Smith		2,153	500	1844-5		740	Norman: cup, trs, brk
Burslem, St Paul	L. Vulliamy	Separate trades	10,018	7,763	1828-9	994	1,043	Perp: twr. Reblt 1874; dem
Burton-on-Trent, Ch. Ch.	J. Mitchell		3,215	400	1843-4	256	744	E.Eng: W stpl, trs
Chesterton, Holy Trinity	H. Ward & son	A. & G. Holme	2,024★	150	1851-2	158	327	E.Eng: twr

CHURCHES BUILT WITH THE AID OF THE SECOND PARLIAMENTARY GRANT

Church	Architect	Contractor	Cost £	Grant £	Date	Accommodation		Style & Remarks
						Pews	Free	
Coseley, Christ Church	T. Lee	Samuel Buxton	10,784	8,632	1827-9	816	1,156	Gothic: twr. Rest 1883
Darlaston, St George	T. Johnson	Messrs Higham	2,554	300	1851-2	152	521	C13. Alt 1885; NW stpl
Edensor (Longton), St Paul	H. Ward & son		2,542	300	1853	306	499	Dec
Etruria, St Matthew	H. Ward & son		2,200	250	1847-9	221	497	Early Dec: b-t. Rest
Hope (Hanley), H. Trinity	H. Ward & son		2,850	325	1847-9	204	446	Anglo-Norman: turr
Lane End (Longton), St James the Less	T. Johnson	James Trubshaw	9,773	10,273	1832-4	1,102	908	Gothic: twr. Reblt 1878
Mow Cop, St Thomas	T. Stanley		1,665	300	1841-2	185	327	E.Eng: twr, stone
Moxley, All Saints	W. Horton		2,770	260	1850-1	189	446	E.Eng. Stpl 1877
Newcastle-under-Lyme, St George	F. Bedford	Aaron Sant (save painter)	7,977	4,952	1827-8	617	671	Perp: twr, pinnacles. Add
Northwood, Holy Trinity	J. Trubshaw	William Evans	2,714	250	1847-9	67	433	E.Eng: b-t. N twr & sp
Ocker Hill, St Mark	Hamilton & Saunders		2,500	250	1849	108	537	E.Eng, b-g, brk
Pelsall, St Michael	G.E. Hamilton		1,766	250	1843-4	148	484	Gothic Twr 1875, chl 1889
Pennett, St Mark	J.M. Derick[12]	Bramall	6,700	500	1846-9		936	Gothic: twr, trs. Rest 1924
QuarryBank, Christ Ch	T. Smith		3,268	500	1845-6		746	E.Eng: cup, trs, brk. Chl 1897
Reddal Hill (Cradley Heath), St Luke	W. Bourne		3,286	500	1845-7	500	716	E.Eng: trs. Apse 1874
Shelton, St Mark	J. Oates[13]	Separate trades	9,681	9,381	1831-3	1,152	946	Dec: twr. Chl 1868
Silverdale, St Luke	R. Armstrong	Messrs Holmes	2,577	100	1853	239	304	Late C13: stpl, tiled
Smethwick, St Matthew	J. James		2,073*	125	1854-5	250	250	Dec, b-t
Sneyd, Holy Trinity	G.T. Robinson		2,500*	350	1851-2	100	500	C14: twr, sp
Tipton, St Paul	R. Ebbels		4,068	2,000	1838-9	692	574	Gothic: twr. Alt 1899
Tunstall, Christ Church	F. Bedford	Thos Henry Webster	3,146	2,146	1830-1	644	364	Gothic: twr, sp. Chl etc 1885-6
Upper Gornal, St Peter	R. Ebbels	Richard Robinson	2,353	722	1840-1	276	645	E.Eng: 2 W turrs, op rf. Chl, apse 1857, 1865
Wednesbury, St James	W. Horton		3,000	500	1847-8	314	541	E.Eng: twr. Enlgd 1857, 1865, 1885
St John	Daukes & Hamilton		4,000	400	1845	448	552	E.Eng: NW twr, sp. Rest 1883
Wednesfield Heath, Holy Trinity	E. Banks		6,931	220	1850-2	226	443	C14: twr, ashlar
Wellington (Hanley), St Luke	H. Ward & son		2,065*	200	1852-4	246	427	C14: twr
Willenhall: Holy Trinity, Lane Head	W. Horton		3,000*	245	1854-5	112	587	E.Eng
St Stephen	W.D. Griffin		2,926	300	1853-4	194	607	C14: W b-g. Dem 1978
Wolverhampton, St Mark	C.W. Orford	Robinson	4,850	250	1848-9	528	538	E.Eng: W twr, sp. Rednt 1978
St Matthew	E. Banks		3,300	300	1848-9	96	616	C13. Dem 1963
St George	J. Morgan	Samuel Sowter and Samuel Dale	10,268	6,968	1828-30	706	1,332	Doric: twr, sp. rednt 1978
Wordesley, Holy Trinity	L. Vulliamy	Separate trades	7,565	3,818	1829-30	426	1,073	Gothic: twr
SURREY								
Croydon, All Saints, Beulah Hill	J. Savage		5,026	Whole	1827-9	373	632	E.Eng: 4 turrs, brk. Chl 1861
Christ Ch, Broad Green	S.S. Teulon		3,300	10	1851	432	304	E.Eng: trs. Chl enlgd 1860

CHURCHES BUILT WITH THE AID OF THE SECOND PARLIAMENTARY GRANT

Church	Architect	Contractor	Cost £	Grant £	Date	Pews	Free	Style & Remarks
St James, Croydon Cmn	R. Wallace		6,662	1,474	1827-8	800	400	Gothic: belfry. Chl 1881
St Mark, Norwood	Finden & Lewis		1,646	100	1852	98	207	C13: W b-t. Aisles 1864, chl 1869
St Peter, South End	G. G. Scott		6,600	250	1849-51	293	493	C14: twr, sp
Norbiton, St Peter	Scott & Moffatt		4,443	500	1841	386	358	Norman. Chl 1866
Richmond, St John	L. Vulliamy	Wm Baldock Moore[14]	5,633	3,133	1829-31	550	701	Gothic: cup. Chl 1904-5
SUSSEX								
Brighton, Christ Church	G. Cheesman, jun.		3,650	500	1837-8	450	620	Gothic: E twr, sp. Dem
St John, Carlton Hill	G. Cheesman, jun.		5,149	1,000	1838-9	504	707	Doric: stuccoed. Greek Orthodox
St Paul, West Street	R. C. Carpenter	Geo Cheesman & son	9,036	1,000	1846-7	499	701	Early Dec: twr. Sp 1874; narthex 1887
St Peter	C. Barry	William Ranger	17,392	4,858	1826-8	879	1,119	Dec: W twr. Chl 1906
Hove, St John B.	W. G. & E. Habershon		7,847	5	1853	452	479	Dec. Twr & sp 1859; mixed use
WARWICKSHIRE								
Attleborough, Holy Trinity	T. L. Walker		2,629	250	1841	164	347	Gothic: twr, sp
Balsall Heath, St Paul	J. L. Pedley		3,600★	300	1852-3	500	613	C13: twr. Enlgd 1868
Birmingham:								
All Saints, Handsworth	Rickman & Hutchinson		3,820	1,020	1832-3	506	668	Gothic: turrs. Chl 1881; dem
St Jude	C. W. Orford		3,300	500	1850-1	300	1,002	C13: b-t. Dem
St John Ev., Ladywood	S. S. Teulon		4,887★	267	1851-4	517	551	Dec. Chl & trs 1881
St Matthias	J. L. Pedley		3,500★	380	1855-6	410	741	Dec: b-t. Bom; dem 1952
Coventry, Christ Church	Rickman & Hutchinson	John Walthew	10,081	8,986	1830-2	563	943	Gothic; only medieval twr remains after bombing
St Peter	R. Ebbels		3,810	800	1840-1	559	695	E.Eng: W twr
St Thomas	Sharpe & Paley		3,450	230	1848-9	120	456	Gothic: NW turr. Dem
Foleshill, St Paul	J. L. Ackroyd		3,295	500	1840-1	508	580	E.Eng: twr. Bom; dem
Keresley, St Thomas	B. Ferrey		2,845	300	1844-5	100	320	E.Eng: W twr, sp. Dem 1980
Saltley, St Saviour	R. C. Hussey		5,413	300	1848-50	212	582	C15. Sp 1871
Stratford-on-Avon	J. Murray		2,520★	80	c.1854	171	344	C14. NW twr & sp 1875-93
WESTMORLAND								
Kendal, St George	G. Webster	Separate trades	4,242	878	1839-41	376	878	Gothic: 2 belfry turrs. Chl 1911
WILTSHIRE								
Derry Hill, Christ Church	Wyatt & Brandon		2,342	250	1839-40	108	392	Perp: twr, sp
Dilton Marsh, H. Trinity	T. H. Wyatt		3,262	400	1844	102	500	Norman: crossing twr, trs
Leigh (Bradford-on-Avon) Christ Church	G. P. Manners		3,365	350	1841	219	559	Perp: twr, sp. Chl 1878
Shaw Whitley, Christ Ch.	T. H. Wyatt		1,480	400	1836-8	130	320	E.Eng. Stpl 1905
Trowbridge, Holy Trinity	A. E. Livesey	Chas & Richard Gane	5,251	1,676	1837-8	501	525	Gothic: twr, lancets
Warminster, Christ Ch.	J. Leachman	James Provis	3,130	1,755	1830-1	150	672	Gothic: twr. Chl 1871, nave arcades 1881
WORCESTERSHIRE								
Catshill, Christ Church	H. Eginton		1,750	200	c1838	132	414	E.Eng: twr, ashlar. Chl 1887

CHURCHES BUILT WITH THE AID OF THE SECOND PARLIAMENTARY GRANT

Church	Architect	Contractor	Cost £	Grant £	Date	Accommodation		Style & Remarks
						Pews	Free	
Claines, St George	J. Lucy[15]	Cook & Rowlands	3,589	2,195	1829-30	354	358	Gothic: twr. Dem 1894
Eve's Hill, St James the Gt	W. Bourne		3,300	750	1838-9	261	746	E.Eng; W twr. Chl 1869
Freebodies, St John	W. Bourne		3,200	750	1838-9	261	746	E.Eng; W twr
Langley, Holy Trinity	W. Bourne		1,520*	150	1851-2		400	C14: b-g, stone. Dem 1968
Kidderminster, St John B.	G. Alexander		4,075	200	1842-3	396	861	Norman; twr, sp, brk; reblt 1890-4 save twr & sp
Oldbury, Christ Church	T. Johnson		4,507	3,142	1840-1	783	725	E.Eng: NW twr, brk. Chl 1867, twr 1888; conv
YORKSHIRE (EAST RIDING)								
Bridlington Quay, Ch. Ch.	Scott & Moffatt		2,546	100	1840	291	320	Gothic. Enlgd 1857, twr 1859
Hull, St James, Myton	Hansom & Welch	William Exley	5,373	3,591	1829-31	600	603	Gothic: twr, sp. Bom; dem
St Mark, Sutton	H. F. Lockwood		3,871	500	1841-2	812	246	Gothic: twr, sp. Bom; dem
St Paul, Sculcoates	W. Dykes		4,000	500	1846-7	540	541	Gothic: stpl. Bom: dem
YORKSHIRE (NORTH RIDING)								
Whitby:								
St John, Baxtergate	J. B. & W. Atkinson		3,148	750	1848-9	380	840	C13; b-g; pl.rib-vault
St Michael	J. B. & W. Atkinson	Separate trades	3,300	150	1847-8	201	500	E.Eng: b-g, op rf. Consecrated 1856; dem
Scarborough, Christ Ch.	Atkinson & Sharp	Separate trades	6,692	4,733	1826-8	600	600	Gothic: twr. Chl 1873; rednt 1977
YORKSHIRE (WEST RIDING)								
Barkisland (Halifax), Christ Church	Mallinson & Healey		1,350*	150	1852-3	150	296	C14: b-g
Batley Carr, Holy Trinity	R. D. Chantrell		1,828	300	1840-1	296	334	Dec: W twr. Add 1895
Battyeford, Christ Church	I. Bonomi	Separate trades	1,769	691	1839-40	350	348	Gothic: W twr. Dem 1971 after fire
Birkenshaw, St Paul	Atkinson & Sharp	Separate trades	3,310	Whole	1829-30	393	315	Gothic: twr, sp. Chl 1892
Bradford:								
St Andrew, North Horton, (Lister Hills)	Mallinson & Healey	Separate trades	2,425*	200	1851-2	324	482	C14: NE twr. Sp 1863; dem 1965
St Matthew, Bankfoot (Carr Bottom Lane)	Mallinson & Healey		1,867	200	1848-9	140	350	Dec: b-g, spirelet
Brampton Bierlow, Ch. Ch.	Pritchett & sons		3,000*	125	1854-5	295	235	Dec: twr, chl
Brighouse, St Martin	L. Hammerton	Separate trades	3,605	Whole	1830-1	572	558	E.Eng: twr. Chl 1905
Clayton (Bradford), St John Baptist	Mallinson & Healey	Separate trades	1,903	1,031	1849-50	210	592	C14
Cleckheaton, St John	Atkinson & Sharp	Separate trades	2,632	Whole	1830-1	296	307	E.Eng: twr. Chl 1864; dem save twr
Cowling, Holy Trinity	J. B.Chantrell		1,896	500	1844-5	178	355	Gothic: twr
Cragg, St John Baptist	C. Child	Separate trades	1,888	452	1838-9	348	380	E.Eng; W twr
Crosland, South, H. Trin.	P. Atkinson	Separate trades	2,588	2,272	1827-9	378	322	E.Eng: twr
Cross Stones, St Paul	Pickersgill & Oates	Separate trades	2,840	1,840	1833-5	648	372	Gothic: small twr
Cullingworth, St John Ev.	Perkin & Backhouse		1,660*	500	1851-3		564	C13: twr, sp. Rest 1902
Denholme, St Paul	Chantrell & Shaw		3,700	500	1843-6	100	543	C13: twr, sp. Rednt 2002
Dewsbury, St Matthew, West Town	Bonomi & Cory		2,361	250	1847-8		527	Perp: massive twr. Restd

CHURCHES BUILT WITH THE AID OF THE SECOND PARLIAMENTARY GRANT

Church	Architect	Contractor	Cost £	Grant £	Date	Accommodation		Style & Remarks
						Pews	Free	
Dodsworth, St John	B. Taylor		2,518	250	1843-4	260	243	Norman: twr. Restd
East Knottingley, Ch. Ch.	C. Vickers		2,166	200	1847-8	196	561	E.Eng: b-g. Dem
Eastwood, St Mary V.	Perkin & Backhouse		1,523*	230	1854-5	482	465	C13: b-g. Dem
Eccleshill, St Luke	W. Rawstorne	Separate trades	2,634	1,114	1846-8		336	Perp: twr, sp. Chl 1913
Embsay, St Mary V.	T. Shaw		1,500*	150	1852-3		317	Perp
Farsley, St John Ev.	W. Wallen		1,531	300	1842-3	198	252	Gothic: twr. Twr reblt 1895
Golcar, St John	P. Atkinson	Separate trades	3,133	Whole	1828-9	520	430	E.Eng: W twr, sp. Chl 1862
Gomersall, St Mary V.	Jeremiah Dobson		2,466	180	1850-1	125	341	Dec: twr. Trs 1864
Greasborough, St Mary	Watson, Pritchett & Watson	Trades[16]	5,077	2,000	1826-8	370	415	Dec: W twr
Halifax, St James	J. Oates	Separate trades	4,196	Whole	1830-1	779	427	Gothic: 2 W turrs. Dem 1955
St Paul, King Cross	R. D. Chantrell		3,650	300	1844-6	232	364	Gothic: twr, sp. Repl 1912, save stpl
Hebden Bridge (Mytholm) St James the Great	J. Oates[17]		3,047	Whole	1832-3	648	372	E.Eng: W twr. Chl 1876
Heckmondwike, St James	Atkinson & Sharp	Separate trades	2,805	Whole	1830-1	365	324	Gothic: twr, sp. Chl 1906
Hopton, St John	Bonomi & Cory		1,245	100	1844-5		317	Gothic: W twr
Hoyland, St Peter	Watson, Pritchett & Watson	Trades[18]	2,076	1,000	1830	125	374	Gothic: twr, sp
Huddersfield, St Paul	J. Oates	Separate trades	5,700	Whole	1828-30	863	380	Gothic: W twr, sp. Chl 1883
Idle (Bradford), H. Trinity	J. Oates	Separate trades	3,115	Whole	1828-9	604	416	E.Eng: twr, sp.Vestry 1895
Ingrow, St John Ev. (Paper Mill)	W. Rawstorne		2,167	500	1841-2	408	356	Lombard: W twr
Kimberworth, St Thomas	M. Habershon		1,561	600	1841-2	195	407	E.Eng: W twr. Chl 1882
Kirkstall, St Stephen	R. D. Chantrell	Separate trades	3,206	Whole	1828-9	500	500	E.Eng: W twr, sp. Enlgd 1864, 1874
Knaresbrough, H. Trinity	J. Fawcett		3,200*	300	1854-6	204	612	C13: twr, sp
Leeds:								
All Saints, York Road	Mallinson & Healey		3,166	300	1849-50		756	C14: sp. Dem
St Andrew, Cavendish St	Scott & Moffatt		3,972	300	1843-4	149	581	E.Eng: W b-t. Dem
St Barnabas, Brewery Field	J. T. Fairbank		1,660*	250	1854-5	50	484	C13. Dem
St John B, New Wortley	Jeremiah Dobson	Separate trades	3,457*	350	1852		700	Dec: NE twr, sp. Dem
St Jude, Hunslet (Pottery Field)	Burleigh & Boyce		2,671	300	1852-3		603	Gothic. Dem
St Matthew, Camp Road (Little London)	C. W. Burleigh		2,851	200	1850-1	250	450	Dec: SW twr, sp, trs. Dem
St Matthew, Holbeck	R. D. Chantrell	Separate trades	3,735	3,349	1829-30	606	596	E.Eng: W twr. Sp etc 1860; dem
St Michael, Buslingthorpe	C. W. Burleigh		2,170	300	1852-4		610	Early C14. Dem 1969
St Philip, Wellington St, (Bean Ing)	R. D. Chantrell		3,371	300	1845-7	443	144	Early Dec: twr, sp. Dem 1931
St Stephen, Burmantofts	Jeremiah Dobson	Separate trades	2,685*	200	1853-4		605	Dec: b-t. Dem
Lindley, St Stephen	J. Oates	Separate trades	2,714	Whole	1828-9	408	459	E.Eng: W twr, sp
Linthwaite, Christ Ch.	Atkinson & Sharp	Separate trades	3,135	3,035	1827-8	600	200	E.Eng: W twr, sp. Chl etc 1895
Lockwod, Emmanuel	R. D. Chantrell	Separate trades	3,147	3,047	1828-9	522	398	E.Eng: W turr. Chl 1899
Morley, St Peter	R. D. Chantrell	Separate trades	2,968	Whole	1829-30	576	424	Gothic: twr, sp. Chl 1885

CHURCHES BUILT WITH THE AID OF THE SECOND PARLIAMENTARY GRANT

Church	Architect	Contractor	Cost £	Grant £	Date	Accommodation		Style & Remarks
						Pews	Free	
Morton, St Luke	Perkin & Backhouse		1,550	500	1849-50	100	311	Rest
Mount Pellion (Halifax), Christ Church	Mallinson & Healey		1,360*	125	1853-4		273	Dec: SW twr. Enlgd
Mytholmroyd, St Michael	Mallinson & Healey		1,739	300	1847-8		480	Gothic: W twr. Chl 1887
Netherthong, All Saints	R. D. Chantrell	Separate trades	2,867	2,557	1829-30	382	318	Gothic: W turr. Chl 1877
New Mill, Christ Church	P. Atkinson	Separate trades	3,715	3,525	1829-30	588	412	E.Eng: twr. Reb 1882
Oakworth, Christ Church	W. Wallen		2,019	500	1845-6	276	319	Gothic: belfry
Ovenden (Halifax), St John	C. Child	Separate trades	1,070	200	1838	264	86	E.Eng: W twr
Oxenhope, St Mary V.	Bonomi & Cory		1,199	250	1849		437	Norman: W twr
Paddock, All Saints	J. Oates	Separate trades	2,706	Whole	1828-9	408	459	As Lindley, Gothic: twr, sp. Rednt
Pateley Bridge, St Cuthbert	Woodhead & Hurst	Separate trades	6,612	2,000	1825-7	371	432	Gothic: twr. Rednt 1982
Pudsey, St Paul	Perkin & Backhouse		1,570	200	1855-6	120	399	E.Eng
Queenshead (Halifax), Holy Trinity	J. Mallinson		2,613	500	1842-3	400	402	Gothic: twr. Chl 1885; twr reblt 1906
Robertown, All Saints	Chantrell & Shaw		2,077	300	1844-5	362	138	Gothic: b-t
Sheffield:								
Christ Church, Pitsmoor	Flockton & Lee		2,312	232	1849-50	266	576	Early Dec: W twr. Add 1895
St Jude, Eldon	J. Mitchell		2,070	250	1848-9	204	526	Gothic. Dem 1947
St Jude, Moorfields (1)	J. Mitchell		1,750*	—	1849-52			Twr fell on nave: reb as next
(2)	Flockton & son		3,363	350	1854-5	314	591	C13: b-t. Dem
St Matthew, Carver St	Flockton & son		2,820	200	1854-5	273	458	C15: W stpl. Chl 1884
St Thomas, Brightside	Flockton & son	Gregory & Turner	1,527*	100	1852-4	199	241	Late Gothic; SW twr, sp. Conv
Shelf, St Michael & A.A.	Mallinson & Healey		1,745	250	1849	148	345	C14: b-g
Shepley, St Paul	W. Wallen		1,404	100	1845-8	90	203	Chl 1868
South Ossett, Christ Ch.	Mallinson & Healey		2,000	200	1850-1	196	407	C13: twr. Later sp
Stannington, Christ Ch.	Woodhead & Hurst	Separate trades	2,820	Whole	1828-9	356	366	Gothic: W turr
Thornes, St James	S. Sharp	Fawcett & Woodhead	2,020	1,000	1829-30	320	250	Roman Doric: W twr
Thurgoland, Holy Trinity	W.Hurst & Moffatt		1,300	150	1841-2	403	104	Gothic: belfry. Repl 1870
Upper Thong, St John (Holmfirth)	E. H. Shellard		4,340	200	1846-8	262	438	Perp: huge S twr, trs. Chl 1875
Wakefield, St Mary	C. Clapham	Pickles & Clarke	1,863*	300	1853-4		620	Dec: SW twr, sp. Enlgd 1887
Woodside, St James	C.W. Burleigh		1,916	200	1846-8		384	Gothic
Wyke, St Mary	Mallinson & Healey		3,050	500	1846-7		704	E.Eng: twr, sp
Yeadon, St John Ev.	W. Rawstorne		1,605	300	1843-4	216	375	Gothic. Chl 1893
York, St Thomas, The Groves	G. F. Jones	Separate trades	1,970*	50	1853-4	249	252	E.Eng: b-t on W gable

WALES AND MONMOUTHSHIRE

ANGLESEY

Church	Architect	Contractor	Cost £	Grant £	Date	Pews	Free	Style & Remarks
Holyhead, St Seiriol, Maesclaled	C. Verelst		4,200*	185	1854	358	378	Gothic: sp

CHURCHES BUILT WITH THE AID OF THE SECOND PARLIAMENTARY GRANT

Church	Architect	Contractor	Cost £	Grant £	Date	Accommodation		Style & Remarks
						Pews	Free	
CARDIGANSHIRE								
Aberystwyth, St Michael, Llanbadarn	E. Haycock	R. James	3,789	1,289	1830-2	567	634	Gothic: b-t. Repl 1890
CARMARTHENSHIRE								
Carmarthen, St David	E. Haycock	W. & T. Rowland	4,107	3,000	1835-6	564	498	Gothic: twr. Enlgd
Cwmaman, Christ Church	R. Ebbels		1,075	400	1841	46	499	E.Eng: twr
Llanelly, St Paul	G. G. Scott		2,460	250	1849-50		503	Late C13
CAERNARVONSHIRE								
Llanllechyd (Glanogwen) Christ Church	T. H. Wyatt		3,850	300	1855-6		646	C12: stpl
DENBIGHSHIRE								
Brymbo, St Mary	J. Lloyd		1,180	600	1838	200	400	Dem c.1870
Denbigh, St David	T. Penson		3,600	250	1838-40	402	426	Twr 1855-8
Gwersyllt, Holy Trinity	T. Penson		2,405	150	1850-1		384	C13: stpl
Pontfadog, St John Baptist	F. Wehnert[19]		849	100	1845-7		322	E.Eng: twr
Rhosllanerchrugog, St John	T. Penson	Ebenezer Thomas	2,200	200	1852-3	36	388	Norman: b-t
FLINTSHIRE								
Bagillt, St Mary	J. Lloyd		2,167	300	1837-9	248	516	Gothic
Bistre, Emmanuel[20]	J. Lloyd		1,092	200	1841-2	207	449	Gothic: square b-t; rest 1881
Brynford, St Michael	T. H. Wyatt		2,060*	125	1851-2	72	278	C12: b-t
Gwernafield, Holy Trinity	J. Lloyd		800	300	1838	170	354	'Without architectural features'.[21] Repl 1871-2
GLAMORGAN								
Aberdare, St Elvans	A. Mosely		4,000*	250	1852-3	240	560	Gothic, sp
St Fagan, Trecynon	T. T. Bury		1,795*	200	1851-3	17	658	E.Eng: b-g. Burnt down 1855
Cardiff, St Mary	T. Foster	Geo. Monk & son	5,724	1,663	1841-3	642	1,162	Norman: 2 W twrs
Clydach, St John	W. Whittington		1,600	200	1845-7	200	300	Lancets, N twr with turrs
Glyntaff (Newbridge)	T. H. Wyatt		2,500	414	1838	90	710	Norman: twr
Maesteg, St David	E. Moxham		1,045	100	1852-3		220	Lancets, b-g
Merthyr Tydfil, St David	Wyatt & Brandon	Joshua Daniels	4,110	1,204	1846-7	600	600	E.Eng b-t
Pont-y-Rhun	J. Prichard		1,355*	100	1851-2	96	209	C13: b-t
Rhondda Valley, St David	C. E. Bernard		1,050*	60	c.1853	36	227	
Skewen	E. Moxham[22]		1,050	125	1849-50	72	252	Early Dec, op rff
Swansea, St Peter	R. K. Penson		1,495*	85	1856		307	E.Eng: b-t
MONMOUTHSHIRE								
Abertillery, St Michael	J. Norton		?	125	1853-4			Repl 1898
Nant-y-Glo, Holy Trinity	J. Daniels	Joshua Daniels	1,253*	100	1852-4	216	319	E.Eng: b-t

CHURCHES BUILT WITH THE AID OF THE SECOND PARLIAMENTARY GRANT

Church	Architect	Contractor	Cost £	Grant £	Date	Accommodation		Style & Remarks
						Pews	Free	
Newport, St Paul	T. H. Wyatt	Separate trades	5,024	1,350	1835–6	555	745	Gothic: twr, sp
Pilgwenelly, H.Trinity	J. H. Langdon		2,700	250	1851–2	248	401	C14
Tredegar, St George	J. Jenkins	Thomas Griffiths	3,061	1,042	1835–6	614	394	Saxon or Early Norman: twr
Trevethin (Abersychan), St Thomas	E. Haycock	John Lane	1,746	1,155	1831–2	60	493	Gothic: b–t
MONTGOMERYSHIRE								
Newtown, St David	T. Penson	John Baggaley	4,837	2,000	1843–5	400	800	Gothic: twr
PEMBROKESHIRE								
Pembroke Dock, St John	J. P. Harrison		3,774	400	1846–8	150	651	Gothic: twr

Notes

1 J. Green was called in to survey the church after completion because of the architect's death.

2 Completed by William Slater after Carpenter's death.

3 The Lancashire & Yorkshire Railway Company required the site in 1848, so a new church was built at their expense, with the Commissioners' approval, in twelfth-century Gothic style by A. H. Holme.

4 For purchase. The original cost of the building was £10,000.

5 So reported to the Commission, but it was built in Gothic.

6 Became bankrupt, and work taken over by Henry Charles Holland.

7 Contractor's tender.

8 Covers both pews and free seating.

9 A dispute between the Commission and the parish over the site of the second church caused the works to be suspended; when resumed in mid-1850, a new contract was made with Thomas Smith.

10 At first referred to as 'St Mark'.

11 Plans modified and executed by Samuel Smith and son.

12 Derick was discharged for 'misconduct' and superseded by Lewis Stride.

13 Completed after his death by M. Oates and T. Pickersgill.

14 Francis and Edmund Charles Richman were the original contractors, but performed only £260 worth of the work (CBC, SR, III, 86).

15 Lewis Belling completed the building after Lucy's death.

16 Lord Fitzwilliam's workmen carried out the work.

17 J. Oates having died, the work was superintended by M. Oates and T. Pickersgill.

18 Lord Fitzwilliam's workmen carried out the work.

19 Completed by R. K. Penson because of Wehnert's bankruptcy (D.R. Thomas, *History of St Asaph* (1874)).

20 Modelled on Casterton church, Westmorland (Thomas, op. cit.).

21 Thomas, op. cit.

22 First designs in 1848 by R. C. Saunders (ICBS).

APPENDIX 2

Architects employed on Commissioners' Churches

Together with a list of their churches, and the authority for each ascription. The reference ICBS is to the records of the Incorporated Church Building Society, viewable on-line at www.churchplansonline.org . Many other CBC churches, having also received a grant from the ICBS, will be found on this web-site.

AKROYD, JAMES LLOYD, *fl.* 1838-49
Foleshill (Warks) CBC, SR, V, 28
AITKIN, REV. R., incumbent of Pendeen
Pendeen (Corn) CBC, BC, MB 17
ALEXANDER, GEORGE, d. 1884
Herne Hill (London) CC file: Kidderminster (Worcs), St John CBC, SR, 221
ALLOM, THOMAS, 1804–72
Highbury (London), Christ Church CC file 18106
ANDERSON, JOHN, *fl.* 1825-32
(Durham), West Rainton CC file 18120; Hetton-le-Hole CBC, SR, II, 242
ARMSTRONG, RICHARD, d. *c.*1909
Silverdale (Staffs) CC file 18203
ARNOLD, VERNON
Kennington (London), Christ Church CC file 20453
ASHPITEL, ARTHUR, 1807-69
(London), Homerton CC file 18096; Greenwich, St John, Blackheath LCC, metrop. bldgs reg.
ATKINSON, JOHN BOWNAS, 1807-74, and WILLIAM
(N Yorks), Whitby, St John CBC, SR, VII, 10; St Michael CC file 16240
ATKINSON, PETER, jun., *c.*1776-1843
(All, save Manchester, in Yorks, and ascriptions from CBC, SR): Stanley★ I, 81; Alverthorpe★ II, 81; Leeds St Mark★ II, 80; Scarborough★ II, 95; Linthwaite★ II, 113; Crossland II, 163; Golcar II, 164; New Mills II, 214; Manchester, St Andrew★ III, 1; Birkenshaw★ III, 10; Cleckheaton★ III, 9; Heckmondwike★ III, 9 (★in partnership with Richard Hey Sharp, 1793-1853).
ATKINSON, THOMAS WITLAM, 1799-1861, and CHARLES
Hyde (Ches), St George CBC, SR, II, 226
BADDELEY, JOHN
Wrockwardine Wood (Salop) CC file 17771
BANKS, EDWARD, *fl.* 1844-74
(Staffs), Wolverhampton, St Matthew CBC, SR, VII, 1; Wednesfield, Holy Trinity CBC, BC, MB 17
BARRY, CHARLES, 1795-1860
Stand (Lancs) CBC, SR, II, 161: Manchester, St Matthew SR, II, 160: Brighton II, 134: (London), Islington, Holy Trinity II, 93; St John II, 111; St Paul II, 106; Saffron Hill III, 152
BARRY, EDWARD MIDDLETON, 1830-80
South Hampstead (London) CC file 12170, pt I
BASEVI, GEORGE, 1794-1845
Stockport (Chest) CBC, SR, I, 98: (London), Greenwich, St Mary I, 142; Chelsea, St Saviour IV, 225; St Jude ICBS
BEATSON, WILLIAM, b. 1808
Rotherhithe (London), St Paul CBC, SR, VII, 45
BEDFORD, FRANCIS OCTAVIUS, 1784-1858
(London), Camberwell St George CBC, SR, III, 199; Lambeth, St John I, 6; Norwood, St Luke I, 61; Newington, Holy Trinity I, 126; Lambeth, St

Mary the Less II, 87: Newcastle-under-Lyme (Staffs) II, 114: Riddings (Derbys) II, 235: Horwich (Lancs) III, 3: Tunstall (Staffs) III, 80: St Giles-in-the-Fields (London), Holy Trinity III, 221

BELLAMY, THOMAS, 1798-1876

Camberwell (London), Emmanuel CBC, MB 54

BERNARD, CHARLES E.

Rhondda Valley (Glam) CBC, SR, VII, 111

BLORE, EDWARD, 1787-1879

Battersea (London), St George CBC, SR, II, 167: Plaistow (Essex) II, 168: Warrington II, 222: Waltham Cross (Herts) III, 88: Stratford (Essex) III, 117: Croft (Lancs) III, 128: Westminster, St Mary IV, 82; St Luke IV, 160: Lambeth (London), Holy Trinity IV, 212: Barkingside (Essex) IV, 226

BONOMI, IGNATIUS, 1787-1870

Winlaton (Durham) CBC, SR, II, 175: (W Yorks): Battyeford IV, 192; Hopton★ ICBS; Dewsbury St Matthew★ ICBS; Oxenhope★ CBC, SR, VII, 20. (★ in partnership with John Augustus Cory, 1819-87)

BOURNE, WILLIAM, fl. 1838-55

(Worcs), Eve's Hill CBC, SR, IV, 186; Freebodies IV, 186; Langley VII, 7j: Reddal Hill (Staffs) CC file 16049

BOWMAN, HENRY, 1814-83, and CROWTHER, JOSEPH STRETCH, d. 1893

Portwood (Ches) CC file 21706

BOYCE, PHILIP (probably an assistant or partner of C. W. Burleigh)

Leeds: St Michael, Buslingthorpe; St Jude, Hunslet respective CC files

BROWN, JOHN, 1805-76

Greenwich (London), Christ Church ICBS

BROWN, THOMAS, d. 1840. A partner of W. HAYLEY, q.v.

BROWNE, ROBERT PALMER, c.1802 -72

East Peckham (London), St Mary Magdalen CBC, SR, IV, 224

BURLEIGH, C. W.

Leeds, Woodside CBC, MB 64; St Matthew, Camp Road SR, VII, 64; St Michael, Buslingthorpe★ VII, 91; St Jude, Hunslet★ CC file 21988. (★P. Boyce (q.v.) signed letters 'for C. W. Burleigh', and signed the consecration certificates for these churches. CC files)

BURTON, DECIMUS, 1800-81

Tunbridge Wells (Kent) CBC, SR, II, 114

BURY, THOMAS TALBOT, 1811-77

Aberdare (Glam), St Fagan CBC, SR, VII, 89: Battersea (London), Christ Church VII, 32

BUTTERFIELD WILLIAM, 1814-1900

Stoke Newington (London) CBC, SR, VII, 105

CARPENTER, RICHARD CROMWELL, 1812-55

Brighton, St Paul ICBS: Milton (Kent), Christ Church (completed by W. Slater, q.v.) ICBS

CARTER, OWEN BROWNE, 1806-59

Southampton, St Peter CC file 16120

CARVER, RICHARD, c.1792-1862

(Som), Bridgwater CBC, SR, IV, 172; Coxley IV, 209: Easton V, 180.

CHAFFER, THOMAS

Trawdon (Lancs) GR

CHANTRELL, JOHN BOHAM

Denholme Gate (W Yorks) (in partnership with T. Shaw) CC file 15573

CHANTRELL, ROBERT DENNIS, 1793-1872

(W Yorks), Leeds, Christ Church. CBC, SR, II, 100; Kirkstall II, 208; Lockwood II, 207; Netherthong II, 137; Morley II, 224: New Mills (Derbys) II, 214: (W Yorks), Holbeck III, 20; Batley Carr V, 86; Robertown (in partnership with T. Shaw ,q.v.; probably J. B. Chantrell worked in the same firm) CC file 16061; King Cross (Halifax) GR; Leeds, St Philip Bean Ing ICBS

CHEESMAN, GEORGE, fl. 1828-48

Brighton: Christ Church CBC, SR, IV, 147; St John Ev. IV, 223

CHILD, CHARLES, d. 1862

(W Yorks), Cragg CBC, SR, 1V, 112; Ovenden V, 76: Walsden (Lancs) MB 65

CHRISTIAN, EWAN, 1814-95

(London), Marylebone St Luke GR; Sydenham, Christ Church ICBS: Somercotes (Derbys) ICBS

CLAPHAM, CHARLES

Wakefield, St Mary CBC, SR, VIII, 122

CLARKE, JOSEPH, 1819-88

East Crompton (Lancs) ICBS: Dukinfield (Ches), St Mark CBC, MB, 66: Lumb, Whalley (Lancs) ICBS: Danebridge (Ches) CBC, BC, MB 17: (Lancs), Pinfold SR, VII, 154; Golborne BC, MB 17: Lambeth (London), St Barnabas (in partnership with James Humphreys) GR

CLAYTON, ALFRED BOWYER, 1795-1855

Kennington (London), St Mark (nominally D. R. Roper, q.v.) GR

CLUTTON, HENRY, 1819-93

(London), Bethnal Green, St Jude GR; Paddington All SS GR; Limehouse CBC, SR, VII, 100

COCKERELL, CHARLES ROBERT, 1788-1863

Westminster, St George Regent St ('Hanover Chapel') CBC, SR, I, 115

CORSON, WILLIAM REID

Tonge (Lancs) successor to J. E. Gregan, decd CBC, SR, VII, 170; CC file 16176

CUFFLEY, A. D.

Glodwick (Lancs) GR

CUNDY, THOMAS, jun., 1790-1867

Westminster, St Paul, Wilton Place CBC, SR, V, 128; Paddington, Holy Trinity *DBA.*

DANIELS, JOSHUA

Nant-y-Glo (Mon) CBC, SR, VII, 130

DAVIES, John, 1796-1865

Winchmore Hill (Middx) CBC, SR, II, 110

DAUKES, SAMUEL WHITFIELD, 1811-80

Gravesend (Kent) CBC, SR, VII, 40; (London), St Marylebone; St Andrew ★ ICBS; St Stephen★ ICBS: Wednesbury (Staffs), St John★ (★in partner-ship with Hamilton)

DEASON, JAMES, *fl.* 1855-68

 Isleworth (Middx), St John Baptist CC file 11578

DERICK, JOHN MACDUFF, 1810-61

Pensnett (Staffs) CC file 16024: superseded by L. Stride

DICKSON, T., and BRAKSPEAR, WILLIAM HAYWARD

Ashton-under-Lyne (Lancs), Christ Church CC file 16538

DOBSON, JEREMIAH, *fl.* 1849-70

(W Yorks), Gomersall CBC, SR, VII, 44; Leeds, St Stephen, Burmantofts VII, 140; St John B, New Wortley VII, 113

DOBSON, JOHN, 1787-1865. See *Memoir* by M. J. Dobson, 1885

Newcastle upon Tyne, St James Benwell CBC, SR, III, 129; St Peter V, 112: (Durham), Monkwearmouth CC file 4727; Bensham; Benfieldside; Hendon CC file 15757

DONALDSON, THOMAS LEVERTON, 1795-1885

Brompton (London), Holy Trinity CBC, SR, II, 108

DUESBURY, H. (also DEWSBURY), *fl.* 1840-50

Dalston (London) CBC, SR, V, 75

DUNLOP, ROBERT

Thornley (Durham) CC file 25080

DYER, CHARLES, 1794-1848

Bedminster (Som) CBC, SR, II, 127

DYKES, WILLIAM HEY, *fl.* 1845-58

Sculcoates (E Yorks) GR

EALES, CHRISTOPHER, *c.*1809-1903

Charlestown (Corn) CBC, SR, VII, 4

EBBELS, ROBERT, d. 1860

(Staffs), Tipton, St Paul CBC, SR, IV, 69; Upper Gornal, IV, 174: Coventry, St Peter V, 76: Cwmaman (Carm) V, 118

EDMUNDS, WILLIAM

(Kent): Margate, Holy Trinity CBC, SR, II, 73; Dover, Holy Trinity III, 185

EDWARDS, FRANCIS, 1784-1857

Hoxton (London), St John CBC, SR, I, 196

EGINTON, HARVEY, 1809-49

Catshill (Worcs) GR

ELLIOTT, JOHN, *fl.* 1832-68

Newtown (Hants), St Luke CC file 15988

ELLIS, EDWARD, *c.*1817-90

Edmonton (Middx) CC file 17924

FAIRBANK, JOHN TERTIUS, *fl.* 1846-56

Leeds, St Barnabas, Holbeck CBC, SR, VII, 133

FAWCETT, JOSEPH

Knaresborough (W Yorks) CBC, BC, MB, 17

FERREY, BENJAMIN, 1818-80

(London), Southwark, St Mary Magd. CBC, SR, V, 171; St Giles-in-the-Fields, Christ Ch. ICBS: Keresley (Warks) ICBS: Barnstaple (Dev) ICBS: Morpeth (Northumb) ICBS: Bethnal Green (London), St Simon Zelotes GR: South Banbury (Oxon) CBC, SR, VII, 99: (Devon), Devonport, St Michael CC file 15581; Sutton St John CBC, SR, VII, 94: Lambeth (London), St John, Angell Town GR

FINDEN, THOMAS, c.1785-1861, and LEWIS, THOMAS HAYTER

Croydon (Surrey), St Mark CC file 18211

FLOCKTON, WILLIAM, 1804-64, and SON (THOMAS JAMES, 1825-99)

Sheffield, Christ Church, Pitsmoor CBC, SR, VII, 27; St Thomas, Brightside VII, 112; St Matthew, Carver St. VII, 151; St Jude, Moorfields (rebuilding) VII, 133

FORBES, John B. b. c.1795

Cheltenham, St Paul CBC, SR, II, 237

FOSTER, JAMES, c.1748-1823, and SONS (JAMES, jun., and probably JOHN, d. c.1880, and THOMAS, q.v.)

Kingswood (Glos) ICBS

FOSTER, THOMAS, c.1793-1849

(Glos), Stroudshill CBC, SR, IV, 158; Whiteshill V, 38: Cardiff, St Mary V, 63 (with JOHN, ICBS)

FOSTER, JOHN, jun., c.1786-1846

Liverpool, St Martin CBC, SR, I, 155

FOULSTON, JOHN, 1772-1842

Plymouth, St Paul, Stonehouse CBC, SR, III, 51

FOWLER, CHARLES, 1791-1867

Paddington (London), St John CBC, SR, III, 32

FOWLER, FRANCIS E. H., fl. 1842-78

Woolwich (London), St John 1845 CC file 16279, Pt. 2

FRANCIS, FREDERICK JOHN, 1818-96, and HORACE, 1821-94

(London), Paddington, St Stephen CC file 17811, pt. 2; Christ Ch. Craven Hill (Lancaster Gate) CC file 17806

FRANCIS, FREDERICK JOHN

Whitechapel (London), St Jude CBC, MB 60

GABRIEL, SAMUEL BURLEIGH (fl. 1848-60), and HICKS, JOHN, fl. 1836-68

Bristol, St Simon, CC file 15317; St Michael ICBS.; St Jude ICBS; St Clement (with Hirst) GR

GANDY-DEERING, JOHN PETER, 1787-1850

Westminster, St Mark, N Audley St. CBC, SR, II, 96

GODWIN, GEORGE, 1815-88

Kensington, St Mary the Boltons CBC, SR, VII, 46

GOLDICUTT, JOHN, 1793-1842, and GUTCH, GEORGE, c.1790 -1874

Paddington (London), St James CBC, SR, V 107; 154

GOODRIDGE, HENRY EDMUND, 1797-1864

Frome Selwood (Som) ICBS

GOODWIN, FRANCIS, 1784-1835

Stepney (London), St Philip (nominally J. Walters, q.v.) SM Corr. 2 X E, 3: Southsea (Hants), St Paul CBC, SR, II, 22: Bordesley (Warks) II, 21: Ashton-under-Lyne (Lancs) St Peter II, 57: Kidderminster (Worcs), St George II, 49: West Bromwich (Staffs) III, 50: Derby II, 70: Hulme (Lancs) II, 56: Bilston (Staffs) II, 162: (Lancs), Oldham II, 109; Pendleton (in partnership with R. Lane, q.v.) III, 2

GOUGH, ALEXANDER DICK, 1804-71

(London), Islington, St Matthew CBC, SR, VII, 89; St Mark VII, 125; St Jude VII, 155: Chatham (Kent), St Paul VII, 132

GRANVILLE, WALTER LONG BOZZI, c.1819 -74

Hatcham (London), St James CBC, SR, VII, 107

GREEN, JOHN, 1787-1852

(Northumb), North Shields CBC, SR, III, 77, Seghill GR

GRIFFIN, WILLIAM DARBY fl. 1853-68

Willenhall (Staffs) St Stephen CC file 18202, pt 5

GRIFFITHS, ROBERT, fl. 1839-57

Little Dawley (Salop) CBC, MB 59

GWILT, JOSEPH, 1784-1863

Charlton (Kent) St Thomas CBC, SR, VII, 38

HABERSHON, MATTHEW, 1789-1852

Belper (Derbys) CBC, SR, I, 72: Kimberworth (W Yorks) IV, 170

HABERSHON, WILLIAM GILLBEE, c.1818-91 and EDWARD, d. 1901

Hove (Sussex), St John ICBS

HAKEWILL, EDWARD CHARLES, 1812-72

(London), Hackney, Clapton CBC, SR, V, 111; St John of Jerusalem MB 61

HAKEWILL, HENRY, 1771-1830

Westminster, St Peter, Eaton Sq. CBC, SR, I, 128

HAMILTON, GEORGE ERNEST, *fl.* 1828-49

(Staffs), Pelsall CBC, SR, V, 191; Ocker Hill (in partnership with H. C. Saunders, q.v.) CC file 12822

HAMMERTON, LEES (completed churches by T. Taylor q.v.)

(W Yorks), Dewsbury Moor; Earlsheaton: Leeds, St Mary; Brighouse CBC, SR, III, 31

HANNAFORD, JOSEPH, *c.*1769-1847

Bransgrove (Bransgore: Hants) CBC, MB 8

HANSOM, JOSEPH ALOYSIUS, 1803-82

Myton (Hull), St James CBC, SR, III, 44: Toxteth Park (Lancs) III, 29 (both in partnership with E. Welch, q.v.)

HARDWICK, PHILIP, 1792-1870 (Philip seems to have taken over his father Thomas Hardwick's practice *c.*1824, as he is ultimately referred to as architect of the father's churches then unfinished)

Stretton (Ches) CBC, SR, II, 104

HARDWICK, PHILIP CHARLES, 1822-92

Haggerston (London) All SS CBC, SR, VII, 171

HARDWICK, THOMAS, 1752-1829

(London), St Luke, Old Street, St Barnabas CBC, SR, I, 48; St Marylebone, Christ Church I, 55: Workington (Cumb) I, 75: (Lancs), Bolton I, 69; Farnworth I, 115

HARRISON, JAMES PARK, b.1817

Pembroke Dock (Pembs) ICBS

HASLAM, REV. WILLIAM

Truro (Corn), St George CC file 17862

HAYCOCK, EDWARD, 1790-1870

Shrewsbury, St George CBC, SR, III, 1: Trevethin (Mon) III, 89: Llanbadarn (Cards) III, 20: Carmarthen IV, 54

HAYLEY, WILLIAM, 1827-71

(Ches), Bollington★ CBC, SR, III, 44; Norbury★ III, 123: (Lancs), Newtown★ IV, 150; Tong★ IV, 115; Manchester All Souls, Ancoats V, 95; Stretford V, 179: Macclesfield (Ches) ICBS: Heaton Norris (Lancs) ICBS (★in partnership with Thomas Brown, d. 1840)

HAYS, WILLIAM BENNETT, *fl.* 1847-68

Bermondsey (London), Christ Church (with George Allen) ICBS

HAYWARD, JOHN, 1808-91

Carnmenellis (Corn) CC file 15426

HEDGELAND, CHARLES

Starcross (Devon) CBC, SR, II, 74

HEMSLEY, HENRY, *c.*1764-1825

Ramsgate (Kent) CBC, SR, II, 27 (completed by H. E. Kendall, q.v.)

HIGHAM, ALFRED BURDAKIM, *fl.* 1848-60

Walker (Northumb) ICBS

HOLDEN, ISAAC, d. 1884, and HOLDEN, JAMES PLATT, 1806-90

Ramsbottom (Lancs) CC file 16044

HOLME, ARTHUR HILL, 1814-57

Bevington (Lancs), St Alban CBC, SR, VII, 55; Liverpool, St Matthias (rebuilding) CC file 20467; All Souls, Vauxhall, CC file 17623

HOPKINS, JOHN DOUGLAS, d.1869

Woolwich (London), Holy Trinity, Pevsner

HORNER, HENRY PETER, *fl.* 1840-75

Burnley (Lancs), St James ICBS

HORTON, WILLIAM, *fl.* 1847-55

(Staffs): Wednesbury, St James ICBS; Moxley CBC, SR, VII, 56; Willenhall, Holy Trinity MB 67

HOWARD SAMUEL

Rainow (Ches) GR

HURST, WILLIAM, 1787-1844, and MOFFATT, WILLIAM LAMBIE, 1808-82

Thurgoland (W Yorks) ICBS. Hurst was previously in partnership with Woodhead, q.v.

HUSSEY, RICHARD CHARLES, 1806-87 (partner of T. Rickman 1835-8, and successor to his practice)

Saltley (Warks) CBC, SR, VII, 5

HUTCHENS, CHARLES, *c.*1781-1834

(Corn), St Day CBC, SR, II, 106; Chacewater II, 106; Redruth II, 161

INWOOD, WILLIAM, *c.* 1771-1843, and INWOOD, HENRY WILLIAM, 1794-1843

St Pancras (London), St Peter CBC, SR, I, I3; St Mary I, 11

IONS, JOHN

Gateshead Fell (Durham) CBC, SR, I, 129 (design modified by I. Bonomi (q.v.) CBC, MB 16)

JACKSON, GEORGE, *c.*1805-42

Pelton (Durham) CC file 16020, pt. I:2

JAMES, JOSEPH, 1828-75

Smethwick (Worcs) CBC, SR, VII, 136

JENKINS, JOHN, d.1844

Tredegar (Mon) CBC, MB 45

JOHNSON, JOHN 1808-79

Stratford Marsh (Essex) CBC, SR, VII, 11: St Pancras (London), St Paul, Camden Rd (in partnership with F. W. Ordish) CC file 11880

JOHNSON, THOMAS, 1794-1865

Lane End (Staffs) CBC, SR, IV, 63: (Lincs), Gainsborough, Holy Trinity V, 177; East Stockwith ICBS; Morton ICBS: (Staffs), Darlaston CBC, SR, VII, 90; Bilston St Luke VII, 9: Oldbury (Worcs) MB 52

JONES, GEORGE FOWLER, *c.*1817-1905

York, St Thomas CBC, SR, VII, 153

JONES, THOMAS

Trefonnen (Salop) CBC, MB 10

KEMPTHORNE, SAMPSON, 1809-73

(London), Rotherhithe, All Saints. CBC, SR, V, 21; Holy Trinity IV, 167

KENDALL, HENRY EDWARD, sen., 1776-1875

revised and executed Ramsgate (Kent) after death of H. Hemsley (q.v.)

KENDALL, HENRY EDWARD, jun., 1805-85

Kensal Green (London) ICBS

LAMB, EDWARD BUCKTON, 1806-69

Clerkenwell (London), St Philip CBC, SR, III, 92

LANE, RICHARD, 1795-1850

Salford (Lancs), St Simon ICBS; in partnership with F. Goodwin (q.v.) designed Pendleton (Lancs)

LANGDON, JOHN HARRIS, d. 1853

Pilgwenelly (Mon) CBC, SR, VII, 69

LAPIDGE, EDWARD, 1793-1860

Hammersmith (London), St Peter CBC, SR, II, 134: Hampton Wick (Middx) III, 35

LEACHMAN, JOHN, b. *c.*1795

Warminster (Wilts) CBC, SR, II, 234

LEE, THOMAS, jun., 1794-1834

Netherton (Worcs) CBC, SR, III, 202: Coseley (Staffs) II, 77

LIDDELL, THOMAS, 1800-56

Heworth (Durham) CC file 17595

LIDSTONE, THOMAS

Lower Brixham (Devon), All SS CBC, MB 14

LITTLE, THOMAS, 1802-59

(London), St Pancras, St Mark, Albert Rd. CBC, SR, VII, 77; Paddington, St Saviour, Warwick Ave CC file 17811, pt 2

LIVESAY, AUGUSTUS FREDERICK, *c.*1807-79

Trowbridge (Wilts) CBC, SR, IV, 121: (Hants), Portsea, Holy Trinity IV, 187; Milton, St James V, 98

LLOYD, JOHN, *c.*1793-1867

Brymbo (Denbighs) CBC, SR, IV, 143: (Flints), Bistre V, 80; Gwernafield ICBS

LOCK, ALFRED GEORGE, and DUCKETT, JOHN S.

Southampton, Christ Church, Northam CC file 15993

LOCHNER, WILLIAM CONRAD, *c.*1780-1861

Enfield (Middx), St James CBC, SR, Ill, 83

LOCKWOOD, HENRY FRANCIS, 1811-78

Hull, St Mark CBC, SR, V, 136

LOWDER, JOHN, 1781-1829

Bath, Holy Trinity CBC, MB 3, 7 Mar. 1820

LUCY, JAMES, d. 1829 or 1830

Claines (Worcs), St George (completed by Lewis Belling) CBC, SR, II, 201

MALLINSON, JAMES, 1819-84, and HEALEY, THOMAS, 1809-62

(W Yorks), Queenshead CBC, MB 60; Wyke MB 63; Mytholmroyd ICBS; Bradford, St Matthew, Bankfoot CBC, SR, VII, 6: Shelf VII, 9; Leeds, All SS, York Rd VII, 40; St John B, Clayton VII, 65; South Ossett VII, 66; North Horton VII, 81; Barkisland VII, 93; Mount Pellon ICBS

MANNERS, GEORGE PHILIP, *c*.1789-1866

Bath, St Mark, Lyncombe CBC, SR, II, 218: Leigh (Wilts) V, 176

MATTHEWS, JOHN

(Ches), Byley CC file 15389; Minshull Vernon CC file I5950; Elworth CC file

MAWLEY, HENRY

Hounslow (Middx) CBC, SR, II, 167

MEREDITH, MICHAEL

All SS, Skinner St (London) CBC, SR, II, 221

MIDDLETON, JOHN, d. 1885

(Durham), Hartlepool CBC, BC, MB 17; Darlington CC file 17798

MITCHELL, JOSEPH, *fl.* 1841-66

Burton-on-Trent (Staffs) ICBS: Charlesworth (Derbys) ICBS: Sheffield, St Jude, Eldon ICBS; St Jude, Moorfields, (first building) CBC, SR, VII, 123, 133

MOFFATT, WILLIAM BONYTHORN 1812-87 (the early partner of G. G. Scott)

Milford (Derbys) ICBS

MOFFATT, WILLIAM LAMBIE, 1808-82. See Hurst, W. and

MOORE, Thomas, *fl.* 1839-68

Ayres Quay (Durham) CBC, SR, V, 110

MORGAN, JAMES, *c*.1773-1856

Wolverhampton (Staffs), St George CBC, MB 32

MOSELEY, ANDREW, *c*.1811-1906

Aberdare (Glam), St Elvan CBC, SR, VII, 128

MOXHAM, EGBERT, 1822-64

(Glam), Skewen CBC, SR, VII, 36; Maesteg VII, 108

MURRAY, JAMES, 1831-63

Stratford-on-Avon (Warks) CBC, SR, VII, 161

MYLNE, WILLIAM CHADWELL, 1781-1863

Clerkenwell (London), St Mark CBC, SR, I, 156

NASH, JOHN, 1752-1835

(London), St Marylebone, All Souls, Langham Place; Haggerston, St Mary CBC, MBs

NEWMAN, FRANCIS B., *fl.* 1852-8, and JOHNSON, JOHN, *c*.1807-78

Islington (London), St Andrew CBC, SR, VII, 101

NORTON, JOHN

Abertillery (Monmouths) ICBS

OATES, JOHN, 1793-1831

Buckley (Flints) CBC, SR, I, 32: (W Yorks): Shipley I, 127: Wilsden I, 178: Idle II, 205: Lindley II, 72: Paddock II, 173: Huddersfield, St Paul II, 223: Halifax, St James III, 30: Shelton (Staffs) II, 237: Hebden Bridge (W Yorks) III, 31

OATES, MATTHEW. See T. PICKERSGILL

ORDISH, FREDERICK WEBSTER, 1821-85

Cheltenham, St Luke ICBS: St Pancras (London), St Paul, in partnership with J. Johnson (q.v.) CC file 11880

ORFORD, CHARLES WYATT

Wolverhampton (Staffs), St Mark ICBS: Birmingham, St Jude CBC, SR, VII, 41

OWEN, JACOB, 1778-1870

(Hants), Portsea, All SS CBC, SR, I, 118; Forton in partnership with his son, T. E. Owen CBC, MB 36

OWEN, THOMAS ELLIS, 1804-1862

Portsmouth, St Mary CBC, SR, IV, 144

PALMER, JOHN, 1785-1846

Blackburn, St Peter CBC, SR, I, 85

PARSONS, WILLIAM, 1796-1857

Leicester, St George CBC, SR, I, 116

PEARSON, JOHN LOUGHBOROUGH, 1817-98

Westminster, Holy Trinity, Bessborough Gardens GR

PEDLEY, JAMES LYNDON

Balsall Heath (Warks), CBC, SR, VII, 98: Birmingham, St Matthias VII, 145

PENNETHORNE, JAMES, 1801-71

Holborn (London), Holy Trinity, Gray's Inn Road CBC, SR, IV, 146

PENSON, RICHARD KYRKE, 1816-85

Pontfadog (Denbighs), executed F. Wehuert's design ICBS

PENSON, THOMAS, c.1790-1859

Denbigh ICBS: Newtown (Montgom) CBC, SR, V, 124,/MB. 60: (Denbighs) Gwersyllt SR, VII, 54: Rhos VII, 98

PERKIN, WILLIAM, d.1874, and BACKHOUSE, ELISHA

(W Yorks), Cullingworth CBC, SR, VII, 30; Morton ICBS; Pudsey, St Paul CBC, SR, VII, 75; Eastwood VII, 67

PICKERING, GEORGE

Birtley (Durham) CBC, SR, VII, 21

PICKERSGILL, THOMAS, c.1807-69 and OATES, MATTHEW: completed churches by J. Oates (q.v.) unfinished at his death:

Cross Stones (W Yorks) CBC, SR, IV, 54

PINCH, CHARLES

Tatworth (Som) CBC, SR, V, 182

PINCH, JOHN, d. 1849

Bath, St Saviour CBC, SR, II, 236

PORDEN, CHARLES FERDINAND, 1790-1863

Lambeth (London), St Matthew, Brixton CBC, SR, I, 20

JOSEPH POTTER, c.1766-1842

Sheffield, St Mary CBC, SR, II, 70

POYNTER, AMBROSE, 1796-1886

Cambridge, Christ Church CBC, SR, IV, 169; St Paul V, 114: Westminster, Christ Church, Broadway V, 207

PRICHARD, JOHN, c.1818-86

Pont-y-Rhun (Glam) CBC, SR, VII, 93

PRITCHETT, GEORGE EDWARD, 1824-1912

Hockerill (Herts) CBC, SR, VII, 69

PRITCHETT, JAMES PIGOTT, (in partnership for some years with W. Watson, q.v.), 1789-1868, and SONS

Brampton Bierlow (W Yorks) CBC, SR, VII, 137

RAILTON, WILLIAM, c.1801-77

Bethnal Green (London), St Bartholomew CBC, SR, V, 164

RAMPLING, CLARK, 1793-1875

Birch (Lancs) CBC, MB 26

RAWSTORNE, WALKER, c.1807-67

(W Yorks), Ingrow CBC, SR, V, 170; Yeadon V, 232; Eccleshill V, 219: Burnley (Lancs), St Paul ICBS

REED, CHARLES, alias VERELST, d. 1859

Chorley (Lancs), St Peter CBC, SR, VII, 37: Maesclaled (Anglesey) VII, 161

REEVES and BUTCHER, LOUIS(?) GEORGE

Coalbrookdale (Salop) CC file 17949

REPTON, GEORGE STANLEY, 1786-1858

Westminster, St Philip, Regent Street, CBC, MB 5 (13 Nov. 1821); also Britton and Pugin *Public Buildings of London,* 1, 102-6 (1825)

RICKMAN, THOMAS, 1776-1841

Barnsley (W Yorks)★ CBC, SR, 1, 89: Birmingham, St George★ I, 81; St Peter★ II, 28; St Thomas★ II, 90; All SS★ III, 114: Erdington (Warks) I, 60: Carlisle, Christ Church★ II, 133; Holy Trinity★ II, 139: (Lancs:) Preston, St Peter★ 1, 114; St Paul★ 1, 141: Chorley, St George★ I, 27: Lower Darwen★ II, 75: Over Darwen★ II, 75: Mellor★ II, 76: Whittle-le-Woods★ II, 208: Pemberton★ II, 236: Haigh★ III, 5: Tockholes★ III, 190: Bristol, Holy Trinity★ II, 231: Coventry, Christ Church★ II, 137: Loughborough (Leics) IV, 64: Sneinton (Notts)# IV, 139 (★ in partnership with William Henry Hutchinson (c.1800-31): # in partnership with Richard Charles Hussey, q.v.)

ROBINSON, GEORGE THOMAS, 1828-97

Sneyd (Staffs) CC file 12547

ROGERS, WILLIAM, d. 1858

Lambeth, St Michael, Stockwell CBC, SR, V, 42; All SS, York Rd *Builder,* xv, 716; xvi, 26

ROPER, DAVID RIDDALL, c.1773-1855

Kennington, St Mark CBC, SR, I, 47: II, 83 (A. B. Clayton may have been responsible for the design (GR), but Roper signed the works' certificates (CBC, MB 8)

ROPER, ROBERT, 1757-1838

Houghton (Lancs) CBC, BC MB 4, 311

RUSSELL, JOHN

Stockingford (Warks) CBC, SR, I, 166

ST AUBYN, JAMES PIERS, 1815-95

Devonport (Dev), St Paul CBC, SR, VII, 29; St James the Great VII, 39; St Mary VII, 53: (Corn), Godolphin VII, 8; Penponds VII, 70

SALVIN, ANTHONY, 1799-1881

Ulverston (Lancs) CBC, SR, II, 171: King's Lynn (Norf), St John GR: Hammersmith (London), St Stephen, CBC, SR, VII, 24

SAMBELL, PHILIP

Truro (Corn), St John CBC, MB 26

SAUNDERS, HENRY CAULFIELD, 1820-66. A partner of G. E. HAMILTON, q.v.

SAVAGE, JAMES, 1779-1852

(London), Chelsea, St Luke CBC, SR, I, 24; Holy Trinity II, 202; Bermondsey, St James I, 194: Croydon (Surrey), All SS II, 112: Tottenham (London) II, 169: Ilford (Essex) II, 218: Westminster, St Michael, Burleigh Street III, 124

SCOLES, JOSEPH JOHN, 1798-1863

Great Yarmouth (Norf), St Peter CBC, SR, III, 99

SCOTT, GEORGE GILBERT, 1811-78

Bridlington Quay (E Yorks)★ GR: Norbiton (Surrey)★ CBC, SR, V, 204: Turnham Green (Middx)★ ICBS: Halstead (Essex)★ ICBS: Leenside (Notts)★ CBC, SR, V, 233: Leeds, St Andrew MB 57: Antrobus (Ches) CC file 15059: Westminster, St Matthew CC file; St Andrew CC file: Llanelly (Carm) VII, 33: Kingsley (Ches) VII, 35: Croydon, St Peter (Surrey) ICBS: Denton (Lancs) CBC, SR, VII, 102: Edgehill (Lancs) VII, 66: Forest Gate (Essex) VII, 70: Leicester, St John the Divine VII, 110: Lee Park (Kent) GR: Leavesden (Herts) CC file 21770 (★ in partnership with W. B. Moffatt, q.v.)

SHARP, SAMUEL, 1808-74

Thornes (W Yorks) CBC, SR, II, 51

SHARPE, EDMUND, 1809-77

(Ches), Dukinfield St John CBC, SR, IV, 193; Stalybridge IV, 163: (Lancs), Bretherton V, 39; Farrington IV, 220: Scholes V, 39; Blackburn, Holy Trinity V, 228: Coventry (Warks), St Thomas★ ICBS: Ringley (Lancs)★ CBC, SR, VII, 67 (★ in partnership with E. G. Paley (1823-95)

SHAW, GEORGE, b.1810

(Lancs), Birtle ICBS; Healey CBC, SR, VII, 35; Werneth, St Thomas CC file 17466

SHAW, JOHN, jun., 1803-70

(London), Holy Trinity, Gough Sq. CBC, MB 47; Christ Church, Watney St SR, V, 61

SHAW, THOMAS, fl. 1840-68 (in partnership with R. D. Chantrell (q.v.) c.1844 CC file 16061)

Embsay (W Yorks) CBC, SR, VII, 90

SHELLARD, EDWIN HUGH, 1815-85

Whitfield (Derbys) CBC, MB 59: (Lancs), Leesfield ICBS; Audenshaw ICBS; Blackley ICBS; Failsworth ICBS; Droylsden ICBS; Waterhead ICBS; Coldhurst ICBS; Shuttleworth ICBS; Godley-cum-Newton ICBS; Hurst ICBS: Paddington ICBS; Musbury CBC, SR, VII, 53; Hulme St Mark VII, 82; Werneth, St John CC file 21744: Upper Thong (W Yorks) ICBS: Bredbury (Ches) CC file 21728

SLATER, WILLIAM, 1819-72

Completed Christ Church, Milton (Kent) after R. C. Carpenter's death. CC file 15947

SMIRKE, ROBERT, 1781-1867

Chatham St John (Kent) CBC, MB 2: (London), Wandsworth MB 2; St Marylebone St Mary MB 2; W Hackney CC file 18120: Bristol, St George (Glos) CC file 15292: (Lancs), Salford St Philip CBC, MB 4: Tyldesley MB 4

SMITH, GEORGE, 1783-1869

Noak Hill (Essex) CC file 16065

SMITH, HUGH

Daventry (Northants) CBC, SR, V, 84: St Pancras (London), St John Ev. Pevsner

SMITH, SAMUEL, 1766-1851 and SON

Wrockwardine Wood (Salop), altered and executed plans by J. Baddeley CC file 17771

SMITH, THOMAS (probably the 'son' of previous entry: both are 'of Madeley')

(Salop), Ironbridge GR; Wellington CC file 16223: (Staffs), Brockmoor GR, Quarry Bank GR

SMITH, THOMAS, 1798-1875

West Hyde (Herts) ICBS

SOANE, JOHN, 1753-1837

(London), Newington, St Peter: Bethnal Green, St John, St Marylebone, Holy Trinity. S.M.

STANLEY, THOMAS

Mow Cop (Staffs) CC file 17901

STEWART, DANIEL

(Lancs), Burscough Bridge CBC, MB 38; Liverpool, St Matthias (first church), in partnership with J. A. Picton, CC file 20467

STEVENS, Henry Isaac, 1807-73

Ashby-de-la-Zouch (Leics) CBC, SR, IV, 220: (Notts), Ison (Hyson) Green ICBS; New Radford ICBS: (Derbys), Hazelwood ICBS; Cotmanhay ICBS; Bridgehill ICBS; Idridgehay CBC, SR, VII, 1561: Mansfield (Notts) VII, 155

STREET, GEORGE EDMUND, 1824-81

Treverbyn (Corn) CBC, BC, MB 17

TAYLOR, BENJAMIN, d. 1848

Dodsworth (W Yorks) CBC, SR,V, 118

TAYLOR, GEORGE LEDWELL, 1780-1873

Walham Green (London) CBC, SR, II, 108: Sheerness (Kent) IV, 73

TAYLOR, THOMAS, c.1778-1826

(W Yorks), Pudsey, St Lawrence CBC, SR, 1,86; Attercliffe I, 94; Sheffield, St Philip I, 57; Hanging Heaton 1, 99; Dewsbury Moor I, 100; Earlsheaton II, 20; Leeds, St Mary I, 113

TEULON, SAMUEL SANDERS, 1812-73

Bermondsey (London), St Paul ICBS: Croydon (Surrey), Christ Church GR: Birmingham, St John Ev. CBC, SR,VII, 138: Lambeth (London), St Andrew VII, 167

TRAVIS, HENRY, *fl.* 1848-64, and MANGNALL,WILLIAM, *fl.* 1846-58

Rooden Lane (Lancs) CBC, SR,VII, 62

TRIMEN, ANDREW

Werneth (Lancs), St Thomas CBC, SR,VII, 131. (Became insolvent; replaced by G. Shaw)

TRUBSHAW, JAMES, 1777-1853, and TRUBSHAW, CHARLES, 1811-62

Congleton (Ches) ICBS: Northwood (Staffs) ICBS: Macclesfield, St Peter (Ches) CBC, SR,VII, 28

UNDERWOOD, HENRY JONES, 1804-52

Oxford, Holy Trinity CBC, MB 59

VERELST, see REED

VICKERS, CHARLES, *fl.* 1820-50

East Knottingley (W Yorks) ICBS: Northampton, St Edmund CBC, SR,VII, 92

VULLIAMY, LEWIS, 1791-1871

(London), Sydenham, St Bartholomew CBC, SR, II, 101; Kensington, St Barnabas II, 110: Burslem (Staffs) St Paul II, 164: Richmond (Surrey), St John III, 35: (London), Highgate III, 97;Woburn Sq. III, 98:Wordesley (Staffs) II, 187: (Lancs),Wuerdle III, 76: Todmorden III, 75: Spotland III, 76: Habergham Eaves IV, 68: (London), Bethnal Green, St Peter V, 105; St James the Less CC file 15158; St Thomas CBC, SR,VII, 22; Kensington, St James MB. 60: Westminster, All SS SR,VII, 2

WALKER, PETER

Didsbury (Lancs) GR

WALKER,THOMAS LARKINS, d. 1860

Attleborough (Warks) CBC, SR,V, 122: Bethnal Green (London), St Philip V, 120

WALLACE, ROBERT, c.1790-1874

Croydon, St James CBC, SR, II, 98

WALLEN,WILLIAM, 1807-53

(W Yorks), Farsley CBC, SR,V, 235; Shepley VII, 23; Oakworth R. Holmes, *Keighley Past and Present*

WALTERS, JOHN, 1782-1821

Stepney (London), St Philip *Gent. Mag.* XCI, ii, 374

WARD, HENRY, and SON

(Staffs**)**, Etruria ICBS: Hope ICBS: Wellington ICBS: Edensor CBC, SR,VII, 107: Chesterton MB. 65

WATSON,WILLIAM, c.1770-1836 (in partnership with his son and J. P. Pritchett (q.v.)

Greasborough (W. Riding) CBC, SR, II, 178: Hoyland III, 212

WEBSTER, GEORGE, 1797-1864

Kendal CBC, SR, IV, 198

WELCH, EDWARD, 1806-68 (a partner of J. A. Hansom q.v.)

Adlington (Lancs) CBC, MB 47

WELCH, SAMUEL THOMAS, *fl.* 1843-68

Bristol, St Luke CBC, SR,V, 181

WHICHCORD, JOHN, 1790-1860

Maidstone (Kent) CBC, SR, II, 137

WHITE,WILLIAM, 1825-1900

Baldhu (Corn) *Ecclesiologist,* IX, 262, and ICBS

WHITTINGTON,WILLIAM, 1769-1849

Clydach (Glam) ICBS

WIGHTWICK, GEORGE, 1802-72

Plymouth, Holy Trinity CBC, SR,V, 29; Christ Church MB. 60

WILD, JAMES WILLIAM, 1814-92

(London), Greenwich, Holy Trinity CBC, SR, IV, 217; Streatham, Christ Church V, 150: Coates (Cambs) V, 151

WILKINS,WILLIAM, 1778-1839

Nottingham, St Paul CBC, SR, I, 4

WILSON, JAMES, 1816-1900
Milton (Kent), Holy Trinity ICBS
WOODHEAD, JOHN★, d. 1838, and HURST, WILLIAM★, 1787-1844
(W Yorks), Sheffield, St George CBC, SR, I, 25; Pateley Bridge II, 129; Stannington II, 206; Brampton (Derbys) III, 46 (★completed Sheffield St Philip after T. Taylor's death q.v.)
WOODYER, HENRY, 1816-96
Lydbrook (Glos), CBC, SR, VII, 68: Winchester (Hants), Holy Trinity CC file 17915
WYATT, PHILIP WILLIAM, d. 1835
Bishopwearmouth (Durham), St Thomas CBC, SR, II, 241
WYATT, THOMAS HENRY, 1807-80
Newport (Mon), St Paul CBC, SR, IV, 86: Shaw Whitley (Wilts) IV, 124: Newbridge (Glam) IV, 124: (London), Bethnal Green, St Andrew★ V, 126; St Matthias GR: Derry Hill (Wilts)★ CBC, SR, V, 24: Merthyr Tydfil (Glam)★ CC file 21744, pt. 19: St Pancras (London), Holy Trinity★ CBC, SR, VII, 22: Brynford (Flints) VII, 91: Llanllechyd (Glanogwen, Caernarvon) GR (★ in partnership with David Brandon)
YOUNG, WILLIAM, d.1877
Leigh (Lancs), St Paul ICBS

APPENDIX 3

List of Members of
H.M.'s Commission for Building New Churches in Populous Places, 1818-1856

Commissioners were appointed by Letters Patent on three occasions – in 1825 and 1845, as well as in 1818. Their names are therefore preceded by the date of appointment. A large number of Ministers and heads of departments were entitled to sit on the Commission ex-officio: a list of such offices is given after the nominal list, in which their holders, as such, do not necessarily appear. Certain ecclesiastical dignitaries were entitled to ex-officio seats from 1825, and these too are listed.

1818 Bathurst, Charles Bragge (1754-1831) chancellor of the Duchy of Lancaster 1812-23.

1825 Blomfield, Charles James (1786-1857) bishop of Chester 1824, of London, 1828.

1818 Burton, Francis (c.1744-1832), M.P.

1818 Cambridge, George Owen (1756-1841) Archdeacon of Middlesex.

1818 Colchester, Charles Abbott, 1st Lord (1757-1829), Speaker 1802-17.

1828 Copleston, Edward (1776-1848) Bishop of Llandaff and Dean of St Paul's from 1828.

1818 Cornwallis, James (1742-1824) Bishop of Lichfield and Coventry.

1825 D'Oyly, George (1778-1846) Rector of Lambeth from 1820.

1818 Eldon, John Scott (1751-1838), 1st Earl of Eldon, Lord Chancellor 1807-27.

1818 Eyre, John (1758-1830) Archdeacon of Nottingham.

1845 Gladstone, William Ewart (1809-98).

1818 Grenville, William Wyndham Grenville, 1st Lord (1759-1834).

1845 Hale, William Hale (1795-1870) Archdeacon of London from 1842.

1818 Hardwicke, Philip Yorke, 3rd Earl of (1757-1834).

1845 Harrison, Benjamin (1808-87) Archdeacon of Maidstone from 1844.

1818 Harrowby, Dudley Ryder, 1st Earl of (1762-1847) Lord President of the Council 1812-27.

1818 Headlam, John (c.1768-1853) Archdeacon of Richmond (Yorks).

1818 Howley, William (1766-1848) Bishop of London 1813, Archbishop of Canterbury from 1828.

1845 Inglis, Sir Robert Harry, 2nd Bart (1786-1855) M.P. for Oxford University.

1818 Ireland, John (1761-1842) Dean of Westminster.

1845 Jelf, Richard William (1798-1871) Principal of King's College, London.

1827 Kaye, John (1783-1853) Bishop of Lincoln from 1827.

1818 Kenyon, George, 2nd Lord (1776-1855).

1818 Law, George Henry (1761-1845) Bishop of Chester 1812, of Bath and Wells from 1824.

1818 Robert Banks Jenkinson (1770-1828), 2nd Earl of Liverpool, First Lord of the Treasury 1812-27.

1825 Lonsdale, John (1788-1867) Principal of King's College, London 1839, Archdeacon of Middlesex 1843, Bishop of Lichfield from 1843.

1825 Lushington, Stephen (1782-1873) Judge of the Consistory Court of London from 1828.

1818 Manners-Sutton, Charles (1755-1828) Archbishop of Canterbury.

1818 Manners-Sutton, Charles (1780-1845) Speaker of the House of Commons 1817-35 (cr. Viscount Canterbury 1835).

1818 Mant, Richard (1776-1848) Rector of St Botolph Bishopsgate, London to 1820, Bishop of Killaloe 1820-23, of Down and Connor from 1823.

1845 Musgrave, Thomas (1788-1860) Bishop of Hereford 1837, Archbishop of York 1848.

1818 Nicholl, Sir John (1759-1838) Dean of the Arches.

1818 North, Brownlow (1741-1820) Bishop of Winchester.

1818 Outram, Edmund (1765-1821) Archdeacon of Derby.

1825 Pelham, George (1766-1827) Bishop of Lincoln.

1845 Pepys, Henry (1783-1860) Bishop of Worcester.
1818 Pott, Joseph Holden (1759-1847) Archdeacon of London 1813-42.
1825 Robinson, Sir Christopher (1766-1833) Judge of the Consistory Court of London from 1821.
1845 Ryder, Dudley (1798-1882) Lord Sandon, 2nd Earl of Harrowby from 1847.
1825 Ryder, Henry (1777-1836) Bishop of Lichfield and Coventry 1824.
1818 Scott, Sir William (1754-1836) Judge of the Consistory Court of London to 1821; Master of the Faculties (cr. Lord Stowell 1821).
1818 Sidmouth, Henry Addington, 1st Viscount (1757-1844), Home Secretary, 1812-22.
1845 Sinclair, John (c.1800-75) Archdeacon of Middlesex from 1843.
1826 Sumner, Charles Richard (1790-1874) Dean of St Paul's and Bishop of Llandaff 1826, Bishop of Winchester from 1827.
1828 Sumner, James Bird (1780-1862) Bishop of Chester 1828-48, Archbishop of Canterbury from 1848.
1818 Tomline, Sir George Pretyman (1750-1827) Bishop of Lincoln 1787-1820, Bishop of Winchester from 1820.
1842 Turton, Thomas (1780-1864) Dean of Westminster 1842, Bishop of Ely from 1845.
1825 Van Mildert, William (1765-1836) Dean of St Paul's and Bishop of Llandaff 1820, Bishop of Durham from 1826.
1818 Vansittart, Nicholas (1766-1851) Chancellor of the Exchequer 1812-23 (cr. Lord Bexley 1823).
1818 Vemon, Edward Venables (1757-1847) (assumed surname Harcourt) Archbishop of York.
1818 Watson, Joshua (1771-1855).
1818 Whitaker, Thomas Dunham (1759-1821) Vicar of Whalley and Blackburn.
1818 Wollaston, Francis John Hyde (1762-1823) Archdeacon of Essex.
1818 Wordsworth, Christopher (1774-1846) Rector of Lambeth to 1820, Master of Trinity College, Cambridge 1820-41.

List of Offices

In 1818 the holders of the following offices were appointed by name to sit on the Commission; in 1825, the holders of these offices for the time being were appointed *ex officio*.

Lord High Chancellor
Lord President of the Council
First Lord of the Treasury
Secretary of State for the Home Department
Chancellor of the Exchequer
Chancellor of the Duchy of Lancaster
First Commissioner of Woods and Forests (Woods and Works after 1832)
Speaker of the House of Commons
Dean of the Arches
Master of the Faculties
Judge of the Consistory Court of London
Surveyor-General of the Board of Works[1] (abolished 1832)

The following ecclesiastical appointments also received a permanent seat on the Commission in 1825:
Archbishops: Canterbury, York
Bishops: London, Winchester, Lichfield and Coventry, Chester, Lincoln
Deans: Westminster, St Paul's

To these were added in 1845:
Bishop of Ripon
Archdeacons: London, Middlesex
Principal of King's College, London

Secretaries
1818-29 George Jenner
1829-54 George Jelf
1854-56 Thomas Beachcroft

[1] Benjamin Charles Stephenson (d. 1839) Major-General, knighted 1832.

APPENDIX 4

Church Building Acts, 1818–1856

1818   58 Geo. III. c.45 for building and promoting the building of additional Churches in populous Parishes.

1819   59 Geo III. c.134 to amend and render more effectual the 1818 Act.

1822   3 Geo. IV. c.72 to amend and render more effectual the two earlier Acts.

1824   5 Geo. IV. c.103 to make further provision, and to amend and render more effective the earlier Acts.

1827   7 and 8 Geo. IV. c.72 to amend the Acts – extended Commission's powers to 20 July 1838.

1828   9 Geo. IV. c.42 to abolish Church Briefs, and to provide for the better collection and application of voluntary contributions for … enlarging and building churches and chapels. Incorporation of Church-Building Society.

1832   1 and 2 Wm. IV. c.38 to amend 7 and 8 Geo. IV. c.72, to provide more effectually for the improved Pastoral Superintendence - dealt with Patronage.

1833   2 and 3 Wm. IV. c.61 to render more effectual 1819 Act – episcopal jurisdiction over certain new districts.

1837   7 Wm. IV. and 1 Vic. c.75 to prolong for ten years the Commission.

1838   1 and 2 Vic. c.107 to amend and render more effectual the Church Building Acts – chiefly concerned with Patronage.

1839   2 and 3 Vic. c.49 to make better Provision for the Assignment of Ecclesiastical Districts, etc.

1840   3 and 4 Vic. c.60 to further amend the Acts – subdivision of Districts.

1844   7 and 8 Vic. c.56 to remove doubts about marriages in certain places.

1845   8 and 9 Vic. c.70 for the further amendment - further facilities for forming districts.

1846   9 and 10 Vic. c.68 Burial Service in certain cemeteries.

       9 and 10 Vic. c.88 Patronage.

1848   11 and 12 Vic. c.37 to amend the Law relative to the Assignment of Ecclesiastical Districts.

       11 and 12 Vic. c. 71 to continue the Commission till 1853.

1851   14 and 15 Vic. c.97 Patronage, fees, etc.

1854   17 and 18 Vic. c.14 to continue the Commission until 1856.

       17 and 18 Vic. c.32 concerning leasehold land acquired under the Acts.

1856   19 and 20 Vic. c.55 for transferring the Powers of the Church Building Commissioners to the Ecclesiastical Commissioners for England.

Illustration Acknowledgements

Photographs

The following holders of copyright or reproduction rights are gratefully acknowledged in respect of the following plate numbers:

By courtesy of Bath Preservation Trust: 4. By courtesy of Geoff Brandwood: 16, 46, 77, 78, 187, 237-9. By courtesy of Bristol City Council (Bristol Record Office), 182. By courtesy of R. Castell: 2, 8, 9, 11-13, 185. The Church Commissioners for England: 60, 118, 128, 195, 196, 198, 245. By courtesy of English Heritage/National Monuments Record: 6, 19, 20, 31, 33, 34, 39, 40, 41, 42, 43, 51, 57, 61-4, 66, 72-5, 80, 83, 96, 100-2, 104, 111, 114, 125-7, 134, 135, 137, 140, 143, 144, 147, 149, 153, 155, 157, 160, 161, 169, 172, 184, 193, 194, 199, 200, 203, 204, 207, 209, 215, 216, 221, 224-6, 228, 229, 231, 232, 234-6, 240-4, 246-9. By courtesy of David Hunt/Alistair Hodge: 120. Cameron Newham: 1, 52, 53, 58, 72, 81, 88, 95, 106, 112, 115, 119, 121, 122, 130, 138, 141, 151, 165, 167, 168, 173, 174, 177, 181, 210, 212-4, 218, 220, 222, 223. Incorporated Church Building Society: 185. Nottingham City Council (Arts and Leisure Services/North East Midland Photographic Record), 45, 145. M. H. Port: 7, 10, 54, 76, 107-10, 113, 116, 117, 123, 129, 132, 142, 148, 162, 163, 166, 170, 171, 201, 211. Royal Institute of British Architects: 14, 22-9, 93, 105, 189-91, 217, 230. By courtesy of the Trustees of Sir John Soane's Museum: 21, 35, 37, 38, 56, 103. Michael Slaughter: 55, 79, 94, 112, 133, 202, 205, 206, 208. By courtesy of Wakefield Diocesan Board of Finance: 89, 92, 158, 159. By courtesy of Christopher Webster: 131, 175, 176, 178-80.

Illustrations from periodicals and books:

Gentleman's Magazine: 68, 71, 84, 85, 152, 219.

J. Britton, *Architectural Antiquities of Great Britain* (5 vols, 1807-26): 15, 17, 90, 150.

J. Britton and A. Pugin, *Illustrations of the Public Buildings of London* (2nd edn by W. H. Leeds, 1838): 65, 99.

E. Churton, *Memoir of Joshua Watson* (Oxford & London, 1861): 5.

J. Elmes and T. H. Shepherd, *Metropolitan Improvements* (1827): 18, 30, 32, 36, 44, 47-9, 59, 66, 124, 136, 139, 146, 154, 192.

G. Godwin, *The Churches of London* (2 vols, 1838-9): 3, 233.

Meyler's Bath Guide (Bath, 1817): 183.

P. Nicholson, *New and Improved practical Builder* (1837): 97, 98.

W. Odom, *Memorials of Sheffield: Its Cathedral and Parish Churches* (Sheffield, 1922): 69, 70, 82.

W. H. Pyne, *Lancashire Illustrated* (1831): 86, 197.

S. Rayner, *History and Antiquities of Pudsey*, ed. by William Smith (1887): 87.

H. Roberson, *An Account of the Ceremony ... at Liversedge* (Leeds, 1813): 164.

R. Tress, *Modern Churches. Designs, Estimates and Essays* (1841): 227.

Bibliography

Manuscript sources

The records of the Church Building Commission, 1818-56 (Church of England Record Centre):
  - Board Minute Books: 1 (28 Jul. 1818-16 Mar. 1819), 3 (29 Feb. 1820-18 Jul. 1820), 5-10 (8
    May 1821-3 Jun. 1823), 12 (9 Dec. 1823-16 Mar. 1824), 14-17 (1 Jun. 1824-12 Jul. 1825), 19-
    28 (22 Nov. 1825-19 Feb. 1828), 30-40 (22 Apr. 1828-17 Apr. 1832), 42-61 (22 Jan. 1833-23
    Jun. 1846), 63-67 (9 Mar. 1847-9 Dec. 1851).
  For some period after 1820 a series of Supplementary Minute Books, containing letters, etc.,
  was kept, but these have disappeared.
  - Building Committee Minute Books: 4-7 (6 Nov. 1821-2 Aug. 1823), 9 (6 Mar. 1824-23 Nov.
    1824), 17 (8 May 1849-24 Nov. 1856).
  - Division Committee Minute Books: 1-3 (6 May 1825-15 Dec. 1843).
  - Surveyor's Reports: 7 vols, 1821-56 (vol. 6, 1843-8, is missing).
  - Rules and Regulations, etc., 1818.
  - Cases and Opinions, 1818-25.
  - CC files:
        9881, pt 1 Consolidation and amendment bills [1845, 1848, 1850,1858].
        12058 General [regulations, select vestries, continuation of CBC in 1837, etc.].
        12107 Drawbacks, general.
        12131 Accounts.
        21507 Office establishment, 13 Great George Street.
        21744 Miscellaneous papers.
        21745 Establishment, organization, etc.
        21819 Architect and Surveyorship.
        23735 General file [continuation of church-building grants by Ecclesiastical
        Commissioners].

Records of the Church Commissioners for England (Church of England Record Centre):
  Church-building files for particular parishes.

Incorporated Church Building Society (Lambeth Palace Library):
  Minutes of proceedings leading to the foundation of the society, 1815-18.
  Church-building files for particular parishes (accessible on-line at
  www.churchplansonline.org).

C. R. Cockerell, diary (RIBA Library).

Thomas Rickman, diary 1807-34 (RIBA Library).
  Rickman's work-books 1821-37 (British Library, Add. MSS 37793-802).

John Soane, correspondence and architectural drawings (Sir John Soane's Museum).

Architectural drawings:
  At RIBA Drawings Collection, Victoria & Albert Museum, by
  Bedford. F.; Blore, E.; Dobson, J.; Edwards, F.; Ferrey, B.; Goodwin, F.; Gregan, J.; Habershon,

M.; Hardwick, P.; Lamb, E .B.; Livesay, A. F.; Lloyd,J.; Mallinson & Healey.; Nash, J.; Pickering, G.; Rickman, T.; Repton, G. S.; Scott, G. G.; Shellard, E.; Smirke, R.;Vulliamy, L.;Watson, Pritchett & Watson;Woodhead & Hurst.
At Victoria & Albert Museum, Department of Prints and Drawings: C.R. Cockerell, John Soane

Blomfield Papers, Lambeth Palace Library.
Harrowby MSS (1st Earl, and Bishop Ryder) at Sandon Park, Staffordshire.
Howley Papers, Lambeth Palace Library.
Liverpool Papers, British Library, Add. MSS 38261, 38265-73, 38299, 38328, 38574.
Manners-Sutton Papers, Lambeth Palace Library.
Peel Papers, British Library, Add. MSS 40377-8, 40412, 40521.

H.M.'s Office of Works, Letter Books, 1818-31 (ref. Work 1 and Work 6) at National Archives, Kew (formerly PRO).

Parliamentary Papers
Reports of the Church Building Commissioners to Parliament:
1821 (29) X, p. 1 ff.
1822 (605) XI, pp. 1ff.
1823 (573) VII, pp. 1ff.
1824 (430) IX, pp. 1ff.
1825 (511) XV, pp. 91ff.
1826 (422) XI, pp. 1ff.
1826-27 (533) VII, pp. 1ff.
1828 (566) IX, pp. 1ff.
1829 (326) V, pp. 1ff.
1830 (677) XV, pp. 1ff.
1831 (336) IX, pp. 1ff.
1831-32 (687) XXIII, pp. 309ff.
1834 (400) XL, pp. 33ff.
1834 (585), XL, pp. 43ff.
1835 (622) XXXV, pp. 23ff.
1836 (574) XXXVI, pp. 171ff.
1837 (523) XXI, pp. 1ff.
1837-38 (619) XXVIII, pp 1ff.
1839 (516) XVI, pp.319ff.
1840 (640) XXVIII, pp. 145ff.
1841, sess. 2 (30) I, pp. 193ff.
1842 (582) XXV, pp. 43ff.
1843 (565) XXIX, pp. 1ff.
1844 (615) XXXI, pp. 85ff.
1845 (615) XXVII, pp. 67ff.
1846 (689) XXIV, pp. 447ff.
1847 (693) XXXIII, pp. 217ff.
1847-8 (663) XXVI, pp. 275ff.
1849 (580) XXII, pp. 439ff.
1850 (628) XX, pp. 439ff.
1851 (611) XXII, pp. 553ff.
1852-3 (279) XL, pp. 49ff.
HL Sess. Pps 1852-3 (417) [Not printed in Commons series because of administrative confusion on change of ministry]
1854 (478) XIX, pp. 131ff.
1854-5 (532) XV, pp. 167ff.
1856 (390) XVIII, pp. 65ff.

Account of Charges and Expenses paid by the Commissioners for building New Churches:
1819-21 1821 (428) XVI, p. 135.

1821-2 1822 (385) XXI, p. 87.
1822-3 1823 (543) XIII, p. 387.
1823-4 1824 (409) XVIII, p. 63.
1824-5 1825 (497) XXI, p. 31.
1825-6 1826 (419) XI, p. 17.
1826-7 1826-7 (528) XX, p. 591.
1827-8 1828 (532) XXI, p. 529.
1828-9 1829 (265) XXI, p. 57.
1829-30 1830 (670) XIX, p. 7.
1830-1 1830-1 (357) VII, p. 9.
1831-2 1831-2 (615) XXX, p. 1.
1832-3 1833 (731) XXVII, p. 327.
1833-4 1834 (550) XLIII, p. 223.
1835-6 1836 (542) XL, p. 1.
1836-7 1837 (505) XLI, p. 449.
1837-8 1837-8 (547) XXXVIII, p. 151.
1838-9 1839 (516★) XLI, p. 11.
1839-40 1840 (262) XXXIX, p. 23.
1840-1 1841, sess.2 (2) II, p. 327.
1841-2 1842 (469) XXVI, p. 559.
1842-3 1843 (531) XXX, p. 511.
1843-4 1844 (522) XXXVIII, p. 87.
1844-5 1845 (603) XXXV, p. 281.
1845-6 1846 (569) XXXII, p. 7.
1846-7 1847 (698) XLIV, p. 297.
1847-8 1847-8 (632) XLIX, p. 185.
1849-50 1850 (523) XLII, p. 139.
1850-1 1851 (423) XLII, p. 525.
1851-2 1852 (436) XXXVIII, p. 331.
1853-4 1854 (324) L, p. 129.
1854-5 1854-5 (374) XLI, p. 81.
1855-6 1856 (217) XLVI, p. 147.

Reports and papers:

HL 1811 (48 and 75) XLVI, pp. 1ff., Return of the number of Places of Divine Worship ... in every Parish containing a Population of 1,000 and upwards ...

HL 1812 (99) LVI, pp. 128ff., Account of the Number of Parishes and their Population, Number of Churches ... and their Capacity, ... in each Diocese ...

HL 1816 (116) LXXIX, pp. 128ff., Account of the Population, and Capacity of Churches and Chapels, in all Benefices or Parishes wherein the Population consists of 2,000 and upwards, and the Churches will not contain One Half.

HL 1816 (118) LXXIX, pp. 271ff., Comparative Statement of the Population, and Capacity of Churches and Chapels, in all Parishes in which the Population exceeds 4,000, and the Churches or Chapels will not contain One Fourth.

1818 (4) XVIII, pp. 93ff., Accounts of the Population of certain ... Parishes, with the Capacity of their Churches.

1818 (5) XVIII, pp. 137ff., Account of the Number of Benefices and their Population; Number and Capacity of Churches ...

1819 (327) XVII, pp. 1ff., Account of Church Briefs ... 1805-19.

1824 (175) XVIII, pp. 55ff., Account of Number of Churches ... built under Direction of Commissioners...

1824 (465) XVIII, pp. 65ff., Return of Expenditure for building new Churches ...

1826-7 (524) XX, pp. 487ff., Account of Church Briefs ... 1819-27.

1826-27 (527) XX, p. 589, Return by Trustees for building New Churches in Parish of Newington ...

1828 (446) IV, Report from the Select Committee on the Office of Works.

1829 (95) XXI, p. 59, Application to Commissioners ... for Advance of Money for ... new Church in ... Liverpool.

1829 (330) XXI, pp. 61ff., Applications for building Chapels ...

1830 (476) XIX, pp. 5ff., Applications for building Chapels ...

1831-2 (272) VII, pp. 5ff., Return of Grants by Commissioners ...

1831-32 (708) XXX, pp. 3ff., Return of Official Applications to Bishops for ... Building of Additional Churches ...

1836 (301) XL, pp. 26ff., Drawbacks and Duties allowed on Materials for Building Churches in Scotland.

1837 (87) XLI, Accounts of all Sums charged ... upon the Church Rates ... due ... to the Church Building Commission.

1837 (437) XLI, pp. 429ff., Account of the Sums expended under the Direction of the Commissioners for Building Churches ...

1837-8 (325) XXXVIII, pp. 141ff., Return of Amount of Drawback allowed on Building Materials used in Erection of Places of public Worship in Great Britain, 1817-37.

1840 (262) XXXIX, pp. 131ff., Amount expended ... since 15 May 1837.

1840 (620) XXXIX, pp. 47ff., Churches and Chapels consecrated in the last Ten Years ...

1845 (322) XXVIII, pp. 261ff., Return of Amount of Drawback ... 1837-45.

1850 (in 628) XX, p. 47, Places where new churches are building, towards which the Commissioners have made grants ...

1850 (1224), XX, pp. 181ff., Second report from Division of Parishes Commissioners, with need for 600 new churches.

1851 (527) XLII, pp. 519ff., Return of the Number of Free Sittings established in the several Churches built ... with the Aid of Grants from the Church Building Commissioners ...

1852-3 (51) LXXVIII, pp. 23-60., Particulars of information received by sub-committee of the Parishes Commissioners regarding the immediate want of 600 new churches.

1852-3 (125) LXXVIII, pp. 61ff., Accounts of the Sums expended ... since 26 March 1840 ..

1854 (399) L, pp. 131ff., Copies of Correspondence of the Ven. Archdeacon Allen with the Church Building Commissioners ...

1856 (387) XLVI, pp. 129-33, A Return of all Sums ... Granted ... within the last Ten Years, in Aid of the Erection of Churches ...

1857-8, IX, pp. 59ff., HL select committee report on deficiency of places of worship.

1861 (557) XLVIII, pp. 3ff., Returns of Parishes Divided and Districts assigned ... 1818-56.

1876 (125-I) LVIII, pp. 553ff., Number of Churches (including Cathedrals) ... built or repaired at a cost exceeding £500 since the year 1840.

1876 LVIII, pp. 657-8, Convocation of Canterbury Return.

HL1876 Grants promised by the late Church Building Commissioners and paid by the Ecclesiastical Commissioners up to 31 Oct.1876.

HL 1877 XII, pp. 71-5., Return of the church-building fund that devolved on the Ecclesiastical Commissioners.

Parliamentary Debates

Parliamentary Debates, 1803-20, 41 vols, 1803-20

Parliamentary Debates, New Series, 25 vols, 1820-30

Parliamentary Debates, 3rd series, 350 vols, 1830-91

Newspapers and Periodicals

The Times

Gentleman's Magazine

Quarterly Review

Companion to the Almanac

Magazine of the Fine Arts

British Critic

Architectural Magazine 1834-8

The Ecclesiologist 1841-68

The Builder from 1842

Articles and theses

Bannister, T., 'The Earliest Architectural Uses of Iron', *Architectural Review*, 127 (1950), pp. 231–46.

Bullen, J. B., 'The Romanesque Revival in Britain, 1800-1840', *Architectural History*, 47 (2004), pp. 139-58.

Carlos, E. J., Reviews of new churches in *Gentleman's Magazine*:

1823, pt 1, p. 4; *1824, pt 2*, pp. 129, 217 (Architecture of the New Churches), 294 (Observations on the New Churches III); p. 489 (Camden Town Chapel). *1825, pt 2*, p. 393 (Trinity, Newington); p. 577 (Hanover Chapel and Christ Church, Marylebone). *1826, pt 1*, p. 201 (St Luke, Chelsea). *1826, pt 2*, p. 9 (All Souls, Langham Pl., & St Philip, Regent St); p. 201 (St Peter, Walworth). *1827, pt 1*, p. 9 (St George, Camberwell, & St Mark, Kennington); p. 209 (St John, Hoxton, & St Barnabas, King Sq.); p. 393 (St John, Waterloo Road, & St Luke, Norwood). *1827, pt 2*, p. 9 (St Mary, Bryanston Sq., Marylebone); p. 201 (Trinity, Bordesley); p. 393 (St Mary, Somers Town); p.577 (St Mary, Haggerston). *1828, pt 1*, p. 393 (St Peter, Regent Sq.); p. 443 (Hanover Chapel, Regent St). *1828, pt 2*, p. 105 (St George, Battersea). *1829, pt 1*, p. 9 (St John, Upper Holloway & St Paul, Balls Pond); p. 297 (Trinity, Marylebone, & St Peter, Pimlico); p. 405 (Trinity, Cloudesley Sq.); p. 577 (St Matthew, Brixton, & St Mark, Clerkenwell). *1829, pt 2*, p. 393 (St Mark, N. Audley St, & St Mary, Greenwich); p. 577 (St Anne, Wandsworth, & Stepney Chapel). *1830, pt 1*, p. 577 (St John, Walham Gr., & Trinity, Brompton). *1830, pt 2*, p. 297 (St James, Bermondsey). *1831, pt 1*, p. 105 (St Peter, Hammersmith, & St John, Bethnal Gr.); p. 297 (St Mary, Lambeth, & Trinity, Sloane St); p. 386 (West Hackney). *1831, pt 2*, p. 9 (St Barnabas, Kensington). *1832, pt 1*, p. 9 (Trinity, Little Queen St). *1833, pt 2*, p. 9 (St James, Croydon).

Carr, G. L., 'The Commissioners' Churches of London, 1818-1837. A Study of religious art, architecture and patronage in Britain from the formation of the Commission to the Accession of Queen Victoria', Univ. of Michigan Ph.D. thesis, 1976 [copy in RIBA Library].

Cooney, E. W., 'The origins of the Victorian Master Builders', *Economic History Review*, 2nd series, VIII, no. 2 (1955), pp. 167ff.

Draper, P., 'The Bane of Consistency: Nineteenth-Century Legacies in the Study of Gothic Architecture', in Salmon, F., ed., *Gothic and the Gothic Revival* (26th Symposium of Society of Architectural Historians of Great Britain, 1997), 1998.

Fedden, R., 'Thomas Hopper and the Norman Revival', *Studies in Architectural History*, 2 (1956), pp. 58-69.

Gentleman's Magazine. Anon. articles on St George, Frankwell, Shrewsbury (1832, pt 2, p. 589); and St George, Sheffield, and St Thomas, Brampton (1833, pt 1, p. 577).

Hopkins, E., 'Religious Dissent in Black Country Industrial Villages in the first half of the Nineteenth Century', *Journal of Ecclesiastical History*, 34 (1983), pp. 411-24.

[Leeds, W. H.], 'On the Architecture of the New Churches', *Magazine of the Fine Arts*, May 1821, pp. 130-8.

Liscombe, R., 'Economy, Character and Durability: Specimen designs for the Church Commissioners, 1818', *Architectural History*, 13 (1970), pp. 43-57.

Mather, F. C., 'Georgian Churchmanship Reconsidered … 1714-1830', *Journal of Ecclesiastical History* (1985), pp. 255-83.

Maynard, W. B., 'The Response of the Church of England to Economic and Demographic Change: the Archdeaconry of Durham, 1800-1851', *Journal of Ecclesiastical History*, 42 (1991), pp. 437-62.

Mole, D. E. H., 'Challenge to the Church. Birmingham, 1815-65', in Dyos, H. J., and Wolff, M., *The Victorian City. Images and Realities* (1973), vol. 2, pp. 815-36.

Mole, D. E. H., 'The Victorian Town Parish: Rural Vision and Urban Mission', *Studies in Church History*, 17 (Oxford, 1979), pp. 361ff.

Mowl, T., 'The Norman Revival', in *Influences in Victorian Architecture*, ed. Macready, S., and Thompson, F. H., (1985).

Parry, T. M., 'The Incorporated Church Building Society 1818-1851', Oxford M.Litt. thesis, 1984.

Port. M. H., 'Francis Goodwin, 1784-1835', *Architectural History*, 1 (1958), pp. 60-72.

Port, M. H., 'The Office of Works and early nineteenth-century building contracts', *Economic History Review*, 2nd series, XX (1967), pp. 94-110.

Quarterly Review, 27, no. 54 (Jul. 1822), 'Application of the various Styles of Architecture'.

Saint, A., 'Anglican church-building in London, 1790-1890: from state subsidy to the free market', in Brooks, C., and Saint, A., *The Victorian Church. Architecture and Society* (Manchester and New York, 1995), pp. 30-50.

[Southey, R.], 'New Churches'. *Quarterly Review*, 23, no.46 (July 1820), pp. 49-91.

[Southey, R.], 'New Churches - Progress of Dissent', *Quarterly Review*, 31, no. 61 (Apr. 1824), pp. 229-54.

Walsh, J., 'Methodism at the end of the eighteenth century', in Davies, R. and Rupp, G. eds, *A History of the Methodist Church in Great Britain* (1965), vol.1, pp. 288 ff.

Welch, P. J., 'The Significance of Bishop C. J. Blomfield', *The Modern Churchman*, XLV (1955), pp. 336-44.

Ward, W. R., 'The Cost of Establishment: Some Reflections on Church Building in Manchester', *Studies in Church History*, III, (Leiden, 1966), pp. 286ff.

'Z', 'On the building of new churches', *Monthly Magazine*, LIV (1822), pp. 211ff.

Books and pamphlets (The place of publication is London unless otherwise stated)

Addleshaw, G. W. O., and Etchells, F. *The Architectural Setting of Anglican Worship* (1958).

Anon. *Church Extension in relation to the present national crisis* [n.d., 1841].

Archer, J. H. G. *Art and Architecture in Victorian Manchester* (Manchester, 1995).

Bayliss, A. *Life and Works of James Trubshaw* (Stockport, 1978).

Beckwith, F. *Thomas Taylor, Regency Architect, Leeds* (Leeds, 1949).

Best, G. *Temporal Pillars. Queen Anne's Bounty, the Ecclesiastical Commissioners, and the Church of England* (Cambridge, 1974).

Bewes, W. A. *Church Briefs* (1896).

Biber, G. E. *Bishop Blomfield and His Times. An Historical Sketch* (1857).

Bingham, N. *C. A. Busby. The Regency Architect of Brighton and Hove* (1991).

Blomfield, C . J. *Proposals for a fund to be applied to the building and endowing of additional churches in the Metropolis* (1836).

Bolton, A. *The Works of Sir John Soane, R.A.* (1924).

Bowdler, T. *The Life of John Bowdler* (1825).

Britton, J., and Pugin, A. C. *Illustrations of the public buildings of London* (2 vols, 1823, 1828); (2nd edn, enlarged, by W. H. Leeds, 2 vols, 1838).

Brooks, C. *The Gothic Revival* (1999).

Brooks, C., and Saint, A. (eds) *The Victorian Church. Architecture and Society* (Manchester, 1995).

Brose, O. J. *Church and Parliament. The Reshaping of the Church of England 1828-1860* (Stanford, 1959).

Chadwick, O. *The Victorian Church* (2 vols, 1966, 1970).

Churton, E. *Memoir of Joshua Watson* (2 vols, Oxford, 1861).

Clarke, B. F. L. *Church Builders of the Nineteenth Century. A Study of the Gothic Revival in England* (1938).

Clarke, B. F. L. *The Building of the eighteenth-century church* (1963).

Clarke, B. F. L. *The Parish Churches of London* (1966).

Clifton-Taylor, A. *The Pattern of English Building* (2nd edn, 1965).

Colvin, H. *Biographical Dictionary of British Architects* (3rd edn, New Haven & London, 1995).

Cornish, F. W. *History of the English Church in the Nineteenth Century* (2 vols, 1910).

Crook, J. M. *John Carter and the Mind of the Gothic Revival* (1995).

Crook, J. M., and Port, M. H. *History of the King's Works, VI, 1782-1851* (1973).

Cudworth, W. *Round about Bradford* (Bradford, 1876).

Dalton, H. W. *Anglican Resurgence under W.F.Hook in Early Victorian Leeds. Church Life in a Nonconformist Town, 1836-1851* (Thoresby Society, 2nd series, no. 12, Leeds, 2002 for 2001).

Darley, G. *Sir John Soane. An Accidental Romantic* (New Haven & London, 1999).

Dobson, E. *Rudiments of the Art of Building* (1849).

Doll, P. *After the Primitive Christians. The Eighteenth-Century Anglican Eucharist in its Architectural Setting* (1997).

Dowell, S. *A History of Taxation and Taxes in England* (4 vols, 2nd edn 1888).

D'Oyly, C. J. *Memoir of George D'Oyly, D.D.* (2 vols, 1847).

Eastlake, C. L. *The Gothic Revival* (1872).

Elmes, J. *A Letter to the Rt Hon. the Earl of Liverpool on ... Deficiency in the Number of Places of Public Worship ...* (1818).

Elmes, J., and Shepherd, T. H., *Metropolitan Improvements* (1827-31).

English, H.S. *The Laws respecting pews or seats in churches* (1826).

Friedman, T. *Church Architecture in Leeds 1700-1799* (Leeds, 1997).

Friedman, T. *The Georgian Parish Church* (Reading, 2004).

Gay, P. *The Geography of Religion in England* (Worcester, 1971).

Gilbert, A. D. *Religion and Society in Industrial England. Church, Chapel and Social Change, 1740-1914* (1976).

Godwin, G., jun., *The Churches of London* (1839).

Goodhart-Rendel, H. S. *English Architecture since the Regency* (1953).

Gray, D. *Spencer Perceval, 1762-1812, the Evangelical Prime Minister* (Manchester, 1963).

Hammond, P. C. *The Parson and the Victorian Church* (1977).

Haydon, B. R. *New Churches considered with respect to the Opportunities they offer for the Encouragement of Painting* (1818).

Hempton, D. *Methodism and Politics in British Society 1750-1850* (1984).

Hempton, D. *Religion and political culture in Britain and Ireland* (Cambridge, 1996).

Hints to Churchwardens ... relative to the Repair and Improvement of Parish Churches (1825).

Historical MSS Commission, XIV Report (1894), *App. 4, MSS of Lord Kenyon*.

Hitchcock, H.-R. *Early Victorian Architecture* (New Haven, 2 vols, 1955).

Hole, R. *Pulpits, politics and public order in England 1760-1832* (Cambridge, 1989).

Incorporated Church-Building Society. *Suggestions from the Society for ... the Enlargement and Building of Churches ... for the consideration of persons engaged in such undertakings* (1819; rev. 1842).

Ison, W. *The Georgian Buildings of Bath* (1948).

Leatherbarrow, J. S. *Victorian Period Piece* (1954).

Lee, C. E. *St Pancras Church and Parish* (1955).

Lewis, S. *Topographical Dictionary of England* (4 vols, 1831).

Linstrum, D. *Historic Architecture of Leeds* (Newcastle upon Tyne, 1969).

Linstrum, D. *West Yorkshire Architects and Architecture* (1978).

Malet, W. W. *On Church Extension or, An Enquiry, What should the State do? or, What can the Church do, unless her Rights are restored, and her efficiency upheld (1840).*

Mann, H., *Sketches of the Religious Denominations abridged from the official report* (1851).

Mann, H. *Religious Worship* (1854).

Mansbridge, M. *John Nash. A complete catalogue* (1991).

Mant, R. *Church Architecture considered* (Belfast, 1843).

Mathieson, W. L. *English Church Reform 1815-1840* (1923).

Nicholson, P. *The New Practical Builder and Workman's Companion* (1823).

Nockles, P. B. *The Oxford Movement in Context. Anglican High Churchmanship, 1760-1857* (Cambridge, 1994).

Noel, B. W. *The State of the Metropolis considered in a letter to the Rt Hon. And Rt Rev. the Lord Bishop of London* (3rd edn, enlarged, 1835).

Odom, W. *Memorials of Sheffield: Its Cathedral and Parish Churches* (Sheffield, 1922).

Overton, J. H. *The English Church in the Nineteenth Century, 1800-33* (1894).

Palmer, W. *An Enquiry into the possibility of obtaining means for Church Extension without Parliamentary Grants* (1841).

Parker, C. S. *Sir Robert Peel from his Private Papers* (3 vols, 1891-9).

Pellew, G. *The Life and Correspondence of ... Viscount Sidmouth* (3 vols, 1847).

Pevsner, N. *Some Architectural Writers of the Nineteenth Century* (Oxford, 1972).

Pevsner, N. (and others), *The Buildings of England* (from 1950, by counties, many revised).

Phillpotts, H. *A Pastoral Letter to the Inhabitants of Plymouth* (1844).

Pocock, W. F. *Designs for Churches and Chapels* (1819).

Port, M. H. *The Commissions for Building Fifty New Churches*, London Record Society 23 (1986).

Prey, P. de la R. du, *Sir John Soane. Catalogues of Architectural Drawings in the Victoria and Albert Museum. Sir John Soane* (1983).

Rayner, S. *History and Antiquities of Pudsey*, ed. W. Smith (Pudsey, 1887).

Rickman, T. *An Attempt to Discriminate the Styles of English Architecture* 1817.

Rickman, T. M. *Notes on the Life ... of Thomas Rickman* (1901).

Royal Institute of British Architects, Drawings Collection Catalogues, 19 vols (Farnborough, 1972-89, var. editors, composite index).

Russell, A. *The Clerical Profession* (1982).

Satoh, A. *Building in Britain* (Aldershot, 1995).

Shaw, J. *A Letter on Ecclesiastical Architecture as Applicable to Modern Churches Addresed to the Rt rev. the Lord Bishop of London* (1839).

Shepherd, T. H. See Elmes, J.

Soloway, R. A. *Prelates and People. Ecclesiastical Social Thought in England 1783-1852* (1969).

Stroud, D. *Sir John Soane, Architect* (1984).

Stroud, D. *The Architecture of Sir John Soane* (1961).

Summerson, J. *Sir John Soane* (1953).

Summerson, J. *Georgian London* (1945; rev. edn by H.Colvin).

Summerson, J. *Heavenly Mansions and other essays on Architecture* (1949).

Summerson, J. *Architecture in Britain 1530-1830* (Harmondsworth, 2nd edn, re-arranged, 1955).

Summerson, J. *The Life and Works of John Nash Architect* (1980).

Survey of London, XXIII, The Parish of St Mary Lambeth, pt 1, South Bank and Vauxhall, ed. W. Godfrey (1951).

Survey of London, XXV St George's Fields, ed. I. Darlington (1955).

Survey of London, XXVI The Parish of St Mary Lambeth, pt 2, Southern Area, ed. F. H. W. Shepherd (1956).

Taylor, A. *The Websters of Kendal. A North-Western Architectural Dynasty*, ed. J. Martin (Cumberland & Westmorland Antiquarian & Architectural Society, Record Series XVII, Kendal, 2004).

Tress, R. *Modern Churches. Designs, Estimates and Essays* (1841).

Trimen, A. *Church and Chapel Architecture* (1849).

Virgin, P. *The Church in an Age of Negligence. Ecclesiastical Structure and Problems of Church Reform 1700-1840* (Cambridge, 1984).

Ward, J. R. *Religion and Society in England 1790-1850* (1972).

Warne, A. *Church and Society in Eighteenth-Century Devon* (Newton Abbott, 1969).

Watkin, D. *Life and Work of C. R. Cockerell* (1974).

Watkin, D. *Sir John Soane. Enlightenment Thought and the Royal Academy Lectures* (Cambridge, 1996).

Watson, R. *Anecdotes of the life of Richard Watson bishop of Llandaff* (1817).

Webster, A. R. *Joshua Watson* (1954).

Webster, C. R. D. *Chantrell, Architect. His Life and Work in Leeds* (Leeds, 1991).

Whiffen, M. *Stuart and Georgian Churches. The Architecture of the Church of England outside London 1603-1837* (1947-8).

Whiffen, M. *The Architecture of Sir Charles Barry in Manchester and its Neighbourhood* (Manchester, 1950).

Wood, R .J. *Church Extension in Leeds* (Leeds, 1964).

Worsley, G. *Architectural Drawings of the Regency Period 1790-1837* (1991).

Yates, N. *Buildings, Faith and Worship. The liturgical Arrangement of Anglican Churches 1600-1900* (Oxford, 1991).

Yates, N., Hume, R., and Hastings, P. *Religion and Society in Kent 1640-1914* (Woodbridge, 1994).

Yates, R. *The Church in Danger. A Letter to Lord Liverpool* (1815).

Yates, R. *The Basis of National Welfare* (1817).

Yeomans, D. T. *The Trussed Roof: its history and development* (Aldershot, 1992).

Yonge, C. D. *The Life and administration of ... 2nd earl of Liverpool* (3 vols, 1868).

Young, E. and W. *Old London Churches* (1956).

Index

Bold figures indicate illustrations of the subjects, or works by the architect(s) named.
The appendices are not included in this index.